DEFENDING THE HOLY LAND

—

A Critical Analysis of
Israel's Security & Foreign Policy

ZEEV MAOZ

With a New Preface and Afterword

THE UNIVERSITY OF MICHIGAN PRESS
Ann Arbor

First paperback edition 2009
Copyright © by the University of Michigan 2006
All rights reserved
Published in the United States of America by
The University of Michigan Press
Manufactured in the United States of America
⊗ Printed on acid-free paper

2012   2011   2010   2009   5   4   3

A CIP catalog record for this book is available from the British Library.

Library of Congress Cataloging-in-Publication Data

Maoz, Zeev.
    Defending the Holy Land : a critical analysis of Israel's security
and foreign policy / Zeev Maoz.
        p.   cm.
    Includes bibliographical references and index.
    ISBN-13: 978-0-472-11540-2 (cloth : alk. paper)
    ISBN-10: 0-472-11540-5 (cloth : alk. paper)
        1. Israel—Foreign relations.   2. National security—Israel.
3. Arab-Israeli conflict.   I. Title.

    DS119.6.M32   2006
    327.5694009'045—dc22   2005030218

ISBN-13: 978-0-472-03341-6 (pbk. : alk. paper)
ISBN-10: 0-472-03341-7 (pbk. : alk. paper)

In memory of

AVNER YANIV

Preface to the Paperback Edition

Thomas L. Friedman's first rule of Middle East reporting is "Never lead your story out of Lebanon, Gaza, or Iraq with a cease-fire; it will always be over by the time the next morning's paper is out."[1] This rule applies not only to journalists who write about things as they happen; it applies not only to cease-fire reporting; it is equally valid advice for scholars who write about the more general aspects of Middle East politics. Events in the Middle East have a tendency to overtake those who write about them—including those who study general patterns rather than specific episodes. Even the history of the region—or rather our understanding of that history— evolves and changes over time. Naturally, this requires authors to revisit their research as time passes.

The research and writing of *Defending the Holy Land* were completed in the summer of 2004. I did a number of limited revisions in the winter of 2005, including limited references to what appeared to be then an Israeli plan to withdraw from the Gaza Strip and dismantle the Jewish settlements in this area. The book itself was published in May 2006. Two months later, Israel initiated yet another war against Lebanon in retaliation to a Hizballah kidnapping of two Israeli soldiers. During the war I appeared in a number of media venues and wrote a number of op-ed pieces criticizing Israeli conduct of the war on moral, political, and strategic grounds.[2] At the outset, I realized that this war was going to become a

---

1. Thomas L. Friedman, "Ballots and Boycotts," *New York Times*, January 13, 2005, A35.

2. The articles can be read on my Web site: http://psfaculty.ucdavis.edu/zmaoz/recent_op.htm. Some of the articles were widely cited ("Morality Is Not on Our Side," published in *Ha'aretz* on July 25, has over 2,700 hits on Google and was translated into more than twenty languages).

fiasco, but my warnings, like those of other—rather few—Israeli experts, fell on deaf ears. The same applies to writings about the Israeli conduct (or rather misconduct) of the Intifada, the continued building of illegal settlements in the West Bank, and the persistent dominance of security concerns and the security establishment over Israel's foreign policy and diplomacy. One can say similar things about the shortsightedness, folly, and recklessness of Israel's enemies—principally the Palestinians and Hizballah. But this too is not an excuse for the continued malfunctions in Israel's diplomacy and military strategy.

Unfortunately, the events over the last two years since the book was published vindicated most of the arguments I had made in the book. There is very little that required revising. In fact, the recommendations of the Vinograd Inquiry Commission that the Israeli government appointed to investigate the political and military conduct of the Second Lebanon War read a lot like chapter 11 of *Defending the Holy Land*. It is important, however, to cover very briefly the Second Lebanon War and the continued conduct of the Intifada. Also, the continued WMD escalation in the region requires some discussion. Accordingly, I have added a brief afterword that discusses these events. A more extensive study of these processes will be published subsequently, but the general themes that I have emphasized in the original version of the book have not changed. Perhaps it is naive to expect they would. Nevertheless, the events of the last two years indicate that an alternative approach to Israel's security and foreign policy is urgently needed before another catastrophe takes place.

Preface

This book has been brewing in my mind for nearly three decades. I have closely followed Israel's national security and foreign policy over the years. Like for many other Israelis—scholars and laypersons—who followed these policies, this was not a detached and distant scrutiny. It was an anthropological process of participating observation. I have both taken part and had major stakes in many of the events and processes that are discussed in this book. As a soldier I participated in three of the wars that are discussed herein: I served as a young soldier in the War of Attrition, fighting in the northern section of the Suez Canal. As a reserve officer I participated in the Yom Kippur War and the Lebanon War. I also did numerous tours of duty (in both my standing army career and my reserve duty) in the occupied territories. In the early 1990s I had a brief stint on a team advising Yitzhak Rabin on strategic affairs.

For the most part, this process of observation was rather depressing; only a few years during this period offered rays of hope. What bothered me more than specific episodes of ineptitude, folly, and deception—and there were many of these over the years—were two aspects of policy-making that have not received sufficient attention. First, I was concerned by the persistent failure of the policy community to learn from Israel's mistakes. This lack of self-inspection applied not only to politicians and bureaucrats but also to a significant portion of the scholarly community in Israel, the Israeli media, and—of course—public opinion. In too many areas of policy, Israel has experienced persistent and repeated failures. Yet, many of these failures were explained away or covered up as something else. Even when they were recognized as failures, no meaningful reforms were undertaken. Things remained pretty much as they had been before the fiascos.

Second, I became increasingly uncomfortable with the uncritical treatment by most Israelis of the foundations of Israel's national security doctrine. Although Israelis are generally a critical and cynical breed, there is an underlying consensus on many fundamental security and foreign policy issues. There is a general agreement on the underlying assumptions of Israel's security and foreign policy (for example, on the elements of the threat to Israel's security). There is a general consensus on some fundamental principles of Israel's security doctrine (e.g., the need to rely on an offensive and escalation dominant doctrine). And there is a fairly consensual interpretation of certain outcomes of these policies (e.g., that Israel's nuclear policy has been a phenomenal success). Consensus is a good thing if it is based on correct assumptions and principles. My feeling was that too many of the foundations of Israel's security and foreign policy doctrine have become religious principles rather than propositions that need to be tested against the empirical facts. Because almost nobody bothered to examine whether this general consensus is based on a correct reading of Israel's environment and policies, there was a significant void in the literature dealing with Israel's national security and foreign policy. There were almost no efforts to evaluate the various contours of these policies. This book is an attempt to systematically examine and review both the foundations of these policies and their operational expressions.

Several institutions and individuals helped me in the process of writing and rewriting this book. First and foremost, much of the data used in this study is derived from the project of the Quantitative History of the Arab-Israeli Conflict, which was partially funded by the United States Institute of Peace. In the course of writing the book I have discussed ideas and have shared some of the writings with colleagues in Israel and abroad. I have received numerous comments and suggestions on my nuclear chapter (see acknowledgments in Maoz 2003a, 44) and on my chapter on Israeli interventions in intra-Arab affairs (see acknowledgments in Maoz 2001, 137). Discussions and correspondence with Haim Assa, Gad Barzilai, Isaac Ben-Israel, Michael Brecher, Avner Cohen, Yair Evron, Azar Gat, Orit Kamir, Jack Levy, Benny Miller, Alex Mintz, Ben Mor, Zeev Segal, J. David Singer, Abrasha Tamir, and Lesley Terris have enriched my understanding of the intricacies of the various issues discussed in this book. The second part of the book (chaps. 7–14) was completed while I was a visiting professor of political science at the University of Michigan. The final round of revisions was influenced by the suggestions of Michael Barnett, the other reviewers for the University of Michigan Press, and University of Michigan Press editor Jim Reische. I am thankful to all those individuals and institutions for their comments, suggestions, and encouragement. Needless to say, none of these institutions or individuals necessarily agrees with or endorses the ideas and arguments of this book. I bear sole responsibility for its contents and substance.

My deepest thanks, as always, go to my family. Zehava, my wife, was an infinite source of encouragement and support. My children, Inbal and Omry, have been critical sounding boards, challenging many of my ideas. Inbal made a great number of useful substantive and editorial comments on the manuscript. One cannot ask for more.

My friend and colleague Professor Avner Yaniv was the person whose views and insights I missed the most in the process of writing this book. Avner—whose writings on Israel's security feature prominently in the coming pages—would probably have disagreed with many of my observations and conclusions. But his knowledge and understanding of Israeli foreign and security affairs, and of the close linkage between domestic and security affairs, went much beyond his writings on these matters. Avner passed away prematurely in June 1992. Twelve years later, I still miss the conversations and debates we had about these matters. I dedicate this book to Avner's memory.

—Davis, California, August 2004

Contents

PART I

Foundations

— I —

The Israeli Security Puzzle

Conceptions, Approaches, Paradoxes

I. INTRODUCTION

On May 12, 1948, a group of nine men and one woman met in Tel Aviv to decide on the establishment of a new state. Around them, a ferocious civil war had been going on for the past six months. The British mandate was to expire in two days. The ten members of the Provisional State Council of the Jewish Agency faced a tough dilemma. The United Nations (UN) resolution of November 29, 1947, decreed that Palestine was to be partitioned into a Palestinian state and a Jewish state. The Arabs and the Palestinians had rejected this resolution, threatening to invade Palestine if the Jews declared their own state. The Palestinians— aided by irregular forces from various Arab states—had been fighting the Jews since late 1947. As long as the British forces were in Palestine, there was a semblance of a government. Now that they were about to leave, it seemed necessary to somehow fill this vacuum.

The inclination of the Jewish leaders was to proclaim the formation of the Jewish state. But that would bring about an invasion by the armies of the Arab states. On the table for consideration was an American proposal to delay the declaration of independence, accept an armistice, and allow for a mediation process by the international community in an effort to find a mutually acceptable solution to the Palestine problem. The representatives of the security organs of the Yishuv—the prestate institutions—presented a bleak assessment of the coming war. They expected at

3

least three and as many as seven Arab states to send armies into Palestine. The Jewish population, numbering some 650,000 people, was being mobilized. By May 1948, the newly established army of the Jewish organizations amounted to some 80,000 recruits (Ostfeld 1994, 54). However, they were poorly equipped and required considerable training before they could be sent to the front. The military commanders anticipated as many as 120,000 Arab soldiers equipped with armor, airplanes, and artillery to participate in the invasion of Palestine (Ostfeld 1994, 23–24). The military commanders estimated the chance of survival of the Jewish state as even at best (Sharef 1959, 83–84; Shlaim 2000, 33).

With the support of six members against four opposed, the Provisional Council decided to proclaim a Jewish state and call it the state of Israel. The Provisional Council would henceforth become the provisional government of Israel, until such time that elections could determine the permanent government.

As David Ben-Gurion, the interim prime minister, had anticipated, on May 14, 1948, a combined invasion of a Jordanian and Egyptian army started. The Syrian and the Lebanese armies engaged in a token effort but did not stage a major attack on the Jewish state. Other states sent volunteers, but the combined strength of the Arab armies and the irregular forces fighting the Jewish state was far less than anticipated. The balance of forces in terms of military personnel was in favor of the Israeli army (Golani 2002, 158–68). Initially the Jews had far less advanced military equipment than the Arab armies, but this changed quickly when Israel signed a weapons deal with Czechoslovakia. Other weapons deals through private sources also enabled the new state to tilt the balance of hardware in its favor (Ilan 1996, 181–200). After nearly seven months of fighting (interrupted by two UN-decreed truces), Israel defeated decisively all the Arab states, crushed the Palestinian resistance, and signed a series of armistice agreements with all of its Arab neighbors.

The War of Independence exacted a heavy toll on the Jewish state. A total of sixty-five hundred soldiers and civilians died in the war, 1 percent of the entire Jewish population. The economy of the new state was in extremely bad shape, having been totally mobilized for the war effort. While the war was raging, thousands of Jewish refugees were flowing into the country. They needed food, homes, work, language training, and other social benefits. But the end of the war brought a great deal of hope and optimism to the new state. Many Israelis believed that the armistice agreements would soon be converted into peace treaties that would stabilize and legitimize the new state's boundaries (Segev 1984; Yaniv 1995,

37–38; 1987a, 38). Ben-Gurion thought otherwise. He believed that the Arab rejection of Israel was fundamental and irrevocable. They were defeated in the first round, but there would be other rounds of warfare. Next time, the Arabs would be better prepared, better equipped, and—with the memory of the humiliating 1948 defeat in their minds—possibly better motivated. Israel had to be ready to fight again (Ben-Gurion 1969, 480–92).

Ben-Gurion was right about the need to fight again, but he probably did not expect his prophecy to be fulfilled to such an overwhelming extent. Over the fifty-five-year period between 1948 and 2004, Israel fought 6 interstate wars, fought 2 (some say three) civil wars, and engaged in over 144 dyadic militarized interstate disputes (MIDs) that involved the threat, the display, or the use of military force against another state.[1] Israel is by far the most conflict-prone state in modern history. It has averaged nearly 4 MIDs every year. It has fought an interstate war every nine years. Israel appears on top of the list of the most intense international rivalries in the last two-hundred-year period (Maoz 2004a).

Fifty-five years after its independence and after peace treaties with two of its most bitter enemies, Israel still lives by its sword. One out of ten Israelis in the age group of fifteen to forty-nine wears an army uniform on a daily basis. One out of every eight dollars that Israelis produce goes to defense every year.[2] As this book goes to press, Israel continues to fight a bitter civil war with the Palestinians, the end of which is nowhere to be seen.

One could claim—indeed, many already have—that a fundamentally hostile environment, one that has yet to accept the Jewish state into the community of nations, imposed on Israel the need to become the "Sparta of modern times." However, some of the factual realities behind Israel's policies do not add up to a picture in which Israel plays the victim's role. For example, Israel signed a peace treaty with its most powerful enemy, Egypt, in 1979. This treaty seems stable even twenty-five years later. Yet, the size and scope of Israel's Defense Forces (IDF), the continued high defense spending, and its proclivity to use excessive force have not declined. They did not decline even after another peace treaty was signed with Jordan in 1994. Israel continues to maintain and—quite probably—continues to expand its nuclear capability, clinging to the policy of "nuclear ambiguity." Israeli and foreign strategists repeatedly claim that Israel is quantitatively and qualitatively superior to any combination of enemies in the region (e.g., Cordesman 2004, 2002; Gordon 2003). Yet, Israel keeps building and exercising its military power on a regular basis.

The frequent use of massive air power and armored force in an attempt to quash the Palestinian uprising during the last four years is a vivid example of Israel's proclivity to amass and use excessive military force despite diminishing threats. It also suggests how futile this policy may be.

Is Israel forced to live by its sword, or does it want to live that way? Is the militarization of Israeli society a fact imposed by its hostile environment? Or is it a device by which its elite mobilizes the society to confront the domestic challenges that Israeli society has faced since its inception? Have Israel's military strategy and diplomacy responded to the challenge of survival in a highly complex, often hostile, and always challenging international environment? Or have these strategies been determined by internal considerations, structures, and people driven by personal and collective ambitions and drives?

Those who are looking for a single and elegant explanation and for clear answers to these questions would do best to turn to another book. I do not intend to provide direct answers to these questions, although some ideas could be gleaned from this study. Instead of trying to explain what made Israel the Sparta of modern times, I examine the goals its leaders set for the country's foreign and security policy. I investigate whether and to what extent the policies Israel has pursued over the years helped accomplish these goals. And—most important—I evaluate the central policies and strategies that Israel has applied over time and explain how they came about and why they succeeded or failed.

The observations offered by the present study about Israel's security and foreign policy are neither simple nor elegant. Many of them are quite controversial. This book is primarily an attempt to evaluate these policies, by asking a simple set of questions that connect goals to policy and policies to outcomes. Specifically, I examine the following questions:

1. What were the—explicit and hidden—goals of decision makers in key foreign and security matters?
2. How were the policies selected by decision makers supposed to accomplish these goals?
3. Were these goals accomplished?
4. If they were, how was the policy related to the outcomes?
5. If these goals were not accomplished, why not?
6. Did various policies have side effects, that is, outcomes that were not intended or were not foreseen by the policymakers?
7. If so, to what extent were these side effects in accordance with, or in

contradiction to, the broader goals of Israel's security, foreign, and domestic policy?

In the present chapter I outline the goals of the study, its scope, its structure and approach, and the key themes that emerge in the coming chapters. Before going into these matters, however, we must outline the fundamental building blocks of Israel's security and foreign policy. In the next section I present the basic assumptions underlying Israel's security and foreign policy since 1948. On the basis of these assumptions I present the principal tenets of Israel's security conception and the derivative foreign policy. I emphasize the notion of a *derivative foreign policy* because—as I will document in the following chapters—Israel's foreign policy has always been a servant of Israel's security policy.

The third section provides a brief overview of the scholarship on Israel's security and foreign policy. This overview is necessarily general and superficial. It is intended only as a broad outline of various strands of thought in the study of Israeli history and security matters. Much of this literature will be used extensively in the chapters that follow. In the fourth section I discuss the theoretical and methodological principles that guide this study. The fifth section lays out the structure of this study and the key themes it invokes.

2. THE BUILDING BLOCKS OF ISRAEL'S NATIONAL SECURITY POLICY

The foundations of Israel's national security conceptions were laid down by David Ben-Gurion in the late 1940s and the early 1950s. Many Israeli strategists view these doctrinal foundations to be valid at present as well (Ben Israel 2001, 269–71; Tal 2000, vi). Ben-Gurion's ideas not only are widely accepted among the members of the Israeli security community but are widely shared by the Israeli public (Arian 1995, 65–66, 173–86, 254–71). I present these principal ideas and discuss them very briefly here.[3] In subsequent chapters I reexamine many of these ideas in a more critical fashion.

Israel's security policy is based on a set of assumptions about Israel's regional and international environment. These assumptions define the basic threat perception that Israel is said to have experienced over the years.

1. *The Arab world is fundamentally hostile toward Israel. It would attempt to destroy the Jewish state given the right chance.* The Arabs—Palestinians,

Egyptians, Syrians, or even more remote peoples such as the Algerians, Libyans, or Iraqis—have never accepted the formation of a Jewish state in Palestine. They might accept it as a (possibly temporary) fact, but they have never internalized the fact that Jews have the right to a national homeland in the Middle East. Therefore, the Arabs harbor a permanent and powerful motivation to annihilate the Jewish state. The only thing that prevents them from doing so is their awareness of the futility of this mission and/or their awareness that the price of such an attempt would be exorbitant. The implication is that Israel is destined to live for a long time under an existential threat. In the short term (the short term being the foreseeable future) its policies and actions can only affect the Arab cost-benefit calculus; they cannot affect Arab motivation. In the long run this motivation may change, but this is not certain, and the long run may be very long indeed.

2. *Fundamental asymmetries exist between Israel and the Arab world.* No matter how widely or how narrowly we define the boundaries of the Arab world, Israel faces enemies that are much more populous, have vastly larger territory, possess more natural resources, and are better networked with the outside world than is the Jewish state. Even if these resources are not spent directly on the mission of destroying Israel, the pool of resources at the disposal of Arab leaders creates a threat of vast magnitude.

3. *The international community is an unreliable ally.* Israel is dependent on the outside world to survive economically and militarily. As an advanced society, it also requires ties with the outside—mostly Western—world for cultural, educational, and social purposes. Israel is also dependent on the world because, up to the early 1990s, most of the Jewish population resided outside of Israel. Its spiritual, social, and economic ties to the Jewish community are an essential component of the Israeli national identity. Israel is also dependent on the outside world for weapons. At the same time, Israel cannot rely on the outside world to ensure its survival and defense. Ultimately, Israeli men and women will have to risk their lives to defend their country. Nobody else will do it for them. Moreover, both the experience of the Holocaust and the short history of the prestate and state periods suggest that the international community is an unreliable source of political and military support. It is at times of dire need that the international community—even Israel's closest friends and allies—has consistently disappointed Israel. Israel can ultimately rely only on itself to ensure its survival, not on the pledges of others, no matter how well intentioned they may be. The concept of "a

people that dwells alone" is a clear expression of this perception of international isolation.

4. *Israel's geography is a major constraint on its ability to fight.* The map of Israel (see maps 1.1 and 1.2) shows how small Israel is in relation to its neighbors and how narrow the country's "waist" has been in the area immediately north and east of Tel Aviv—especially before the occupation of the territories during the Six Day War. This implies that an attack by one or more Arab states could split the country into several slices almost instantly. Moreover, Israel's population centers are within the range of light arms fire and certainly artillery fire of its enemy. A jet plane taking off from Syria, Jordan, and even Egypt can reach Israel's population centers in a matter of minutes. The Israeli civilian and military airfields are within the range of tactical Syrian missiles and a short flight from Egyptian bases in the Sinai and from Jordanian air bases. In the era of complex maneuvering jet fighters, Israel's planes do not have even enough room to circle around over Israeli airspace in order to practice or land in their bases. For Israel, losing territory means risking its very survival.

5. *The Iron Wall offers the long-term hope for the Jewish state.* The concept of an "Iron Wall," developed in Zeev Jabotinsky's famous articles of 1923, represents a vision that entails both short-term hardships and a long-term ray of hope. This concept was implicitly adopted by Ben-Gurion, Jabotinsky's great political rival (Shlaim 2000, 19). The Iron Wall theme suggests that Israel has a number of things working for it in the long run: its staying power, the military blows it hands the Arabs every time they try to attack it, and the development of a model society that outperforms Arab societies. All these factors, along with Israel's viability and prosperity as a democratic and advanced society, will work to convince the Arabs of the futility and the illogic of their dreams. Over time, the Arabs will come to accept the Jewish state and to make peace with it. Initially, this would be a peace of realists, that is, a peace of acceptance but not reconciliation. As this peace bears fruits, the Arabs will realize that they stand to benefit far more from peaceful and open relations with the Jewish state than from conflict or boycott. When that happens, reconciliation would follow. It is impossible to develop a long-term national vision on the basis of this bleak reality. Why should Jews come to settle in Israel so that they or their children would be driven into the sea by a mass of Arabs bent on genocide and politicide, while the international community stands idly by? Even the most optimistic scenario suggests that Israel would have to live by its sword for a very long time—

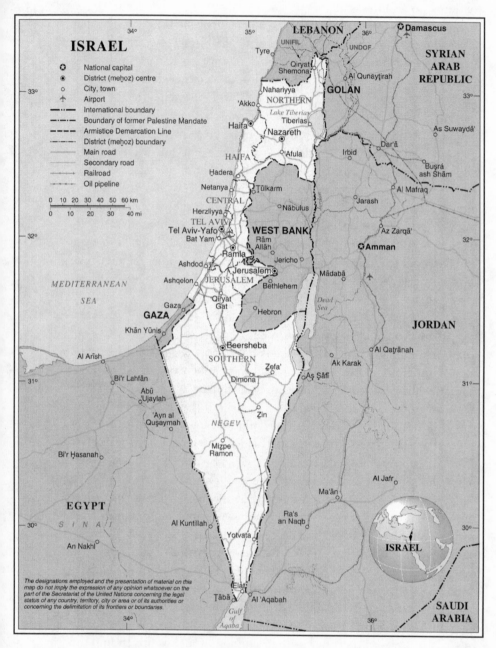

Map 1.1. Israel. (Reprinted by permission of the United Nations Cartographic Section. Israel, Map No. 3584 Rev. 2, January 2004.)

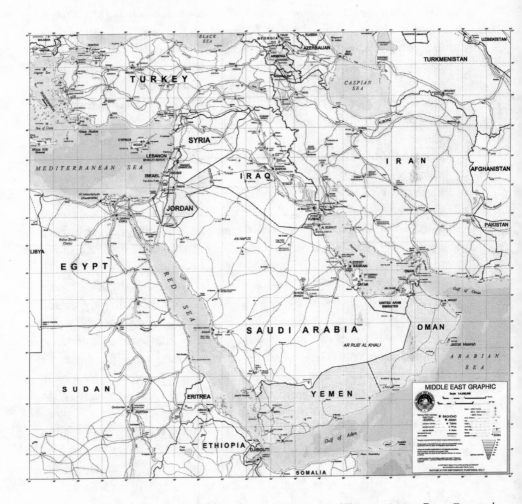

Map 1.2.　The Middle East, 2003. (Courtesy of the University of Texas at Austin, Perry-Castañeda Library Map Collection.)

perhaps several generations. The Zionist leaders had to provide a ray of hope in that vision. The concept of the Iron Wall provides this long-term optimistic vision and the rationale for Israeli resilience and staying power despite the lack of a short-term relief.

As noted, these assumptions remained largely stable over time. Some of the more operational contours of these assumptions may have undergone changes in different periods. For example, the scope of the threat had originally been limited to the Arab world. States such as Iran and Turkey were excluded from the circle of enemies for a long time because they were not considered "Arab." Turkey's status has remained unchanged in this respect. Iran, however, has become one of the most potent enemies of Israel since the 1990s due to the fundamental hostility of the Islamic regime in Tehran, its long-range missiles, and its nuclear program. The economic threat—especially that element based on Arab oil resources— became much more prominent in the list of resources that could be mobilized against Israel after the 1973 Arab oil embargo. Finally, the key fear of Israeli leaders in the 1950s and 1960s was of an all-out attack by a mass of Arab armies. This danger may have diminished somewhat, but it is still a significant threat. However, the new concern that takes up much of the time of the Israeli security community is the acquisition of weapons of mass destruction (WMDs)—especially nuclear weapons—by one or more of Israel's enemies. So there is an added technological threat that has become an important element in Israel's list of nightmares.

The basic tenets of Israel's security doctrine that emerge from these assumptions reflect a set of ideas concerning the general principles for dealing with these threats and structural constraints over the long haul. These tenets are not listed in any particular order, as there is no clear hierarchy among them.

1. *The principle of qualitative edge.*   Israel must rely on a large margin of qualitative advantage to offset the quantitative advantages of the Arab states. The strength of the Jewish state lies in the quality of its manpower, in its technological and educational capability, and in the social cohesion and motivation of its population. This qualitative edge is expressed in both military and nonmilitary terms. In military terms it is translated to hardware and software. Israel must be able to develop and/or acquire far more modern and capable weapons systems than the Arabs. The quality of manpower ensures that Israeli pilots, sailors, tank crews, artillery gunners, and even infantry and special operations soldiers outperform their Arab counterparts by a wide margin. Even when the weapons systems are evenly matched in terms of their technical specifications, the difference

in manpower quality ensures that the Israelis should always have better soldiers than the Arabs. The same applies to military generalship; to tactical command quality; and, of course, to the synergy among weapons systems, support systems (e.g., logistics, communication, intelligence), people, and mission. In terms of nonmilitary elements of power, Israeli society should be able to provide the armed forces with cohesive and high-quality human, economic, social, and political reserves. This would enable the military along the borders to operate free of concerns as to what is going on at the home front. Therefore, national leaders should seek—to the extent possible—to pursue policies that rely on a high degree of public support in matters of national security. This implies, among other things, opting to go to war only under circumstances of no choice. Purely aggressive wars may erode public support for national security policies and thus reduce the willingness of Israeli society to contribute to a long-term national security stand necessary to sustain the Iron Wall in the long run.

2. *A nation at arms.*   Israeli society must be fully mobilizable in times of crisis and ready and willing to extract all of its resources for the struggle for survival. At the same time, Israel should be able to provide its people with welfare, freedoms, and basic rights akin to that of any advanced democratic society. Israeli society must be able to function as a "normal" society during times of relative peace in order to be a true haven for the Jews around the world. Since the transition from peace to war may be very quick, the society must be able to transform itself quickly into a fully mobilized entity. This dictates a large conscript military force as well as a substantial reserve component that is well trained and equipped and that can be mobilized quickly.

3. *The principle of strategic defensive and operational offensive.*   Israel's political and strategic posture is status quo–oriented; yet its operational doctrine is offensive. At any given point in its history, Israel's decision makers accepted the territorial status quo. Therefore they always claimed that Israel had no territorial ambitions. Nevertheless, for the reasons discussed later, Israeli political leaders believed that Israel could not afford to fight defensive wars. The preference for an offensive strategy was never due to proactive political ambitions; it was an outgrowth of structural constraints. Some of these constraints are listed subsequently.

4. *The principle of short wars aimed at quick decision.*   Israel cannot afford to fight long and drawn-out wars. It has to engage in short and decisive military campaigns. The focus on short wars is dictated by three fundamental constraints.

a. Social and economic constraints. A fully mobilized military force implies bringing Israeli economy and society to a screeching halt. The opponents may wear Israel out not by imposing one massive military strike but rather by overdrawing its human and material resources beyond their breaking point. Also, defensive strategies yield to the enemy the strategic advantage; Israel's enemies can decide when, where, and how to attack. This can tip Israeli society beyond its economic breakpoint due to the need to maintain full mobilization. Short and decisive wars allow Israel to maximize its capabilities, to achieve military decision, and then to release its reserve forces so that its society could continue to function. Israel has to slice up its strategic marathon against the Arab world into a series of one-hundred-meter dashes.

b. Geographic constraints. Israel's small territorial margins, its narrow waist, and the small distance between the border and Israel's population centers prohibit defensive postures. Defending a given territory effectively must allow the defender some room for maneuver within its own lines (Luttwak 2001, 147–57), which Israel does not have. Therefore Israel must rely on an offensive strategy and transfer the fighting to the enemy's territory. This may require a willingness to use a first-strike doctrine and to initiate preventive or preemptive wars. Even when the enemy launches the first strike, Israel must strive to seize the strategic initiative by moving to an offensive and into the enemy's territory as quickly as possible.

c. International constraints. The international community is likely to intervene quickly and decisively in order to bring an end to the fighting. If Israel wants to reach a military decision in the war for purposes of cumulative deterrence (see later discussion), it must do so before the international community imposes on the combatants a cease-fire or even a political agreement. Israel's tenuous international standing requires it to be in a position of military and territorial strength at the start of negotiations. Thus, Israel must be the one to determine the scope, speed, and nature of the war through its own actions.

5. *The principle of major power support for war.* Israel must ensure the explicit or tacit support of at least one major power before going to war. In the past, Israel's leaders had to deal with the duality in their perception of the international community. On the one hand, they recognized the basic dependence on the outside world for both material and diplomatic support. On the other hand, they were utterly suspicious of the willingness and ability of the international community to support Israel during severe existential crises. The resolution of this seeming contradiction was

typically framed in the previous maxim. The support of a major power would ensure that Israel would, at the very least, receive enough weapons and munitions to replenish those expended or destroyed during the war. Major power support is also instrumental for fending off diplomatic attacks and sanctions through the UN Security Council, but this is seen as secondary to ensuring a constant source of weapons supply. The implication of this principle is that Israel should try to avoid or delay wars for which it cannot secure the support of a major power.

6. *Autonomy of action before alliance.* Israel should prefer independence of action over binding alliances that might limit its freedom of action. The pursuit of allies to bolster Israel's security has always been an important desire of Israel's leaders. In practice, however, Israel has never faced a practical dilemma where its leaders had to choose between an offer of a formal defense treaty with another state and a prospect of losing its autonomy to act when, where, and how it seemed fit. Nevertheless, the hypothetical possibility was often discussed in policy circles. The prevailing view has always been that Israel is better off keeping informal ties and defense cooperation with other nations rather than signing a binding alliance treaty. Israeli policymakers generally considered the liabilities of a defense pact—the constraints it would impose on Israel's freedom of action and the questionable reliability of even the friendliest state—to outweigh the benefits of such an alliance. A defense pact would contradict the other elements of Israel's security conception. Thus, Israel is seen to be better off without such an alliance than with it.

7. *The principle of cumulative deterrence.* Israel's long-term security doctrine rests on three principles: cumulative deterrence, limited military decision, and excessive use of force in both limited conflict settings and general wars. Israel cannot impose on the Arabs a peace through a massive and total military victory (Kober 1995); it can only hope to persuade the Arabs to accept peace due to their war weariness. The Arab states must come to understand that they cannot destroy Israel and that the price of continued conflict is more than they can bear. This implies that Israel has to brace for a protracted conflict punctuated by a—possibly large—number of short wars and limited encounters. The principle by which Israel can hope to convert over time the Arab motivation to continue the conflict into a readiness to make real peace with it is the concept of cumulative deterrence (Almog 2004, 1995; Bar Joseph 1998). Cumulative deterrence means successive and effective uses of force in both limited and massive military encounters. Such successful demonstrations of force are designed to convince the opponent of the futility of

military force in the long term. Cumulative deterrence assumes frequent failures of both general and specific deterrence.[4]

Whenever the more "conventional" form of deterrence fails, Israel must launch a decisive military operation that would bring about a relatively unambiguous military decision within a short time frame. In the cases of more limited challenges of low-intensity conflict (LIC) or limited military engagement, Israel should be able to dominate the process of escalation and maintain the strategic initiative, so as to bring the opponent to the point of exhaustion and defeat. The accumulation of what Almog (2004, 6) calls "assets in a victory bank" would serve to persuade the Arabs that they cannot win. As Lieberman (1995, 63) puts it: "Short-term deterrence failures may be a necessary condition for long-term deterrence success."

8. *The Samson Option.* This principle concerns ambiguous nuclear deterrence in situations of last resort. If conventional deterrence fails and Israel finds itself in a situation wherein it might be defeated in a major military confrontation, or if the Arabs engage in actions that threaten the very survival of Israel (e.g., use WMDs against population centers or basic infrastructures), Israel threatens to use its nuclear weapons. This threat is ambiguous, however, because Israel has never openly admitted to possession of nuclear weapons. The conception that Israel has sought to convey—through veiled threats and signals of various kinds—is that its nuclear weapons serve as an ultimate insurance policy designed to deter the annihilation of the state by massive force. Hersh's (1991) term—the Samson Option—is an apt characterization of the role of nuclear deterrence in Israel's security policy.

9. *Settlements as determinant of borders.* Israeli settlements will determine Israel's final boundaries. This tenet does not appear in the standard list of the basic tenets of Israel's security conception. It has become, however, a cornerstone of Israeli security conception both before the occupation of Arab territories in the Six Day War and even more so since 1967. Even before 1948, the leading Zionist leaders strongly believed that the outcome of any political settlement in Palestine would be determined by the demographic distribution of the ethnic groups residing in it. The drive to bring in Jewish immigrants and settle them in distant areas in an effort to form Jewish population centers in all parts of Palestine was due not only to the vision of Palestine as a Jewish homeland but also to the wish to affect the boundaries of the Jewish state. Settlements form a human and physical fait accompli. They show the determination of a nation to hold on to a given territory and signal to both friends and foes

that they will be defended by force. Thus, settlements were always seen as a pillar of national security.

Taken together, these nine tenets form a fairly coherent and stable national security conception. This conception was never published in an official document (and even when there was an attempt to frame it in terms of an official policy it was never approved by the cabinet or the presiding defense minister at the time; see chap. 11). Yet, there is enough official, semiofficial, and scholarly writing to suggest that this is the doctrine Israel has been using all along. The principal aims of this conception is to enable Israel to overcome the need to cope with fundamental threats to its survival on the one hand and to develop as a "normal" society that will attract Jews from all over the world on the other hand.

Both the assumptions on which this doctrine rests and the principles of which the doctrine is composed are part of a belief system shared by politicians, experts, and laypersons. However, they are neither valid as a description of objective reality nor accurate characterizations of Israel's actual behavior. In fact, I will show throughout this book that many of the foundational assumptions of these conceptions have been fairly removed from reality. I will also show that in many cases Israel violated its own doctrinal principles. In other cases, the rigidity of these doctrinal canons has been detrimental to Israel's security and welfare; some of these principles may well have undermined Israel's ability to make peace with its neighbors. At this point, however, my intent is to present the elements of Israel's security-related belief system as shared by most Israelis. This belief system serves as the basis for the evaluation of Israel's policies in the coming chapters.

3. ISRAELI SCHOLARSHIP ON NATIONAL SECURITY AND FOREIGN POLICY

This overview is intended as a way of positioning the present study in relation to other studies on the subject. I do not claim originality in most of what is covered in this book. Nor do I claim neutrality and perfect objectivity with respect to the issues I study. I make explicit observations about the wisdom, effectiveness, benefit, or even ethical standing of various policies. Because this is an evaluation study, I also make prescriptive points and normative judgments. Thus, it is important to be explicit about where this book stands in relation to the large and sometimes polarized literature on these topics.

The centrality of security affairs in Israeli society, politics, and economics is probably unparalleled in the world, certainly in the democratic world. Accordingly, the list of scholarly works on these matters is extremely large. Although we do not have a precise way of measuring it, it is plausible to assume that the number of per capita publications by Israelis on security and foreign policy far surpasses that of any other nation in the modern world.

Another book would be needed solely to review these publications. Therefore, I do not intend to even start doing that here. Rather, I wish to provide a very general characterization of this literature. I divide the literature into four classes of works: ideological, historical, analytical, and prescriptive. The boundaries among these categories are rather vague; many studies cross several classes. Nevertheless, each work—at least those I know and cite in the coming pages—tends to fall into one primary class or another.

3.1. The Ideological Literature

As with any ideological work, the studies belonging to this genre emerge primarily from a set of beliefs and seek to maximize or realize certain norms or values. These works have a marked target—a certain vision they seek to realize—and a marked path—a policy, position, or strategy they consider as most suitable, moral, or expedient for the realization of this vision. Typically, this literature does not deliberate very much on the nature of the vision—its morality, its consistency with other values or the values of other groups, and its internal logic and consistency. Nor does this literature consider, in many cases, alternative paths to accomplishing this vision. For the most part, this literature focuses on advocacy. Many of the programmatic writings of Zionist thinkers—for example, Jabotinsky's Iron Wall essays mentioned earlier—as well as the writings of other Israeli politicians belong to this genre. A few other works by scholars also fall into this category. I will mention just a few representative writings. They in no way reflect the entire spectrum, but they give the reader a general flavor of this literature.

Ideological writings on national security and foreign policy can be placed along a left-right (or, more accurately, along a hawkish-dovish) spectrum. A number of important writings of David Ben-Gurion (e.g., Ben-Gurion 1971, 1956) deal with Israel's security and foreign policy; Moshe Sharett—Israel's foreign minister under Ben-Gurion and the second prime minister—also wrote an ideological booklet (Sharett 1958). More recent works include Netanyahu's (2000) hawkish vision of Israel's international standing and Peres's (1993) vision of Israel in a regional system characterized by peace, development, and progress.

3.2. Historical Studies

The vast majority of the studies of Israel's security and foreign policy are historical. These range from accounts of distinct episodes to broad historical surveys of long periods, from autobiographies and biographies of political and military figures to case studies and accounts of specific episodes in Israel's history. The distinct characteristic of historical studies and biographies or autobiographies is that they tell a story of a period, an event, or an aspect thereof from the subjective perspective of the people who participated in them. Many of these works rely on primary sources, such as transcripts of government sessions, diplomatic and personal correspondence, and directives by various political and military officials to subordinates. These are supplemented by interviews with the key players in those episodes or secondary accounts by other scholars.

Over the last two decades, however, a growing number of works have raised critical issues about various aspects of Israel's history and the political and military management of its security. Many of these critical studies stem from a deliberately anti-institutionalist perspective. Many of them start out from a fundamentally different epistemological and ideological perspective. This alternative perspective challenges many of the fundamental axioms of the traditional historiography of Israel. These critical scholars are called "new historians" or "post-Zionist." Whatever their collective label, their writings have challenged conventional wisdom about a number of basic facts in Israel's history. For example, they challenged the widespread myth of a miraculous victory in the War of Independence. Israel, contrary to popular belief—supported by quite a few traditional historians—was not militarily inferior to the Arab states that had attacked it. On the contrary, at almost every step of the way, Israel enjoyed a significant advantage in both manpower and equipment (Flapan 1987; Pappe 1992). Second, in contrast to the belief that the Palestinian Arabs fled from Palestine during the War of Independence due to the urging of the Palestinian leadership, these historians showed that Israeli official and unofficial policy had encouraged and actually participated in driving out Palestinians of the areas it occupied during the war. Israel bears considerable responsibility—though hardly the exclusive blame—for the Palestinian refugee problem (Morris 2004). Third, the Jewish leadership in Palestine attempted to strike a number of deals with

King Abdullah of Transjordan in a "collusion" designed to solve the Palestinian problem between the Jewish state and Transjordan at the expense of the independent Palestinian state authorized by the UN partition resolution (Shlaim 1988). More general revisionist reviews of Israel's history include Shlaim's (2000) study of Israeli-Arab relations and Morris's (2001) and Kimmerling and Migdal's (2003) studies of Israeli-Palestinian relations.

Clearly, these departures from conventional writings invoked quite a few efforts to defend the institutional positions (Shapira 2003; Gelber 2003; Karsh 1997). Beyond the name calling and the personal attacks that these debates invariably entailed, the debate between traditional or institutional historians and revisionist historians revived Israeli historiography and rendered it more relevant socially. As new archives are being opened and new documents are being declassified, this debate is paradoxically intensifying. Many aspects of this debate are reflected in the coming chapters, but—as I point out in the next section—my perspective is going to be different in terms of both methodology and approach from both the revisionist and the institutional perspectives.

3.3. Analytic Studies

The focus of analytic studies is on the explanation of Israel's security and foreign policy. Such studies may be very general and cover a broad array of issues and problems, or they can be more specific—focusing on a specific issue, policy, or episode. In this case, too, the number of studies on security affairs far outweighs those on foreign policy. The single most comprehensive analytic study on Israel's foreign policy is Brecher 1972. Other books include Klieman's (1990) study of Israel's foreign relations and Shaham's (1998) survey of Israeli relations with the world. General work on Israel's strategic affairs includes studies by political and military decision makers (e.g., Allon 1968; Tal 2000) or by scholars (e.g., Yaniv 1995, 1987a; Handel 1995, 1973; Ben-Horin and Posen 1981; Levite 1989).

More specific analytic studies focus on such issues as decision making (Brecher 1975; Brecher, with Geist, 1980; Maoz 1997a); nuclear policy (Aronson, with Brosh, 1992; Evron 1994); limited use of force (Shimshoni 1988; Kuperman 1999, 2001); public opinion and national security (Arian 1995); or civil-military relations (Perlmutter 1969; Ben Meir 1995).

In this area, too, much of the literature in the past was primarily in line with the conventional wisdom shared by Israeli politicians and the security community. If there was criticism, it was directed at specific episodes or decisions. Not much of the criticism was structural. In addition, the literature was generally compartmentalized. Many of the studies focused on the level of the bureaucracy and the political elites. Not too many empirical and analytical connections were made between processes operating at the bureaucratic or political levels and wider social trends.

Here, too, in the last decade a growing number of Israeli political scientists and sociologists have started challenging conventional views, offering more structural connections between security and social processes. Traditional scholars emphasized the nation-building role of the military in Israeli society. The IDF was seen as the "melting pot," a major agent of socialization of immigrants from all over the world into the Israeli society. In the last decade, a group of sociologists provided a different perspective of the role of the IDF. This scholarship showed that the militarization of Israeli society by the leading political and economic elites served to advance economic and political interests of these elites and to perpetuate the stratification of the Israeli society (Barzilai 1996; Ben-Eliezer 1998; Levy 2003). Critical studies of Israel's legal system have also shown how the Israeli courts—notorious in Israel for their (sometimes excessive) liberalism—have actually served to legitimize the government's policy on security affairs largely at the expense of fundamental human rights and personal and collective liberties (Hofnung 1996; Kretzmer 2002; Barzilai 2003).

3.4. *Prescriptive Studies*

Prescriptive studies differ from ideological studies in that they do not have a specific ideological vision and a clearly preferred path to accomplishing it—at least not visibly so. Rather, these studies offer policy recommendation on the basis of a more analytic study of various policy problems and on the basis of consideration of several options toward redressing these problems. The prescriptive part of the study rests heavily on the analytic part of the study. Perhaps the most persistent scholar who emphasized prescriptive ideas is Yehezkel Dror (1989, 1998). Dror's work emphasizes both doctrinal and structural reforms in policy-making and in institutional design. Emmanuel Wald—a former senior officer in the IDF strategic planning branch—has been both an ardent critic and a passionate prescriber of reforms in military structures and doctrines and decision-making processes (1987, 1992). Milstein (1999), a highly conservative historian, offered a hawkish security doctrine. Feldman (1983) proposed an overt nuclear deterrence policy for Israel, while Evron (1994) supports continued nuclear ambiguity.

The prescriptive studies are highly analytic, but their analysis is—for the most part—based on rather limited examination of historical and empirical data. Most studies have been rather narrowly focused on one or a few issue areas, and most of them have made a fairly clear distinction between domestic or social issues and foreign or security issues. In this genre, we do not find clear revisionist alternatives to the fairly mainstream prescriptions of much of the existing literature.

How does the present book relate to the existing literature? First, it builds on all four classes of work. It considers and employs both traditional approaches to Israel's history and revisionist ones. It considers both mainstream analytic studies and more critical studies. It considers in passing ideological works only to examine perceptions of leaders but does not delve too much into the psychological or philosophical roots of these writings. And it also considers some of the ideas embedded in the prescriptive writings.

Second, the book's approach differs from most of the literature on Israel's security and foreign policy in that it attempts to provide a comprehensive and critical assessment of Israel's national security and foreign policy. Its distinguishing characteristics are fourfold:

1. This book's starting point is evaluative. It attempts to examine the extent to which the goals of Israel's security and foreign policy have been served by its doctrines, policy decisions, and actions. It attempts to understand the logic behind the grand strategies (to the extent that such strategies existed) or specific policies. At the same time I match the underlying—overt and hidden—goals of certain policies with their implementation and with their consequences. I also apply policy evaluation criteria to examine these policies, as well as their side effects.

2. The book's approach is critical. It challenges the fundamental assumptions that have guided the founding fathers of Israel's national security and foreign policy and their successors. It suggests that these assumptions were not matched with the empirical realities in the region. In many cases, gloomy assumptions about Israel's strategic environments, held by Israeli decision makers, had self-fulfilling properties. They forced Israel to act in a manner that exacerbated regional conflicts and raised the costs of such conflicts both for Israel and for its opponents.

3. The book ties together different aspects of Israel's foreign and security policy that have not traditionally been connected in other studies on

the subject in an attempt to find an overarching logic and common strands across issues and policies.

4. The book connects history, policy, theory, and methodology in a manner that I describe as "strategic." This approach seeks to integrate these fields under a common roof in order to enhance our ability to understand processes and to evaluate them. It uses history in an attempt to understand policies and events from the perspective of the participants. It uses theory to put these perspectives and actions in a more general and abstract context that looks for patterns and logic behind seemingly unexplained or unrelated issues. In this context, it attempts to uncover and explain basic trends and patterns in Israeli foreign and security policies. Finally, I examine the relationship among basic assumptions, plans, policies, actions, and outcomes from the end to the beginning. This approach allows us to assess the quality of policies, to derive lessons, and to offer amendments to existing policies or alternative ones.

In order to explain how I plan to integrate history, policy, theory, and methodology in an effort to evaluate various aspects of Israel's national security and foreign policy-making, I discuss the general approach and methodology of this study in the next section. Readers who are interested in the substance of the book may skip the next section without significant loss.

4. EVALUATING POLICY: THEORETICAL AND METHODOLOGICAL CONSIDERATIONS

4.1. *An Outline of the Evaluation Methodology*

The purpose of this book is primarily evaluative. To evaluate Israeli national security and foreign policy, we must understand the connection between the goals of Israeli decision makers and the policies they pursued. We need to explore the connection between the policies and their—intended and unintended—outcomes. This would enable us to explain why some policies succeeded while other failed. The key aim of policy evaluation is to draw lessons from these successes and failures so that policy can be improved. But beyond that, a closer inspection of various policies may give us a better look at the underlying logic of policy-making across a large number of issues. If we find common patterns in how policies are made across issues, we may be able to develop a more general understanding of policy problems and pitfalls. Similar disconnects among policy objectives, policy choices, policy implementation, and policy outcomes suggest structural problems. If such structural problems exist, their identification and treatment may improve policy across a large number of issue areas.

It is important to note at the outset that the best process of policy evaluation is conducted as part and parcel of the policy-making and policy implementation process (Mark, Henry, and Julnes 2000; Nagel 1998). Ideally, when a policy is planned, a program and methodology designed to evaluate its performance and outcomes is attached. This program is applied in parallel to the implementation of the policy and provides policymakers an ongoing feedback on how this policy performs with respect to their goals and objectives. Such feedback allows decision makers to fix bugs in the policy as it is implemented. This minimizes damage to the policy, reduces expenses, and allows policy shifts if it turns out that the policy is not the right one. Unfortunately, a policy evaluation of this kind is not applicable in our case. Most of the policies we examine in this book were applied a long time ago. Most of them have never been fully evaluated; and many of them have not been evaluated at all. What we can do is engage in second-best evaluation strategies, those that are done in retrospect. In this section I discuss how I intend to apply retrospective evaluation to Israeli national security and foreign policy.

Policies are designed to solve problems. Thus, evaluating a public policy must be based first on inspecting the problem that it is intended to solve. Once we understand the nature of the problem, it is possible to specify the goals that the policy is designed to accomplish. In light of these goals, it is then possible to assess the policy in terms of whether and to what extent it was instrumental in accomplishing its stated objectives. However, the evaluation of a public policy in terms of its direct effects on the original problem is incomplete. A policy may have side effects, that is, consequences that were not part of the key goals of the policy but that nevertheless were affected by its implementation (Leeuw 1995; Mohr 1995; Nachmias 1979). Finally, as in the case of administering medicine to a patient, it is important to assess whether the medicine does more damage than good and whether the patient would have fared better without it than with it.

Methodologically, the preferred design for policy evaluation is the comparative interrupted time-series design wherein two groups are compared over time: a "control" group and an "experimental" group. Both groups are identical in all aspects but one. The control group is one on which the policy (or treatment) is not administered, whereas the experimental group is the one on which the policy is administered. Each group is examined prior to the implementation of the policy, during the implementation process, and after it is implemented. The impact of the policy on the experimental groups is assessed both in terms of a before-after comparison and in terms of comparison to the control group.

In strategic affairs (in contrast to domestic policy areas), the evaluation of policies—certainly of grand strategic undertakings—is a difficult task. One of the key problems concerns the difficulty in examining the impact of an alternative—counterfactual—policy on a given historical process (Mohr 1995, chap. 1).[5] Clearly, this evaluation design is irrelevant here. However, other evaluation schemes can be applied. For example, we can use an (interrupted time-series) analysis that entails a comparison of the problem before the policy was implemented to the situation after the policy was applied (Mohr 1995; Nachmias 1979; Nagel 1998). This design uses the goals of the policy as the guiding evaluation standard. It looks at the characteristics of the problem—for example, the magnitude, the frequency with which the problem occurs, or the costs due to the policy problem—before the policy is implemented. It then treats the implementation of the policy as the "interruption" due to treatment. Finally, it examines the outcomes of the policy—both the direct outcomes and the side effects. It then compares the postpolicy features of the problem to the prepolicy features.

While it is impossible to tell from this kind of analysis whether the policy that was actually applied was the "super optimal" one (Nagel 1998, 10–12), other—quite significant—observations can be made. First, it is possible to say whether and to what extent the policy that was applied accomplished its goals. Second, it is possible to evaluate the extent to which the postpolicy features of the problems were reduced in comparison to the prepolicy features. Third, the analysis of side effects can tell us a great deal about the extent of the decision makers' foresight and about other outcomes of the policy that can serve as additional—exogenous—criteria for evaluating the policy.

We cannot say what would have happened to the problem if no policy or an alternative policy had been implemented. But we can glean from these observations other conclusions about the quality of the policy. First, we know that there is something problematic about the policy if it did not accomplish its objectives. If the magnitude, severity, frequency, or costs of the problem after the implementation of the policy are similar to or

higher than the same features of the problem before the policy was implemented, then we can reasonably argue that the policy was problematic.
Finally, even if the policy remedied some aspects of the original problem
but—at the same time—generated adverse side effects, then the policy is
problematic. Thus, the direct benefits of a given policy must be analyzed
in relation to its side effects.

When a policy accomplished its professed goals, and when some or all
of the features of the problem are redressed by the policy, a positive evaluation cannot be ruled out even if there may be a more efficient and effective alternative policy. Thus, in both cases—when the policy seems to
have accomplished its objectives and when it did not—it is possible to
make at least a limited assessment of the value of the policy.

So when looking at an event—such as a war—or a policy—such as
nuclear policy or peace diplomacy—from an evaluative perspective, we
need to identify several elements.

1. *The nature of the problem and its features.* What were the key problems that the decision makers faced? Answering this question not only
requires examining how the decision makers perceived the problem (as
one would attempt if one wanted to conduct historical or analytical
research that attempts to explain how a policy was selected) but also
requires exploring the "objective" features of the problem. Sometimes
there may be a gap between the decision maker's understanding of the
problem and the actual parameters of the policy dilemma. Problematic
policies may be selected because decision makers think they want to
resolve a problem whose features are rather different from the ones they
need to address. Such gaps often results in adverse side effects of the policy that is eventually selected. Understanding the problem requires
examining its key parameters. How severe was the problem? With what
frequency did it occur? What kind of damage or what extent of cost did it
inflict on the decision makers (or, in our case, on the state of Israel)?
What were the expected implications of the problem if it were not
addressed?

In the realm of politics in general, and in foreign and security policy-
making in particular, understanding problems strictly in terms of what
decision makers say they are may be misleading. Very often decision makers frame problems in ways that are convenient for them, hiding features
of the problem that they do not feel comfortable verbalizing. For example, decision makers very rarely admit that they applied public policies to
address domestic political problems (such as slippage in polls and pressure
from interest groups). So, the problem identification stage must go

beyond the decision maker's account; we must probe deeper into the context in which the policy arises and apply objective criteria to evaluate policy problems.

2. *The objectives of the decision makers.* Beyond the stated objectives of a given policy, we need to go below the verbal surface to identify hidden goals and agendas that affect policy selection. The policy objectives are clearly the benchmark against which the outcomes of the policy must be evaluated. Therefore, hidden objectives are important parameters that need to be identified. Sometimes decision makers may continue to pursue policies that do not appear to resolve the publicly stated problems and that do not accomplish their professed goals. They might do it because the policy seems to be effective in addressing hidden goals and to resolve unstated problems.

3. *The logic connecting the specific policy to the—stated and unstated—objectives.* We must understand just how the policy was supposed to accomplish the—explicit and hidden—objectives set forth by the decision makers. If we cannot stipulate a logical connection between a given policy and stated objectives, it is possible that this policy was supposed to address hidden objectives. The opposite, however, is not necessarily true. There may be a straightforward logical connection between a policy and a set of explicitly stated goals. This does not preclude the presence of a hidden agenda. Therefore, we must be careful to articulate all possible connections between the policy and the objectives of the decision makers. This allows us to trace decision makers' expectations from a given policy. This should help us connect the policy to its intended or unintended outcomes. Policy outcomes that are not in line with these expectations are treated as side effects.

4. *The process of policy implementation.* Very often there exist gaps between the intended and actual implementation of policies, even at the most crucial moments in a nation's life (Allison and Zelikow 1999, 158–60). The road to the public policy hell may be paved with particularly good intentions, much more so than in other areas. Therefore, it is important to separate poor policy planning and policy design from poor policy implementation. In strategic studies, the Clausewitzian concept of "friction" refers to factors operating beyond the control of the decision makers, which may affect the outcome of the decision. A good policy takes friction into account, but no matter how well a policy is designed it cannot foresee or take account of all friction-related problems. Thus, it is important to separate policy problems that result from unanticipated friction from problems that result from poor planning or poor implementation.

It is also important to separate policy problems from paradoxes (Maoz 1990b, 9–21). In a policy context, a paradox is defined as "a causally-induced contradiction between expectations and the consequences of behavior resulting from them" (13). This means that a policy that is tailored to generate outcomes that are in line with a set of expectations produces contradictory results. The key feature of paradoxes is that they are typically unsolvable; decision makers cannot afford to pursue different policies even if they know that the consequences of the policies they do pursue are the opposite of those they want to accomplish. To avoid paradoxes, decision makers need to revise the entire logical system upon which a policy relies—including reassessment of their objectives, the underlying assumptions, and the logical connections between goals and policies. Implementation of a policy that is paradoxical in nature would yield adverse results almost by definition. Identifying a paradoxical policy is therefore an important issue in evaluating it.

5. *Analysis of direct outcomes and side effects.* Identifying the outcomes of the policy is probably the most important operation of the evaluation process. Part of this step is straightforward: policy outcomes are defined in terms of the parameters of the problem that the policy was designed to solve and in terms of the policy objectives. Did the policy reduce the manifestation of the problem, its magnitude, severity, or frequency? Did the policy accomplish the goals it was designed to achieve? This, in essence, is the before-after comparison. Positive results—that is, the parameters of the problem after the implementation of the policy are less severe than before—suggest that the policy was not a bad one. It may not have been the best policy (because we did not compare its results to the results of other policies that have not been applied), but it certainly is not a deficient policy. Likewise, if the before-after comparison yields negative results—the policy did not accomplish its objectives or the parameters of the problem did not change for the better or have even gotten worse—then the policy is problematic. This is so even though it may have been a better policy than any conceivable alternative.

Side effects are more difficult to identify and evaluate. It is more difficult to establish a direct connection between a given outcome and a policy if this outcome was not part of the problem that the policy was supposed to address. Likewise, if a given outcome is not a direct part of the intended policy objectives, it is not immediately obvious that it was affected by the policy. Nevertheless, in many situations it is possible to identify a causal link between a policy and an outcome, even if it had not been intended. This is so if policymakers or scholars who study the policy establish such a link in their statements and writings. In this case, the evaluation is done in terms of the effect this outcome has on the general goals of the decision makers. An outcome may be termed good or bad not in terms of the direct objectives assigned to the policy (otherwise it would not be identified as a side effect); rather, it may be evaluated in terms of more general objectives, such as security, peace, welfare, and economic stability.

The key problem in this analysis of outcomes concerns possible discrepancies between the direct outcomes of the policy and its side effects. If the direct outcomes and the side effects of the policy point to the same direction (both are positive or both are negative), then this problem of evaluating the policy does not arise. Yet, in many cases, a policy may have positive results, in that it accomplishes its goals and/or remedies the problem it was designed to solve. At the same time it generates side effects that are negative. Conversely, a policy may have negative results in terms of the problems it was designed to solve, but it has positive side effects. How do we evaluate the outcomes of this policy? There is no simple answer to that question. Any physician who prescribes a medicine that has side effects needs to grapple with this kind of dilemma. The rule of thumb in this kind of situation is to prescribe the less damaging treatment overall. If the direct outcomes of a policy were more substantial in terms of their impact on the goals of the decision makers than the side effects, then the direct outcomes offset the side effects. And if the side effects were more substantial than the direct outcomes, then the side effects offset the direct outcomes. The idea then is to subtract the value of the side effects from the value of the direct results of the policy. Net evaluation therefore is based on this difference between direct and indirect policy outcomes (weighted—of course—by the relative importance of each of the policy outcomes).

6. *Assessment of general tendencies and trends.* Since I am concerned here with several policy issues, I identify common denominators across different policies. While the evaluation is done with respect to each policy taken in isolation, I identify common patterns across policies. If such common denominators exist, and if they are related to common policy problems, then we may well be dealing with structural policy hazards. A remedy for a given policy would probably not be effective as a systemic corrective mechanism; the system as a whole must be somehow reformed. If, however, no general trend exists, then each set of problems on a given policy requires a specific solution that is custom tailored to the specific issue area in which they arise.

This approach could be applied systematically if a policy is in place for a long time and if it is applied in a fairly consistent manner. Several policies that are discussed in this book render themselves to a more analytic application of such an evaluation: Israel's nuclear policy, Israel's use of limited force, Israel's peace diplomacy, and Israel's covert intervention in Arab affairs. In other cases a more limited evaluation will be attempted, because policies have been more ad hoc in nature and their results differed from one case to another. Nevertheless, the general approach outlined previously will be applied to all policies and events discussed in this book. In some cases—for example, in the case of Israeli covert diplomacy of intervention in the internal affairs of Arab states or in the case of Israel's peace diplomacy—I will offer specific evaluation criteria as I discuss these policies.

4.2. The Strategic Perspective versus the Historical Perspective

I have already mentioned briefly the differences between the strategic perspective and the historical perspective, but it is important to elaborate on the general approach I take in this study. We must differentiate the strategic approach from the historical perspective that many analysts have used, even when their studies attempted explanation rather than description. The strategic approach that I employ in this study uses history in a somewhat roundabout and perhaps devious manner. Historians attempt to understand what happened in terms of the perspective of the participants in the events and processes they study. In a manner of speaking, a good historian identifies with his or her characters. The better the ability to identify and "enter into the mind" of one's characters, the more accurate and genuine the historical account. For a historian there is no counterfactual reality (except if the characters had considered alternative realities in their discussions and writings); he or she sees only what the characters taking part in the events saw.

A good historian does not judge his or her characters; he or she must understand them. This is so even if the values, visions, aspirations, and beliefs of the characters are fundamentally different from those of the historian. A good historical analysis is not only one in which the cast of characters is authentic; it is one that captures the "spirit of the time," the mood, the mentality, the way of thinking, and the social atmosphere that engulfs the characters. In a manner of speaking, a good historian creates both authentic characters and authentic scenes. It is typically not acceptable to judge characters in terms of values, principles, and standards that are not part of the period or of the environment in which they lived and operated. A good historical analysis may be critical of the characters included in it. However, this criticism must be based on an understanding of the beliefs, values, and information available to the characters and on the spirit of the time. The principal goal of the historian is to understand what happened and why.

In contrast, the principal goal of the strategist is to derive lessons from what has happened in the past in order to improve or change behavior in the future. The strategist plays the role of a Monday morning quarterback or of a coach who looks at a video of a football game to learn the mistakes of the teams. The strategist attempts to understand not only what the cast of characters knew, believed, thought, and wanted and how these things were translated into action. He or she must also understand what it was they should have known, how they should have considered their reality, and *how they should have acted*. The strategist must impose the wisdom of hindsight to derive lessons, thus constantly criticizing, judging, and evaluating the actual behavior of the characters.

The historian's insights can extend only as far as the documents allow him or her to go. He or she is not supposed to make inferences on the basis of things that were not said or written. The strategist cannot work without written or verbal documentation of events, but he or she is not bound by them. Strategic analysis requires moving beyond the available documentation; it requires making inferences on the basis of the evidence that goes beyond the evidence. The strategist must figure out not only what happened but also what did not happen and what should or could have happened had people acted differently. The historian cannot be diverted by counterfactuals; the strategist cannot do without them. Clearly, the task of the strategist is far more complicated and tricky than that of the historian, because the strategist must impose some basic assumptions in the analysis that the historian need not use. For example, strategic analysis must rely on the assumption of rationality. This does not mean that strategists assume that political and military decision makers are invariably rational. Rather, strategists must assume that rationality is a normative benchmark for evaluating actual behavior (Maoz 1990b, 5–6, 327–29). Examining actual behavior in terms of whether and to what extent it deviated from what should have been the rational behavior helps the strategist in the task of policy evaluation. It serves as a foundation for policy prescriptions that are based on the analysis of historical events and processes.

Finally, for the historian time moves in a linear sequence, from the more remote past to the more recent past (and in some cases to the pres-

ent). The timeline of the historical narrative is an important element in
the explanation of events; the order of things is a key determinant of
cause and effect. For the strategist, the order of things may sometimes be
reversed. Very often, the last event is the first thing that the strategist
examines, because this tends to be the outcome, just as the end of the
game is the starting point of the coach's or the analyst's examination. The
strategist often works backward, from the last to the first event. The por-
trayal of events, the linkages between them, and the outcomes to which
they lead may often be used by the strategist to uncover unseen patterns,
goals, considerations, and complex—sometimes paradoxical—relationships between intentions and outcomes. In some of the chapters, I challenge the more conventional explanations of certain historical events by
using this kind of approach. I show that it is unlikely that decision makers pursued certain goals or strategies—typically attributed to them in
historical analysis—given the kind of behavior they displayed. Starting
from these discrepancies, I reconstruct different goals or strategies that
make more sense given the observed behavior, and I show a better consistency between these hidden goals or agendas and behavioral patterns.

Embedding an evaluative perspective within a strategic conception
makes this study particularly complex and controversial. I evaluate several things that are bound to raise questions. First, I question the goals of
the decision makers. Historians that rely solely on available documentation may miss some hidden goals because they are not expressed in writing or in oral addresses. The strategic approach and the assumption of
some level of rationality—at least in the sense that decision makers consistently try to match policy with some objectives—establish some logical
grounds by which I can challenge expressed motives and goals in a way
that historians might find it difficult to do. Second, I question the notion
of uniqueness of explanations. The fact that a given behavior has a good
explanation in terms of the prevailing circumstances and the ad hoc calculus of decision makers does not make this explanation sufficient or even
best. If a pattern of behavior is repeated across issue areas and circumstances, then a more general explanation is required. Of course, not all
behavior assumes generalizable patterns. And even things that may
appear to be part of a pattern may be just a random set of discrete events.
But there is reason to suggest that patterns are observed due to some more
general processes and considerations. In trying to trace patterns and
explain them in more general terms I depart from the historical analysis
yet again by building bridges across events, issue areas, policy domains,
and time periods. These bridges allow me to make some general observa-

tions about the structure and process of Israel's national security and foreign policy. Hopefully, these observations, even if they turn out to be controversial, may inspire debate and discussion among both interested observers and professional participants.

A word about data sources is essential. The study relies on a number of data sets that were compiled by the project Quantitative History of the Arab-Israeli Conflict (QHAIC), which I developed when I served as head of the Jaffee Center for Strategic Studies at Tel Aviv University. Additional data that I have used are referenced by their sources. Much of the actual material I use and most of the discussion in the book are based on historical material, primary and secondary sources. The nature of the issues I discuss in this book is such that the analysis is necessarily case based and qualitative. In some instances, however, I rely on quantitative data. These data help shed more systematic light on the substantive points that are based on a more traditional qualitative analysis. More sophisticated statistical analyses of some of the policies discussed in this book will appear in journal articles.

A final methodological note concerns objectivity. Readers of the following chapters will undoubtedly discover that Israeli policies are sharply criticized. Evidence of both deliberate aggressive designs and deficient policies that are due to incompetence and folly is amply provided in the following pages. Since much of the book is centered on the Arab-Israeli conflict, one may justly ask, What about the Arabs? Isn't it possible that, however problematic Israel's policies have been, much of what happened over the course of the Arab-Israeli conflict is due to far more incompetent, aggressive, and short-sighted policies of the Arab states and the Palestinians? It is impossible to provide a truly objective evaluation of Israel's policies without addressing the interactions between these policies and the policies employed by the Arab states and by the Palestinians. A book that evaluates just Israeli policies without attempting to evaluate the other side is not only unfair; it is scientifically suspicious because it provides a one-sided picture of reality.

There is no question—at least in my mind—that the Arabs have been far more incompetent, short sighted, and malicious than have been the Israelis. In fact, I repeatedly make this argument throughout the book. In chapter 13, I show the effect of the malice, folly, and incompetence of Arab leaders on Arab states and societies and argue that much of Israel's success in state building was due to Arab folly and incompetence. This, however, does not diminish the responsibility of Israel for its own policies. On the contrary, it makes Israel's mistakes more pronounced. It is one thing to make bad security policy when you confront a highly competent and resourceful adversary. In such cases, at least some of the blame can be attributed not to your incompetence but to the adversary's behavior. But if policies are bad in the face of incompetent adversaries, then there is something seriously wrong with them. Playing against a strong and competent football team with a strong defense would cause even a highly skilled offense to fumble the ball or be intercepted. A good offense on the opponent side would penetrate even a competent defensive side. Yet, fumbling the ball and throwing interceptions against a weak defense or letting a weak offensive rival gain significant yardage suggests significant problems in one's game, even if our side won.

More important, Arab mistakes do not explain why Israeli policies were deficient across so many issue areas and why these deficient policies are not fixed and thus recur despite clearly adverse results. I will come back to these points toward the end of the book. At this point, however, it is important to acknowledge the limitation of this analysis—due to its focus on Israeli policies and its limited treatment of Arab policies. It is also imperative that we make it clear that Arab folly cannot absolve Israeli decision makers from responsibility for their mistakes and for repeating these mistakes so many times and across so many issues.

5. AN OVERVIEW OF THE BOOK

This book focuses on several key questions that address various aspects of Israel's security and foreign policy.

1. What are the key characteristics of the Israeli use of—massive and limited—force? What were the objectives underlying the policies of military force? What functions did various strategies of using force serve? Have the objectives of various strategies of high-intensity conflict and LIC been accomplished? What accounts for the pattern and outcome of Israeli strategies of using military force?

2. What were the goals of Israel's nuclear policy? What was the underlying strategic logic behind the development of Israel's nuclear weapons and the policy of nuclear ambiguity? To what extent where these goals accomplished? What are the—intended and unintended—strategic implications of this policy?

3. What is the pattern of Israeli covert and overt intervention in the internal affairs of the Arab states and the Palestinians? What func-

tions were these interventions intended to serve? Did they accomplish their intended objectives?

4. What are the principal characteristics of Israel's peace diplomacy over time? Has Israel—as its leaders claimed—persistently extended its hand for peace only to be repeatedly rejected by the Arabs? Has Israel been as daring in its peace diplomacy as it has been in its military strategy, or has Israel been risk averse when it comes to negotiating peace agreements that entail security risks? What factors account for the principal characteristics of Israel's policy?

5. Are there structural similarities across different areas of policy? Are the key patterns of the Israeli use of force and their underlying reasons similar to those that characterize Israel's overt and covert diplomacy? Are there structural factors that explain similar patterns of behavior in different areas of policy? If so, what are these factors?

6. If significant problems are identified in Israel's national security and foreign policy, how can we account for Israel's successful performance in military, economic, and social affairs despite enormous security challenges?

7. What are the implications of these patterns in Israel's national security and foreign policy for the future of the Middle East and for Israel's place in the region?

The book is divided into five parts that address these questions. Part I—the present chapter—lays out the foundations of the analysis. What follows is a brief outline of the contents and key themes of the book.

5.1. Part II: The Use of Force

Part II discusses the logic, pattern, process, and implications of the Israeli use of force over time. The major theme is that most of the wars in which Israel was involved were the result of deliberate Israeli aggressive design, flawed decision making, or flawed conflict management strategies or were avoidable. Israel's war experience is a story of folly, recklessness, and self-made traps. None of the wars—with a possible exception of the 1948 War of Independence—was what Israel refers to as *Milhemet Ein Brerah* ("war of necessity"). They were all wars of choice or wars of folly. Israel's limited use of force strategy emphasized escalation dominance and excessive force. This policy was also largely ineffective. In some cases it caused major escalation, while in other cases it did not prevent terrorism or LIC. Despite this tragic experience, no self-inspection took place in Israeli security policy. Many cases of both high-intensity conflict and LIC were due to mismanagement at both the military and the political level, reflected lack of proper political oversight over the actions of the IDF, and avoided a sober assessment of the benefits and liabilities of the excessive reliance on military force to manage the conflict with the Arabs.

Chapter 2 examines the origins of the 1956 Sinai War. This war was the result of the persistent drive of Ben-Gurion and Dayan to a second confrontation with the Arabs. The Sinai War was unavoidable because Israel sought every avenue to start a war. Domestic opposition—principally Moshe Sharett—prevented the initiation of a war sooner. Once Sharett was removed from office, there was no domestic opposition to the war coalition in the cabinet and the IDF. Nasser helped Israel by providing it with both a strategic pretext (i.e., the Egyptian-Soviet weapons deal of September 1955) and a diplomatic pretext (i.e., the nationalization of the Suez Canal on July 26, 1956) that enabled the collusion with France and Britain. The aim of the war was none of the official reasons given by Israel. Rather, it had been the overthrow of Nasser and the rearrangement of the Middle East. In this regard, the operation backfired.

Chapter 3 focuses on the causes and course of the Six Day War of 1967. It discusses three "conventional" explanations of the outbreak of the Six Day War. The domestic politics explanation focuses on internal determinants of the Israeli, Syrian, and Egyptian policies that brought about the crisis and led to its escalation. The inadvertent war explanation focuses on the dynamics of mutual deterrence and crisis management that have been applied to avoid war but have backfired. The psychological slippery slope explanation focuses on the emotional and cognitive aspects of crisis decision making in Cairo and in Jerusalem, arguing that stress, wishful thinking, and misperception drove the parties into a war nobody wanted. In contrast to these explanations, I argue that the origins of the war can be found in Israeli adventurist policy vis-à-vis Syria, the lack of proper political control over the military, and domestic political competition in Israel. These same factors put enormous pressure on the government during the crisis and the war itself, bringing about a process of unwanted escalation and expansion of the war beyond the original intentions of the political elites. The implications of these events have been far reaching in terms of the Arab-Israeli conflict to the very day.

Chapter 4 examines the War of Attrition of 1969–70. It traces the origins of the war to two principal factors: the Israeli decision to deploy its forces on, and prohibit shipping in, the Suez Canal and the lack of interest in a political settlement following the Arab summit in Khartoum.

Despite the fact that Nasser did plan for and consciously decided on a war of attrition by mid-1968, Israel's deployment along the canal and its excessive use of force caused this war to exact heavy costs from both Israel and Egypt and brought Israel to a head-on collision with Soviet soldiers, eventually driving it to an uneasy cease-fire. In this chapter I also evaluate the Israeli policy of deep penetration bombing in the context of the prevalent tendency of Israeli strategy to overreact to uses of force by the Arabs. I argue that this approach was especially self-deceiving. Not only did it cause major escalation of the war, but it also generated a false sense that this campaign compelled Egypt into accepting the cease-fire, thereby enhancing Israeli deterrence. In fact, it caused just the opposite.

Chapter 5 examines the 1973 Yom Kippur War. If there was an unnecessary and avoidable war in the Middle East, the Yom Kippur War was it. This is a prime example of where a little bit of diplomatic foresight and a little less political and military arrogance could have prevented the most severe war in the Middle East since 1948. This chapter does not discuss the diplomatic fiasco in failing to prevent the war (this is discussed in chap. 10). Rather, it focuses on the confusion and mismanagement of Israeli military strategy after the War of Attrition. The leading theme in the extant literature on the war is that the key folly in this war, from an Israeli perspective, was a major intelligence failure. In contrast, I argue that the key Israeli faults were in trying to fight the old war under entirely different strategic, topographic, and political conditions. The IDF failed in understanding the doctrine of the Egyptians and Syrians, failed to apply its own operational plans, and misused its air force during the first few days of the war. Had it not been for major political blunders by the Egyptian and Syrian leaders and for the support of the United States, Israel would have suffered a humiliating defeat. Even so, the costs of war were far higher than they should have been had Israel used its strategy properly and its forces effectively.

Chapter 6 focuses on Israel's invasion of Lebanon and the long-term occupation of parts of this country over the 1982–2000 period. This war was the outgrowth of a grand design of Ariel Sharon that sought to kill four birds with one war: first, to destroy the political and military capacity of the Palestinian Liberation Organization (PLO) so as to kill nationalist Palestinian sentiments in the West Bank and Gaza Strip; second, to humiliate and defeat the Syrian forces in Lebanon and to drive them out of that country; third, to create a Christian-dominated state in Lebanon that would, fourth, sign a peace treaty with Israel. I trace the evolution of the grand scheme from its beginning to the tragic conclusion of the unilateral Israeli withdrawal from Lebanon in May 2000. I examine the manner in which Sharon manipulated the cabinet as well as the entire Israeli society into a deep and long-lasting trap. I analyze the process of entrapment in the Lebanese swamp and the establishment of the security zone in southern Lebanon. This process of entrapment was facilitated by the evolution of an ideology led by the IDF regarding the strategic importance of the security zone. Finally, I discuss how a process started by a nonpartisan group of Knesset members, as well as a small pressure group of several women, brought about a withdrawal from Lebanon despite the resistance of the IDF. I examine why the political and social systems of oversight and control failed to save Israel from the long-term process of entrapment and the repeated military failures in Lebanon.

Chapter 7 examines the strategic and tactical logic of Israel's never-ending struggle against terrorists and guerrillas. It focuses on several facets of this policy: limited military actions against Arab states, LIC in a context of guerrilla war, the struggle against terrorism, and strategies for dealing with mass protests by Palestinians. I first discuss the evolution of Israel's limited conflict strategies over time. On the basis of this discussion the chapter offers a critical examination of the effectiveness of these policies and their political, moral, and strategic ramifications. I argue that many of these policies have been notoriously unsuccessful yet most of them continue to be employed by force of inertia. The most effective measures were the least popular ones, and the most popular measures, which entailed excessive use of force and punishment, turned out to be the least effective ones. I examine the different functions of limited use of force policies, arguing that in many cases limited force strategies were used to foster escalation and to bring about high-intensity shooting wars. In other cases, the mismanagement of limited engagements resulted in inadvertent escalation to full-blown wars. The factors that motivated Israeli uses of limited force were varied, and many of them involved domestic political and social considerations.

5.2. Part III: Israel's Nuclear Policy

Chapter 8 evaluates Israeli nuclear policy from its inception to the present. Most students of this policy rated it as an unqualified strategic success. Specifically, the policy is said to have effectively deterred an all-out Arab attack, while the posture of nuclear ambiguity allowed Israel to maintain strong strategic ties with the United States and to fend off pressures for joining the Non-Proliferation Treaty (NPT) regime. In addition, the policy is said to have generated two positive side effects. First, it is thought to have effected a shift in Arab operational planning from general to limited war scenarios. Second, it is considered to have been instrumental in bringing the Arab states to direct negotiations and to peace agreements with Israel.

My analysis suggests that the evidence upon which these arguments rely is tenuous at best. Israel's nuclear policy did not deter the Arabs from attacking it; nor is there evidence that it imposed limitations on Arab operational planning. Finally, both Israel's cumulative conventional deterrence and—more important—increased Israeli flexibility following the Yom Kippur War were far more significant factors in the Arab-Israeli peace process than Israel's nuclear policy. On the other hand, Israel's nuclear policy had several adverse side effects. First, it was a major factor in accelerating a conventional arms race and in igniting a nonconventional arms race in the Middle East. Second, the regime of secrecy surrounding it prevents an open and reasoned debate about its stabilizing and destabilizing features. In sum, the balance sheet of Israel's nuclear policy appears to be negative rather than positive. In light of this evidence I argue that Israel should use its nuclear policy as an important bargaining chip in bringing about a weapons of mass destruction free zone (WMDFZ) in the Middle East, in the context of a comprehensive regional security regime.

5.3. *Part IV: Foreign Policy: Shadow and Open Diplomacy*

Chapter 9 examines Israeli intervention in intra-Arab affairs. Israeli intervention in the internal affairs of other Arab states and the Palestinians has been quite frequent and has taken on many forms over the years. Yet this policy has not been systematically explored within the more general context of this nation's security policy. The chapter reviews the logic underlying the policy of clandestine and overt intervention in the internal affairs of Arab states. It examines the history of these efforts since the 1953–54 "mishap"—the activation of a spy network in Egypt in an effort to sabotage the British intention to pull its forces from Egypt—to the efforts to suppress Hamas following the Oslo Accords (1993–2000). I review the underlying logic of action in each of these cases and the implications of interventionist policies for Israeli-Arab relations and for Israel's security. The argument is that this interventionist policy was pursued persistently despite the fact that not one instance contributed significantly to Israel's security. On the contrary, in most cases the policy of intervention backfired, damaging Israeli-Arab relations, and even resulted in unintended consequences directly opposite to those intended.

The implications of these arguments for Israel's future security policy are examined in the concluding section.

Chapter 10 examines Israeli peace diplomacy as a series of missed opportunities. I argue that over time Israel was as responsible for the lack of peace with Arab states as were the Arabs themselves. In the process, Israel has gradually been forced to accept agreements that it could have accepted at lower cost and under better terms than it did eventually. I review a number of peace-related opportunities ranging from the Zionist-Hashemite collusion in 1947 through the collapse of the Oslo process in 2000. In all those cases I find that Israeli decision makers—who had been willing to embark upon bold and daring military adventures—were extremely reluctant to make even the smallest concessions for peace, sometimes insisting on minor and insignificant issues to the point where such stubborn positions brought about the collapse of carefully designed peace processes. I also find that in many cases Israel was engaged in systematic violations of agreements and tacit understandings between itself and its neighbors. The factors that are responsible for those missed opportunities are largely the same as those responsible for all other aspects of Israeli policies: structural barriers that accord to military considerations a significant priority over diplomatic ones, fundamental psychological barriers that cause both leaders and the public to vacillate between paranoia and arrogance, improvisation at the expense of strategic thinking, lack of political control over military strategy, and the excessive influence of militarism on Israeli diplomatic thinking.

5.4. Part V: Causes and Implications of the Mismanagement of National Security and Foreign Policy

Chapter 11 analyzes the structural aspects of foreign and security policy-making in Israel as one of the central explanations of the patterns of Israeli policy-making in national security and foreign affairs. I focus on the effect of formal and informal structural factors on the making of Israel's policy. Security policy has consistently dominated foreign policy. In virtually every major decision process, security considerations superseded diplomatic considerations. The only organization with a discipline of staff work is the IDF. All other organizations involved in the making of foreign and security policy—the Foreign Ministry, the Defense Ministry, and even the treasury (which has a very effective staff on every subject except defense matters)—have traditionally relied on the IDF staff work. I examine the formal and informal mechanisms that are supposed to oversee and evaluate national security policy, including the Knesset, the judiciary, and the National Security Council (NSC), and find that they have consistently failed in their mission.

The dominance of the security establishment in Israeli political affairs is reviewed through the analysis of the excessive involvement of former military personnel in almost every aspect of Israeli political, social, and economic life. An "old boys' network" was formed within the Israeli political elite, composed of former generals who have entered political life across the entire left-right continuum. Despite the significant political and ideological differences among its members, this network is char-. acterized by a shared set of basic political and military beliefs—which largely follow Ben-Gurion's strategic philosophy. Most of them accept the important role of the IDF in Israeli society; they generally support a fairly free hand to the IDF on budgetary and research and development (R&D) matters, as well as on matters of deterrence and the development and acquisition of WMDs. Efforts at establishing informal institutions that would oversee security and foreign policy, or that would offer an alternative public discourse of these policies, have been largely unsuccessful. This chapter sums up the structural implications of the empirical analyses in parts II–IV of the book and concludes that the basic rigidity of Israeli security and foreign policy will continue as long as no fundamental shift takes place in the formal and informal structure of the machinery that produces these policies.

Chapter 12 reviews the findings of the study. It examines how plausible the axioms were that form the basis of Israel's security doctrine and the basic tenets of this doctrine that were outlined in this present chapter. It lays out the key problems we have uncovered in Israel's security and foreign policy. On the basis of these findings, the chapter concludes by discussing possible reforms in the structure, process, and substance of Israeli foreign and security regime that may move Israel toward a more rational and adaptive future.

Chapter 13 examines a key puzzle that emerges from this critical analysis of Israel's national security and foreign policy. An objective view of basic data concerning Israel would almost certainly describe the country as an unqualified success story: It started out as a society of about 650,000 Jews and was born into a war that killed 1 percent of its Jewish population. Over time, however, Israel increased its population tenfold and was converted into a modern democratic, economically prosperous, militarily powerful, and technologically sophisticated society. Israel won four major wars against considerably more powerful enemies. Its per capita income is four times the average per capita income in the Middle

East. Its armed forces are considered to be among the most efficient and powerful of all the world's armies. Its scientific community is considered among the leading in the world. And it was able to maintain an open, democratic, and pluralistic political community in spite of the external threats. Yet the book's argument is that Israeli security and foreign policy has had numerous problems, that it has been run by many incompetent individuals and rigid organizations, and that this rigid structure has been responsible for quite a few fiascos and has generated many unintended results that carried significant ramifications. If that is the case, then how can we account for the Israeli success story?

The answer to this question is threefold. First, despite numerous blunders, Israel was able to flourish because its opponents were far less competent—or far more incompetent and corrupt—than the Israeli elite. While the Israeli elite used the Arab-Israeli conflict as a mechanism for state building and social integration within a democratic system, Arab elites used the Arab-Israeli conflict as a mechanism for maintaining authoritarian control and for perpetuating social and economic underdevelopment. Even the more progressive and daring Arab leaders in terms of Arab-Israeli peace (e.g., Sadat, Hassan of Morocco, King Hussein of Jordan, and Yasir Arafat) have maintained a closed, highly hierarchical, and largely corrupt political and economic system, thus preventing it from properly reaping the economic and social fruits of peace. This duality has exacerbated the political and economic problems of the Arab regimes, thus rendering the Israeli success story especially spectacular in comparison to the poverty, corruption, underdevelopment, and lack of political and social freedom in the Arab world.

Second, for much of Israel's history, continued conflict with the Arabs had important benefits for the development of the country. It enabled the ruling elite to use—and even to cultivate—the state of continued conflict as a mechanism for forging a fairly unified society and to use the IDF as a basic mechanism for socialization and politicization of the Israeli public. It also allowed this elite to shove under the rug a large number of social, economic, and ethnic problems that arose from the immigrant and multi-ethnic structure of the society. The continued state of conflict allowed the elite to extract extremely high material and human resources for national goals from the population and to justify policies of exploitation on the one hand and of selective preferentialism on the other. However, when the costs of conflict became too high to absorb, the elites shifted toward more peaceful policies. Once the peace process started, many underlying social and political tensions began to surface. With the economic benefits of peace came the social, economic, and political calls for equality among different Israeli sectors as well as among Arab Jews.

Third, a deeper examination of the "Israeli success story" reveals not only that Israel's economic, social, and educational performance was suboptimal but that it deteriorated over time. Israel's economic growth is slow compared to both most advanced industrialized societies and comparable societies that also live under a severe security threat—such as Taiwan, South Korea, and Singapore. Israel's educational system is rapidly deteriorating at the elementary and secondary school levels. Israel's infrastructure is also in a state of rapid decay. While there is clearly no direct effect of conflict on these processes of relative decline, the indirect effects are significant and increasing. This chapter explores the interrelationships between security policy and social policy in Israel and discusses the implications of the tensions between the two.

Chapter 14 concludes the study by offering an analysis of where Israel may be going in the future. It outlines four scenarios. These scenarios are neither mutually exclusive nor do they exhaust all possible worlds. The future may also entail sequential movement from one scenario to the other(s).

Escalation scenario. This scenario envisions a possible escalation and expansion of Israeli-Palestinian or Israeli-Syrian conflicts, the militarization of conflicts between Israel and outer-ring states such as Iran, or the emergence of radical Islamic regimes in one or more of Israel's immediate neighbors. A possible evolution of this kind would entail the outbreak of regional wars and the possible use of WMDs. This scenario carries major adverse military, economic, social, and political consequences for states in the region and for the international community as a whole.

Conflict unending scenario. This scenario envisions a continued state of conflict between Israel and its neighbors but one that simmers rather than explodes. Crises and possibly limited wars may continue to erupt sporadically, with growing costs to both sides. Repeated clashes raise basic dilemmas and risks to all actors in the region, as well as to Europe, the United States, and east Asia, yet international efforts at resolving the conflict are unsuccessful.

Cold peace scenario. This scenario envisions limited and partial settlements between Israel and the Palestinians and/or between Israel and Syria and Lebanon. However, significant issues or other conflicts are not resolved. Other regional problems such as economic underdevelopment, demographic pressure, environmental decay (particularly water), regime stability, and arms control and regional security agreements are not addressed. Each one of these issues may give rise to new conflicts that may either reopen underlying tensions or reverse previous peace efforts.

Regional peace scenario. A comprehensive process of regional, bilateral, and domestic change takes place in the Middle East. This process entails resolution of most or all outstanding international conflict in the region. Regional and extraregional actors engage in a process of establishing a set of regional institutions designed to foster cooperation and joint problem solving on security, economic, social, and environmental affairs.

This chapter outlines the main characteristics of these scenarios, the conditions leading to each, and their implications for the region and for the international community. It also discusses the implications of each scenario for Israel's security and economic well-being. This chapter concludes by addressing how Israel could help avoid the more dangerous scenarios and increase the probability of the more favorable scenarios and identifies avenues of future research on Israel's security and foreign policy.

PART II

The Use of Force

— 2 —

The Sinai War

The Making of the Second Round

I. INTRODUCTION

On October 29, 1956, Israel carried out an unprovoked attack on Egypt. This attack was coordinated with Great Britain and France, according to a predesigned plan that had been signed at a conference held in the city of Sèvres near Paris six days earlier. This plan entailed the following scenario. In the first stage, the IDF would raid deep into the Sinai by parachuting a battalion next to the Mitla pass—some thirty kilometers east of the Suez Canal. This would bring about a military clash between large-size Israeli and Egyptian forces deep in the Sinai Peninsula. In the second stage, Great Britain and France would issue an ultimatum, calling both parties to withdraw their forces, a demand that would be met by Egyptian defiance. This would serve as a pretext for the third stage: large-scale bombing raids by British and French planes on the Egyptian air force and the landing of French and British forces in the Suez Canal Zone.

If there ever was an aggressive design for a coordinated attack on a sovereign state, this was it. What kind of justification can one give to this war? Is there a version of the story in which Israel could be at least partly absolved from a charge of unprovoked aggression? Can the war be justified in terms of the perceptions of Israeli leaders at the time that the initiation of this unprovoked attack was designed to prevent a far greater evil? Can the war be justified—if not in terms of its causes then at least in terms of its consequences?

47

From the perspective of Great Britain and France, the war can only be described as an act of utter folly of two declining imperial powers trying to cling to their remaining imperial possessions. Both powers sought to contain threats emanating from rising anti-imperialist forces in the Middle East. In retrospect, there is no other way to characterize this misadventure. Nasser's defiance of the West had included acts such as signing a weapons deal with the Soviet Union in 1955, leading the fight against the British-dominated Baghdad Plan (Podeh 1995), participating in the new nonaligned bloc established in Bandung in 1955, and supporting the Algerian rebels. Most important, Nasser's decision to nationalize the Suez Canal posed a seemingly major threat to Western interests. The collusion with Israel was their way of dealing with this threat.

From the Israeli perspective, however, the collusion with Great Britain and France was an opportunity that had arisen due to Nasser's anticolonialist and pro-Soviet politics. According to conventional wisdom, the roots of the war were embedded in national security calculations of the national survival variety. Israeli motivations were seemingly far more fundamental and complex and had nothing to do with colonial designs. The traditional explanation of the origins of the Sinai War is found in much of the Israeli official writings, as well as in the writings of many Israeli historians and strategic analysts. I first outline this explanation and discuss the logical and empirical flaws entailed in it. Traditional accounts of the Sinai War are problematic not only because they fail to depict correctly the calculus and perceptions of Israeli decision makers. They are further flawed because they tend to convert these calculations and perceptions into an objective reality; they fail to deal with the deeper underlying motivations of the Israeli decision makers; and they ignore the gap between the formal justifications of the Sinai War and the actual reality that preceded it.

My explanation of this war focuses on the motivated biases of the Israeli elites at the time, biases that helped convert their perceptions and predictions into self-fulfilling prophecies. I argue that the Israeli behavior was the key factor that fomented escalation along the Israeli-Egyptian border. This behavior was backed by aggressive design of the security elite in Israel. It derailed prospects for coordination and de-escalation along the border; it converted a series of tactical menaces that posed no major threat to Israel's security into a perceived strategic threat of major magnitude. Israeli decision makers who have written about the war, and quite a few academic scholars, suggest that the key goal of the war was to remove the threat caused by the Egyptian-Soviet weapons deal of 1955. In this sense, the Sinai War is often seen as a preventive war. Yet by the time the decision to go to war was made, the so-called strategic threat was significantly diminished. The Israeli attack on Egypt developed by design and by inertia rather than as a strategic necessity. Even in terms of its consequences, the Israeli attack had paradoxical effects on Israeli national security. It fueled a process of strategic escalation that, in many respects, paved the way for a magnified arms race and for the next war.

2. THE CONVENTIONAL EXPLANATION OF THE SINAI CAMPAIGN

The conventional account of the Sinai War emerges from the autobiographical writings of political and military decision makers (e.g., Ben-Gurion 1969, 1959; Dayan 1967, 1976) or of the biographers thereof (Bar-Zohar 1977; Tevet 1971). Quite a few scholarly studies adopted the key elements of this version (e.g., Sachar 1981, 72–111; Brecher 1975, 225–317). This story contains several elements that—taken together—depict the Sinai campaign as a preventive war, a war born out of a fundamental shift in the balance of power in the region (Levy and Gochal 2001). Israel was forced into the war to prevent the outbreak of a far more destructive war in the future.

This narrative starts with the continued menace of repeated Fedayeen infiltrations to Israel from the Gaza Strip and the West Bank, infiltrations that caused the death of numerous Israelis, significant economic damage, and substantial demoralization of the Israeli society. Moshe Dayan (1967, 9) argued that

> initially, the Israeli government regarded these infiltrations as the residual damage caused by the 1948 war, and even though it demanded the Arab states to comply with the armistice agreements, it had adopted a policy of tolerance and patience. Yet by the second half of 1954, the acts of infiltration into Israeli settlements and terror attacks on Israeli citizen increased, and several months later it became clear to the Israeli government that these are not isolated incidents that stem from personal motives, but rather an organized act, committed with the knowledge of Arab states, and as a result of Egyptian initiative.

From that perspective, the government was under increased pressure to curb these infiltrations and to reduce the number of casualties of these perpetrations.

True, the infiltrators did not come only from the Gaza Strip, which was under Egyptian control; quite a few of these infiltrations came out of the West Bank, which was under the control of the Transjordanian army. Yet, many in the Israeli security establishment believed the new Egyptian regime entered the business of instigating terrorism by using the frustration, anger, and poverty of the Palestinian refugees in the Gaza Strip as the fuel for a war of attrition against Israel. In the inaugural speech of his new government on November 2, 1955, Ben-Gurion referred to the growing threat stemming from these infiltrations (1959, 23):

> the war against us continues in other ways: through means of boycott, through blockade, and through infiltrations by murderers and terrorists from time to time, across the border. Recently, Egypt has placed itself at the helm of this guerrilla warfare. The infiltrations from the Gaza Strip alone caused us a total of 153 casualties, in killed and wounded.

This change in Israeli perception was not unrelated to the ascendance of the charismatic Gamal Abd-el Nasser to power in Egypt. Ben-Gurion (then still on leave of absence in Sdeh Boker) and the security elite—the minister of defense, Pinhas Lavon; the chief of staff (COS); Dayan; and the head of military intelligence, Benjamin Givli—came to believe that Nasser's rise to power indicated a substantial shift toward radicalism in Egypt. This radicalism was both vehemently anti-Israeli and anti-Western. The Israeli security elite regarded with growing concern the rise in anti-Israeli rhetoric in Egypt, but, more important, they became increasingly alarmed when the new Egyptian regime started negotiating in earnest the withdrawal of the remaining British forces from the Suez Canal area. This suggested that, once the British pulled their forces out, there would be no buffer zone between the Egyptian armed forces and the Israeli border (see chap. 9).

A number of political acts by the newly founded military regime in Egypt, such as the prevention of free passage by Israeli vessels in the Suez Canal and the closure of the Tiran Straits to Israeli shipping, supported the growing Israeli threat perception. These acts were seen by the Israelis not only as an outright violation of the armistice agreement but also as an indication that Egypt was trying to strangle Israel economically by preventing its natural right of free passage in international waterways.[1] In his November 2, 1955, speech, Ben-Gurion (1959, 23) stated:

> The Egyptian government violated a basic international law regarding the freedom of navigation in the Suez [Canal], on which there exists

an explicit resolution by the UN Security Council. This Egypt[ian government] is now attempting to blockade the way to Israeli ships in the Red Sea—in violation of the international principle of freedom of navigation. This unilateral war must stop, because it cannot remain unilateral for long.

Yet these two problems diminish in importance compared to the threat invoked by the August 1955 arms deal between Egypt and the Soviet Union, which radically transformed the balance of power in the region.[2] Once this deal materialized and the weapon systems started pouring into Egypt, the threat from the Israeli perspective was life threatening. Israeli decision makers believed that, once the Egyptian army absorbed these weapons and adjusted its doctrine, it would be in a position to handle Israel a massive blow anytime it chose to do so. Since Israel was still subject to severe restrictions on weapon acquisition imposed on it by the Tripartite Declaration of 1950, it had little choice but to attack Egypt before this threat materialized. The problem was to find the right pretext and the right international constellation to minimize the adverse political damage of such an attack. But the strategic imperative of a preventive war was clear to the Israeli leadership.[3]

This explanation portrays the attack on Egypt as stemming from a significant rise in threat perception by the Israeli elite. This rise was based on the strategic developments on the ground. The rise of a radical regime in Egypt that was committed—as evidenced by its rhetoric—to the destruction of the state of Israel established the intent. The Egyptian-Soviet weapons deal provided the capability. This combination of capability and intent was potentially deadly. The Sinai campaign was an offensive war launched for defensive purposes (Yaniv 1995, 136).

According to this explanation, the aims of the Sinai campaign were fourfold:

1. Reestablishing an acceptable military balance between Israel and Egypt by destroying the Egyptian army and the weapon systems it had acquired from the Soviet Union.
2. Putting an end to the infiltrations from Egypt into Israel by occupying the Gaza Strip.
3. Ensuring freedom of navigation in the Gulf of Suez by occupying the Sharm a-Sheikh area and the Tiran Straits.
4. Establishing a deterrence equation that would prevent, or delay significantly, the Arab planning of a decisive military campaign against Israel.[4]

Thus, war was seen as a strategic imperative. While some activists—especially IDF COS Moshe Dayan—wished to launch it as soon as possible, Ben-Gurion did not want to start it in a manner that would be depicted by the international community as naked aggression. The diplomatic ramifications of an unprovoked and unilateral Israeli attack would be unacceptable. However successful such a war would be from a military point of view, it was bound to turn into a diplomatic nightmare if Israel embarked upon it without significant international backing. The need to lay out the diplomatic foundations imposed significant delay on the timing of the war.

Fortunately for Israel, Nasser's pan-Arab ambitions played into its hands. Nasser positioned himself as the anti-imperialist champion in the region by successfully derailing U.S.-British efforts at establishing an anti-Soviet alliance in the Middle East (Podeh 1995, 192, 195–97; Sela 1998, 43–45). American and British efforts to lure Nasser into the Western fold by offering him economic and military aid as positive inducements proved futile. Nasser ended up making the deal with the Soviet Union (Hahn 1991, 155–210; Bowie 1989; Sayed-Ahmed 1989, 97–121; James 1990; Kelly and Gorst 2000). This, of course, placed Nasser's Egypt in the "bad guys" camp, but apparently it was not sufficient to admit Israel to the "good guys," pro-Western club. Nasser's decision of July 26, 1956, to nationalize the Suez Canal was the straw that broke the British and French backs, and from that point on, the road to the Sèvres collusion was wide open.

3. HIDDEN AND NOT SO HIDDEN AGENDAS: PROBLEMS WITH THE CONVENTIONAL EXPLANATION OF THE SINAI CAMPAIGN

It is important to state at the outset that the evidence suggests that Israeli threat perceptions were genuine. The frequent terrorist infiltrations were indeed a menace, causing quite a few casualties. The blockade of the Tiran Straits and the prevention of shipping in the Suez Canal were indeed a blatant violation of international law and of UN Security Council resolution. And certainly the Soviet supply of advanced weapons to Egypt created a significant threat to Israeli security. However, these threat perceptions tell only part of the real story. Moreover, the kind of preventive war that Israel had planned does not appear to have offered a real solution to these problems. The conventional explanation suffers from some serious logical and empirical problems. Let us discuss some of these weaknesses.

First, how grave were the terrorist attacks on Israel from Egypt? Figure 2.1 provides the figures on Israeli casualties (both dead and wounded) due to military and terrorist operations against Israel from the beginning of 1949 through the end of 1956.[5] As these figures suggest, Israel indeed suffered numerous casualties from both nonstate and state-instigated violence over this period. A state of roughly 1.5 million people (average population over the period) suffering between 150 and 300 casualties per year was clearly paying a high price for its security.[6] No responsible government could ignore these infiltrations. Yet, if we examine the sources of this violence, we can see that violence against Israel emanating from Egypt—mostly from the Gaza Strip—accounted for anywhere between a quarter and a sixth of these violent acts. This is true for the entire period. What is more important, however, is that infiltrations and military actions from the Gaza Strip did not increase significantly in 1953 and 1954. Indeed, there is a slight increase in 1955 and a major jump in the amount of casualties in 1956, but—as we will soon see—this is due to a fundamental increase in the volume and scope of Israeli military actions rather than to a change in Egyptian policy toward infiltrations.

Figure 2.2 tells a similar story. The years 1953–54 witnessed a significant rise in the number of military incidents directed at Israel. Those emanating from the Egyptian border, however, showed only a small rise and accounted for anywhere from a sixth to an eighth of all incidents. Thus, the gravity of the terrorism problem was indeed high, but the major culprit was not Egypt; nor was it the new Egyptian regime. Rather, a vast majority of all incidents (and the violence inflicted by these infiltrations) came from the Jordanian border. As noted elsewhere (Maoz and Mor 2002a, 180–84), the Israeli-Syrian border was somewhat turbulent in 1951, but between 1951 and 1955 the border was relatively calm, so that only few acts of violence emanated from Israel's northern boundaries.

In contrast to Ben-Gurion's claims, up until early 1955 the Egyptian regime in general, and the Egyptian armed forces in particular, neither encouraged nor got directly involved in violence against Israel. Despite numerous claims that Egyptian military intelligence was in the business of staging infiltrations to Israel, the bulk of the evidence suggests that "with few exceptions Egyptian policy consistently opposed infiltrations" (Morris 1993, 86).[7] Yaari's (1975) study—relying on documents captured

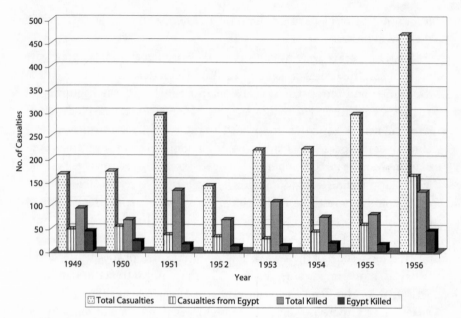

Fig. 2.1.   Israeli casualties due to infiltrations and state violence against Israel, 1949–56

by the IDF during the Sinai campaign and on transcripts of interrogation of Egyptian prisoners—also suggests that the Egyptian military had orders to curb infiltrations to Israel, and during 1953 and 1954 they made serious efforts in this regard.[8]

In the second half of 1954 and in the early months of 1955, a fundamental change took place in Israeli policy toward Egypt. This shift was masterminded by Defense Minister Pinhas Lavon and the IDF COS Moshe Dayan. This change involved two significant events. First, in July 1954 Israeli military intelligence activated a spy network composed of Egyptian Jews in a series of bombings of public places in Alexandria and Cairo. The objective of these terrorist operations was to bring about a chain reaction that would derail the Anglo-Egyptian negotiations over the transfer of control over the Suez Canal to Egypt and the evacuation of the British troops stationed in the canal area. Shortly after these bombings started, the Egyptian security forces rounded up and imprisoned most of the members of the Israeli spy ring (see chap. 9). This clumsy Israeli intervention in Egyptian internal affairs resulted in a significant breakdown of trust between Israeli and Egyptian diplomats, who had been

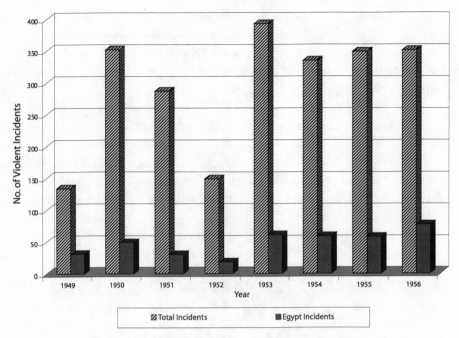

Fig. 2.2. Number of terrorist and military incidents directed at Israel, 1949–56

negotiating directly and indirectly in an effort to bring about a peace agreement or some modus vivendi between the two states.

Second, in February 1955 Ben-Gurion ended his leave of absence and returned to the Defense Ministry. The first operational plan presented to him upon his return was a large-scale attack on an Egyptian army base in the Gaza area. This attack was framed as a reprisal for a number of attacks emanating from Egypt over the months of January and February, leading to the killing of three Israelis (Golani 1997, 658–61; Morris 1993, 92–93). The attack went forward and resulted in thirty-eight Egyptian and eight Israeli fatalities and has been, as Sharett observed, "the bloodiest operation on the Egyptian front since 1949" (Sheffer 1996, 786).

The precise motivations and forces behind the conception, the planning, and the actual execution of the Gaza raid have been documented elsewhere.[9] This operation may have been deliberately designed to send a strong message to the Egyptians, or it may have escalated beyond the original plan due to complications on the ground (Michelson 1994; Dayan 1976, 142). Be that as it may, the raid had a profound impact on the Egyptians. First and foremost, it brought home to Nasser the extreme weakness and incompetence of the Egyptian armed forces. The Egyptian soldiers and their equipment were no match against the superior Israelis. While conversion of this army into a fighting force of some significance would be a long process, Nasser's lesson was that the army needed modern weapons and quickly.[10]

Second, the raid caused an immediate escalation along the border. The Egyptian forces in the Sinai had been upgraded and expanded (Michelson 1994, 21; Morris 1993, 344). The Egyptian army abandoned its efforts to restrain the Palestinian raids. In fact, Egyptian units started engaging Israeli forces and even participated in attacks on Israeli citizens—for example, a raid on a wedding celebration in the village of Patish on March 24, 1955 (Morris 1993, 347–48; Golani 1997, 35–36). While there is no evidence to suggest that Egypt pursued escalation, the Israeli raid ignited a spiral process that entailed both an accelerated arms race and heightened military escalation along the border. In this sense, the raid played into the hands of the activist camp in Israel that—for a long time—had been looking for a pretext to launch a "second round."

The evidence suggests that the infiltrations from Egypt were not a real cause of war. The Israeli policy of reprisals was more instrumental in bringing about escalation than the infiltrations into Israel from the Gaza Strip. The Israeli policy of reprisals aimed at a stimulus-response chain reaction was designed to pave a spiraling escalatory path to war.

But what about the preventive logic discussed previously? Even if it had been indeed the Gaza raid that pushed Nasser to sign the massive weapons deal with the Soviet Union, the outcome of the deal raised considerably the stakes for Israel. Most political and military leaders believed that the deal transformed the balance of power in the region. From this perspective, an attack aimed at the destruction of the Egyptian army and its newly acquired weapon systems would indeed have been defensible as a preventive war. But was the balance of power tilted in Israel's disadvantage when the war started?

Had Israel been subject to the weapons embargo established by the Tripartite Declaration by the start of the war, the Egyptian-Soviet weapons deal would indeed have tilted the balance of power in Egypt's favor. Yet, by July 1956—four months before the war—Israel was no longer in dire shortage of sophisticated weapons. Both in terms of quality and quantity of available weapon systems, Israel was almost evenly matched with Egypt.[11] Table 2.1 provides the balance of military power prior to the Sinai War.

As we can readily see from table 2.1, the numerical balance of forces was slightly tilted toward Egypt, but it was not nearly as bad as the Israeli politicians had claimed. In fact, by mid-1956, Israel was receiving fairly sophisticated weapon systems from France and Germany, including Mystère jets (with promise of top-of-the-line Super Mystère fighter planes and Votour fighter bombers). On July 4, 1956, French foreign minister Pineaut informed the Israeli ambassador to Paris, Yaacov Tsur, that all restrictions on weapons shipments to Israel had been lifted (Sachar 1981, 99). So, by the fall of 1956 the seemingly life-threatening strategic imbalance caused by the Egyptian-Soviet arms deal of a year earlier had diminished to a slightly uncomfortable strategic equation. This equation too was about to change in Israel's favor even without the need to launch a military attack.[12]

A more careful inspection of the strategic planning and management of the Israeli-Egyptian conflict, however, provides additional support to the argument that the Sinai War was not principally about reinstalling a stable balance of power by destroying the Egyptian army. Two important issues are relevant here. First, operational plans for attacking Egypt existed and had been proposed much prior to the Egyptian-Soviet weapons deal of September 1955. Second, the nature of the operational plan contradicts the fundamental logic of a preventive strike aimed at destroying Egyptian newly acquired capabilities.

The planning for a major military confrontation with Egypt started long before the Egyptian-Soviet arms deal. Various operational plans were raised at different points in time. A plan for a forceful breakup of the Tiran and Suez Canal blockade was presented by the COS Dayan and Defense Minister Lavon to the government as early as January 1954 (Sheffer 1996, 715; Golani 1997, 63–71). Prime Minister Sharett confronted Dayan with the question, "Do you realize this means war with Egypt?" Dayan replied, "Of course I do." The government summarily

TABLE 2.1. Egyptian-Israeli Balance of Forces on the Eve of the Sinai War

Weapon System	Egypt	Israel	Comments
Combat aircraft	200	134	French Mystères of the IAF were superior to the Soviet Mig-15, -17, and -19 of the Egyptian air force
Transport aircraft	55	21	
Total aircraft	255	155	Only 60 Egyptian fighters, 10 bombers, and 55 transport aircraft operational
Tanks	530	400	
Artillery pieces	500	150	
Armored personnel carriers	200	450	
Personnel dedicated to fighting	50,000	50,000	

Source: Principal sources for data include Dupuy 1978, 212; Dayan 1967, 183–97.

rejected the plan. Other plans based on different scenarios and other targets for attack were also rejected before reaching any operational level, but the itching for war was there all along.

Possibly the first realistic version of an operational plan was ignited following the grenade attack on the Patish wedding ceremony of March 24, 1955. Ben-Gurion presented three questions to Dayan: (1) How long would it take to occupy the Gaza Strip? (2) Is the IDF prepared for a war with Egypt? (3) Is the IDF prepared for a general war against (all or several) Arab states? Following these questions, Ben-Gurion brought to the cabinet a proposal to occupy the Gaza Strip in retaliation for this terrorist attack, but the government rejected the proposal (Golani 1997, 37–38; Bar-Zohar 1977, 1139–40).[13] Later that year, preparations were made for an operation designed to capture Sharm a-Sheikh and the Tiran Straits. Operation Omer, the planning of which was set in motion in October 1955, called for a forceful opening of the blockade in the Gulf of Suez under the assumption that this would lead to a general war with Egypt (Golani 1997, 71–72).

Ben-Gurion's position regarding war between Israel and the Arab world was ambivalent—mostly due to his awareness of the international repercussions of an aggressive war. Dayan, however, had no such qualms. He was convinced that such a war was inevitable and that Israel would be better off militarily if it fought such a war at a time, place, and on terms of its choosing. His challenge was to muster the domestic and international circumstances that would provide Israel with a pretext for war. Up to the Egyptian-Soviet weapons deal, the only two areas that were of concern to Israeli decision makers—and could also be used to boost Israel's case in the international community—were the infiltrations into Israel's territory and the continued blockade on its southern waterways. Unfortunately for Dayan, Sharett adopted a policy of restraint as long as he was prime minister. Moreover, most of the infiltrations came from Jordan; it would have been difficult to justify a strike against Egypt as a large-scale reprisal for infiltrations. Also, Dayan's relationship with Defense Minister Lavon was strained and based on mutual mistrust and suspicion, even though they agreed on many political and strategic issues. Up to February 1955, there was a solid majority in the government against war. However, the return of Ben-Gurion to the Defense Ministry restarted the planning process for a war in earnest.

The operational plan of attack contradicted the logic of preventive strike aimed at destroying the Egyptian army. The IDF did not have plans to attack Egypt's territory beyond the Suez Canal. However, the main body of the Egyptian forces was west of the Suez Canal. According to Israeli intelligence, Egyptian forces in the Sinai included two divisions, one Palestinian division, one border guard battalion, and one armored brigade-size regional reserve force. This order of battle was less than one-third the total size of the Egyptian forces. Also, only a small fraction of the Egyptian air force was stationed in the Sinai (Dayan 1967, 183; Dupuy 1978, 213). Unless the Israeli Air Force (IAF) planned a comprehensive long-range operation designed to destroy the Egyptian air force on the ground—as was done in 1967 with a far more modern air force—the damage to Egyptian air power would have been minimal.[14] Even if the Israelis had wanted to launch such a dismantling aerial strike, the range of the planes at their disposal in 1954 and 1955—in fact up to July 1956—was too short to make the trip to Egypt and back.

The kind of operation that had been planned by the IDF was incapable of accomplishing the objective of destroying the Egyptian armed forces and their newly acquired equipment. This was clearly the case before the Sèvres Agreement. The Sèvres Agreement rendered this objective more realistic in one respect, in that it enabled the destruction of the Egyptian air force on the ground. But it rendered this objective less realistic in another respect. Under a bilateral war scenario, an Israeli attack in the Sinai would have forced Nasser to move his main forces into the Sinai. This would have enabled a direct confrontation between the Israeli armored divisions and the Egyptian ones on the terrain of the Sinai Desert. However, confronted by the threat of a joint French-British attack, Nasser would have been forced to concentrate his forces in Egypt itself. This would have prevented a direct clash between the main bodies of the Israeli and the Egyptian armies. What would have happened to the Egyptian army in the confrontation with the French and British troops was anybody's guess. The troops allocated by the major powers to Operation Musketeer were too small and limited in their weapons to allow for a major confrontation. The major powers viewed this as a limited operation, designed to capture the canal area. The plan was to reach a rapid military outcome and to bargain for a political solution. Either way, the prospect of actually destroying the Egyptian armed forces through this kind of operation was a tenuous one. Unless there was a fundamental change in the Egyptian regime following the war—a change that would have implied a marked improvement in Israeli-Egyptian relations—the strategic threat to Israel following the envisioned war would have been no less than before the war.

4. THE UNDERLYING CAUSES OF THE SINAI WAR

The immediate causes of the Sinai War may have been the need to curb infiltrations, the drive to remove the blockade on Israeli southern waterways, and the pressure to rectify the balance of power between Israel and Egypt. But these were not the only causes, nor were they the most important ones. What then were the underlying causes of the Sinai War?[15]

4.1. The Self-Fulfilling "Second Round" Prophecy

Perhaps the most basic cause of the war was the belief among Israeli elites that a second round of war between Israel and some combination of Arab states was inevitable. This belief evolved in the early 1950s as the armistice agreements failed to transform into full-fledged peace agreements. This expectation of a second round of war was based on the continued anti-Israeli rhetoric in the Arab world and on statements calling for retribution for the 1948 war. It was also based on continued infiltrations into Israel from Jordan and the Gaza Strip, as well as on conflict over the demilitarized areas in the Israeli-Syrian border (Maoz and Mor 2002a, 140–41).[16] This notion of a second round was not focused on an Egyptian scenario. Most offensive aspirations of Israeli leaders entailed dreams of occupation of the West Bank, controlled by Jordan (Morris 1993, 9–12; Gelber 1994, 15). This belief gave birth to ideas of taking advantage of local military engagements as a pretext to starting a war. The "second-round" conception found support among various activist political parties (e.g., the right-wing Herut Party and the left-wing activist Ahdut Ha'Avodah Party). But, in addition, leading members of the ruling Mapai Party also toyed with these ideas (Sheffer 1996, 694–95).

Romantic notions about a second round that would "convert Israeli Eastern border into a straight line"[17] notwithstanding, the second-round logic rested primarily on strategic foundations. These foundations are attributable to Ben-Gurion's thinking. While Ben-Gurion had major reservations about the notion of preventive war, he did feel—even in the early 1950s—that by 1956 the Arab states would amass enough military power to attempt to launch a second round of fighting (Sheffer 1996, 690). Accordingly, while serving as minister of defense up to his retirement, he spent considerable time both on the organization of the IDF and on doctrinal issues that were based on the assumption of an imminent second round. His successor, Pinhas Lavon, shared the same ideas, but, in contrast to Ben-Gurion, he was less concerned about the diplomatic repercussions of a preventive war.

From a territorial perspective, Jordan was the principal target of the second-round idea. From a strategic and political perspective, however, Jordan was the less preferred target. Up to 1955, the Transjordanian Legion was managed and trained by the British; the de facto commander of the legion was General John Glubb. An Israeli-initiated war against Jordan would risk—at the very least—a harsh diplomatic reaction and—more probably—a military clash with the British army. Moreover, as Yaniv (1987a, 47) notes, "the presence of the Jordanian forces in the West Bank was not a threat; to some extent, indeed, it was a source of confidence. Controlled by Britain, a weak and intimidated Jordan would not launch a war against Israel. At the same time, British control over the Arab Legion turned this force, in effect, into an instrument of Israeli policy, almost a tactical Israeli surrogate."

Egypt was a different matter altogether. From a strategic perspective it constituted the primary threat to Israel, regardless of the regime in power. The size of the Egyptian armed forces was larger by a factor of four compared to the Syrian and Jordanian armies and by a factor of two compared to the Iraqi army. The Egyptian army was better equipped than the Syrian army (although the Jordanian Legion was better trained and equipped). In terms of military potential and political clout, Egypt was the key to both peace and war with the Arab world. Egypt was also not under the political protection of any major power. So, the logic of the second round—framed in cold strategic terms rather than in terms of romantic aspirations—envisioned Egypt as the prime target of a military strike designed to establish deterrence.[18]

The belief that a second round was fast approaching, combined with the perception of fundamental territorial and demographic asymmetries between Israel and its Arab neighbors, gave rise to the notion of "offensive defense" (Bar-On 1992, 56). In Dayan's perception, this meant using the policy of retaliation as a vehicle for strategic escalation.[19]

The belief that Israel had to ensure that the second round would start on terms that are strategically favorable to Israel was intertwined with other elements of threat and opportunity that evolved over the 1953–56 period. Preparing the IDF for a second round of major war was at the heart of all Israeli military plans and strategy in the mid-1950s. This, of course, had the effect of a self-fulfilling prophecy. It acted to boost a spirit of activism and overreaction to infiltrations. After Ben-Gurion's return to the Defense Ministry in February 1955, the use of limited reprisals as a tool of escalation became policy (see chap. 7). It was also an instrument for magnifying the threat to a point where threat perceptions—expressed in intelligence estimates within the IDF and the Defense Ministry, as well as in the policy community—were only remotely related to the actual strategic realities on the ground. Up to the Egyptian-Soviet weapons deal, the quantitative balance of power in the region was fairly even, while the qualitative balance was overwhelmingly in Israel's favor. The Jordanian and Syrian armies did little to develop an offensive capability that could threaten Israel. The same applied to the Egyptian army for much of the period.

Taken as a whole, the second round was set in motion in the minds of key players in the political and military elite in Israel from the early 1950s on. The question was how to find the right time, pretext, and international arrangement to make it happen.

4.2. The Nasser Factor

The Free Officers' coup in Egypt on July 22, 1952, was seen in Israel initially as a good thing. The Israeli perception of Egypt's goals in the 1948 war was rooted in a scapegoating perception: the decadent Egyptian monarchy trying to divert attention from the country's troubles by instigating hostility toward Israel. Israeli decision makers interpreted the commitment of the new regime to economic and political reforms as implying a willingness to substitute the retribution agenda for a more conciliatory one (Bar-On 1992, 36). However, this perception changed radically, especially after the official ascendance of Nasser to power in 1954. Having read Nasser's 1954 pamphlet *The Philosophy of the Revolution*, Ben-Gurion concluded that the new leader of Egypt constituted an existential threat to Israel by virtue of his grand designs. Egypt, as depicted in that pamphlet, had leadership aspirations in the inter-Arab, African, and broader Middle Eastern arenas. These aspirations necessarily coincided with the basic anti-Israeli attitude reflected by some sections of this pamphlet. Israel was dealing no longer with a leader committed to internal reform but with a leader bent on sweeping regional change. Israel would be a key element in these plans.

In his speech to the Knesset on January 2, 1956, Ben-Gurion stated:

> The Egyptian dictator published a pamphlet entitled *The Philosophy of Revolution*. . . . [T]he author expounds sincerely three ambitions that seem to guide him: (1) to lead the Arab peoples, (2) to become the

leader of the Islamic peoples, and (3) to become the spokesman of the African peoples. The internal reforms—the termination of national tribulations, the education of the [Egyptian] people, the development of the country, the uplifting of the [Egyptian] farmers—slogans on which the revolution was justified—were seemingly postponed for the distant future. They were replaced by foreign political ambitions. . . . The rulers of Egypt must have come to the conclusion that it is easier to grab victories in the realm of foreign policy than to fix the pitiful state of affairs in the domestic sphere, and to win hegemony among the Arab peoples; it seems that the Cairo dictators have concluded that the easiest and cheapest means is an attack on the state of Israel. (1959, 41)

The interpretation of events since the 1952 coup—or, more specifically, since the assumption of formal power by Nasser—was now couched in the grand strategy that the Israeli leaders attributed to Nasser. Against this backdrop, we can reformulate the key aim of the coming war: to thwart the establishment of a radical Arab coalition bent on an all-out effort at destroying Israel (Golani 1997, 16). The idea was to bring about a chain of events that would result in the overthrow of the radical Nasserist regime in Egypt. In this context we can understand the convergence between Israeli interests and the Franco-British ones.

Bar-On (1991, 39–40) presents verbatim the directive of Dayan to members of the general staff on October 23, 1955.[20]

The basic solution to Israel's security problem is the removal of Nasser's regime in Egypt. Other measures may ease the situation temporarily, or delay the decision, but no solution other than the complete overthrow of Nasser from the leadership of Egypt will remove the underlying factor of the threat to the state of Israel.

In order to overthrow Nasser's regime, we must bring about a decisive confrontation with Egypt in the nearest possible future, before the process of weapons absorption in the Egyptian armed forces will render this military operation overly difficult, or maybe even impossible.

A. We must take every possible measure to acquire additional weapons and ammunition until such time as the confrontation will occur, but we should not condition one [the confrontation] upon the other [weapons acquisition].

B. Despite the points made above, this conception rejects the notion of a preventive war. Such a war means an aggressively initiated attack by Israel. With all the significance we attach to the overthrow of Nasser's regime, Israel cannot afford to confront the whole world, being accused of aggression. This kind of accusation would prevent the full realization of the war aims due to the intervention of the superpowers. . . .

C. This confrontation should be brought about through the method of gradual deterioration. . . . Israel cannot bring about the deterioration through overt provocation. But Israel does not require a provocation [to justify an attack on Egypt]. In the state of present conflict with Egypt, Egypt herself provides the provocations on a daily basis. Israel can respond through a method of detonation— that is, to insist on its rights without any concession and to respond decisively to any Egyptian aggression. The aim of such a policy is to bring about a direct confrontation. . . .

D. The practical imperative deriving from these assumptions is the conduct of an active and noncompromising policy, relying judicially and diplomatically on the demand of full compliance with the armistice agreements and international law. Nasser will indeed do whatever he can to avoid an all-out confrontation in the immediate future, but we must assume that he will not be able to tolerate severe damage to his prestige due to Israel's activities. There will be a limit to his restraint, and at a certain point he will have to "lose his cool" and respond in force. Under the worst case, when Nasser's self-restraint is higher than expected, the activist security policy of Israel will fulfill at the very least its [other] objectives in all fields under contention, and will buy for Israel a position of power and realistic achievements, before the increase in the power of the Egyptian army will make such achievements difficult.

E. The military implications of these matters are:

(1) Israel will respond forcefully and in large scale to any attack on Israeli forces or settlements. On any sharpshooting or attack of an Israeli patrol or position in the Gaza Strip, Israel will occupy the [Egyptian] post that launched this attack, using heavy weapons and armor, if this is tactically necessary.

(2) On any sabotage, mining, or murder by the Fedayeen, there will be an Israeli raid in the depth of the Gaza Strip against the barracks of the Egyptian army there.

(3) Every Egyptian post that extends to Israeli territory in the Nitzana area will be occupied and destroyed.

(4) If Burns[21] fails in his effort to reduce the Egyptian troop concentrations in the Abu Ageila region, the IDF will capture the

Nitzana region, will fortify it, and will convert it into a "solid" military base.

(5) If the Egyptians do not guarantee the freedom of passage in the Eilat Straits, Israel will occupy the entire area and will hold it as a guarantee for freedom of navigation necessary.

F. ... Nasser might "swallow" all the above actions, except one—the occupation of the Eilat [Tiran] Straits. Reprisals, Israeli invasion of the Nitzana area, or a policy of excessive force along the border are passing events, but the occupation of Egyptian territory and holding it for a long time is a provocation that one cannot accept lying down. One must assume, therefore, that the occupation of the Eilat Straits by the IDF is the detonator that will blow up the entire powder keg.

This is the essence of the policy of "deterioration,"[22] as well as a clear exposition of the linkage between the goal of overthrowing Nasser and the operational plans of escalation. Indeed, this policy was beginning to roll, with raids on the Egyptian base at Kuntillah on October 26–27 and in Sabha on November 2, 1955 (resulting in the death of over one hundred Egyptian soldiers in both raids). The IDF presented to the government plans for the occupation of the Tiran Straits. The government, still with a majority of moderates led by Sharett, rejected the plan. Also, Nasser responded with restraint to the repeated Israeli provocations.

The objective of overthrowing Nasser came up repeatedly in discussions between the Israelis and their would-be allies in 1956. By spearheading the struggle against the Baghdad Pact, by starting an anti-French campaign with respect to Algeria, and—most important—by nationalizing the Suez Canal, Nasser positioned himself as the key anti-Western leader in the region. Both Britain and France marked Nasser as a key target. The plan of Operation Musketeer was designed to trigger a process leading to a change from within Egypt, one that would result in a negotiated settlement with a new, and more acceptable, Egyptian regime (Thornhill 2000, 22–24; Gorst 2000, 36–37; Bar-On 1992, 234–35).[23]

4.3. The Domestic Imperative

Domestic factors are typically seen as a minor aspect of the Sinai campaign. Historians view the major domestic aspect of this war in terms of the Sharett–Ben-Gurion controversy. Sharett represented a conciliatory line that emphasized diplomacy, while Ben-Gurion represented the activist approach. Actually, in-depth analyses of this controversy reveal considerable overlap in their approaches, as well as fundamental dis-

agreements.[24] One of the key differences between the two leaders concerned their attitude toward a second-round war initiated by Israel. As
noted, Ben-Gurion was in favor of such a war but wanted to find the right
international constellation that would minimize the diplomatic fallout of
such a war. Sharett, on the other hand, was adamantly opposed to such a
war.

By June 1956, the moderate element in Ben-Gurion's government
vanished with the resignation of Moshe Sharett as foreign minister. Even
during the last months of 1955 and the first half of 1956, Sharett's
influence on government policy diminished considerably. Despite that,
his opposition to Ben-Gurion's proposals of late October and early
November 1955 to occupy the Sharm a-Sheikh area was sufficient to
block these plans. Ben-Gurion's tactic was to try to outmaneuver Sharett.
For example, the decision on the Kinneret raid of December 1955 (see
chap. 7) was made while Sharett was in the United States trying to negotiate a weapons deal. The removal of Sharett paved the way for the secret
collusion with Britain and France. The government was made privy to
the whole Sinai operation just one week before it broke out. With the
leader of the moderate faction in the government removed, Ben-Gurion
was able to secure government support for the operation without much
difficulty.

Tracing the effects of domestic political factors on the road to the
Sinai War is a difficult task, mostly because much of what went on was
done without real government oversight and because the Ben-Gurion
crowd was very successful in marketing panic in Israel. We have no public opinion data to examine the extent of public support of the government's security and foreign policy. Yet, on the basis of somewhat sparse
information—such as Knesset debates and elite perceptions of public
opinion—it is possible to speculate on the effect of domestic factors on
the decision processes leading to the Sinai campaign.

Understandably, the key issue up to September 1955 in the discourse
on foreign and security policy in Israel was the problem of infiltrations.
Israeli decision makers were as concerned about public perceptions of
both the infiltrations and Israeli reprisals as they had been about international reactions to their reprisal policy. Both the older and ideologically
motivated Kibbutzim and the new immigrant villages (Moshavim)
exerted considerable pressure on the government to find solutions to the
problem of infiltration (Morris 1993, 31–34). The situation got worse as
the infiltrations became more numerous and daring and as the number of
Israeli casualties began to mount. Debates in the Knesset during the early

1950s reveal strong criticism of government policy both from opposition parties (e.g., Herut) and from activist parties within the government (e.g., Ahdut Ha'avodah).

Following Ben-Gurion's departure in 1953, the domestic scene became more turbulent. Increased parliamentary attacks and critical articles in the Israeli press berated Sharett's policy of restraint (a policy that was itself somewhat of a facade). Pressure also mounted from within the military elite and the activist circles within the government and the Mapai Party leadership. Ben-Gurion kept pressing for his pessimistic view of the Arab world even from his retreat at Sdeh Boker (e.g., Sheffer 1996, 714, 723, 732–34). Sharett repeatedly clashed with Lavon over seemingly adventurist schemes that the latter was advocating (Sheffer 1996, 720–23). Sharett's dovish views of the conflict and the policy of restraint encountered considerable criticism from within and outside his party. There was constant counting of incidents of infiltrations and casualties, in repeated efforts to extract from Sharett approval for reprisal raids. More seriously, Defense Minister Lavon authorized several reprisals without consulting with Sharett—something that even Ben-Gurion tried to avoid (at least until the previously mentioned Kinneret raid of December 1955).

The "mishap" added to the internal rift in the government and in those political circles that had been in the loop of knowledge of the extent of the military and political elite involvement in this fiasco. Sharett was furious that such a critical action—involving sensitive political and international considerations—was conducted without his knowledge and approval (which would not have been granted). The "mishap" brought about the resignation of Lavon and the return of Ben-Gurion. Ben-Gurion's second reign as defense minister was far more dangerous than Lavon's. Lavon was a dangerous adventurist, but had little military authority. Ben-Gurion commanded the respect and admiration of his political peers and was considered a major authority on security matters by the military elite. Nobody dared circumvent Ben-Gurion.

Despite the fact that Sharett still had considerable influence among his cabinet colleagues—thus using it to abort such initiatives as the March 1955 proposal by Ben-Gurion to occupy the Gaza Strip—his influence was fast dwindling. The July 1955 elections resulted in Mapai losing 5 percent of its seats, while the newly founded activist party Ahdut Ha'avodah won ten new seats in the Knesset. This was a clear sign that the Israeli public—still largely ignorant of the nature of the "mishap"— did not appreciate Sharett's policy of restraint. Ben-Gurion, who now was tasked with forming a new government, included two ministers from the Ahdut Ha'avodah Party in it, and the new activists in the government added to his relative freedom of maneuver. In the first eight months of the new government, the rift between Sharett and Ben-Gurion became unbridgeable. By June 1956, Sharett was effectively stripped of any meaningful influence in the government and was forced to resign. The domestic constraints on military action were removed.

The rhetoric of panic and despair that the activists pushed in the media and the Knesset provided for a convenient setting for public support of the war option. Bar-On (1992, 27) describes the public's mood following the Egyptian-Soviet weapons deal.

> In terms of the public awareness in Israel during the fall of 1955, it will not be an overstatement if we conclude this chapter by saying that the skies have darkened and were covered with heavy clouds of doubt and concern. Not everybody in Israel agreed with the policy of reprisals chosen by Ben-Gurion and Dayan in 1955, and the role of this policy in escalating the tension was not negligible, but all agreed that Israel faced existential risks.
>
> A historian must regard with suspicion such generalizations about the moods of large publics, since very often such moods and such feelings are in fact shared by only small elite groups. Yet in the present case, it is difficult not to be impressed by the general scope of the alarm and concern, which extended to various public strata. Moreover, these public concerns within a few weeks since information about the Czech weapons deal was published were extremely powerful, and the elite groups must have been influenced by them. Therefore, understanding of this feeling of emergency serves as a necessary infrastructure for the understanding of the actions taken by decision makers.

It is possible that, as Bar-On notes, decision makers were influenced by a general sense of threat invoked by the Egyptian-Soviet weapons deal. More likely, however, the sense of alarm was filtered to the public by the perceptions of the elites, which interpreted for the public the risks involved in the shift in the strategic balance. Even after the signature of the weapons deal with France in June 1956, and when the weapon shipments started arriving to Israel, Israeli decision makers kept arguing that the balance was still heavily tilted in favor of Egypt and that the existential risk was not removed.

On October 15, 1956, after considerable amounts of weapons had been delivered to Israel, and on the eve of the imminent war, Ben-Gurion stated in the Knesset:

I will say that there has been a change for the better in the ability of the IDF [following the French weapon shipments], although I must stress—with utmost concern—that Egypt alone is still significantly superior. It has heavy tanks—British, Czech, and Soviet. It has Soviet jet planes and Bombers of quality and quantity that are superior to what we possess, and if we add to this the growing armaments of the other Arab states—our concern will grow further. . . . I do not want to say that effective, sufficient, and modern weapons have no critical value. I am confident, as is each and every one of the IDF commanders, that in a confrontation with the Egyptians or with the other Arab armies we will eventually prevail. But we want to prevent a war and to ensure our rights, our standing and our security, and there is only one way to accomplish all this: if we are given by our friends and allies a sufficient amount of defensive weapons that will not be inferior to the weapons possessed by our enemies. Even if the quantities of weapons at our disposal do not match those of our enemies, if the weapons we have are of a superior quality, this will deter our enemies from attacking us, from depriving us of our rights, and from endangering our status. (Ben-Gurion 1959, 198)

The magnification of the threat even in light of reassuring information was a ploy to boost public support for war. Throughout the fall of 1955 and the spring of 1956 the slogan in the media and political discourse was "there will be a war next summer." The political leaders who had been seeking a pretext for a war in the fall of 1955 were disappointed both by Nasser's refusal to fall into the "deterioration" trap and by opposition in the government to the Gaza Strip and the Tiran Straits schemes pushed by Ben-Gurion. The solution was to frame public expectations by making a war imminent. The idea sold to the Israeli public sphere was that the Egyptians would start the war sometime in the summer of 1956.

When the summer came and went and no war broke out, the rhetoric slightly changed; war was just postponed. Nasser was now focused on confronting the West, but the imminence of the war did not subside. What was created during this period was a mutually reinforcing process. The political elites who were interested in a war created a public mood of fear and concern. The public mood then affected other politicians, who—even if they had not been in favor of an aggressive war—could not confront the concerned public.

Thus, when Ben-Gurion returned from Sèvres, he started a series of consultations with the parties making up his coalition government regarding the imminent war. It is unclear to what extent these ministers were told of the precise contents of the Sèvres agreement (Golani 1997, 397–98). Ben-Gurion brought up the war proposal to the cabinet meeting on October 28, one day before the war was scheduled to start. By then all the ministers were primed to accept the decision without much debate. Of course, nobody seriously discussed the real political objectives of the war or its desired political outcomes.

5. POLITICAL OBJECTIVES AND OPERATIONAL PLANS: THE LOGIC OF THE SINAI CAMPAIGN

We have seen that, if the stated objective of the Sinai War from an Israeli perspective was to restore a favorable balance of power to the region, the operational plans that had been proposed—both prior to and during the Sèvres collusion with the French and British—were ill suited for this objective. The Israeli elite had been primed for war long before the Egyptian-Soviet weapons deal. The key objective of this war was to overthrow the Nasser regime, and this provides a better explanation of the operational plans. The deterioration theory that had been expounded by Dayan was designed to lure Nasser into launching a large-scale attack against Israel. His defeat in this war would bring about a chain of events in Egypt (the nature of which was not entirely clear) that would result in the overthrow of the military regime. Since Israel could not face a worse regime than the Nasserist one, any political alternative was preferable.

The same applies to the Sèvres scheme. In a conversation between the director general of the French Ministry of Defense, Abel Tomas, and Ben-Gurion during the Sèvres Conference, Tomas said to Ben-Gurion: "One of these days, the Sèvres Conference will become public knowledge. It is up to us to determine whether it would be remembered as the second Yalta Conference, or as the Munich Conference of the Middle East" (Bar-On 1992, 276). The notion that Sèvres had the potential of Yalta—the framing of a new world order—was deeply embedded in the collective psyche of the participants.

Ben-Gurion's remarks at the opening session of the conference are even more revealing of the scope and nature of this perception:

> Jordan is an artificial entity, and has no future. Lebanon suffers from an excess of a Muslim population, and would be quite happy to get rid of those parts where this population is located. Jordan must, therefore, be dismantled, the East Bank [of the Jordan River] should be annexed to Iraq, in return for an Iraqi commitment to settle the Palestinian

refugees in the Arab states and to make peace with Israel, and the West Bank should be organized as an autonomous area, connected with Israel economically, while Israel manages its foreign and security affairs. The areas south of the Litany River must be torn out of Lebanese control and annexed to Israel. The Suez Canal area must be internationalized, and Israel must be allowed to control the sea entrances to the Gulf of Eilat. A precondition for any agreement is the overthrow of Nasser and the establishment of a democratic pro-Western regime in Egypt that would also be willing to make peace with Israel.

This arrangement will be in line with everybody's interests. Great Britain will return to a position of hegemony in Iraq and in Transjordan, and its oil-related problems will be alleviated once Nasser is removed, and the muddy wave of ultra-nationalism that he instigates in the region would diminish, and the Suez Canal would become an international waterway. France would establish its hold in the Middle East through Israel and Lebanon, which—as a state with clear Christian majority—would be able to return to internal stability and to its pro-Western orientation. Also the problems that France faces in North Africa may be resolved. The Americans would benefit too once the Soviet penetration into the region is stopped, and the democratic regime in Egypt would guarantee a pro-Western orientation of the entire Middle East

Israel's benefits need not be specified, as this arrangement could bring about the desired peace. This plan sounds fantastic [unrealistic], but Israel is used to seeing many fantastic plans come true. (Bar-On 1992, 253)

Ben-Gurion was known to drift in his speeches into the realm of wishful thinking writ large. This is also evident from his Knesset speech following the Sinai War, where he talked about the "third Kingdom of Israel." But even so, this presentation reflects the hidden aspirations behind the operation. The British and French were taken aback by this far-fetched vision, but they also shared it to some extent. Young (2000) notes that, in spite of widespread opposition within the diplomatic and the civilian security communities to the scheme that had been cooked up by the British politicians, many of the civil servants shared the view of Nasser as a modern Hitler, and the memories of the British appeasement policy of the mid- and late 1930s were fresh in their minds.

Given these perceptions, how could these plans bring about a chain of events that would overthrow the Nasserist regime? Operation Musketeer was designed in three stages, based on logistical and political constraints on the British and subsequently on the French forces. First, the operation called for an aerial strike on the major military airports of the Egyptian army. Second, it called for the launching of "psychological warfare," that is, a combination of the dropping of leaflets, radio broadcasts, and aerial strikes on economic targets, designed to induce the Egyptian army to lay down its weapons (or to induce a coup d'etat). Third, the plan called for the landing of paratroops and commandos in Port Said and Port Fuad.[25] The plan was based on two alternative scenarios. One was that the psychological warfare would have the desired effects, in which case the large-scale invasion and occupation of the Canal Zone would have been unnecessary. The British military command viewed this scenario as unlikely, however (Gorst 2000, 40). Thus, a large-scale invasion was seen as an essential element of the operation. Moreover, the plan assumed that—once significant ground forces had landed in Port Said or captured Egyptian airports—the joint British-French forces would have to move on Cairo itself.

Despite the warning by the British and French general staffs that a significant ground operation would be necessary to accomplish these goals, the political elites—possibly including the Israelis—believed that the psychological warfare would be effective in bringing about the overthrow of the Nasserist regime. The hidden assumption was that the United States would go along with the scenario, once it unfolded, or that it would be too slow to react due to the presidential elections scheduled for the first week of November. The politicians also assumed that international efforts to prevent the joint French-British operations would be slow or ineffective. By the time everybody woke up, Cairo would have been taken by the Franco-British ground forces and the change of regime would have been under way (Kyle 1989, 129; Bowie 1989, 209; Amery 1991, 119).

This scheme failed for various reasons.[26] Most important, the entire design manifested substantial political and/or military miscalculations. None of the plans had a clear vision of the alternative regime in Egypt. There was no discussion of how the new regime would be established, who would be the leading figures, and how it would be accepted by the Egyptian public, given that it had been established by colonial intervention. The time and effort spent by military planners on the military campaign, and the time and effort spent by diplomats on planning the political scheme that would start the joint operation at Sèvres, were in direct opposite to the amount of time and effort spent on determining the political endgame of the crisis.[27] This, of course, is not atypical of war planning in other cases, where most of the effort is spent on the outbreak of the war and only little effort is spent on planning how it will end.[28]

The Israelis spent even less effort than the British and the French connecting the military operation with the desired political outcome. Ben-Gurion and Dayan had far-reaching visions, all of which depended on the overthrow of Nasser. However, the prospect of Nasser's downfall became a realistic outcome of the war only at Sèvres. The Israeli plans that entailed unilateral action—the occupation of the Gaza Strip in March 1955 or Operation Omer, the occupation of the Sharm a-Sheikh area and the Tiran Straits of October–November 1955—had a very low probability of overthrowing Nasser. There was a vague conception that, following a military defeat in the war, which was bound to evolve out of these military operations, Nasser's opposition in Egypt would triumph. However, nobody had a clue as to the nature of such an opposition, its power, and the relationship between defeat in war and the overthrow of the regime.

Thus, everybody believed that the initiation of a war would change the Middle East dramatically. Everybody believed that this change would serve their interests. Nobody had the foggiest idea how the war would be connected to those changes. More important, before the Sèvres collusion, no decision maker spent any time considering how an Israeli-initiated war would be accepted by the international community. Would there be any political circumstances under which Israel would be allowed to maintain its occupation either of the Gaza Strip or of the Sharm a-Sheikh area? So, even if Israel had succeeded in its military campaign, it would have been more than doubtful that it could preserve the territorial fruits of its victory. There was also no guarantee that Nasser would commit his troops to a war before they were ready. Even if Israel did launch the Gaza Strip operation or Operation Omer, Nasser could have used diplomacy rather than military means to defeat the Israeli scheme. Israel would then have been even more isolated than it was in 1955.

There were also inherent strategic contradictions in Israeli military planning. As noted, Ben-Gurion was extremely concerned by the possibility of an aerial Egyptian strike at Israeli population centers. Therefore, during the Sèvres Conference he insisted on French air cover and on a French-British air strike against the Egyptian air force as soon as possible (even prior to the seaborne invasion of Port Said). Had Israel acted unilaterally—especially in December 1955 or January 1956—this scenario would have been more realistic.[29] Moreover, nobody had any inkling of how to deal with the roughly three hundred thousand Palestinians in the

Gaza Strip if it were occupied or how to secure the Sharm a-Sheikh area from Egyptian aerial or seaborne attacks if the Omer Operation were approved by the government.

The French connection, to a large extent, saved Israel from its own hair-brained schemes. Not only did it provide Israel with much needed weapons systems, but it created a closer connection between the political aims of the war and the operational plans. The flaws in the French-British plan notwithstanding, the role assigned to the Israelis was much better defined and more closely fitted to Israel's capabilities than Israel's own plans prior to this trilateral collusion.

6. CONCLUSION: THE ROAD TO WAR
AND ITS IMPLICATIONS

The Sinai War is typically depicted as a preventive war even by external observers (e.g., Levy 1987; Levy and Gochal 2001). The wish to prevent a more difficult and costly war in the future may have been indeed in the background of the Israeli decision to initiate the war. The menace of the repeated infiltrations and the blockade on Israeli shipping were significant problems. But these were not the key causes of the war. The main observation of this chapter is that a war would have broken out in the Middle East even if the Egyptian-Soviet weapons deal did not materialize. It would have been initiated by Israel, perhaps as a limited operation that escalated or as an incident of hot pursuit of infiltrators across the Jordan border. The Israeli leadership had been itching for war since the early 1950s. The only problem was to find the right pretext and the right international circumstances to start one. Initially the principal target of the war had been Jordan, but this target shifted to Egypt after the rise of Nasser in 1954. Several considerations and beliefs guided the Israeli drive to war.

1. A large number of people in the military and political elite believed that a second round of war was inevitable and even desirable. This elite believed that the outcome of the 1948 war had not been decisive either in providing Israel with defensible borders or in reducing the Arab motivation for another round. Both military and political leaders viewed the borders created by the armistice agreements as strategically untenable and politically unacceptable. They were actively searching for an appropriate pretext to occupy the West Bank. This belief was coupled with a concern that such a war might break out when the strategic and political circumstances were extremely difficult. Most Israeli leaders were

convinced that the Arabs were actively preparing for the next round. This belief rested on shaky empirical foundations. There was no sign that the Arab armies had operational plans for such a war. Nor was there evidence of active preparations for such a war. The Arab armies were in a process of stagnation, their leadership focused more on domestic power struggles than on preparations for a military engagement.

2. The belief that a second round of war was inevitable and even desirable primed military and political elites to escalate reprisals to the point where such beliefs became self-fulfilling. The policy of escalation prompted actions such as the Gaza raid, which brought about a change in the Egyptian attitude toward the Fedayeen and drove Egypt to upgrade its army for fear of an Israeli strike. This created, in turn, an acute threat perception in Israel as a result of the Egyptian-Soviet deal and furthered the escalatory schemes of the proponents of war in Israel.

3. Activist leaders in Israel shifted their strategic ambitions from Jordan to Egypt in 1954, shortly after Nasser's rise to power. Nasser was perceived as an extremely dangerous leader who was intent on, and capable of, sweeping the Middle East into a concentrated effort aimed at destroying Israel. Disregarding the sorry state of the Egyptian and other Middle Eastern armies, and downgrading Nasser's efforts at trying to find some modus vivendi with Israel, Ben-Gurion, Dayan, Lavon, Givli, and others marked unseating Nasser as a major objective for Israeli strategy. This changed the political objective of the planned war: from occupation of territory that would make Israel's borders more defensible to the overthrow of the Nasserist regime in Egypt.

4. The Egyptian-Israeli balance of power that had seemingly shifted in Egypt's favor as a result of the Egyptian-Soviet weapons deal of September 1955 was no longer as disadvantageous to Israel by July–August 1956. The opportunity to collude with France and Great Britain in a scheme of regional proportions was a driving force for Israeli elites, once Nasser decided to nationalize the Suez Canal.

5. These schemes were driven by a military-political coalition that had been in partial or full control of the government since the early 1950s—especially with the appointment of Moshe Dayan to the position of the COS of the IDF in 1953. This coalition was restrained for several years by a moderate group of ministers led by Moshe Sharett. By 1955, however, the militant coalition was able to tilt the balance of political power in its favor, with the return of Ben-Gurion to the Defense Ministry and—later that year—to the prime minister's office. By mid-1956, the moderate elements were purged from the government and the activist

coalition could operate without any effective oversight by more moderate and level-headed politicians.

6.   The linkage between the political aims and the operational planning of different versions of attack on Egypt was extremely tenuous. Israeli strategists spent much time and effort on the first stage of the war. Yet prior to the collusion with the British and French they did not have a clue how this first stage would bring about the desired objectives. Nor did they have an inkling of how to end the war.

A myth was developed concerning Ben-Gurion's strategic perspective. Many scholars suggest that Ben-Gurion's conception required securing international support for Israeli war-related ventures.[30] This myth was enunciated even by such close associates as Moshe Dayan (Dayan 1967, 12–15). The truth of the matter seems to be that Ben-Gurion was ready to embark on rather risky military initiatives without consulting, let alone obtaining, the support of key major powers. Some of the actions taken in October 1956—especially the Israeli raid on a police station in the city of Qalqilya in the West Bank on October 10–11—brought it to a head-to-head collision with Great Britain. Up to June 1956, it was the Sharett coalition in the government that prevented a number of military initiatives proposed by Ben-Gurion from becoming government decisions.

Once the French and British came into the picture, the linkage between operational plans and political end results became more explicit and logical. Yet, the loopholes in the strategic architecture—principally the international coordination aspects—brought about the undoing of the plan once it was implemented.[31]

What were the implications of the war? For France and Great Britain, the fiasco had profoundly negative domestic and international implications (Bellof 1989; Vaisse 1989; Watson 1989). For Israel, paradoxically, the consequences were seemingly positive. After a short period of basking in pipe dreams of holding onto the Sinai Peninsula, Israel was forced to withdraw to the prewar international boundaries. However, in the process, it was ensured a number of things that contributed to its security for over a decade. First, a UN force entered into the Gaza Strip to ensure that there would be no infiltrations from there and into the Sharm a-Sheikh area to ensure the freedom of navigation in the Gulf of Eilat. While Israel did not renew its effort to send ships through the Suez Canal, the southern sea route to Eilat was open. Israel was now free to develop the Eilat harbor and the city itself. Second, Israel also received verbal assurances from the United States that the latter would organize an international force to reopen the Tiran Straits if Egypt once again decided to restrict the freedom of navigation in the Gulf of Eilat. Third, the Sinai Peninsula became de facto demilitarized. This reduced friction between the Israeli and Egyptian armies, a process that had been also a source of trouble in the mid-1950s.

The subsequent ten years after the Israeli withdrawal from the Sinai were the most peaceful years Israel had experienced since its inception. The Israeli-Egyptian border was notoriously quiet, and the conflict between the two states was converted from a shooting and bleeding confrontation to a contest of words and propaganda, but without military clashes. The Egyptian army established tight control over the Palestinian population of the Gaza Strip, preventing any attempt to infiltrate Israel. Terrorism emanating from the Gaza Strip was renewed only after the Israeli occupation of the area in 1967.

Diplomatically, Israel was subject to considerable international pressure during and immediately following the Sinai War—including a threat of military intervention by the Soviet Union. However, Israel's international standing improved considerably after its withdrawal from the Sinai. First, Israeli-French ties deepened. Israel was assured of a relatively free flow of modern weapons. The French agreed to provide Israel with a nuclear reactor, which developed into the Israeli military nuclear capability in the late 1960s. The French also agreed to develop ballistic missiles for Israel (see chap. 8). The balance of power that emerged out of the Sinai War was clearly and significantly in Israel's favor. This shift of the strategic balance to Israel's advantage became irreversible. Second, contrary to the conventional wisdom that the Eisenhower administration turned a cold shoulder to Israel and considered it to be a strategic liability, recent research suggests that "the Eisenhower years were an 'incubation period' during which the ground-work was laid for the eventual American-Israeli alliance" (Ben-Zvi 1998, 136). The way in which Israel handled itself during the postwar negotiations may well have contributed to this process.

Third, the military success in the war made Israel a model of successful development and thus an attractive partner to many ventures among newly emerging states in Asia and Africa. Consequently, Israel became a hot commodity for both agricultural and military training projects. Its economic and military ties with African states widened considerably.

These accomplishments are important and unintended side effects of the Sinai War. A more comprehensive assessment of the implications of the war suggests, however, that the picture is decidedly mixed. First,

Nasser arose from his military defeat like a phoenix. He successfully downplayed the significance of the defeat of his forces by the Israelis in the Sinai, while at the same time presenting the Israeli attack as blatant and unprovoked aggression. More important, however, he managed to portray the fighting against the British and French troops along the Suez Canal as a major military victory of the forces of liberation and freedom against colonialism.

The collusion between Israel and the two colonial powers helped Nasser depict Israel as a vanguard of superpower colonial design in the Middle East. He, on the other hand, emerged as a leader of anti-imperialistic forces. This boosted his image as the champion of pan-Arabism. Nasser skillfully converted a military defeat into a diplomatic victory and was out to reap the fruits of that victory. Several ventures taken by Egypt in the late 1950s raised concern among Israeli decision makers. Egyptian intelligence agencies and its diplomats in several Arab countries—principally, Jordan, Lebanon, Syria, and Iraq—started instigating internal unrest, seeking to replace the conservative regimes in these countries with radical pan-Arab and pro-Nasserist elements.

The defeat of colonialism in the Sinai War was also an opportunity for Soviet penetration into the region. The Soviet Union's unqualified support of Egypt during the war—including the famous letters by Prime Minister Bulganin to France, Great Britain, and Israel threatening the use of nuclear weapons in defense of Egypt—increased its prestige and reputation among the "forces of progress" in the region. Thus, when the regional coups took place in Syria and Iraq, Soviet influence in these countries replaced the previous British and French influence.

If the goal of the Sinai War had been to bring about Nasser's downfall and to restore Western influence in the region, the outcome of the war was the complete opposite. The nineteen years between 1955 and 1974 witnessed the growing involvement of the Soviet Union in regional politics—typically of a military and diplomatic nature—and the extension of the superpower cold war into the Middle East. Superpower competition in the region had acted as much as an escalatory factor as it played a restraining or cooperative role (Miller 1995, 125–221).

In terms of Arab-Israeli relations, the efforts at reaching an Arab-Israeli settlement slowed down following the Sinai War. While indirect envoys kept going between Cairo and Jerusalem in the late 1950s and 1960s, the possibility of a settlement between the two states diminished significantly. This applied equally to Israeli-Syrian relations (M. Maoz 1995, 62–71).

As I argue in chapter 8, the Sinai War had a paradoxical effect on Israeli threat perception. Rather than reducing Israeli threat perception, it acted to increase it in some important ways. Egyptian defense spending in the immediate postwar period somewhat stabilized, yet Israeli defense expenditures continued to rise at an average pace of 15 percent per annum over the 1957–62 period. Following 1962 Egypt began increasing its defense expenditures more rapidly and significantly (Safran 1969). To a large extent, one of the key consequences of the Sinai War was the launching of the Israeli nuclear project. This had both a threat and an opportunity impetus to it, both closely related to the war. The opportunity was the close Israeli-French ties that spilled over to the nuclear realm and to missile technology. The threat was the conclusion derived by the Ben-Gurion crowd from the period leading up to the Sinai War and from the postwar regional processes that, over the long run, Israel had to obtain a nuclear "insurance policy" to counter and deter the emergence of a grand Arab coalition backed by the Soviet Union that set upon an all-out multiple-front war aimed at the destruction of the Jewish state.

Taken as a whole, the Sinai War was a military success. It had some strategic and diplomatic implications that served Israeli security. It did manage to accomplish most of the professed aims of the war. However, it also had adverse effects on Arab-Israeli relations, on Israel's regional standing, and on Israeli threat perception. And—most important—in terms of the grand regional strategic design of the war, that is, making the region safer for Israel and the West, it accomplished just the opposite.

— 3 —

The Six Day War

Playing with Fire

I. INTRODUCTION

The typical study of the events and processes leading up to the Six Day War covers the following sequence. During the winter and spring of 1967, Israeli-Syrian relations escalated significantly. Exchanges of artillery fire, infiltrations of Palestinian guerrillas from Syria into Israel, and concentrated efforts by each state to derail irrigation and water projects of the other became a daily matter. The war of words between the two states also intensified. On April 7, 1967, the Israeli Air Force (IAF) shot down seven Syrian Mig-21 jets, some of them over Damascus.

In late April and early May 1967, Soviet intelligence informed Egypt that Israel was concentrating its troops near its northeast border facing Syria. Israel flatly denied these rumors. However, the Syrians—convinced that the Israelis were preparing a major strike against the Ba'ath regime—called upon Egypt for help. On May 15, 1967, in response to the Syrian and Soviet warnings, two Egyptian brigades crossed the Suez Canal into the Sinai Peninsula. This move was a violation of a tacit understanding between Egypt and Israel—established following the Israeli decision to withdraw from the Sinai in 1957—that the Sinai Peninsula would remain demilitarized.

The initial Israeli response to the Egyptian violation of the post–Sinai War understandings was to put the standing army on alert. Israeli diplomats kept reassuring the outside world that Israel had no aggressive designs against Syria. At the same time, the Arab press—particularly in Jordan and Syria—began pounding Nasser for "hiding behind the UN apron" and called on Egypt to remove the UN force. Indeed, on May 18, Nasser demanded UN secretary-general U-Thant to reposition the UN forces out of the Gaza Strip. U-Thant not only agreed to do so without argument but also removed voluntarily the UN force from the Sharm a-Sheikh area. More significant, Israeli intelligence reported that Egypt was pulling its troops out of Yemen. At that point, the government decided on partial mobilization of reserve units.

The West was alarmed by the escalation of Egyptian-Israeli relations. American, British, and French diplomats met with the region's leaders in an attempt to calm things down. However, just the opposite happened. On May 22, Nasser announced the closure of the Tiran Straits to Israeli shipping. The closure of the straits constituted an official Israeli casus belli, thus leading to a general mobilization of Israeli reserve forces. Israel—invoking the tacit understanding that had been established between the two states in 1957—demanded that the United States act diplomatically or militarily to reopen the straits for Israeli shipping.

While diplomatic efforts to defuse the crisis continued, two parallel processes took over. First, a tremendous amount of rhetoric from all over the Arab world called for an all-out Arab attack aimed at destroying the Jewish state. A flurry of Arab diplomatic activity brought about greater coordination between various states contiguous to Israel. The peak of this activity was the establishment of the Egyptian-Jordanian joint command on June 1 and the beginning of the transfer of Egyptian commando units to Jordan immediately thereafter.

Second, the sense of an existential threat in Israel grew considerably. Out of a population of slightly over 2.5 million Israelis, the mobilized strength of the Israeli armed forces included some 275,000 soldiers, about two-thirds of them reservists. One-fifth of Israel's labor force was mobilized. The Israeli economy came to a screeching halt. Strategically, all of the "red lines" Israel had established as part of its deterrence policy after the Sinai campaign were violated by Egypt (Yaniv 1987a, 81–87). The Israeli government came under severe domestic criticism for its timidity. There was growing pressure on Prime Minister Eshkol to bring into the government people with significant strategic experience, such as Ben-Gurion and Dayan. The IDF also put considerable pressure on the government to launch a preemptive strike.

The government continued its quest for a diplomatic solution to the crisis. On May 28, it decided to delay military action in order to give diplomacy another chance. The Johnson administration—despite its best efforts—failed in its efforts to organize an international flotilla that would reopen the Tiran Straits. The domestic pressure on the government forced Eshkol to form a national unity government with the RAFI and GAHAL opposition parties. Dayan was appointed defense minister. Israeli diplomacy now focused on securing support from the United States for military action. While the United States did not explicitly endorse the Israeli action, the Johnson administration hinted that it would not impose sanctions on Israel and—moreover—would contain any Soviet military intervention in the conflict.

On June 4, the Israeli government authorized the IDF to launch a pre-emptive strike designed to remove the existential threat to Israel. On the following morning, the IAF launched an all-out attack on the air forces of its major Arab adversaries. Most of the Arab air forces were destroyed within six hours. At the same time, the IDF started its ground attack in the Sinai. Jordanian forces, operating under the belief that the Egyptian army was gaining ground in the war, opened fire on Israeli targets in Jerusalem and other areas of the Israeli-Jordanian border. King Hussein agreed to allow Iraqi forces to enter Jordan and move toward the West Bank. Israel immediately responded by launching a massive attack on the West Bank. Within four days of the outbreak of the war, Israel was in control of the Sinai Peninsula and of the West Bank, including Jerusalem. During this period, Syrian forces fired on the Israeli settlements in the border areas but did not attempt to advance into Israel. A debate raged in the Israeli government on the possible occupation of the Golan Height. The government delegated this decision to the minister of defense. On the night of June 9–10, hours before the cease-fire was due to begin, Dayan directed the IDF to occupy the Golan Height. By late June 10, Israeli forces were in control of the Golan Height, up to the city of Kunaytra. A new cease-fire was set for June 11. The war was over.

These appear to be the basic facts of the crisis leading to the Six Day War. However, because the crisis erupted seemingly out of the blue and because it appears that none of the parties linked to this crisis—directly or indirectly—was interested in a war, explanations diverge on the factors contributing to the escalation process that led to the war. I start out by presenting three general explanations of the origins of the war, then I discuss some of the drawbacks of each of these explanations, and finally I offer an alternative explanation of the origins of the war. This explanation suggests that Israel's policy had an important impact on the process that led to the Six Day War. Israeli misconduct during border conflict with Syria was to a large extent responsible for the process of escalation that evolved into the May–June 1967 crisis. Moreover, the dominant role of the IDF in foreign and security affairs had important implications for the management of the crisis and for the outcomes of the war. I conclude this chapter with some implications that can be derived from this episode.

2. THE CONVENTIONAL WISDOM ON THE ORIGINS OF THE WAR

The description just given of the chain of events leading up to the war depicts it as purely preemptive. Israel faced a clear and present danger of a military attack by Egypt or by a coalition of several Arab states. Israel's basic options were to absorb the first strike or to strike first. Israel chose preemption, but it was strategically as well as morally justified in doing so (e.g., Walzer 1977). This explanation centers on the May 15 crisis starting with the movement of Egyptian troops into Sinai. Israel's actions during this crisis seem to be almost recklessly prudent; its political leaders did everything to avoid war, but this prudence was interpreted by the opponent as signs of weakness and indecision. Israel was forced to act only after all diplomatic efforts had been exhausted. The war was a clear act of self-defense. The blame for this war rested squarely on Egypt. This explanation characterizes the memoirs of the key Israeli players and many other Israeli writers (e.g., Dayan 1976, 391–93; Rabin 1979, 133–53; Weizman 1975, 255–58; Braun 1997, 15–16).

Scholarly studies of the causes of the Six Day War provide a more nuanced picture. Several alternatives have been suggested. These explanations are not mutually exclusive. Each focuses on a different set of factors, but all seem to complement each other. Three principal explanations characterize the literature: the domestic politics explanation, the inadvertent war explanation, and the psychological slippery slope explanation.

2.1. *The Domestic Politics Explanation*

The key puzzle that these explanations address concerns the rapid deterioration of Israeli-Egyptian relations from a cold war that had persisted for ten years to a shooting war. This is even more puzzling in light of several Egyptian statements suggesting that the conditions for an Arab-Israeli war had not yet been fulfilled (e.g., Sharabi 1970, 53; Heikal 1978, 58; Nutting 1972, 97).

The first explanation relies on the diversionary theory of war (Levy 1989b). In a nutshell, this theory asserts that political leaders facing domestic problems will attempt to divert public attention from domestic policy to populist foreign policies. Such foreign policies often entail finding or uplifting an external "scapegoat" through the initiation of crises or by escalating dormant disputes to a boiling point. The diversionary explanation of the origins of the Six Day War examines not only the domestic political problems of the actors involved and their effect on the process of escalation to war; it also explores the connection between inter-Arab disputes and the road to war.

All principal actors in the Six Day War drama were experiencing considerable domestic problems. The newly formed Ba'ath regime in Syria confronted violent demonstrations and acts of sabotage on a daily basis, as the Islamic and Sunni opposition to the ruling Alawite elite increased (Bar-Simantov 1984, 147–65; Lawson 1996, 34–51; M. Maoz 1995, 95; Seale 1988, 104–16). The domestic struggle in Syria grew into a competition in radical rhetoric vis-à-vis Israel. Jordan and Egypt refused to let guerrillas from the newly formed Palestinian Liberation Organization (PLO) operate from their territory. In contrast, the Ba'ath regime in Syria provided both logistical and practical support to the PLO. Most infiltrations to Israel after 1965 originated from the Syrian border. Syria also increased its own military actions against Israel by shelling Israeli settlements in the border area. These actions entailed significant costs, as Israeli artillery and air force repeatedly pounded Syrian positions on the Golan Height. Yet, as long as Israel's responses were limited and did not involve any raids on Syrian positions, this was an acceptable price for the struggling regime in Damascus.

By the fall of 1966 and the spring of 1967, things seemed to be getting out of hand. Israeli-initiated encroachments into the demilitarized zones (DMZs) along the Syrian border became more frequent and intense. Israeli leaders made repeated statements to the effect that the Syrian regime was directly responsible for the border clashes and that Israel may act directly against the Syrian regime.

At this point Egypt entered into the picture. Egyptian elites, aware of their military inferiority vis-à-vis Israel, had been urging prudence in the dealings with Israel. However, by the end of 1966, Egyptian leaders faced a tenuous domestic and inter-Arab situation. First, the Nasserist ideological radiance was beginning to fade as the Egyptian economy continued its stagnation (Beattie 1994, 5–7; Waterbury 1983, 98–99; Barnett 1992, 103–27). Second, there was Egypt's involvement in the Yemen civil war that had been raging since 1962. With sixty thousand Egyptian troops stationed in Yemen, the war imposed a heavy burden on an already overdrawn economy (Sachar 1981, 138; Gawrych 2000, 3–5). More important, the Yemen civil war split the Arab world right down the middle, pitting conservative states such as Saudi Arabia and Jordan against Egypt. Criticism of Nasserist prudence vis-à-vis Israel and his seeming abandonment of the Palestinian cause became a growing issue in inter-Arab rhetoric (Sela 1998, 69–70; Kerr 1971, 129–50).

When the Israeli-Syrian clashes became increasingly intense, Syria asked for Egypt's assistance. Nasser, pressed between his reluctance to escalate and the mounting inter-Arab and domestic pressure, agreed to sign a defense pact with Syria on November 6, 1966. At the same time, he repeatedly warned the Syrians against dragging everyone into a war (Nutting 1972, 391–92, 395).

The Soviet Union also acted under considerable pressure. By the mid-1960s it appeared that the Soviet brand of communism was losing ground in the global arena. Hints of a Sino-Soviet rift started to surface. The Chinese decision to go it alone on nuclear weapons and the growing Chinese revolutionary propaganda suggested that something was rotten in the communist camp. Soviet Middle East policy also seemed to have been making little strides. In addition, an internal rift in the Kremlin regarding the extent of support the Soviet Union ought to grant to anti-imperialist forces in the Middle East increased the pressure on Soviet leaders (Ben-Tzur 1975, 121–53; Sachar 1981, 139–42; Golan 1990, 55, 58).

The Israeli political and economic situation in the mid-1960s was also fluid. The Israeli economy was in deep recession in 1966 and 1967, with an unemployment rate of roughly 12 percent. The economy was stagnated (declining from an average growth rate of 6 percent per annum in the early 1960s to 2 percent in 1966 and 0 percent in 1967).[1] The Eshkol government was under constant criticism for both its foreign policy and its domestic policy from the opposition parties. On November 13, 1966, the IDF raided the village of Samu, south of Hebron, in retaliation for repeated infiltrations. As had often happened in the past, the operation escalated, leaving seventeen Jordanian soldiers dead. Quite a few people berated the government for having been afraid to hit Syria, which had been responsible for these infiltrations, and for choosing to attack the weak and defenseless King Hussein (Aronson 1978, 59–60; Yaniv 1995, 201–2).

Thus, all actors involved were in domestic trouble, and all tried—in one way or another—to find external scapegoats to ease these problems.

While all sides were interested in keeping the scapegoating strategy on a back burner, things got out of hand. Syrian instigation of infiltrations into Israel and its shelling of Israeli settlements in the border area put the heat on the Israeli government, forcing it to respond with the use of armor, artillery, and air power. Moreover, the rhetoric used by Israeli leaders invoked perceptions of significant threat among Syrian leaders. They found themselves trapped between the fear of a large-scale Israeli retaliation and the domestic competition in anti-Israeli policy. The Syrian recourse was to call on the Egyptians to bail them out of the quagmire.

Nasser's warnings that the Syrian activities vis-à-vis the Israeli settlements would risk unwanted escalation fell on deaf ears. But the events of spring 1967 suggested to Nasser that Syrian concerns regarding a major Israeli strike were not far fetched. On April 7, the IAF shot down six Syrian Mig-21 jets, two of them over Damascus. Second, Israel intended to hold its nineteenth independence day parade in Jerusalem, in an apparent show of strength, across the street from Jordan. Third, a number of interviews by Israeli leaders contained explicit threats directed at the Syrian regime. Finally, the Soviets provided Egypt with intelligence suggesting large Israeli troop concentrations in the north.

Nasser knew that, if Egypt did not come to Syria's help in the event of an Israeli attack, the domestic and inter-Arab implications would be disastrous. His insertion of troops into the Sinai was a precautionary measure. Yet, the public nature of this move significantly constrained Nasser's ability to withdraw these troops—as had been the case in 1960 (Bar Joseph 1996). Nasser sent Egyptian COS General Fawzi to Syria to investigate the reports regarding Israeli troop concentration. But even when Fawzi indicated that these reports were unfounded, Nasser could not bring himself to back up. Oren (2002, 65) notes:

> A major share of the [Egyptian] army was now in the Sinai; to call it back now would be humiliating in the extreme at a time when Nasser could ill afford further humiliations. Continuing the buildup, on the other hand, could greatly enhance his status. Reactions to the move throughout the Arab world were enthusiastic, even ecstatic; years have passed since Nasser had been so hailed.

The inter-Arab pressure began to mount. Jordanian and Saudi newspapers ridiculed Nasser for "hiding behind the United Nations Emergency Force (UNEF) apron." There was also internal pressure on Nasser to push further. Field Marshall Amer, the Egyptian war minister, pressed

Nasser to allow his units to be positioned in the Sharm a-Sheikh area but could not do so unless the UNEF was withdrawn (Oren 2002, 66–67). Accordingly, he demanded the UNEF commander, Gen Rikhye, to redeploy UN troops in the Sinai.

Nasser may have well hoped that the UN would either refuse his request, delay its response, or—at worst—redeploy UNEF in new positions but leave them in the Sinai. UN secretary-general U-Thant decided, however, to completely withdraw the UN troops. Once this happened, the domestic and inter-Arab pressure on Egypt logically dictated the closure of the Tiran Straits. From there on, the crisis assumed a course of its own. Yet, up to the outbreak of the war, Nasser was interested in finding a ladder to climb down from the tall tree he found himself on. But this ladder had to be extremely elegant; for each step he climbed up, the more difficult it became to descend without being humiliated domestically and in the Arab world.

The domestic political explanation emphasizes three related factors that formed this pressure on Nasser: First, Egypt was in deep economic trouble, due to a growing external debt, suspension of U.S. wheat shipments as of 1965, and high unemployment (Oren 2002, 21–22). This created a strong pressure for scapegoating. A report by Lucius Battle, U.S. ambassador to Egypt, stated that "Nasser's grim domestic situation would soon compel him toward some dramatic act abroad." David Ness, the U.S. chargé d'affairs, in a dispatch on May 11, 1967, noted that Nasser had reached "a degree of irrationality bordering on madness, fed, of course, by the frustrations and fears generated by his failures domestic and foreign" (Oren 2002, 42).

Second, Nasser's standing in the Arab world was in constant decline. This created pressure on Nasser to move his troops into the Sinai and constrained his ability to break the slide toward escalation from that point on. Nasser's advisers—particularly Field Marshall Amer—argued that the Egyptian army was in very good shape and in a high state of readiness, so that if the Israelis attacked, Egypt would be able to repel the attack or to enter into a static war, one that would soon be stopped by outside intervention (Oren 2002, 56–57).

In Israel, the initial reaction to the Egyptian move was very cautious. But as the crisis progressed, domestic pressure began to mount. Despite this domestic pressure, Eshkol was determined to exhaust the diplomatic route before initiating war. However, during the crisis the IDF became a critical pressure group for war. Following the government's decision to delay action on May 28, Eshkol confronted an angry and rebellious group of generals, almost openly defying the government's authority (Oren 2002, 132–34).

The combination of public pressure, political lobbying, and the "near putsch" of the IDF general staff was too powerful for Eshkol and the moderate majority in the government. By June 1 Eshkol was forced to form the national unity government and to appoint Dayan as the minister of defense. From there, the road to war was open.

2.2. The Inadvertent War Explanation

The inadvertent war explanation focuses on two related dynamics: first, the dynamics of (direct and extended) deterrence, wherein one side attempts to prevent an adversary from attacking oneself or a third party;[2] and second, the dynamics of crisis management, wherein each side tries to demonstrate both resovle and prudence at the same time, in an effort to get the opponent to back down.[3] The inadvertent war explanation attempts to answer two questions. First, why did the process of escalation begin, when it appears that nobody had been interested in escalating? Second, why did the crisis escalate to a war that nobody wanted and all parties concerned tried to prevent? The domestic politics explanation explores the domestic roots of the crisis. The inadvertent war explanation requires us to review the strategic context within which this crisis emerged.

Israel. After a long period of relative calm along Israel's borders, tensions began to flare up following its decision to complete the Kinneret-Negev irrigation project (Maoz and Mor 2002a, 184–85). Syria expressed the most vocal opposition to this project, pressing the Arab League to adopt a joint strategy aimed at derailing the Israeli project. However, Nasser was instrumental in inducing moderation in the Arab summits of 1946 and 1965 (Sela 1998, 69–74). In 1965, the Syrians started a diversion project of the Hatzbani River, which runs into Lake Kinneret. The Israelis responded by encroaching into the DMZs, thereby provoking the Syrians into firing on Israeli farmers. In retaliation, Israeli tanks destroyed the Syrian diversion equipment. This process repeated itself several times in 1965 and early 1966. By February 1966, the Syrians abandoned their diversion project (Bar Yaacov 1967, 148–49; Khouri 1968, 229; Maoz and Mor 2002a, 185).

This process convinced the IDF that it was possible to compel Syria to stop its support of Al Fatah guerrillas and to limit, if not end, its habit of shelling Israeli settlements along the border. And it was seemingly possible to do so without escalating the conflict. However, by 1966 the number of border incidents increased, and so did their intensity. The Israelis concluded that an effective compellence strategy required escalating their actions. The range of artillery fire on Syrian positions was increased, and the Israelis applied air power more frequently. In September 1966 COS Rabin stated: "The reaction to Syrian acts, whether they be terrorism, diversion, or aggression on the border, must be aimed at the perpetrators of that terrorism, and at the regime that supports it. . . . The problem with Syria is, therefore, a clash with its leadership."[4]

When Israeli-Syrian clashes continued into 1967, the IDF decided to issue a stronger signal. The shooting down of six Syrian Mig-21 jets on April 7 was intended as a deterrent message to the Syrians. The consequence of these actions and statements was just the opposite (Stein 1991a, 127–29); they served to light all the red lights in Damascus. The Syrians conveyed to the Soviets their perception of an imminent Israeli strike. They also requested urgent help from Egypt. The Soviets forwarded to the Egyptians false information about the Israeli troop concentrations.

As noted, the Israeli response to the insertion of the two Egyptian divisions into the Sinai was prudent. A state of alert was declared in the IDF southern command, but no mobilization of reserves took place in the first few days. IDF commanders interpreted this move—quite correctly—as an Egyptian effort to deter Israel in view of the Soviet reports about Israeli troop concentrations in the north.[5]

The Egyptians' request of the removal of the UNEF troops and U-Thant's compliance with this demand imposed on Israel a new dilemma: Israeli deterrence—based on a policy of "red lines" or casus belli (Yaniv 1987a, 81–87)—preconditioned Israel's responses to the Egyptian actions. The IDF command was not too worried about an Egyptian surprise attack. Rather, the key question was how to restore the credibility of Israeli deterrence (Stein 1991a, 139–43). The incentive to preempt was a combination of two factors: the Israeli need to restore deterrence and the concern that the deployment of Egyptian troops in the Sinai would enable them to stage a surprise attack sometime in the future.

The Soviet Union. Considerable speculation and debate exist among experts as to the logic guiding the Soviet behavior during the crisis. We know two things. First, the Soviets provided Egypt with a false report about Israeli troop concentrations on the Syrian border. They refused to retract their claim even when the Egyptians knew that this had not been the case.[6] Second, during the crisis, the Soviets did their best to restrain the Egyptians in order to avert war. Soviet pressure may well have prevented the launching of an Egyptian combined aerial strike on Israeli targets on May 28 (Oren 2002, 117–21). This duality in the Soviet behavior is clearly puzzling.

Some accounts suggest that the Soviets purposely fabricated the report about Israeli troop concentrations on the Syrian border for several reasons. First, they may have been misled by the Syrians and simply repeated Syrian claims without double-checking their accuracy. Second, Soviet intelligence did a poor job of analyzing information without double-checking it. Third, the Soviets may have been trying to improve Nasser's standing within the Arab world by a seemingly harmless military-diplomatic maneuver.[7] However, if the Soviet leaders believed that Israel had been planning to hit the Syrian regime, then their actions can be seen as an effort to deter Israel through their Egyptian proxy rather than by issuing a direct threat to Israel—which could have provoked American intervention.

Once the crisis escalated, the moderate faction in the Kremlin—led by Prime Minister Kosygin—put pressure on Egypt to let diplomacy run its course. It would have been counterproductive, from a Soviet perspective, if Egypt had started the war. Thus, the Soviet Union was also playing a deterrence game with both its regional adversaries and its allies.

Egypt. The Egyptian troop movement into the Sinai was an act of extended deterrence. Nasser wanted to send the Israelis a simple message: back off Syria (Stein 1991a, 129–31). This was the same message he had sent the Israelis in February 1960 following the Israeli raid on the Syrian village of Tawfiq. If it had stopped there, then this would have been an effective exercise in deterrence, whether or not the Israelis had intended to attack Syria. Israeli decision makers responded cautiously to the initial Egyptian move. Arab sources argued that Nasser had been signaling to the international community all along that he had no aggressive design. However, this message got garbled by the UN secretary-general, who had actually—according to one account—challenged Nasser to demand the removal of the UN troops. So here, too, deterrence appears to have backfired. But this time it did not backfire because it was misperceived by the target of the deterrence attempt. Rather, it failed due to a combination of factors that neither the challenger (Israel in this case) nor the defender (Egypt) had intended.

Thus the process of escalation leading up to the Egyptian troop entry into the Sinai was the result of the Israeli policy that sought to compel Syria into putting an end to the military clashes along the border. This policy invoked existential fears among members of the military junta in Damascus. The Syrian calls for help, supported by false Soviet reports about Israeli troop concentrations in the north, prompted Nasser into an exercise in extended deterrence. Nasser's subsequent actions placed Israel on a horn of a strategic dilemma: to respond diplomatically to the crisis would kill Israel's deterrence, even if diplomacy succeeded in defusing the crisis and returning the status quo ante. To escalate would mean war—possibly associated with severe diplomatic repercussions. Deterrence logic combined with the failure of diplomacy prevailed, and Israel went to war.

This account provides a reasonable explanation for the first stage of the crisis—the circumstances leading up to the Egyptian troop movements into the Sinai. It also explains the Israeli decision to preempt. What it does not explain is the set of Egyptian decisions during the crisis itself that caused the crisis to escalate. To account for these decisions, several authors have invoked the crisis management explanation.

Crisis management has a logic of its own. As George (1991, 22) notes,

> Confrontations between adversaries can be easily managed and terminated—indeed avoided altogether—if either side is willing to back away from a confrontation and accept damage to its interests. Yet, once a crisis is set into motion, each side feels impelled to do what is needed to protect or advance its most important interests; at the same time, however, it recognizes that it must avoid utilizing options and actions for this purpose that could trigger unwanted escalation of the crisis. This is the policy dilemma of crisis management.

We noted that the first element of escalation took place not necessarily with the insertion of Egyptian forces into the Sinai but rather with the Egyptian demand to remove the UNEF troops from some of the border areas. U-Thant's response to Nasser's request to redeploy UNEF troops was of an all-or-nothing nature (Oren 2002, 70). This pushed Nasser into a corner. To withdraw his request would result in public humiliation. He thus had no choice but to demand the withdrawal of the UNEF. This action pushed the Israelis into large-scale mobilization of reserves. At that point, restoring the status quo ante would have been an act of even greater humiliation. Now, Nasser's goals in the crisis were changed by the facts on the ground. Rather than deterring the Israelis from attacking Syria, now the goal was to preserve some of the fait accompli that had already been accomplished over the past few days. To do that, Nasser had two options: to stay put and let diplomacy bring about a peaceful end to the crisis or to escalate, thus putting further pressure on Israel. The fact that the Sharm a-Sheikh area was left empty after the withdrawal of UNEF troops called for the next step. So did numerous media articles in the Arab press. If Nasser escalated further, by closing the straits, a compromise deal could be struck to reopen them in exchange for remilitarization of the Sinai Peninsula. This could be shown as a major achievement (Mor 1991).

Nasser believed that he could escalate the crisis up to a point, giving Israel the "last clear chance" to avoid war.[8] For Israel, each additional step Nasser took was another nail in the coffin of deterrence. Israel's demand for restoring the status quo ante was no longer moved primarily by the wish to avoid war; it was motivated by the need to demonstrate that Israeli threats were credible. Israel had to match the Egyptian moves with its own moves. Yet, once the entire reserve force was mobilized and sitting in the border areas for nearly three weeks, the basket of options for demonstrating resolve without further escalating the crisis was fundamentally empty. The only option remaining was to initiate war. By June 1, 1967, both sides faced a choice between launching a war and backing down. Egypt could wait a little longer. Israel, due to its precarious economic and political situation, could not.

2.3. The Psychological Slippery Slope

The psychological slippery slope explanation focuses squarely on the Egyptian decision-making process during the crisis. The initiation of the May–June crisis is seen as a rational step—assuming that Nasser believed the information about Israeli troop concentrations. However, the process of escalation is inconsistent with the prudent positions Nasser had expressed during the 1960s and with his warnings to the Syrians that their provocations against Israel might lead to an unwanted war. So there is a need to account for the logic underlying the subsequent decisions that Nasser made during the crisis.

The psychological explanation focuses on two themes. The first suggests that Nasser started out in a prudent manner but was drawn into a dream world by the burst of support in Egypt and the Arab world. This interacted with a self-deception process inflamed in part by Nasser's own rhetoric and by the reaction it invoked. Each move Nasser made was accompanied by demonstrations of support and elation in the Arab world and in Egypt itself. As the crisis unfolded, Nasser become increasingly detached from reality and developed a tendency toward wishful thinking along with a feeling of personal and national invincibility.[9]

The second theme focuses on the interaction between Nasser and Field Marshall Amer. Nasser was led astray by his most trusted adviser, who either believed himself or provided his superior with false information regarding the balance of forces and the effectiveness of the Egyptian army. Based on these data, Nasser believed that he could afford to escalate. Even if fighting did break out, the Egyptian army would be able to fight it out effectively until a cease-fire was declared. Here Nasser plays the role of a victim rather than that of a villain or a reckless gambler.[10]

The psychological explanation of the Israeli decision-making process emphasizes the conditions of extreme stress. The level of stress under which the Israeli government operated increased with each step the Egyptians took. Despite this acute stress, however, Israeli decision makers exhibited fairly rational behavior (Brecher 1975, 318–453; Stein and Tanter 1980; Brecher, with Geist, 1980; Oren 2002).

Egypt. As noted, Nasser's behavior during the May–June crisis was uncharacteristic of his past prudent behavior. It is also difficult to explain the contradiction between two fundamental facts about Nasser's crisis management. First, most observers seem to agree that Nasser did not want a war. At the very least it is clear that he was not interested in initiating one. However, with every move he made, he acknowledged repeatedly that the probability of war increased. Several days before the war broke out, he was certain it would (Parker 1993, 59; Mor 1991).

It is clear that Nasser's recklessness increased as the crisis unfolded. For example, while authorizing the insertion of Egyptian troops into the Sinai and approving the recommendation of Amer to demand the withdrawal of the UNEF, he nevertheless consulted with his foreign policy advisers regarding the drafting of the letter to General Rikhye, the UNEF commander. He asked Amer to rephrase several paragraphs in the letter, so as to prevent an irreversible process of extraction of the entire UNEF. For example, he accepted the advice of his foreign policy advisers to redraft the demand for the *withdrawal* of *all* UN forces to *redeployment of UN forces* (Parker 1993, 64–67; Oren 2002, 67). However, when U-Thant issued the all-or-nothing reply, Nasser chose the former.

The key puzzle concerns the decision to close the Tiran Straits. Nasser admitted that the closure of the straits increased the probability of war to 80 percent. This decision—in contrast to other explanations—was not a direct derivative of U-Thant's decision to withdraw the UNEF from

Sharm a-Sheikh (Parker 1993, 73–76). Finally, what clinched for the Israelis the decision to go to war was the Egyptian-Jordanian pact of June 1 (Oren 2002, 127–32; Mor 1991; 1993, 138–41). This action was completely antithetical to the notion that Nasser did not want a war.

Nasser's initial aim in the crisis was clearly to deter Israel from attacking Syria. There is almost no dispute on this point. The insertion of troops into the Sinai was in line with this goal. However, in contrast to the February 1960 Rotem crisis, wherein the Egyptian troop movements were done secretly—in fact, so secretly that the Israeli intelligence discovered the troops only after they had reached their designated positions on the border (Bar Joseph 1996)—on May 15, 1967, the Egyptian troops marched through the center of Cairo and went across the Suez Canal in the open and in broad daylight, all accompanied by radio statements and by media coverage.

This kind of public display may well have been due to organizational standard operating procedures (SOPs), as a deliberate display of deterrence power or as a private initiative by Amer, without consultation with Nasser himself or with the foreign policy advisers. Nevertheless, the Egyptian troop movement invoked a wave of reactions in Egypt and the Arab world. The supporting reactions that Egypt was finally moving to an overt confrontation with Israel were mixed with criticism of Egypt's "hiding behind the UNEF apron" and with expectations that Egypt demand its removal. This reaction had been anticipated by Egypt's military planners at the time they made the decision to move troops into the Sinai (Parker 1993, 64–65; Oren 2002, 66; Stein 1991a, 131–33). Yet, Nasser had not anticipated that his move would be challenged in the manner that it was by U-Thant. The UN all-or-nothing challenge was semipublic and imposed on Nasser a no-choice situation. He could not afford to back down in front of an energized Arab world.

Once UNEF was withdrawn from both the Sinai and the Sharm a-Sheikh area, the domestic and inter-Arab cost of restraint became higher than the potential benefits of escalation. Leaving Sharm a-Sheikh demilitarized would signal to the entire Arab world that it was Nasser's fear of Israel, rather than the UNEF, that prevented confrontation. Yet, Nasser was still cautious. He fully understood the strategic implications of closing the Tiran Straits. Thus, he turned to Amer for an assessment of the military situation. In a meeting of the Supreme Executive Council of Egypt (equivalent to the cabinet in the Egyptian regime) that took place on the night of May 21–22, just before the announcement of the closure of the Tiran Straits, Nasser asked Amer if the armed forces were ready.

Amer responded: "on my neck be it. Everything is in tip top shape" (Parker 1993, 72; Sadat 1977, 172; Oren 2002, 83). This perception that Egypt had the capability to carry out this gamble and get away with it was also based on the seemingly conciliatory Israeli response to the withdrawal of UNEF.[11]

Again, the combination of outburst of public support all over the Arab world and the relatively moderate Israeli response to the closure of the Tiran Straits moved Nasser further down the slope of wishful thinking and self-propelling rhetoric. But beyond these psychological mechanisms, there were a number of factual (or seemingly factual) elements that increased his confidence in his ability to turn this crisis into a diplomatic coup. First, he received repeated assurances—especially from Amer—regarding the ability of the Egyptian armed forces to win or withstand a war. In fact, on May 28, the Egyptian army planned a combined aerial attack on Israeli cities and on the Dimona nuclear reactor and a ground attack aimed at cutting off the city of Eilat and the southern Negev from the rest of Israel (code-named Operation Dawn) (Oren 2002, 92–97, 118–21). Despite skepticism among members of the Egyptian armed forces regarding the ability of the Egyptian air force and ground forces to pull off this operation, Amer was pushing for this attack with Nasser.[12] Moreover, when asked what would happen to the Egyptian air force if it were attacked by the Israelis, the air force commander estimated a loss ratio of about 10 percent (Sadat 1977, 174; Stein 1991a, 135; Parker 1993, 57).[13]

Second, on May 25, Nasser had sent Shams Badran with a delegation to Moscow in order to secure Soviet military and political support. Badran's talks with the Soviets produced an ambivalent picture. His talks with Brezhnev (the secretary-general of the Communist Party), Marshall Grechkov, and other politicians and military figures led Badran to expect a more active Soviet involvement in the event of a war. While the Soviets thought that the message to Nasser meant supporting Egypt by supplying it with weapons and other equipment, Nasser had reason to believe that the Soviets would actively intervene if things turned out for the worse (Parker 1993, 30–33). This would clearly be the case if Egypt became the target of an attack rather than the initiator of the war.[14]

Third, Nasser could reasonably believe that, if war broke out, Israel would have to fight on multiple fronts. Since the Syrians were the instigators of the crisis and had been threatened by Israel anyway, they would enter the fight in the north. While he had not received explicit pledges of military support from other Arab states, the Iraqis were moving troops to the Jordanian and Syrian borders. Since the decision to close the straits, Nasser's most bitter rivals in the Arab world—King Hussein of Jordan and Faisal of Saudi Arabia—had completely reversed their public propaganda from bitter cynicism and accusations to unqualified support (Oren 2002, 84). Moreover, massive demonstrations in Baghdad, Amman, Riyadh, and the North African states suggested that public pressure on the Arab governments to support Egypt would impose on these governments active military and economic aid to Egypt in the war. This pressure was especially effective when it came to King Hussein. Hussein had been trying to prevent war privately, but publicly he sided with Nasser (Oren 2002, 127–29; Kam 1974, 44–45).

Taken together, these facts convinced Nasser that Egypt could get away with the gamble. Nasser considered two possible scenarios. First, it was still possible to avoid a war altogether if international diplomacy came up with a deal that would constitute a diplomatic victory for Egypt. Second, if war did break out, Egypt could fight it out along with several Arab states. Given the belief conveyed by his generals regarding the readiness of the Egyptian army and given the pledges of support by the Soviets and the other Arab states, a war became less of a threat and more of an opportunity.

Thus, from this perspective, Nasser was led astray not only by his own personality but also by his trusted military commanders and by his misreading of the diplomatic scene and of the military capability of the opponent. Part of the image of invincibility he developed as the crisis evolved was based on what he had perceived as cautious Israeli responses. This indicated to him that the Israelis were not as confident in their military might as had been the case ten years before.

The combination of these factors led Nasser to believe that Egypt could absorb an Israeli first strike and still win the war or at least hold out long enough to allow for superpower intervention, as had been the case in 1956. In retrospect, this belief seems out of touch with reality, but at the time, such perceptions seemed utterly plausible.

Israel. As noted, most of the studies suggest that Israeli decision makers behaved quite rationally during much of the crisis. However, it is also clear that they operated under extreme stress, and there is some evidence to suggest that such stress may have impaired their performance to some extent. Two episodes come to mind. First, on May 25, two days after the closure of the straits by Nasser, IDF COS Rabin went to visit David Ben-Gurion at his home in Kibbutz Sdeh Boker. Ben-Gurion admonished

Rabin for placing Israel at grave risk. Apparently distraught by Ben-Gurion's accusations, Rabin called Ezer Weizman, the IDF chief of operations, and told him that he felt responsible for having brought on Israel this grave danger and that he wished to resign his post and have Weizman take over the IDF. Weizman (1975, 211–12) refused to take Rabin's post at that time and asked Rabin to rest and reconsider. After a period of forty-eight hours, Rabin returned to function, albeit not as self-confident as he had been in the past.

The second episode concerns Eshkol. On May 28, after the cabinet decided yet once more to give diplomacy a chance and to delay the attack, Eshkol went on the radio to deliver a message to the nation. As Oren (2002, 132) notes,

> He was desperately short on sleep, had a nagging chest cold and an artificial lens in one eye—the result of recent cataract surgery—that kept shifting. Compounding this physical state was the condition of the script that he received only upon entering the studio, finding it crisscrossed with corrections and last-minute additions, which he now had to deliver live. The outcome was a stuttering, rambling, barely intelligible reading that listeners interpreted as a sign of exhaustion and panic.

While all these technical factors may have contributed to what is known in Israel's political history as "Eshkol's stuttering speech," there seems to be little doubt that psychological pressure was much at work here. We can surmise this pressure from the facts provided by the domestic politics explanation as well. Eshkol was facing not only fundamentally existential dilemmas but also considerable pressure from opposition parties and from his own generals. The May 28 meeting with the general staff was as close to a military coup d'etat as Israel ever came.

Despite these episodes that affected the quality of decisions, the system appears to have functioned reasonably well under the circumstances. Thus, in contrast to the Egyptian side, where the system served to create compound misperceptions, miscalculations, and wishful thinking, the Israeli decision-making system under crisis performed quite well.

3. DEFICIENCIES IN THE EXISTING EXPLANATIONS

The discussion of these three explanations reveals that they are not mutually exclusive. In fact, they seem to complement each other quite well. The domestic politics explanation covers the internal arenas of the two sides, showing the constraints under which both sides were operating prior to and during the crisis. It does not account for the interactive structure of the crisis, nor does it account for the strategic logic that affected the evolution of the crisis. These aspects are discussed in the inadvertent war explanation. However, here, too, the state of mind of the politicians, military commanders, and diplomats is not well understood, and their shift from cautious to reckless policies is not well explained. This aspect is covered by the psychological explanation.

But these explanations share several problems. First, they gloss over the origin of the crisis—namely, the Soviet and Syrian claims of Israeli troop concentrations along the Syrian border. The literature on the crisis is in agreement that these reports were false and that the Egyptians were well aware of this. Fawzi's report to Nasser that the troop concentration reports had been false should have defused the crisis prior to the withdrawal of the UNEF troops. Several authors (e.g., Ben-Tzur 1975; Parker 1993, 3–35; Oren 2002, 54n51) have explored the question of why the Soviets issued those false reports to Egypt, coming up with inconclusive answers. If Soviet behavior was a result of deliberate machinations or if it was due to the utter incompetence of its intelligence agencies, then the interpretations of the subsequent stages of the crisis according to the three explanations make sense. If, however, these reports reflected a genuine Soviet concern of an impending large-scale Israeli attack on Syria, then the roots of the crisis that led up to the Six Day War lie elsewhere.

Second, these accounts of the crisis ignore to a large extent the Syrian perspective. Because they focus largely on the set of events starting around May 13–14 (the Egyptian decision to introduce troops into Sinai), the state of mind of the Syrian leadership and the reasons the Syrians inflamed the crisis appear immaterial to the evolution of the crisis itself. Yet, no complete account of the crisis can ignore the policies pursued by Syria, the perceptions of the Syrian decision makers, and their domestic and international situation. Moreover, the writings on the origins of the war fail to incorporate the Israeli-Syrian border war with the May–June events in a coherent fashion.

The existing literature also does not link the political and military circumstances in Israel to the management of the May–June crisis itself. Most of the blame for the outbreak of war is placed on Nasser and the Egyptian decision-making process. A small share of the blame is put on the Soviets for inflaming the crisis in the first place. Israel's conduct during the process gets fairly good marks by most analysts. Because the decision-making process during the crisis was fairly rational, Israel is absolved of the blame for its escalation. Israel faced an existential challenge and handled the crisis well. The victory in the war is also seen as a logical outgrowth of Israel's prudent crisis management strategy. However, here, too, the focus on Israeli behavior during the May–June 1967 crisis ignores the underlying causes of the war. To understand these causes, we must examine the military and political background of the crisis. We must examine the roots of the Israeli-Syrian crisis, as well as other strategic and political developments during the 1960s. It is only in light of these processes that we can understand certain elements of the crisis itself, such as the collapse of Rabin during the crisis and the near putsch of the Israeli generals, as well as the political atmosphere that led to the formation of the national unity government.

4. THE ISRAELI SLIPPERY SLOPE EXPLANATION

The following explanation I develop does not contradict the explanations I discussed previously. It builds upon and expands the domestic politics explanation. But it differs from these explanations in three important respects. First, it goes back several years into the past in order to identify the underlying roots of the war. Second, it examines Israeli policy not only in terms of military behavior but in terms of a fundamental change in military strategy that took place during those years. Third, it focuses on factors emphasized by the domestic politics explanation but interprets the working of these factors quite differently from the previous explanations. In short, it emphasizes the context that enables us to better understand the behavior of groups and of individuals during the crisis.

The roots of the Six Day War are to be found in both strategic and political events that took place in Israel in the late 1950s and the early 1960s. The first important background process was the Israeli decision to embark on a nuclear weapons project in the early 1960s (see chap. 8). This project raised the threat perception of Egypt for several reasons. First, it was the most powerful Arab state and as such constituted the main strategic challenge for Israel. Second, as was evidenced by the 1956 war, Egypt had already been the target of an unprovoked Israeli attack in collusion with two Western powers.

Third, Egyptian ties to the Soviet bloc rendered it a prime target of the Western powers. A nuclear rival on its border meant not only having to face Israel but having to face a spearhead of Western imperialism. The fact that the reactor was given to Israel by France—who had recently fought another Arab nation in Algeria—served as strong evidence for this concern (Levite and Landau 1994, 39–42). Fourth, Egypt would be the key target of a nuclear offensive. The risk of radioactive fallout on Israel in the event of an Israeli nuclear attack on Jordan or Syria would be extremely high due to the short distances between some of the population centers of these states and Israeli territory. In contrast, Egypt's population centers were separated from Israel by 200 kilometers of desert. Moreover, once the Aswan dam was built, Egypt would be vulnerable to a total disaster if the dam were blown up by nuclear weapons.

Nasser tried to confront this new threat in a number of ways. First, he embarked on an ambitious surface-to-surface missile (SSM) program, with the help of German scientists. Yet by 1964, this project was dead in the water.[15] Second, in his diplomatic dealings with the West, Nasser tried to warn whoever wanted to listen regarding the disastrous consequences of the Israeli nuclear project and threatened from time to time to launch a preemptive strike against Dimona. Third, the Egyptian general staff developed operational plans for attacking the Dimona reactor. The aerial attack of the Dimona reactor became a key element in Amer's Operation Dawn. Egyptian jets overflew the reactor four times during the May–June crisis, apparently for reconnaissance purposes, without being intercepted even once by the IAF.[16]

Another important element in the background of the crisis involves political changes in Israel in the early and mid-1960s. Ben-Gurion decided to retire as prime minister and defense minister in 1963, and Levi Eshkol—who had served as finance minister—was selected to replace him in both posts. Eshkol, a mellow and able politician with substantial knowledge and experience in economic matters, knew very little about security affairs. As long as Ben-Gurion's loyal seconds—Shimon Peres and Moshe Dayan—remained in the government, he could rely on their experience, knowledge, and political support to handle security matters.

However, by 1965, the political situation in Israel changed dramatically with the rift in the Mapai Party. Ben-Gurion left Mapai over a debate regarding the political ramifications of the 1954 "mishap" and formed a new party, RAFI. Dayan and Peres, as well as a large number of loyalists, left with him. As a result, a new security-oriented political front opened, challenging the leadership of Eshkol in security matters.[17] Eshkol had to rely increasingly on his Ahdut Ha'avodah coalition partners, especially Yigal Allon, Israel Gallili, and Moshe Carmel, three people with substantial security background during the prestate era and the War of Independence. In day-to-day management of security affairs, Eshkol gave the IDF a free hand that had never existed before. Itzhak Rabin, the COS appointed in 1964, had a very good rapport with Eshkol. During the years 1963–67, the Israeli defense budget increased by an average of 30 percent per annum, and the defense burden (military expenditures divided by gross domestic product [GDP]) increased from 5 to 11 percent. At no time in the past did the IDF enjoy so much growth. Brigadier General Israel Lior, Eshkol's military secretary, succinctly describes the relations between Eshkol and Rabin (Haber 1987, 97).

> The extensive security-related activities occupied much of Eshkol's time during the day. Naturally, he had an important support base during these days: chief of staff Itzhak Rabin. . . . Rabin, both due to his role and to his personality stood above all the others. Every Friday, during the meetings of the Defense Minister's staff, Rabin led the discussions from beginning to end. Eshkol accepted his views almost without questioning. I would say that [Eshkol] followed him [Rabin] with closed eyes.
>
> "I don't know much about military affairs," Eshkol used to say more than once. "I was never in the army." Eshkol knew his limitations about military matters. He was very careful about military assessments.

While Rabin was generally loyal and asked for Eshkol's approval of military operations, there were almost no instances where the defense minister did not approve the COS's recommendations. The IDF became used to almost blank-check approval of its operations, and the general staff knew it could operate almost free of political constraints. This did not mean that the IDF was bent on military adventurism, as had been the case during the Dayan era. But it did imply that the IDF was cleared to develop a strategy of military engagement without being worried too much about the political implications. This latitude translated directly into the management of the conflict with Syria.

When Syria embarked on the Hatzbani diversion project, it acted pretty much on its own. The decisions of the Arab summit in Cairo in 1964 to launch a diversion project were never implemented. In 1965 it became clear that, other than providing moral and diplomatic support to the Syrian diversion project, other Arab states had no intention of causing undue escalation at that time. This fact was clear to the Israelis as well. Yet, Israel's wish to derail the Syrian diversion project had to be reconciled with the need to maintain good relations with the United States, which viewed the solution to this problem as diplomatic rather than military (Rabin 1979, 127–30).

The Israeli military approach to this dilemma was deceptively simple.

Israel would take nonmilitary actions in the DMZs, which would provoke Syrian military retaliation. In response, Israeli artillery, armor, and—if needed—air force would destroy the heavy equipment the Syrians brought in to divert the Hatzbani River. For example, after the Syrians started diversion work in the Banyas area, an Israeli patrol entered the Tel-Dan area on March 17, 1965. Syrian positions opened fire on the patrol, using rifles and machine guns. In retaliation, Israeli artillery and tank fire destroyed the Syrian diversion equipment. The Syrians moved their diversion site to a location opposite the Bnot-Yaacov Bridge some 32 kilometers south. The same pattern repeated itself on May 13, and the Syrian heavy equipment was again destroyed by Israeli armored fire. The Syrians began to learn the pattern and decided to move their equipment further into their own territory outside of tank cannon range, hoping that Israel would not be able to find the pretext to escalate.

However, Israel did manage to find a pretext. Twice (on July 14 and August 12) it used its air force to attack the Syrian diversion project, destroying again the heavy equipment. Between August 1965 and February 1966, work on the diversion project came to a halt. The heavy equipment was removed, and most of the effort was invested in paving new roads in the area in which diversion was supposed to take place (Bar Yaacov 1967, 148–49; Khouri 1968, 229). Syria shifted its emphasis from active preparation of the diversion project to indirect support of the PLO, especially the Al Fatah guerrilla operations inside Israel, and to minor incidents of exchanges of fire along the border.

Yet, the Israeli military activity along the border continued and even escalated throughout 1966. Using similar tactics for triggering incidents, the Israelis continued to provoke the Syrians. The IDF responded disproportionately every time the Syrians opened fire on Israeli tractors working in the DMZs or on police boats disguised as fishing boats getting close to the northeast shore of Lake Kinneret. The principal aim of this "controlled" escalation was to dissuade the Syrians from supporting PLO operations. Once the psychological barrier of activating the IAF was passed in 1965, both the military constraints and the political constraints on applying air power to the limited conflict were removed. Thus, on several occasions during 1965 and 1966, the IAF was activated. Over this period, seven Syrian jets were shot down in dogfights. None of the Israeli jets was damaged (Haber 1987, 110–13).

In a rare and revealing interview ten years after that period, Moshe Dayan discussed this pattern of Israeli behavior with the journalist Rami Tal (1997).

Dayan: I know how at least 80 percent of all those incidents there [along the Israeli-Syrian border] got started. In my opinion, more than 80 percent, but let us talk about 80. It worked like this: we would send a tractor to plow some place in the demilitarized zone where nothing could be grown, and we knew ahead of time that the Syrians would shoot. If they didn't shoot, we would tell the tractor to move deeper [into the DMZ], until the Syrians got mad eventually and fired on it. And then we would activate artillery, and later on the air force. . . . I did it, and Laskov [Haim Laskov, Dayan's successor as COS], and Chera [Zvi Zur, Laskov's successor], and Rabin too when he was there [as head of the northern command], but it seems to me that the one who enjoyed most these kinds of games was Dado [David Elazar, the head of the northern command in 1965–67].

Rami Tal: I am quite stunned by what you are saying. And for what was all this?

Dayan: Well, looking back, I can't say there was a well-defined strategic conception on this issue. Generally speaking, I'll tell you this. When the War of Independence ended, we signed armistice agreements with the Arabs. We were smart enough to understand that these agreements were not peace agreements, but we were not smart enough to understand that the armistice agreements that had been signed under the auspices of the UN and which were supported by the great powers . . . were very serious agreements that form something with a significant political value. What do I want to say by this? We thought then, and it lasted for a long time, that we can change the armistice lines by a series of military operations that are less than war, that is, to snatch some territory and hold on to it until the enemy would give up on it. . . .

What I want to say is that we had thought about the armistice lines as temporary boundaries. On the other side, the Arabs too argued that they did not recognize these boundaries, since they did not recognize the state of Israel, at any lines, not even the lines of the United Nations General Assembly resolution of 1947. And this, too, contributed to the fact that nobody took the armistice lines seriously. . . .

Israel Lior, Eshkol's military *aide de-camp*, put a different spin on this idea.

In the north, fairly heavy fighting persisted on the water sources [of the Jordan River]. This war was managed by the chief of staff Rabin

along with the head of the northern command, Dado Elazar. I had a
bad feeling about this matter. I thought that Itzhak Rabin suffered
from what I used to call the "Syrian syndrome." This Syrian syndrome
seems to have afflicted almost anyone who served at one point or
another in the Northern Command. I [suffered from it] too at some
point in time. The service on this front, opposite the Syrian enemy,
aroused a special kind of hatred toward the Syrian army and the Syrian people. There is no comparison, I think, between the attitude of
the [average] Israeli to the Egyptian or Jordanian army, and his attitude towards the Syrian army. . . . Rabin and Dado were very aggressive in their military operations on the northern sources of water. The
incidents on the sources of the water and on the control of the demilitarized zones have become an inseparable part of the [security]
agenda. (Haber 1987, 95–96)

While in the mid-1960s there was no evidence of a deliberate Israeli
effort to encroach into the DMZs, the IDF did regard these areas as a Syrian soft spot and capitalized on this sensitivity to provoke Syrian
response. In this respect, Rabin and Elazar emulated to a large extent
Dayan's "deterioration" policy of late 1955, without being aware that this
was indeed a policy of deterioration. It is not clear, as Dayan points out,
that the IDF's actions were guided by a coherent strategy. Yet most IDF
commanders—as well as Israeli politicians—thought the limited engagement policy was played out by both parties under a strict set of rules that
minimized the prospect of unwanted escalation. Stein (1991a, 127–29)
claims that Israeli policy was a mix of deterrence and coercive diplomacy.
However, the fact remains that Israel initiated most of the incidents
along the border over that period, so the extent to which compellence
was working was questionable at best.

By 1966, Israeli actions became more frequent and intense. Israeli
rhetoric was stepped up as well. During 1966, statements by a number of
Israeli officials—diplomats and generals—threatened action against the
Syrian regime. For example, on the eve of Rosh Hashana on September
12, 1966, Rabin stated in an interview to Ba'Mahane, the IDF weekly
magazine, that

Syria decided to lead [the region] to war, thus the response to Syrian
actions must be both against those who commit terrorist actions and
against the regime that harbors terrorism and acts to divert [the Jordan
sources]. Here, the objective must be to change the [Syrian] regime's
decision and removal of the motivation for these acts. . . . The prob-

lem with Syria is fundamentally a clash with its regime. Here we can find some parallel to Israeli-Egyptian relations during 1955–56, although I do not put much weight on historical analogies. (quoted in Gilboa 1969, 60)

What happened in 1966 that changed the rate of Israeli actions vis-à-vis Syria and the escalation in the antiregime rhetoric of Israeli decision makers and military leaders? Two important processes come to mind: the Ba'ath coup of 1966 and the growing political and economic instability in Israel. In February 1966, a group of young officers ousted the old Ba'ath elite that had ruled the country. The composition of the group and its radical ideology brought back memories of the officers' coup in Egypt back in 1952. As was the case in the past, the new regime confronted significant domestic unrest. The regime's commitment to anti-Israeli action was thus seen as part of its effort to establish itself (Bar-Simantov 1984; Lawson 1996, 43–51). This provided the IDF with both a motive and an opportunity to try to put pressure on the new Syrian regime.

The November 1965 elections in Israel resulted in the emergence of the RAFI Party. Made up of former Mapai members, RAFI challenged virtually every move that the government had made, in both domestic and foreign affairs. In contrast to the GAHAL right-wing party, whose criticism of the government became part and parcel of the political game between a permanent ruling party and a permanent opposition party, the contest between Mapai and RAFI was both ideological and personal. The RAFI leadership was security oriented and challenged Eshkol on almost any move he made. Eshkol spent more time trying to fend off the "Ben Gurion crowd" than working on any other political struggle during his tenure of the prime minister post (Oren 2002, 50).

By 1966 the Israeli economy, which up to that year had experienced remarkable growth, went into serious recession, with economic growth declining sharply and unemployment rising rapidly. This had been the first major economic downturn since the early 1950s. Here, too, the government was subject to sharp criticism (Brecher 1975, 326).

There is no evidence to suggest a scapegoating scheme by Eshkol or members of his government. However, the implications of the worsening of the domestic political and economic situations for the management of the LIC in the north were twofold. First, Eshkol was increasingly busy in managing political and economic crises and thus provided even more leeway to the military elite in managing the conflict in the north. Second, the security elite within the government and the IDF, largely made up of people from the Ahdut Ha'avodah Party,[18] was trying to establish its credentials vis-à-vis the opposition security elite. Allon was revising the new edition of the central treatise on Israel's national security (Allon 1968).[19]

The debate between the Ahdut Ha'avodah elite and the RAFI elite centered—among other things—on fundamental disagreements regarding Israel's nuclear policy. While the nuclear program had been in full swing by 1966, the debate continued—now across the rows of the Knesset. These debates served to push the military leaders to embark on a more daring and adventurous course of action vis-à-vis the Syrians.

A key turn of events took place in November 1966 following the Samu raid of November 15. This raid invoked considerable political criticism in Israel. Critics argued that the target of this raid should have been Syria rather than the Hashemite regime, which had been putting a great deal of effort into curbing infiltrations. Moreover, if Israel intended to use this raid as a signal of resolve vis-à-vis the November 4 Egyptian-Syrian defense pact, then it picked the wrong target (Gilboa 1969, 77).

Interestingly, the RAFI criticism regarding the management of the LIC by the government had been that the government was inflaming the crisis beyond what was required and that things might get out of hand. The reaction of the activists in the government and the IDF was to bolster their strategy by escalating. The April 7, 1967, dogfight was intended as a signal to Syria and to the domestic opposition that either the strategy worked or that the Syrians would suffer even more.

Following the April 7 incident, either in anticipation of some Syrian retaliation or as an effort to underscore the point made through the use of air force, Israel probably redeployed secretly some tank units along the border (Brecher, with Geist, 1980, 45). On May 7, 1967, the Israeli government decided that, if all public and private warnings to the Syrians demanding them to stop support of the PLO and the shelling of Israeli villages failed, Israel would undertake a retaliatory raid (Brecher, with Geist, 1980, 36, 45). The decision was to undertake a set of public and defensive measures designed to bring about reduction in the tensions in the north. However, if these measures failed, the government would authorize a raid. Eban (1973, 164) notes that, even if all else failed, the retaliatory raid was to be a limited and demonstrative one. However, this was not the way the plan was presented in the series of public statements that followed this decision.

On the official level, a number of statements by Israeli diplomats (see Brecher 1975, 360–61) threatened that Israel would take measures that were "no less drastic than those of April 7." On May 14, *Ba'Mahane* published yet another Rabin statement to the following effect: "Israel's response to Jordan and Lebanon is appropriate only for states that are not interested in terrorist attacks launched against their will. With Syria, the problem is different, because the regime is sponsoring the terrorists. Therefore, the essence of the response to Syria must be different . . . Since the Syrian regime is behind the acts of terrorism, it had better take measures to curb these actions, and the sooner, the better" (Oren 2002, 52; Gilboa 1969, 101).

An unidentified official source[20] stated that "Israel would take limited military action designed to topple the Damascus army regime if Syria continues launching sabotage raids inside Israel." The United Press International report added, "Military sources said such an offensive would fall short of all-out war but would be mounted to deliver a telling blow against the Syrian Government" (quoted in Brecher 1975, 361).

Was there a definite commitment in the Israeli government to launch a large-scale operation? It may well have been a case of cheap talk, empty threats, or even deliberate disinformation (Parker 1993, 19). However, several facts indicate that such an operation may have been in the making. Between April 8 and May 14, there were sixteen incidents of exchanges of fire, mining, and infiltrations along the Israeli-Syrian border. As we have seen, a government decision pledged a retaliatory act. Some troop movements did take place in the north, although there is no direct evidence of substantial troop concentration of the size discussed in the Soviet and Syrian reports. It is possible that the government did not exactly know about these troop movements given the nature of the relationship between Eshkol and Rabin. There is sufficient evidence to suggest that Syrian concerns were not without factual foundation, although they were clearly exaggerated.

Thus, both domestic politics in Israel and a lack of political control over military actions contributed to the process of escalation in the north. The IDF operated rather free of political constraints. The IDF's recommendations for military action were uniformly approved by Eshkol's cabinet, even when Eshkol had serious reservations (Haber 1987, 116–17; Yaniv 1995, 200–202). And the IDF had been pushing— ever since the Samu raid—for escalation vis-à-vis Syria.

This chain of events and statements could not have come at a more fluid time from the perspective of the Syrian and Egyptian regimes. As we have seen in the domestic political explanation, both regimes operated under significant domestic and inter-Arab pressures. The domestic weakness of the Ba'ath regime in Syria caused it not only to try to divert attention from its internal problems by fueling anti-Israel rhetoric but to magnify Israeli military actions and verbal threats. Syrian leaders took Israeli statements about planning to strike at the Damascus regime quite literarily and personally. Israeli actions and statements fed rather well into the paranoia of the Ba'ath officers in Damascus. Israeli adventurism also served to inflame Arab public opinion in the face of the lack of effective response by other Arab leaders, especially Egypt. The interaction between Israeli military "controlled escalation" and the domestic Syrian problems and inter-Arab struggles is, therefore, the key to understanding the Six Day War as emanating from a process of unwanted escalation.

It is in this context of extremely loose political oversight of the IDF management of the border warfare with Syria that we can understand some of the puzzling aspects of civil-military relations during the May–June 1967 crisis. The IDF commanders had the feeling that they could escalate the limited encounter with Syria further without risking Egyptian intervention. The broad discretion given to the IDF was evident to people such as Ben-Gurion and Dayan. These people were concerned with the possibility of inadvertent escalation. They suspected, though they did not know for sure, that the IDF was actually preparing yet another step in this ladder.

Thus, when the crisis broke out, Ben-Gurion admonished Rabin for putting Israel at risk (possibly before the nuclear project produced weapons) through irresponsible provocations of the Syrians (Bar-Zohar 1977, 1588–90; Rabin 1979, 150; Oren 2002, 51). A subsequent encounter of Rabin with Minister Moshe Haim Shapira, leader of the National Religious Party (NRP), also put considerable pressure on him (Rabin 1979, 156–58), prompting him to tell Ezer Weizman, "I have dragged Israel into the hardest and biggest war Israel has ever known, because of a series of mistakes I had made. . . . I believe that one who had made mistakes must go. Will you accept the position of the Chief of Staff?" (Weizman 1975, 259).

Rabin spent the next two days in bed with a combination of a bad case of exhaustion, nicotine poisoning, and guilt. When he came back he was not his old confident self (Haber 1987, 174–75; Weizman 1975, 261). But both during Rabin's absence and toward the peak of the crisis (especially on May 28), other generals in the IDF general staff almost performed a military coup d'etat when the government decided on yet another delay in military action. Weizman is reported to have taken down his rank insignia and thrown them on the table in front of Eshkol, stating that he could not be held responsible for the consequences of failing to attack on time.[21] Despite the government's May 28 decision to delay the attack, the IDF maintained full mobilization of reserves (Oren 2002, 124–25). Only when Dayan was appointed defense minister did the IDF calm down. By then it was clear that the green light for attack had been given.

During the war, Dayan himself got a taste of the dishes he had been serving the politicians as COS in the mid-1950s. On several occasions during the war, the IDF defied the defense minister's directives. Dayan instructed the IDF not to reach the Suez Canal but rather to stop eight to sixteen kilometers east of it. He reasoned that allowing the canal to operate while the parties negotiated some postwar arrangement would be preferable to a situation whereby the two armies faced each other across the canal (Oren 2002, 248; Haber 1987, 246; Brecher, with Geist, 1980, 261; Dayan 1976, 443). However, the IDF forward units reached the Suez Canal by June 7 and positioned themselves there, thereby creating a fait accompli that would have profound implications afterward.

More important, Dayan opposed proposals to occupy the Golan Height. He feared that this operation would bring Israel to a head-on collision with Syria and would create a fundamental acrimony beyond that which had previously existed between Israel and Syria (Brecher, with Geist, 1980, 261–62; Oren 2002, 195, 261; Haber 1987, 248–50; Tal 1997, 107–8; Dayan 1976, 444–45). He had been able to convince the cabinet first to oppose a decision to launch a ground attack on Syria. The government was confronted by the formation of an ad hoc lobby for the occupation of the Golan Height that included the settlers of the Kibbutzim facing the Syrian border. This lobby also included a number of cabinet ministers and—most important—the commander of the northern command, General David (Dado) Elazar. Elazar air transported a delegation of the northern Kibbutzim to the cabinet room to plead their case to the government. Elazar, who commanded the futile and meaningless limited war in the north that started the whole mess, exploded in his meeting with Eshkol on June 8:

> "I don't need more forces, I don't need anything. I can go up today, to occupy and move forward. . . . We will probably have casualties, but this will not be lethal. We can do it."
>
> "Is that what the Chief of Staff thinks as well?" asks Eshkol.
>
> "As far as I know—yes. This is what I have understood from him, and he had also told you that."
>
> Eshkol ignores this answer by Dado, and puts forth another question: "And why is the Defense Minister against it?"
>
> "I don't know. Today I did not talk with the Defense Minister. I

don't know his reasons, but they clearly are not operational or tactical." (Bartov 1978, 133)

The following day in his discussions with Dayan and Rabin, Elazar called the decision to refrain from occupation of the Golan Height *Bechiya Ledorot* ("a mistake for generations to come"), and Dayan had to warn him against taking action on his own: "I know you and understand what you want, but nevertheless I know you are a disciplined guy, and you would not do anything that contradicts what we had decided" (Bartov 1978, 134). Eventually, the pressure on Dayan was too much, and on the night of June 9–10 (in fact, after the Syrians had announced their agreement to a cease-fire), he authorized the IDF to occupy the Golan Height, a decision he regretted ten years later (Tal 1997).[22]

5. CONCLUSION

The Six Day War was an inadvertent war. Everybody could have done much to prevent it; instead, almost every action taken by each of the parties accomplished just the opposite—making the war inevitable.[23] Yet, the "everybody was guilty" notion serves only to minimize the role of Israeli policies and practices in the process leading up to the crisis and the management of the crisis itself. My argument focuses on several points.

1. Israel carries a major portion of the blame for the deterioration and escalation of Israeli-Syrian relations. Over the period 1965–67, the IDF staged numerous provocations, including deliberate violations of the DMZs and the Syrian zone on the northeast shore of Lake Kinneret. The escalation in provocative actions was accompanied by inflammatory rhetoric by politicians and generals. This escalation caused the Syrians and the Soviets to think that Israel was planning to topple the regime in Damascus through a large-scale military action.

2. These actions may have been designed to compel Syria to stop the diversion project and the Al Fatah raids into Israel. However, the evidence suggests that by early 1966 the Syrian diversion project was no longer operative. The number of Al Fatah infiltrations from the Golan Height was limited, causing few casualties. Syria did not pose any serious strategic threat to Israel. Therefore, there was nothing to deter and little cause for compellence.

3. Israeli adventurism was affected by three principal factors. First, it was facilitated by significant loosening of political control over the military during the Eshkol era. This reduced control entailed blanket

approval of most operations and the almost unrestricted deployment of air power as an element of conflict management. Second, the political competition between the Eshkol government and the political opposition fostered a climate of activism that enabled the IDF to operate rather freely in the north. Third, this adventurism was characterized by overzealous use of power by the IDF vis-à-vis the Syrians, accompanied by loose tongues and threatening messages in the media. Some military planning and political decisions on a large-scale operation—which were probably intended as contingency measures—may have leaked out to the Soviets and Syrians (Parker 1993, 19–20).

4.   A key conclusion of this analysis is that Israeli military adventurism vis-à-vis Syria fed into, and interacted with, the domestic weaknesses of the Syrian regime and the inter-Arab political competition that drove Nasser into escalation. It also accounts for the domestic political pressures that acted upon the Israeli politicians and affected much of their thinking and behavior during the crisis. Israeli policies were not the only (and perhaps not the major) culprit in the process of deterioration toward war. But neither was Israel a victim or an innocent bystander in this process. It is most important to reiterate the conclusion of most scholarly accounts of the crisis: this was a process of unwanted escalation, which everybody wanted to prevent, but all were responsible for making this escalation unavoidable.

5.   The reduced political control over the military backfired during the crisis and in the conduct of the war. The IDF general staff became the chief pressure group that pushed the government to initiate the war. During the war, the IDF commanders actually continued their pressure to expand the war—especially to the Golan Height. The positioning of the IDF forces along the Suez Canal in spite of Dayan's intention to avoid closure of the canal had profound implications for the future of the conflict on the southern front.

The war ended in an overwhelming military victory. The kill ratio in terms of human fatalities was almost twenty to one in favor of Israel. The kill ratio in terms of armor and airplanes was ten to one (Dupuy 1978, 309). The end of the war found Israel in control of the Sinai Peninsula, the West Bank of the Jordan River, and the Golan Height. Israel's deterrence was reestablished big time. In contrast to the Sinai War, where the international community united to force Israeli withdrawal from the Sinai, Israel was able to cling to the territories it had occupied for a very long time. At best, Israel could use these territories to expand its size by settling Jews in them. At worst, it could use these territories as bargaining

chips for a contractual peace. The war also caused a significant strengthening of Israeli-American relations. The United States became the chief
arms supplier of Israel, which continues to the present day. Israel became
a reliable ally of the United States. According to some analysts, the U.S.-
Israeli alliance has been extremely beneficial to both sides (e.g., Organski
1988).

So, even if the war was a result of miscalculation and multiple blunders, many of them committed by the Israeli political and military elite,
its consequences were paradoxically beneficial for Israeli foreign and
security policy. It is not the purpose of this chapter to delve into the
implications of the Six Day War, but some implications have a bearing
on the following chapters. First, Israeli threat perception following its
dramatic victory did not diminish. In fact, it increased. This increase in
threat perception was expressed in accelerated defense spending, defense
procurement, and an increase in military personnel. Israel's defense burden went up from an average of 6 percent over the preceding decade to an
average of 14.1 percent over the 1968–73 period. Israel's military personnel went up by an average of 30 percent in the period 1968–73 compared
to the 1957–67 period. Israel's dollar-per-soldier ratio went up from an
average of $1,875 during the 1957–67 period to an average of $9,554 over
the 1968–73 period (see chap. 8). Second, there are several indications
that the production of nuclear weapons and their potentially operational
deployment took place during these years (Hersh 1991; Barnaby 1989).

Third, the war had a tremendous psychological effect on Israeli society and on its decision makers. The initial approach of the Israeli government to the occupation of the territories was that of a bargaining chip.
Yet this approach soon changed into one of possession of at least
significant portions of the territories. Fourth, a growing dependence of
Israeli society on Arab labor took place during this period. Fifth, and perhaps most significant, a new polarization of Israeli society evolved, largely
on issues pertaining to the control and management of the occupied territories. This split lasts to the very day. As I will argue in subsequent
chapters, the Six Day War was not only born in sin; it had profound
ramifications—most of them negative—for Israeli policy and society for
years to come. The war both exacerbated conflict between Israel and its
neighbors and polarized the Israeli body politics and its society. How
exactly this worked is the topic of the subsequent chapters.

— 4 —

The War of Attrition

The First Payment for Arrogance

I. INTRODUCTION

The War of Attrition is said to have resulted from an Egyptian decision to launch a static war against Israel in March 1969. Most accounts suggest that Egypt launched this war to accomplish three objectives. First, Nasser wanted to demonstrate to the Egyptian people that Egypt was down but not out of the conflict following the Six Day War. Second, Egypt wanted to send a signal to the Arab world and to the major powers that they needed to put pressure on Israel in order to bring about its withdrawal from the occupied territories. Third, from a military perspective, Nasser wanted to prepare the defeated Egyptian army for another round, in which Egypt would take the offensive initiative.[1]

The key criticism of Israeli behavior prior to and during the war centers on the decision to escalate the war, through deep penetration bombing of infrastructure and civilian targets in Egypt. The deep penetration bombing caused a major escalation in Soviet involvement in the war. It brought about at least one aerial clash between Israeli jets and Egyptian jets flown by Soviet pilots in July 1970. It had the potential of converting the conflict into a Soviet-Israeli military conflagration. This escalation could have even drawn the United States into direct military involvement in the conflict (Parker 1993, 125–26). The course and consequences of this war carry important political and strategic implications for the process leading up to the Yom Kippur War of 1973.

113

This chapter discusses three aspects of the War of Attrition that bear on the general argument of this part of the book. First, in contrast to much of the literature that dates the beginning of the war to March 1969, I trace the origins of the war to the first few months following the termination of the Six Day War. Second, I discuss the Israeli management of the war, focusing on the strategic aspects of the fighting along the Suez Canal and the deep penetration bombing strategy. Third, I discuss the implications of the war.

In the previous chapters, I reviewed the conventional wisdom explanations regarding the origins of those wars, criticized them, and offered alternative explanations. In this case, there clearly was an Egyptian decision to launch a war of attrition along the Suez front. The goals of this war are also fairly transparent. However, the Egyptian decision to launch the war tells us, basically, what the Egyptians had in mind given the situation that had materialized along their new border with Israel. It is important to explain, however, why this situation evolved and how it affected the Egyptian decision to start a war of attrition. We must look, therefore, at the events that transpired along the Egyptian front following the termination of the Six Day War.

The management of the War of Attrition highlights important features of the overall Israeli approach to the use of force, as well as the limits of this approach. The War of Attrition was the first Arab-Israeli war that ended without a clear victor and vanquished. It was the first—but not last—war Israel had not won, at least not in terms of clear territorial and/or strategic achievements. As we will see, the Israelis were the last to realize this and to draw the right lessons from the war. But the War of Attrition had profound implications for subsequent events in the Arab-Israeli conflict. Hence, it is important to evaluate Israeli performance in this war.

2. THE ORIGINS OF THE WAR OF ATTRITION

The Six Day War ended with the Israeli forces spread on the Suez Canal and the Gulf of Suez overlooking Egypt. This was in violation of Dayan's directive to the IDF to stay away from the Suez Canal. However, once the IDF reached the Suez Canal, Dayan refrained from ordering redeployment. From the IDF perspective, this new border appeared ideal because of the natural water hurdle separating the two armies. This rendered the new border seemingly "defensible."

The first major postwar incident along the Suez Canal occurred in late

June 1967. The Egyptians established a symbolic post east of the canal in the Port Fuad area, the only part of the Sinai Peninsula that the IDF had not occupied during the Six Day War. The Israelis attempted to attack and drive the Egyptian force back, but the IDF force got trapped in the muddy ground in the area (Rabin 1979, 209). The heavy battle that ensued, labeled by the Egyptians as the "battle of Ras el Ush," was decided in favor of the Egyptians. This provided Egypt a first indication that the IDF was not invincible after all (Korn 1992, 89–90; Dupuy 1978, 348; Gamassy 1993, 99).

The Suez Canal was closed for shipping by Egyptian decree, but the possibility of reopening it existed. The Israelis, however, wanted to take advantage of their presence on the East Bank by claiming their partial sovereignty of the canal. It is unclear whether there was a conscious political decision, but by early July the IDF launched several small boats into the canal in the Qantara area (the central sector of the canal). The Egyptians fired on these boats; the Israelis hit Egyptian targets in Qantara and Ismailiya with artillery and tank fire. Egyptian artillery responded, and soon the IAF was brought in to establish its superiority in the area. The clash lasted three days (July 14–16, 1967), during which the Egyptians lost six jets. Israeli casualties in this incident included fifteen soldiers killed and sixty-nine wounded. Egyptian casualties were estimated in the hundreds.[2]

Similar incidents, albeit on a smaller scale, continued sporadically over the summer and early fall of 1967. The script was similar: the Israelis sent small boats into the canal, the Egyptians fired on these boats with light weapons, and the Israelis responded with light and mortar fire. These incidents were limited, however, causing only few casualties on both sides. But the Israelis established a new set of rules: "If we can't use the Canal, neither can you" (Dupuy 1978, 348–49).

On October 21, 1967, two Soviet-made Egyptian Komar missile boats sank the Israeli destroyer *Eilat,* killing forty-seven Israeli sailors. In retaliation, the IAF bombed the Egyptian oil refineries in Suez City. By that time, the civilian population in the canal area had dwindled gradually, owing to the occasional Israeli fire on civilian targets. Following the Israeli attack on the refineries, the Egyptian government began evacuating the civilian population along the Suez Canal (Korn 1992, 96–97; Schueftan 1989, 125–26). By October 31, over 350,000 Egyptians were evacuated from Ismailiya and Suez. Korn (1992, 97) notes: "The import of all this could hardly have been missed: Nasser was clearing the decks for war, and in that war he was ready to sacrifice the cities of the Suez Canal."

Yet, following the destruction of the oil refineries, the area calmed down for almost a year. The next serious military incident took place on September 8, 1968. Why did Nasser wait so long before starting the war? The conventional answer is that Egypt had to rebuild its military forces before embarking on a war. If the Israelis decided to attack across the Suez Canal, Egypt would be ready (Schueftan 1989, 65–66, 126–27; Korn 1992, 56–57).

A number of other measures taken by Nasser over this period render credence to this proposition. First, Nasser instructed Muhammad Fawzi, the newly appointed minister of war, to prepare a plan for retaking the Sinai by 1970 (Schueftan 1989, 64–65; Korn 1992, 93). "Plan 200" was beginning to take shape by January 1968. It called for three operational stages. The first, the "steadfastness" stage, was scheduled from June 1967 to March 1968. The second, the "confrontation" stage, was supposed to extend from March 1968 to the beginning of 1969. The third, the stage of "deterrence and victory"—the Egyptian attack to recapture the Sinai—would be implemented from 1969 to sometime in 1970.[3]

Second, Nasser needed extensive Soviet support to rebuild Egypt's army in terms of equipment, training, and logistics (Heikal 1978, 191–92; 1975, 39–45). Third, Nasser needed financial support from the oil-rich Arab states to help him in the reconstruction of the Egyptian armed forces and in making up for the loss of the revenues of the Suez Canal and the Suez oil refineries (Gawrych 2000, 101; Korn 1992, 97).

So 1968 was to be used for rebuilding the armed forces, for securing Egypt's strategic supply from the Soviet Union, and for obtaining support from the Arab world. On the diplomatic front, Nasser adopted a seemingly uncompromising stand, best illustrated by the following statement of his: "that which was taken by force shall be returned by force" (Korn 1992, 72). Accordingly, he seemingly rejected any effort to negotiate an Israeli withdrawal from the Sinai. This was his reaction to the American message regarding the Israeli offer to withdraw to the international boundaries in return for a formal peace treaty and security arrangements (Schueftan 1989, 41–42; Korn 1992, 13–15). He argued that recognition of Israel or a partial agreement with it would reward the Israelis for their aggression (Riad 1981, 47).

This explanation for the lull in the hostilities between October 1967 and September 1968 is quite tenuous, however. First, it assumes that these were the Egyptians who had deliberately avoided confrontation. In fact, the Israelis were equally "guilty" of the relative tranquility that characterized this period. Once its deterrence was established by destroying the oil refineries, and once both parties tacitly accepted the principle of a closed canal, Israel had little incentive to escalate. Second, by early 1968, the Egyptian armed forces not only regained all of their lost and destroyed equipment from the Soviet Union but were considerably stronger in overall size and hardware than they had been in June 1967 (Korn 1992, 56).

Third, both during the Khartoum Conference of August 28–31, 1967, and during the October–November UN negotiations leading up to Security Council Resolution 242, Egypt sent out numerous signals that it was interested in a negotiated settlement (see chap. 10). Nasser was willing to consider a political settlement (even a separate one) with Israel, based on full Israeli withdrawal in return for an Egyptian pledge of non-belligerency. He was hoping for U.S. pressure on Israel toward such an agreement. Another possibility he considered was an Israeli withdrawal out of the Suez Canal Zone as a gesture of goodwill that would allow the opening of the canal and the reconstruction of the Suez refineries. The lull in the fighting was Nasser's way of signaling to Israel and the United States that he was open to discussing possible agreements (Meital 1997, 58).

The renewal of the fighting along the canal in September 1968 was, among other things, a result of lack of political progress in the diplomatic arena. Nasser felt that the United States was not willing to press Israel into territorial concessions. Gunnar Jarring, the UN special representative appointed following Resolution 242, produced no meaningful results. Nasser also sensed—quite correctly—that the Israeli position regarding the return of the Sinai to Egypt had undergone fundamental change. There were several small incidents in June 1968, which included exchanges of fire across the canal and the interception of an Egyptian patrol in northern Sinai, near Roumani (Parker 1993, 129). Heavier fighting started on September 8 and October 29. This was Nasser's way of signaling to the Israelis and the Americans that lack of political progress would lead to further escalation quite soon (Bar-Simantov 1980, 43–45; Parker 1993, 129; Schueftan 1989, 130–31).[4]

The Israeli government interpreted the Khartoum resolution to imply that there was no partner for negotiations for a "land for peace" deal. Instead of treating the occupied territories as a bargaining chip, as the June 19, 1967, decision implied, the Israeli government began treating the territories in terms of "strategic depth" and "defensible borders." The IDF was instructed to treat the Suez Canal as the stopping line of Egyptian military activity. During the first half of 1968, the IDF held relatively few units along the Suez Canal, building fairly superficial fortifications.

The Canal Zone became a tourist attraction for both the Israelis and their guests (Korn 1992, 98; Gawrych 2000, 103; Parker 1993, 129). Even after several incidents in June and July, when several Egyptian reconnaissance commando units were spotted or intercepted in the Sinai, the IDF's deployment did not change.

The incidents of September and October 1968 took the IDF by surprise.[5] Israel's reaction was a daring commando raid into Upper Egypt. On the night of November 1, an Israeli paratroop force destroyed two bridges across the Nile and a power transformer in the Naj Hamadi area. This was meant as a signal that Israel was capable of hitting deep into Egyptian soil. By that point, however, Nasser was determined to start the War of Attrition in earnest (Bar-Simantov 1980, 43–45; Schueftan 1989, 134–36).

The War of Attrition was an integral part of an Egyptian strategy designed to restore the honor and pride of the Egyptian army; it was one stage in a long-term plan to recapture the Sinai (Schueftan 1989, 63–95; Gamassy 1993, 10–23; Shazly 1980, 15). Nevertheless, Israeli policies contributed to the decision to initiate the war in several ways. First and foremost, Israeli presence along the canal and Israel's actions both contributed to the closing of the canal and to the evacuation of the Egyptian population in the cities. This removed any civilian constraints on escalation. Had there been a buffer between Egyptian troops and the Israeli troops and had there been international pressure on both Israel and Egypt to keep the Suez Canal open, it may well have compelled the two sides to think twice before escalating.

Second, Israeli presence along the canal was a constant menace and humiliation to the Egyptians. Israeli behavior—launching boats and swimming in the canal, as well as converting various sites opposite Qantara and Ismailiya into tourist sites—may not have been a matter of policy. Yet, the arrogant nature of these behaviors and the psychological impact they were bound to have on the Egyptians went unnoticed by Israeli policymakers. In addition, the deliberate Israeli intervention to prevent the pulling out of thirteen ships—some of them American—that had been stranded in the Suez Canal since June 1967 did not help to alleviate tensions. This kind of arrogant and uncompromising behavior was instrumental in fomenting Egyptian resolve to take a limited military initiative in order to redeem at least part of its self-esteem.

Third, Israeli attitudes hardened over time. The Israeli interpretation of the Khartoum resolutions was very negative. As a result, the initially flexible policy position toward an agreement with Egypt and Syria, and the acceptance of the land-for-peace formula pronounced in Resolution 242, was replaced by a position that demanded direct negotiations toward full peace as a precondition for considering territorial compromises.[6] The Israelis adopted the English version of Resolution 242, clearly indicating that Israel was seeking territorial modifications on all fronts. Throughout 1968, the Israelis repeatedly turned a cold shoulder to Gunnar Jarring. Jarring represented for Israel an organization that betrayed its mission when it pulled out the UN observers in May 1967. The Israelis never saw Jarring as a serious emissary capable of delivering anything meaningful.

Fourth, the IDF continued its policy of disproportionate use of force in retaliation of minor Egyptian violations of the cease-fire agreement, thereby provoking the Egyptians and helping remove their restraints. This may have well resulted from local initiatives or SOPs carried over from the pre–Six Day War engagements along the Syrian border. The Egyptian sinking of the Israeli destroyer *Eilat* and the resulting Israeli destruction of the Suez oil refineries are a case in point. The Israelis argued that the *Eilat* was outside of the 21-kilometer Egyptian territorial water; yet the Egyptians argued that *Eilat* entered Egyptian territorial water. The habit of sending ships to areas overlooking Egyptian cities was part of a pattern of provocations that the Israelis had applied since the war. It is possible that Egypt would have launched the war regardless of these Israeli actions, but it seems plausible that Israeli actions removed any inhibitions Nasser may have had about such a war.

3. ISRAELI STRATEGY, PHASE I:
ATTRITION AND TIT FOR TAT

Up to February 1970, the Israeli response to the Egyptian War of Attrition was essentially to do more of the same of what it had been doing since 1967. This strategy consisted of three elements: first, fortification of the Suez front and quid pro quo management of the static war; second, occasional incursions into Egyptian territory, through small-scale or large-scale raids; third, paralysis on the diplomatic front and rejection of proposals for settlement and/or withdrawal.

As the Egyptian use of artillery fire across the canal intensified toward the late fall of 1968, the IDF general staff began to reconsider its deployment and fortifications along the canal. The number of casualties on this front also began to mount to a level where the Israeli public started taking notice. On October 29, 1968, Dayan informed the Knesset that, in the sixteen months since the Six Day War, Israel had suffered a total of

101 fatalities and about 300 wounded on the southern front (Gawrych 2000, 103; Parker 1993, 131).

The deliberations in the IDF and the government produced two conclusions. First, a decision was made to increase the light infantry presence on the canal itself and to place IDF troops in fortified bases along the canal. Each such fortified position (called *Maoz*—or "small fortress"—in Hebrew) contained a force ranging from a platoon to a company. These fortified positions (*Maozim*) were separated by open spaces a distance of about eight to sixteen kilometers, and these distances were covered by light patrols that were designed to prevent incursions by Egyptian commandos and to secure the supply roads to the Maozim. In order to protect the patrols and supply vehicles from direct fire from across the canal, a dirt ramp was built all along the eastern bank of the canal. The total force immediately overlooking the canal never exceeded one infantry brigade.[7] As a second line of defense, the IDF built concrete fortifications stationing armored units in locations of eight to eleven kilometers east of the canal and in positions about midway between the Maozim. From these positions—called *Taozim*—tanks could move forward to prepared tank ramps along the dirt ramp and fire at Egyptian positions (Korn 1992, 99–101; Bar-Simantov 1980, 62–63; Dupuy 1978, 358–61).

The artillery duels along the Suez Canal raged on a daily basis. The Maozim and the Taozim helped reduce Israeli casualties. Yet, supply vehicles and Israeli patrols were open targets to Egyptian snipers and to occasional commando raids. In April 1969, the IDF counted no less than 475 incidents. Over the period of March to December 1969, over 138 Israelis died in the Canal Zone (Schueftan 1989, 440). Egyptian commando units raided some of the Maozim, and one of them was almost taken on April 19 (Korn 1992, 117). Another Egyptian commando attack on a Maoz ("The Pier") near Suez City on July 12 resulted in 10 Israeli fatalities.

The IDF launched a return raid on Naj Hamadi on April 24, a raid on Souhaj on June 30, and a commando raid on the fortified Green Island on July 19. Another emerging pattern involved growing use of the IAF. On June 17, two Israeli Mirage jets overflew Nasser's residence in Cairo, causing a supersonic boom over Egypt's capital. During June and July, Israeli jets shot down over twenty-one Egyptian jets (Schueftan 1989, 189–90). In general, however, Israel played by the rules dictated by the Egyptian strategy, emulating to a large extent Egyptian patterns. This tendency to reply in kind began to confront increased criticism inside and outside the government. The IDF raids were depicted as heroic achievements and served to boost the IDF image in the world, but they had no effect on Egyptian strategy and resulted only in additional casualties (Bar-Siman-tov 1980, 68–70; Korn 1992, 116–19). There was a growing awareness among Israeli decision makers that their strategy of responding in kind to the Egyptian attrition strategy was not working (Gawrych 2000, 110). Yet, this kind of war could not go on without significant damage to Israeli military strategy, the domestic support for the government, and Israel's international standing. It was time to revise Israel's strategy.

4. ISRAELI STRATEGY, PHASE II: ESCALATION

The revision process of Israel's war strategy was not systematic; it emerged from numerous debates and was implemented in a piecemeal fashion. Two options emerged: to persist in the tit-for-tat strategy or to escalate. Weizman (1975, 309–10) notes:

> A country with a strong standing army, which has only recently defeated its foes in a war of movement excellently waged, if it chooses to fight by means of commando raids and not to make use of its full strength, does so for one or two reasons: either it does not believe it can make use of its strength to the full extent . . . or . . . due to the self-deluding belief that this or that commando action would solve the problem.[8]

There was a third option. This option was beginning to make rounds among some circles in Israeli public opinion (at that time a tiny minority) and among a small number of government officials. This option was to launch a peace initiative that would signal to the Egyptians willingness to compromise. This option came up in a debate between Finance Minister Pinhas Sapir and Defense Minister Dayan in late 1968 and early 1969 regarding the integration of the West Bank and Gaza Strip economies with that of Israel (Korn 1992, 133–35). It reflected a divergence of views regarding the general approach to the conflict and to some extent is reminiscent of the old Sharett–Ben-Gurion debates in the 1950s. Sapir's conception was that the conflict was temporary and that the territories should be taken as a bargaining chip in future negotiations with the Arabs. Any unilateral steps by Israel to render its hold over the occupied territories permanent would be self-defeating or would even threaten the very existence of Israel as a Jewish state. As long as Levy Eshkol was alive, this view held considerable credence in the Labor Party. However, following Eshkol's death on February 26, 1969, and his succession by the hard-liner Golda Meir, the militant position in the cabinet gained the upper hand. The mere notion of initiating a peace proposal appeared to be akin to treason (see chap. 10).

By the fall of 1969, the dilemmas associated with the handling of the War of Attrition intensified. The key dilemma was presented by and to the decision makers as a choice between potential losses. Continuing the tit-for-tat strategy entailed a certain but low cost. The other option—escalating the war—either could result in a risky prospect of inadvertent escalation, due to direct Soviet involvement, or could end the war. This framing rendered the latter option far more attractive than the former.[9] The escalation option emerged gradually, and its adoption was an evolutionary process. Quite a few military planners suspected that the activation of the IAF may lead to increased Soviet intervention (Schueftan 1989, 197–98). The dense Egyptian antiaircraft defenses along the canal also raised concerns about significant IAF losses. Yet, IAF operations in July 1969—seen as a pilot test of a large-scale air campaign—were judged to be a significant success. The aerial raids were thought to have caused severe damage to the entire Egyptian deployment along the canal, including to its air defense systems.

The relative success of the Israeli aerial operations notwithstanding, the idea of using the IAF as a key element of an offensive strategy was slow in gaining political support. Dayan's concerns regarding the possibility of direct Soviet intervention in the conflict were pitted against the growing frustration among central members of the IDF general staff—such as Weizman—due to the perceived futility of the static ground war. In August and September, the IAF continued to conduct limited operations, mostly in support of ground raids, but the basic strategy did not change in the summer and fall of 1969.

Two events that were only indirectly related to the developments in the Suez Canal tipped the balance in favor of the offensive aerial strike strategy: the Rogers peace plan and the supply of F-4 Phantom jets to Israel by the United States.

Throughout the spring and summer of 1969, Joseph Sisco, assistant secretary of state for Near Eastern and south Asian affairs, and Nikolai Dobrynin, Soviet ambassador to the United States, held a series of talks aimed at drafting a joint U.S.-Soviet plan for peace in the Middle East. After prolonged negotiations, the American team drafted a ten-point proposal. The proposal called for full Israeli withdrawal from the Sinai in return for Egyptian-Israeli negotiations toward a contractual peace agreement and freedom of navigation for Israeli shipping in the Suez Canal and the Gulf of Aqaba. The proposal was submitted to the Soviets on October 28, and copies of it were handed to Israel and Egypt.[10]

Egyptian response to the Rogers proposal was formally negative. Informally, however, Egypt did not turn it down. In Israel the Rogers Plan was seen to present grave risks. It clearly stated that the United States viewed a complete Israeli withdrawal from the Sinai as part of the solution. However, what concerned Israeli decision makers more than the terms of the proposal was the process by which this proposal emerged. This proposal was seen as an attempt by the superpowers to impose a settlement on Israel. Israeli decision makers felt that the continued war created incentives for the superpowers to propose an imposed solution. This added increasing pressure on Israel to change strategy in order to bring about an end to this war. Accepting the proposal, even in principle, was unacceptable to the Meir government. This was not only because of the threat of the collapse of the national unity coalition. Rather, it ran contrary to the basic conviction of Meir, Dayan, and Gallili—the key players in the Labor Party.

Yitzhak Rabin, Israel's newly appointed ambassador to the United States, emerged as one of the more important players in the decision-making process. Rabin reported to the Israeli government that the U.S. national security adviser, Henry Kissinger, was opposed to the Sisco-Dobrynin talks. Kissinger, according to Rabin, had argued that the stalemate in the Middle East worked in favor of American interest and that it was counterproductive to impose a settlement on the parties (Korn 1992, 153–58). Kissinger predicted that a superpower plan would not work, because the indigenous parties would reject it. Second, if the United States were to intervene, it would have been only after the Egyptians ended the Soviet involvement (Kissinger 1979, 368–69, 373–77). Rabin also argued that leaving the Suez Canal closed to shipping was an important asset to the United States, because it would deny the Soviets a quick route to supplying the North Vietnamese. Rabin suggested that the United States would not be opposed to a deliberate Israeli escalation of the war (Margalit 1971; Rabin 1979, 261; Korn 1992, 171–74).

Bureaucratic politics were also operative, however. By August 1969, Israel received its first shipment of F-4 fighter-bombers. The Phantom jets were considerably more sophisticated and multipurpose weapon systems than anything else that existed in the region thus far (Korn 1992, 63; Schiff 1970, 176; Gawrych 2000, 114). The arrival of the first batch of Phantoms increased considerably the belief in the IAF that Israel could strike deep in Egyptian territory with near impunity (Shlaim and Tanter 1978).

Bar-Simantov's (1980, 117–18) assessment reflects the near consensual view of most analyses of the Israeli decision to escalate the war.

> Israel . . . chose to put military considerations before political ones. This choice was mainly the outcome of the strategic gains secured earlier [in the previous cases of activating the IAF along the canal]. . . . It was thought that the strategic superiority asserted by Israel at the end of 1969 would enable it to "teach the Egyptians a lesson" for having started the War of Attrition and would also bring the war to an end by deciding the outcome both militarily and politically.

This balance of military considerations prior to diplomatic ones is characteristic of the Israeli tendency to try to solve that which does not render itself to a forceful solution, by the application of an even more forceful strategy. But here political considerations did not present a real trade-off. This decision, as Bar-Simantov (1980, 118) observes, "appeared to be an opportunity to prevent the imposition of a political settlement not to Israel's liking."

Finally, deep penetration bombing appeared expedient in early 1970 because it had become feasible from an operational perspective, given the upgrade in Israeli air power. The technical and tactical concerns that had accompanied the deployment of the IAF in the second half of 1969 were removed. "We should do it because we can" is the phrase that best characterizes this logic (Shlaim and Tanter 1978).

Thus, on January 7, 1970, Israel started to apply a systematic strategy of hitting military, economic, and civilian targets deep inside Egypt. Most of the Egyptian casualties were military, but occasionally Israeli planes also hit civilian targets, causing an enormous amount of human and material damage.[11] The aerial attacks can be divided into two phases. The first phase (January–February) focused on military targets near the main cities of Egypt, including several raids in the immediate vicinity of Cairo. The second phase (March–April) focused on the Nile Delta area (Bar-Simantov 1980, 132).

A key issue in the deliberations regarding the escalation of the War of Attrition during the fall of 1969 was the question of direct Soviet intervention. Dayan, known for his obsessive concern with this issue, had a good reason to expect such intervention. Soviet involvement in the rehabilitation of the Egyptian armed forces after the Six Day War, the number of Soviet advisers in Egypt, and the political support that the Soviet showed toward the Arab cause were clear indicators of the growing level of direct Soviet involvement in the conflict. Deep penetration bombing would challenge Soviet commitment to their Egyptian friends. However, most experts in the intelligence community and in the government discounted the prospect of direct Soviet involvement. The argument was based on several factors. First, the Soviets had been extremely reluctant to involve their own personnel in local conflicts, due to the risk of escalation to a global conflagration. Second, the Soviets would be weary of getting entangled in their own version of Vietnam. They would be facing a more potent military force than the one they could bring to bear in the region, and their forces would be handed a humiliating defeat. Third, the history of the cold war suggested that the Soviets were extremely reluctant to intervene directly in conflicts outside the Soviet bloc. The only case where they had embarked on such an adventure—Cuba in 1962—must have taught them about the futility of such an effort (Bar-Simantov 1980, 126–30).[12]

Another issue in the government's deliberations on deep penetration bombing was the question of U.S. response. Here, Rabin's view dominated the debate. Rabin argued that not only would Washington not oppose the Israeli decision to escalate, but it would tacitly support it. Rabin argued that Washington was interested in a decisive Israeli victory. First, it would hand the Soviet client another humiliating defeat, despite all of the hardware the Soviets had been pouring into Egypt since 1967. Second, the Nixon administration believed that yet another humiliation of Nasser would send a signal to other regimes in the Middle East that Egyptian nationalism was the wrong tree to climb on (Korn 1992, 171–73; Bar-Simantov 1980, 130–32).

On both the Soviet issue and the American issue the government was deeply divided. The most influential voice in this debate, however, was Rabin, a civil servant who had no formal business advocating policy. His opinions weighted heavily with Golda Meir. Golda's position was crucial, because she could have tilted the balance either way. But it appears she had no real dilemma. She felt that something had to be done in order to bring an end to this unfortunate war. She was prepared to accept the intelligence estimates and the assessments of her favorite ex-general Rabin and discount the reservations of other—not less knowledgeable and experienced—advisers and support the deep penetration strategy.

Here, too, military considerations dominated political ones. But in this case, a number of political and international considerations converged to make the case for the deep penetration bombing policy. The growing domestic discontent with the government's policies and the concern with the Rogers Plan were powerful incentives to escalate. This may have offset the risk of Soviet involvement in the minds of some cabinet ministers.

5. ISRAELI STRATEGY, PHASE III: DECLARING VICTORY AND ENDING THE WAR

The deep penetration bombings wreaked havoc in Egypt, causing numerous fatalities, severe economic damage, and grave concern among the Egyptian leaders. Their plan to fight a war of attrition under mutually acceptable limits on the rules of engagement seemed to have collapsed. Nasser's concern with the course the war had been taking started before the Israeli decision on deep penetration bombing. The collapse of the air defense system along the Canal Zone in the fall of 1969 forced Nasser to send his top aides to Moscow in December. The Egyptians asked for long-range bombers and SA-3 missiles in order to enable Egypt to withstand Israeli aerial attacks and to retaliate with long-range bombing of its own. The Russians turned down Egyptian requests for long-range bombers but agreed to provide Egypt the SA-3 missiles (Korn 1992, 183; Schueftan 1989, 250–51). The new surface-to-air missiles (SAMs), however, had a highly complex operating system that required training Egyptian teams for a period of over six months before they could become operational under Egyptian personnel.

Nasser had been extremely concerned with this development. Accordingly, on January 22, 1970, he flew to Moscow. In his presentation before the Soviet leadership, Nasser threatened resignation and reorientation of Egypt towards the United States if his requests for Soviet weapons and intervention were not met (Heikal 1975, 83–88). This threat had a powerful effect on the Soviet leadership. The Soviet politburo decided on January 25—for the first time in its history—to involve Soviet personnel in a shooting war outside the Soviet bloc. The Soviets decided to send to Egypt, within a month, (1) a division of SA-3 missiles and peripheral equipment, manned by Soviet soldiers and technical personnel; (2) three flights of Mig-21J jets with Soviet pilots and ground personnel, in addition to fifty Sukhoi 9 and ten additional Mig-21J planes sent for training purposes along with training personnel; and (3) four 15-B radars and crews, designed to provide support for the existing Egyptian air defense systems. These systems were never before supplied to anyone outside of the Soviet bloc (Korn 1992, 191; Schueftan 1989, 257–59; Heikal 1975, 88).

In addition, the Soviets agreed to train eighteen hundred Egyptian pilots, technicians, and antiaircraft officers in the Soviet Union. The

Soviets would operate the new SAMs and the Mig-21J jets until the Egyptians were sufficiently trained to operate these systems themselves. This commitment clearly marked a new phase in the Arab-Israeli conflict, with potentially explosive implications.

The installation of the new SA-3 system was constantly interrupted by Israeli air attacks, killing hundreds of Egyptian workers who had been digging the depots for those systems (Schueftan 1989, 262). Both American and Israeli intelligence began to pick up on the magnitude of the direct Soviet involvement in February. However, the size and precise nature of the Soviet involvement did not become clear before the second half of March. On March 20, in a speech to Israeli television, Moshe Dayan discussed for the first time the possibility of air clashes with Soviet pilots. He hoped, however, the IAF would continue to have relative freedom of operation along the Suez Canal, without direct engagement with the Soviet-flown jets (Korn 1992, 195–96).

The first Israeli-Soviet confrontation occurred on April 18, when Israeli reconnaissance planes were nearly intercepted by a team of Mig-21J jets. This incident prompted the IDF to stop its deep penetration bombings, although the IAF continued to bomb targets along the Suez Canal (Korn 1992, 197–98; Schueftan 1989, 266; Bar-Simantov 1980, 151). Although there was some debate in the cabinet regarding the gravity of the threat posed by Soviet intervention, Dayan's more prudent approach was adopted by the government (Bar-Simantov 1980, 153–54).

More important, however, was the question of the implications of an Israeli-Soviet clash. Yigal Allon claimed that the Soviets would do all in their power to avoid a confrontation for fear of American intervention and for fear of being shown as a paper tiger by IAF pilots or IDF fighters. Dayan believed that such a confrontation would have just the opposite effect. The possibility that Israel would find itself isolated and facing a major power was a clear and present danger rather than a theoretical scenario. Dayan argued:

> Since Israel is dealing not only with the SA-3's but with the Soviets, I want to state in all simplicity that we have no capability for an all-out confrontation with the Soviet Union. If the USSR decides to enter into the Middle East conflict "fully" and if the USA fails to restrain [the Soviet Union] and refuses to help Israel, we shall be in a very difficult situation. (quoted in Bar-Simantov 1980, 153)

The key Israeli problem now became finding a way to continue fighting while avoiding a direct clash with the Soviets. It was evident that the

Egyptians would not stop the War of Attrition on their own. In fact, the Egyptians were also receiving close support by Soviet advisers on handling the artillery duel along the Suez Canal. The accuracy and concentration of Egyptian artillery during these months improved significantly, causing heavy casualties to the IDF (Korn 1992, 203; Schueftan 1989, 440; Bar-Simantov 1980, 170–71; Schiff 1970, 219). Neither the IDF nor the politicians had any idea of how to continue the fighting in any effective manner without endangering confrontation with the Soviets.

From a diplomatic point of view, the natural strategy was to turn to the United States. The first and most obvious Israeli request to the United States was to speed up the supply of Phantom jets and other military material to Israel. The second request was more complicated: to have Washington find ways to restrain the Soviets. More specifically, the Israelis wanted a firm American commitment to issue an extended deterrence threat to the Soviets that the United States would aid Israel in the case of direct military clashes with Soviet forces (Bar-Simantov 1980, 156–59; Korn 1992, 198–202). To Israel's utter surprise, both of these requests were turned down by the Nixon administration. Although there had been a serious debate in the administration regarding the dispatch of additional weapons to Israel, there was little or no debate regarding the deterrence request. The United States was not willing to get involved in this war (Bar-Simantov 1980, 159).

Meanwhile, Soviet penetration into Egypt deepened. By May 1970 there were more than ten thousand Soviet military personnel in Egypt, providing the Egyptians with both direct support and advice on a wide range of Egyptian military operations (Bar-Simantov 1980, 160; Korn 1992, 198). The SA-3 batteries were deployed close to the Canal Zone, so that the IAF's operations along the canal were now being limited (Bar-Simantov 1980, 161–63; Korn 1992, 230; Pollack 2002, 94). The deployment of the Soviet missiles rendered a clash between Israeli and Soviet personnel unavoidable. Things started heating up in late June after the Soviets managed to devise a new way of deploying SAM batteries that proved effective against IAF attacks. In early July there were a number of clashes between IAF planes and Soviet-manned SAM batteries. The IAF lost three Phantom jets but destroyed three missile batteries, damaging two others (Bar-Simantov 1980, 163). But more significantly, there were a number of aerial clashes in July, the most severe taking place on July 25, as a pair of IAF Skyhawks were chased by two Soviet-flown Mig 21Js, with one of the Skyhawks being damaged by a Soviet hit.

Israeli response to this situation was typical: escalation. The Israelis decided to initiate an aerial showdown to demonstrate Israel's resolve. Previous Israeli responses to the Soviet challenges were restrained and motivated by the wish to avoid a direct confrontation. These limitations were reciprocated neither by the Egyptians nor by the Soviets. This signaled to the Israelis that the self-imposed restraints may have been interpreted by the other side as a sign of weakness. In a June 25 speech in Benghazi, Nasser stated that Egypt was bent on continuing or even stepping up the war (Bar-Simantov 1980, 237n59). Thus, the entire strategy of relying on the massive use of air power to decide the war was in danger of collapse (Korn 1992, 233). On July 30, an IAF ambush shot down five Soviet-flown Migs. Neither the Israelis nor the Soviets made public this aerial clash, but the Israeli message was seemingly delivered.

The clash with the Soviets can also be interpreted as a decision to declare victory and end the war. Throughout the spring and summer months of 1970, the United States sought different avenues to bring about a cease-fire between Egypt and Israel. Soviet intervention intensified these efforts, as the direct military involvement of the Soviets started to raise concern in Washington. On May 2, Nasser sent a telegram to Nixon offering to establish a dialogue with the United States. In spite of Kissinger's objections, Secretary of State William Rogers and the assistant secretary for Near Eastern and Asian affairs, Joseph Sisco, launched an initiative for a cease-fire. This proposal was presented to the Israeli government on June 19 (Brecher 1975, 489–90). On June 21, the Israeli cabinet rejected the proposal. There were several reasons for this decision. Acceptance of the cease-fire would end the national unity government. Strategically, many ministers felt that failing to end the war as its clear and undisputed victors would harm Israeli deterrence. An important element in this decision was an assessment—probably backed up by IDF intelligence—that Nasser would also reject it, thus rendering the Israeli rejection irrelevant. However, on July 21, Nasser announced that he accepted the cease-fire proposal.

In addition, on July 23, Richard Nixon sent a special dispatch to Golda Meir. The Nixon dispatch pledged to renew the weapons shipments to Israel that had been suspended since February 1970. Most important, Nixon promised that the United States would not force Israel into withdrawal against its will. An agreement would have to be mutually acceptable to the indigenous parties of the conflict. The United States would not impose a settlement.

Israel asked the United States for further clarifications in the wake of the Nixon dispatch. While less than a full backing of Israeli views, these assurances had the requisite impact on most Labor ministers (Brecher 1975, 495–96). In the GAHAL Party, several liberal ministers and Parliament members tried to persuade Menachem Begin that acceptance of the cease-fire proposal by the Israeli government should not cause him to resign from the government. Meanwhile, Dayan was trying to work out formulas for the government to have its cake and eat it too—that is, to respond favorably to the U.S. initiative without bringing about a breakdown of the national unity government (Maoz 1990c, 98–100). On July 30, the cabinet met and—after a long and heated debate—decided to accept the cease-fire proposal. The GAHAL ministers left the national unity government, but the government survived.

The Israeli decision to accept the cease-fire allowed an end to the War of Attrition. On August 7, 1970, the guns across the two sides of the Suez Canal fell silent. However, a new crisis emerged immediately thereafter, threatening new hostilities. Under the cover of the cease-fire agreement, the Egyptians moved their antiaircraft missile batteries to the west bank of the canal. Israel regarded this move as a blatant violation of the cease-fire. Yet the government was divided on how to deal with the new crisis. The doves (including Foreign Minister Eban and Minister of Justice Haim Zadok) argued that Israel should do nothing, as this move would have taken place with or without the cease-fire. Attacking the missiles would restart the war (Yaacobi 1990a, 41). The hawks, led by Moshe Dayan, favored a strike to destroy the newly deployed missile sites. Their argument was that letting this violation pass would signal to Nasser that he had a permit for future violations of the cease-fire agreement.

However, most of the ministers favored a diplomatic response to the Egyptian violation. Israel Gallili, a close confidant of Golda Meir, proposed that the government seize this opportunity to suspend the Jarring mission. This option would demonstrate some Israeli resolve but would not cause a renewed rift in American-Israeli relations. It would also give Israel a bargaining chip with Washington when it came to American weapons shipments to Israel. On September 3, 1970, Israel announced the suspension of the Jarring mission.

6. THE IMPLICATIONS OF THE WAR OF ATTRITION

The War of Attrition fundamentally altered the national euphoria that engulfed Israel following the Six Day War. During the war, a number of new phenomena entered the Israeli political and military scene. For example, the prolonged War of Attrition started to invoke severe skepticism regarding the wisdom of holding onto the territories. A few, seemingly extreme left-wing groups at the margin of the Israeli political spectrum raised this skepticism. However, elements of this criticism of the government's status quo policy began filtering into Israeli public opinion in unprecedented ways. The Israeli Cameral Theater produced and presented a satirical show called "The Queen of the Bathtub,"[13] ridiculing the government's foreign and security policy. In the spring of 1970, a group of high school students about to get drafted into the IDF issued a widely publicized letter questioning their motivation to serve in light of the continued intransigence of the government. These were initial signs of the extent of public rift over the occupied territories and Israel's peace policies. This rift was to deepen and intensify over the coming years, but in 1970 it was just beginning to surface into the public's conscience.

But this rift was only a by-product of the War of Attrition. The implications of the war were more far-reaching than the growing domestic discontent. Unfortunately, the government and the IDF failed to derive meaningful lessons from it. The discussion of the implications of the war emphasizes the gaps between the actual implications and the kind of lessons derived by the Israeli foreign policy and security establishment.

6.1. The Strategic Implications of the War of Attrition

The first and most important implication of the War of Attrition concerned the Egyptian motivation and "will to suffer" (Rosen 1972). This war proved that the Egyptian army, political system, and society were not willing to accept the occupation of the Sinai lying down. Moreover, the Egyptians were prepared to pay a heavy price in order to change the status quo. The total number of Egyptian fatalities—military and civilian— in the war is not known for sure. Reliable estimates, however, put this number at over five thousand soldiers and about two thousand civilians (Small and Singer 1982, 94; Dupuy 1978, 369). Even in the most difficult hours, during the deep penetration bombing and the intensification of the fighting along the canal, the Egyptian army did not break down. On the contrary, it intensified its operations toward the final months of the war (Korn 1992, 275). Egyptian resolve compensated for its inferiority in air power and probably for its inferiority in tactical and operational capabilities (Pollack 2002, 93–96). Egyptian resolve during the war should have suggested to the IDF the tenuous status of Israeli deterrence. Paradoxically, Israel's success in the Six Day War and its overwhelming superiority in air power did not have a debilitating effect on Egypt. The Egyptian decision to launch the War of Attrition should have indicated to

Israeli decision makers the extent of Egypt's commitment to the recovery of the Sinai.

Related to the demonstrated Egyptian resolve was the significant improvement in Egyptian combat performance (Pollack 2002, 95–96). This improvement was not at the same rate in different fields, but the overall change since the Six Day War was significant. During the Six Day War, the Egyptian air force did not have a fighting chance, given the destruction of about 70 percent of its order of battle on the ground within the first hours of the war. The few dogfights that took place immediately after the war ended almost always with the downing of Egyptian jets. Israel lost on the Egyptian front less than ten jets, half of them due to antiaircraft fire.[14] During the War of Attrition, the IAF lost over thirty planes, about two-thirds of which were shot down by antiaircraft fire.[15] The Egyptian air force did not improve considerably in terms of its fighting ability during the War of Attrition. The asymmetry in the combat skills of the two air forces was preserved, if not widened, during the war, because a new generation of Israeli pilots received combat experience and because the F-4 Phantoms represented a significant leap forward in aerial combat.

On the other hand, the antiaircraft defense systems underwent a revolutionary change. This was the case even before the deep penetration bombings, and it was even more pronounced after February 1970. The Soviet-Egyptian agreement involved intensive training of SAM personnel and pilots. While the skill level of the Soviet pilots was not all that high—as evidenced by encounter with the IAF—the Soviets developed an outstanding capacity in antiaircraft warfare, and they transferred this knowledge to the Egyptians. The IAF was not able to effectively counter this new capability.

The IAF was far from oblivious to the problem that the SAMs presented. Developing operational measures to destroy the SAM batteries became a top priority of the IAF after the cease-fire agreement. What went unnoticed, however, was that the SAMs were a problem not only for the IAF but for the entire IDF. The SAMs enabled the Egyptian army to overcome the tremendous disadvantage that it had in the air. As such, the antiaircraft systems—typically seen as a defensive weapons system—were converted into an offensive support system in the new Egyptian doctrine.

Another major improvement that went almost unnoticed was the ability of the Egyptians to employ limited offensive moves across the canal almost at will. Many of the Egyptian incursions into the eastern bank of the Suez Canal were quite successful. Egyptian commandos were able to hit Israeli convoys, capture prisoners, and almost occupy an Israeli Maoz. In most of these raids Egyptian forces were able to return successfully to the West Bank. Clearly, the road from sporadic commando raids across the canal to an all-out crossing of the canal by large forces is long and hard. Yet, these raids should have served as an indication of a developing technical and doctrinal capability to cross the canal and attack with force.

The overall command and control of the War of Attrition by the Egyptian general staff suggested a significant improvement in the ability to manage large-scale operations (Pollack 2002, 97–98). In the Six Day War, the entire command structure of the Egyptian military virtually collapsed. Despite the fact that Nasser told his military commanders that an Israeli attack was "certain" (Mor 1991; Oren 2002, 158–59), the entire Egyptian air force was exposed to Israeli attack. Moreover, once the Israeli ground forces entered the Sinai, much of the Egyptian command structure collapsed, and within two days the entire Egyptian force was in total disarray, with convoys of soldiers withdrawing eastward. The central lesson derived by the Egyptians was the need to develop a new and improved command and control structure (Gamassy 1993, 90–91). This structure was put to test during the War of Attrition and functioned fairly well, despite the fact that some senior officers—including the Egyptian COS Lt. Gen. Abd Al Mun'im Riad—were killed during the war. The intensive training program of the Egyptian officer corps and the overall improvement in the armed forces were felt during the war. Yet, in almost none of the Israeli writings prior to the Yom Kippur War do we observe a reference to the change in the quality of Egyptian command and control and to the overall improved performance of Egyptian commanders during the War of Attrition. The IDF did not change its image of the overall strategic quality of the Egyptian armed forces and its command and control structure following the War of Attrition.

The lack of a sober and critical learning process from the War of Attrition was due to an overall feeling in the Israeli security community that Israel had, in fact, won the war. The overriding belief was that Israeli escalation, through the deep penetration bombings and the cumulative damage caused by the IAF, had forced Nasser to accept the cease-fire. Writing in the immediate wake of the War of Attrition, Zeev Schiff, the dean of the Israeli military commentators and a world-renowned expert on military affairs, argued:

The cease-fire exposed the depth of the Egyptian defeat in the War of
Attrition. From day to day it became increasingly evident that the
Egyptians were on the verge of total collapse. Their casualties in the
front went sky high; way beyond what it was estimated in Israel during
the fighting. The intensive bombings of the IAF have virtually driven
mad the Egyptian soldiers along the front. Later, the Egyptian president, Anwar Sadat, admitted that the Egyptian troops suffered thousands of fatalities. The Egyptian people, who are generally indifferent
to their own troubles and sufferings, found it difficult to cope with
these terrible [military] blows. The Egyptian elite was forced to accept
the cease-fire in order to stop the bloodshed in the War of Attrition
which they had themselves started less than a year and a half ago.
(Schiff 1970, 233–34)

Ezer Weizman (1975, 319) corroborates this perception of victory:

During the three years between 1970 and 1973 [we have] nourished
the self-delusion that we had won the War of Attrition, thereby causing our senses to fall asleep. Instead of saying: "We had failed in dismantling the [SAM] missile systems; let us find ways of eliminating
them, because these systems would play a decisive role in the next
war"; we said: "We had won, we had succeeded. The Egyptians were
again in need of American help in order to bail them out." (And they
[the Egyptians] were in dire straits, no doubt about it!) Thus have we
nurtured a myth instead of facing the facts. We have perhaps served
public morale, but we have done that at the expense of the *need* to
draw lessons.

Korn (1992, 274, 308n4) notes that, even in a 1990 interview with
Haim Bar-Lev, the COS during the War of Attrition, the latter claimed
that the Egyptian army had "broken first."[16]

The failure to derive the military implications of the War of Attrition
due to the perception of the outcome as an unqualified success had dire
consequences. The forward deployment of the SAM sites along the canal
by the Egyptians, in violation of the cease-fire agreement, did cause a
great deal of concern in the IDF. Weizman and others have viewed the
Israeli decision to avoid destroying these missiles as a key factor that
helped the Egyptian crossing of the canal in 1973. There may be some
truth to this argument. Yet, as I argue in the next chapter, the failure to
draw lessons was far more profound and far more general than merely the
lack of political will to violate the cease-fire by attacking the SAM-3
sites.

Not only was there lack of learning due to a false sense of victory, but there was also a significant degree of false learning. First, the War of Attrition reinforced the Israeli belief in the effectiveness of the strategy of excessive force. This notion was at the heart of the deep penetration bombing strategy. Israeli strategists believed that the deep penetration bombing compelled Egypt to accept the cease-fire agreement. This interpretation boosted the IDF's commitment to a strategy of disproportionate retaliation and entrenched the notion that the post-1967 boundaries were indeed defensible. Second, Israeli strategists and politicians also continued to believe that they could continue transferring the fighting to the enemy's territory with relative impunity.

6.2. *The International Implications of the War*

The Egyptian resolve in the War of Attrition should have lit red lights among the political leadership. The question of the cost of holding onto the Sinai should have come up immediately after the War of Attrition. Some Israeli politicians, especially Eban and Dayan, did take notice of this fact. Most others did not. The dominant belief was that Israeli military superiority would offset the Egyptian motivation to recover the Sinai. This had major implications for Israeli diplomacy in the early 1970s (see chap. 10).

The War of Attrition sent mixed signals to Israeli politicians in terms of U.S.-Israeli relations. On the one hand, there was a growing sense of American-Israeli cooperation due to a seeming convergence of interests vis-à-vis the Soviet Union. This entailed the false perception that the United States was interested in keeping the Suez Canal closed to Soviet weapons shipments to North Vietnam. The increasingly intimate ties between Egypt and the Soviet Union during the War of Attrition signaled to Israel a tightening of U.S.-Israeli friendship. Israeli politicians believed that the Nixon administration had a deep interest in upgrading American-Israeli relations. Kissinger's conception of the Arab-Israeli conflict in terms of U.S.-Soviet relations seemed to have indicated a tolerant view of Israeli ambitions, policies, and military actions.

On the other hand, U.S. regional diplomacy during the War of Attrition suggested that the State Department under William Rogers and Joseph Sisco developed a position that Israel should withdraw from most—if not all—of the territories it had occupied during the Six Day War. The Rogers Plan of 1969 was seen by Israeli decision makers as an imposed superpower plan to bring Israel back to the 1967 boundaries. The struggle over the Rogers cease-fire plan was conducted to a large extent under the shadow of this prospect (Brecher 1975; Margalit 1971; Medzini 1990, 372–73). The possibility that going along with this plan may have been in Israel's interest did not occur to the Israelis. In their negotiations over the cease-fire agreement—which should have been seen first as an Israeli interest—a prime Israeli concern was to secure an American commitment not to impose an agreement calling for Israeli withdrawal.

The reading of the signals from Washington during the war was largely incorrect. Israel confronted a number of unpleasant surprises in March and April 1970 when the Nixon administration decided to delay an additional shipment of F-4 Phantom jets to Israel. Israeli policy in the post–War of Attrition period was predicated on the assumption that the United States, though in disagreement with Israel's policy on the occupied territories, would nevertheless side with Israel as long as there was no fundamental change in Egypt's policies and its ties with the Soviet Union.

What served to reinforce this perception was the Israeli-American management of the September 1970 crisis in Jordan. This crisis erupted due to King Hussein's decision to challenge the PLO presence in Jordan (Dowty 1984). At the height of the crisis, Syrian forces invaded northern Jordan in order to help the PLO. In his predicament, Hussein called for American help. Since it would have taken the United States considerable time to deploy a military force in Jordan, the United States called on Israel to help. Israeli decision makers, having debated the wisdom of such action, eventually called for a general alert in the IDF, concentrating its forces in the Jordan Valley across the Jordanian-Syrian border. Partly because of this action, but mostly because the Jordanian army effectively defeated the invading Syrian column, the Syrian forces withdrew from Jordan and the king was able to reestablish his hold over the country. This rendered the Israeli intervention superfluous. However, the Israeli willingness to intervene was welcomed in Washington, and Israel was seen to become an even closer ally than it had been thus far (Rabin 1979, 314–15).

Thus, the Israeli perception was that the War of Attrition served to form a stronger and more secure alliance with the United States. The threat coming from the State Department's initiatives to move the peace process forward was a real one. Yet, Israeli decision makers basked in the belief that the White House was not going to pressure Israel as long as the Soviets were deeply involved in Egypt.

The confrontation with the Soviet Union was an entirely different matter, however. Dayan, who had suffered from a serious case of acute paranoia concerning the Soviets, proved to his skeptical colleagues that even a paranoid has enemies. The government allowed the IDF to make a point vis-à-vis the Soviets on July 30, 1970, but at the same time understood that continued escalation would lead to an inevitable clash with the Soviets. Such a clash could not end well, since the United States was unwilling to intervene directly, nor did it intend to provide the IDF a capability to fight the Soviets. This signaled to the decision makers that Israel's capacity to escalate had its limits, beyond which Israel would find itself confronting a hostile superpower, probably alone. Again, the failure to recognize the limits of the use of force proved fairly costly three years later.

6.3. *The Social and Domestic Political Implications of the War*

All of Israel's previous wars represented a classical "rallying around the flag" syndrome. Even during the Sinai War, which was a blatantly aggressive war, there were almost no voices in the Israeli public questioning its goals or morality. The Six Day War was also interpreted by most Israelis as a defensive war, imposed on Israel by Nasser's actions. All of these reflected numerous examples of national unity. Israelis flew from abroad to take part in these wars. Those who were not drafted to active duty engaged in volunteer work. If there was a criticism of policy, this was directed at what seemed to be hesitant and indecisive behavior by the government. Almost nobody criticized the government in 1948, 1956, or 1967 for escalating too fast and too much.

Although the military and political objectives of these wars were never fully spelled out, the government was applauded for the military victory. The Israelis were not too bothered by the fact that none of these victories was translated into political achievements. The percept that the Arab-Israeli conflict was a long struggle in which Israel could not afford to lose a single war was accepted without too much debate. Since Sharett's resignation in 1956, there was no meaningful moderate faction in the government. GAHAL, the major opposition party, was even more activist than the parties inside the government. Thus, there was no dovish alternative to the government's policy.

During the War of Attrition, however, some Israelis started questioning government policy from the left. As the war began to drag on, and as there was no reprieve in sight, the morale in Israel started sagging. The government's outright rejection of the Rogers Plan and its escalation of the war began invoking criticism. However, this criticism was low key, shared by few, and resented by many. More important, the survival of the national unity government was maintained by diplomatic paralysis. "The decision not to decide" was the term coined with respect to the lack of any peace policy. This criticism became more vocal during the last months of the war. However, public opinion was generally supportive of the government's policies.

The decision to accept the cease-fire offer was controversial mostly within the government. The debate was fierce and extremely emotional (Margalit 1971; Brecher 1975, 493–96). Dayan attempted to manipulate the government decision so that the GAHAL ministers would accept the cease-fire and stay in the government (Maoz 1990c, 98–101). Once the GAHAL Party left the cabinet, the key opposition to the government came from the right wing.

Nevertheless, the Israeli public accepted the government's policy, almost at face value. A study that examined the relationship between the government's policy and Israeli public opinion during this period (Kiss 1977) found that public opinion followed government policy very closely throughout these years, no matter what shifts occurred in that policy. It appears that government policy reflected the mainstream public views. Moreover, the government effectively manipulated public opinion. Israel did not withdraw from the canal; it compelled Egypt to accept the status quo. The adherence of Egypt to the status quo during the following three years was interpreted by the Israeli public as a sign of Egyptian weakness. It was also interpreted as an indication of successful deterrence. The public was willing, therefore, to accept and support what appeared to be the government's decision of political indecision. The Israeli public, the Israeli press, and most academics fell asleep on their watch. The awakening was to be fundamental and extremely costly.

7. CONCLUSION

The War of Attrition was initiated by Egypt. It was part and parcel of an Egyptian plan to prepare its armed forces for the next round of mobile warfare with Israel. It seems that this war was imposed on Israel by Egypt. Israel was not responsible for starting the war, but its strategy is thought to have had a major effect on its termination.

My argument in this chapter is that Israel may have played more than a small part in the outbreak of the war. Israel's handling of the war had an important impact on its length, on its costs, on its escalation, and on its outcome. Most important, Israel's strategy during the war had long-term implications for Israeli-Egypt diplomacy, in particular, for the failure to reach an agreement with Egypt during the 1971–72 period. Its strategy had also implications for the outbreak and management of the Yom Kippur War of 1973.

Israel's military strategy and its political and diplomatic conduct during the War of Attrition were characterized by the rule of thumb that the more aggressive you are on the battlefield, the more intransigent we will be in the diplomatic arena. The notion that Israel could be forced to make political concessions because of continued violence was an anathema to all Israeli prime ministers. But Golda Meir brought this notion to an extreme. The Eshkol government adopted a reasonable diplomatic position immediately following the Six Day War, treating the occupied territories as a bargaining chip that should be traded for peace. This was replaced in the Meir government by an uncompromising position viewing the occupied territories as strategic assets that were preferable to peace. The default position of nondecision with respect to the future of the territories was the dominant policy plan. Moreover, when the government was confronted with policy proposals by outside parties (e.g., the Rogers Plan of 1969), its response was instinctively defiant. It took a great deal of American pressure—a typical combination of a few sticks and many carrots—to sway the government into accepting an American-initiated cease-fire that should have been, in the first place, in its own interest.

Even if Israel did not start the War of Attrition, its diplomatic and military handling and, more important, the lessons it drew from the war suggest that Israeli policymakers and, to a large extent, most of the Israeli public were living in an incubated reality of their own making, one that did not appreciate either the limits of Israel's power in preserving the post-1967 status quo or the determination of its opponents to change it. Neither did Israeli diplomacy understand the opportunities that were present to move toward a peaceful solution of the Israeli-Egyptian conflict. It would take another, extremely costly war to draw Israel out of its self-made illusion of power and righteousness.

— 5 —

The Yom Kippur War

The War That Shouldn't Have Been

I. INTRODUCTION

At 2:00 p.m. on October 6, 1973, a massive artillery barrage coming from the Egyptian side hit Israeli soldiers stationed along the Suez Canal. At precisely the same time, an all-out barrage from the Syrian side hit Israeli targets on the Golan Height. Egyptian and Syrian units moved across the cease-fire lines in a coordinated attack on Israeli positions. This action started what came to be known in Israel as the Yom Kippur War. This war was the costliest and most difficult war since the 1948 War of Independence. Israel's fatalities in that war amounted to nearly three thousand soldiers in seventeen days of fighting. The war ended in an Israeli victory, but this victory was not translated into political achievement. Israel had to concede its control over the Suez Canal. It also was forced, in contrast to its prewar position, to concede territory it had captured in 1967 in the Golan Height, including the city of Kunaytra.

Domestically, the Yom Kippur War sparked a major political crisis. The Labor Party lost 5 percent of its seats in the Knesset in the December 1973 elections. Public opinion eventually forced the Meir government to resign. In the longer run, the war contributed to Labor's fall from power in the 1977 elections.

The Yom Kippur War is depicted as a war of self-defense. Israel was attacked simultaneously by two Arab states, without any provocation on its part. There is no debate regarding the defensive nature of the Yom

140

Kippur War. There is, however, a growing debate on other issues. First, was it really a war of no choice? Was there something Israel could have done to prevent it? The conventional wisdom and the institutional position is that Israel did all in its power to prevent the war; there simply was no viable diplomatic way to prevent the war. A growing body of scholarship suggests, however, that the war could have been averted by diplomacy and that Israel bears the major burden of this diplomatic failure.

The second debate concerns the sources of the strategic surprise under which the war started. Was it merely a failure to anticipate the actual outbreak of the war or its precise timing, or was there a more profound surprise that entailed a failure to understand Egyptian and Syrian strategy? Who is to blame for failing to provide the political leadership with early warning? What were the implications of the strategic surprise for the conduct of the war? Most Israeli studies of the surprise attack implicitly or explicitly assume that, had Israel not been caught unprepared, it could have either prevented or delayed the war or that it would have won a decisive victory at a considerably lower cost. However, is it possible that the problem was in the failure to understand *how* rather than *when* Israel's adversaries would attack? Did Israeli intelligence fail to understand the political purpose of the attack, not only its military characteristics?

A third debate concerns the lessons of the war. What can be learned from the war regarding Israel's security predicament? Are there any lessons to be learned regarding the contribution of the occupied territories to Israel's security? One argument, advanced by many on the Israeli right, is that this war demonstrated the significance of strategic depth. What would have happened had Israel been caught by surprise on its 1967 borders? Had the Egyptians and Syrians succeeded to attack Israel within its 1967 borders, they could have split Israel into several parts in a matter of hours. The counterargument is that it was precisely the Israeli insistence on holding onto the territories that formed the motivation for a high-risk attack. Moreover, the only thing that the war demonstrated is that Israel requires significant DMZs around it so as to reduce the prospects of surprise attack.

Fourth, the war demonstrated a major deterrence failure. But what exactly were the sources of this failure? Was it the failure of Israeli decision makers to respond by force to the Egyptian violation of the 1970 cease-fire agreement by moving its SAM batteries to the Suez Canal Zone? Was the deterrence failure tied directly to the intelligence failure? Alternatively, was it a more fundamental failure, one inherent in the exclusive reliance on strategic deterrence as the sole instrument of policy?

In this chapter I deal very briefly with the question of the avoidability of the Yom Kippur War. I discuss this issue only insofar as it impinges on the other questions. A more elaborate discussion of this issue is given in chapter 10. Here I focus on the strategic management of the war and on its implications. My points are the following.

1.   The surprise of the Yom Kippur War was not only a failure of the Israeli intelligence to forecast the timing of the Egyptian-Syrian attack. Egypt and Syria would have most probably launched the attack, and possibly with greater ultimate success, even if Israeli reserves had been mobilized. Rather, Israel's strategic problem was its failure to grasp the extent to which Egypt and Syria were committed and willing to bear the costs of a major war designed to change the territorial and political status quo in the region. Israel's security community failed in reading the military and doctrinal implications of such commitments.

2.   The Yom Kippur War represents a strategic Israeli defeat. It was the first, but not the last, war in which Israel's strategy failed. Israel achieved a nominal military victory not because it managed the war successfully but despite military mishaps at most stages of the war. Israel's victory in this war was not due to the successful application of strategy. Rather, it benefited from major military and political blunders of its opponents. If Sadat's initial success did not go to his head, causing him to exceed his own political plan of war, there is a distinct possibility that the war would have ended in an unequivocal Egyptian victory. If Sadat had not embarked on a major diplomatic deception vis-à-vis the Syrians, the Syrians could have also achieved significant territorial gains over that same period. Israel was bailed out by its enemies, not by the wit and creativity of its own strategists.

3.   The roots of these strategic failures can be traced back to the implications of the War of Attrition and to the 1971–72 period. I discuss the linkage between Israeli military arrogance prior to the war and the panic that engulfed many of its political and military leaders during the war, up to the point of arming its nuclear weapons, on the one hand, and proposing a cease-fire in place on October 12, on the other.

4.   Paradoxically, the war had contradictory implications for Israel's security and foreign policy. For the first time since 1948, several Israeli political leaders began doubting the reliance on military power as the exclusive strategy for sustaining Israeli security and well-being. These perceptual changes were instrumental for the flexibility that was required in order to bring about the postwar disengagement agreements with Egypt and Syria and the subsequent peace process leading to the Egyptian-

Israeli peace agreement of 1979. Following the Yom Kippur War, Israeli policymakers were willing to accept almost everything they had rejected prior to the war. On the other hand, the war deepened Israeli paranoia. Following the war, Israel entered into massive investments in military power, both conventional and nuclear, lifting defense spending up to 25 percent of its GDP. This paranoia was also converted into a significant upgrade of Israel's nuclear program.

I also examine the political implications of the war. I analyze the impact of the war on Israeli strategic thinking and on the practice of security conceptions in the postwar period. In addition, I focus on Israeli-American relations following the war and in light of the effects of the war on American Middle East policy.

2. SURPRISE? WHAT SURPRISE?

The Yom Kippur War sparked a large number of studies on strategic surprise.[1] This intelligence fiasco is typically defined as the failure of the intelligence community to warn the political decision makers that an all-out attack was imminent. Consequently, much of the blame for the costs of the war and for the failure to achieve a decisive military victory of the Six Day War style is placed at the doorstep of the IDF intelligence community.

The argument is simple: had Israeli intelligence provided timely warning of the imminent attack to the decision makers, the latter would have called up for a full mobilization of the reserve forces. The IDF could have either foiled the entire Egyptian crossing effort or launched an effective counteroffensive that would have destroyed the two attacking armies within a few days. The counterfactual argument (i.e., what would have happened if the IDF had sufficient warning time) is so persuasive that few have challenged it. The focus on the intelligence failure tends to blur other aspects of the war. The Agranat inquiry commission that was appointed to investigate the events leading up to the war focused mostly on the intelligence failure. It did deal to a limited degree with the management of the war on the southern front, finding the commander of that front, Major General Shmuel Gonen (Gorodish), responsible for several faulty decisions. However, this was a minor digression from the commission's main focus. Indeed, most of the people found responsible for the fiasco were directly or indirectly involved in the intelligence failure.[2]

The severity of the intelligence community's failure to forecast the Egyptian and Syrian attacks cannot be overestimated. It failed first in having reassured the military and political leaders that it would be able to provide them with early warning of an impending attack at least ninety-six hours prior to the actual attack (Bar Joseph 2001, 117–18). Second, it failed in making good on this promise. The actual warning time was less than ten hours. However, the most fundamental failure of the intelligence community is hardly acknowledged, and it consists of two elements. First, the intelligence community failed to recognize the political motivation behind the Egyptian decision to go to war and the operational implications thereof. Second, it failed to decipher the changes in the operational doctrine of the Egyptian and Syrian armies and to provide the IDF with an analysis of their implications for Israel's operational doctrine. This had an adverse effect on the general staff and profoundly affected the management of the war.

The intelligence's assurance that the IDF and the political leaders would have ample warning time was a typical product of the post-1967 arrogance in the IDF. This arrogance had absolutely no foundation in the past record of the IDF intelligence. The crisis preceding the Six Day War was a huge intelligence failure, in many respects more serious than the 1973 fiasco. IDF intelligence's annual national intelligence estimate (NIE) of April 1967 predicted that Egypt would not go to war within the next several years because its forces were far too embroiled in the fighting in Yemen and because Nasser was aware of the unfavorable balance of force in the region (Haber 1987, 95). As we saw in chapter 3, IDF intelligence failed to consider the threatening impact of Israel's actions on Arab intentions.

Another major failure concerned the IDF intelligence's discounting of the probability of direct Soviet intervention in the War of Attrition following Israeli deep penetration bombing (see chap. 4). Both fiascos took place under the glorified reign of Major General Aharon Yariv as head of IDF intelligence. In both cases, the intelligence community was well aware that it had fouled up, but nobody was willing to draw the lessons. Another fiasco, the magnitude of which became evident only long after the 1973 war, concerned the intelligence assessment of Sadat as a weak, unreliable, and unstable leader. This assessment supported Golda Meir's intransigent stance vis-à-vis the peace initiatives of Egypt in 1971.

How could the intelligence community survive these debacles without taking serious stock of the causes of these failures in estimates? The 1967 fiasco went unnoticed because the IDF had a lot of warning time due to the demilitarization of the Sinai and due to Nasser's decision not to attack first. Concomitantly, field intelligence collection was of extremely high quality, providing the IDF with excellent knowledge of the deployment of the Arab armies and air forces. The gratitude expressed by the IDF commanders to the intelligence community—largely directed at the quality of field intelligence—spilled over into the research branch of IDF intelligence, which had failed miserably to predict the crisis.

In 1970, the same story repeated itself. Good field intelligence compensated for incompetent research and assessment. However, by 1970, Yariv had established a reputation as "Mr. Intelligence," achieving a status within the IDF general staff and with the political leadership that was unsurpassed by any head of military intelligence before him or after him. Because of that, he could fend off criticism (to the extent such existed) without really addressing it. This image deceived even competent and observant scholars who studied this period. Bar Joseph (2001) gives high marks to IDF intelligence under Yariv (who retired in 1972) compared to the extremely poor marks he gives to IDF intelligence under Eli Zeira—Yariv's successor. Israeli military intelligence (AMAN) under Zeira clearly deserves most of the slings and arrows that Bar Joseph hurls at it. However, the arrogance that characterized many people in the research branch during Zeira's reign was inherited directly from Yariv's reign. So was the tendency to shove under the rug major failures in intelligence assessment.

But there were other, perhaps more fundamental, intelligence failures. The intelligence community failed to understand the enemy's operational doctrine. The failure to comprehend and interpret correctly a military doctrine has profound implications for war fighting, irrespective of how the war breaks out. In September 1939, the Polish army was ready for war with Germany. The German attack did not come by surprise. However, the Polish army fought the German Panzer tanks with cavalry. And the result is well known.

In the final stages of the 1970 War of Attrition, the IAF encountered serious problems with the SAM-3 batteries in Egypt (Weizman 1975, 319; Korn 1992, 275; Schiff 1970). The IAF was extremely concerned by the advance deployment of the SAM batteries along the Suez Canal following the August 7 cease-fire and put strong pressure on the politicians and the COS to destroy those batteries. The government, however, decided to refrain from authorizing such an attack, because of a combination of pressure and inducements coming from Washington.

The SAM threat to IAF operations registered very well with air force intelligence. IAF commander Major General Benny Peled thought he had a firm approval by Defense Minister Dayan and by two successive COSs, Bar-Lev and Elazar, to allow the IAF exclusive concentration on destroying the SAM batteries. The next mission of the IAF would be to destroy the Egyptian air force, and only then would it be free to support the IDF ground operations (Gordon 2000).

In contrast to the IAF, the ground forces failed to understand the implications of the Egyptian reliance on antiaircraft systems as part and parcel of the operational doctrine of the Egyptian ground forces. Two fundamental changes occurred in the Egyptian doctrine, which went unnoticed in Israel. First, Egypt decided to rely on its SAM and other antiaircraft capabilities as a substitute for air power. Second, Egypt planned to use its SAM capability as a defensive screen for its ground forces, shielding them from IAF attacks in their offensive operations. This imposed some geographic limits on the depth of the attack. Specifically, the ground attack would be restricted to a distance of about eleven to sixteen kilometers east of the canal (Shazly 1980, 31–36; Gamassy 1993, 138–39; Pollack 2002, 102–3).

Israeli intelligence believed that, unless Egypt acquired sufficient aerial capability to offset the IAF advantage, it would not dare to attack. This was a sound conception. However, nobody bothered to check whether such an offsetting capability would have to imply more or better aircrafts or other measures. There was no shortage of information in Israel regarding the SAM capabilities or the training schedule of the SAM personnel. The failure was in interpreting what all this information revealed about the Egyptian doctrine. Specifically, IDF intelligence did not understand that the SAMs assumed the role of a support system for a ground offensive by providing a protective umbrella for ground forces.

Another fundamental change involved the Egyptian concern with the superior capability of the Israeli armored units. Both in the Six Day War and in a number of military operations during the War of Attrition, Israel had demonstrated its vast superiority in mobile armored warfare. Egyptian military planners knew that their armored and infantry units would be exposed to massive counterattacks by armored divisions. The entire Egyptian campaign depended on the ability of the Egyptian ground units to repel the Israeli counterattack. With their back to the water, the Egyptian forces would be particularly vulnerable in terms of their ability to maneuver. In order to overcome this deficiency, instead of acquiring better tanks and developing better mobile warfare capability, the Egyptians opted for a technological substitute. This substitute was antitank warfare by infantry units carrying Sager missiles. Forward infantry units carrying these missiles would dig in the immediate vicinity of the Canal Zone and hit the Israeli tanks on the move. The antitank missiles were to serve as a shield against ground-based attacks on Egyptian forces.

IDF intelligence knew about the Sager missiles and followed closely the training of the antitank units. Many of the exercises were conducted along the West Bank of the canal, under IDF observation. However, nobody interpreted correctly the fundamental change in Egyptian operational doctrine of armored combat. Nobody was able to read this change as an adequate Egyptian response to the Israeli superiority in armored warfare. And nobody in the IDF thought that the Egyptians could withstand a major Israeli counteroffensive once they crossed the canal (Lanir 1983, 48–49; Wald 1992, 107–10).[3]

Much of the Israeli scholarship on the Yom Kippur War assumes that things would have developed much differently had the IDF been fully mobilized. Bar Joseph (2001, 384–404) claims that the surprise attack had grave psychological effects on the IDF general command, forcing it to abandon well-prepared and well-practiced contingency plans for just such a scenario. Major General Benny Peled also argued that the IAF was ordered to concentrate most of its effort on supporting the IDF ground operations in the Canal Zone and in the Golan Height rather than dealing with the SAM batteries. As a result, the IAF lost a third of its best jets in the first days of the war. Only after it had been allowed to remove the SAM missile threat was the IAF able to establish complete control of the skies and help turn the tide of battle in Israel's favor (Gordon 2000).

These arguments may be quite valid. They do not, however, lead to the conclusion that the outcome in the first days of the war would have been different. In fact, I will argue in the next section that, if the IDF had indeed carried out its predesigned plans, the Israeli defeat would have been complete and the political damage would have been even more severe than it had actually been. If the IAF had been given a free hand to concentrate on the SAM batteries, there would have been even less support to the ground forces trying to prevent the Egyptian crossing of the canal, so that the Egyptian ground forces would have been able to complete their crossing more successfully than they actually did and with fewer casualties. Second, the IAF did not have effective antimissile measures in the first few days of the war. Only as a result of the massive American airlift starting on October 14 did the IAF receive some antimissile measures that enabled it to overcome the SAM problem. Third, one of the most important missions of the Israeli ground forces that crossed the canal westward on October 16 had been to destroy the SAM batteries on the ground. The fact of the matter is that there were numerous operational SAM batteries even after the IAF did its best to destroy them. In fact, the IAF kept losing planes due to SAM missiles until the last quarter of the war, although the losses were lighter, mainly due to the IAF's avoidance of the dense SAM areas (Adan 1980, 319–20).

Would the result of IDF ground operations have been different had the IDF been fully mobilized on the eve of the attack? There are three possible counterfactual scenarios that assume full IDF mobilization. One is that the IDF would have put considerable effort in trying to prevent the Egyptians from crossing the canal, and the implication is that it would probably have succeeded in doing so. The second scenario suggests that the IDF would have let the Egyptians cross the canal and then attacked the crossing forces with their backs to the water. The third scenario suggests that the IDF would have ordered a retreat of the infantry forces from the Maozim. The armored IDF units would have waited for the Egyptians about twenty kilometers deep into the Sinai. Once the Egyptian units tried to attack eastward, they would have exposed themselves to the entire capability of the IDF armor. Let us consider each of these counterfactual scenarios in turn.

In order to prevent the Egyptians from crossing, the IDF would have had to move its two armored divisions westward in a manner similar to what actually happened during the October 8 counteroffensive.[4] This would have exposed the tanks to the antitank missiles of the Egyptians just as it did on October 8. Moreover, the initial crossing by the Egyptians, during the afternoon and evening hours of October 6, was done by infantry units, the main purpose of which was to capture the Maozim along the canal and to secure the ground for the crossing of the canal by the two Egyptian armies. These same units operated most of the antitank weapons. Many of these units crossed the canal on rubber boats; the bridges allowing the transfer of heavy vehicles were built after the bridgeheads were secured. The crossing was done under heavy cover of Egyptian artillery. On the other hand, most of the IDF artillery in the Sinai was based on standing army units, hence operating at almost full capacity. The failure of the Israeli artillery to prevent the creation of a solid Egyptian bridgehead on the eastern bank of the canal during the first few hours of the war had little to nothing to do with the absence of IDF reserve units in the Sinai.

Moreover, the Egyptians clearly overestimated the extent of resistance the IDF could muster during the first few hours of the war, expecting much more effort, time, and casualties to complete the crossing (Shazly

1980, 252–53; Pollack 2002, 101–2). This implies a very strong commit-ment to achieving this goal. The combination of a determined army equipped with effective antitank weapons, shielded by the SAM umbrella, would probably have resulted in the same outcome of the actual Israeli counterattack on October 8. One of the few critics of the Israeli strategy assesses the effect of the initial surprise attack on the Israeli fail-ure to counterattack the Egyptians:

> Just as it was impossible to prevent the Egyptian crossing of the Canal
> even if there had been no surprise, so was it impossible for the coun-
> terattacks to have ended differently if the Israelis had not been taken
> by surprise. Furthermore, the excuse of "the way the war began,"
> which does not explain the tactical defeats on the Canal at the outset,
> certainly does not justify the subsequent failures in counterattack.
> Defects in operational implementation of the armored shock doctrine
> . . . undoubtedly aggravated the situation on the ground. But they in
> no way explain the basic drawback of the shock doctrine or cover up
> for it. In practice, the counterattacks had no chance of success, and
> they would have failed even if the implementation had been flawless;
> the IDF had no tactical answer to the Egyptian offensive/defensive
> doctrine, in general, or to the tactical challenges of the integrated
> land battle. (Wald 1992, 110)

Suppose the IDF would have waited, letting the Egyptians complete their crossing of the canal. Once the Egyptian forces were situated with their backs to the canal barrier, the IAF would have blown the bridges along the canal and the IDF would have launched a counteroffensive, hitting the Egyptians with all of its firepower. It is not clear that the IDF would have fared better under this scenario. The Egyptians were pro-tected by the SAM missile shield, so that the IAF's costs would have been exorbitant—as it indeed was in the war itself. These forces were also pro-tected by the antitank missiles. The IDF—having been fully mobilized by then—did not dare launch another counteroffensive between October 9 and October 16. This suggests that there was no real response to both missile shields. The tide of the war started turning only when Israel received—through the American airlift—the kind of technology that enabled the IAF and the IDF to deal better with the SAMs and the anti-tank missiles.

Let us now consider the third counterfactual scenario. Suppose the IDF would have waited for the Egyptians to get out of their missile cover and move forward, as they did on October 14, and then the IDF armored forces would confront the Egyptian armored forces in a moving battle on open ground. This scenario sounds more plausible than the other two counterfactuals. However, there are several problems with this argument. We know that the IDF commanders were very much concerned about losing ground in the first few days of the war. The key concern was not how to draw the Egyptians out of their missile cover but how to avoid the loss of the territory already controlled by the Egyptians without returning a good fight (Van Creveld 1987, 211–12). In other words, letting the Egyptians complete the first move entailed the risk that it would have become also their last military move. The Egyptians would declare victory and call for a cease-fire in place. The IDF would have been humiliated completely, and the entire structure of Israel's deterrence would have collapsed. The IDF could simply not afford to let the Egyptians decide the next move. A massive counteroffensive was both a strategic and a political imperative. Elazar's dilemma was this:

> The political constraint is well engraved in our minds in this early morning hour [of October 7]: how many days of fighting will be handed to us before the Arabs succeed in mobilizing the UN Security Council and imposing a cease-fire? Can we patiently wait until the IDF completes its mobilization of reserves, go to a counteroffensive [with its full strength] and uproot the enemy from its newly established forts? Would the cease-fire preempt us and will convert these [temporary] accomplishments of our enemy into permanent accomplishments? The political issues will continue to be a central element in the overall calculations of the Chief of Staff, with respect to the operational goals of the war, with respect to establishing the strategic order of priorities, and with respect to the time table. The war was managed with a stop-watch in hand. (Bartov 1978, 2:58)

The argument that the surprise attack was a decisive factor in the Syrian front appears, at first blush, to have more credence than in the south. First, the strategic depth of the Golan Height is minimal: the width of the Height is roughly twenty to thirty kilometers. The terrain on the Golan Height is fairly flat, with a few hills spread in different locations. This terrain allows for fairly free movement of armored vehicles. On the eve of the war, there were elements of two armored brigades stationed on the Golan Height. Another armored brigade was sent to the height on October 5, barely reaching its destination when the war started. The force ratio between the Israelis and the Syrians at the start of the war was more than one to ten in favor of the latter (Dupuy 1978, 439–44; Herzog 1975,

69–71; Pollack 2002, 1, 482–84). Outmanned, outgunned, and with their backs to the northern Galilee, with a Jewish population of roughly two hundred thousand, the IDF forces were able to hold off the Syrians and to turn the tide of war in their favor within three days of fighting. To be sure, the death toll was extremely heavy, but the IDF performed much better against the Syrians than it had against the Egyptians.

Nevertheless, the reasons that the Syrian attack failed despite the overwhelming quantitative advantage the Syrian enjoyed were precisely the same as those that account for the failure of the IDF counterattack in the south. First, the Syrians had to engage in a war of movement and fire, a type of war in which the IDF was considerably more competent. Second, because of the rapid advance, the forward Syrian units were separated from their logistical base (Dupuy 1978, 445–61; Van Creveld 1975). Third, although the Syrian artillery and the infantry equipped with Sager missiles also inflicted heavy casualties on IDF forces, they were not sufficiently organized or sufficiently effective in providing cover to the Syrian tanks. It might be the case that the IDF reserves that started arriving tipped the balance in favor of the IDF during the counteroffensive of October 9, but it was the force that was on the ground on October 6 that was primarily responsible for stopping the Syrians.[5]

This fighting on the Golan Height suggests that, when Israel applied its doctrine of mobile armored warfare against an army that did the same, its tactical and operational advantages more than compensated for the fundamental numerical inferiority (Pollack 2002, 505–9). However, the application of this doctrine against the Egyptian SAM and antitank missile shield failed miserably. The problem, then, was not only the initial surprise. It was the fundamental failure to read the entire structure of the political plan, the operational doctrine, as well as the more tactical aspects regarding the timing of the attack that characterizes the conduct of this war (Lanir 1983).

3. VICTORY? WHAT VICTORY?

The war ended in a major military victory for Israel. Israel entered the war on terms that were extremely unfavorable and finished it 101 kilometers east of Cairo and less than 40 kilometers southwest of Damascus. The Third Egyptian Army was completely surrounded, and, but for the forced cease-fire, the envelopment of the Second Egyptian Army would have taken place as well. The kill ratios in 1973 were considerably lower than they had been in 1967, but they were nevertheless impressively in favor of Israel (Dupuy 1978, 608–9). The inability to convert the military victory into a significant achievement on the negotiating table epitomizes Israel's precarious diplomatic position. This does not detract, however, from the significance of the military outcome of the war.

But how much of the credit for the victory goes to Israel? I suggest that Israel's victory was due far more to the follies of its adversaries and to the help of the United States than to the military or political ingenuity of the Israeli leadership. There is good reason to suspect that, had the Israeli leadership been left to its own devices, the war would have ended in a humiliating defeat. In a previous study (Maoz 1990b, 175–77, 186–90) I examined this aspect of the war in terms of the relationship between the successful application of the Egyptian-Syrian surprise attack and their ultimate failure in the war. Here I examine both the Egyptian and Syrian strategy and the Israeli behavior during the war.

As noted, Sadat felt that the superpowers, eager to solidify the new sense of peaceful coexistence—the détente—developed an interest in a stable Middle Eastern status quo. Consequently, they agreed not to rock the territorial and political boat in the region. This implied for Egypt that, unless something drastic happened, the Israeli occupation of the Sinai would be perpetuated by superpower concert. The war was designed to shake up this superpower complacency. Accordingly, the war was defined as an instrument for shaking the status quo. Of course, the war was also designed to uplift Egyptian morale and to show to the entire world that Egypt was capable of standing up to the seemingly invincible Israelis. But it was the international objective of the war that shaped its operational contours. Thus, the plan consisted of an Egyptian drive to occupy a limited strip of land east of the Suez Canal, hold onto it, call it a victory, and sue for a cease-fire.[6]

Sadat knew that this idea was a hard sell to his potential partners in this venture, such as the Syrians. Therefore, he decided to engage in a deception campaign vis-à-vis his would-be ally (Seale 1988, 194–200). The plan he had showed to the Syrians was Granite I, a plan that entailed an initial thrust to the Mitla and Gidi passes in the first phase of the war and a second phase that entailed the occupation of the entire Sinai Peninsula. This plan had been shelved back in 1972 because the Egyptian command deemed it as unrealistic. But the Syrians operated on the notion that the Egyptians would try to reoccupy the Sinai in its entirety. Seale (1988, 197) suggests that, had Asad known that the Egyptian plan called for a limited offensive, he would probably have not gone along with the Egyptian scheme. Syria's plan consisted of the occupation of the Golan Height; there were no operational plans to go down to the Galilee once this goal was accomplished (Pollack 2002, 481).[7]

Thus, in both cases, the operational objectives of the two allies were fairly limited. The plan had been to do just what Elazar had feared: to call for a cease-fire through the UN (see this vol., p. 150). Both Egypt and Syria went to this war believing that the risks they were running were extremely high, that they would pay a heavy cost in casualties and possibly in physical damage to their infrastructure, and that their territorial accomplishments would be limited under the best scenario. Both states invested a major effort in a deception campaign designed to accomplish surprise. However, neither believed that the surprise would be as deep and profound as it actually was. Both leaders believed that their armies would confront substantial resistance in the first stages of the war. Sadat expected fifty thousand casualties in the crossing effort.[8] We do not know precisely what Asad's expectations were in terms of casualties or damage, but—as Moshe Maoz (1995, 129–30) points out—he instructed hospitals and graveyards in Syria to prepare for a large number of clients.

The Israeli victory in the Yom Kippur War was affected by two principal factors: the Israeli strategy and the Egyptian and Syrian behavior during the war. As we have seen, Israeli strategy in the first phases of the war was dictated by four factors: (1) the shortage of forces due to the surprise of the Egyptian-Syrian attack; (2) the need to make hard choices about the activation of the air force in support of the ground forces rather than its predesigned missions; (3) the need to repel the Syrian attack in the Golan Height before turning to a decision on the Egyptian front; and (3) the political risks associated with an impending cease-fire.

Up to October 10, Israeli strategy met mixed results. On the Golan Height, the IDF stopped the Syrian thrust, and its counteroffensive was pushing them back. In the Canal Zone, however, the October 8 counterattack was a disaster. It resulted in a large number of casualties and did not change the territorial status quo even one iota. The failure of the counterattack completely overshadowed the fact that the Syrian attack had been repelled. Herzog (1975, 179–80) describes the gloomy meeting of COS Elazar, Defense Minister Dayan, and Prime Minister Meir on the night between October 8 and 9. Braun (1992, 126–35), who provides a generally favorable portrait of Dayan's handling of the situation, also notes the atmosphere of despair and pessimism that characterized the cabinet's meeting. The perception of threat was so deep that—as Hersh

(1991, 225–27), Aronson (with Oded Brosh 1992, 139–49), and Cohen (2005) suggest—during that night, the Israeli cabinet decided to arm its nuclear warheads.

Equally significant was the fact that Israel's losses in equipment over the last several days were staggering. Kissinger (1982, 492) was told by the Israelis that the IDF had lost over fifty planes and four hundred tanks during the last three days. Besides the urgent need to replace its losses, Israel faced considerable shortages in ammunition, electronic equipment for the IAF, and antitank weapons. Israeli diplomats made an urgent appeal to the United States to provide Israel with an airlift that would enable it to continue the war.

Israel's accomplishments in the Golan Height during October 10–11 notwithstanding, the sense of despair in the Israeli government persisted. On October 12, the Israeli ambassador to the United States, Simcha Dinitz, informed Kissinger that Golda Meir was willing to consider a cease-fire in place (Kissinger 1982, 509, 512–13).[9] This initiative may have been due to a feeling that the Egyptian positions along the canal were impenetrable and that the Israeli counteroffensive in the Golan Height would offset the losses in the Canal Zone (Bartov 1978, 2:161–62; Braun 1992, 166). Thus, during the period of October 11–14, Israel would have probably accepted the status quo on both fronts if its enemies had also been willing to do so. Ironically, on the first four days of the war, Israel fought against time, trying to throw in everything it had to minimize the damage of the initial attack. On the next four days of the war, Israel fought under the assumption that the loss of the Suez Canal was unavoidable and that it would have to accept a cease-fire in place.[10]

Why did the Egyptians and Syrians fail to call for a cease-fire in place when they had the chance? Had Egypt and Syria agreed to call for a cease-fire during these days, they would have been left with all (Egypt) or some (Syria) of their initial achievements. The answer to this question is complicated. First, there are conflicting Egyptian accounts of the ultimate military objective of the war. Some claim that this objective was the occupation of the Mitla and Gidi passes (e.g., Gamassy 1993, 270). Others (e.g., Hafez Ismail, Sadat's national security adviser) argue differently:

> Our forces had, in the preceding period, accomplished their specific mission. Through my conversations with General Ahmad Isma'il before the war began, I knew that he did not intend to advance to the mountain passes. The instructions from the general command that the goal was the occupation of the passes . . . all this was meant to moti-

vate the lower-ranking officers during the bridgeheads stage to continue to work towards a well-defined target.[11]

It is not the subject of this book to examine the Arab decision-making
process. But in this case, it is important to understand what happened on
the Arab side. The Egyptian-Syrian decision-making process is a typical
example of the answer to the key question I will pose in chapter 13: Why
did Israel fare well despite repeated blunders, incompetence, and political
and military follies? One of the answers to this question has to do with the
blunders, incompetence, and follies of its enemies. In this case, Egypt and
Syria's strategic and political failures helped save Israel from herself. In
effect, the follies of Israel's enemies are what made the difference between
a humiliating Israeli defeat and a seemingly brilliant, but costly, Israeli
victory in the Yom Kippur War.

By October 9, the Soviets started putting pressure on the Egyptians to
accept a cease-fire in place. The argument was simple and reasonable
(Gamassy 1993, 257–59).

> (1) the time had come to consolidate the gains achieved through a
> ceasefire and to shift the struggle to the political arena for a solution;
> (2) deteriorating conditions on the Syrian front had encouraged Pres-
> ident Asad to ask for matters to move towards a ceasefire; (3) the Syr-
> ian's army failure would allow Israel to concentrate its forces on the
> Sinai front, which would complicate the situation for the Egyptians
> there; (4) . . . continued Soviet objections to any ceasefire resolution
> would make it difficult in the future to achieve such a resolution if
> developments required a ceasefire to the advantage of the Arabs.
> (258)

However, both leaders strongly opposed the Soviet offer. Several reasons account for this paradoxical behavior. First, for Asad, the sunk cost
paradox (Maoz 1990b, 276–82) was at work. Asad's key effort after October 10 was to recover his losses. He felt betrayed by the Egyptian static
position along the Suez Canal, because it enabled Israel to concentrate
on the Syrian front. His main effort over the next four days was to talk
Sadat into launching an offensive effort. At first, especially during October 12–14, he felt optimistic about the prospects of an Egyptian attack
that would take the heat off the Syrian front. After the failure of the
Egyptian attack of October 14, Asad's major goal was to repel the Israeli
counterattack, which—by that point—began entering Syrian territory
east of the purple line. Instead of trying to minimize his losses, Asad was

trying to recover them. It was only after he had been absolutely con-vinced that the situation could not get better and would only get worse (especially after Sadat had agreed to a cease-fire on October 21) that he made the same decision.

The Egyptian approach to a cease-fire resolution is more complex. Several factors were at work here. Egyptian political and military decision makers provide a confused account of these matters. Some leaders believed that, once the Egyptian forces consolidated their positions east of the canal, the war would be converted into a static war of attrition, forcing Israel to agree to a settlement that entailed an additional with-drawal, perhaps to the Mitla and Gidi passes (Riad 1981, 245, 248). Another belief (Heikal 1975, 219–25) was that the Egyptian forces would try to capitalize on their initial success, following the abortive Israeli counterattack of October 8, and capture the Mitla and Gidi passes. Ismail Ali argued that Egypt had to help take the pressure off the Syrian front (Shazly 1980, 248).

What these explanations do not tell us is the psychological state of mind of the Egyptian political and military leadership in those first few days of the war. The atmosphere in the political and military circles was ecstatic. The canal crossing went much better than expected, resulting in much fewer casualties than the most optimistic projection. By October 9, over one hundred thousand Egyptian soldiers had crossed the canal east-ward (Shazly 1980, 233). The Egyptians had also won the battle of Octo-ber 8, repelling the Israeli counteroffensive with far less casualties than expected and without losing any significant hold over the territory acquired over the previous two days.

Now the key question facing the Egyptian leadership was, What next? There were three general options. The first was the political route: call it a victory—which it clearly had been—and ask for a cease-fire in place. If this succeeded, the war would be over and both its military and political objectives would have been accomplished to the fullest. If the Israelis did not agree and/or the United States did not impose such a cease-fire on the Israelis, at least Sadat would have gained a number of diplomatic merits in the international arena and could have pursued one of the other two options.

The second option was to stay put and let the Israelis initiate the next move. The successful operations of October 8 suggested that the Israelis may try again, but as long as the Egyptian forces were covered by the com-bined SAM and antitank missile shields, they could hold their own per-haps long enough to convince the Israelis of the futility of their effort to retake the canal. Given the Israeli vulnerability to casualties, this seemed a fairly realistic assessment. The downside of this option was that there was a possibility that the Israelis would be able to penetrate the Egyptian lines and even cross the canal (Gamassy 1993, 264). However, this risk was seen as relatively manageable because of the capability of the Egyptian forces and their ability to activate reserves rather flexibly in such an event.

The third option was to capitalize on the initial success and move eastward toward the Sinai passes. This apparently was the recommendation of the military commanders (Gamassy 1993, 264–65; Shazly 1980, 243–44).[12] The argument here was that the Israelis were exhausted and demoralized and that their mobilization was not as yet complete. Letting them get organized would make the offensive far more difficult and costly than hitting immediately. A successful thrust would bring Egyptians to control the passes. If the attack failed, the Egyptians could always resort to one of the other two options.

Over the period of October 9–14, the Egyptians combined the first and second options, delaying decision on the third. Hafez Ismail sent a message to Kissinger, demanding a cease-fire in place and an Israeli pledge to commence withdrawal to the international border within a pre-specified time frame (Kissinger 1982, 496; Heikal 1975, 228–29; Gamassy 1993, 261). This position was intended to set the basic tone of the negotiations. The Egyptians were in no hurry. However, Sadat was not willing to authorize a premature attack. On October 10 the first Egyptian infantry brigade was ordered to move along the Suez coast to occupy Ras Sudar. Outside of the SAM cover and the antitank cover, it incurred heavy casualties. Overwhelmed by Israeli air attacks and by armored and infantry forces, it was forced to withdraw without even getting close to its target (Shazly 1980, 241–42). This should have indicated to the Egyptian military and political command the risk of diverting from their initial strategy.

Thus, the days between October 9 and 13 were used to consolidate Egyptian positions along the eastern bank of the canal and to prepare for the offensive. The fact that the Israelis did not launch any significant attacks during those days served to increase Egyptian self-confidence, thus bolstering the assessment that the Israelis were demoralized to the point that they effectively had given up hope of recapturing the Canal Zone. This overconfidence that spread among the political leaders was at odds with the realistic pessimism of the field commanders.[13] Simultaneously, the situation on the Syrian front was getting ominous. Asad sent urgent messages to Sadat asking Egypt to relieve the Israeli pressure off Syrian forces by launching an attack. Asad—who was led to believe that Egypt's objectives included the occupation of the entire Sinai—did not understand why Egyptian forces remained in place. Egyptian writers agree that Sadat and Ismail were sympathetic to the Syrian appeals for help (Heikal 1975, 230). However, there was no agreement among the political and military decision makers whether the Syrian appeals justified an attack that—as some generals argued—would almost certainly fail.

Ismail informed the military commanders that political considerations determined the decision to launch an offensive. These considerations, presumably, overrode the military concerns (Shazly 1980, 246–48; Gamassy 1993, 270).[14] It is plausible to suggest, therefore, that the actual decision of an offensive on October 14 was a combination of over-confidence and submission to Syrian appeals for help.

The Israeli success in repelling the Egyptian attack on October 14 had a tremendous effect on Israeli self-confidence and de facto altered Dayan's pessimistic assessment of the prospects of a renewed Israeli offensive. On the other side, the costly defeat of the Egyptian offensive should have sent a signal to the Egyptian leadership that the tide of the war may well be turning and that this was perhaps their best opportunity to call it quits. If the message from the battlefield was not enough, the message from the Soviets was persistent. The Israelis were beginning to receive replacement weapons from the United States. Their army was in full force, and the situation on the Syrian front was going from bad to worse (Heikal 1975, 237). The messages from the Soviet ambassador appeared to fall on deaf ears, prompting the Kremlin to send Soviet premier Aleksei Kosygin on October 16 to Cairo.

By that time, the Israeli forces had already crossed the canal westward. The extent of the "breach"—as this Israeli incursion was labeled by Gamassy (1993, 281)—was still limited, however. It was just the arrowhead of the division commanded by Ariel Sharon that managed to cross the canal and was beginning to open the way for the crossing of the entire division, as well as for the next division commanded by Avraham (Bren) Adan. Kosygin's team, armed with aerial photographs taken by Soviet satellites, warned Sadat that, if Egypt did not agree to an immediate cease-fire, the Israelis could encircle the third and second armies and threaten Cairo. Still, Sadat did not buy. Nor did he heed the advice of the military commanders to withdraw some of the Egyptian forces stationed east of the canal in order to fight the Israeli forces on the West Bank (Shazly 1980, 260–63; Gamassy 1993, 292). Only on October 21 did

Sadat agree to a cease-fire. By that time, two full Israeli divisions had been fighting west of the canal in a major envelopment maneuver designed to encircle the Third Egyptian Army. The entire SAM system that had shielded the Egyptian troops so well was by then almost completely destroyed. While the Egyptian army did not break, its defeat was beginning to reach much larger proportions.

In examining this sequence of events, several interesting observations emerge. First, during the period of October 9 to October 14 (or even October 15), Egypt had a unique opportunity to bring the war to an end under very favorable circumstances and under highly unfavorable circumstances for Israel. The Soviets were well aware of this window of opportunity and did their utmost to convince Sadat of the need to call for a cease-fire in place.

During this period, Israel was willing to accept such a resolution. Had the Soviet Union initiated this call for a cease-fire, it would have been very difficult for the United States to block it. Under this scenario, the war would have ended a week or so after it had started. With two armies east of the canal, having beaten a major Israeli counteroffensive, this would have been a huge morale-boosting victory for Egypt. Israel could have consoled itself with some minor achievements on the Syrian front, having driven the Syrian forces back to the purple line and even encroaching into Syrian territory in some places. But the overall picture from a military and diplomatic point of view would have been bleak.

Yet another scenario could have prevented an Egyptian defeat in this war. The October 14 attack, which cost nearly two whole tank brigades, weakened Egyptian position by destroying some of their best forces. Had the Israelis attempted their attack when the Egyptian forces were fully prepared and in their full power, the outcome of this attack would have been the same as the outcome of the attack of October 8 (Shazly 1980, 250–51). Moreover, had the Egyptians reacted timely and correctly to the Israeli incursion into the West Bank of the canal by withdrawing some of their forces westward, the IDF force would have suffered major casualties, which would have made it impossible to sustain the encirclement effort. Israel would have been forced to accept a cease-fire in place.

American policy was a crucial factor in preventing the Egyptians from seizing a full-size victory. Henry Kissinger was not willing to accept Israeli defeatism during the first week of the war. Kissinger realized that, paradoxically, the Yom Kippur War offered a unique opportunity for jumpstarting a peace process in the region. Sadat, in Kissinger's view, launched the war in order to invite the United States to mediate between itself and

Israel (Kissinger 1982, 467–68). However, if the war ended in a clear one-sided victory, the defeated party would have revenge—rather than diplomacy—on its mind, while the victor would want to reap the full diplomatic fruits of the military victory. Thus, the war had to end in a stalemate if both sides were to make the necessary concessions it would take in order for mediation to be effective (Kalb and Kalb 1974, 479; Golan 1976, 46). Thus, a cease-fire in place was not in U.S. interests (Kissinger 1982, 494–95). Kissinger managed to fend off a number of Israeli ideas that would have undermined the new goals of the United States, such as launching an initiative for a cease-fire in place or sending Golda Meir in a secret visit to the United States to plead for arms.

Egyptian mistakes happened on two levels. On the military level, the departure from the original war plans by launching the October 14 attack exposed Egyptian weaknesses and boosted Israeli morale. Another mistake entailed the failure to withdraw Egyptian forces to the western bank of the canal in order to counterattack the invading Israeli force during the first two days of the Israeli crossing. This was probably due to Sadat's failure to realize the gravity of the situation that had developed since October 16 (Shazly 1980, 262–63). On the diplomatic level, Sadat, overcome with euphoria due to the Egyptian offensive during the first days of the war, refused to agree to Soviet pleas of a cease-fire. Only after the Israeli maneuver on the western bank of the Suez Canal threatened to encircle the Third Egyptian Army did Sadat agree to a cease-fire. By then, Israeli victory was only a matter of magnitude.

This was a Pyrrhic victory for Israel. It was facilitated by the help of its major ally, which helped to save Israel from its own follies. And it was made possible by the blunders of its enemies, which had been fooled by their own initial military successes. Israeli strategy and its military capability had also some impact on the military outcome of the war, but it had a considerably smaller part on the final outcome than the other factors mentioned previously. Israeli strategy would have been of little help even if Israel had not been surprised by the outbreak of the war and even if there had been less mismanagement and confusion during the initial phases of the war than there actually was.

4. THE IMPLICATIONS OF THE YOM KIPPUR WAR

The immediate political outcome of the Yom Kippur War was a series of agreements that entailed withdrawal of Israeli troops from areas that the Israeli public had been led to accept as strategically important and as part and parcel of the Israeli notion of "defensible borders." The superpower crisis toward the end of the war, which involved a nuclear alert by the United States, demonstrated once again the potential link between a Middle Eastern war and a global conflagration.

As is the case with most traumatic events of a similar magnitude, the Yom Kippur War resulted in a fairly thorough reckoning and soul-searching in Israel. Questions such as "What went wrong?" "Who is responsible?" and "What are the lessons of the war?" were raised repeatedly in the scholarly literature, in the media, and by various elements of the Israeli body politic and the public. As I noted at the beginning of this chapter, a plethora of studies by Israeli academics on strategic surprise is an indication of this soul-searching process. I now focus on several implications of the Yom Kippur War for Israeli strategy, Israeli foreign policy, and Israeli society and politics.

4.1. Strategic Implications

Israeli military strategy was more affected by this war than by any other previous war. These implications can be identified in four key areas of strategy.

4.1.1. Air Warfare

The heavy losses inflicted by the Egyptian and Syrian SAM missiles on the IAF led to a shift in the focus of both technological solutions and operational doctrine in the post–Yom Kippur War (Gordon 2000, 231–36). During the war itself, the IAF received air-to-surface missiles that helped it fight the SAM batteries. These missiles improved the ability of the IAF to operate in the combat zone during the first crucial days of the crossing. However, most of the SAM batteries on the western bank of the canal, as well as inside the Syrian part of the Golan Height, were destroyed by Israeli infantry and special forces. The SAMs not only presented a problem for the freedom of operation of the IAF but also prevented it from providing close support to the Israeli ground forces. Since 1973, the IAF focused its R&D efforts on anti-SAM measures (Bonen 2003; Brom 2003). These measures were tested—with profound success—in 1982 in Lebanon.

In contrast to the Six Day War, this was not the IAF's finest hour. The IAF did have an important impact on the overall outcome of the war, but it was not as dominant a role as it had in 1967. Its attrition rate in this war was fairly high, losing a third of its capability. The IAF had been instrumental in knocking down Syrian logistical support to the armored and infantry divisions that had penetrated the Golan Height. It also did some damage to the Iraqi division on its way to the Golan front. Yet, it did not prevent it from reaching the front and actually confronting the Israeli armor in one of the major tank battles of the war.

The IAF did maintain its nearly absolute supremacy in aerial combat. The ratio of shoot downs of planes in air-to-air combat was forty to one in favor of the IAF (Ben Eliyahu 2003).[15] The need to secure Israeli airspace was minimal, as there was no real threat to Israeli population centers from enemy warplanes. The Syrians indeed fired several FRUG missiles in the general direction of the Israeli air base of Ramat David. However, they stopped this type of warfare after the IAF bombed Syrian military headquarters in Damascus.

The IAF failed in creating meaningful damage to the Egyptian ground forces, both during the canal crossing and during the subsequent ground operations. By 1973, the IAF should have been quite familiar with tactics of close ground support operations through helicopter gunships that were used extensively by the U.S. military forces in Vietnam. However, this aspect of warfare was not incorporated into the IAF until the early 1990s. Helicopters were used primarily as transport vehicles for special operations inside Egypt and Syria but were not deployed in battle.

4.1.2. Ground Warfare

Both the IAF and the ground force of the IDF failed to draw the correct lessons from the War of Attrition. However, the ramifications of this failure were probably more severe for the ground forces than they had been for the IAF. Two fundamental issues were at stake here. One issue concerned the failure to interpret correctly the Egyptian new doctrine of antitank warfare and the static tactic of limited offense and defense under the cover of SAMs and antitank weapons. The other issue concerned the oscillation between an offensive and defensive strategy in the period between the War of Attrition and the Yom Kippur War. Each of these issues carried different implications, and each of these issues was addressed differently in the coming years.

The shock of antitank warfare was enormous, and the IDF immediately understood the need for a drastic change in this field. This change consisted of several shifts. First, antitank missiles were among the first items the IDF acquired from the United States during the war. The TOW antitank missiles and LOW personal antitank weapons that came with the American airlift were hardly used during the Yom Kippur War. Nevertheless, a direct consequence of the war was the significant insertion of a number of different antitank elements into the ground forces. Tactics enabling close cooperation between infantry and armored forces in battle were also upgraded. This was basically a lesson learned from the enemy. Israeli tacticians inserted new techniques and new approaches into the integrated land battle. These changes were not fundamental, however. Rather, they constituted marginal improvements in both techniques and technology.

A longer-term effect of the armored warfare fiasco was the clear message that the Israeli weapons development establishment got from the IDF: focus on the development of precision-guided munitions with ground warfare applications. The entire project on the technology of ground warfare took more than two decades to reach fruition, but the R&D work on this area was—if not initiated by the surprising conduct of land warfare by the Egyptians and Syrians in the Yom Kippur War— greatly augmented by this war (Cohen, Eisenstadt, and Bacevich 1998, 24–25).

In the meantime, and largely until the last decade of the millennium, the overall strategy of ground warfare of the IDF did not change much. This is well reflected in the military strategy of the Lebanon War of 1982. The IDF invested heavily in both upgrading its tank force qualitatively and enlarging it quantitatively. On the eve of the Yom Kippur War, Israel had roughly two thousand tanks of all kinds (Dupuy 1978, 608). By 1982, Israel had roughly thirty-six hundred tanks, much improved in quality compared to their 1973 predecessors (Maoz 1996a, 82–84; Cohen, Eisenstadt, and Bacevich 1998). This number increased to roughly forty-two hundred by 2000. One of the key efforts centered on the development of a new tank—the Merkava—that would bear specifications addressing the challenges posed by the warfare of 1973.[16] Some people in the IDF bitterly criticized the "more and more sophisticated tanks is better" conception (Wald 1992, 122), but their advice was not heeded.

The same logic of "more is better" applied to the overall manpower of the IDF. First the IDF resolved to boost significantly the fighting capacity of the standing army, so that it would be better equipped and better manned to absorb a surprise attack in the future. The IDF standing military personnel—most of it in the ground forces—increased from roughly 100,000 in 1972 to 160,000 by 1975 and to 170,000 by 1980, a 70 percent increase in the course of seven years. A similar increase took place in the size of the reserve forces. In 1973, the reserve force amounted to roughly 210,000 people. By 1980, it increased to 310,000. While the length of service in the standing army did not change for men (it remained three years of service), the IDF dug deep into the manpower of the Israeli society, upping its mobilization capacity. At the same time, it also increased the duration of reserve service per year. Reservists averaged forty-five days of service for regular soldiers and noncommissioned officers and up to sixty days a year for officers over the next decade.

4.1.3. Naval Warfare

Naval warfare was the only area of warfare where Israel had made important strides based on good lessons of past experiences. The sinking of the destroyer *Eilat* in October 1967 and the disappearance of the submarine *Dakar* on February 1968[17] were two huge blows to the Israeli Naval Force (INF). A painstaking reassessment ended in a major change in strategy. The INF switched from large ships and submarines to a small naval armada made up of quick and elusive missile boats, equipped with the sophisticated—Israeli-made—Gabriel sea-to-sea missile. This combination proved lethal during the Yom Kippur War. Israeli missile boats hit Egyptian and Syrian ports, conducted several naval encounters, and sank fifteen Egyptian and Syrian boats, with only one damaged missile boat on the Israeli side (Dupuy 1978, 567–75, 609). The naval war, however, had little impact on the overall conduct of the war. Nevertheless, the INF strategy was vindicated by this war, so it continued to pursue this strategy after the war as well.

4.1.4. Nuclear Weapons and Nuclear Strategy

The military trauma caused by the war ignited a great deal of R&D work in Israel. However, nowhere were the ramifications of the war felt as much as they were in terms of Israel's nuclear strategy. The details on what went on in this realm are shrouded in secrecy. Open sources, however, make for a reasonably reliable picture. Israel armed its nuclear warheads on at least two occasions during the war: October 9 and October 23 (see chap. 8). We do not know just what Israel had in its arsenal at that point, but it is reasonable to suppose that it had two to three dozen bombs and a dozen or so nuclear warheads on its Jericho missiles. The war led to a major upgrade of the nuclear reactor in Dimona and to accelerated production of nuclear weapons of all kinds (Barnaby 1989, 55; Hersh 1991, 239–40; Cohen 2005).

No less important than the actual acceleration of the nuclear weapons production was the escalation of the verbal nuclear threats, in line with Israel's policy of ambiguity. Israel's president, Ephraim Katzir, stated on December 1, 1974, that "Israel now has nuclear potential" (Cohen 1998,

21–22). Moshe Dayan, by then removed from the government, stated that he believed Israel must have the option—the knowledge and operational capability—to produce nuclear weapons (excerpts of this interview in *Yediot Aharonot*, November 17, 1976). The notion that Israel must increasingly rely on a nuclear deterrent to supplement and even replace its conventional deterrent became a favorable notion in Israel's security establishment. However, Yitzhak Rabin, who replaced Golda Meir as prime minister, had always been skeptical of the value of nuclear weapons for security (Inbar 1999, 119–22). He continued to emphasize conventional deterrence over the nuclear option. Yet, he did allow a fairly free hand to his defense minister and nuclear enthusiast, Shimon Peres, to pursue aggressive production and expansion of the nuclear program (Maoz 2003a, 71–72).

Details about changes in Israel's nuclear strategy are far more veiled, but if we can draw inference from alleged patterns of weapons development it is not unreasonable to suggest that strategic planners began thinking about the tactical use of nuclear weapons in battle conditions (Evron 1994, 190–92). Originally, these weapons were to be used only under the direst circumstances. After the Yom Kippur War, it is quite plausible that some military planners started treating the weapons as designed to prevent a major defeat in a conventional war, and thus they began to treat nuclear weapons as usable weapons in limited military engagements. This turn of conception went almost unnoticed, certainly without any meaningful debate or political oversight.

4.1.5. The Financial Burden

All these postwar investments required a great deal of financial effort. Just as the IDF dug deep into its manpower pool, the Israeli government following the war dug deep into the nation's pockets to extract money for the defensive effort. Figure 5.1 displays the changes in the human and material defense burdens imposed by the Yom Kippur War.

It can be clearly seen that the Yom Kippur War affected a significant upward jump in both human and material burdens. The defense burden rose from less than 15 percent of the nation's GDP to over 25 percent, the largest in the world at that time (Berglas 1986, 176; Lifschitz 2003, 89). The human burden rose to about 8 percent. This implies that between 1974 and 1984 roughly nine out of every one hundred Israelis (not including Israeli Arabs, as they are not drafted into the military) served on active military duty at any given point in time. It took the Israeli economy a long time to recover from the financial and human implica-

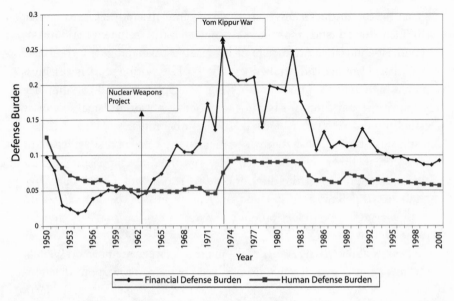

Fig. 5.1.   Human and material defense burdens, 1950–2002

tions of the rebuilding of the IDF following the Yom Kippur War (Berglas 1986).

4.2.   The Foreign Policy Implications of the War

The war had paradoxical implications for Israel's foreign policy. On one level, it improved Israeli relations with the United States. On another level, it caused significant erosion in Israeli international standing. This trend had been happening since the Six Day War but received a huge boost by the Yom Kippur War. On a third level, the war did not do much to change the adverse balance between the foreign policy establishment and the security establishment. The latter continued to dominate the former.

The most important foreign policy implication of the war was the growing Israeli diplomatic and military dependence on the United States. The war also accentuated the linkage between military support and diplomatic cooperation. The U.S. warning issued to Israel on the eve of the war not to launch a preemptive strike clearly influenced Golda's directive, over the objection of COS David Elazar, not to authorize a preemptive strike against the Egyptians and Syrians. The—possibly deliberate—delay of the airlift to Israel during the period of October 6–14 (Golan 1976) was another example of this linkage. Finally, American pressure on

Israel to stop its operations in the Canal Zone and in the Golan Height on October 22 and 23 stopped Israel short of some major military achievements. Israel's dependence on U.S. peace diplomacy increased as well. Israel was led kicking and screaming into the disengagement agreements with Egypt and Syria. It can be said that the Yom Kippur War marked the domination of U.S. diplomacy on Israel's peace policy, a domination that is still prevalent at present (Spiegel 1985, 312–14).

Israel's dependence on the United States also increased amid the weakening of the Israeli position in the international community. First, a tidal wave of suspension of diplomatic relations with Israel swept through the African states, many of which had received considerable economic, technical, and even military aid from Israel in the past. Second, this trend was expressed in a number of anti-Israeli resolutions in the UN General Assembly, including the resolution equating Zionism with racism and the decision to grant the PLO an observer status in the General Assembly (Klieman 1990, 10–16). This international isolation lasted in one form or another until after the Oslo Accords of 1993. This trend of hostile UN resolutions made Israel increasingly dependent on U.S. diplomatic support, especially in the UN Security Council, to block various initiatives calling for economic and diplomatic sanctions against Israel. The price of this diplomatic dependence had been the necessity to go along with U.S. peace initiatives in the region, which invoked a great degree of (possibly unjustified) concern in Israel.

The irony is that the first war that represented a deliberately initiated and unprovoked Arab attack since 1948 resulted in a greater isolation of Israel than either the Sinai War or the Six Day War, both initiated by Israel. One explanation for this isolation is that Israel was beginning to pay the price for its political intransigence, a trend that started with the French embargo of 1967 and the wholesale Eastern European suspension of diplomatic relations in Israel following its attack on the Golan Height toward the end of the Six Day War. The Yom Kippur War marked the growing legitimacy accorded by the international community to the PLO. After 1973, many states established semidiplomatic relations with the organization, and it received a growing level of international legitimacy.

As noted, the domination of the security establishment on the making of Israel's foreign policy did not change following the war, despite the tremendous criticism of this establishment's failure to provide early warning. The key lessons of the war have been military. It took quite a few years before Israelis (and even then only a handful) came to realize that the key failure of the war had been the failure to prevent it through diplomatic means. One of the recommendations of the Agranat inquiry commission was to establish multiple advocacy systems in national security affairs, especially—but not exclusively—on matters of intelligence assessment. The Rabin government attempted to institute a number of reforms in the intelligence community, but these changes did not alter the fundamental structure of this community. IDF intelligence continued to dominate the field, and no real body dealing with policy planning emerged outside of the military community (see chap. 12).

The domination of the security establishment on the foreign policy establishment was also suggested by the growing ties Israel had been forging with other pariah states such as South Africa, Turkey, and Iran. These ties were based primarily on security cooperation. We do not have evidence that the ties with Iran were criticized by the Foreign Ministry, but the Israeli–South African axis certainly did not help increase Israel's international standing, especially in Black Africa.

Finally, nobody interpreted the war as a fundamental diplomatic failure to reach agreement on an interim agreement back in 1971–72. The foreign policy of Israel—at least in the eyes of the foreign policy establishment—was vindicated by the war (Gazit 1983, 148–52). Sadat was seen as not ripe for real peace, and until such a shift occurred, Israel was justified in holding onto the territories. The territorial concessions in the postwar agreements were explained as concessions to the United States, rather than as an intrinsic Israeli interest.

4.3. The Domestic Political Implications of the War

The principal implication of the Yom Kippur War was the shattering of the consensus on the Arab-Israeli conflict in Israeli society. This had two major aspects. First, the war induced a growing polarization of the Israeli public. The national security and foreign policy debate in Israel became increasingly heated and polarized. Second, the war started a gradual process of shift of Israeli public opinion and of the entire spectrum of political parties away from the notion of greater Israel that had been prevalent prior to the war.

This trend seems paradoxical in terms of the political events of the mid- to late 1970s. Specifically, it appears that the erosion in the dominant standing of the Labor Party since December 1973 (and its ultimate electoral defeat by the right-wing Likud Party in May 1977) seems to suggest just the opposite. This is not the case, however. The public supported consistently the political agreements signed by both the Labor and Likud governments with Israel's neighbors. All of these agreements entailed territorial concessions by Israel, as well as political concessions on territories not ceded. This shift away from the greater Israel concept continues to the very day, despite the seeming turn to the right in terms of electoral results (Arian 1995; Shamir and Shamir 2000, 164–83).

This does not mean that Israeli policymakers abandoned their basic perceptions. On the contrary, for many hawks, the war seems to have proved the need for "defensible borders," defined in terms of territorial depth. The Arabs were bent on the destruction of the state of Israel, and if the surprise attack had been launched prior to 1967, with Israel in its narrow borders, the war would have resulted in a possibly disastrous outcome to Israel. A growing number of strategists, however, realized that the territories occupied by Israel in 1967 represented a trap rather than a security guarantee. For one thing, they increased Arab motivation to fight. Second, they forced Israel to hold significant armed forces vis-à-vis the main bodies of the Arab forces, thus exposing them to surprise attacks of the sort launched in 1973. With the main bodies of the two armies standing opposite to each other for a long time without a significant land barrier separating them, one army can easily shift from routine to offensive deployment, thereby surprising the other.

Third, the territories required Israel to fight in external lines, due to the need to mobilize reserves and transfer large amounts of manpower and material across large distances. The shift of emphasis from one front to another in the context of a multifront war required a huge logistical effort and—at the very least—took a great deal of time (Van Creveld 1998, 240–41). The debate on the security-related value of the occupied territories was slow to develop, but develop it did. And it continued throughout the period during which Israel started to sign agreements involving withdrawals from territories occupied in 1967.

The public treated the Yom Kippur War as a de facto military defeat. The December 1973 elections were too early after the war to affect a significant shift in electoral preferences, but the Labor's share of seats declined from 46.7 percent in the prewar Knesset to 42.5 percent. On the other hand, the Likud Party increased its share of the seats from 21.7 percent in 1969 to 32.5 percent in 1973. But the real change in public attitude was seen in a new wave of extra-parliamentary public activism. Public opinion forced the government to appoint an inquiry commission to investigate various issues related to the Yom Kippur War. This commission, headed by Supreme Court judge Shimon Agranat, issued its report on February 1974. The report called for the resignation of the COS,

Elazar; the head of military intelligence, Zeira; a number of other senior officers in the military intelligence; and the commander of the southern front, Gonen. The commission chose not to delve into the decisions of political leaders concerning the events leading up to the war. Its argument was that political decisions are to be judged by the court of public opinion. The public responded to that with large demonstrations calling for the resignation of Moshe Dayan. Ultimately, these demonstrations brought about the resignation of Golda Meir and her replacement by Yitzhak Rabin. Dayan was left out of the government.

The trauma of the Yom Kippur War still rests with the Israeli public and politicians. And this, to a large extent, is for the wrong reasons. It is boosted by considerable research on what is seen as the key problem of the war: the surprise attack. However, gradually a growing number of studies have identified diplomacy as the key failure of the war. Paradoxically, a war that could have been avoided began changing the public mood toward moderation, because both policymakers and ordinary people began to consider the price of continued conflict as excessive and because more people started questioning the Iron Wall conception that seems to have characterized Israeli diplomacy and security policy thus far.

— 6 —

The Lebanese Swamp,
1981–2000

I. INTRODUCTION

By now it is widely recognized that the Lebanon War was a disaster for Israel, a minor one perhaps, but a disaster nevertheless. The only one person who fails to admit it is Ariel Sharon, the chief architect of that war. But the scope and nature of the debacle in Lebanon have never been fully explored. This chapter examines the roots, dimensions, and implications of the fiasco that was ironically labeled "Operation Peace for Galilee."

The high-intensity part of the war lasted roughly three weeks. If we include in that phase the limited military operations, termed the "creeping occupation," undertaken by the IDF during the months of July and August, then the war lasted from June 6 to August 22, 1982, about two and a half months. Even if we mark the end of the war by the landing of the U.S. and French marines in west Beirut in September, the actual shooting war was fairly brief. Israel's involvement in Lebanon, however, had only begun, extending for eighteen more years. The Lebanon War really ended only on May 29, 2000, when the last IDF soldier left Lebanese soil. From August 1982 to May 2000 Israel fought a different war, a guerrilla war, and this war exposed Israel to a large array of strategic, social, and political problems.

There is no question that the Lebanon War was a war of Israeli aggression. Israelis prefer to use the "war of choice" understatement, but the

meaning and import of that term are just the same. The consensus about
the aggressive nature of the war makes a discussion of the war seemingly
superfluous. We can clearly use this war to document the argument that
it was made possible by the two common conditions that were at the root
of previous wars: the emergence of a revisionist and aggressive scheme by
elements of Israel's leadership and the stupidity, miscalculation, and
incompetence of the highest order in other sectors of Israeli political
leadership and its social and political institutions.

The Lebanon War presents a number of puzzles. One is "the paradox
of power and conflict outcomes" (Maoz 1989; 1990b, chap. 8; Maoz and
Felsenthal 1987). The paradox is that Israel lost the war not *despite* the
fact that it is more powerful but *because* it is more powerful. The gaps in
military capability between Israel and all players in the Lebanese political
arena were overwhelming. Yet, Israel was forced to leave Lebanon with
its tail between its legs. This did not happen in previous wars, when the
balance of capabilities was seemingly in favor of the Arabs or when the
balance in favor of Israel was not as lopsided as in the 1982–2000 period.
Why the vastly more powerful side lost the war is difficult to explain, and
quite a few alternative accounts exist (e.g., Merom 2003; Levy 2003,
146–70).

Another puzzle concerns what I call "the sunk cost paradox." This
paradox concerns the difficulty of a state to extract itself out of a losing
situation even though it is aware that it cannot win a war and even if it is
well aware that it is going to lose. Therefore, it takes more time and casualties for a would-be loser to end the war than to admit defeat (Maoz
1990b, 290–94). When that study (Maoz 1990b) was published, Israel's
withdrawal to the security zone in southern Lebanon seemed to have
ended this misadventure. It turns out that the loser's paradox was exacerbated in the ensuing period. The continued Israeli occupation of
Lebanese territory brought about a bitter conflict between Israel and the
Hizballah. The Galilee, for which the war was supposed to ensure peace,
was actually subjected to repeat shelling by Hizballah. Most important,
over 350 Israeli soldiers and civilians were killed during this period. Israel
finally withdrew from Lebanon in May 2000 in a manner that accentuated the depth of the military and political defeat in the war.

Thus, we need a more elaborate explanation of the Israeli entrapment
in Lebanon. The role of the army and intelligence community in this
episode was never fully analyzed. Neither do we have an explanation for
the silence of various elements of Israeli public opinion. The severity of
the sunk cost paradox is illustrated by the fact that the Israeli withdrawal

from Lebanon was not a result of a decision by a visionary political leader or of a fundamental change in the behavior of the other side. Rather, it was ignited by a grass-roots movement originating with a group of women who turned out to be both smarter and more effective than the entire IDF machinery (Levy 2003, 204–7).

Finally, Sharon's ability to maneuver the Begin government into carrying out the same plan that it had flatly rejected only a few months before the war is a classic case of political manipulation (Maoz 1990c, 105–8). This feature of the war deserves a closer look, not the least because for fifteen years the Israeli public, the security community, the political system, the media, and the academic community in Israel were led to believe that Israeli withdrawal from southern Lebanon would spell disaster for the Galilee. Five years later, the border with Lebanon is nearly as calm as the Israeli-Egyptian, Israeli-Jordanian, and Israeli-Syrian borders. The only thing that occasionally inflames the border is the continued Israeli overflights of Lebanese territory (Sobelman 2003).

Viewed in isolation, each of these puzzles can be explained through a different set of factors. However, taken together, these puzzles—as well as quite a few additional ones—represent a chain in a long history of malice, folly, and incompetence. In this chapter I examine the Israeli experience in Lebanon as a prolonged military and political failure, not merely one that is limited to a set of bad decisions—though there were some exceptionally bad ones in the process.[1] Rather, the Lebanese case suggests that stupidity can be both contagious and rather chronic. The present chapter attempts to highlight several key aspects of the war and the long occupation of the security zone.

1. *The origins of the war.* An implicit argument in many studies (an argument made explicit in Yaniv and Lieber 1983) is that the processes that were taking place within Lebanon and between Syria and Lebanon imposed on Israel a security dilemma (to use Yaniv and Lieber's language) that was impossible to resolve without resorting to force. The Begin government only happened to stumble onto a problem created by others. Any other responsible government would have dealt with the Lebanese problem in much the same way. I challenge this thesis. The Lebanon War was not really a war about Lebanon. It was part of a grand scheme aimed at creating a new order in the occupied territories designed to perpetuate Israeli occupation of the West Bank and Gaza by destroying the PLO. This scheme evolved in the mind of Ariel Sharon and was shared, at least partially, by Menachem Begin. Lebanon was nothing less than a war made by two individuals who dragged the entire Israeli society into a

costly adventure. Given the role Sharon is playing in Israeli politics at present, this point is of major significance.

2. *The politics of the war and the politics of withdrawal.* A number of studies examine the politics of the war and the politics of withdrawal. I will discuss some of the aspects that have been covered in the literature, such as the decision-making process and the changing public and elite attitude toward the war. However, my focus here is on the relations between the government and the IDF in general and the intelligence community in particular. I argue that this process can be explained largely by the lack of meaningful mechanism for oversight and control of the security community by political and social institutions.

3. *The politics of entrapment.* In May 2000, the last Israeli soldiers left Lebanon. Since then, more than five years have passed. Contrary to the doomsday predictions of IDF intelligence, the Hizballah have not engaged in shelling of the northern borders of Israel. The northern Galilee has been a very quiet border. However, for fifteen years after the security zone was established, Israelis were led to believe that a withdrawal from southern Lebanon without an agreement with Syria and Lebanon would spell disaster. During this period, over 320 Israeli soldiers and 20 civilians were killed in southern Lebanon and in the upper Galilee. Since May 2000, however, only five people have been killed (Sobelman 2003). How could an entire country be fooled by a baseless assessment? Israel had no territorial claims to southern Lebanon, so what caused this process of entrapment? I explore the logic of entrapment from the perspective of a military and political doctrine emphasizing the excessive use of force for deterrence purposes. I also examine how and why all of the watchdogs in Israel fell asleep while on guard duty. The lessons of the Lebanon War are highly significant in terms of Israeli foreign and security policy because the failure in this war was not only military or political; it was also a social and moral failure of significant proportions. I derive the lessons of this war by examining the consequences of entrapment.

2. THE ORIGINS OF THE WAR

Quite a few Israeli politicians never really internalized the Israeli-Lebanese border. More important, the political makeup of Lebanon seemed peculiar and unnatural not only to Syrian leaders dreaming of "Greater Syria" (Pipes 1990); it also seemed unnatural to some Israelis. In a meeting that took place in February 1954, Ben-Gurion proposed a plan of dismantling Lebanon and creating a Christian Maronite state that would become Israel's ally (Sharett 1978, 377–78). Ben-Gurion's reference to Lebanon in his opening address at the Sèvres Conference of October 1956 (see this vol., p. 71) is a typical example of this reasoning. But this line of thinking did not have immediate operational implications. The armistice agreement between Israel and Lebanon contained no ambiguity as to the international border. Consequently, neither side had territorial claims. Lebanon did nothing to aid Egypt in 1967, thus providing Israel no pretext to occupy its territory. Finally, the Israeli-Lebanese border was generally quiet up to the late 1960s. Thus Israeli leaders saw little need for retaliatory action. During the 1949–70 period, when Israel had to worry about security threats emanating from its other borders, the relative tranquility of the Lebanese border was a source of reassurance.

During 1968, a number of infiltrations from Lebanon to Israel caused several Israeli casualties. In addition, the first hijacking of an Israeli plane to Algiers (on July 22) and an attack on an El Al airplane in Athens originated from Beirut. In retaliation, the IDF raided the Beirut airport on the night of December 26–27, blowing up fourteen civilian planes. Subsequently, the IDF launched a number of small raids into Lebanon in retaliation for Palestinian attacks on Israeli border settlements.

The increased activity of the PLO from Lebanon and the resulting Israeli raids created conflict between the Palestinians and the Lebanese government. A number of military engagements between the Palestinian guerrillas and the Lebanese security forces in 1968 and 1969 led to the Cairo agreement of November 3, 1969, which provided the PLO with significant autonomy in southern Lebanon. In exchange, the PLO agreed not to interfere in Lebanese politics. The agreement also constrained PLO activities in southern Lebanon, so as to prevent Israeli retaliation raids (Dupuy and Martell 1986, 28–30).

The mass exodus of the Palestinian guerrillas from Jordan in September 1970 and June 1971 shifted the center of gravity of the Palestinian operations against Israel to Lebanon. As we can see in figure 6.1, the number of infiltrations and attacks on Israeli targets originating from Lebanese territory increased markedly in 1970 and remained high in 1971 and 1972. The number of Israeli raids also climbed during the same time. As the situation was beginning to get out of hand, the Lebanese government once again imposed its authority on the PLO. In 1972 another agreement was signed between the PLO and the Lebanese government, but this time the PLO agreed to accept strict limits on its operational freedom (Brynen 1990, 61). Indeed, the number of incidents went down in 1972 and 1973. Even during the Yom Kippur War, the PLO did not do much to provoke the Israelis.

After the Yom Kippur War, the number of incidents emanating from Lebanon increased. In 1974 and 1975 the number of PLO attacks resulted in a large number of fatalities and caused considerable concern in Israel. The civil war that broke out in Lebanon in 1974 allowed the PLO considerable freedom of operation because the Lebanese government had lost control over the country. Paradoxically, the Syrian intervention in Lebanon in 1976 significantly brought down the number of PLO raids into Israel. The Syrians engaged the PLO in battle and severely restricted the PLO's freedom of movement. Southern Lebanon was free of Syrian control due to its tacit agreement with Israel (Evron 1987, 46–48; Rabinovich 1984, 101–4). Thus, the PLO could stage raids into Israel from there. Yet, the PLO's preoccupation with the Syrians and the restriction on its movements in northern and central Lebanon made such raids logistically difficult to carry out.

On March 11, 1978, a group of PLO terrorists from Lebanon staged a major attack, killing thirty-eight Israelis. Israel retaliated by launching a large-scale attack on PLO bases in southern Lebanon. Operation Litany, as this raid was labeled, lasted roughly four months. UN Resolution 425 of March 19, 1978, allowed the withdrawal of Israeli forces in return for the insertion of a peacekeeping force into southern Lebanon (Naor 1993, 244–46; Yaniv 1987b, 71–75). This arrangement seemed to work reasonably well. The frequency and severity of clashes along the Lebanese border went down significantly. In the spring of 1981, a crisis erupted between Israel and Syria as a result of provocations by the Christian militias against Syrian forces in Zahle. The Syrians landed commando units, using transport helicopters—arguably an infringement on the 1976 agreement between Syria and Israel (Rabinovich 1984, 116–17; Evron 1987, 89–96; Yaniv 1987b, 85–89).

Israel's response was swift. On April 28, 1981, Israeli jets shot down two Syrian helicopters carrying supplies to the Syrian troops south of Zahle. Asad retaliated by inserting SAMs into Lebanon and deployed additional SAMs along the Syrian-Lebanese border (Evron 1987, 94–96; Yaniv 1987b, 86–87; Sharon 1989, 429). The Begin government authorized an air strike to destroy Syrian missile batteries; however, the attack was postponed due to bad weather (Rabinovich 1984, 118–19; Schiff and Yaari 1984, 35). In an effort to defuse the crisis, President Reagan sent a special envoy, Philip Habib, to mediate between Israel and Syria. Habib's mission did not bring about an agreement, but things calmed down. Israel

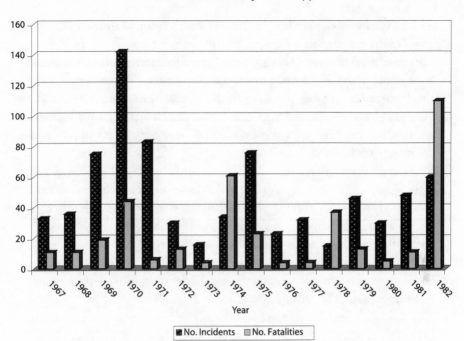

Fig. 6.1. Number of terrorist attacks emanating from Lebanon, 1967–82

accepted, at least temporarily, the presence of Syrian missiles on Lebanese soil. Syria, for its part, halted its attack on the Christians.

The crisis in Lebanon shifted from an Israeli-Syrian struggle to a confrontation between Israel and the PLO. The PLO's freedom of action in southern Lebanon, where Syrian troops could not enter, allowed it to increase its power in terms of armed personnel, weapon systems, and the evolution of a command and control structure. Evron (1987, 107) notes,

> From late 1981 official Israeli spokesmen have tended to exaggerate the dangers inherent in the PLO presence there. . . . Israeli leaders pointed out that the PLO was in the process of developing a conventional military capability, and particularly emphasized the increased number of artillery pieces acquired by the PLO since 1981. It seems, however, that most Israeli military leaders, when referring to the increase in PLO military capabilities, were concerned about its potential ability to harass Israeli settlements in northern Israel, rather than its constituting a strategic threat to Israel.

In July 1981, Israel decided to launch a major air raid on PLO bases in southern Lebanon and in west Beirut. This raid resulted in over one hundred killed and about six hundred wounded (Schiff and Yaari 1984, 36). The PLO responded in a massive shelling of northern Israel. This mini-war of attrition lasted for about ten days, resulting in few Israeli casualties but causing many of the residents of the city of Kiryat Shmona to flee the city. Ambassador Habib returned to the region to mediate between the PLO and Israel. This time the shuttle diplomacy yielded an agreement whereby the PLO committed itself to refrain from attacks on Israeli civilian targets (Schiff and Yaari 1984, 36–38).

By that time, Begin—having won narrowly the elections of July 1981—purged his new government of most moderate ministers and appointed Ariel Sharon to the defense minister's post. Sharon had already started drafting his plan of attacking Lebanon before the election. He had supported the planned attack on the Syrian SAM batteries in April and pushed for the large-scale attack on the PLO in July.[2] His new position provided him with new bureaucratic and political powers that facilitated the implementation of his grand design.

Thus, neither the PLO operations nor the Syrian activities in Lebanon posed a significant threat to Israel. It was principally Israeli actions (or the actions of the Christian Phalanges, indirectly supported by the Mossad; see chap. 9) that escalated things on the Israeli-Lebanese border. What was Sharon's motivation for launching the war in Lebanon? Since his first posting in the Begin government in 1977, Sharon had been obsessed with the growing PLO's influence in the occupied territories. As minister of agriculture, Sharon masterminded an ambitious plan for establishing numerous new settlements in the occupied territories (Sharon 1989, 355–72; Benziman 1985, 206–12). Yet, as long as Dayan and Weizman were in the government, their presence had a modifying influence on Israeli settlement policy. Once these two politicians resigned from the government, Sharon was free to operate. He did so both by continuing an aggressive settlement policy and by attempting to manipulate Palestinian politics (see chap. 9).

Sharon perceived Begin's autonomy plan as a highly risky venture. Tensions in the occupied territories began to mount as the autonomy talks started in 1980 and continued throughout 1981. Sharon felt that the PLO was imposing its nationalist agenda on the local population. The expulsion of the mayors of Hebron and Halhoul in 1980 only served to aggravate things. Sharon viewed this as a prelude to a popular uprising to be staged by the PLO. He realized immediately the risks associated with this kind of uprising to the vision of Israeli control of the West Bank and Gaza.

There were other disturbing signs from Sharon's perspective. First, the

PLO was constantly gaining points in the world's public opinion. Arafat appeared at the UN in 1974 and was becoming a regular guest in many Western capitals. The peace between Israel and Egypt, paradoxically, increased the salience of the Palestinian issue. Begin's presentation of an autonomy plan for the Palestinians—however restricted—was an admission of the impossibility of realizing the dream of annexation, long harbored by the Likud Party (Benziman 1985, 205). As Sharon (1989, 402) himself noted,

> My own reaction [to Begin's autonomy plan] was that the plan was loaded with danger. It could easily, I said, become a Balfour Declaration for the Palestinians and might well lead to a second Palestinian state (in addition to Jordan), something no Israeli with any regard for the country's safety could agree to.

Sharon did not object to the plan in the government but rather tried to circumvent a meaningful implementation of the autonomy plan by establishing new civilian settlements in the West Bank. As he pointed out, the primary "precaution" Israel had to take against the risks associated with the autonomy plan was "to insure that we keep in our hands the vital strategic terrain and prevent any future possibility that it would fall into someone's else's hands. . . . From our historical experience we knew that only settlements could secure a claim to land" (Sharon 1989, 403).

Second, Sharon believed that the presence of the PLO in southern Lebanon contributed significantly to its influence in the occupied territories. The PLO could demonstrate to the Palestinians under occupation that active resistance to Israel offered hope. Sharon was also critical of Operation Litany in Lebanon. This operation yielded few tangible results. The PLO guerrillas refrained from direct engagements with the Israeli forces, retreating once the Israeli forces entered southern Lebanon. When the Israelis withdrew, the guerrillas returned to their previous positions. The United Nations Interim Force in Lebanon (UNIFIL) served to constrain Israel rather than the Palestinians (Sharon 1989, 425–26). Third, Sharon was deeply disturbed by the 1981 cease-fire agreement between Israel and the PLO. Not only did this cease-fire put a political damper on any plan to initiate a head-on clash, but it also constituted a diplomatic victory for the PLO. For the first time in the history of the Israeli-Palestinian relations since 1948, an Israeli government signed an agreement—albeit indirect—with the PLO. This was bound to have an effect on the Palestinians in the occupied territories (Sharon 1989, 432–33; Schiff and Yaari 1984, 37).

These factors suggested to Sharon that it was imperative to hand the PLO a severe blow so as to diminish its influence on the Palestinians within the occupied territories. Repeating Operation Litany would not do. The PLO could always withdraw to central Lebanon. The PLO head-quarters in Beirut would not be damaged. After Israel was forced to with-draw from Lebanon, the PLO would return as if nothing had happened. For Sharon, the 1981 Mount Sanin crisis with the Syrians represented a real blow to Israeli deterrence: Syria had blatantly violated the 1976 understandings by inserting SAMs into Lebanon. Israel did not respond to this violation, which could have tempted the Syrians to engage in a creeping erosion of the 1976 agreements. Syrian presence in Lebanon prevented any meaningful change in that country. This implied that it would be impossible to launch a large-scale offensive against the PLO without a direct engagement with the Syrian forces.[3]

But handing a blow to the PLO and to the Syrians would accomplish nothing if the civil war in Lebanon continued. The political vacuum in the country would draw in hostile elements. This revived the old Ben-Gurion dream of a Christian-dominated state that would be aligned with Israel. Only such a process would effectively convert the military achieve-ment of the planned war into a favorable political outcome. This required, however, very close coordination with the Christians. Already in November 1981, Sharon informed Bashir Gemayel—the leader of the Christian Phalanges who had just announced his candidacy to the presi-dency of Lebanon—that Israel was planning a large-scale attack on the PLO and Syrian forces in Lebanon. "Curiously enough, this message made Bashir privy to information that the Israeli Cabinet did not even suspect!" (Schiff and Yaari 1984, 46).

In January 1982, Sharon paid a secret visit to Lebanon, meeting with the Christian leaders. Sharon discussed openly the possibility of the Christians occupying west Beirut (Schiff and Yaari 1984, 49–51; Sharon 1989, 439–42). The deal was deceptively simple: Israel would create a military situation that would enable the Christians to occupy west Beirut, thus facilitating the election of Bashir Gemayel as president of Lebanon. As Sharon viewed it, the Christian end of the bargain would be twofold: occupy west Beirut and—after Bashir's election as president—begin for-mal negotiations with Israel, leading to either a peace agreement or a nonbelligerency agreement. This would cement the political achieve-ment of the war. "We will make Bashir President," exclaimed Sharon to his aides who accompanied him to Beirut (Schiff and Yaari 1984, 51).

The basic scheme of the Lebanon War, as it evolved in Sharon's mind, was fourfold.

1. Destroy the PLO infrastructure in Lebanon, including the PLO head-quarters in Beirut. The physical destruction of the PLO human and material assets in Lebanon, including the killing of the PLO leader-ship, was a top priority. But expulsion of the PLO from Lebanon would also be an acceptable achievement.

2. Drive Syrian forces out of Lebanon. Sharon knew that this could not be accomplished without a full-scale confrontation with the Syrians. It would have been preferable if the Syrian forces had started shooting at the Israeli forces, because this would provide Israel with the politi-cal pretext for attacking the Syrians. However, if the Syrians did not play by the Israeli rules, Israel would have to initiate a direct attack on the Syrians.

3. Install a Christian-dominated government in Lebanon, with Bashir Gemayel as president. This would ensure that the military accom-plishments of the war would be preserved by a political ally who could end the civil war and would ensure a strong state that was capable of making and enforcing its policies on the population, including the ter-mination of Syrian presence in Lebanon.

4. Sign a peace treaty with the Lebanese government that would solidify the informal Israeli-Christian alliance and convert it into a binding agreement. If this were not possible—due to the political constraints under which the Christians found themselves in the Arab world—a nonbelligerence agreement would also be acceptable.[4]

This scheme had gaping holes in all of its aspects. In contrast to other war scenarios in Israel's history, almost everybody in the military estab-lishment who had been privy to this scheme had major reservations. This did not bother Sharon and Eitan too much. They were in a position to impose their will on their subordinates and would not let these reserva-tions interfere with the basic scheme.[5]

Sharon's scheme was not a secret. Sharon's intense lobbying for the defense minister's post in 1981 brought about a series of objections from a number of politicians from inside and outside the Likud. Many of those opposed to Sharon's appointment to the post—such as Deputy Prime Minister Simcha Erlich, Deputy Prime Minister Yigael Yadin, and former foreign minister Moshe Dayan—warned Begin that Sharon would embroil Israel in an aggressive (and possibly costly) war in Lebanon (Naor 1993, 259–63). Sharon had already indicated his beliefs that the "solution" to the Palestinian problem may be found in Lebanon and that it would take a war to accomplish this task. Even hard-liners who viewed the threats emanating from the PLO's presence in Lebanon as significant did not believe that an aggressive war was the solution.

The war in Lebanon was not about peace to the Galilee. The Galilee was not under threat by the Palestinians or the Syrians. The evidence on PLO operations in Lebanon since Operation Litany in 1978, and even more so since the July 1981 cease-fire, suggests that the PLO was exercising considerable restraint along the border. The massive bombardment of the PLO in July 1981 came in direct response to an Israeli decision to launch a large-scale air raid against PLO headquarters in Beirut (Schiff and Yaari 1984, 35–36). The decision to launch this attack was a typical example of how a weak cabinet succumbs to military considerations. Some people in the Israeli government—such as Begin and Sharon—and in the IDF—principally Rafael Eitan—had sought ways to escalate the situation in Lebanon ever since the Syrian introduction of SAMs in April 1981. The attacks on the PLO headquarters in Beirut in July can be seen as an attempt to escalate the conflict to the point of direct confrontation leading up to an all-out war against both the PLO and the Syrians.

Sharon's key objective was to hand a deadly military and political blow to the PLO. The defeat of the PLO in Lebanon would end the Palestinian dream for a homeland in the West Bank and Gaza Strip. Sharon viewed the solution to the Palestinian problem within the confines of Jordan (Sharon 1989, 552–53; Shlaim 2000, 477). As long as the Palestinians in the occupied territories harbored any hope for a Palestinian state in the occupied territories, they would continue resisting Israeli settlement policy and would raise hell with world public opinion. Destroying the PLO in Lebanon would convince the Palestinians to find the solution to their problem in Jordan.

> There was no objective military urgency in acting before the renewal of such activities [repeated heavy bombardment of Israeli cities in the north by the PLO]. . . . It is much more likely that the leading Israeli decision makers were concerned about another issue relating to the PLO; namely, their perception of the PLO as an effective political constraint against Israeli plans in the West Bank and Gaza. . . . Complete destruction of the PLO, as it was argued, would undermine its power and international recognition and pave the way for the com-

plete subordination of the West Bankers. . . . It could be speculated that the war in Lebanon was perceived by some [Israeli decision makers] as creating an option for a process which might lead to the transformation . . . of the relationship between Jordan, the West Bank, and Israel. This transformation might then bring about the emigration of many of the West Bank inhabitants to the eastern side of the Jordan River. The way would then be clear for the final annexation of the West Bank. (Evron 1987, 107–8, 110)[6]

Kimmerling (2003, 81) offers this interpretation of the underlying goals of the Lebanon War:

after the Palestinian refusal to adopt Sharon's equation of "Jordan is Palestine," only their politicide could, from Sharon's point of view, resolve the conflict. . . . The politicide of the Palestinians might include destroying their institutional and military infrastructure in southern Lebanon and possibly annihilating Fatah and other top PLO political and military organizations. This new political reality would . . . force Palestinians in the West Bank and Gaza strip into accepting any solution dictated by the Israelis.[7]

It may appear that the notion of occupying an Arab country and its capital and risking war with the entire Arab world in order to destroy a guerrilla or terrorist organization was utterly megalomaniac. Yet this was not at all exceptional in terms of Israeli history of the use of force. The Sinai-Suez scheme of Ben-Gurion and Dayan during 1956 was not less ambitious. The difference was that in 1956 the task of occupying Egypt and rearranging its political system was up to the British and French. Israel was only to play the role of aggressor that provided the British and French with the pretext of intervening in the conflict. In Lebanon, Israel took upon itself the role both of the provocateur and of the political architect of an Arab country.

3. THE POLITICS OF THE LEBANON WAR

3.1. *The Politics of War Initiation, March 1981–June 1982*

As noted, Sharon's master plan had a number of gaping holes in it, resting on several flawed assumptions. However, it was also a carefully calculated plan. In order to address the politics of war initiation and war management in Lebanon, it is important to analyze some of the aspects of this plan.

Operation Big Pines consisted of several aspects. Israel would invade an Arab country and put its capital under siege (perhaps even occupy Beirut). It would also engage the Syrian forces in Lebanon, thus fighting not only against a guerrilla or terrorist organization but against another Arab country. This would be an extremely risky venture. First, it would put the recently signed Israeli-Egyptian peace treaty to test. Egypt might "fail" the test and abrogate the treaty after it had gained the whole Sinai back. More important, Syria might open another front on the Golan Height, thus increasing the risks to Israel. Other states might send troops—in particular Iraq, which had been harboring aspirations of revenge following the destruction of its Osirak nuclear reactor in July 1981. The oil-rich Arab states might renew their oil embargo, thus bringing about strong pressures by oil consumers on Israel.

Second, unless the United States was on board—at least diplomatically—Israel might find itself isolated in the international community. It could face UN sanctions and might even see its weapons shipments suspended. The Reagan administration had briefly suspended the shipments of F-15 aircrafts to Israel after the bombing of the Osirak reactor. This was the first time such a drastic act had happened during the Begin government. Naor (1993, 256) points out that, while the Carter administration was very critical of Israeli policy verbally, the Reagan administration showed a willingness to hit Israel where it really hurt. Risking a major diplomatic confrontation with that administration would be a very costly affair.

Third, it was unclear how the Israeli public would deal with an offensive war. The Begin government had won the elections of July 1981, but this was a very narrow victory. Long-term entanglement in Lebanon and high levels of casualties might turn the public against the war and against the government that had initiated it.

Minimizing the risks of the invasion of Lebanon was not enough to ensure success of the grand design, however. Israel had to ensure that the underlying assumptions of the attack would be met. The PLO would have to be physically destroyed. The Syrians would have to be engaged so that their withdrawal from Lebanon would be ensured. Bashir Gemayel had to be elected as president of Lebanon. Finally, the Christians had to cooperate with Israel during the war by entering west Beirut so as to prevent the image of Israeli forces entering a capital of an Arab state. They also were expected to initiate a peace or nonbelligerency treaty with Israel. These were tenuous assumptions, and the violation of any one of them could topple the entire deck of cards that represented Sharon's grand design.

It is not entirely clear when Sharon began to formulate his plan. Schiff and Yaari (1984, 37–38) argue that Sharon and Begin were willing to agree to the July 1981 cease-fire with the Palestinians because by then they had been convinced that a major showdown in Lebanon was inevitable. Sharon began communicating his ideas in operational terms to his advisers and to IDF functionaries as soon as he entered the Defense Ministry in August 1981. While he found COS Eitan and Begin to be eager and loyal allies, Sharon faced at least three formidable obstacles: the cabinet, some senior IDF officers, and the United States.[8]

Sharon and Begin hoped to win the cabinet's approval for Operation Big Pines. On December 20, 1981, they presented the plan to the cabinet. A number of ministers scowled at the plan. They demanded more discussion before voting on it. Bewildered by this unexpected opposition, Begin decided to adjourn the meeting without taking a vote (Naor 1993, 268, Yaniv 1987b, 107; Schiff and Yaari 1984, 47–48). The opposition in the cabinet to Operation Big Pines was a devastating blow to Sharon, not the least because the plan he had presented to the cabinet was only a small portion of the grand design. He focused only on the military dimension of the war, avoiding completely the political aspects of the entire plan. The engagement with the Syrian forces was not mentioned. The occupation or encirclement of Beirut was not mentioned. Sharon only noted that the IDF was designated to reach the Beirut-Damascus highway. Yet, even this minimalist version of the plan did not invoke enough support in the cabinet.

But the December 20 cabinet session was also educational to Sharon because it alerted him to the kind of obstacles he had to overcome if he were to win approval of the cabinet for initiating the Lebanon War. In problems of the sort wherein a political leader wishes to advance an aggressive scheme in the face of political opposition, he can bring to the discussion a number of loyal allies from the IDF, most principally, the COS, the head of military intelligence, and the commander of the relevant regional arena. Sharon indeed had the COS squarely on his side, but the other two officers had major reservations regarding various aspects of the plan.

The view of Major General Yehoshua Saguy, head of military intelligence (AMAN), was shaped by an atypically accurate analysis of his research branch. Saguy deeply doubted the loyalty of the Christian Phalanges and discounted their fighting skills and resolve. He repeatedly argued that the Christians were unreliable allies and would betray Israel the first chance they got. This assessment of AMAN ran in direct contrast to the assessment of the Mossad, headed by Major General (Ret.) Yitzhak Hoffi. The Mossad had been responsible for forging the relations between Israel and the Christian Phalanges. Already in April 1981, Saguy warned Begin that the Phalanges were creating a provocation in Mount Sanin that would draw Israel into a confrontation with the Syrians (Schiff and Yaari 1984, 33–34, 49–51; Naor 1993, 240). Saguy repeatedly warned Sharon and other IDF commanders of any significant reliance on Bashir Gemayel. He frequently clashed with Hoffi, and Sharon used this confrontation to adopt the Mossad's view of the Phalanges over that of AMAN.

In addition, and in contrast to Sharon's optimistic assessment of the amount of time that would be required for the IDF to stay in Lebanon, Saguy envisioned a fairly prolonged stay in Lebanon. He also raised significant concerns about the diplomatic backlash of such a war, especially in terms of U.S.-Israeli relations (Schiff and Yaari 1984, 47–51). Finally, Saguy may have also had major reservations about the Lebanon-occupied territories linkage.

Major General Amir Drori, the commander of the northern front, shared Saguy's skepticism about the Phalanges' fighting skills. He pointed out to Eitan that it was "out of the question to depend on the Christians. From a military standpoint, they're in very poor shape. Their capability is limited solely to the defensive, and they cannot be expected to participate in a mobile war" (Schiff and Yaari 1984, 46).

Thus, from Sharon's perspective, bringing these officers to the cabinet meeting in order to help sway the opposition to the plan ran a number of major risks. Beyond the risk that these officers would undermine Sharon's and Begin's efforts, there was a chance that the entire scope of the plan would be revealed. Officers would have to answer hard questions about the scope of the attack, about the fact that the IDF was actually preparing for a direct clash with the Syrian forces, and about the coordination with the Phalanges.

While it seemed both expedient and feasible to conceal the key elements of the plan—including its principal objectives—from cabinet ministers, it was impossible to do so as far as the IDF was concerned. It was both impractical and self-defeating to delude the IDF that a confrontation with the Syrian forces was somehow avoidable. It was essential that the IDF be fully aware of the territorial scope of the war, including the need to encircle Beirut, so as to prepare plans and deploy forces for these operations. The IDF had to be intimately involved in the coordination with the Christians. Finally, the IDF—at least the key commanders—had to be made privy to the need for deception of the cabinet by Sharon.

From a military point of view, and considering the political and territorial contours of the planned attack, it was best to confront the Syrian forces at the beginning of the war, in order to prevent them from bringing in reinforcements or starting a second front on the Golan Height. Moreover, a landing of troops north of Beirut seemed necessary to ensure the encirclement of the city and to prevent a fleeing of the PLO leadership and troops to northern Lebanon. Saguy's and Drori's reservations about the effectiveness and reliability of the Phalanges implied that the IDF would have to prepare a major amphibious force for this purpose. The original version of Operation Big Pines therefore involved major elements that had not been part of the plan presented to the cabinet on December 20. It involved a direct and large-scale confrontation with the Syrians. And it entailed a major amphibious operation in the Beirut-Junieh area (Schiff and Yaari 1984, 51–53).[9] Moreover, in order to force a quick Syrian retreat, the IDF would have to land a contingent in the Beirut-Damascus highway area (Schiff and Yaari 1984, 109).

The reluctance in the cabinet to approve even a downscaled version of Operation Big Pines necessitated major modifications in the plan. First, the IDF would have to forgo its intention of an early confrontation with the Syrians; this would have to "emerge" out of the confrontation with the PLO and would be put off to several days after the initial plunge into Lebanon. Second, the IDF would have to rely on the Phalanges in the Beirut area. The Phalanges would have to confront the PLO or put a siege on west Beirut. The IDF would attempt a more limited encirclement operation by landing troops in the Sidon area, some forty-eight kilometers south of Beirut. The basic contours of Operation Big Pines would be preserved, but the government would be presented with a downscaled plan, called Little Pines. This plan envisioned a limited confrontation with the PLO up to the Litany River, some forty kilometers north of the Israeli-Lebanese border. It also suggested that it may be possible to accomplish these goals without a confrontation with the Syrian forces.

Sharon's strategy vis-à-vis the cabinet also changed. In essence, Israel would use PLO provocations—whether or not these had been real violations of the July 1981 agreement—to launch large-scale air strikes in Lebanon. These strikes would entice the PLO to resume bombardments on the Galilee, thereby paving the way to approval of the Little Pines plan by the cabinet. As Naor (1993, 268) puts it:

The strategy [Sharon devised] for the approval of the [Big Pines] plan was a manipulation of stimulus and response: the Cabinet would be presented each time with a proposal for an operation of modest and limited objectives, but when the terrorists responded by firing Katyusha rockets and artillery on the settlements in northern Israel, the government would be forced to approve a drastic military operation. Such a move can be a "small" plan . . . which, during its implementation, would accomplish the original objective of the "big plan." The military planners received directives for the planning of operations according to various options of limited scope. But whoever understood the internal logic of such plans and read the picture of the aerial battle could have deciphered, already at the beginning of the winter [of 1982], what was about to happen.

The first opportunity for implementing this strategy presented itself in late January 1982. A group of six PLO guerrillas was captured in the Jordan Valley, trying to infiltrate from Jordan into the West Bank. Begin admitted that the infiltration was from Jordan and that this incident was not a breach of the 1981 agreement with the PLO. Nevertheless, he allowed Sharon and Eitan to propose to the cabinet a large-scale strike against PLO targets in Lebanon. Surprisingly, again the majority of cabinet ministers—led by Begin's deputy, Simcha Erlich—rejected this proposal (Yaniv 1987b, 108; Naor 1993, 269–70).

Sharon wanted to get the process started before the final phase of Israeli withdrawal from the Sinai—scheduled for April 26, 1982—which entailed dismantlement of the Rafah settlements (Yaniv 1987b, 108; Naor 1993, 270). His hope was that, if Egypt abrogated the peace treaty with Israel as a result of the attack in Lebanon, Israel would at least remain in possession of a portion of the Sinai and would not have to dismantle the Rafah settlements. Therefore, in March Sharon increased his pressure on Begin to intensify the provocations against the PLO so as to garner cabinet approval for the first phase of the war. However, it became evident that "not only 'doves' like Erlich and Burg, but also 'hawks' like Begin and Shamir wished to avoid combining the Lebanese problem with the implementation of the peace treaty with Egypt" (Naor 1993, 270).

Twice during the month of March, Sharon and Begin presented to cabinet ministers truncated versions of the plan. On both occasions, a majority of the group rejected the proposed plan. However, opposition to the idea of a large-scale operation in Lebanon was gradually eroding. On April 11, following a shooting on an Israeli diplomat in Athens, Begin proposed a massive Israeli attack on PLO bases in Lebanon. While there was now a majority support for the action in the cabinet, no less than nine ministers still opposed the operation. Among them were Simcha Erlich and David Levy, two deputies to the prime minister (Yaniv 1987b, 108; Evron 1987, 121–22). Begin proposed the establishment of a six-member cabinet subcommittee that would decide on the manner and scope of retaliation. On April 21, five days before the final Israeli withdrawal from the Sinai, the first Israeli air strike in southern Lebanon took place (Evron 1987, 122; Sharon 1989, 447). The PLO did not react.

Israeli provocations continued. On May 9, the IAF was again activated against PLO targets in Lebanon. This time the PLO responded by a Katyusha and mortar barrage. The PLO fire did not hit any Israeli settlement. The PLO was signaling that it could not restrain itself for long if Israeli provocations continued (Schiff and Yaari 1984, 55; Evron 1987, 122; Naor 1993, 273). On the next day, the cabinet met again. Sharon and Eitan presented a watered-down plan of attack on Lebanon. The running estimate in the IDF was that this operation would require three to six months of IDF presence in Lebanon. When presenting this plan to the cabinet, Sharon indicated that Israel would make every effort to prevent a clash with the Syrians. He presented this plan as a "policing operation." When asked how long this action would take, he responded that it would take twenty-four hours (Naor 1993, 273). To Begin's and Sharon's utter dismay the government was deadlocked, with seven ministers voting in support of this operation and seven in opposition. Erlich and Levy were again in the latter camp (Naor 1993, 273–74; Yaniv 1987b, 109; Evron 1987, 123; Schiff and Yaari 1984, 55–56).[10]

The big opportunity came when, on June 3, the Israeli ambassador to Great Britain, Shlomo Argov, was gunned down by a Palestinian terrorist. Within hours, it was established by the Israeli intelligence that the assassination attempt was carried out by the Abu Nidal group. This faction, a splinter group from the PLO operating in close cooperation with Iraqi intelligence, was dedicated among other things to the overthrow of Arafat and the creation of an alternative to the PLO. In a cabinet meeting on June 4, Avraham Shalom, the head of the Israeli General Secret Service (GSS, or SHABAK, to use its Hebrew acronym), informed the ministers that the attack had been carried out by the Abu Nidal organization. However, Begin interrupted Shalom by saying, "they are all PLO." He then proceeded to recommend a large-scale air strike against PLO headquarters in Beirut. Everybody in the cabinet meeting immediately understood the implications of approving this action. In fact, both Eitan and Saguy informed the cabinet that this time the PLO was sure to respond in force to the Israeli attack. Given the previous course of events, it was evident that, if the air attack on the PLO headquarters were approved, the war could no longer be avoided.

Once the PLO responded as predicted, the cabinet was convened again on June 5 to discuss the proposed plan of operation, "Peace for Galilee." Sharon and Eitan presented the plan of attack as a limited operation extending forty kilometers north of the Israeli-Lebanese border, up to Sidon in the west and Lake Karoun in the east. Most of the ministers accepted this plan as a reasonable response to the PLO barrage. Nevertheless, a dissenting voice did arise. Minister of Communications Mordechai Zipori raised a number of significant reservations to the proposed plan. A former brigadier general and commander of the armored corps, Zipori was the only person in the second Begin government, other than Sharon, with military experience. He immediately understood that this plan entailed a direct confrontation with the Syrians. He also suspected that the scope of the operation may be wider than that presented by Sharon and Begin. Other ministers, principally Erlich, Berman, and Burg, also expressed reservations and abstained in the vote (Naor 1993, 282–92; Schiff and Yaari 1984, 102–6; Sharon 1989, 456–57; Yaniv 1987b, 110–13; Evron 1987, 123–29). As Naor (1993, 281) points out, Sharon saw in this decision a de facto approval of the first stage of the larger plan and indeed directed the IDF to prepare for the occupation of the areas surrounding Beirut.

Sharon's strategy throughout the period starting December 20 and ending with the June 5 decision to go to a limited military operation involved an extremely elaborate process of political manipulation, labeled the salami tactic (Maoz 1990c, 90–91).

> This tactic is a continuous effort at structuring a series of decisions. Each "small" decision may accord with the group's preferences and may result from careful analysis of data and considerations of costs and benefits. But if the group had known that each decision would lead to another logical extension of the policy and these decisions, taken together, were part of a pattern whose end was undesirable, most of its members would not have supported even one decision in the chain.

Realizing that there was little or no support in the cabinet for the grand design he had worked out with Begin and Eitan several months earlier, Sharon sliced down his plan into several small pieces. He presented increasingly modest versions of Operation Big Pines to the cabinet. Even with Begin's unfailing support, these truncated versions of the invasion plan were too much for many of the ministers. One of Sharon's major problems was convincing the ministers of the necessity of a large-scale operation against the PLO given the restraint the latter had displayed since July 1981 (and even then, some ministers had understood that the PLO had been merely reacting to an Israeli provocation). Sharon's conclusion was that the PLO needed to be provoked into firing on civilian settlements.

Since March 1982 he concentrated his efforts on getting the cabinet to authorize an air strike against PLO targets, using any attack on Israeli targets abroad and in the occupied territories as a pretext for such an operation. Sharon finally got his wish in early April, after the shooting of an Israeli embassy official in Paris—also by the Abu Nidal faction. Once this first step was approved, getting the government to approve further air strikes became just a matter of procedure. All he had to do was to get approval for gradual escalation of these air strikes. Begin, of course, was a willing ally in this process by blowing each terrorist incident out of proportion and by attributing each incident to the PLO.

Even so, Sharon had to deal, among other things, with skeptical generals in the IDF who viewed the grand scheme as resting on crooked foundations. Some of these generals were constant participants in the cabinet meetings. Their reactions to questions by ministers who had nagging suspicions regarding Sharon's ultimate scheme could derail the entire plan. One of the key puzzles in this rolling decision-making process was the failure of Saguy to voice his concerns in cabinet meetings. Schiff and Yaari describe Saguy's stern warnings in the meetings of the IDF general staff regarding the slippery slope entailed in Sharon's grand design. Yet, faced by indifference from his two immediate superiors (Eitan and Sharon) to his concerns,

> gradually, Saguy fell silent, withdrew into himself, acquiesced in the self-serving realities of other men. His tragic flaw, the inability to stand before the prime minister and his Cabinet in Sharon's presence and tell them what he told his colleagues in the army with such cogency, turned Saguy, the one man who had fought Ariel Sharon almost every step of the way, into an accomplice in Sharon's effort to divide and rule. For Yehoshua Saguy participated in almost all the Cabinet meetings before and after the outbreak of the war; unlike most of the ministers, he understood precisely what was going on, but held his peace. (Schiff and Yaari 1984, 57–58)

A possible explanation for this was that Saguy simply feared for his job. Speaking up and challenging his superiors in front of the cabinet would have created a confrontation with Sharon and Eitan, the outcome of which would have been unknown. Saguy had already discussed his concerns with Begin back in March. According to Schiff and Yaari (1984, 53–54), Begin was influenced by Saguy's concerns and had indeed shifted his preferences from an unequivocal support of Sharon's grand design to a more limited operation. But this was not at all evident from Begin's treatment of the dissenting ministers during cabinet meetings. Begin's outbursts against Zipori—insinuating that Zipori's reservations about the Sharon scheme were due to the fact that he had not been appointed defense minister (Schiff and Yaari 1984, 59)—could only cause a greater inclination for self-censorship.

This was neither the first nor the last time in which a senior officer suppressed his opinion and applied self-censorship in the face of strong commitments of his superiors to a certain course of action. But, as we will see, Saguy is the most tragic figure in this sad episode, because he had foreseen with great accuracy the depth of Israeli entanglement in the Lebanese mess. He was treated very harshly (but also fairly) by the Kahan Commission that investigated the Sabra and Shatilla massacre for precisely this point: his failure to fulfill his duty by voicing his concerns in the cabinet.

Other officers who had reservations about the military aspects of the plan did not even have an opportunity to be heard by cabinet ministers. Sharon and Eitan barred their access to the prime minister until the latter stages of the operation. At that point, Israel was already deeply embroiled in Lebanon and the government was already committed to a disastrous policy in a way that made it impossible to affect a drastic change of course by the very same people who had submerged Israel into this swamp.

The cabinet and some of the senior IDF officers were tough nuts to crack. Yet Begin, Sharon, and Eitan manipulated these two groups by a combination of deceptive and bullying tactics. This could not be easily done with the United States, the third element of the equation that had to be solved before the war could get under way. Sharon and Begin were aware that the United States would not support the grand design envisioned in Operation Big Pines and that its intelligence agencies could spot the preparations for this plan in the IDF. Moreover, the Israelis had already sprung several military and diplomatic surprises on the Reagan administration. These included shooting down the Syrian helicopters in March 1981, the bombing of the Osirak reactor in June, the attack on the

PLO headquarters in July, and the decision in December to apply Israeli law on the Golan Height (Schiff and Yaari 1984, 63).

Sharon's strategy vis-à-vis the Americans was to some extent similar to his deception campaign in the Israeli cabinet. He realized early on that the U.S. secretary of state, Alexander Haig, would be a valuable ally. Haig and Sharon shared many ideas in common, and the latter was prepared to explore this affinity to the fullest. According to Schiff and Yaari (1984, 65), Sharon used a sophisticated "drip method" to "furnish the Americans with selected details of his military antidote to the PLO presence in Lebanon, stopping well short of revealing the whole plan or its timing." Sharon employed various tactics that together composed a sophisticated strategy of manipulating the Reagan administration into tacit support of his scheme without fully understanding where it was leading. First, he continuously claimed that the PLO's actions were making a "mockery of the July 1981 ceasefire and that sooner or later Israel would have to react with a resounding blow. His aim was to establish in principle Israel's right to respond through a military offensive without having to specify its scope" (Schiff and Yaari 1984, 65).

Second, Sharon consistently downplayed the likelihood of an Israeli-Syrian engagement. After the capture of the group of Palestinian guerrillas that tried to infiltrate Israel from Jordan, Begin sent Saguy to brief Haig and to convince the secretary of state to support the new Israeli interpretation of the cease-fire agreement. Saguy was remarkably successful. He got Haig to agree that any violation of Israeli borders by the Palestinians would be considered a breach of the July 1981 cease-fire agreement (Schiff and Yaari 1984, 67–68; Spiegel 1985, 413–14).

By March 1982, the American intelligence community had pieced together most of the details of the grand design. Details of this intelligence were leaked to the press. On April 8, John Chancellor of NBC outlined the general contours of the planned Israeli campaign in Lebanon. Despite these facts, there were no specific warnings—at least not official ones—coming from the United States about the repercussions of an Israeli military action in Lebanon. The Reagan administration, through its ambassador to Tel Aviv, Samuel Lewis, issued some indirect warnings to different ministers. But these were seen as a private venture by the ambassador rather than official policy.

Encouraged by the administration's lack of reaction to the emerging crisis in Lebanon, Sharon set to Washington in May. He was denied a meeting with the president, but this was of little concern to Sharon. It was Alexander Haig whom he wanted to persuade. During his discussions with Haig Sharon revealed more of his plan than he had revealed, or had intended to reveal, to the Israeli cabinet. Schiff and Yaari (1984, 72–74), probably relying on transcripts of this meeting, indicate that Sharon did not dismiss the possibility of a military encounter with the Syrians, although he said Israel would not initiate such an encounter. He also did not indicate that Israel would restrict its operation to the forty kilometer zone. Haig and Habib, however, insisted that Israel would be justified in acting militarily only in the face of an "internationally recognized provocation" by the PLO. Even then, a disproportionate military strike would "create the most severe consequences for the United States" (Sharon 1989, 451). Sharon and Moshe Arens, the Israeli ambassador to Washington, reported that the Americans had understood the Israeli position and—even if they had not provided an official approval of the plan of attack—seemed to have resigned to accept it. Haig reportedly told Sharon that if there was no choice "he would expect the reaction [to the PLO provocation] to be swift and to illustrate his point he used the metaphor of a lobotomy—a quick, clean neutralizing operation" (Schiff and Yaari, 73–74). Sharon came out very encouraged from this trip, and he conveyed this impression to Begin upon his return.

Some red lights should have been lit, however, when on May 28 Begin received a letter from Haig. Haig's letter—while reiterating Israel's right to defend its people from terrorist attacks—nevertheless urged Israel to exercise utmost restraint. In a meeting between Arens and Haig the following day, the latter apparently received assurances that if an area of forty kilometers in southern Lebanon were cleaned of terrorists, it would be possible to convert it into a buffer zone and the United States would be willing to deploy American troops to ensure the preservation of peace in this region (Naor 1993, 278). These mixed signals were interpreted by both Sharon and Begin as an equivalent to an American "green light" to Israel to launch its offensive. The three pieces of the puzzle were now in place. All Israel had to do was to find the right "provocation" to start the attack.

3.2. The Politics of War Management, June–September 1982

The task of bringing the horse to the water—getting the cabinet to approve the war—was far more difficult than having it drink the water, even when the water turned out to be murky. Once the cabinet approved the war, it became automatically committed to reaping any fruits out of it. Now Sharon could frame decisional dilemmas as gambles involving only risks, thereby exploiting the tendency of decision makers to make risky choices (Kahneman and Tversky 1979). More important, once the field commanders were busy in managing the war, Sharon and Eitan became the sole authority in the cabinet for interpreting what was going on at the battlefield. They could now color the reality any way they wanted.

Sharon's first task was to receive authorization for a confrontation with the Syrian forces. For that purpose, on June 7 he ordered the central division of the IDF force to move toward the Syrian positions in the Dahr al-Baidar area (Schiff and Yaari 1984, 114, 155; Dupuy and Martell 1986, 115–17). This maneuver brought the IDF into contact with the Syrians and created a threat on the Syrian forces. A limited clash occurred on June 7, and Sharon, seizing this opportunity, brought to cabinet two options.

> One is to abandon the conception that the Syrians are not involved in the war and attack them directly. The second possibility is to move further up north and try to push them, or approach them from the rear, assuming that it is possible that the risk of their encirclement would lead them to withdraw. Our recommendation is not to approach this area [near Jezzin] and to try to move further north. Perhaps the risk of becoming encircled would force the Syrians to withdraw. (Naor 1993, 293–94)

The possibility that the IDF could complete its mission on the front with the PLO without approaching the Syrian forces in the first place did not occur to the cabinet ministers. Faced with these two options, the cabinet adopted Sharon's recommendation. Sharon, of course, knew that threatening the Syrians with encirclement would only increase the likelihood of engagement. In response to a question of whether this maneuver would cause the IDF to exceed the forty kilometer line, Sharon answered in the affirmative. Thus by approving the maneuver to the north, the government in fact overrode its previous decision limiting the operation to a forty kilometer zone (Naor 1993, 294; Schiff and Yaari 1984, 112–14). Once the central division of the IDF started moving north toward the Beirut-Damascus highway, the Syrians—immediately realizing the final target—started redeploying their SAMs and their forward positions in the area between Jezzin and the Beirut-Damascus highway. This provided the IDF with the pretext for an attack on the Syrian forces (Naor 1986, 66).

On the night of June 8, Sharon urged the IDF commanders to push into the Jezzin area, telling them that "a confrontation with the Syrians is unavoidable" (Schiff and Yaari 1984, 159). In the meeting with his commanders, Sharon confronted criticism by several generals, including Moshe Levi, the deputy COS. They argued that the concentration of forces against the Syrians and the push north contradicted the cabinet's decisions. Sharon used a combination of threats and soothing words. "'Relax' he told the doubters and worriers. 'Whoever's feeling the heat can pour a pail of water over his head'" (Schiff and Yaari 1984, 164).

In the cabinet meeting of June 9, Sharon proposed attacking the Syrian SAM batteries. Playing on the ministers' sensitivity to casualties, he described the IDF position as topographically inferior to those of the Syrians. The Syrian SAMs would prevent the IAF from providing air support to the ground troops if the Syrians chose to attack. This would endanger the IDF force, which had already moved much beyond the forty kilometer range in the Jezzin area. Sharon presented the dilemma as follows: "We must act quickly in order to provide our forces the [air] support they need and to get them out of the difficult situation that they have found themselves in" (Naor 1986, 69). That the "difficult" situation was a result of the movement of the troops in the so-called flanking maneuver that the government had itself approved the day before was not lost on the ministers. So despite their severe reservations and the growing perception of several of them that they were being entrapped by Sharon, the cabinet approved the IAF attack on the Syrian SAM batteries (Schiff and Yaari 1984, 164–66; Naor 1986, 69–71).[11]

Once Sharon realized that this pattern of manipulation was working, he pressed on. Using sheer intimidation and veiled threats against reluctant IDF generals who had raised objections to various steps of war expansion and had questioned whether Sharon was operating under cabinet authorization, Sharon was able to overcome objections within the IDF to specific moves of "crawling advance" toward Beirut. More important, however, the spectacular success of the IAF attack on the Syrian SAMs and the major aerial fight that ensued—in which Israeli jets shot down sixty Syrian Migs without a single IAF loss—boosted Sharon's standing with Begin. Because Begin had grave concerns about the IAF casualties during the attack, he viewed this success as a major sign of a strategic shift in the war that—up to this point—had been going not as well as expected (Naor 1986, 72).

By that time, and without the knowledge of the cabinet, IDF forces in both the eastern and western sectors of Lebanon were moving toward Beirut, but they were not able to reach the Beirut-Damascus highway, nor were they able to reach the outskirts of Beirut in the west. By June 10 a letter from President Reagan expressed his deep concern of the advance of the Israeli troops beyond the forty kilometer line and requested that Israel agree immediately to a cease-fire by 6:00 a.m. on June 10. The cabinet met at 4:00 a.m. to consider a response to Reagan's letter. Sharon urged his colleagues to turn down the cease-fire ultimatum "on both moral and practical ground" (Naor 1986, 77). The government decided to accept the request for a cease-fire "in principle" but to reject the timetable and impose conditions on its acceptance of a cease-fire.

In a subsequent meeting of the cabinet on the same day, Sharon requested approval for the capturing of positions along the Beirut-Damascus highway. He explained that one of the divisions was placed again in inferior positions vis-à-vis the Syrian armor and that capturing positions along the highway would bring the Syrians to the conclusion that they would have to withdraw (Naor 1986, 81–82; Schiff and Yaari 1984, 170). Again, making similar arguments to those he had made when he had requested approval for the attack on the Syrian SAMs on the previous day, Sharon was able to receive this authorization despite the growing realization by some ministers that they were being led by the nose.

On June 11, the government—believing that the major objectives of the IDF had been achieved—decided on a unilateral cease-fire to start at noon that day. This cease-fire held for no more than two hours, possibly due to its breach by the IDF itself. The paratroop brigade in the west had received orders to advance to the Beirut-Aley road (Naor 1986, 87; Schiff and Yaari 1984, 181–82). By that time, due to the advance of the Syrian third division to Mansuriyeh to cover the flanks of the forces stationed there, Eitan had ordered an attack on the Syrians and at the same time had ordered the paratroop brigade to advance to the outskirts of Beirut. Thus while the government thought it had ordered a cease-fire, the IDF had actually continued its crawling movement toward the Lebanese capital. Late on June 12, Israeli tanks surrounded the presidential palace in Ba'abdeh at the outskirts of Beirut. The IDF forces and the Christian forces met near Ba'abdeh. Begin himself learned about the IDF's presence in Beirut only the next day and not from his defense minister but rather from the American mediator, Philip Habib. Begin's first inquiries with Sharon and Eitan led him to deny Habib's accusation, but after several inquiries he found out that the Americans were correct and that he had been deceived by his own people (Naor 1986, 86–88; Schiff and Yaari 1984, 193–94).

Sharon's argument that he had briefed the cabinet and informed the ministers about the progress of the war, so that the "political echelon would maintain firm direction of the battlefield" (Sharon 1989, 464), is obviously false. On the other hand, Sharon is correct in arguing that it had been the cabinet's decisions that allowed the IDF to reach Beirut. By allowing an engagement with the Syrians and by stipulating conditions for the cease-fire that could be easily violated, the cabinet had given a green light to the IDF's advance to Beirut. Now, Sharon's task was to tighten the rope around the PLO in west Beirut. His original plan had been to have the Christian Phalanges do it. However, his meeting with Bashir Gemayel in Beirut on June 11 was extremely disappointing. Bashir refused committing his troops to attack the PLO in west Beirut (Schiff and Yaari 1984, 188–90; Sharon 1989, 471–72). For Sharon, reaching Beirut only to allow Arafat and the fourteen thousand PLO guerrillas in the city escape unharmed would convert the military success of the war into a political defeat. Arafat could present any outcome short of a military defeat as a victory—the Palestinian guerrillas repulsing the Israeli tanks and airplanes.

For that reason Sharon urged Begin and the government to reject Habib's efforts to bring about a disengagement of forces. His argument was now based on opportunity: the IDF was in a position to put a siege on west Beirut in order to get rid of the PLO. The IDF COS, Eitan, now changed the assessment of the relationship between the invasion of Lebanon and terrorism, claiming that "it was impossible to eliminate the threat of terrorism without the elimination of the PLO in Beirut" (Naor 1986, 93). Even Begin became convinced that the IDF's position in east Beirut created an opportunity for far-reaching political consequences (Naor 1986, 93–94). This opportunity could be best realized if the Christian Phalanges fulfilled their pledge to attack west Beirut. For that reason, Begin joined Sharon in opposing a separation of forces and was willing to allow the IDF to employ artillery in support of a Christian attack of west Beirut. He was not willing, however, to allow the use of air support for the Christians (Naor 1986, 94; Schiff and Yaari 1984, 199).

Bashir, however, was not willing to engage the PLO in west Beirut. This left the Israelis on the horns of a dilemma: enter west Beirut by themselves or put a siege to it and maintain constant pressure on the PLO by a combination of artillery shelling and air attacks. A third possibility—declare victory and withdraw to the forty kilometer line—did not even occur to the cabinet. The sunk cost logic, coupled with the perception of opportunity to rid Israel of the PLO, were powerful incentives. Even opposition leaders such as Yitzhak Rabin—while criticizing the process by which the IDF got so far in excess of the forty kilometer zone—supported the siege of west Beirut (Sharon 1989, 468).

Throughout the siege of west Beirut, Sharon continued to delude the government, using the same salami tactics as before. Some of the ministers came to understand that they had been victims of manipulation by Sharon. During the June 11 cabinet meeting, Yitzhak Berman, the energy minister, noted to Sharon: "Arik, perhaps you'll be good enough to tell us what you're going to ask us to approve the day after tomorrow, so that you can secure what you're going to ask us to approve tomorrow morning" (Schiff and Yaari 1984, 187). Nevertheless, the cabinet continued to play along for the most part, approving the incursions into Beirut even ex post facto. Since Begin himself was willing to live with ex post facto approval of IDF actions, other ministers were willing to go along with this as well.

In his dealings with the IDF, Sharon continued to rely on his bullying tactics. However, stories about growing opposition within the IDF to the creeping advances into Beirut began leaking to the press. Reports about the situation in west Beirut were getting to the government through indirect channels.

Paradoxically, however, this process of salami escalation of the siege of west Beirut produced the desired effects on the United States and on the PLO. Philip Habib helped negotiate an agreement leading to the evacuation of Lebanon by Arafat and some fourteen thousand PLO guerrillas that had been under siege in Beirut. The United States and France pledged to introduce forces into Beirut to separate the sides and enforce the cease-fire. Israel agreed to stay out of Beirut. By August 22, all of the PLO leaders and most of their armed forces left Lebanon. This was apparently the event that was supposed to vindicate Sharon, because it proved that his plan was working. He had moved a reluctant cabinet and a hesitant IDF to do what he had wanted all along. More important, he got the United States to play along by negotiating the agreement, resulting in the deportation of the PLO. Finally, the presidential elections in Lebanon that were to be held at the beginning of September were almost certain to bring Bashir Gemayel to power, precisely in line with Sharon's script.

As noted at the beginning of this section, Sharon's grand design anticipated a number of risks, and its implementation rested on the belief that many of these risks would not materialize. By the beginning of September 1982, it appeared that Sharon had been right on the mark on virtually all of the issues. The Arab states did not intervene in the war. There were no economic sanctions on Israel and no oil embargo on the West. Even when the Syrian forces in Lebanon were attacked without any provocation, and even when the PLO was under siege in Beirut, no Arab state lifted a finger to help them. Egypt did not abrogate the peace treaty with

Israel, although it did recall its ambassador from Israel. More important, despite considerable pressure from the United States, and despite the fact that Israel's main ally in the Reagan administration, Alexander Haig, had been dismissed, the United States went along with the Israeli scheme. It appeared that Sharon's military campaign would become the first war in Israel's history that was converted into a significant diplomatic achievement.

There was one more piece of the puzzle that needed fitting. Sharon had to ensure that Bashir Gemayel would be elected president of Lebanon. There could not be a more rigged election if one were to invent one: "Squads of armed Phalangists equipped with walkie-talkies drove the delegates to the site of the vote at a military barracks in East Beirut. Some of the delegates took the precaution of coming with their own bodyguards, and at least one of them asked his Phalangist escort to press a gun into his back so that others would believe that he was being brought there by force" (Schiff and Yaari 1984, 233). Bashir was elected president on August 23, two days after the PLO began its exodus from Lebanon.

Bashir did not survive long as president of Lebanon. But during the short time that he did, it became abundantly clear that he was not going to honor his commitment to play by the Israeli line. In several meetings with Israeli leaders (with Begin on August 24 and with Sharon on September 12) Bashir deliberately stonewalled the Israelis' offers of a public visit to the Knesset. He was deliberately vague on the possibility of a Lebanese-Israeli agreement, asking for more time to stabilize his regime and to bring about the complete withdrawal of the remaining PLO and Syrian forces in Lebanon (Schiff and Yaari 1984, 233–46; Naor 1986, 143–44).[12] Be that as it may, on the afternoon of September 14, Bashir was assassinated. With this event, the undoing of Sharon's grand design in Lebanon commenced.

"The assassination of Bashir Gemayel threatened to demolish the politico-military structure that directed the entire war" (Naor 1986, 150).[13] This statement clearly suggests one of the most fundamental flaws in Sharon's design: that it rested upon an alliance with one person and that it depended either on Bashir's highly questionable credibility or on his survivability. Sharon suspected that about two thousand armed PLO members stayed behind in west Beirut and were threatening, along with some seven thousand militiamen of the Muslim Sunni faction, to prevent the emergence of a Christian-dominated regime in Lebanon (Naor 1986, 150).[14] In his conversations with Begin, however, Sharon tried to push for the IDF's entry into west Beirut on humanitarian grounds: he argued that the Christians were out for revenge and that there was a real threat of chaos and massacre following Bashir's assassination. The entry of the IDF to west Beirut was essential in order to create a barrier between the Christians and the Muslims in the city (Naor 1986, 151–52; Schiff and Yaari 1984, 253). This appealed to Begin's sense of responsibility to the population under Israeli control, and he approved the IDF's entry into west Beirut. No cabinet meeting was convened to approve this rather dramatic violation of the Habib agreement.

In the next thirty-six hours, Sharon put pressure on the Phalange militia to enter the refugee camps of Sabra and Shatilla, presumably to uproot any remaining PLO guerrillas who were hiding in these camps. The Phalanges, thirsty for revenge, agreed to do so. By the time the cabinet met on September 15, the Phalanges had already been inside the refugee camps. The cabinet's approval of the entry of the Phalanges into the camps—just like its approval of the IDF's entry into west Beirut—was done ex post facto. In his briefing to the cabinet, Sharon explained the need to enter the refugee camps in order to pull out the suspected PLO guerrillas but also the need to get the Phalanges involved in the fighting. The preference for the Phalanges was explained in terms of preventing IDF casualties (Maoz 1986; Naor 1986, 162–63). The Phalange militias entered the refugee camps and spent nearly three days there. When they left the camps, some eight hundred men, women, and children were left dead in the streets. This massacre took place under the eyes of the IDF commanders who had been stationed on the roofs overlooking the camps. While there were rumors of a massacre during these two days, no concrete evidence was available to suggest that the Phalanges had engaged in systematic killing of civilians.

The Sabra and Shatilla massacre shook Israeli public opinion. Demands for the appointment of an independent inquiry commission that would investigate the massacre came from all parts of Israeli society. The government's effort to block these demands was met with utter indignation. A demonstration of four hundred thousand people—the largest in Israel's history—and a critical speech by Yitzhak Navon, the president of Israel, forced the government to appoint the inquiry commission, headed by Supreme Court chief justice Kahan. The commission heard hundreds of witnesses—including testimonies from Begin, Sharon, most cabinet ministers, and the key military commanders, as well as various people in the refugee camps. It issued its report on February 9, 1983. The report was penetrating on a number of points but extremely superficial on others. It addressed the personal responsibility of both politicians and military commanders for the massacre. Its most important recommendation was that Sharon resign and, if he refused, that he be dismissed by the prime minister. Both Begin and Shamir were sharply criticized by the commission. The commission would have recommended the dismissal of COS Eitan, except that he was due to step down anyway. The commission recommended removing from his post the head of AMAN, General Yehoshua Saguy, who had continuously warned of the murderous tendencies of the Phalanges.

This ended Sharon's direct influence on the decision-making process with regard to Lebanon. Sharon agreed to resign as defense minister but stayed in the government as minister without a portfolio. Sabra and Shatilla may have been the first sign of defeat in the war, but at that point very few in Israel were willing to recognize the depth of the Lebanese fiasco. It took almost three more years before a dramatic change would take place. And even then the war was far from over.

We can now attempt to take stock of the politics of the war. That this was a war of naked and senseless ambition on the part of one person is abundantly clear. Sharon's grand design was extremely daring and risky. Most people in the IDF who were privy to this design had significant doubts about its feasibility and realism. Only a few had spoken against it clearly and plainly, and those who did addressed only a few elements of it—such as the reliability of the Phalanges. The notion that Israel could establish a new order in Lebanon was not really subject to an open and comprehensive challenge. Sharon's treatment of the opposition in the IDF was brutal bullying, consisting of the dismissal of dissenting views and voices and the reliance on Eitan as the principal executioner of his plan and the suppressor of cautionary voices. This approach was both essential—from Sharon's point of view—and possible. It was essential because the key commanders of the IDF could not be kept out of the picture entirely. And because Eitan was a loyal ally, he could impose his authority on his reluctant subordinates.

But the dissent in the IDF was both minimal and subdued. Most military commanders found the grand design quite attractive from a military point of view. None had a moral or political problem with the initiation of an unprovoked war. None had a major problem with the siege or occupation of an Arab capital. None had a major problem with the unnecessary killing of hundreds of innocent civilians in the course of fighting with the PLO or during the massive bombing of west Beirut. This applies not only to senior commanders but also to lower-ranking infantry, armored, and artillery commanders and to air force pilots. Unlike the case of the Al Aqsa Intifada (see chap. 7), there was no case of conscientious objection among senior commanders until the siege of west Beirut. The case of Colonel Eli Geva, a tank brigade commander who protested the siege and was dishonorably discharged from the IDF, was the exception that proved the rule.

Quite a few people in the government had suspected from the start that they were being fed the grand design in small slices. But most of them raised only technical objections to specific decisions. The first to resign from the government that initiated the war and went along with Sharon all the way was Yitzhak Berman in September 1982, in protest of Begin's attempt to stonewall the appointment of the inquiry commission. None of the ministers who complained that they were denied information and that they were required to approve ex post facto actions that the IDF had already carried out chose to resign. None of the coalition members of the Likud Party threatened to bring down the government over what had been a series of blatant violations of government practices. More important, time and again all of the ministers went along with each element of Sharon's scheme. As the war developed, the ministers' trust in Sharon's accounts of the battlefield and political situation eroded significantly. Yet, most of the decisions during the war were reached by consensus. Ministers were willing to accept the fait accompli that Sharon repeatedly established. Despite their protests, most cabinet members supported virtually every option that Sharon presented. In none of the decisional occasions starting June 4 and ending September 17, 1982—with the exception of the August 12 decision by the cabinet to strip Sharon of his power to use the IAF—did any minister present alternative courses of actions to those proposed by the defense minister. And given the lack of nonviolent alternatives to Sharon's proposals, most ministers saw no point in opposing these proposals.

Not only were Sharon's proposals left unchallenged for much of the time, but his assessment of the situation was unchallenged by anybody from the government. During the September 15 cabinet meeting that authorized the entry of the Phalanges into the Sabra and Shatilla refugee camps, David Levy remarked that there may well be a massacre there, as the Phalanges were driven by feelings of revenge. Nobody reacted to this comment, and even Levy himself supported the decision to insert the Phalanges (Maoz 1986).

Menachem Begin's behavior during the war is perhaps the most puzzling aspect of this continuous process of government failure. Begin's supporters depict him as a person alternating between moods of decisiveness

and self-righteousness, on the one hand, and benign neglect and complacency, on the other. In general, most observers agree that Begin had been
systematically misled by Sharon during the war, having been forced, over
and over, to go along with Sharon even after these deceptions had been
discovered. While this may be true to some extent, Sharon's deceptions
fail to account for significant aspects of Begin's behavior. Begin strongly
supported Operation Big Pines and tried to push it in the cabinet. He was
briefed of Sharon's and Eitan's meetings with Bashir Gemayel, so he must
have known that these talks entailed a demand of the Phalanges to take
west Beirut. He was also aware that the planned IDF amphibious landing
at Junieh was also discussed in the Sharon-Gemayel meeting. Thus, he
had been aware of the discrepancy between the limited plans that Sharon
presented to the cabinet and the preparations for a larger engagement.

Begin was also engaged in the deliberate misrepresentation of the
scope of the July 1981 cease-fire agreement with the PLO. As noted, he
agreed on some occasions that the agreement did not cover PLO attacks
abroad. At the same time, he argued that, in accepting the cease-fire
agreement, the PLO had in fact agreed to suspend all guerrilla and terrorist operations against Israel. There is no question that he, like Sharon,
sought a convenient pretext for starting the war. The question is what
kind of war he had in mind. Naor (1993, 268) and Yaniv (1987b, 100)
claim that, while he had been aware of Sharon's grand design—and may
have even supported it initially—he came to recognize the pitfalls of this
plan and shifted his preference to a more limited operation. Schiff and
Yaari argue that there is evidence to support this notion, but there is also
considerable evidence to support the notion that Begin not only was
aware of Sharon's grand design but supported it all the way. Their conclusion is that "[t]he truth lies somewhere in between, on the assumption
that Begin had been assured, or had somehow convinced himself, that the
upcoming operation was not really a war at all but a sharply defined and
contained ground action" (Schiff and Yaari 1984, 60–61).

This is inconsistent with Begin's own authoritative personality and
his willingness to consistently accept the "surprises" that Sharon landed
on his desk almost every day between the outbreak of the war and the
Sabra and Shatilla massacre. As noted, the most drastic action he took to
curb the defense minister's almost absolute authority to micromanage the
IDF's operations during the war was the August 12 decision to deprive
Sharon of his ability to use the IAF directly. But other than that, he supported Sharon almost every step of the way. While it is utterly plausible
that other ministers could have been manipulated by Sharon in support-

ing the very same plans they had opposed all along, it is inconceivable that a shrewd and experienced politician like Begin would have been subject to a similar manipulation. There is reasonable ground to expect that, had Begin opposed any of Sharon's moves during a given stage in the war, the cabinet would not have supported Sharon. Moreover, in contrast to other ministers, Begin was directly responsible for the Mossad, which was deeply involved in the coordination with the Phalanges. He was briefed regularly by the head of the Mossad, Yitzhak Hoffi, of the developments on the ground. Thus, Begin's continued support was a key to Sharon's ability to get his plan implemented. And Begin's support of Sharon's plan was not that of a sick man who could be easily deluded.

Begin's interaction with the Reagan administration prior to and during the war suggests continuous support for a large-scale war. Begin's letter to Reagan on June 6 specified the forty kilometer line as the territorial objective of the war (Naor 1993, 291; Schiff and Yaari 1984, 106). And Begin was a man of honor and integrity who would not have given his word in writing and done something altogether different. But personal integrity is one thing and political expediency is quite another thing. The letter to Reagan may well have been necessary in order to secure American support and to enable the U.S. intervention on Israel's side at the UN Security Council. Israel needed U.S. support in blocking any premature initiatives for a cease-fire. The fact that Begin seemingly agreed to accept U.S.-initiated cease-fire proposals only to violate them several hours after they had been established lends credence to the proposition that Begin was a willing participant in Sharon's deception campaign and served as Sharon's firewall vis-à-vis the United States. The depiction of Begin as a man of honor and integrity is inconsistent with his failure to restrain and reprimand his defense minister. It also does not fit his habit of constantly harassing any dissenting voices in the cabinet throughout the war. Begin did not allow an open and frank discussion at any time during the war.

The politics of the war in Lebanon reflect a collusion between the prime minister, the defense minister, and possibly the foreign minister, Yitzhak Shamir. The COS, Eitan, was their loyal executioner of the military plan. This coalition was extremely effective in blocking, sidestepping, or manipulating anybody within the IDF, the cabinet, and the Israeli political system who opposed the war or its operational contours. It was also effective in withstanding international pressure to avoid the war or to limit it once it started. This coalition enabled Israel to engage in an aggressive war that led to the occupation of most of the territory of an

Arab state, to the death of roughly ten thousand people—Palestinians and Lebanese—and to massive destruction of portions of an Arab capital. The war was made possible by deceiving an entire country about its scope and goals.

What made this coalition effective was not its own power. Rather, it was the weakness of the opposition it confronted at home and abroad that allowed this coalition to succeed in its schemes. As we have seen, both the cabinet and the IDF had been utterly docile. The main political opposition, the Labor Party, went along with the initial part of the war, even though its key leaders suspected that Sharon was aiming for more than forty kilometers. Moreover, Rabin ended up supporting the siege of Beirut after the fact. Other elements of Israeli society did not show active signs of protest either against the outbreak of the war or against its expansion.[15] The only meaningful mass protest was not an antiwar demonstration per se but rather a public outcry at the Sabra and Shatilla massacre. There were very few and sparsely populated antiwar demonstrations in Israel.

The Reagan administration, both with Haig as secretary of state and afterward, went along, albeit grudgingly, with the Israeli attack. The United States consistently blocked anti-Israeli resolutions in the UN. Reagan did not demand an immediate Israeli withdrawal from Beirut and went along with Israel on the plan to expel the PLO from Lebanon. The United States continued to support the Israeli presence in Lebanon not only during the war but throughout the period during which Israel occupied the territory of Lebanon.

The watershed event in this war was the Sabra and Shatila massacre of September 15–17, 1982. But it took a very long time to get Israel out of Lebanon. By the end of September 1982, Israeli fatalities in the war amounted to roughly 235 soldiers. More than 700 additional soldiers would die before the Israeli misadventure in Lebanon was over. Just why this was the case is the topic of the next two sections.

3.3. *The Politics of Sunk Costs: The Long Road to Withdrawal, September 1982–June 1985*

Despite the assassination of Bashir Gemayel and the Sabra and Shatilla massacre, and despite the slowly eroding public support for the expanded war, most cabinet ministers felt that the war was a major success. To cement this "success," a political agreement had to be signed with the new government in Lebanon. Bashir's brother, Amin Gemayel, was elected president of Lebanon on September 21, 1982, and immediately

Israeli and American delegates began pressing him to reach an agreement with Israel that would allow a simultaneous pullout of both Israeli and Syrian forces from Lebanon. Amin, however, was not enthusiastic about cooperating with the Israelis. Nor was he willing to risk his relations with Syria by signing anything that could be interpreted as a peace treaty with Israel. Yet, pressured by both the Israelis and the Americans and concerned about the continued Israeli occupation of much of Lebanon, Amin nevertheless agreed to enter into negotiations with Israel.

The Israeli government aimed for an agreement that would entail three elements: (1) the simultaneous withdrawal of the Israeli and Syrian forces from Lebanon; (2) security arrangements in southern Lebanon, including early warning stations and Israeli military presence, as well as special security privileges to Major Sa'ad Haddad, Israel's ally in the south; and (3) a political agreement entailing elements of "normalization" if not full peace with the government of Lebanon. Israel also insisted that negotiations would be conducted along two parallel tracks: a public track and a secret one. The purpose of the latter track would be to reach secret understandings on matters that the Lebanese government could not agree on publicly (Yaniv 1987b, 163–65; Schiff and Yaari 1984, 289).

The official talks opened on January 3, 1983. The Israelis tried to push their agenda, but the Lebanese gradually managed to trim the Israeli demands to a bare minimum. After five months of nerve-wrecking negotiations, the Israelis modified most of their demands, narrowing this agreement to a very limited set of understandings. Many of these understandings did not even make it to the formal part of the agreement and were appended as exchanges of letters between the delegations. Most important, the implementation of the agreement—particularly the Syrian withdrawal from Lebanon—depended exclusively on Syrian goodwill. The signing of the agreement on May 17, 1983, and its approval by both the Lebanese Parliament and the Israeli Knesset fooled nobody: the chances of this agreement being implemented, even on a partial basis, were extremely slim. Schiff and Yaari (1984, 297) note that "in Israel everyone knew that the outcome bore only the faintest resemblance to the dream that had fueled the whole foray into Lebanon a year earlier."

But even so, Israel could use the agreement as an opportunity. By declaring victory and withdrawing from Lebanon, Israel could cut its losses and end this tragic affair. By May 1983, the IDF was bogged down in Beirut and in the Shouf area, often findings itself between a rock and a hard place in the internal struggle among different factions in Lebanese politics. The May 17 agreement could provide the Israeli government with a convenient pretext to depart at least from these areas if not from all of Lebanon. The government, of course, would hear none of it. Faced by an outright Syrian defiance of the agreement, it chose to stick to its guns. Yaniv (1987b, 184–85) points out the dilemma confronting the Begin cabinet.

> But what about a complete withdrawal? Such a move would have been greatly welcomed by the Israeli left, including segments of the Labor party. For this reason alone such a move was totally unacceptable for a government led by Menachem Begin which had taken the country into this war in the first place. . . .
>
> Seen from this perspective a complete, abrupt, and unilateral Israeli withdrawal would make no sense even if ultimately there was no alternative and even if it was taken for granted that an orderly phased-out withdrawal would entail heavy casualties. An abrupt uni-lateral retreat could be assumed to lead to a dangerous vacuum in the areas to be vacated and subsequently to a return there of precisely those forces that Israel had attempted to drive away. This could not be proven, but it was plausible to assume that it would happen.

Elsewhere (Maoz 1990b, 276–82), I have labeled this kind of dilemma as the sunk cost paradox. This paradox refers to cases where states "can accumulate tremendous losses not because [they] mistakenly think [they] can win, but because [they] correctly expect to lose. In [their] efforts to minimize the costs of defeat, [they] actually maximize them." By May–June 1983 it was evident to most observers that only one of the four key goals of the war was accomplished: the PLO was expelled from south-ern Lebanon and from Beirut. Driving out the Syrian forces from Lebanon, establishing a Christian-dominated government, and negotiat-ing a full-fledged peace treaty were not accomplished. The sensible thing would be to cut losses and get out of Lebanon as soon as possible.

This government, however, wanted to salvage some of its losses from the war. The problem was that, "when all was said and done, the success or failure of the policy embodied in the May 17 agreement depended on Asad's goodwill, and he, for very good reasons, had none" (Yaniv 1987b, 182). The government faced three choices: to renew the confrontation with the Syrian forces stationed in the Beqa Valley; to stay put in its cur-rent deployment in Lebanon, thereby pressuring the Lebanese to force the Syrians to withdraw; or to withdraw by itself. Engaging the Syrians meant resumption of the war. This was both internationally and domestically costly. Complete withdrawal—the logical thing to do—was both politically and psychologically unfeasible.

Now the new argument was that the vacuum created by an IDF withdrawal would be filled by the PLO. Israeli withdrawal could take place only if the Lebanese army entered the areas evacuated by the IDF to ensure that no elements hostile to Israel return to those areas (Yaniv 1987b, 185). There was no evidence that the PLO would return to Lebanon, but this new argument became the holy grail of the Israeli presence in Lebanon through the final withdrawal of May 2000. Moreover, the expectation that the Lebanese army would replace the IDF was nonsense, of course. The Lebanese army could only survive as long as it was confined to its barracks.

The initial inclination of the government was to stay put in the same positions in Beirut and the Shouf area. But the costs of continued policing of Lebanon were beginning to pile up. Menachem Begin, apparently shaken both by the costs of war and by the death of his wife, announced his resignation on August 27, 1983. This was perhaps the first honest admission of failure in the war. He was replaced by Yitzhak Shamir, who immediately implemented—together with Moshe Arens, the new minister of defense—the first IDF withdrawal from the Beirut area to the Awali River. The new IDF deployment was born out of a compromise among different factions in the government. It was large enough to show that the government was responsive to domestic and international pressure. And it did convey a message to Lebanon and Syria that if they were willing to fulfill their part of the May 17 agreement so was Israel. It was sufficiently limited, however, to prevent a warranted impression of a rushed escape and to suggest to the Lebanese and Syrians that Israel had staying power and that it would continue to occupy Lebanese soil as long as there was no "guarantee" to its security in the south (Yaniv 1987b, 216).

But the very argument that served as the strategic reason for preferring a very limited withdrawal to a significant withdrawal—the need to guarantee security in southern Lebanon—turned out to be the root of Israel's predicament in Lebanon over the next seventeen years. By the beginning of 1983, a new Shi'ite resistance group had formed with the financial and ideological backing of the new Islamic regime in Iran. The Hizballah initiated a series of suicide bombings against Israel and the United States. On October 23, 1983, a car loaded with explosives crashed into the U.S. marines' compound in Beirut. The explosion left 241 marines dead. Simultaneously, another car drove into the French headquarters, causing over 150 casualties (Yaniv 1987b, 221; Dupuy and Martell 1986, 206).

Shortly thereafter, President Reagan decided to pull out the international force from Beirut (Dupuy and Martell 1986, 210). The U.S. decision, as embarrassing as it may have seemed (Tanter 1990), was the rational thing to do. The administration realized that there was no realistic chance to restore order in Lebanon and that any foreign force would be exposed to numerous guerrilla attacks. Israel should have paid close attention to the logic of cutting costs that guided the American decision. It did not, and it paid the price.

On November 4, a truck loaded with explosives crashed into the Israeli headquarters in Tyre, killing sixty people. This started a rampage of attacks on IDF forces, mostly in southern Lebanon. The very same Shi'ite population that had greeted the invading IDF forces with rice (a gesture of hospitality and welcoming) now engaged the IDF in guerrilla warfare. Between September 4, 1983, and the actual decision to withdraw from Lebanon, a total of 250 Israeli soldiers were killed in guerrilla operations, by then most of which were carried out by Hizballah operatives.[16]

Wishing to "guarantee" security in southern Lebanon, Israel exposed itself to a large dose of insecurity. However, the Shamir government—the same government that got Israel into this mess (minus Begin, who had resigned)—was incapable of bringing itself to withdraw from Lebanon. For this government, withdrawal spelled defeat of the Likud in the coming elections. From a strategic perspective, this would invite attacks on Israel from southern Lebanon. This perception was now backed by the IDF intelligence. The scenario that followed was that the Hizballah either would allow the return of the PLO to southern Lebanon or would take over the task of harassing Israeli settlements by itself (Yaniv 1987b, 258–59). Bolstered by IDF concerns, Shamir and Arens led the campaign for continued entrenchment in the Lebanese swamp (Yaniv 1987b, 259–61).

The Labor Party's decision of June 1983 calling for the complete withdrawal of the IDF to the international border acted as a constraint on the Shamir government. Withdrawal would mean carrying out Labor's policy. Shamir was forced to call for early elections scheduled for July 1984. With the Labor Party leading in the public opinion polls, the Likud's only hope was to stick to its guns and actually use the information about the accelerated attacks on the IDF as a justification for its position (Yaniv 1987b, 250–54).

This tactic appears to have worked. The July 23, 1984, elections ended in a virtual tie between the two blocs, forcing them to negotiate a national unity government on the basis of a rotation arrangement between Shamir and Shimon Peres. More important, any decision in the tied cabinet would have to be made by a majority vote; a draw would preserve the status quo. This reality spelled stalemate with respect to Lebanon, as long as both the Likud and Labor stuck to their traditional positions.

This prevented a rapid decision on the matter of withdrawal. The only way out of this political deadlock was to effect a defection of one of the Likud representatives in the cabinet to the pro-withdrawal faction. In fact, it took nearly six months before the issue was brought up for decision by the entire government. Yitzhak Rabin, the new defense minister, understood that proposing an immediate and complete withdrawal would only defeat the proposal. Hence, he employed the same salami tactic that Sharon had used in dragging the cabinet into the Lebanon War; only this time he used it to get Israel out of Lebanon. He directed the IDF to prepare a plan for withdrawal in three stages, spread over a period of six to nine months. The last stage would take the IDF out of Lebanon completely, leaving only a few Israeli advisers in southern Lebanon (Yaniv 1987b, 274–75).

The sequencing of the withdrawal over a relatively long period of time finally convinced one of the key members of the Likud Party, David Levy, to support Rabin's plan. The government decided in favor of withdrawal. There was one modification in the Rabin plan, however. In the final stage, Israel would not withdraw completely from Lebanon. Rather, it would maintain a small contingent in the area south of the Litany River that would work with the Southern Lebanese Army (SLA) to thwart threats from the Hizballah or to prevent the return of the PLO guerrillas. In terms of the politics of the moment, Rabin's plan appeared both sensible and politically fitting. In retrospect, the commitment to maintain an IDF presence in southern Lebanon was a recipe for disaster.

From a military point of view there was no problem in pulling the IDF out of Lebanon within a matter of days. The problem was political: to prevent an image of hurried and desperate escape. However, the decision of the government and the phasing of the withdrawal process backfired.

The pending withdrawal of the IDF created an irresistible temptation for everybody in the south—Shi'ites, Sunni Lebanese, Sunni Palestinians, even Christians—to engage in attacks against the retreating army. For former collaborators with the IDF this was an opportunity to absolve themselves of the charges of collaboration. . . . For the militants this was a way of leading their underground operations to a final, bloody crescendo. Internal competition among different factions must have also encouraged such an attitude, as did the evident impression that the decision to withdraw was born out of an Israeli sense of defeat, that the IDF was "broken," and that Israeli soldiers would do anything not to have their names added to the bottom of the soon-to-be-closed list of Lebanon war casualties. (Yaniv 1987b, 278–79)

The wish to prevent an image of stampede withdrawal created just that. In an effort to salvage some of the IDF's image of deterrence, Rabin announced an "Iron Fist" policy: Israel would raid Shi'ite villages in retaliation to attacks on the IDF, entering villages, arresting suspected Shi'ite guerrillas, and blowing up their houses. Again, this policy backfired. The Hizballah responded with a barrage of suicide attacks (Pappe 2003, 357) that resulted in further IDF casualties. This tit-for-tat-policy continued until the IDF completed its withdrawal in June. This escalation, however, created both a political necessity and a perception of strategic imperative to maintain an IDF contingent inside southern Lebanon. This decision, again, had profound effects on Israel.

3.4. The Politics and Strategy of Muddling Through, June 1985–May 2000

The IDF security zone in southern Lebanon was born as a result of a political compromise, and it was supposed to be a temporary arrangement. The original purpose was to have the SLA become increasingly responsible for order in southern Lebanon. But since the actual SLA was heavily based on the Christian population, and since it had been financed, trained, and advised by the Israelis, it became a threat to the other ethnic groups. Like many temporary arrangements, the security zone became a trap that lasted fifteen years.

I discuss the strategic aspects of the Israeli entrapment in southern Lebanon in chapter 7. In this section, I examine why it took Israel so long to withdraw from the security zone. I also analyze the price Israel paid for this fundamental failure to realize the futility of its continued presence in southern Lebanon.

Pappe (2003, 348, 357) notes that between July 1985 and November 1986 there were sixteen incidents of suicide attacks staged by the Hizballah. Most of these attacks were directed at SLA targets. The number of incidents was much larger, but the trend was the same; most Hizballah attacks were directed at the SLA.[17] Israel should have gotten the message: the Hizballah wanted removal of the SLA and termination of the Israeli symbolic security zone. Throughout the period of 1985–92, there were very few limited exchanges between Israeli and Hizballah or Amal forces in southern Lebanon. With the exception of 1988, during which twenty-one Israeli soldiers were killed (fourteen of them in two separate suicide bombings), the number of Israeli fatalities per year over this period was in the single-digit figure.

This seemed an acceptable price for what IDF intelligence and the Mossad claimed was a threat to the Galilee if Israel withdrew to the international border. This reality changed dramatically on February 16, 1992, when Israeli helicopters killed the Hizballah leader Abbas Mussawi. This assassination sparked a series of clashes in Lebanon (in addition to the bombing of the Israeli embassy in Buenos Aires on March 17). Israeli fatalities in Lebanon reached a high of thirty-seven, including the first two civilian fatalities since the invasion of Lebanon ten years earlier.

The assassination of Mussawi led to escalation of the conflict between Israel and the Hizballah. The Hizballah increased targeting of IDF positions in Lebanon and renewed shelling of Israeli towns. The irony was that the key purpose of the security zone—prevention of shelling of Israeli targets—was defeated by Israel's own actions. The Hizballah developed a simple decision regime (Kuperman 1999): firing on targets inside Israel in retaliation for the killing of Lebanese civilians by the IDF. In all other cases, the IDF contingent in the security zone, as well as the SLA militiamen, were the key targets. This strategy should have suggested to the IDF intelligence that the key objective of the organization was to end IDF occupation in Lebanon. Its extremist rhetoric calling for the destruction of Israel notwithstanding, the Hizballah's goal was liberation of Lebanon.

The post-Mussawi escalation reached its first peak in July 1993. The Israeli government, engaged in secret talks with the PLO and in complex and sensitive negotiations with the Syrians, was facing a militant opposition. Suspecting that he would have to reveal to the public a sharp policy turnaround in terms of its relations with the PLO or with Syria, Rabin decided to demonstrate resolve, directing the IDF to launch Operation Accountability. Over the course of ten days, the IDF pounded southern Lebanon with a massive barrage of artillery, tanks, airplanes, helicopters, and missile boats. The operation yielded no meaningful result. Faced with widespread criticism, Israel was forced to put a halt to its operation. The Hizballah continued its guerrilla operations against the IDF within the security zone in pretty much the same manner as before.

An almost identical process repeated itself in April 1996. Faced with a barrage of suicide terrorism carried out by Hamas and the Islamic Jihad in Tel Aviv and Jerusalem and with a critical election coming up in May 1996, Shimon Peres authorized Operation Grapes of Wrath. This operation was designed to compel Hizballah to reduce its activity against the IDF and SLA by putting pressure on the Shi'ite population in southern Lebanon. As in 1993, the IDF launched a campaign of fire and destruction. As Van Creveld (1998, 305) notes:

> To the initiated, the firepower put on display during "Operation Grapes of Wrath" was nothing short of awe inspiring, the more so because it was carried out uninterrupted day and night. In the air and on the ground, in many ways it was more sophisticated than anything the Coalition forces deployed as recently as 1991 in the Persian Gulf.
>
> Had the targets been Syrian armored divisions . . . no doubt they would have been annihilated. After sixteen days during which 13,000 rounds were fired and hundreds of strikes by fighter-bombers and attack helicopters took place, between six (says Hizballah) and fifty (says the IDF) persons were killed. Meanwhile the Katyushas, though perhaps no longer as numerous or well-aimed as during the first days of the operation, kept coming, bringing life along the border to a halt, demolishing thousands of houses, and causing damage of approximately $30 million.

What put an end to the operation was not Hizballah's capitulation. Quite to the contrary; the IDF spokesman reported that Hizballah had launched over six hundred Katyusha rockets on the Galilee. Rather, it was a humanitarian disaster. An IDF tank barrage on Kfar Qana resulted in the killing of 109 Lebanese men, women, and children. Warren Christopher, the U.S. secretary of state, worked out a cease-fire and a series of understandings between Israel and the Hizballah. Ironically, these understandings legitimized the Hizballah operations against the IDF in the security zone, as well as the firing of Katyushas on civilian targets inside Israel in retaliation to the hitting of Lebanese civilians by the IDF.

The Israeli entanglement in southern Lebanon was complicated by the peace negotiations with Syria. Israeli decision makers believed that the Syrians maintained a de facto veto power in Lebanese politics. Hence the Israeli notion was that Asad has turned the Israeli-Lebanese negotiations hostage to the Israeli-Syrian negotiations. Accordingly, the Israeli government came to understand that the route out of Lebanon must go through Damascus. By the mid-1990s, a small number of Israeli politicians began contemplating the idea of unilateral withdrawal (Beilin 1998). But the debate on the Lebanon policy was limited to a few people and was overshadowed by the Israeli-Palestinian and Israeli-Syrian negotiations. The IDF kept pounding the politicians with doomsday scenarios regarding the risks of withdrawing from southern Lebanon. All these factors made the notion of unilateral withdrawal a marginal item on the public agenda.

What started bringing about change in the public mood toward the notion of unilateral withdrawal was, ironically, a helicopter accident. On February 4, 1997, two helicopters—carrying IDF soldiers returning from vacation to their security zone outposts—collided in midair, killing seventy-seven soldiers. This accident gave the movement for unilateral withdrawal from Lebanon a major push; it highlighted the absurdity of the whole setup in which the IDF had to sneak troops into the security zones like thieves at night, just to ensure the safety of the incoming and outgoing troops. A group of women, mothers of soldiers who had served in Lebanon, going by the name "Four Mothers" started a public campaign for unilateral withdrawal. Public opinion also started shifting. By April 1997, already 41 percent of the Israelis favored this idea (Arian 1997). Once planted, this idea was hard to uproot.

The movement for unilateral withdrawal from Lebanon still faced an uphill battle, however, against a determined IDF and a dormant public opinion. This idea did not become a preferred policy due to a rational process of the reassessment of pros and cons. Rather, it became a policy as a result of political competition. The 1999 election campaign pitted the incumbent prime minister, Benjamin Netanyahu, against Ehud Barak. In February 1999 Netanyahu was leading Barak in the polls by as much as seven percentage points. Barak, looking for an issue that would change the tide of the electoral battle, announced on March 1 that, if elected, he would lead the IDF out of Lebanon within one year, through an agreement with Syria or through unilateral withdrawal (Drucker 2002, 129–30).

Barak, as COS and as a Knesset member, had been unequivocally opposed to unilateral withdrawal (Drucker 2002, 130), but he realized that this issue would help him in his campaign. When Barak came to power he repeated his pledge in almost every public speech. Barak, however, was faced with significant opposition in the IDF general staff. The leading opponents were the COS, Shaul Mofaz; the head of AMAN, General Amos Malka; the head of the research division, Amos Gilead; and the commander of the northern front, General Gabi Ashkenazi. These generals launched a not so subtle political campaign of apocalyptic predictions regarding the outcomes of unilateral withdrawal (Drucker

2002, 131–32; Edelist 2003, 152, 208–9, 289) in an attempt to fight Barak's intention to withdraw.

As a former COS, however, Barak was able not only to contain the IDF's anti-withdrawal campaign but also to use the growing support in the Israeli public of this idea. When it became evident by late March that the Israeli-Syrian agreement was dead in the water, Barak directed the IDF to withdraw by the end of May. Within a fortnight, the eighteen-year occupation of Lebanese territory ended.

4. THE LESSONS OF THE LEBANON WAR

The lessons of the war and occupation in Lebanon cover strategic-military, political, and social issues. It is commonly assumed that the process of deriving lessons from failures is more thorough and effective than doing so from successful episodes. In the Lebanese case, a key problem—which explains why there has been no systematic review of the consequences of this war to the very day—is the admission of failure. There is still a considerable ambiguity in Israel over the outcome of this war. Quite a few people in the political system believe that this was a just and successful war. More important, quite a few past and present military figures believe that the unilateral withdrawal from Lebanon was a mistake. These "experts" argue that the unilateral withdrawal encouraged the Palestinians to launch the Al Aqsa Intifada, believing that they could extract from Israel wide-ranging concessions through a long-drawn struggle, just as the Hizballah managed to do in Lebanon.

In light of this ambiguity, it is important to point out clearly some of the key aspects of the Israeli failure in Lebanon.

1. Israel accomplished none of the key objectives it set for itself in the Lebanon War.
2. Israel accomplished none of the objectives it set for itself in the security zone in southern Lebanon.
3. The functioning of the principal military systems—including the general staff, the intelligence community, and the operational command of the northern front—was defective throughout the 1982–2000 period.
4. The functioning of the political system was defective throughout the period.
5. The watchdogs of the Israeli political and social system performed poorly throughout the period.

I discuss each of these aspects briefly and then examine some of the key lessons that can be drawn from this failure.

4.1. *The Objectives of the Lebanon War: Expectations versus Outcomes*

As noted, most of the Israeli public, the political system, and quite a few members of Begin's cabinet believed that the key goal of the war was to liberate northern Israel from the constant harassment of the PLO. This mission seems to have been accomplished: the PLO was driven out of Lebanon; its military and political infrastructure in the country was completely destroyed. Yet, this apparent success is completely over-shadowed by the fact that—while Israel rid itself of one enemy in Lebanon—it arranged for itself another enemy. The perception of threat emanating from the Hizballah after the Lebanon War—whether it is based on reality or on fiction—is not much different from the threat perception that served as a political and diplomatic justification of the Lebanon War.

However, "peace to the Galilee" was not the real objective of the war. The war was aimed to destroy the nationalist sentiments in the West Bank and Gaza, inspired primarily by the PLO. In fact, it caused just the opposite: the defeat of the PLO in Lebanon was instrumental in foment-ing a new kind of Palestinian nationalism, and it had little effect on the extent of secular nationalism in the occupied territories. The post-Lebanon religious nationalism represented by the rise of the Hamas movement was far more extreme and far more motivated to armed strug-gle than its PLO counterpart (Mishal and Sela 2000; Kurz, with Tal, 1997). And both the religious and secular nationalists were increasingly motivated to resist the Israeli occupation in the West Bank and Gaza. This became the first intifada (Schiff and Yaari 1990, 11–12).

Syrian military presence in Lebanon ended only in 2005. It continues to maintain indirect influence on Lebanese politics. (Rabil 2003, 78–80). Throughout the 1990s, Syria effectively blocked every effort to bring about a separate peace treaty between Lebanon and Israel. In fact, many people in the Israeli security community believed that Syria was alternat-ing between encouraging and restraining Hizballah attacks on the IDF on the basis of developments in the Israeli-Syrian peace talks (Rabinovich 1998, 109–10).

The establishment of a Christian-dominated state in Lebanon that would sign a peace treaty with Israel was clearly not accomplished. The dream of a peace treaty with Lebanon died right at the birth of the May

17, 1983, agreement. Such a treaty is probably not going to happen in the near future and independently of an Israeli-Syrian peace treaty.

Israel went into this war with open eyes. This war represents neither a remarkable military victory nor a political one. Israel withdrew from Lebanon with its tail between its legs, and it withdrew eighteen years too late. There can be no clearer failure of policy than the case of the Lebanon War. The first and most important reason for the failure to accomplish the objectives of the war is that the goals were both overly ambitious and unrealistic. Writing in late 1983, Schiff and Yaari (1984, 301) put it very aptly.

> Born of the ambition of one willful, reckless man, Israel's 1982 invasion of Lebanon was anchored in delusion, propelled by deceit, and bound to end in calamity. It was a war for whose meager gains Israel has paid an enormous price that has yet to be altogether reckoned; a war whose defensive rationale belied far-reaching political aims and an unconscionably myopic policy. It drew Israel into a wasteful adventure that drained much of its inner strength and cost the IDF the lives of over 500 of its finest men in a vain effort to fulfill a role it was never meant to play.

The realization that these goals were in the realm of pipe dreams rather than realistic political objectives came fairly early in the process. The fact that Israel remained in occupation of Lebanese soil for eighteen more years represents a fundamental failure of a large number of systems in the Israeli political system, its bureaucracy, and its society at large. We need to analyze in greater detail the nature of this systemwide malfunction.

4.2. The Intelligence Failure

The Lebanon War presented the Israeli intelligence community with a complex challenge. It was required to assess, over a relatively long period of time, the intentions and behavioral patterns of a large number of actors that made up the Lebanese political and social system. Some of these actors were loosely organized communities; others emerged as a result of the Israeli involvement in Lebanon. The nature of the Lebanese system compelled the intelligence community to resort to nineteenth-century methods, relying primarily on human intelligence (HumInt), which is more difficult to acquire, far less reliable, and more difficult to interpret and analyze than electronic and visual methods of intelligence gathering.

The prewar period was characterized by considerable dissent within the intelligence community regarding the upcoming invasion. The Mossad leadership believed that it was possible to forge a credible alliance with the Christians in Lebanon. AMAN, however, consistently argued that this alliance was both unfeasible and unreliable. Moreover, as early as April 1981, AMAN argued that the Christian Phalanges were deliberately trying to draw Israel into an active involvement in the Lebanese civil war.

During the planning phases of the war, Saguy consistently warned his colleagues that IDF would get embroiled in a futile struggle in Lebanon. He was not afraid to voice his views in the IDF general staff forum but kept quiet in the cabinet, thus becoming an unwilling accomplice to Sharon's and Eitan's deceptions and manipulations. Begin, Sharon, and Eitan chose the convenient assessment of the Mossad regarding the alliance with the Christians and the possible outcome of the war.

Between 1982 and 1985, AMAN continued to assess correctly the abysmal prospects of a meaningful Israeli-Lebanese agreement. AMAN also argued that Syria employed local proxies to foil anything that would diminish its dominant role in Lebanon. These assessments also turned out to be correct. What the Israeli intelligence community failed to realize was that the Israeli schemes in Lebanon would actually backfire. The intelligence community failed to foresee and to warn against the feelings of frustration and the perceptions of threats of the Druzes, the Sunnis, and particularly the Shi'ites by the Israeli-Christian collusion. It failed to foretell the rise of the Hizballah and the turning of Amal against Israel in southern Lebanon. Yaniv (1987b, 229) notes:

> The quick change in the south of Lebanon from a relatively hospitable territory [for the Israelis] to an extremely hostile one was among the greatest failures of national intelligence estimates that Israel has ever known. No one, not even the most persistent opponents of the war, had ever raised this possibility. Although it developed gradually, in the final analysis it shook the Israelis no less than the entry of Egyptian forces into the Sinai in January 1960 and May 1967 or the launching of the Egyptian-Syrian surprise attack on Yom Kippur, 1973.

The crux of the intelligence failure was the inability to assess the impact of the Israeli occupation on the various communities in Lebanon. In January 1985, when the government decided on the phased withdrawal and on the security zone, AMAN failed to anticipate the long-term implications of the continued occupation of Lebanon.

This failure was the first among a whole series of intelligence debacles over a period of fifteen years. Three years of occupation of Lebanese territory and the continued attacks on the IDF should have lit up all of the red lights in AMAN regarding the response of Hizballah to the IDF presence in the security zone and to the continued support of the SLA. Instead, a new "conception" evolved in the intelligence community: that the Hizballah would continue to fight against Israel when it withdrew from southern Lebanon. The implication was that Israel should not withdraw from the security zone as long as it was not assured that the Hizballah was disarmed and the Lebanese army established an effective hold on southern Lebanon.

This fatalistic assessment relied exclusively on analysis of the rhetoric of Hizballah leaders and ignored completely the Hizballah's modus operandi against the IDF and the SLA. This assessment remained fixed over the fifteen years of Israeli presence in southern Lebanon and served as the foundation of numerous military and political decisions regarding southern Lebanon. It was the foundation of the IDF's opposition to unilateral withdrawal. It also accounts for the post-withdrawal myth that the PLO's decision to launch the Al Aqsa Intifada was based on the PLO's analysis of the episode of unilateral withdrawal.

An additional intelligence fiasco was the failure to foresee the effects of the escalation of IDF actions in Lebanon—in particular, the kidnapping of Sheikh Ubeid and Mustafa Dirani and the assassination of Abbas Mussawi—on Hizballah's behavior. The IDF also failed to foresee the ineffectiveness of Operation Accountability and Operation Grapes of Wrath in reducing Hizballah's activity.

These debacles represent perhaps more profound and substantial intelligence failures than any other intelligence errors in Israel's history—the Yom Kippur fiasco included. First, as Bar Joseph (2001) shows, the intelligence failure in the 1973 case was due to a unique personal configuration that took place in AMAN. In the Lebanese case we are dealing with a consistent, long-lasting, and self-amplifying failure.

Second, the 1973 intelligence fiasco was due to the fact that AMAN's head imposed a faulty conception of the enemy's intention on a wide array of practical indicators that pointed in a completely different direction. The most important lesson that AMAN should have drawn from the Yom Kippur fiasco was that intelligence must be based on practical indicators—the actual behavior and physical activity of the enemy. Such indicators should guide assessment not less (and perhaps more) than assessments of intentions, which—by nature—are based on ambiguous information. The failure of the intelligence community in Lebanon was, to a large extent, a replication of the failure of Yom Kippur: here, too, the principal conclusion was based on an analysis of intentions, which itself was based on the interpretation of texts and verbal statements rather than on actual behavior.

Third, in contrast to the unique personal and organizational conjunction that facilitated the Yom Kippur fiasco, in Lebanon this failure encompassed five COSs of the IDF, six heads of AMAN, a similar number of heads of the research division of AMAN, and four heads of Mossad. It is impossible to account for this persistent failure of estimate in terms of specific personal or organizational conjunctions.

Finally, the organizational and methodological refinements in the research division that were established following the Yom Kippur earthquake—the control unit and the devil's advocate—did not present serious challenges to the institutional intelligence assessment. The research units in the Mossad and in the Foreign Ministry were also partners to this fiasco. Any internal set of control mechanisms that is based on people who grew up in the AMAN system, and whose advancement is based on decisions by the very same people whom they are supposed to criticize, is utterly impractical.

The Lebanon War demonstrates a fundamental difficulty inherent in the process by which the intelligence community forms assessments within an interactive and dynamic setting. An intelligence agency that is legally prohibited to engage in an assessment of the effects of our behavior on the behavior of the enemy will invariably fall into a trap wherein it is institutionally required to view—and therefore will make it a habit of doing so—the enemy's behavior in deterministic and noninteractive terms. In the Lebanese case, the major factor that affected Hizballah's and Amal's behavior was Israel's behavior in southern Lebanon. The tendency to see Hizballah's behavior as motivated by its ideology and by instructions from Iran contributed significantly to the intelligence failure.

4.3. *The Failure of Strategy*

Israeli military strategy in the Lebanon War can be divided into two parts: the offensive strategy that dominated the first stage of the war up to the occupation of Beirut and the antiguerrilla strategy on which Israel relied thereafter. The Lebanon War was a *deluxe* war. It was a single-front war; Israel enjoyed overwhelming numerical and qualitative advantage; the IDF was highly prepared because it had planned the war for a long time; and it enjoyed the advantages of the first strike. Israel exploited those advantages to the fullest.

From a strictly military point of view it was a brilliantly executed military operation, carried out with precise coordination between major branches of the Israeli Armed Forces. . . . Meticulous planning and execution accounted for the lightning advance into Lebanon's difficult, mountainous terrain, often ahead of schedule. . . . In less than three startling weeks the PLO war machine in South Lebanon and in Beirut, with its modern weapons and equipment . . . was destroyed. . . . According to unofficial figures nearly 1,200 PLO guerrillas were killed in action and some 3,700 wounded.

Syria, too, had to bow to the superb performance of the Israeli forces, especially its air force and armor. . . . Syrian troops suffered heavy losses and retreated along the entire front. Unconfirmed Syrian losses were about 1,000 killed and nearly 3,700 wounded. (Dupuy and Martell 1986, 141)

The most significant achievement in the Lebanon War was that of the IAF, which successfully destroyed the Syrian SAM batteries in the Beqa Valley and shot down over eighty Syrian Migs in the air without losing a single plane. The Israeli navy also performed well, establishing complete command of the sea and effectively blocking any attempt of the PLO to move people through the sea during the siege of Beirut.

The political constraints on the execution of the optimal strategy by the IDF impeded the ability to accomplish the key military objective. The need to delay the encounter with the Syrian forces enabled the latter to reinforce their troops and redeploy them in a manner that made it difficult for the IDF to complete the encirclement operation. The IDF was able to push the Syrian forces in the Beirut area and to drive them out of the Beirut-Damascus highway. But the Syrians effectively resisted the IDF's effort to drive their forces out of the Beqa Valley. The cease-fire allowed the Syrians to further reinforce their troops. An engagement with these reinforced troops would have been exceedingly costly. The battle of Sultan Yaaqub demonstrated this difficulty (Schiff and Yaari 1984, 174–80; Dupuy and Martell 1986, 123–29). The Syrians were beaten but not entirely defeated militarily.[18]

The failure of Israeli strategy in the second, long phase of the war is therefore all the more disturbing in comparison to the effectiveness of the Israeli offensive strategy in the first phase. The numerical and qualitative advantage that Israel enjoyed in the second stage was overwhelming. The guerrilla warfare that the IDF encountered in Lebanon was a new form of warfare for the IDF, but it was not a new form of warfare in history. Yet, the IDF operated in Lebanon as a cumbersome, heavy-handed, and non-adaptive bureaucratic organization. The relatively low rate of IDF and civilian casualties during the 1985–2000 period is deceptive. It does not tell us of the effectiveness of the IDF. Rather, it teaches us of the self-imposed constraints of the Hizballah.

The IDF strategy in the second stage of the war included limited territorial possession (the maintenance of several outposts inside Lebanon), reliance on local mercenaries (SLA), an emphasis on sea and aerial operations, controlled escalation in several junctures, and strategic restraint vis-à-vis Syria. With the significant exception of Israeli naval strategy, these elements were employed in a manner that suggests a fundamental misunderstanding of the nature of low-intensity conflict (LIC). It highlights the failure to understand the linkages between strategy and tactical operations and the failure to cope with the challenge posed by guerrilla warfare to the grand strategy of Israel (Van Creveld 1998, 304–6).

The IDF deployment in the security zone of southern Lebanon emerges from the old maxim that one must be able to establish physical control of a territory via static outposts. The only advantage of this deployment is symbolic: the IDF controlled the territory. But this advantage was more than offset by the liabilities of static defense in LIC. The IDF outposts became sitting ducks and subject to attacks by the Hizballah, which maintained a mobile posture. The more casualties were sustained by the IDF as a result of Hizballah attacks on the outposts, the more resources were invested in fortifying them.

These outposts forced the IDF to ferry food, ammunition, and people. The roads leading to these outposts became targets of roadside bombs. The replacement of troops in these outposts became a complicated logistical problem. Instead of controlling the territory, IDF troops became de facto prisoners of the Hizballah. The Hizballah determined the timing of entry and exit to these outposts more than did the IDF.[19] The activation of special forces and ambushes of the IDF from these outposts became a problem because Hizballah operatives could monitor the activity in these outposts without being detected.

There is no rational explanation for the clinging of the IDF to the anachronistic conception of static outposts. Mobile patrols that are inserted and extracted in surprise and that use a variety of methods (e.g., helicopters, crossing from the international border, disguise, amphibious landing) and move without a specific pattern could have been much more effective in tracking down and confronting Hizballah guerrillas. Such operations did take place, but they were limited in scope, primarily because of the prioritization of the static outposts in terms of physical, logistical, and human resources. Here, too, bureaucratic inertia and folly prevailed over reason and strategic and tactical creativity.

The reliance on local mercenaries turned out to be a major liability. The SLA operated not out of ideological motivation but rather due to financial incentives. In all too many cases SLA operatives betrayed their patrons in order to ensure their own safety. When it became evident that Israel would withdraw from Lebanon, SLA people provided the Hizballah with valuable intelligence that led to a number of successful attacks on the IDF.[20] The SLA completely evaporated once the IDF started its withdrawal from Lebanon.

IDF strategy in Lebanon was dictated less by the nature of the problems it confronted on the ground and more by the availability of resources and technologies. The IDF misused sophisticated technologies by applying them blindly to LIC situations where they were utterly unsuitable. Instead of developing tactics and adapting resources to the conditions of warfare and to the nature of the enemy in Lebanon, the IDF attempted to insert heavy and sophisticated weapons suitable for conventional warfare. The activation of the air force, the armored corps, and heavy artillery in Lebanon not only failed to bring about any significant achievements but in many cases backfired. The use of massive fire platforms can be effective when there are well-defined targets. When used against populated areas they are bound to inflict heavy collateral damage, even if the level of precision of these platforms is high. In fact, virtually all cases of escalation in fighting were due to the IDF's infliction of civilian casualties through area bombardments.

Paradoxically, during the fifteen years in which the IDF made extensive use of artillery, tank fire, and aerial bombing, the scope and intensity of Hizballah operations increased significantly. Thus these operations not only failed to impair Hizballah's freedom of operation, but they may have in fact contributed to Hizballah's motivation to operate and to inflict casualties on the IDF. The Hizballah Web site provides statistics about its operations over the 1996–2000 period.[21] While one should take some of these data with a grain of salt, they are nevertheless indicative of the scope of Hizballah operations over the period. The Hizballah reports a total of 995 operations in 1996, resulting in the death of sixty so-called martyrs; 889 operations in 1997, resulting in the death of fifty-six "martyrs"; 1,519 operations in 1998, resulting in the death of thirty-seven "martyrs"; a total of 1,250 operations in 1999, resulting in the death of forty-two "martyrs"; and around 400 operations over the January–May 2000 period, with an unknown number of fatalities. The size of the

Hizballah stood—according to various estimates—at roughly eight hundred guerrillas at its peak (Feldman and Shapir 2004). IDF forces in southern Lebanon reached a level of two reduced brigades (roughly two thousand soldiers) in the late 1990s.

As the IDF's use of massive bombardments that caused civilian Lebanese casualties increased, so did Hizballah's attacks on Israeli settlements. The IDF Web site reports that, from Operation Accountability in 1993 to the IDF withdrawal in May 2000, the Hizballah fired over one thousand Katyusha rockets and mortars at Israeli settlements, and over six hundred of these were fired at the peak of the use of massive aerial and artillery bombing during Operation Grapes of Wrath in April 1996. Nevertheless, the IDF continued this policy of massive use of firepower up to the point of hitting infrastructural targets in 1999.[22]

One type of criticism directed at the IDF strategy in Lebanon was that it was too "soft." This criticism implied a notion that "whoever is not compelled by force is bound to be compelled by more force."[23] Many in the Israeli security establishment urged the application of massive force, hitting infrastructural targets—such as electricity, water, and even hospitals—so as to compel the Lebanese population to put an end to Hizballah operations. This kind of strategy was not fully explored during the second phase of the Lebanon War, but it is not difficult to imagine that it would have had little effect. The two cases of massive use of firepower in an effort to compel the civilian population to restrain the Hizballah—Operation Accountability and Operation Grapes of Wrath—failed to yield such restraint.

The IDF became a slave of high-end technology and hardware instead of relying on tactical creativity and initiative. The vast resources invested in R&D designed to deal with low-intensity threats (e.g., the Nautilus system designed to destroy Katyusha rockets, devices for detecting roadside explosives, and devices for protecting troops in moving vehicles and in stationary outposts) proved to be strategically meaningless. Even if they did improve the IDF's capacity to deal with known threats, the Hizballah proved more resourceful in developing new techniques against which these systems were completely irrelevant.

Beyond the systemwide malfunctions of the Israeli strategy in Lebanon, it is important to point out some specific problems that are typical of more general fallacies in Israeli LIC and antiterrorist strategy (see chap. 7). The policies of kidnapping and assassination resulted in rampant escalation and, in fact, deepened IDF's entanglement in Lebanon. In addition, these operations led to two major terrorist attacks on Israeli tar-

226 I DEFENDING THE HOLY LAND

gets in Buenos Aires. All of these operations were designed for domestic consumption and had absolutely no strategic purpose. Their results were far reaching, however, and not in line with the IDF's expectations. Unfortunately, these consequences were never seriously evaluated and no lessons were drawn.

The IDF in Lebanon performed in a cumbersome, maladaptive manner. It was commanded by conservative generals entrenched in anachronistic strategic thinking. It attempted to cover up its failure to develop an effective counterguerrilla doctrine by creating myths about the Hizballah and entrenching its stay in Lebanon. The social and political watchdogs of the executive branch that operate in a democratic system should have detected this strategic blunder much earlier. But these systems in Israel seem to have fallen asleep on watch duty.

4.4. Israeli Society in the Lebanese Swamp

The argument that the women's organization Four Mothers was largely responsible for the Israeli final withdrawal from Lebanon may be true. But it may also create a misleading impression that the Israeli political and social systems performed an effective oversight on the IDF. The question is not why Israel withdrew from Lebanon in 2000. Changes in public moods in a democratic society will have an impact on political decision making. The key question is why it took Israel so long to finally get out of the Lebanese mess. How can we explain a seemingly rational and intelligent society that is willing to absorb year after year fatalities of an unnecessary and immoral occupation? How is it possible that such a society goes on for years without questioning the IDF and the government's claim that the security zone protects the northern border of Israel, even when Katyusha rockets land in the thousands on these northern settlements?

A political and social analysis of the Israeli presence in Lebanon must examine the failure of the social and political mechanisms of oversight and control over this period. Why did the political system, the media, the academic establishment, and the attentive public fall asleep while on guard duty, as far as the Lebanese mess was concerned? The full impact of such voluntary groups as Four Mothers on the final decision to withdraw can only be understood against the backdrop of the complacency of these systems of oversight and control. The understanding of what happened to these systems in the Lebanese case is an important case study for anybody who wants to understand the functioning of the Israeli foreign and security system.

Israeli public opinion on Lebanon is characterized by two similar waves. The first wave covers the period of June 1982–June 1985, and the second covers the period of July 1985–May 2000. Each wave started with strong public support of the government's policy on Lebanon. Over time, as costs accumulated, public opinion started moving away from the government position. But this movement was very slow, and for most of the period a stable majority still supported the official position. Table 6.1 provides some figures that substantiate this trend.

It is fair to argue, therefore, that public opinion was not an extremely powerful factor in forcing the government to change its strategy in Lebanon. This applies both to the policy of continued presence in Lebanon during the 1983–85 period and to the IDF's presence in the security zone during 1985–2000. Even in 2000, after Ehud Barak announced his intention to withdraw from Lebanon, public opinion supported the notions pushed forth by the IDF that (a) the security zone brings quiet to the north of Israel (75 percent support) and (b) the security zone is an important bargaining chip in the Israeli-Syrian negotiations (79 percent support) (Arian 2000, 25). In fact, with respect to Israel's policy in Lebanon the public was fairly complacent and bought into official government positions for much of the time.

The slow turnaround in public opinion in both periods was due to different factors, however. The 1983–85 period was accompanied by some meaningful acts of public protest, including several large demonstrations (the largest was the one following the Sabra and Shatilla massacre). In the late 1990s, the shift was due to changes in the positions of some political

TABLE 6.1. Israeli Public Opinion on the Lebanon War and the Security Zone

Question	1982	1984	1985	1987	1995	1997	1998	2000
Support (justification) of Lebanon War	77%[a]	41%[b]	27%[d]	27%[c]	NA	NA	NA	NA
Support of Israeli presence in Lebanon (pending proper security guarantees)	79	51	39	NA	NA	59[c]	56	NA
Security zone provides security to northern Israel	NA	NA	NA	NA	77	72[c]	64	75
Support of unilateral withdrawal from Lebanon	20[e]	35[e]	53[e]	NA	NA	41[c]	44	62

Sources:
[a]Merom 2003, 182, cites PORI and Barzilai 1996, 149–50.
[b]Yaniv 1987b, 194, unspecified public opinion polls.
[c]Arian 1997, 12; 2000, 24–25. Data refer to security zone only.
[d]Arian 1985.
[e]Data refer to withdrawal from Lebanon excluding the security zone.

leaders, not so much to the human and material price Israel was paying. The Lebanese case is marked by a significant degree of public conformism.

An analysis of journalistic and academic writings on the Lebanon War and on the Israeli occupation of the security zone shows a great deal of conformity and complacency as well. Quite a few opinion leaders criticized the Lebanon War: both the mere conception of a "war by choice" and the expansion of the war beyond the forty kilometer zone. It is quite possible that these elements—together with pressure from institutionalized political circles—facilitated the decision to withdraw from most of Lebanon (Yaniv 1987b, 246–54, 268–84; Barzilai 1996, 148–52; Merom 2003, 177–93, 209–26). Yet, during the 1985–2000 period, there was little criticism by opinion leaders in the media and the academic community of the IDF operations and strategy, of the morality of the continued occupation, and of the benefit of it. Most public opinion leaders failed to ask critical questions and to identify fundamental inconsistencies and weaknesses in the official positions of the IDF and the political leaders. Criticisms against IDF actions in Lebanon centered on specific episodes (e.g., the ambush of the naval commando in 1998, the helicopter collision of 1997, and incidents of friendly fire in the security zone). No comprehensive critique exists of Israeli policy in southern Lebanon over the entire period of 1985–2000.

Most opinion makers bought into the IDF rhetoric, accepted the flawed intelligence assessments of AMAN about the possible consequences of withdrawal, and viewed the security zone as "an important bargaining chip in the negotiations with Syria," thus tying—as the political establishment did—withdrawal from the security zone to a peace treaty with Syria.[24]

Parliamentary debates also suggest a fundamental and systematic malfunctioning of the legislative oversight over the executive operations in Lebanon. From June 1985 to May 2000, there were only fifteen parliamentary debates dealing with the Lebanon problem, ten out of those in the last six years (1994–2000).[25] Out of these cases, there were only two government presentations explaining policy—both cases occurring in the course of Operation Accountability. In none of these cases did the parliamentary debate result in an operational decision or legislation. None of the key decisions during this period—such as the escalation of warfare due to kidnapping and assassination raids or the two large-scale military operations in 1993 and 1996—was thoroughly debated in the Knesset. Moreover, in most policy debates concerning southern Lebanon, criticism was leveled at the government policy for being too "soft." None of these debates contained presentation of statistical data on casualties or costs. Paradoxically, even the decision to withdraw from Lebanon did not receive a specific scrutiny by the Knesset.

All incumbent governments during that period had a vested interest in suppressing public and parliamentary debate of their policy to cover up the continued strategic failure in Lebanon. However, it was a built-in interest of the political opposition to use the Lebanese fiasco as a tool for criticizing government policy. This did not happen. The leading opposition parties never presented a meaningful and institutionalized alternative to the government policy in Lebanon. In this sense, the two leading parties—when they were both in the coalition and in the opposition—were perpetrators and accomplices to the same crime.

5. CONCLUSION

The Lebanon War demonstrates, perhaps more than any other war in Israel's history, some of the key ideas of this part of the book.

1. It was an aggressive war born out of a belief that Israel's strategic problems are best solved through decisive use of military force. And it was the first war that demonstrated the futility and folly of this conception.

2. The precise contours of the war may have been conceived by one "willful, reckless man" (Schiff and Yaari 1984, 301). But it was executed according to this plan only because quite a few influential people in the government and the IDF went along with it, while others slept on watch duty.

3. The management of the high-intensity conflict and LIC by the IDF reflects fundamental problems of doctrine and generalship. The war reveals major problems in national intelligence. IDF intelligence performed an accurate analysis in the prewar period. At the same time, the commanders of the IDF intelligence failed to convince policymakers of the adverse implications of Israel's actions. The second part of the war (1984–2000) reveals a mega intelligence failure that extended over a very long period and across many different people and administrations.

4. The war represents a basic failure of the democratic systems of oversight and control of the executive branch and of the IDF. This failure was not an aberration; it continues to the present. The architect of the Lebanon calamity has been elected twice to lead the country in yet

another bitter conflict with the Palestinians. Nor is this a failure of one isolated element of the system; it is systemic. The established system of oversight and control in the Knesset and in the bureaucracy, as well as the informal watchdogs of government policy—the media, the academic community, and public opinion—failed to monitor the executive failures.

5. There is, nevertheless, an optimistic side to this prolonged misfortune. This is the fact that a small body of parliamentarians was able to overcome the strong barriers of a rigid party system and present, perhaps for the first time in Israel's history, a bipartisan alternative to government policy. It also concerns the ability of a grass-roots movement to affect policy in a rational direction. This group was started by several concerned mothers without any political experience and leverage and expanded into an effective pressure group that finally won the ears of policymakers and saved the institutionalized state of Israel from itself.[26]

The war shattered the myth of Israel as a state fighting a defensive battle for its survival. It demonstrated to many in the mainstream political and social spectrum in Israel that Israel can be blatantly aggressive and that the role of David and Goliath in the Arab-Israeli conflict may well be reversed. Quite a few sociologists and political scientists suggest that the Lebanon War was a watershed event in the attitude of many Israelis toward the IDF and government policy. This war is also considered to have had major implications for the relations between the IDF and the Israeli society (e.g., Levy 1997, 179–83; 2003, 146–70; Ben-Eliezer 2003, 34–35; S. Cohen 2003, 110–11; Barzilai 1996, 149–65). This fact, however, was not translated into a thorough self-inspection of the many layers of failure and malfunction that this war unveiled.

This war was also unique in that it started out as a conventional war— a sustained series of battles between large military (and quasi-military) formations. It was soon converted into a prolonged LIC and turned out to be the first clear-cut defeat of the IDF. Paradoxically, this defeat occurred under the most favorable military conditions in Israel's history. Interestingly, this defeat was not fully recognized by the IDF or by many elements in the political system. Because it was converted into a prolonged LIC, the outcome of the war does not look as severe as it would have looked had Israel lost a conventional war. Nevertheless, the implications of this war are far reaching. Some of these implications—those that relate to the limited use of force by Israel in the second part of the war—are discussed in chapter 7.

— 7 —

The Unlimited Use of the Limited Use of Force

Israel and Low-Intensity Warfare

I. INTRODUCTION

As I mentioned in part I, Israel has been involved in 166 dyadic militarized interstate disputes (MIDs) short of war throughout its history. The dyadic MID data set (Maoz 2005) and the updated MID 3.1 data set[1] suggest that there was only one year out of fifty-six years of history in which Israel did not engage in acts involving the threat, display, or limited use of force with its neighbors. The only year in which Israel did not engage in a militarized conflict was 1988, when Israel was deeply immersed in fighting the Palestinian uprising, the intifada. So it is fair to say that during each and every year of its history Israel was engaged in violent military actions of some magnitude. Dayan's book recounting the 1977–78 Israeli-Egyptian peace negotiations was entitled *Shall the Sword Devour Forever?*[2] The answer to Dayan's question appears, thus far, to be decidedly affirmative.

One possible explanation for Israel's constant fighting is that the continuous use of limited force is the only rational Israeli response to the continued Arab threat to its survival. Israel could not impose a military decision of the conflict through an all-out use of force (Kober 1995). Nor was it able to convert its military victories into a political victory at the negotiation table. As I argue in the next chapter, Israel cannot impose

231

peace through the threat of nuclear weapons. Thus, the use of limited force appears to be Israel's only rational response to the fundamental security challenges it has faced since its inception.

The underlying long-term objective of this policy is what we described as "cumulative deterrence" in chapter 1. The cumulative impact of numerous instances of limited use of force is designed to convince the Arabs of the futility of their quest for the destruction of the Jewish state. The limited use of force enabled Israel, according to this conception, to maintain a continuous posture of military preparedness, side by side of the development of a society, an economy, and a democratic political system.

But the Israeli limited use of force strategy had additional functions. Rather than serving as a device for limiting conflict, it was used for far more diverse goals. My argument regarding the Israeli strategies of limited force is threefold.

1. Israeli political and military leaders employed its strategy of limited use of force to accomplish both strategic and domestic political goals. In some cases, this strategy was a major tool of deterrence designed to prevent war. In other cases it was used for strategic escalation intended to provoke the Arabs to initiate war. It was also perceived as a major mobilization device, not only to boost public support for the government but—more broadly—to mobilize a heterogeneous society with little or no military background for national security goals during times of relative tranquility.

2. As with high-intensity conflict strategies, Israeli low-intensity strategy was based on escalation dominance, that is, disproportionate responses to provocations, as well as military initiatives not in response to specific provocations. At the same time, Israeli strategy tried to walk a fine line between outmatching the challenge with excessive force, on the one hand, and deflecting blame for escalating minor incidents to all-out wars, on the other.

3. This strategy, for the most part, was largely unsuccessful. First, even when it was intended to foster deterrence, it resulted in inadvertent escalation. Israel's low-intensity strategy was at the root of all wars since the 1948 War of Independence—save the Yom Kippur War. Second, as a strategy of deliberate escalation, it did bring about the intended escalatory process, but it forced Israel—rather than the Arabs—to launch aggressive wars. Third, the strategy generated adverse side effects. It was a key factor causing escalation of Arab actions against the Israeli population, converting these actions into a "strategic threat."[3] Finally, the Israeli image of successful management of the conflict was substantially

eroded by the inability to address low-intensity challenges because it proved ineffective in curbing Arab violence against Israel.

There still exists a great deal of consensus in the Israeli security establishment, the political system, and public opinion about the fundamental wisdom of Israel's limited use of force strategy. It is viewed as a necessary evil and, as such, phenomenally successful. Consequently, despite critiques of specific elements of this strategy, there was little discussion of the different variants of this strategy and its implications. If a debate existed, it was often between those who advocated employing this strategy within strict parameters and those who advocated further escalation. The moderates in this debate believe in the notion of cumulative deterrence through the persistent (and slightly disproportionate) yet limited use of force. The other faction advocates moving from a limited use of force strategy to massive use of force aimed at military decision. One almost never hears in Israeli strategic circles that perhaps the reliance on military force as the principal (or even the only) instrument of policy is fundamentally misconceived. At best, we hear that force alone would not solve the problem of low-intensity warfare or of terrorism. The notion that force in fact exacerbates anti-Israeli violence is not part of the strategic discourse in Israel.

In this chapter, I document these themes and discuss their implications. In order to do that, I focus on four forms of low-intensity warefare. First, I discuss acts of limited violence against Arab states, in what came to be known as the strategy of reprisals. Second, I discuss guerrilla warfare, especially in the Lebanese context during the 1985–2000 period and the Al Aqsa intifada of 2000–2003. Third, I discuss the variations in Israel's antiterrorism policy. Fourth, I examine Israeli strategy vis-à-vis acts of civil disobedience and popular rebellion during the two episodes of the intifada. Following this review, I explore the explicit and latent functions of the Israeli limited use of force strategy. Finally, I suggest alternative approaches to effective performance in low-intensity warfare. These approaches are partly of a military nature but mostly of a political and diplomatic one.

2. A BRIEF HISTORY OF ISRAEL'S
LIC EXPERIENCE, 1949–2004

Any analysis of the Israeli policy of reprisals must begin with a discussion of the evolution of this policy in the early 1950s. The principles that were established during the period define to a large extent the nature of this policy to the very day. As I document in the remainder of this chapter, this strategy did not change in any fundamental way over time.[4]

2.1. The Origins of the Policy of Reprisals, 1949–56

The need to respond to low-intensity challenges arose immediately following the 1948 War of Independence. Ostensibly, the challenge was repeated infiltrations by Palestinian refugees from the Gaza Strip and the West Bank to Israel. Many of these infiltrations were committed by Palestinians attempting to return to their houses in Israel. Others were simply acts of theft, robbery, or sabotage by desperate Palestinian refugees who had been living on the verge of starvation and despair (Morris 1993, 34–46). These acts were a constant menace to the Israeli population. They were particularly disturbing to the newly arrived immigrants who had been settled in small villages and new development towns that the government had established along the borders. This population was struggling both economically and culturally, trying to assimilate into the new state under difficult conditions. On top of that, they had to deal with the threat of Arab sabotage (Levy 2003, 59–60).

The Israeli government knew that these infiltrations were not orchestrated by the surrounding Arab regimes. Those regimes had also been faced with the refugee problem that had been placed on their doorstep by the 1948 war. The security systems of the Arab states were ill equipped to deal with the hundreds of thousands of Palestinian refugees (Morris 1993, 69–96). There were also occasional incidents involving the Arab Legion's shooting across the border in the Jerusalem area. But these reflected local initiatives or escalation of minor disputes rather than a deliberate Jordanian policy. On the contrary, the Hashemite regime did its utmost to prevent such incidents because it perceived correctly that they might give Israel a pretext to occupy east Jerusalem (Morris 2001, 270; 1993, 70–84).

Israel's initial response to this problem was fundamentally defensive. It attempted to stop or foil these infiltrations using its regular police forces. When this failed, the government established a border police, a special unit put in charge of defending Israel's borders from Palestinian infiltrations. Again, this did not do much to alleviate the infiltration problem. Other acts, including expulsion of Arab and Bedouin communities, had also no apparent effect on the number and intensity of the infiltrations (Morris 1993, 116–72). In 1949, sixty-two Israelis were killed by hostile Arab actions. This figure went down to thirty-eight in 1950 and remained steady during 1951 and 1952.

The policy of reprisals was not born out of a deliberative process of strategy planning. Rather, it emerged as a largely improvised response to domestic pressure on the government. Regional IDF commanders—confronted by criticism and pressure by the civilian population in their jurisdictions—started sending small units to commit acts of sabotage across the border (Golan 2000, 250–64). This was in line with the customary response of Jewish defense organizations to Arab harassment of Jewish settlements prior to 1948 (Kuperman 1999). These responses consisted of raids against Arab villages, destroying their fields or herds in retaliation for Arab raids against Jewish settlements. It was later improved upon by Ord Wingate, a British officer who trained Jewish defense groups to conduct daring raids on Arab villages during the Arab rebellion of 1936–39.

By the early 1950s, however, the reprisal raids were sanctioned by the state and were executed by its armed forces. The initial experience at retaliation was not a good one. The army units charged with the task of retaliating against Arab villages or Arab property were poorly trained and were hardly committed to fulfilling their mission. At the first sign of resistance, they retreated without completing their mission (Morris 1993, 213–15, 236–37; Kuperman 1999). As the Palestinian infiltrations continued, the IDF decided to establish a special commando unit that would specialize in retaliation and deep penetration raids into Arab territories. This unit, known as Unit 101, was established in 1952 under the command of a young major, Ariel Sharon. The formation of this unit marked a shift in Israeli policy toward significant escalation of the reprisals.

Before we continue the discussion on the evolution of the reprisal policy against Palestinian infiltrators, it is important to examine another aspect of the limited use of force in the early days of the Jewish state. A number of military encounters took place between Israeli and Syrian forces on the northern front. As documented elsewhere (Maoz and Mor 2002a, 180–84; 2002b, 7–14), Israel, unsatisfied with the Israeli-Syria armistice agreement, decided to drain the Hulla Swamp by encroaching on the demilitarized zones (DMZs). A number of military clashes with the Syrians ensued. In one particular case, a relatively small Syrian force occupied a small hill in the DMZ on May 4, 1951. A fairly large Israeli force failed to recapture the hill from the Syrians; it took two days and twenty-five Israeli casualties to drive the Syrians out. The battle exposed considerable weakness in the IDF. The Israeli-Syrian incidents subsided, but the military lessons had to be reckoned with.

Thus, the time between the early 1950s up to the formation of Unit 101 reflects a difficult period in the history of the IDF. The IDF's responses to the limited challenges it faced appeared to be either ineffective or outright defective. The formation of Unit 101 shifted the effectiveness balance considerably. The unit engaged in a large number of successful raids into Arab villages. Some of these raids were private projects rather than authorized military activities by the political decision makers (Morris 1993, 237–44), but most raids were authorized by the minister of defense. The Israeli government did not claim responsibility for these raids. Rather, it argued that these raids had been committed by local vigilantes who had responded to the repeated infiltrations by Palestinians. This process of Palestinian infiltrations and Israeli raids into Arab villages continued for the better part of 1952 and 1953.

What turned around Israeli strategy of retaliation—and with it the ex post facto strategic rationale of the policy—was a disastrous raid of Unit 101 on the village of Qibya near Jerusalem on October 15, 1953. In this raid, commanded by Sharon, the unit raided the village and blew up a large number of houses without inspecting whether there were people inside. It turned out that sixty civilians—women, children, and old people—were found among the ruins of the demolished houses the next morning (Morris 1993, 244–55; 2001, 278). Israel was confronted by a wave of criticism, including a vote to condemn it at the UN Security Council. The government denied involvement in the raid, claiming that this had been the act of renegade villagers taking revenge for previous infiltrations. However, nobody bought this fairy tale.

Sharon was not even reprimanded for this massacre, but the policy of retaliation shifted. Two important changes were applied. First, from that point on, the Israeli government assumed official responsibility for all retaliatory raids. Second, the reprisal raids were to be aimed at military installations and regime-related symbols rather than at civilian targets. Civilian Arab casualties continued to accumulate, but after Qibya these were largely unintended and residual casualties. This policy change is well reflected in an IDF directive following the Qibya fiasco.

A. Confrontation will be open and there will be no camouflaging or blurring the identity of the perpetrators [i.e., Israel would admit responsibility for the reprisal and no longer deny knowledge or point to anonymous vigilantes].

B. Arab villages will not be needlessly attacked, and injury to unarmed civilians, women and children will be avoided.

C. The principle of cleaving to the place and method of the [original

Arab] crime—is revoked. We shall hit the enemy where and how we choose, even if the objective does not exactly match the enemy's crime.

D. The speed of the operation [i.e., reprisal] is decisive—the reaction must be as quick as possible and as soon as possible after the crime.

E. The targets chosen [for attack] will be crucial objectives: military centers, [military] camps, police [stations], National Guard concentrations deep behind [enemy lines], the attack upon which will be as painful as possible.[5]

During 1954, however, both the number of reprisal raids and the number of Arab casualties in those raids declined compared to the previous two years. The same applies to the ratio of Arab to Israeli fatalities. This is due primarily to the restraining effect that Sharett—now the prime minister—had on Israeli reprisals. The decline in the number and severity of Israeli reprisals is not all that extreme, however, suggesting that Sharett's influence on the reprisals policy was rather limited. A number of reprisals and intelligence operations were authorized without Sharett's consent. In addition, latent—especially domestic—political considerations forced Sharett to authorize and approve several operations, even when he felt these operations did no actual good. Thus, changes in the general trend of escalation dominance were marginal at best (Morris 1993, 292–316; Sheffer 1996, 725–27).

Ben-Gurion's return to the Defense Ministry in February 1955 marked a fundamental shift in the limited use of force policy. The new policy focused the military-strategic functions of these raids independently of, or even in contradiction to, Israeli diplomacy. From this point on, Israeli raids increased in intensity, scope, and destructiveness, despite a decreased frequency. This trend started with the Gaza raid, the largest raid since 1948 in terms of the order of battle, the target—an Egyptian army camp hosting two companies—and the damage caused by the raid.

The principal aim of the reprisal raids—specifically those directed at Egypt—also changed during 1955 and 1956. Now the principal goal was to incite Egypt into escalating the conflict. As we saw in chapter 2, the "deterioration policy" launched by Dayan in early 1955 became the unwritten law of the IDF in the coming two years. Even though Ben-Gurion did not officially approve of this policy, the practice of reprisals during these years clearly suggests that the aim of the limited use of force was to provoke escalation. In 1955, the number of Israeli attacks was the lowest since 1948, but the number of Arabs—civilians and soldiers—

killed in these attacks was the highest since the 1948 war. This trend intensified in 1956, with the kill ratio going to 4.7 Arabs to 1 Israeli in 1955 and to 5.1 Arabs to one Israeli in 1956. This trick of using reprisals as an escalation trap essentially failed, because the Egyptians would not play the game. It did cause, however, considerable friction with the United Kingdom, especially following the Qalqilya raid of October 1956, just at a time when the Israelis had been trying to work out a trilateral agreement to launch the Sinai War.

With respect to Syria, the period from 1951 to 1955 was relatively quiet (Maoz and Mor 2002a, 182). However, in late 1953 Israel launched a project aimed at creating a series of canals and pipelines diverting water from Lake Kinneret to the southern part of Israel. Since the Syrians held that the eastern shore of the lake belonged to them, they viewed this as a blatant violation of the armistice agreement. As a result, Israel started to snare the Syrians by sending police and naval forces, masqueraded as fishermen, close to the eastern bank of the lake, drawing fire from Syrian positions. Shooting exchanges took place throughout 1954, reaching a peak with the December 1955 Israeli raid on a number of Syrian positions along the eastern bank of Lake Galilee. This raid was larger than the Gaza raid, involving nearly a whole brigade (Morris 1993, 364–65; M. Maoz 1995, 51–52). It also caused significant damage, resulting in fifty-four Syrian military fatalities, thirty prisoners, and an unknown number of civilian fatalities. This raid brought about severe condemnation of Israel by the international community. It may well have been a factor in the derailing of an arms deal with the United States.

2.2. Between Restraint and Brinkmanship: Reprisals Policy, 1957–67

The use of limited force to foster general deterrence diminished following the Sinai War. The stunning success of the IDF during the war established the Israeli military reputation to a degree that made deterrence through reprisals unnecessary. Studies that covered the limited use of force during this period (e.g., Yaniv 1987a, 98–99; Shimshoni 1988, 120–22; Kuperman 1999) suggest that retaliation was made unnecessary by the fact that infiltrations to Israel following the war came to a near complete stop. The facts are somewhat different. Over the period starting in 1957 and ending in 1965, the number of Arab infiltrations and attacks, while significantly lower than before, was far from zero. The number of Israeli casualties from these attacks and shootings was also quite significant (see fig. 7.1). At the same time, it was Israel's policy that

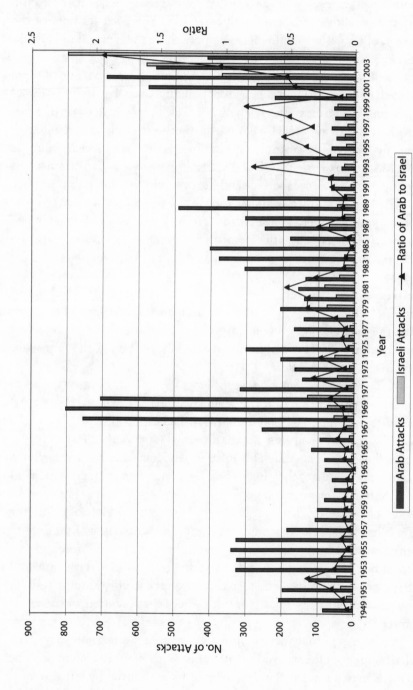

Fig. 7.1.   Number of Arab and Israeli limited military actions, 1949–2004

shifted during this period. The new, perhaps unintended, policy was guided by a philosophy of restraint. As we will see subsequently, the ratio of Arab fatalities to Israeli fatalities—which is a good measure of the notion of escalation dominance—dropped during this period to very low levels, resembling those of the 1949–51 period.

Two significant incidents took place during this period, one of them immediately suggesting the escalatory potential of change in the policy of restraint. The first was the Israeli raid on Tawfiq on January 31, 1960, following several minor clashes on the northern border. It resulted in roughly twelve Syrian soldier fatalities and seven Israeli fatalities (M. Maoz 1995, 70– 71; Bar Yaacov 1967, 185–90). This incident prompted Nasser's decision to send his troops to the Sinai, thus provoking the Rotem crisis (Bar Joseph 1996). The second raid was on the Syrian outpost of Nuqeib in March 1962. Israel's attack caused an unknown number of Syrian fatalities (probably around two dozen) and again resulted in considerable international criticism (M. Maoz 1995, 74; Bar Yaacov 1967, 228–30).

The period between 1957 and 1965 was the most tranquil era in Israel's history thus far. How can we account for this tranquility, given that the fundamental geopolitical realities did not change much following the Sinai War? Several factors account for the post–Sinai War status quo in the region.

1. *The strategic implications of the Sinai War.* The Sinai War carved two important markings in the regional strategic equation. First, it signaled to Egypt, Jordan, and Syria that Israel had both the will and the capacity to start an aggressive war if pushed far enough. Second, it rendered the Gaza Strip vulnerable to an Israeli attack, because the Egyptian main army was out of the Sinai. Thus, Egypt now had an interest in maintaining quiet along the Gaza border.

2. *The diplomatic repercussions of the Sinai War.* Prior to and during the Sinai War, Israel encountered significant international pressure to curb its use of force. The Soviet Union threatened to use force against Israel. Ben-Gurion came to understand the risks associated with the limited use of force, realizing that Israel had better exercise restraint vis-à-vis minor cases of infiltrations than risk a direct confrontation with a superpower.

3. *The shift in Arab political emphasis to inter-Arab processes.* The paradoxical result of the war was the rise of Nasser's status to a national Arab hero. Nasser was seen by many Arabs as a new Saladin by virtue of having confronted two major colonial powers and the Arabs' most hated

enemy and having presumably defeated them. Consequently, Nasser shifted his attention to inter-Arab politics, focusing his efforts on subverting and overthrowing the conservative Arab regimes in Iraq, Jordan, and Lebanon. This led to a series of struggles between Nasser and the conservative leaders in those states (Kerr 1971; Sela 1998, 57–74; Nutting 1972, 271–93; Hussein 1962, 151–96; Bukay 1993). The Israeli-Palestinian issue remained high on the rhetorical agenda of Arab leaders, but it was no longer a unifying device, because Nasser was increasingly prudent in his dealing with Israel.

4. *Arab restraint.* The de facto demilitarization of the Sinai led to significant tightening of the grip over the Palestinians in the Gaza Strip by the Egyptian police. Jordan also learned the lessons of the war and imposed severe restrictions on the Palestinians in the West Bank. The Syrians maintained their restraint along the border with Israel. All these things came together to reduce Arab incentives to challenge Israel militarily. In the absence of such challenges, even if Israel were interested in using limited force to provoke escalation, it would have been difficult to implement such a strategy.

But this period of tranquility did not last long. The escalation was affected by two important turning points in Arab-Israeli relations. One was the establishment of the PLO in the Cairo Arab summit of January 1964 (Morris 2001, 364). Second, the Israeli launching of their Kinneret-Negev irrigation project prompted the Syrians to start a project aimed at the diversion of the headways of the Jordan River in order to deny Israel the ability to divert the Lake Kinneret waters (Maoz and Mor 2002a, 185; M. Maoz 1995, 71–74).

The reescalation of limited warfare had, as we saw in chapter 3, domestic underpinnings. The challenges to Israel's security posed by the Fatah infiltrations and by the diversion project were minor in nature. Yet, they manifested themselves during a period of intense political competition between the Mapai and RAFI Parties. As was the case in the mid-1950s, Israel used limited warfare to deal with the threat to divert the Jordan River headways, seeking to avoid major escalation. By 1965, the Al Fatah organization started to launch a new round of infiltrations to Israel, consisting mainly of acts of sabotage and some mining and resulting in few Israeli casualties. There was no apparent pressure on the government to escalate, because the situation on the Egyptian border offered a relative sense of security. By March 1966, the diversion problem was removed. The repeated shelling of the diversion equipment by the Israelis, the lack of Arab financial and military support of this project, and the domestic political upheaval following the February 1966 military coup of the Ba'ath officers in Damascus combined to convince the Syrians of the futility of the project.

However, by then Israeli military strategists began to like the cat-and-mouse game with the Syrians. The purpose of this strategy was not clear, principally because nobody bothered to document the thinking in the IDF at that time and because the military archives of this period had not yet been opened. The rationale behind the provoked infringements into the DMZs on the Israeli-Syrian border may well have been strategic: this was a low-risk high-benefit strategy designed to foster Israel's image of resolve and determination, something Israeli strategists believed would foster Israel's general deterrence posture.

If this was the case, then the strategy backfired. The escalation process that resulted from this approach formed a yellow brick road toward the crisis that gave birth to the Six Day War. In contrast to the pre–Sinai War period, this process was one of unintended escalation (Maoz 1982b). Neither Israeli military strategists nor Israeli political leaders were aware of the slippery slope that they had paved with their policy of reprisals. Ironically, the people who were most concerned about the dangerous implications of this policy were the two RAFI leaders—Ben-Gurion and Dayan—the activists of the 1950s (e.g., Weizman 1975, 254). But they could not offer a clearly defined alternative strategy. And even if they did, it is likely that the government would have done just the opposite, for political spite.

Were it only for the limited border war, the May–June 1967 crisis would probably not have erupted. What helped bring about the crisis was the vertical and verbal escalation that went along with it. Since early 1966, Israel started using its air force with greater frequency in limited operations. It initiated many overflights over Syrian territory as part of a general pattern of demonstration of resolve and capability (Weizman 1975, 254). These overflights were bound to end up in aerial clashes, once the Syrians sent planes to intercept the Israeli jets. In the fall of 1966, Israel shot down a total of four Syrian Migs (two Mig-19 and two Mig-21) planes. During the Samu raid of November 1966, the IAF shot down two Jordanian Hunters. The biggest clash, however, was the April 4, 1967, dogfight. This raid was a cleverly laid aerial ambush. The Israelis sent a pair of planes as a decoy, and when the Syrians sent a squadron to intercept them, the Mirages that had been waiting in the distance went into action. By the end of the battle, six Syrian Mig-21 jets were shot down.

Alongside this new type of limited warfare, there were quite a few verbal threats by Rabin and Eban. These threats could not have been interpreted by the Syrians as anything other than an Israeli intent at escalating the limited war to an all-out war aimed at overthrowing the Ba'ath regime in Damascus. Here, too, Israeli intent was to compel Syria into stopping its support of the Fatah. Yet, this escalated into a crisis that ended in a major war.

2.3. Limited Warfare alongside and between Wars, 1967–73

Unlike the Sinai War, the Six Day War did not have a calming effect on the Arab-Israeli conflict. On the contrary, the decisive Israeli victory in the war served to strengthen Arab resolve to fight the Israelis. As we saw in chapter 5, it did not take long for the Egyptians to renew hostilities along the Suez Canal. The Syrians also started, as of July 1, 1967, to fire at Israeli posts along the newly established border. The Hashemite regime in Jordan took its defeat quietly, but the Palestinians within Jordan—now confronted with a new wave of refugees from the West Bank— did not.[6] On June 12, the heads of the Palestinian organizations met in Damascus and decided to start an intensive guerrilla campaign against the Israelis (Morris 2001, 365; Tessler 1994, 423).

Yassir Arafat, the leader of Al Fatah, and a few of his associates infiltrated into the West Bank in an effort to organize popular resistance to the Israeli occupation (Tessler 1994, 423–24). The idea was to put military pressure on the Israelis, while minimizing the risk of Israeli reprisals against Arab states, which might turn the Arab states against the Palestinian cause. The attempt to organize popular resistance from within the occupied territories seemed the preferred strategy from this perspective (Morris 2001, 365; Hart 1989, 203–13; Sayigh 1997, 155–58).

Arafat and his men soon learned that the population, though supportive of the Fatah, was not willing to run the risk of confrontation with the Israelis. There was also sudden prosperity in the occupied territories, due to Israeli tourism and trade. There were a number of violent acts against Israelis emanating from the occupied territories, but many of them were ineffective (Morris 2001, 366). More important, the local population did not rise against the occupiers. As time went by, Israeli security forces began to arrest the Fatah infiltrators, putting increased pressure on Arafat (Gazit 1999, 63–64; Mishal 1986, 6–8).

The Palestinian resistance organizations did make significant strides outside the occupied territories, however. First, the various organizations managed to recruit hundreds of volunteers in the refugee camps in Jordan, Syria, and Lebanon. Israeli policy toward the territories was not well defined in the initial months after the war.[7] Hence, it took several months before the Defense Ministry developed a clear policy for managing the occupied territories. Israel's new border with Jordan was not properly guarded. This made it possible to move people and weapons secretly from the East Bank to the West Bank of the Jordan River. The Palestinian organizations started sending into the occupied territories armed squads to attack military and civilian posts. Many of these attacks were aborted or caused only property damage. The number of Israeli casualties due to Palestinian violent attacks in 1967 was less than two dozen (see fig. 7.2). Nevertheless, these organizational and operational activities served to develop both the resolve and the operational competence of the Palestinian organizations and paved the way to other and more daring operations in the following year.

In 1968, the Palestinians switched to guerrilla operations, infiltrations from Jordan through the Jordan Valley and the Bet-Sh'an Valley and, to a lesser extent, from the Israeli-Lebanese border. The damage to Israel was substantial. In 1968, a total of 601 attacks on Israeli targets were committed by Palestinians, out of a total of 754 violent attacks directed at Israel. These resulted in a total of 182 fatalities out of a total of 279 Israeli fatalities in violent clashes. This was a very heavy toll by any standard. The IDF saw with growing concern the development of training and launching bases for Palestinian guerrillas in Jordan and Syria.

The beginning of 1968 also witnessed the renewal of artillery exchanges with Jordan. On February 14–15 a major artillery duel erupted along the entire Israeli-Jordanian border. A hastily mediated cease-fire went into effect on February 16, but the Israeli shelling drove out thousands of villagers in the Ghor area (across the river from the Bet Sh'an Valley).

As the number of infiltrations grew and as Israeli fatalities began to mount, Israel decided to return to its policy of military reprisals. This time it had clear targets—Palestinian bases in Jordan and Syria. On March 21, 1968, the IDF launched a major raid on the village of Karameh in Jordan, the site of the largest Palestinian guerrilla base in Jordan and the headquarters of Arafat and Abu Ayad. The Palestinians had been given advance warning of the impending Israeli raid (Morris 2001, 368–69; Abu Iyad 1983, 95–96). The Fatah leaders decided to stand up and fight, and so did the Jordanian Legion. The Israeli force, three brigade battle groups, met fierce resistance. The IDF lost 33 soldiers, and 161 soldiers were wounded. Over twenty tanks were hit. The Palestinians suffered 151

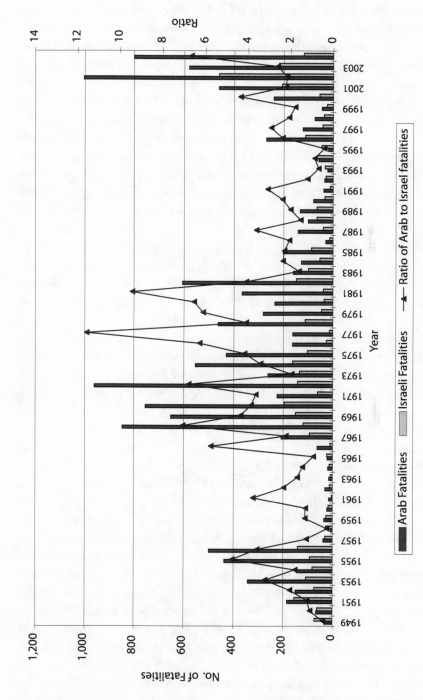

Fig. 7.2. Arab and Israeli fatalities in limited engagements, 1949–2004

fatalities, and 141 guerrillas were captured by the Israelis. The Jordanian army suffered 84 dead and 250 wounded. Two Jordanian jets were shot down by the IAF (Morris 2001, 369; Michelson 1984).

As was the case with the battle of Ras el Ush in the Suez Canal Zone, the Karameh clash—although decided in favor of the IDF—served as a major morale-boosting event for the Palestinian resistance. The Palestinians fought well against a large Israeli force. The Israeli withdrawal was hasty, and this was portrayed by the Palestinians as a major victory, the first victory of a Palestinian force against the Zionists, and a turning point in the Palestinian struggle (Tessler 1994, 425–26; Sayigh 1997, 179). This battle facilitated the recruitment of young refugees to the guerrilla organizations. It also led to initial contacts between Palestinian and European terrorist groups (Karmon 1996). The year 1968 saw also a new trend in the Palestinian tactics. In July 1968, an El Al civilian plane was hijacked by the Palestinian Front for the Liberation of Palestine (PFLP) to Algiers. The Algerian authorities agreed to free the Israeli passengers in exchange for Israeli release of fifteen Palestinian prisoners (Morris 2001, 378). This started a wave of Palestinian hijacking of planes, attacks on Israeli embassies, and attacks on targets abroad.

Israeli response to this new assortment of threats was twofold. Defensively, the IDF instituted a system of ambushes along the border in an attempt to intercept the infiltrators. It also formed a number of units designed to deal with terror attacks in population centers. The Israeli General Secret Service (GSS) placed airborne marshals on the El Al planes. These marshals proved quite effective in foiling subsequent attacks on Israel's civilian carrier. Over time, however, the number of people engaged in antiterrorist activity in Israel began to mount, reaching a figure of about forty-four thousand by the mid-1970s, or roughly 1.3 percent of Israel's population at the time (Alon 1980).

Offensively, Israel continued to rely on the policy of reprisals. The implementation of this policy was complicated, however, by a number of factors. First, Israel had to be careful not to put too much pressure on the Hashemite regime in Jordan by initiating direct confrontations with the legion. Since 1968 Hussein had been struggling to maintain some form of control amid the expansion of the guerrilla activity in Jordan. The Palestinian organizations established an increasingly arrogant presence in Jordan (Astorino-Courtois 1998; Astorino 1994). Hussein's political standing became increasingly fragile. Israeli decision makers did not want to add to Hussein's problems by hitting major regime installations. Second, Israeli decision makers saw Hussein as a possible partner for peace negotiations over the West Bank. In a number of secret meetings between Israeli officials and King Hussein between December 1967 and late 1968 Hussein and his Israeli counterparts discussed various options for a peace settlement between Israel and Jordan (Shlaim 2000, 261–64). Hitting the regime would have derailed this line of communication. Third, by the second half of 1968, the situation along the Suez Canal began deteriorating and diverted the Israeli attention to the southern front.

Given these constraints, the offensive Israeli response was restricted primarily to small-scale raids and numerous ambushes on the East Bank of the Jordan River. The principal objective of the IDF was to engage the would-be infiltrators before they crossed the border. These ambushes were relatively ineffective, as they did not do much to reduce the rate of infiltrations from Jordan to the West Bank. Israel was saved from the infiltrations emanating from Jordan by the Palestinian actions within Jordan rather than by the effectiveness of its antiguerrilla warfare. During 1969 and 1970, the Palestinians established a state within a state in Jordan. Hussein felt powerless to resist the growing Palestinian presence and the increased boldness of their challenge to the stability of the Hashemite regime (Astorino 1994). In September 1970 PFLP terrorists hijacked three airplanes, landing them at the Irbid airport in northern Jordan. The passengers were released, but the terrorists blew up the planes amid the cameras of all the major television networks. This was too much for the king. He ordered his armed forces to confront the PLO. In the civil war that ensued,[8] the Hashemite regime reestablished its complete control over the country, leading to a total ban on infiltrations from Jordan into the West Bank. The PLO guerrillas tried several times to defy this ban, but again the legion hit hard against the Palestinian guerrillas, eliminating completely any institutional and terrorist Palestinian activity in Jordan. The PLO moved its bases to Lebanon. Once again, it was not so much Israeli strategy of counterterrorism but rather the overextension of the PLO's operations inside Jordan that brought about an end to infiltrations from Jordan. This, of course, made Israeli retaliation against Jordanian targets unnecessary.

Israeli responses to the PLO infiltrations from Jordanian territory suggest some interesting points. First, the strategy employed vis-à-vis Jordan represents an exception in terms of the Israeli modus operandi. Israeli actions were either proportionate or even subproportionate to the challenge posed by the terrorists. These practices were exceptional also in that Israel returned to its pre-1953 focus of trying to hit the terrorists rather than the regime that harbored them. Third, whereas Israeli commando raids in Egypt and Syria went deep into the territory of the enemy states, Israeli raids in Jordan stayed close to the border. This was due chiefly to political reasons rather than to military considerations. Fourth, the principal Israeli response to the terrorist challenge emanating from Jordan was defensive rather than offensive. Finally, Israel persisted in these self-imposed restraints despite the increase in the frequency and severity of terrorist infiltrations into the West Bank.

When confronted by infiltrations and limited warfare from Syria, Israel activated both its artillery and air force to attack terrorist bases in Syria. The number and scope of exchanges were, by and large, limited, as Syria kept—generally speaking—a low profile during the Israeli-Egyptian War of Attrition. There were, however, some notable exceptions. In some cases (e.g., on April 3 and June 24, 1970), the artillery clashes resulted in dozens of casualties to the Syrians. On September 8, 1972, a long way into the cease-fire, Israel conducted a major raid deep into Syrian territory using infantry and armored vehicles, destroying a number of PLO and Al Saiqa bases. This battle exacted over two hundred Arab fatalities, half of them Syrian soldiers. Here, Israeli actions followed once again the basic modus operandi of escalation dominance through excessive use of force.

Starting in 1968 Israel confronted terrorism against Israeli targets abroad. Here, too, the initial reaction was primarily defensive. Yet, the attack on the Israeli athletes during the 1972 Olympic Games in Munich, which resulted in the slaying of eleven Israeli athletes, represents a turning point in Israeli strategy vis-à-vis terrorist attacks. Golda Meir, the Israeli prime minister, ordered the Mossad to find and assassinate the leaders of the terrorist organizations everywhere around the world. A series of killings occurred—most of them in Europe and most of them suspected PLO or PLFP terrorists. Twice during this period, once in 1968 and once in April 1973, Israeli special forces raided Beirut, the Lebanese capital. The target of the first raid (December 26, 1968) was the Beirut airport, where the IDF blew up several planes in retaliation for the hijacking of Israeli planes. The second raid was an attack on PFLP headquarters in Beirut in April 1973, where IDF soldiers killed several high-ranking PFLP commanders (Black and Morris 1991, 274–75).

There are several problems with the application of the logic of disproportionality to the struggle against terrorism. First, the targets were elusive. Second, in many cases, they had to be chased and eliminated in friendly states, leading to legal and other complications with the local authorities. The major example of that was the misguided assassination of

Ahmad Bushiki, a Palestinian waiter in the Norwegian town of Lille-hammer, by a group of Mossad operatives. This was a clear case of mis-taken identity, as the Mossad agents intended to assassinate Hassan Salamah, a major figure in the Black September terrorist organization. The group of Mossad agents was captured by the Norwegian authorities and put on trial (Melman and Raviv 1989, 208–11; Black and Morris 1991, 275–77). Third, this form of warfare absolved the Arab states from responsibility for the terrorist acts, because many of these acts were car-ried out in Europe, so the Arab states could make a strong case of plausi-ble deniability.

Overall, even if we exclude the casualties due to the War of Attrition (but we include the actions and casualties associated with the military clashes in Jordan, Syria, and Lebanon), there was a dramatic rise in the number of incidents of limited engagements (including terrorist acts abroad). The number of Israeli casualties due to limited warfare during the 1967–73 period also rose dramatically. The number of Israeli military operations during this period also rose to unprecedented levels. So did the ratio of Arab to Israeli fatalities. This indicates a strong emphasis—dur-ing a time of sustained warfare along all three fronts, as well as the new front of international terrorism—on escalation dominance. The hope that this strategy would deter terrorism was only partly fulfilled, as we will see in the next section.

2.4. The Lebanon Buildup, 1974–82

The Jordanian civil war of 1970 led to de facto elimination of all PLO operations in Jordan. The Palestinian guerrillas moved to Lebanon, with Beirut serving as the headquarters. The major focus of Israeli-Palestinian clashes shifted to the Israeli-Lebanese border.[9] Since I discussed this period at length in the previous chapter, I will not elaborate on it here. But in addition to the clashes along the Lebanese border, Palestinian attacks on Israelis abroad continued, and so did Palestinian efforts to hijack airplanes. In June 1976, a joint operation of the Wadi'ah Haddad faction and the Baader-Meinhoff German terrorist group resulted in the hijacking of an Air France plane en route from Tel Aviv to Paris. Over 160 passengers were on board. The hijackers eventually landed the plane in Entebbe, Uganda. After some negotiations, the IDF launched a daring rescue operation that liberated virtually all of the hostages (Maoz 1981). This raid practically put an end to attempts to hijack planes from or to Israel.

Starting in 1974, Israel developed a new approach to dealing with terrorist attacks from Lebanon. It supported the activity of a local militia made up of Christian Maronites, led by a renegade major in the Lebanese army, Sa'ad Haddad. Israel provided this militia with weapons, trained its people, and even supported it financially. This practice continued after the Lebanon War and throughout the extended Israeli stay in Southern Lebanon. For a long time it was evident that the reliance on a proxy to deal with the PLO or the Hizballah did not work, but nobody in Israel paid attention to the facts.

The escalation in Lebanon over the period 1979–82, as we saw in chapter 6, was due primarily to the fundamental change of agenda of the Israeli government. The PLO presence in southern Lebanon, and its gradual conversion from a loose conglomerate of terrorist and guerrilla groups into a semiconventional army, was actually a positive development for the IDF. Instead of dealing with an elusive guerrilla or terrorist organization, the IDF had identifiable targets if it came to a military confrontation. By August 1981, with the appointment of Sharon to the defense minister's post, the plan of a head-on confrontation started taking shape.

In contrast to Dayan's policy of gradual deterioration in 1955, however, Begin, Sharon, and Eitan did not make this an explicit policy. Rather, they encouraged the IDF and the Haddad militia to launch attacks against the PLO in southern Lebanon in a manner that would provoke them into firing on cities and settlements in northern Israel. Even before his entry into office, Sharon had influenced Begin into using limited force as an escalatory policy. The clear objective was to "cause controlled escalation." After the July 1981 clash with the PLO, Eitan said to his officers: "there is no escape from war; war will break out in the north within six months" (Schiff and Yaari 1984, 35).

The cease-fire agreement that was negotiated by Philip Habib in July 1981 put a seeming damper on the plan to provoke the PLO into a situation that would provide Israel with a pretext for a full-scale war. In order to overcome this hurdle, Sharon and Begin sought to reinterpret the cease-fire agreement in a manner that would make it impossible for the PLO to comply with it, even if it wanted to. They claimed that the cease-fire required the PLO to stop all violent activity against Israel, not just attacks on Israel from the Lebanon border. This meant that any incident in the occupied territories or against Israeli targets abroad would be interpreted as a casus belli. Even if the PLO could control members of the organizations belonging to it—a dubious proposition in itself—it had no way of controlling splinter organizations.

The only question then was one of appropriate timing. Indeed, when on June 3, 1982, terrorists from the Abu Nidal splinter organization shot the Israeli ambassador to England, Begin gave the green light to a massive artillery and air barrage against PLO positions in southern Lebanon. Once the PLO—as expected—responded by shelling Israeli villages in the north, the order was given to the IDF to enter Lebanon. This was no longer a limited use of force strategy. Rather, this war was designed— among other objectives of the war—to provide a comprehensive treatment to the problem of terrorism and infiltrations by physically destroying the entire organization that was behind such acts. By launching this attack, Israel opened a Pandora's box that would haunt it for years to come.

2.5. The Lebanon Experience, 1982–2000

In Lebanon, Israel confronted three new and interrelated challenges: guerrilla warfare in an occupied country, suicide bombings, and Islamic fundamentalist terrorism. All these challenges were to be transferred to the Palestinian-Israeli struggle in the occupied territories to the very present.

The first of these challenges characterized most of the fighting in Lebanon from the end of the war with the expulsion of the PLO from Beirut to the Israeli withdrawal from southern Lebanon in May 2000. Israeli forces in Lebanon discovered that the task of controlling an occupied country against the will of its people was a rather costly venture. In the period from June 6 to September 6, 1982—the end of the PLO withdrawal from Beirut—roughly 200 IDF soldiers were killed in action. From September 1982 to September 1983—when Begin decided to resign and go into forced retirement—another 100 Israeli soldiers were killed in Lebanon. By June 1985, when the Israelis withdrew to the southern Lebanon security zone, the death toll was 666 Israelis (Maoz 1990b, 290). By May 2000, the death toll rose to nearly 1,000 Israelis.

The key Israeli problem in controlling Lebanon was not dealing with the remnants of the PLO guerrillas. Rather, it was dealing with new groups in Lebanese politics. These groups were threatened by the Israeli-Christian alliance in Lebanon even more than they had been by the Palestinians (Maoz 1989, 256–60; 1990b, 239–43). As we saw in chapter 6, Israel faced a major problem in the Shouf Mountains area, finding itself in the middle of a struggle between the Druzes and the Muslims. After the Israeli withdrawal to the Awali River in 1983, its major problem became the newly founded Hizballah organization.

This new militia, unlike the existing semisecular Shi'ite militia Amal, was influenced by the rise of the Islamic republic in Iran and by Ayatola Khomeini's preaching. The Hizballah (Party of God) was composed of radical Islamic elements who adopted the extreme anti-Israeli rhetoric that started coming out of Iran (Jaber 1997; Shapira 2000). Despite its hostile public demeanor, the Hizballah was very careful to aim its attacks at Israeli soldiers and at the Southern Lebanese Army (SLA), Israel's proxy. The Hizballah adopted an explicit policy of retaliating to Israeli killings of Lebanese civilians by firing Katyusah rockets and mortar shells at Israeli villages in the north, but it almost never initiated an unprovoked attack across the border.

The Israeli-Hizballah struggle in Lebanon can be divided into four distinct phases. The first phase is the formative phase from June 1982 to July 1985. The second phase is the security regime phase, which lasted from June 1985 to February 1992, with the Israeli assassination of Hizballah's leader, Sheikh Abbas Mussawi. The third stage is the stage of escalation and includes the period from 1992 to the Israeli withdrawal from the security zone in southern Lebanon in May 2000. The fourth stage is the postwithdrawal stage and extends from May 2000 to the present.

The formative stage was characterized by tight cooperation between the Hizballah, an embryonic organization with undefined character, and Syrian intelligence, at that time bent on driving the Israelis and the U.S. marines out of Lebanon. One of the Hizballah key operators at the time, Imad Murniyah, is said to have been among the planners of the suicide bombing of the U.S. marine headquarters in Beirut in October 1983. Hizballah was also behind the attack on the U.S. embassy annex in Beirut in September 1983. Both of these operations were attributed to Syrian intelligence.

Hizballah's operations in southern Lebanon included ambushes of Israeli buses and trucks carrying soldiers in and out of Lebanon, attacks on isolated posts, and—eventually—some large-scale suicide bombings on IDF headquarters in Sidon in 1983 and on the Israeli border guard headquarters in Tyre in 1984. The diffuse structure of the organization and the elusive character of its operatives made it difficult for the IDF to counter its activities. Israel discounted the significance of the Hizballah activities initially. However, as IDF casualties began to mount, especially after the withdrawal from the Beirut area, the IDF started paying attention to this organization.

Israeli withdrawal into the security zone in southern Lebanon in July 1985 appeared, however, to have been successful. The fear of Katyusha attacks on Israeli towns and villages did not materialize. A security regime of sorts seems to have formed in southern Lebanon. The Hizballah and Amal focused their attacks on the Israeli contingent in the security zone and on the SLA militia. The number of Israeli casualties over the 1986–92 period was relatively small, averaging ten soldiers per year over the 1986–91 period. The Hizballah launched sporadic attacks on the IDF but focused most of its attacks on the SLA. The IDF's small contingent in the security zone focused mostly on training, maintaining, and supplying the SLA. Every day, thousands of Lebanese workers crossed the border to work in Israel. While the situation was not absent of violence, the violence was limited as long as all sides played by the rules. The outbreak of the intifada in December 1987 brought about a wave of solidarity attacks by the Hizballah, which accounts for the sharp rise in Israeli casualties in southern Lebanon during 1988, but the situation stabilized again in 1989 through 1991.

The Israeli government, however, became gradually entrapped in its own propaganda. The national unity government of hard-liner Yitzhak Shamir, faced with the Palestinian intifada, may have wanted to divert attention from the Palestinian scene by portraying Hizballah as an arch-enemy and magnifying the threat it posed to Israel. Pressed into early elections, Shamir authorized the assassination of Hizballah's secretary-general, Abbas Mussawi (who incidentally had been the architect of the modus vivendi regime in southern Lebanon). The assassination of Mussawi had three immediate effects on the Hizballah. First, Mussawi was replaced by the far more extremist Hassan Nasrallah, who advocated a more militant policy toward the Israeli presence in the security zone and also was not—unlike his predecessor—aversive to terrorist acts. Second, the Hizballah stepped up its activity in the security zone, resuming the practice of firing across the international border line. The latter practice, however, was limited to what the Hizballah called retaliatory strikes for Israel's killing of Lebanese civilians. Third, the new Hizballah did not limit its reprisals to Lebanese soil. It moved to engage in international terrorism. It took less than a month for Hizballah to strike back hard at Israel. On March 17, 1992, a car bomb exploded in front of the Israeli embassy building in Buenos Aires, killing 29 people (of whom four were Israelis) and wounding 242 people. The security regime in Lebanon—at least in its existing form—collapsed. And it was Israel's doing that brought about this collapse.

From that point on, Hizballah stepped up its operations in Lebanon, targeting both Israeli forces and the SLA. The Israeli death toll jumped again to 26 in 1992, averaging over 20 fatalities a year (with a peak of 43 fatalities in 1997) through May 2000.

Israel launched two large-scale operations that entailed heavy air and artillery attacks on the Hizballah area in southern Lebanon within and north of the security zone. The first operation, Operation Accountability, was launched on July 25, 1993, as a result of escalating hostilities in southern Lebanon. In this operation, the IAF used blanket bombing on villages and towns in southern Lebanon. Thousands of Lebanese citizens fled the south toward Beirut. The purpose of the operation was yet again to put pressure on the civilian population to dispose of the Hizballah activities in the south. The operation was a total failure. The Hizballah responded by a barrage of Katyusha fire into northern Israel. Over fifty Katyusha rockets landed in Kiryat Shmona and other Israeli settlements. Israel experienced also a flood of refugees from its northern cities to the south, and the population that stayed in the northern cities spent six straight days in shelters. After six days of fighting, the United States arranged for a cease-fire. Nothing had changed on the ground except for general international condemnation of Israel's use of the civilian population of southern Lebanon as hostages.

The second operation, Operation Grapes of Wrath of April 1996, was a rerun of Operation Accountability, only on a larger scale. Again the IAF used blanket bombing of villages, and the Israeli artillery pounded both areas within the security zone and Shiite villages and towns north of the security zone. The images of thousands of refugees fleeing north repeated itself. There were two differences, however. First, the Hizballah was more ready for this kind of operation than it had been three years earlier. It responded with a barrage of over six hundred Katyusha rockets on northern Israel. Israel again experienced the flood of refugees from its northern cities to the south. Second, and more devastating, at the height of the operation, Israeli artillery hit a shelter in Kafar Qana, a village north of the security zone. Over one hundred women, children, and other civilians were killed. This brought about explicit condemnation of Israel in the UN Security Council. Again the United States intervened, and Secretary of State Warren Christopher, in sustained shuttle diplomacy between Damascus and Jerusalem, brought about an agreement among Israel, Syria, and the Hizballah. This agreement, known as the "Grapes of Wrath Understanding," ironically legitimized Hizballah operations against the IDF in the security zone. At the same time, it disallowed hitting civilian targets. However, the clause in these understandings allowing each side to realize its right for self-defense enabled each side to deviate from this principle in retaliation for similar action by the other side.[10] So each side agreed to let its civilian population become hostage to whims and collateral hits on the other side's civilian population. The understandings also established a five-party monitoring group composed of France, the United States, Syria, Lebanon, and Israel. Both Israel and the Hizballah have violated the agreement on a fairly regular basis. From May 1996 to May 2000, over 500 Lebanese civilians and roughly 120 Israelis were killed in the fighting.

The two operations were motivated as much by domestic considerations as by security calculations. In 1993, Israel was engaged in parallel negotiations with the PLO and Syria, and— while the Rabin government displayed considerable flexibility on both tracks—there was a sense that the negotiations were stalemated. The Rabin government also faced considerable criticism from the right wing for its flexibility vis-à-vis Syria. In December 1992, Israel expelled four hundred Palestinians suspected as Hamas activists to southern Lebanon and confronted significant international as well as domestic criticism for blanket violations of human rights. A show of force was seen as a way to ward off domestic criticism of government policy. In February 1966, Shimon Peres, who succeeded Rabin after the latter was assassinated in November 1995, called for early election. In February and March, a wave of suicide bombings inside the cities of Tel Aviv and Jerusalem left over seventy Israelis dead. Peres's lead over his opponent, Benjamin Netanyahu, in the polls had been shrinking rapidly. Peres reasoned that there was nothing like a decisive show of force against the Hizballah to improve his domestic popularity. Here, too, the operation backfired, as Peres lost the May 1996 election by a narrow margin.

As we saw in chapter 6, the IDF—most significantly the intelligence community—was the chief opponent of the notion of unilateral withdrawal. It repeatedly warned that a unilateral withdrawal—not in the context of a peace agreement with Syria and Lebanon—would result in repeated harassment of northern Israel by the Hizballah. When some analysts (myself included)[11] argued that the IDF intelligence not only was off the track on this issue but also had a vested interest in generating gloomy assessments that had no real foundation, the IDF intelligence unleashed former and present officials to denounce publicly these accusations.[12] It has been reported to me that when Ehud Barak, doubling as the prime minister and defense minister, addressed the IDF general staff about his commitment to unilateral withdrawal from Lebanon by June 2000, only two generals expressed support for this policy. All others expressed various degrees of reservation with this policy.[13]

Since the unilateral withdrawal from Lebanon, there have been several incidents between Hizballah and the IDF (Sobelman 2003, 90–91). None of these incidents entailed firing at civilian population centers. Most of these incidents involved firing at IDF positions in the Shab'ah area, an area contested by the Hizballah to belong to Lebanon, or anti-aircraft firing at Israeli jets that violated Lebanese airspace (Sobelman 2003, 64–65).

2.6. The Occupied Territories and the First Intifada, 1973–93

The situation in the occupied territories was relatively quiet over the period of 1973–87. Occasional terrorist attacks, clashes between Jewish settlers and Palestinians, and several incidents of widespread riots that lasted several days—especially in the West Bank—were the typical events in the occupied territories. The PLO and other Palestinian organizations, however, continued their efforts to build and solidify their bases of support in the occupied territories. As a preventive measure, the Israeli government allowed for municipal elections in 1976 in the hope that these elections would provide legitimacy to the pro-Jordan Palestinian groups. The result flew in the face of the Israeli establishment: the election resulted in a resounding victory of the PLO supporters (see chap. 10). This complicated the political task of managing the occupation, but—surprisingly perhaps—it did not raise significantly the level of popular or armed resistance by the Palestinians. Jordan continued to pay the salaries of most public officials in the occupied territories.

In the late 1970s, however, a new phenomenon complicated matters in the occupied territories: a Jewish underground organization was formed. Composed of radical settlers, the Jewish underground launched a series of attacks on Palestinians, presumably in retaliation for Palestinian attacks on Israelis. On June 2, 1979, a series of explosions in the cars of West Bank mayors left several of them maimed. Others were warned by the Israeli security forces in time, thus preventing a greater tragedy. Several days later, a hand grenade was thrown into a Palestinian crowd near a school in Hebron, wounding several people. There were several isolated incidents of shooting and destruction and burning of Palestinian stores over the period of 1980–83.

The scope, magnitude, and frequency of the Jewish underground operations rose considerably after the Lebanon War. On July 26, 1983, a group of men wearing ski masks entered the Islamic Seminary in Hebron and fired at students in the central yard. Three Palestinians were killed and thirty-three were wounded. On January 29, 1984, an alert Palestinian guard on the Temple Mount surprised some suspects who were laying explosives next to the Omar and Al Aqsa mosques. A catastrophe of major proportions was narrowly averted. On March 4, shots fired on a Palestinian bus near Ramallah resulted in eight wounded. Only after the Jerusalem police foiled a simultaneous set of explosions in a number of Palestinian buses in east Jerusalem during the busiest day of the week did the GSS break up the underground and arrest its leaders, all of them public figures and lobbyists for the Jewish settler movement in the occupied territories.

The Israeli government strongly denounced these actions, but it took the GSS five years to break up the Jewish underground and to capture its main operators. Shlomo Gazit, a former IDF coordinator of Israeli activities in the occupied territories, writes about the reason for this lenience of the Israeli security forces.

> The significant delay in exposing and capturing the [Jewish] underground stemmed from the different "rules of the game" [compared to the rules of conduct toward Palestinian suspects]. This time, the GSS was required to investigate while following the Israeli criminal code. It was not possible to apply the [British] Mandate Defence Emergency Regulations of 1945 (which had been applied effectively against Palestinians suspects). In its efforts to expose members of the Jewish underground, no administrative arrests were allowed, the interment of suspects and their isolation for fourteen days was prohibited, nor was there permission to apply any other type of pressure on suspects, or other types of administrative measures (such as demolition of houses).
>
> Since the beginning of the investigation [in 1979], the GSS knew where to look for members of the underground. However, in the absence of unequivocal proof that could lead to indictments, it was not possible to arrest them. The chance of acquiring such proof depended on luck and on time. (Gazit 1999, 100)[14]

Needless to say, all the members of the Jewish underground who had been found guilty of murder and sentenced were quickly pardoned and released after short prison terms.

A significant change during this period concerned the absence of infiltrations into Israeli territory from its Arab neighbors. Israeli presence in Lebanon as well as the strict policy of Egypt, Syria, and Jordan of disallowing terrorist activity from their territory reduced the number of infiltrations to near zero. This shifted the main occupation of the IDF to policing the occupied territories and to guarding the new settlements that were being built at an accelerated rate with the active encouragement of the Likud government.

The PLO was rebuilding itself in Tunis, so its immediate influence inside the occupied territories hinged more on the loyalty of the local elites than on grass-roots activity. The Israeli politicians and the IDF were engaged in their traditional "divide and rule" policy, pitting one Palestinian political faction against the other. By 1982 the autonomy negotiations aimed at an interim settlement in the occupied territories were suspended (see chap. 10). Between 1982 and 1985, there was no meaningful effort at resolving the Israeli-Palestinian conflict.

The Likud government intensified the practices devised in the late 1960s for dealing with suspected terrorists and their supporters (Maoz 1985; Gazit 1999, 88–120). Israel imposed systematically the Defence Emergency Regulations (DER), arresting hundreds of Palestinians suspected as terrorists' supporters, detaining them without trial for years, and deporting many others. It used collective punishments, including the demolition of houses of suspected terrorists, internal deportations, and land expropriation for the purpose of establishing settlements.

The eviction of the PLO from Lebanon began to develop a growing level of grass-roots frustration, especially among younger Palestinians in the occupied territories. The Peres-Hussein London agreement was as threatening to the Palestinians as it was to the Likud Party. As the PLO leadership in Tunis scrambled for various forms of international support, the Hamas activists were beginning to build their support base in the occupied territories through charity and educational work, mostly with victims of the Israeli occupation (Kurz, with Tal, 1997; Mishal and Sela 2000, 16–26). The key challenges to Israeli security forces faced during this period entailed isolated acts of kidnapping of soldiers, shootings on settlers, and occasional placement of explosives in the centers of Israel's major cities. On the international front, the Palestinian organizations attempted to hit Israeli targets abroad. Most of these actions were foiled by Israeli security personnel on site.

By the end of 1987, the pressure pot that had been gathering steam in the occupied territories blew up. An isolated car accident in Gaza was the immediate trigger. In the demonstrations that erupted across the occupied territories, Israeli security forces shot down several Palestinians. The demonstrations spread all over the occupied territories. The Israelis first thought that this episode of popular unrest would soon be subdued by the security forces, as had happened many times in the past. It did not.

The intifada presented the Israeli security forces with a new type of problem: mass demonstrations involving children and women. This problem was one that the IDF had encountered before in limited doses, but both the scope of these demonstrations and their persistence were now a number of degrees beyond what the IDF had been accustomed to. These demonstrators applied new weapons—rocks, burned tires, Molotov cocktails. The Israeli claim of terrorism and violence against innocent civilians no longer worked. The roles of David and Goliath were now reversed, with the release of pictures and television clips showing children with rocks in their hands standing in front of well-armed Israeli soldiers.

When the wave of mass demonstrations did not fade away as initially expected, the IDF was instructed to use brute force against the demonstrators, or as Minister of Defense Yitzhak Rabin put it, "Break their bones," using "might, power, and beatings" (Peretz 1990, 45). The favorite method of the IDF was to smash demonstrations by sheer force, going in with clubs, tear gas, and rubber bullets. This time, however, the demonstrators found ways to evade these measures. More important, whenever one demonstration was quelled in one city, new demonstrations broke out in other cities. Very often, major portions of the population in all of the major cities of the occupied territories were simultaneously engaged in mass protests, road blocks, flaming tires, and the raising of Palestinian national flags. Most important, these demonstration sites were covered by the international press, who captured live pictures of the clashes between unarmed civilians—many of them children—and heavily armed soldiers. As Schiff and Yaari (1990, 116–17) put it:

> It was clear almost from the start that the IDF was quite unprepared for a contest of this sort, for its wealth of its hard-earned experience had come from a very different kind of warfare. . . . What the IDF now had on its hand was a mass civil uprising: not a war fought with tanks, planes, and artillery or a border skirmish with armed men, but a challenge posed without weapons, a contest against bottles, stones, and fire-bombs. And strange as it sounds in retrospect, the prospect of such an uprising was not included among the possibilities that the army was to take into account. . . . And never had [the waves of civil unrest of the past] been so sustained or so closely covered by the media. For the

first time in its history, the IDF encountered a threat that it was quite at a loss to handle—and in an area that it had considered almost a footnote to its operational designs.

The IDF directive to the soldiers in the occupied territories was to avoid live ammunition, except when their own lives were at risk. Yet the number of incidents wherein soldiers used live ammunition increased substantially. The number of Palestinian demonstrators, among them many children who died in the demonstrations, went up. The longer these demonstrations persisted, the more difficult it became to interpret them as a mere outburst of violence by terrorists. The IDF command, perhaps for the first time in Israel's history, joined the statement by Defense Minister Rabin that the intifada could not be suppressed by force alone; a political solution was needed (Schiff and Yaari 1990, 144; Peretz 1990, 44–45).

Over the period of 1988–90, the IDF's primary mission was to act more as an antiriot police than as the mightiest military force in the region. This does not imply that the IDF did not spend a great deal of effort increasing its capabilities vis-à-vis strategic threats. Yet, most of the troops were deployed in the occupied territories attempting to crush the intifada (especially the infantry units and newly created units that were designated to police the occupied territories). This activity put considerable strain on morale and on the motivation to serve. More important, it deepened a trend of "demilitarization," namely, a growing disaffection of significant elements of Israeli society with the armed forces (Levy 2003, 171–80). Fortunately for the IDF, the external threats to Israel's security during this time were reduced significantly. Syria abandoned its plans to reach strategic parity with Israel, and Israel could afford to reduce its defense burden. Moreover, the Lebanese front was relatively calm and the number of casualties in the northern border was negligible.

As time went by, the intifada changed form. Incidents of mass demonstrations became less common. Instead, isolated knifing attacks of Israelis in the occupied territories and the major Israeli cities emerged as the most common tactic of resistance. This was seen increasingly as acts of desperation by individuals. The security organizations were at a loss when it came to dealing with these threats due to their completely random nature and the lack of infrastructure that had traceable characteristics. Just how frustrated the Israeli authorities were with the knifing phenomenon is indicated by the Israeli police's urging of Israelis to carry sidearms. Licenses for carrying weapons were handed out quite leniently.

By mid-1990, the acts of knifing receded, and the popular resistance facet of the intifada diminished. Perhaps the only noticeable period of popular uprising came on October 8, 1990, when a demonstration of Palestinians on the Temple Mount escalated into violence and the Israeli police invaded the mount, killing twenty-two Palestinians and wounding dozens of others. A new wave of demonstrations followed in the West Bank and Gaza, during which several Palestinians were killed. The Gulf crisis, however, soon shifted interest to other matters, and the 1991 war brought the Palestinian intifada to a near standstill. The siding of the Palestinians with the Iraqi regime resulted in the loss of sympathy to the Palestinians not only among many people and politicians in the West but also among the more moderate Arab regimes. Between 1991 and the Oslo Accords, the level of violence aimed at the Israelis went down considerably (see fig. 7.2). So did the level of Israeli responses.

2.7. Suicide Bombings under the Oslo Accords, 1993–2000

The coming to power of the Rabin government in July 1992 represents a watershed in Arab-Israeli relations in general and in Israeli-Palestinian relations in particular (see chap. 10). One of the most difficult challenges to this government—suicide bombing—was due to a change in the strategy of the Islamic organizations who opposed the Israeli-Palestinian peace process. Suicide bombing, as we have seen, was not a new tactic. Both U.S. and French marines in Beirut and the IDF in Tyre and Sidon had been victims of such attacks in 1983 and 1984. The novelty of the suicide bombings starting in 1993 was that they were now being directed at civilian population centers or at "soft" military targets (such as bus stations of soldiers going on vacation). Moreover, the new type of suicide bombings was directed at the most central locations in major cities.

The Oslo Accords were seen by the Islamic organizations—the Hamas and Islamic Jihad—as well as by some PLO affiliate organizations as a sellout of the Palestinian interests by Arafat. Although the PLO affiliates were willing to play by the rules of the soon to be formed Palestinian Authority (PA), the Islamic organizations were not (Kurz, with Tal, 1997). The problem with suicide bombings from the perspective of the IDF was that their planning was relatively unobtrusive and they were seen as undeterrable. Rabin himself was very much affected by the gravity of this problem and began to refer to suicide bombing terrorism as "a strategic threat" (Inbar 1999, 142).

Israel's response to this new challenge was the imposition of closures on the occupied territories as a form of collective punishment. These closures prevented Palestinians from working in Israel and prevented the shipment of goods and exports from the occupied territories to Israel and

to the outside world. They also imposed severe restrictions of the movement of people and goods inside the occupied territories. These closures
became increasingly longer and extensive. Other than having an adverse
effect on the Palestinian economy (World Bank 2003), these closures had
little effect on the scope and extent of suicide bombings. What ultimately
caused a dramatic reduction in the rate of suicide bombings was a decision by Yassir Arafat to clamp down on the Hamas and Islamic Jihad and
to arrest a few key operatives. This served both as a deterrent and as an
effective measure. In contrast to the period of 1994–96, during which an
average of fifty Israeli civilians were killed in suicide bombings, over the
period of 1997–2000, less than twelve Israelis were killed in suicide
bombings overall.[15]

Despite the perceived gravity of the suicide bombings, the government
imposed significant constraints on the use of force by the IDF. The leadership—bound by its obligations to the Oslo Accords—prevented the IDF
from taking harsher measures against the Palestinians. This applied to the
Rabin and Peres governments, as well as to the Netanyahu right-wing government. Netanyahu's success with the PLO (probably due more to the
PLO's self-interest than to Israeli deterrence) was primarily due to Arafat's
belief that he could get out more concessions from the Israelis if he kept
the Islamic militias under leash than if they let them loose. The only case
of massive violence during the Netanyahu era occurred in September
1996, following a decision by the Israeli government to open a cave under-
neath the old city of Jerusalem. These clashes lasted three days, causing
the death of over one hundred Palestinians and about twenty Israeli soldiers. President Clinton quickly intervened and invited Netanyahu and
Arafat to Washington, thereby defusing the crisis.

During the period of 1996–2000, only a few isolated cases of suicide
bombings occurred. Israeli reactions, as noted, were moderate in nature,
thus not destroying the delicate balance of confidence established by the
security organizations of Israel and the PA. Despite the fact that each side
believed that the adversary was consistently violating the spirit—if not
the body—of the Oslo Accords, both tried to maintain a tolerable level
of coexistence. Both sides were aiming for the final round of the political
negotiations—the final status agreement.

2.8. The Al Aqsa Intifada, 2000–2003

The breakdown of Israeli-Palestinian negotiations at Camp David in July
2000 did not immediately ignite violence. The Al Aqsa Intifada broke
out on September 28, nearly three months later. The immediate event

that sparked the violence was a visit to the Temple Mount by opposition leader Ariel Sharon, a visit that had been approved by Prime Minister Barak. This visit was a blatant affront to the Palestinians, especially since one of the key issues that prevented a final status agreement at Camp David had been the control over the Temple Mount.

The IDF and the political elites were not at all surprised by the outbreak of the intifada. IDF intelligence and the GSS kept warning the political leaders that Israel would confront a major wave of violence if final status negotiations broke down. Barak himself had told the Israeli public that his key aim in the negotiations was to expose the true intentions of the Palestinians, insinuating that they were not really interested in peace. However, Israel did not have a clear strategy for confronting a new wave of violence.

The initial features of the Al Aqsa Intifada were similar to those of the first one: mass demonstrations and riots, the blocking of intersections, and the hurling of rocks and Molotov cocktails at Israeli security forces. Beyond these familiar features, however, the Al Aqsa Intifada had fundamentally different underpinnings. These account for the different strategies adopted by both sides. First, the first intifada emerged from the bottom up, born out of growing frustration with the continued Israeli occupation of the territories. It was led by local groups and was not managed by the PLO leadership. The PLO joined the bandwagon only late in the process. The Al Aqsa Intifada was staged by the PA. At least initially, the PA attempted to play a double game. The Palestinian security forces did not take an active part in the fighting against the Israelis, but they also refrained from acting decisively to curb the violence against the Israeli security forces and the settlers. In addition, the PA kept its lines of communication open both with the United States and with Israel. In fact, up to January 2001, Palestinian and Israeli leaders attempted to close the gaps in the final status agreement in Taba. On the other hand, the PA leadership— Arafat in particular—encouraged and even acted to inflame the armed struggle.

Second, almost from the start of the Al Aqsa Intifada, suicide bombings directed at Israeli cities became a key Palestinian weapon. The popular uprising phase of the intifada lasted less than two months. This was replaced by guerrilla attacks on IDF forces and the Jewish settlements in the West Bank and Gaza and attacks on civilian targets in Israel proper. The Palestinian security forces now began to participate in the struggle, engaging both in guerrilla attacks and in terrorist attacks on Israeli noncombatants.

Third, the division of labor among the Palestinian organizations became blurred rather quickly. Initially, the radical Islamic organizations—Hamas and Islamic Jihad—took upon themselves the key burden of suicide bombings. The Fatah and the PFLP aimed their attacks on the IDF and the Jewish settlers. As time went by, a significant radicalization occurred within the Fatah. The Tanzim—the Fatah military movement in the West Bank led by Marwan Barghouti— started planning joint venture suicide bombings with the Hamas and even carried out suicide bombings on its own.

Fourth, and perhaps most important, the difference between the first and second intifada was the magnitude of damage the second one inflicted on both the Palestinian and Israeli populations. During the first intifada, covering the period of December 1987 to the signing of the Oslo Accords in September 1993, a total of 1,124 Palestinians and 75 Israelis were killed in the course of roughly five years. During the second intifada, over a period of nearly four years, a total of 972 Israelis and over 3,000 Palestinians were killed in the wave of violence. The number of clashes between Israelis and Palestinians during the second intifada was roughly five times the number of clashes during the first intifada.[16]

The IDF applied the same measures to confront mass riots and demonstrations as it had done thirteen years earlier. At the same time, Israel was quick to deploy its air force to attack targets of the PA in the West Bank and Gaza Strip. The Israelis maintained that the PA was responsible for curbing violence, and if it did not do so, then it should be punished directly. In this sense, the basic post-Qibya logic of hitting and hurting installations and political symbols of Arab regimes in order to compel them into curbing terrorism was applied to the PA.

A third element of Israeli strategy that was applied almost from the beginning of the intifada was the policy of assassinations, ironically labeled by the Israelis as "targeted killings." The IDF relied principally on its air force—mostly precision-guided munitions (PGMs) launched from attack helicopters—to hit Palestinians suspected of terrorist activity. The frequency of the targeted assassinations increased over time. By August 2004 it became perhaps the principal weapon of the IDF, with over 150 Palestinians killed due to assassinations. This strategy was supposed to accomplish several things—including a demonstration of the capacity for pinpointing and eliminating terrorists, as well as a determination to pursue relentlessly both the leaders and the actual perpetrators of terrorist attacks against Israel.

During the first year of the Al Aqsa Intifada, Israel generally refrained from entering the populated Palestinian areas. Palestinians could move fairly freely within the cities, although their movement from one city to another was highly restricted. Israel increased its presence in the rural and sparsely populated areas of the West Bank but refrained from entering the main cities.

Ariel Sharon, who was elected to the prime minister post by an overwhelming majority, promised a swift and decisive solution to the problem of Palestinian terrorism. Although the general elements of the IDF strategy did not change with the coming of Sharon to power, the relative weight of IDF activities changed considerably. From then on, a gradual effort was made to dismantle the PA. First, Arafat was made the key target of Israeli propaganda. He was portrayed repeatedly as the principal force behind the intifada.

Second, the IDF placed a greater emphasis on targeted assassinations. It also was given a mandate for increased penetration into populated Palestinian areas. Third, the IDF increased its reliance on the air force and armored forces. Sharon and COS Shaul Mofaz, who was into his last year in office, started thinking increasingly in terms of large-scale military action. However, external constraints prevented the IDF from applying this strategy. The terrorist attack of September 11 on the United States changed the Bush administration's fundamental approach to terrorism, and, consequently, some of the external constraints on the Sharon-Mofaz conception were removed. The shock of the September 11 terrorist attack was felt also throughout the Palestinian groups, and those lowered the profile of their attacks. Toward November and December 2001 a self-imposed and undeclared cease-fire was taken by most of the Palestinian organizations. On January 14, 2002, however, the IDF assassinated Ra'ad Carmi, a leading Fatah figure in Tulkarm. In February Israel continued its assassination campaign, killing six Palestinians in two separate incidents. By that time, the IDF troops practically surrounded the Palestinian cities in the West Bank. The Palestinians responded with a barrage of suicide bombings, during which over seventy-five Israelis were killed in the month of March alone.[17]

This provided Sharon the pretext to embark on a large-scale operation. On April 1, 2002, Israel launched Operation Defensive Shield, which included complete occupation of all major Palestinian cities and widespread Israeli presence in the entire West Bank. During the months of March and April alone, over 470 Palestinians were killed by the Israeli security forces. Over 5,000 Palestinians were incarcerated. Over a period of nearly forty-five days, most of the West Bank population was placed under tight curfew, which was lifted only for a few hours per day to allow shopping. This operation was designed to eradicate the Palestinian terror infrastructure by eliminating their capacity to produce explosives. It was also inteded to capture suspected terrorists and their supporters.

Operation Defensive Shield uplifted the morale in Israel and in the IDF but did little to restrain the Palestinians. Suicide bombings continued despite the IDF's heavy presence in the West Bank. So did the attacks on settlers and on settlements. The Israeli government focused now on isolating Arafat and his people in the Muqata'ah, the Palestinian headquarters in Ramallah, threatening his expulsion from the occupied territories. All these actions only increased his crumbling popularity.

On September 17, 2002, U.S. president George W. Bush issued a new proclamation designed to reduce hostilities and to lead to some progress between the parties. The "Roadmap to an Israeli-Palestinian Peace"[18] called for a staged process leading up to a final status settlement. Each side was to undertake a number of obligations, including fundamental political reforms in the PA. Both sides, after considerable hesitations, accepted the guidelines. Implementation was delayed for nearly eight months, however, due to American preparations for an attack on Iraq, which took up most of the Bush administration's time through April 2003.

During this time both sides stuck with their old tactics. The Palestinians launched sporadic suicide bombings inside Israel and attacked Jewish settlements in the occupied territories. The Palestinians in the Gaza Strip had developed fairly primitive rockets, which they started launching at the Israeli cities of Shderot and Ashkelon. While these missiles caused almost no casualties, they did raise the level of alarm. The IDF failed to put a stop to these missiles, despite its heavy presence inside the Gaza Strip.

The Israelis continued their collective punishment policy, targeted assassinations, and occasional incursions into Palestinian cities in the West Bank and the Gaza Strip. Israel's strategy was constrained, however, by the need to maintain a low profile in order not to harm the American plan to attack Iraq. The level of violence declined to some extent but remained fairly constant, with Palestinians averaging about sixty fatalities per month over the period of May 2002–May 2003 and with the Israelis averaging about twenty-five fatalities per month over the same period.

The domestic support for the continued War of Attrition of the third kind was reflected in the seemingly endless supply of suicide bombers among Palestinians and the reelection of Sharon and the Likud Party in

January 2003. This enabled both sides to persist in their strategies. No real alternative to Sharon's and Arafat's strategies emerged. In Israel, the Labor Party's moderate strategy embodied in its candidate to the prime minister post, Amram Mitzna, was defeated flatly by Sharon's promise of peace from a position of strength. Arafat's control over the PA was proven yet again during the summer of 2003, when he succeeded in blocking an American initiative to circumvent him and advance an Israeli-Palestinian cease-fire.

In late spring of 2003, the Bush administration started working toward implementation of the "Roadmap to Peace." American pressure on the PA forced Arafat to appoint a prime minister, Mahmoud Abbas (Abu Mazen). Abbas, a moderate who had viewed the intifada as a strategic mistake, worked out a cease-fire agreement among the various Palestinian organizations and tried to form a government that would engage in negotiations with Israel along the guidelines of the Bush "Roadmap to Peace." Arafat was instrumental in placing major obstacles on Abbas's efforts. Yet, it was not only Arafat who derailed the cease-fire. Some splinters among the Palestinian organizations continued hitting Israeli targets, thus providing yet another pretext to Sharon to continue his assassination policy. This led to two suicide bombings in Jerusalem and Tel Aviv in July and to an Israeli attempt to hit the key Hamas leaders in Gaza. The cease-fire agreement collapsed, and Abbas resigned and was replaced by Ahmed Qureia (Abu Ala). Qureia also failed to form a working government that would revive the PA and resume negotiations with Israel. Sharon, on his end, did not move much toward the Palestinians either.

It was only in early 2004 that a significant change took place in the Israeli approach. Part of this change was induced by grass-roots pressure to build a wall around the West Bank that would prevent infiltrations of terrorists into Israel proper. Sharon was forced to revert to this defensive strategy not due to his free will but because he realized the offensive strategies did not work to diminish Palestinian resolve and their ability to commit terrorist attacks. The notion of a defensive wall was not only an admission of the failure of a military strategy for dealing with the intifada; it was also an anathema to Sharon because of a need to make hard choices about the position of the wall, thereby deciding which settlements would be within the Israeli side of the wall and which would be left inside the Palestinian side. The construction of the wall started in full only in the summer of 2003.

By early 2004, Sharon underwent a perceptual awakening of sorts, announcing a plan for unilateral Israeli withdrawal from the Gaza Strip, including the dismantlement of all Israeli settlements in this area. This plan invoked a great deal of opposition from the right wing as well as from Sharon's own party. At the same time, the plan generated a great deal of support among the center and left wing of the Israeli political spectrum. Partly to demonstrate to the Palestinians that the unilateral withdrawal plan was not an admission of weakness—although, for all practical purposes, it was—the IDF increased its incursions into the Gaza Strip, inflicting significant punishment on the residents of this area, including numerous house demolitions, the killing of Palestinians, curfews, and, mostly, the targeting of the political and military leadership of Hamas in the Gaza Strip. Over the months of March and April 2004, the IDF assassinated the entire leadership of Hamas in Gaza, including Sheikh Ahmad Yassin, the founder of Hamas, and Abdel Aziz Rantisi, his successor. At the time of writing this chapter, both sides continue relying on their strategies without a visible change in sight.

3. TRENDS IN ISRAELI STRATEGY OF LIMITED WARFARE

Clearly, an analysis of the kind of challenges Israel faced over time must serve as the foundation for any discussion of the patterns of Israeli limited uses of force. Table 7.1 provides a summary description of the relationship between the challenges confronted by the IDF and its responses to these challenges. The table also contains an evaluation of the outcomes of Israeli limited use of force strategies.

Table 7.1 suggests that over the years Israel has been subject to a wide variety of challenges, typically considered to be part of its "current security" problem. There were significant variations over time in terms of the challenges and—to a lesser extent—in terms of Israeli responses. Over the twenty-two years since 1948 (up to 1970) most of these challenges entailed infiltrations into Israel from across its borders. The key defensive task was to develop human and physical hurdles that would make it more difficult for would-be infiltrators to enter Israel. The key offensive strategy adopted vis-à-vis this challenge was to hit targets in the host state of those infiltrators. This entailed both hitting targets directly involving infiltrators and their support bases and hitting targets of the host state. Since 1970, most of the challenges have come from within the occupied territories and from Lebanon, many of them following the 1982 invasion of Lebanon.

Over time, Israel came to rely increasingly on defensive and preven-

TABLE 7.1. Israeli Use of Limited Force: Challenges, Strategies, and Outcomes, 1949–2004

Challenge Dates	Type of Challenge	Response Dates	Type of Response	Outcome	Side Effects
1/1949–10/1956	Sabotage, theft of property, killing of civilians	1/1949–10/1953	Reprisal raids: sabotage of property and killing in villages, especially in Jordan	Largely unsuccessful, infiltrations continued and even increased pace	Unclear
		11/1953–10/1956	Reprisal raids against government symbols and targets in Jordan and Egypt	Largely unsuccessful, infiltrations continued, now with support of Egyptian authorities	Escalation of conflict with Egypt, threat of confrontation with UK over Jordan
3/1951–6/1951	Syrian firing at IDF troops in Hamma and Tel al Mutillah, incidents on Lake Kinneret	3/1951–6/1951	Use of air force to bomb Syrian sites, reoccupation of Tel al Mutillah by large Israeli force, raids on Syrian positions overlooking Kinneret	Limited success, led to Syrian encroachment in Lake Kinneret area in retaliation, some raids unprovoked by enemy	International criticism, possible derailing of Israeli-American arms talks
3/1957–1/1964	Occasional infiltrations with little damage to property and life	3/1957–1/1964	No response	Success of policy of restraint	None
12/1959–3/1962	Firing at Israeli fishermen on the lake	12/1959–3/1962	Raids on Syrian villages and outposts	Unclear, but possibly successful for a limited period	Syrian pressure on Arab League to support Jordan Hazbani diversion project
5/1964–5/1967	Mining of roads, damage to Kinneret-Negev project equipment	5/1964–5/1967	Use of artillery and air force to hit Syrian positions on Golan Height, few raids (including to Jordan), threats to Ba'ath regime in Syria	No visible success in curbing Fatah raids and in Syrian shelling of villages in Israel	Escalation to Six Day War
5/1965–3/1966	Syrian attempt to divert Jordan River headways	9/1965–3/1966	Use of artillery, tanks, and air force to hit and destroy diversion equipment	Successful, diversion project stopped by Syrians	Possible contribution to process of escalation to Six Day War
7/1967–12/1967	Fatah effort to organize popular uprising and widespread guerilla warfare in occupied territories	7/1967–12/1967	Use of GSS to track down Fatah activists, no collective punishment activity	Successful, Arafat and his associates forced to escape to Jordan	None immediately visible

(continues)

TABLE 7.1.—Continued

Challenge	Type of Challenge	Response Dates	Type of Response	Outcome	Side Effects
1/1968–9/1970	PLO infiltrations from Jordan	1/1968–9/1970	Ambushes and reprisal raids in Jordan, occasional use of air force to hit targets in Jordan, defensive measures (fence and patrols along Jordan Valley)	Unsuccessful, continued infiltrations, despite Israeli actions	Termination of Jordan infiltrations due to Jordanian civil war (Black September 1970)
6/1968–6/1982	Hijacking of planes, airport and embassy attacks, attacks on Israeli athletes	6/1968–6/1976	Defensive measures, air marshals, embassy guards, airport guards, assassination of terrorist leaders	Defensive measures largely successful, assassination policy failed	Secret agents war assassinations in Europe, no effect on terrorist attacks
10/1970–6/1982	PLO infiltrations from Lebanon, shelling of civilian targets in northern Galilee	10/1970–6/1982	Limited raids, shellings of Palestinian targets	Largely unsuccessful, but limited threats and limited number of casualties	Escalation into Lebanon War (indirect)
9/1982–5/2000	Attacks on IDF troops and on SLA targets by various guerilla groups in various parts of Lebanon (from 1985 in southern Lebanon)	9/1982–5/2000	Antiguerilla warfare, including several large-scale bombing campaigns against civilian targets	Unsuccessful	Unilateral withdrawal from various parts of Lebanon by 1985, from South Lebanon, by 2000, possible encouragement to Palestinians in 2000
12/1987–9/1993	First Palestinian intifada, large-scale demonstrations, riots, attacks on settlers, random stabbings	12/1987–9/1993	Antiriot activity, roadblocks, curfews, collective punishments including destruction of houses, deportation, mass arrests, defensive measures of various sorts	Mixed	Oslo Accords

6/1993–9/2000	Suicide bombings in military and civilian places, buses, and other spots	Preventive measures: intelligence, targeted assassinations, large-scale military campaigns, collective punishments: deportations, mass arrests, closures, curfews; defensive measures: slowdown of peace process	Mixed, most successful measures entailed collaboration with the PA	Terrorism defined as strategic threat, polarization of public opinion regarding peace with Palestinians, election of right-wing government in 1996
10/2000–12/2004	Combination of suicide bombings, popular unrest, guerilla warfare	Preventive measures: intelligence, targeted assassinations, large-scale military campaigns, collective punishment: mass arrests, closures, curfews, defensive measures: fortifications, internal security measures	Mixed, increasingly high percentage of successful foiling, mostly due to intelligence and defensive measures, failure of offensive measures and collective punishment	Growing support of extreme solutions (transfer) and defensive measures (fence)

tive strategies to combat terrorism and guerrilla warfare, although it never abandoned its offensive strategy. Part of the greater emphasis on defensive strategies had to do with the changing nature of the challenge. Since it is difficult—both politically and logistically—to conduct offensive operations in friendly countries, Israel had to resort to defensive measures to protect Israeli (and Jewish) targets abroad. In many cases it had to rely on the security forces of the host states, but it never fully abandoned its own resources in defending Israeli installations abroad. Some of the states that Israel accused of harboring or otherwise supporting terrorism were located too far to launch retaliatory military operations against them. Other states have been already in a formal or informal state of peace with Israel, and both overt and covert operations could have damaged this fragile status quo.[19] Other states (e.g., Iran) were too powerful to risk the escalation that typically resulted from such reprisals.

But part of the growing reliance on defensive measures may well indicate a growing awareness of the limitations both of offensive strategies and of the adverse side effects associated with them. When Israeli decision makers used limited operations as a vehicle for escalation, offensive strategies were extremely useful due to their provocative nature. However, when the principal goal was immediate (rather than cumulative) deterrence, these types of activities were counterproductive.

Third, Israel expended an ever larger proportion of its resources on limited warfare as time went by, in seeming contradiction to the plan of transforming the IDF into an armed force at the front line of the Revolution in Military Affairs (RMA). This is not really the case, however. The IDF indeed spent a great deal of resources on modern technology, but it did not decline in size (Levy 2003, 305–7). Pressures emanating from its own generals, from various social groups, and from the political elites led the IDF to increasingly rely on the standing army to deal with security challenges, largely in lieu of its reserve force contingent. This pressure on the IDF led to privatization of some of the defensive measures related to limited warfare (e.g., security guards in public places, air marshals, and embassy guards).[20] But in dealing with the occupied territories or with the security zone in southern Lebanon, the IDF could not delegate security authority to civilians (except the GSS, whose principal functions were intelligence but not policy implementation). As the challenges to security emanating from the occupied territories increased, a sizable proportion of the IDF was bogged down in dealing with the security threats, largely at the expense of preparation for high-intensity wars (Levy 2003, 173–74, 418–20; Shelah 2003, 99–107).

The diversification of the limited warfare challenges and the resurgence of terrorism required the Israeli security establishment to widen the scope of measures it applied. In the 1950s Israel relied almost exclusively on offensive reprisal raids to Arab territories as the key strategy. Today Israel is engaged in a wide variety of activities, some offensive and some defensive, to combat the Palestinians inside and outside of the occupied territories.

In order to provide a better sense of the magnitude of the limited warfare challenges to Israeli security and of the intensity and scope of Israeli strategies designed to meet these challenges, figure 7.1 provides a graphic description of Israeli and Arab hostilities that are of a limited nature (not involving wars) over the 1949–2003 period.

Figure 7.1 suggests a wavelike cyclical pattern of Arab attacks on Israeli targets and of Israeli actions vis-à-vis Arab states (Israeli policies in the occupied territories are coded only as of September 2000.) Each wave lasts about a decade, and lull periods are also about a decade long. As I show in the next section, Arab actions are highly correlated with Israeli actions, though this correlation is not as straightforward as it appears in the chart.

Note that the ratio of the number of Arab attacks to the number of Israeli attacks is consistently high. Israel averaged less than one attack for every four attacks by Arab guerrillas (or Arab states). This may suggest a remarkable level of restraint on the Israeli side. There is, however, an indication of a declining trend over time, with Israeli attacks becoming more frequent relative to the number of Arab attacks. This is a particular characteristic of the Al Aqsa Intifada. The IDF's offensive responses (including the stepping up of the policy of assassinations) assume an increasingly typical tit-for-tat character (Kuperman 2001). At any rate, the impression of Israeli prudence is reversed when we consider the number of fatalities due to limited military engagements. This is shown in figure 7.2.

The wavelike pattern we saw in figure 7.1 is repeated in figure 7.2 as well. What is different, however, is that the ratio of Arab to Israeli casualties is largely in favor of Israel. The yearly average over the entire period is over three to one. While there were significant fluctuations in the fatality ratio, since the early 1950s it remained significantly in Israel's favor. This is the clearest indication of the escalation dominance principle. Israel did not try to compete with its Arab opponents in terms of the frequency of attacks. Rather, it tried to make sure that its uses of limited military force would count in terms of the physical damage inflicted upon its enemies. An interesting trend started to emerge after the Oslo Accords: Israel displayed prudent behavior in terms of the severity of its actions vis-à-vis the Arab states and the Palestinians. With the exception of Operation Grapes of Wrath in 1996 (mostly due to the Kfar Qana incident), the Israelis-to-Arabs fatality ratio went below one. This changed again in 1997 and remained high in Israel's favor during the Al Aqsa Intifada.

4. THE CHANGING FUNCTIONS OF THE LIMITED USES OF FORCE

The limited use of force strategy of Israel had many objectives. Some of these objectives may have contradicted other objectives. In this section I discuss these objectives and evaluate the extent to which they were served by the various use of force policies.

4.1. General Deterrence

The Qibya fiasco effected a reassessment of the retaliation policy, in terms not only of the targets and methods of this policy but also of its goals. After Qibya, reprisals became a key aspect of Israel's deterrence policy. Dayan explains this in his 1955 article:

> The retaliation raids are designed to set a [high] price for our blood, [a price] that no Arab village, army, or government would feel was worth paying. We could make sure that instead of aiding the [infiltrators], the Arab villages would resist their passing through; [we could ensure] that Arab army commanders would prefer meticulously to carry out their commitments to guard the border [against infiltrators] rather than fail in a clash with our units, and that the Arab governments would desist from confrontation with Israel, which would highlight their weakness. . . . The retaliatory strikes compelled the Arabs to ask themselves from time to time: is the destruction of Israel a realistic programme, or a plan [whose fulfillment] one should despair of? . . . [Moreover,] the . . . clashes in the "border war" would determine how the Israeli soldier was perceived by the Arab public and military.[21]

The conception of reprisals as deterrence implied that the chief purpose of the retaliation raids was not to punish the infiltrators or those giving them shelter but rather to demonstrate the capacity of the IDF to strike hard at the military installations of the bordering Arab states. This demonstration of skill and force had dual deterrence purposes. One was general deterrence; the other was more specific deterrence of future infiltrations.

Concerning general deterrence, Israeli decision makers developed a belief that the success and overwhelming demonstration of force through limited military operations would deter the Arab states from embarking on the path of general war. Yaniv (1987a, 60) notes that "Reprisals . . . constituted an index of mutual deterrence, a method of evaluating the shares of the adversaries in the 'threat exchange,' of measuring the overall balance of forces and resolve in the Arab-Israeli conflict." Shimshoni (1988, 65–66) argues that "Israel's sheer superiority greatly simplified the shared knowledge required for the creation of relevant and credible deterrent threats at the strategic level. . . . In addition, Israel's reputation from the past and intracrisis use of reprisals should have served to settle any lingering doubts." The implication was that more severe challenges to Israel's security would result in a considerably larger "balance of blood" than the one established in the low-level infiltration-retaliation equation.

More recently, Israel Tal, a former deputy COS and a longtime adviser to a succession of ministers of defense from 1974 to the present, noted:

> The deterrent effect of the IDF is enhanced not only by victory in full-scale wars, but by operations between wars, operations that are part of Israel's ongoing defensive activities. Such activities include security measures, painful reprisals, commando raids, special operations deep in enemy territory, and demonstrations of prowess in military technology. Such measures are also employed to increase a sense of frustration in the opposing camp and heighten the deterrent value of the IDF. (Tal 2000, 52)

In order for the deterrent message to sound loud and clear, it was necessary to change the relationship between infiltrations and reprisals. Reprisals had to be measured not in terms of point responses for each and every incident of infiltration but rather in terms of a cumulative balance. This was established through two devices, triggers and proportionality, or—rather— disproportionality. First, as Kuperman (1999, 2001) shows convincingly, the single most important predictor of Israel's retaliation policy throughout the 1949–82 period was an Arab attack that caused Israeli fatalities. Implicitly, a rule was established after Qibya as follows: Israel would retaliate fairly immediately after an Arab infiltration or shooting across the border that resulted in one or more Israeli fatalities. This was not an official policy, but the data clearly show that it was a fairly consistent modus operandi.

Second, since the purpose was to establish a wholly unbalanced balance of resolve, skill, and operational capability, Israel's response to these infiltrations had to be entirely disproportionate to the provocation in terms of targets, damage, scope, and severity of the response. In fact, the provocation now became a convenient pretext for launching raids aimed at establishing general deterrence. While the Jordanian problem was relatively minor, the size of the problem that Egypt posed for Israeli deterrence was exponentially larger (Shimshoni 1988, 103–9). The need to establish deterrence through a demonstration of resolve was much higher.

Accordingly, a linkage had to be preserved between infiltration and reprisals in terms of timing. The timing linkage would support Israel's claim that it was acting in self-defense. Since Qibya, Israel tried, for the most part, to link each and every retaliatory raid to a specific incident of infiltration, shooting, or sabotage. In many cases, this link was made to a series of incidents. On the other hand, Israel adopted—at least officially—a policy labeled later in the 1960s by Prime Minister Levy Eshkol as the "open book policy." The meaning of this was that Israel took note of each and every incident but would respond at the time and place of its choosing. However, the application of this policy—as we will see subsequently—was even more problematic than reprisals that had been linked to specific triggering incidents.

Initially, the same logic of deterrence was applied to the Egyptian border, up to late 1954. However, the emergence of radical Nasserism invoked grave concerns among the Israeli elites. When Ben-Gurion returned to the Defense Ministry, the operational requirements of the concept of "reprisals for general deterrence" regained prominence almost overnight. The Gaza raid of February 28, 1955, was the first of several large-scale raids and military operations against Egypt. The same operational logic also characterized the reprisals in Jordan and Syria. But, whereas the raids into Jordan and the Kinneret raid in Syria were aimed at general deterrence, the raids into Egypt had a different purpose: they were designed to bring about escalation. We will discuss this aspect later.

The Sinai War served to score high in the Israeli self-perception of deterrence. The need to demonstrate resolve and efficacy through limited military operations to prevent the need for full-fledged warfare was diminished significantly after the war. The notion of reprisals as a means of general deterrence arose again in the mid-1960s, when Israel was faced with the dual challenge of renewed infiltrations from Syria and the Syrian diversion project. But these were not existential threats. We do not have clear documentation on the conception of limited warfare as a vehicle for accomplishing general deterrence during the 1960s. The only analysis of Israel's national security problems during this era (Allon 1968) does not explicitly discuss this issue. In his discussion of general deterrence, Allon refers to a general deterrent threat that rested on a series of "red lines," or casus belli, that would provoke a massive Israeli response. One of these casus belli was "a series of limited attacks on Israel [by Arab infiltrators or through guerrilla warfare] at a scope and intensity that is beyond the ability of Israel's measures of passive defense or its reprisal policy to withstand."[22]

Paradoxically, Israel's victory in the Six Day War damaged its ability to deter through the use of limited force. Having achieved an unequivocal military victory of major proportions, the need to employ limited force suggested that its victory in this war did not convince the Arabs of the futility of their struggle. Moreover, the overwhelming victory increased the Arab frustration with the new status quo (Maoz 1990b, 90–96; Maoz and Mor 2002a, 171–72, 220). Nevertheless, Israel's military strategists harbored pipe dreams that the war—by default—would raise the prospects of peace. Allon (1968, 391), for example, argued that "the outcome of the Six Day War gave birth to a 'moment of truth' of sorts, that could lead [leaders], groups, and governments in the Arab states to a second thought and even to the conclusion that Israel is a permanent fact in the region that cannot be removed, and that any additional attempt to attack [Israel] would result in certain failure, and would only bring about further calamity on the heads of the Arab states." This hope was shattered by the resumption of limited military operations against Israel immediately after the war had ended.

Consequently, the idea of renewing the practice of deterrence through limited operations emerged yet again as a preferred strategy, with a renewed focus on escalation dominance. The results ran contrary to the expectations of the Israeli political and military leadership. Large-scale limited operations such as the Karameh raid, the attempt to occupy Ras el Ush in Egypt, the bombing of the oil refineries in Suez, the raid on the Beirut airport, and the Naj Hamadi raid in Upper Egypt were all part of a consistent policy of compellence. The logic behind these operations was to demonstrate how effective "the long arm" of the IDF was. The expectation was that, once the Arabs were convinced of this effectiveness, they would cry uncle. Contrary to the Israeli expectation, the Arab reaction was to initiate the Yom Kippur War.

The Yom Kippur War represented a colossal deterrence failure. Consequently, the Israeli inclination to use limited military operations as a mechanism of cumulative deterrence receded dramatically. The causes of this conceptual shift are not entirely clear, because we do not have clearly articulated discussions of this matter.[23] The empirical fact is, however, that since the mid-1970s Israel has not employed peacetime operations as part of its general deterrence policy. Rather, it has relied increasingly on widening the gap in terms of both the qualitative and the quantitative balance of forces (Almog 1995; Cordesman 2004; Tal 2000, 222–25).

The only significant use of limited force that was aimed at general deterrence after the Yom Kippur War was the 1981 attack on the Iraqi nuclear reactor in Osirak. Back in September 1978, almost three years before the Osirak attack, Ariel Sharon had argued that the development of nuclear potential by an Arab state should be treated as a casus belli requiring preemption (Yaniv 1995, 314). The post hoc justification of the Osirak attack was the Israeli response to the threat of a nuclear Middle East. The inherent contradictions in Israel's own nuclear deterrence policy (see chap. 8) suggested that a balance of terror in the Middle East presents an existential threat to Israel. It was also impossible to remove the Iraqi nuclear threat by an all-out war, principally—but not exclusively—because Israel did not possess the capability (at that time) to carry out a war against noncontiguous states.

Because Israel could not deal with any Arab state that decided to go nuclear through a general war, using surgical air strikes or commando raids (or clandestine, cloak-and-dagger tactics) appeared to be the only viable option of preventing such states from reaching the point of no return. The Begin Doctrine—the statement that Israel would not tolerate the development of WMDs by its enemies—suggested that Israel would use conventional measures to prevent such a threat from materializing (Feldman 1997, 109). This threat remains viable vis-à-vis the Iranian nuclear program (see chaps. 8 and 14).

In this case, however, the threat of preemptive action is seen as the last resort, not the first. It is an action to be taken if all diplomatic and clandestine means have failed, as was the case in the Iraqi nuclear program in the late 1970s and early 1980s. Moreover, the thinking about preemption to thwart the development of nuclear weapons by Israel's opponents is fundamentally different from other uses of limited force to foster general deterrence. Specifically, it is guided by the principle of *underproportionality*. The focus here is on surgical strikes designed to remove the threat and also to demonstrate the ability of the IDF to strike with pinpoint accuracy and limited collateral damage. In contrast, as we have seen, the demonstration of prowess and resolve through limited operations relied on escalation dominance, which required *overproportionality* of response compared to the challenge.

4.2. *Compellence and Specific Deterrence*[24]

The initial attempts (over the period of 1949–52) to deal with the infiltration problem through defensive measures as well as through attempts to pinpoint the infiltrators and punish them directly were as unsuccessful as they were impractical (Tal 1998, 26–39). The number of infiltrations was in the thousands per year (Morris 1993, 28, 46–54, 135–38; Tal 1998, 26). The IDF switched, therefore, rather early to a policy of collective punishment. The basic idea was that, if Israel hit the villages in the general area from which the infiltration had originated, ultimately both the civilian population and the military authorities would curb infiltrations. Israeli decision makers reasoned that the residents of these villages would put pressure both on the Arab governments and on the Palestinian refugees to curb infiltrations. Dayan and Ben-Gurion were the key spokesmen of this logic. Dayan's statement before the Mapai Knesset members of June 18, 1950, makes this point.

> The only method that proved effective, not justified or moral but effective, when Arabs plant mines on our side [is retaliation]. If we try to search for that [particular] Arab [who planted mines], it has no value. But if we harass the nearby village . . . then the population there comes out against the [infiltrators] . . . and the Egyptian Government and the Transjordanian government are [driven] to prevent such incidents, because their prestige is [assailed], as the Jews have opened fire, and they [i.e., the Arab governments] are unready to begin a war. . . . There are no other effective methods [to counter infiltration].[25]

In order for such a policy to work, three assumptions had to be valid. One was that the local residents (as opposed to the refugees who resided in refugee camps) had both the capacity and the will to resist the infiltrators. The second was that local villagers had effective leverage on the would-be infiltrators and on the relevant governments. The third assumption was that the fear of the reprisals would indeed generate the desired response. Whether or not these conditions were met was not really subject to any careful study by the security community. In fact, all three assumptions were quite tenuous. Walter Eitan, the director general of the Foreign Ministry, claimed that reality had proved that "these acts of [military reprisals] are of no real help. After some time, the infiltrations and the acts of theft are repeated." Moshe Sharett claimed that "even those who support these acts [of military reprisals] do not claim that this is a solution to the problem [of infiltrations], because these [infiltrations] are a permanent menace. These acts [of reprisals] do not offer a solution."[26] This applied, as we will see, not only to the first half of the 1950s but to other periods as well.

In practice, however, the Israeli decision makers argued that the reprisals policy was effective even when it was not. When confronted by evidence regarding the continued incidence of infiltrations and even regarding the rise in the number of infiltrations despite the reprisals policy, Israeli decision makers came up with the ultimate response that quells every attempt at evaluating policy: things would be much worse if we did not follow this policy (Morris 1993, 178). Most of the victims of the reprisal raids before Qibya were civilians, many of them women and children. There were quite a few atrocities conducted as well (Morris 1993, 166–72). Even Sharett argued that the underlying logic of the policy of reprisals is compellence: "Every time that the infiltrations reach a high level, we must respond" (quoted in Tal 1998, 68).

The policy change following the Qibya fiasco altered the scope of the reprisals. The Israeli policymakers abandoned the belief that harassment of the Arab villagers would pressure the Arab governments into curbing infiltrations. Now the pressure had to be exerted directly on the Arab governments. This may have created a new dilemma, however, especially in the case of Jordan. Hitting Jordanian military targets too hard could encourage the Palestinians in the West Bank to rise against the Hashemite regime. Shimshoni (1988, 61) notes, "Israel's retaliatory actions . . . indirectly threatened the existence of the Jordanian state. . . . Because Jordan could not threaten Israel with escalation, Hussein adopted the only course available to him: to prevent the provocation of Israeli reprisals."

The focus on military targets led to an increase in the size of the IDF forces carrying out the reprisals. It was no longer possible to conduct military raids with small commando units. Military targets were well defended and therefore required larger forces. Larger forces were more cumbersome and slow in terms of movement, and the engagement with enemy forces meant longer battles. The semblance of proportionality was preserved when the forces carrying out the reprisals were relatively small.

This semblance disappeared completely after Qibya. The Kinneret raid of December 1955 was carried out by a force of an entire brigade. The Sabha operation on November 2–3, 1955, involved a force of a similar size.

The declining significance of reprisals as an instrument of specific deterrence after 1955 eliminated the need to preserve a delicate balance of action-reaction so as to avoid escalation. By mid-1955, the military and political elites were looking for a convenient pretext for war, and the reprisals policy was targeted toward this goal. For that reason, reducing the number of infiltrations through an effective deterrence policy would have defeated the purpose of escalation.

One of the paradoxical properties of using reprisals as a mechanism of compellence is that it has built-in escalatory logic. Initially, reprisals were based on a logic of tit-for-tat proportionality (Kuperman 1999). The reprisal was tailored to fit the act that prompted it in terms of time, place, and scope. The practical constraints on the number of reprisals, on the one hand, and the principle of escalation dominance, on the other, prevented Israel from responding to each and every act of sabotage or violence. But when Israel did respond, it was a far harsher response than the cumulative series of infiltrations that served as the cause of the reprisals. Consequently, the Arabs interpreted this reprisal as a step up a ladder of escalation. As long as the targets of the Israeli reprisals were civilian, and as long as the Arab governments were not directly involved in encouraging infiltrations, and even tried to curb them, the escalatory potential of the Israeli reprisals was not critical. But once the targets of the Israeli reprisals were military, any successful military attack from an Israeli perspective became both an affront and a threat to the Arab regimes. The effect of the Gaza raid of 1955 on the Egyptian strategic calculus (see chap. 2) illustrates this paradox quite well.

Another paradox of unintended escalation stems out of the operational logic of the reprisals policy. Arab military commanders learned over time the operational principles of the Israeli raids. They began to prepare countermeasures. As a result, the military confrontations tended to increase in intensity and in violence. The Qalqilya raid of October 1956 is a good case in point. The Arab Legion studied carefully the tactical standard operating procedures (SOPs) of the Israeli attacks. They knew that, while attacking their primary targets, the Israeli force sent a small unit to block the advance of reinforcements. During the Qalqilya raid of October 1956, the Jordanian Legion ambushed the IDF unit that was designed to block the reinforcements, and this required sending in a larger force to bail out the ambushed units. The escalation in Qalqilya led to a British threat that, if Israel continued to threaten Jordan through the use of massive military force, it would find itself in conflict with the United Kingdom (Morris 1993, 415).

The conception of reprisals to bolster specific deterrence remained rooted in the minds of the political and military elites even after the Sinai War, but the practice of limited use of force for purposes of specific deterrence did not reemerge until the mid-1960s. It is important to note that much of the strategic interaction between Israel and Syria during the period of 1965–67 was not based on conception of specific deterrence. Rather, the key objective of the use of force during this period was to provoke the Syrians so as to provide Israel with a convenient political pretext to remove the threat posed by the Syrian diversion project. The clashes over the Kinneret fishing rights and in the DMZs, as Dayan pointed out later (Tal 1977), were not done with a specific strategic objective in mind.

What did bother the IDF leadership in the mid-1960s were the renewed Fatah infiltrations from Syria. These infiltrations were not nearly as destructive or frequent as the infiltrations of the 1950s. But, as noted in chapter 3, they posed a political problem. The reprisals that started with limited artillery engagements quickly escalated. As we saw in chapter 3, the Samu reprisal (also expanded beyond its intended scope due to a confrontation with the Jordanian Legion) provoked both internal and external criticism. Such criticism, in its turn, was instrumental in the decision to carry out a demonstrative aerial operation in Syria. The downing of the six Syrian Mig-21 jets on April 1967 was a key event in the escalation toward the Six Day War.

The use of limited force for purposes of compellence was resumed after the Six Day War in both the Sinai and the East Bank of the Jordan River. On the southern front, the use of limited force was intended to compel the Egyptians into stopping their military operations along the Suez Canal. With regard to Jordan, the IDF focused on attempting to curb Palestinian infiltrations to the West Bank. In both cases, the policy backfired. In the Suez Canal the Ras Ush operation turned out to be a morale booster for the Egyptian army. In the East Bank, the Karameh operation turned out to be a morale booster for the PLO. In either case, military activity did not stop and even escalated.

These were short-term consequences. In the longer term, the record of these policies is mixed. In the final analysis, the application of this strategy over the period of 1968–70 proved successful in some cases and failed miserably in others. In the Suez Canal, limited use of force quickly converted to manifest escalation. In the case of Jordan, the policy had no real impact on the use of force against Israel. The Palestinian organizations dug themselves their own grave vis-à-vis the Hashemite regime by challenging the king's authority. Israel had little direct impact on this process, although its actions during the September 1970 crisis may have had some impact on the outcome of the civil war (Dowty 1984; Astorino-Courtois 1998; Maoz and Mor 2002a, 188–89). The indirect impact of Israeli military actions against Jordan and the PLO forces in Jordan may have had a cumulative compellent impact on the regime. The king found himself between a rock and a hard place and decided that this state of affairs could not go on. A confrontation with Israel would be more risky for his regime from both a military and a political point of view than one with the PLO. The only reasonable alternative was to confront the PLO (Astorino 1994; Astorino-Courtois 1998).

The effect of compellence was most pronounced in the Syrian case. Syria had no direct way of threatening Israeli population centers, due to the Israeli occupation of the Golan Height. Most of the Israeli settlements in the Golan Height were semimilitary posts manned by soldiers from the Nahal brigade. Therefore, compared to the focus on escalation dominance vis-à-vis Egypt and Jordan, Israel's response to Syrian artillery attacks was restrained. Once the 1970 cease-fire agreement was signed, however, the main threats confronting Israel were removed and it could focus its attention on the Syrian "problem." Between August 8, 1970, and October 4, 1973, Israel launched twenty-four attacks on Syrian targets (as well as on Palestinian training camps inside Syria). These attacks resulted in over 220 Syrian and Palestinian fatalities and over 1,000 wounded. These attacks have probably increased the Syrian frustration with the status quo and contributed to Syria's motivation to engage Israel in an all-out war. But these attacks may also have had a cumulative deterrent impact on the Syrians. Following the Yom Kippur War, the Syrian front became extremely quiet for years to come. The Syrians prohibited PLO operations across the Golan disengagement border. It is unclear whether, and to what extent, Israeli uses of limited force prior to the Yom Kippur War or the results of the war on the Golan Height were responsible for this outcome. It is more likely that it is a combination of both. At any rate, this is arguably the most favorable evidence for the success of the limited use of force strategy since its inception.

The Syrians, the Egyptians, and the Jordanians had a great deal to lose from continued attacks by Israel. Egypt and possibly Syria may have kept a low profile so that they could prepare for an effective all-out effort later on. In the Jordanian case, the regime had to confront the Palestinian guerrillas, lest it would be overthrown by the PLO. Following the Yom Kippur War and the disengagement agreements that followed, it was in the interest of the Arab states to prevent infiltrations to Israel. The Egyptians believed that the postwar settlement held the promise of continued diplomatic progress. There was little reason to provoke the Israelis into fighting when they appeared willing to give back territory for peace. The Syrian case is more complicated, however. Since it is not clear that Asad was ready to resolve the problems with the Israelis around the negotiation table (M. Maoz 1995, 142–44; Seale 1988, 227–28), it is plausible that his policy of reduced profile was at least partially due to the cumulative deterrence effect of Israeli limited operations, as well as to the outcome of the 1973 war.

As long as Lebanon had some kind of government that was capable of deploying its armed forces in order to maintain order, Israeli military operations in southern Lebanon (and in Beirut in April 1973) were designed to compel the Lebanese government into curbing PLO operations. In his instructions to the raiding force preparing to attack the Beirut airport in 1968, Defense Minister Dayan pointed out that the purpose of the raid was to

> make it clear to the Lebanese that they must prevent using the Fatah against our civilian air services. The plane that brought the terrorists to Athens [where they embarked on the El AL plane that they later hijacked] came from Beirut. The terrorists had trained in that country. If the government of Lebanon allows the Fatah to conduct training camps in its territory, it must be punished. It must be clear [to the Lebanese] that they need to think twice before they commit these acts against our airplanes. (Dayan 1976, 545)

These attacks and other military operations may have had some impact on the Lebanese authorities (Yaniv 1995, 249–50). However, the outbreak of the civil war rendered Lebanon nongovernable. The entry of the Syrians into Lebanon helped quell PLO infiltrations into Israel not because of the restrictions imposed by the Syrians on the Palestinians but rather because of the preoccupation of the PLO with the internal fighting in Lebanon. When Israeli military operations started having an effect on the PLO operations in southern Lebanon in the early 1980s, it was, ironically, the exact same time when Israel was interested not in deterring the PLO but rather in provoking it.

The logic of specific deterrence and compellence was applied in southern Lebanon throughout the period of Israeli presence in the security zone. Neither the two large-scale operations (Operation Accountability and Operation Grapes of Wrath) nor the more common strafing of villages had much effect on the motivation of the Hizballah and Amal guerrillas or on their operational capabilities. Again it was shown that a civilian population is a bad target for compellence-related operations, because it typically lacks the will or the capacity to prevent guerrilla attacks from taking place.

4.3. Escalation

Perhaps the most significant function of the limited force operations was that of provoking a process of escalation that would bring about a full-scale war. This is a variation on a concept developed by Lebow (1981)—*justification of hostility crises*. Lebow argues that, in some cases, political leaders want to initiate a war but cannot afford—for either domestic or international reasons—to launch a surprise attack or to be portrayed as the aggressors in that war. For that reason, they initiate a crisis by issuing a demand, displaying force, or initiating a limited force operation. This crisis is intended to provoke the opponent to retaliate. The opponent's escalatory response allows the initiator to put the blame for the beginning of the war on the opponent. At the very least, this process allows sharing the blame for the war with the opponent, if the latter does not escalate or does not strike first.

In at least three instances limited force was employed as a vehicle for escalation. First, in 1955 and 1956, the Dayan doctrine of "deterioration" attempted to incite Nasser into escalation, which would allow Israel to defeat Egypt and bring about Nasser's downfall. Second, in 1981–82 Sharon and Begin sought a pretext for a war in Lebanon. Third, as part of Israel's coping with the Al Aqsa Intifada during Sharon's tenure of power (2001–3), Israel used targeted assassinations to provoke escalation. These cases involved conscious and deliberate provocations through the use of limited operations. In other instances, limited military operations—employing the escalation dominance principle—caused unintended escalation. In such instances, escalation was due to miscalculation and inadequate political control of the use of force by the military. The most obvious case was the use of limited force against Syria during the 1965–67 period that led to the Six Day War. Another, less obvious, case was the escalation of hostilities along the Suez Canal during 1967 and 1968. A borderline case between conscious and miscalculated escalation concerns the decision on deep penetration bombing during the War of Attrition.

The escalatory use of limited force was based on an assumption that the Arabs—be they sovereign states that possess monopoly over the use of force or more loosely structured guerrilla organizations—could not afford to fall much behind the level of escalation dictated by Israeli military actions. Thus, the harsher the Israeli provocation, the harsher the Arab response. This would create a chain of events resulting in a full-scale attack on Israel. Alternatively, this process would escalate to a level at which the initiation of a full-blown war by Israel could be construed—domestically and internationally—as an act of self-defense.

Dayan's directive of October 23, 1955, is the bluntest expression of this logic.[27] Ben-Gurion could not openly use limited operations to foster escalation as long as Sharett was in the cabinet. Yet, the practice of Israeli reprisals policy in 1955 and 1956 clearly suggests a deliberate escalatory pattern. Gideon Rafael (1981, 31), the director general of the Foreign Ministry, explains this logic.

> His [Dayan's] intention, which he later expounded, was to create a situation of such gravity that it would force the Arab states to take up open battle with Israel. He held the view—shared by Ben Gurion—that time worked in favor of the accumulation of Arab strength. . . . In the opinion of Dayan and his associates of the defense establishment, any effective action, open or covert, likely to retard the progress of Arab reinforcement was an unavoidable necessity which would ensure Israel's territorial integrity and political independence.

From August to December 1955, Israel launched eight large-scale raids in which over 240 Arab soldiers and civilians were killed. In the first half of 1956—probably due to the restraining influence of Sharett—only 93 Arabs were killed in twenty-three military operations. In the second half of that year, however, the pace and magnitude of military operations were again stepped up. This resulted in over 400 Arab fatalities in a set of forty-two military operations.

Begin and Sharon also relied on the Palestinian automatic response to Israeli provocations during the summer of 1981 and the winter and spring of 1982. Their hope was that the Palestinians would react to these provocations in a manner that would provide Israel with a diplomatic pretext to invade Lebanon. In both cases where limited force was used as a vehicle for escalation, the Arabs did not react the way the Israeli politicians hoped they would. Both Egypt in 1955–56 and the PLO in 1981–82 displayed considerable restraint in their responses to Israeli provocations. Consequently, Israel had no choice but to launch aggressive wars in 1956 and 1982, thereby facing severe international criticism for its actions.

Israel's principal tactic intended to ignite escalation during the intifada was the policy of targeted assassinations. On four separate occasions Israel violated an implicit cease-fire that the Palestinians imposed upon themselves by assassinations that caused escalation. The first of these cases was the assassination of Dr. Thabet Ahmed Thabet in Tulkarm in December 2000; the second was the assassination of Ra'ad Carmi in Tulkarm on January 14, 2002; the third was the assassination of Salah Shhada in Gaza on July 22, 2002; and the fourth was the wave of assassinations that started on June 2003 during the attempt to form a moderate Palestinian government by Mahmoud Abbas. In each of these cases, the Palestinian response was a wave of suicide bombings that resulted in Israeli encirclement of the major population centers, entry into the Palestinian cities and refugee camps, mass arrests, numerous house demolitions, and long curfews of the Palestinian population. None of these measures served to reduce Palestinian violence against the Israelis, but this was not the key objective, as I will argue later.

But the logic of escalation dominance backfired even when the use of limited military operations was not intended to provide a pretext for a major war. The perceived need to respond to the Fatah infiltrations in 1966 and 1967 and the lack of political oversight on the IDF's provocations against Syria fostered a process of verbal and physical escalation, which gave birth to a belief in Syria that the Israelis were planning an all-out attack aimed at toppling the shaky Ba'ath regime, hence resulting in the May–June 1967 crisis. Likewise, during the first months following the Six Day War, Israeli escalatory actions along the Suez Canal, including the attempt to occupy Ras al Ush, may have had some effect on Nasser's decision to evacuate the canal cities in late 1967 and to launch the War of Attrition in late 1968.

The notion of escalation dominance also backfired in southern Lebanon during the 1992–2000 period. Up to 1992, Israel exercised considerable restraint, and hence the volume of Hizballah actions against the Israelis and their SLA mercenaries was rather low. As we saw in chapter 6, the assassination of Abbas Mussawi in February 1992 resulted in rampant escalation that included terrorist attacks against Israeli and Jewish targets in Argentina, Katyusha attacks on Israeli villages in the north, and escalated operations against the IDF contingent in southern Lebanon. The absurdity of this process was revealed in the "Grapes of Wrath Understandings" of 1996. The rules of the game to which Israel had agreed entailed a well-enunciated escalatory sequence that involved legitimate hits of civilian targets by Hizballah in response to "illegiti-mate" hits of civilian targets by the IDF. The only escape from this com-edy of stupidity was the Israeli withdrawal from Lebanon in 2000.

4.4. *The Domestic Functions of the Limited Use of Force*

Faced with a challenge of repeated infiltrations and unable to find an ade-quate response, the Israeli government confronted growing domestic crit-icism throughout the early 1950s. The policy of reprisals served a dual domestic purpose. First, it showed that Israel was doing something to respond to the infiltrations, thus the government was not completely helpless. Second, it helped develop an ethos of initiative and resourceful-ness that bolstered the kind of militaristic image that the IDF and Ben-Gurion wanted to instill among Israeli youth (Aronson and Horowitz 1971; Levy 2003, 68–78).

As noted by Morris (1993, 185–87) and others (e.g., Aronson and Horowitz 1971; Shalom 1996, 27–33; Tal 1998, 89–90), the policy of reprisals was aimed at creating an impression that the government was "avenging" the casualties inflicted by the infiltrators. Presenting the prob-lem of infiltrations and reprisals as a blood feud was a notion adopted from the ethos of prestate organizations such as Ha'shomer that operated in Palestine before World War I. It was also perceived as part of the ethos of the Jewish immigrants from Arab states, many of whom were settled along the borders. This ethos has been preserved in one way or another to the present day, and it appears to be politically expedient.

Kuperman (1999) found no evidence of the impact of domestic polit-ical considerations on Israeli policy of retaliation. He notes that he could not replicate—using his own data—the findings of Barzilai and Russett (1990), who reported a significant effect of election cycles on the Israeli policy of retaliation. In Kuperman's study, the single most important fac-tor that affected Israeli retaliation policy was the incidence of an Arab attack with Israeli fatalities. This may suggest that the Israeli policy of reprisals was essentially a strategic response to external challenge in a seeming action-reaction fashion.

This is not necessarily the case, however. The incidence of an Arab attack resulting in Israeli fatalities was more likely to get published in the Israeli media and to invoke public reaction. Even without actual expres-sions of outrage by the public (or in Knesset speeches, which is what Kuperman examined as an indicator of domestic criticisms of the govern-ment), the government may well have anticipated the coming domestic criticism, especially in the event that it would fail to respond in force.

Reprisals were used as preemptive responses to domestic criticism before it emerged. The creation of a myth of "heroism" for the reprisals and a mythology around the units carrying out these acts (e.g., Unit 101 and later on the paratroop brigade) helped divert attention from the mere fact that these reprisals had little or no effect on the frequency and severity of subsequent Arab attacks on Israeli targets.

Public opinion was one target of the limited use of force. A threatening political opposition was another. As we saw in chapter 3, the political threat of the RAFI Party was instrumental in fomenting a significant departure from the policy of restraint in the mid-1960s. It was argued that the Israeli decision to bomb the Osirak nuclear reactor near Baghdad in June 1981 was motivated by electoral considerations of the Begin government, which was lagging in the polls. Yet, there is no evidence in support of this claim.

Domestic political functions of limited uses of force may well have become increasingly important over time, particularly as the existential threats to the state of Israel had diminished. The use of limited force became a more appealing option when the government was seen as soft on Israel's enemies, especially when it confronted criticism from security-oriented elites in the opposition. In the mid-1960s, the Eshkol government let loose the IDF on the Syrians because it felt challenged by the RAFI Party members, who had accused the government of irresponsible management of Israel's security affairs.

Perhaps the most significant indication of the impact of public attitudes on policymakers is Yitzhak Rabin's reference to the "strategic" nature of Palestinian terrorism in 1994 (Inbar 1999, 142). Rabin's point was that suicide bombings pose a "strategic" threat insofar as they affect the perception of personal security in Israel. Consequently, they have an impact on foreign investments, on the cost of services in Israel, and on tourism. The fact that this notion was picked up by Israeli leaders after Rabin as a fundamental axiom suggests that responses to such acts were indeed conditioned on the need to deal with actual or potential public criticism.

What is important to note about the domestic function of various strategies for the limited use of force is that there exists no systematic study that attempts to examine the effect of these strategies on public opinion or on parliamentary support for government policy. The impression we get from the rather general survey of the history of the use of force is that offensive strategies had a short-term positive effect on public support for the government, but this effect dissipated as time went by and no meaningful results were in sight. Defensive strategies were not seen as having a short-term domestic benefit, but they were more effective in the long term. The grass-roots movement for the building of the separation wall in the West Bank is an example of this paradoxical pattern.

4.5. Limited Use of Force as a Training Field

The use of limited force—particularly in the 1950s—was motivated by a need to increase the combat readiness of the IDF. This function was twofold. First, limited operations provided a training ground for the forward units of the IDF under realistic battle conditions. Second, these operations served as morale lifters and as an opportunity for "healthy competition" among different units in the IDF, each striving to acquire more prestige due to operational successes. This "training," the morale boosting, and the interunit competition functions remain part of the organizational culture of the IDF to the very day.

The first years of the IDF as the military force of a newly founded state were not happy ones. The IDF went through considerable changes, as it had to adjust to a postwar social and political reality. Many people believed that peace was around the corner (Segev 1984). The standing army was scaled down, and the reserve forces were formed to provide the IDF with manpower support in case of emergency. The huge influx of immigrants in the first few years put a heavy economic burden on the new state,[28] and the defense budget had to be cut significantly (Yaniv 1995, 40–44).

There were also significant morale problems in the postwar IDF, especially in light of the influx of new immigrants. Initially, the IDF did not know how to deal with the problem of new draftees, many of whom spoke only a few words in Hebrew. The social and political value system of these people was not commensurate with the one the IDF tried to instill as part of the Ben-Gurion notion of a state-building military (Yaniv 1993). Moreover, in the first few years after the War of Independence, the IDF encountered a motivational problem. Many of the high school graduates who were drafted into the IDF refused to serve in combat units, opting instead to join service units (Levy 2003, 60). Consequently, many of the combat units were composed of new immigrants with little motivation to endure the strains of combat training. There was also a vast ethnic and sociopolitical inequality in many of these units. While 50 percent of all IDF draftees were of Asian-African origin, only 5 percent of the officer corps was of Asian-African origin. There were also significant cross-unit differences in terms of socioeconomic and ethnic composition. Some IDF brigades were predominantly manned by "oriental" soldiers, while others were predominantly "Western" (Levy 2003, 58).

These problems, along with poor training and the absence of strategic challenges in the postindependence period, combined to make for poor battlefield performance in the first years. The first few acts of reprisals demonstrated deficient military performance. This was also the case in more "conventional" limited encounters with the Syrian army (e.g., the Tel Al Mutillah incident of 1951). This raised considerable concern among the military and political elite (Tal 1998, 83–84). In an analysis of the IDF's performance in the 1949–53 period, Colonel Meir Amit, head of IDF operations, attributed these deficiencies to

> a low level of training, inadequate level of command, low level of manpower, inadequate attention by the [senior] command echelons to these problems. These defective operations were often hidden due to a [cover-up] of the deficiencies and failures by various command echelons. The reporting [of these incidents] was partially faulty and the general staff could not learn about the real situation after the "implementation," and could not rely on efficient implementation of the tasks which it had ordered under the assumption that they would be carried out in full. (quoted in Tal 1998, 85)

The reprisals offered an opportunity to improve the quality of the commanders and of the soldiers, as well as to boost the morale within the IDF. The IDF plan of dealing with this performance problem was to create a "specialized" unit that would carry out the bulk of the reprisals. This was, in essence, the rationale of Unit 101. Unit 101, and later the paratroop brigade, began to perform rather well in these operations. As Dayan noted,

> Most important of all was the lesson that the IDF drew [from these operations]. The government's decisions and the directives of the General Staff were no longer in the realm of wishful thinking, but rather minimal forecasts. Instead of [cases] in the past wherein units had returned and provided excuses why they had not been able to accomplish their mission, the paratroopers had to explain after each operation why they accomplished more than anticipated. A new sense of confidence was flowing in the IDF's arteries. (Dayan 1976, 115)

While the paratroop brigade still carried out the bulk of the reprisals, more and more units were required as the reprisals expanded. The growing level of participation also accounted for a growing level of competition in the IDF and helped inspire a significant boost to the morale of the

IDF. Yaniv (1995, 111) notes: "The reprisal raids accomplished their main military task: the morale [in the IDF] has risen and the norms of combat have improved significantly, and from this perspective, it is evident that the military victory accomplished in Kadesh [the Sinai War] would not have been so easily achieved without the change that had taken place in the IDF . . . as a direct result of the reprisal raids."

The exchanges of artillery and armor fires along the Syrian border in the 1960s also served a similar function. The major players in the 1965–67 adventures were first the armored units and second the IAF. The problems that plagued the IDF infantry units in the early 1950s were very similar to those that afflicted the armored corps in the early and mid-1960s (Tevet 1968, 80–82). The myth of heroism surrounding the paratroopers induced many young draftees—especially from the middle class and settlement movement, which were considered the cream of the crop—to volunteer to the paratroopers and to other infantry units. The armored corps and even more so the artillery units of the IDF were usually left with the remaining draftees. Although the IDF command in the wake of the Sinai War (especially under the leadership of Haim Laskov, who replaced Dayan as COS) invested heavily in the armored corps, the performance of the armored units and of the artillery was extremely poor (Tevet 1968, 82; Bartov 1978, 1:95–99). Most important, these forces needed practice under real-life conditions. Here, too, the principal objective was to foil the Syrian effort to divert the Jordan River headways. But, over time, military decisions about escalation were increasingly affected by the need to practice and to boost the morale of the armored units.

The fact that the commander of the northern front was David Elazar, who had served as the commander of the armored corps in the past, is significant in this context. As Dayan (Tal 1997) suggested and as General Lior stated (Haber 1987), Elazar was particularly eager to play the escalation game in the north. Elazar and Israel Tal, who at that point served as the commander of the armored corps, used to rotate armored and artillery units along the northern front to allow everybody a shot at improving their gunnery skills.

After the Six Day War the IDF had its hands full in military operations, both in the occupied territories and along the new borders. More and more limited operations involved different units. Several large-scale raids into enemy territory during the 1967–73 period were conducted by joint forces from different branches. The IDF also developed a rotation system that provided different units an opportunity to engage in different aspects of limited operations. Moreover, different units—including the armored corps—developed their own commando and reconnaissance forces.

However, given the number of challenges that the IDF had been facing, it was impossible to avoid specialization in limited operations of specific kinds. The growing number of hostage-taking raids required the IDF to develop specialized units to deal with such cases. The elite unit of Sayeret Matkal (a special unit under the command of the head of military intelligence) and later on the special operations unit (SOU) of the border police developed specialized capabilities in this regard. The beginning of the policy of assassinations following the Munich attack led to the development of a specialized unit engaged in assassination-related operations within the Mossad (Melman and Raviv 1989, 204; Black and Morris 1991). The intifada led to the formation of special units in the IDF specializing in covert action within the territories. The second intifada brought about an expansion in the number of such units.

The Israeli presence in Lebanon and the Al Aqsa Intifada also became significant training grounds for high-tech weapons. In Lebanon, the IAF carried out a large number of bombing missions that had absolutely no military rationale, many of them on populated areas. Even after the Israeli withdrawal from Lebanon, the IAF continued to carry out routine reconnaissance missions over Lebanese airspace, most of them without any military significance (Sobelman 2003). The IAF took a major part in the destruction of the police and internal security infrastructure of the PLO during the Al Aqsa Intifada. Many of the targeted assassinations were carried out by IAF jets or helicopters. Since many of these raids resulted in "collateral damage"— the killing of numerous innocent bystanders— the justification for these operations is questionable at best. From a strictly military and intelligence point of view, capturing the targets of the assassination efforts would have been preferable to killing them. Thus, it is plausible that pressure from within the IAF as well as the conception of limited operations as a training ground were key considerations.

4.6. Bureaucratic Inertia

Most limited military operations are calculated and deliberate. The various functions we discussed previously dictated to a large extent the target, the timing, the magnitude, and the intended effect of the operation. But for much of the time, the strategy in its different incarnations was driven by sheer bureaucratic inertia. Israel carried out quite a few operations simply because it was used to doing so.

Kuperman's (1999) study of decision regimes suggests that in many cases, and for substantial periods of time, Israeli decisions on military operations followed a consistent set of procedural and substantive rules. The decision processes leading to a large number of military operation had also been governed by a set of similar characteristics. On paper, political leaders— such as the prime minister or the defense minister—must approve every IDF operation that requires crossing the border. When the operation is more complex and entails possible political complications, larger political forums are required, such as the Ministerial Committee for Security Affairs (the security cabinet) or even the entire government. Hence, it seems that the political echelon has discretion over military operations even of the most limited nature. This seems to suggest that almost any military operation was preceded by a significant process of deliberation involving several political leaders.

Yet we have seen in the preceding chapters just how political decisions have been repeatedly manipulated by military commanders or by political leaders who—by virtue of their expertise and control over information—were able to sway decisions their way. This was the case with regard to major war-related decisions, such as the decisions on the Sinai campaign, the pressure that the military elite put on the politicians during the May–June 1967 crisis, the decision on deep penetration bombing in 1970, and the decision process leading up to and during the Lebanon War of 1982. To a large extent, this process repeated itself during the Al Aqsa Intifada.

More important, many of the security challenges that Israeli politicians have faced have been of a repetitive nature: infiltrations, guerrilla warfare, terrorist attacks on Israeli targets, and suicide bombings. Whenever the nature of attacks on Israeli targets shifted, the Israeli security community had a hard time adjusting to the change. When it did adapt to meet this new challenge, a new pattern of response was established. Once this response pattern was established, however, it became resistant to change even if it did not alleviate the problem. The Israeli policy of targeted assassination is a case in point. As noted previously, the idea was to incapacitate the terrorist organizations by "decapitating the snake." These assassinations had little or no effect on the capacity of the terrorist organizations; this policy may well have even increased the motivation of the Palestinian organizations to carry out attacks. Nevertheless, the policy continued and even intensified during the years of the intifada (Kaplan, Mintz, and Mishal 2004). As the policy of assassination became an integral part of the antiterrorist arsenal of Israeli security organs, they became better at it, and as they became better at it, this measure became a more usable part of their arsenal of responses, regardless of its adverse effects on Palestinian attacks.

The decision-making process concerning limited responses to various challenges had also a fairly standard character (Kuperman 1999). The IDF would often come up with predefined SOPs, without presenting any evaluation of these actions in the past. The politicians, lacking an independent ability to evaluate the effectiveness of these measures, had to rely exclusively on the IDF's analysis. A typical tactic of presenting the case for a given operation to the political decision makers is to offer three alternative courses of action: a "do nothing" option that was unacceptable given previous Arab attacks and the actual or anticipated domestic criticism; a large-scale operation that was sure to provoke international criticism; and a "middle of the road" limited operation. The latter appeared almost always to be the most reasonable course of action under the circumstances. Moreover, each such action was presented as an ad hoc response to a given challenge initiated by the other side. It was almost never suggested and was almost never perceived as part of a repetitive bureaucratic pattern or part of a more general strategy.

The IDF's ability to innovate was constrained by two other bureaucratic practices: the cult of technology and the emergence of a military elite that came out of commando units specializing in hit-and-run operations. The use of high-end technology—such as helicopter gunships and air-to-surface missiles—in LIC operations without a proper understanding of the political consequences of using such weapons is a clear indication of the effect of the cult of technology on LIC and counterterrorist strategies. Beyond the collateral damage caused by many of these operations, they had little effect on the Palestinians' motivations and capacity to continue suicide bombings and guerrilla attacks on Israeli targets. In fact, the use of high-end technologies during the Lebanon conflict and the Al Aqsa Intifada may well have backfired in that it increased the adversaries' motivation to show that they were not incapacitated by Israel's overwhelming technological superiority.

Since the 1973 Yom Kippur War, *all* of the COSs of the IDF came from the paratroop brigade or from Sayeret Matkal: Mordechai Gur (1974–78), Rafael Eitan (1978–83), Moshe Levy (1983–87), Dan Shomron (1987–91), and Amnon Lipkin-Shahak (1995–98) all came from the paratroop brigade, while Ehud Barak (1991–95), Shaul Mofaz (1998–2002), and Moshe Ya'alon (2002–2005) served as commanders of Sayeret Matkal. These units specialized in special operations and had been involved in several assassinations in the past.[29] The organizational culture of those people who had been brought up with the notion that special operations are effective must have affected their propensity to launch these kinds of operations when serving as COSs.

Other people who were brought up in the IDF but in a different organizational culture thought differently. For example, Ezer Weizman commented later about the Abu Jihad assassination: "It does not contribute to the fight against terrorism. It distances the peace process and will bring greater hostility. It also makes us more vulnerable around the world."[30]

The increased public scrutiny of IDF operations in the later 1980s and the 1990s may have imposed significant constraints on the IDF's use of limited force (S. Cohen 2003; Levy 2003, 264–82). The outbreak of the Al Aqsa Intifada, however, lifted the self- and socially imposed constraints on the military, and its commanders returned to their old habit of doing what they thought they had been good at.

5. CONCLUSION

The traditional literature on Israel's strategy typically attributes to limited force and special operations in Israel's strategy deterrence-related functions. These actions are perceived to have been intended to dissuade the Arabs from attacking Israel or to compel them into stopping acts of infiltration, terrorism, and guerrilla warfare. The present study suggests that these limited operations had a considerably broader range of goals. The unlimited use of the limited use of force was intended to accomplish offensive, defensive, and deterrent goals. These strategies were also used as an instrument for boosting society's spirit of militarism, for increasing IDF morale, and for fending off domestic criticism given low-level security challenges. These strategies were conceived as training opportunities to various IDF units and forces between wars. Most disturbingly, the analysis reveals the significant role played by military officers who pushed this policy and contributed to the spiral of violence and counterviolence that characterizes Israel's history from the inception of the state to the very day.

The argument that Israel's limited military operations had a cumulative deterrent value is not supported by this study. Neither can it be rejected by the available data. What is evident here is that these operations had little or no effect on the propensity of nonstate actors to stage attacks against Israelis. Israel's attempts to raise the price for attacks on its citizens and soldiers may have had an ultimate deterrent effect on the

Arab states. Even this came at the price of major escalation. As we have seen, Israeli uses of limited force were at the heart of the process of escalation leading to all wars—save the Yom Kippur War. More important, the wide array of strategies used by Israel to fight terrorist or guerrilla organizations had little or no such effect on the Palestinians or on the Hizballah. The key to reducing the number and severity of nonstate actors against Israel lies in curbing their hostile motivations.

A military policy that is not accompanied with policies aimed at reducing the adversary's motivation for violent action cannot be successful, either in the short or in the long term. Providing enemies with feasible alternatives to the use of force may induce them to reconsider the relative benefits of a strictly violent approach to the conflict. Such a policy should be part and parcel of Israel's strategy. In many cases it was not, and when this was the case, the level of violence declined to a bare minimum.

The first intifada, the guerrilla warfare in Lebanon, and more so the Al Aqsa Intifada suggest that the Israeli concept of escalation dominance cannot be successful if the sole aim of these actions is to reduce the capabilities of and the opportunities available to the liberation movement and guerrilla organizations. When these methods are not accompanied by political action aimed at offering peaceful alternatives to popular resistance, it takes only a few determined groups and limited means to generate a great deal of physical and psychological damage to a society. After two years in which the IDF had most of its standing order of battle and a significant number of reserve contingents deep inside the Palestinian territory, practically surrounding the Palestinian cities, there were still numerous suicide bombings and attacks on Israeli settlers and soldiers. Clearly this strategy took a heavy toll on the Palestinians as well. At the same time, the psychological pressure on Israeli society was also building up. The grass-roots movement for the construction of the fence and for unilateral separation from the Palestinians picked up pace in Israel and forced upon the political leaders decisions that contrasted with their military strategy of escalation dominance. The decision to build the wall around the West Bank and the plan for unilateral withdrawal from the Gaza Strip indicate an admission of fundamental failure of Israel's offensive operations.

The use of limited operations as a device for triggering escalation in the conflict has also been a principal goal in Israeli strategy. In at least two cases it was part of a deliberate process designed to provoke the adversary to escalate to an all-out war or to provide Israel a diplomatic pretext for initiating a war. In both cases the strategy backfired, at least from a diplomatic perspective. In other situations, such actions caused unintended escalation, the implications of which were far reaching. These "hidden" functions of limited operations have not been fully explored in the literature. More important, they have not been truly evaluated.

The lack of sober assessment of the functions and implications of the Israeli use of limited force on Israeli society and on the targets of these actions is all the more disturbing in light of the findings of the present study. At the apex of Israeli military power, which rests on technology and skilled command and control systems, Israel's strategy of limited force demonstrated its poorest showing, highlighting the limits of power and the need to consider alternative courses of action of a diplomatic variety. That the IDF, the principal executioner of these policies, had little incentive to evaluate itself is clear. However, the lack of political and social assessment of the mixed record of Israeli uses of limited force is a symptom of a broader malaise of Israeli society. The poor political and social control of the security establishment is not only in the realm of military operations. Unfortunately, as we will see in the next chapters, the Israeli diplomatic record is largely afflicted by similar malaises.

PART III

Israel's Nuclear Policy

— 8 —

The Mixed Blessing of Israel's Nuclear Policy

I. INTRODUCTION

Most observers of Israel's national security seem to agree on three issues regarding its nuclear policy. First, Israel has acquired significant nuclear capability over a relatively long time. Second, its policy of nuclear ambiguity seems to have been balanced and sound, enabling it to develop its arsenal along with maintaining close relations with the United States and other states committed to nuclear nonproliferation. Third, and most important, the combination of nuclear capability and a policy of ambiguity about its nature and scope has proven itself over time. Israel's nuclear policy may have even exceeded the expectations of the founding fathers of this policy, given its unanticipated positive side effects.

Conventional wisdom has it that Israel's nuclear policy has accomplished three fundamental objectives. First, it has deterred an all-out Arab attack against Israel since 1967. Second, it has been instrumental in modifying Arab military objectives, shifting their operational planning to limited war scenarios. Finally, it was influential in bringing Arab states to the negotiation table, and it was an underlying cause of the various Arab-Israeli peace treaties.

A closer inspection of these propositions suggests, however, that they require a fundamental revision. In contrast to this conventional wisdom, which appears in much of the scholarly research on the subject and which also reflects the prevailing belief in the Israeli security community, I argue that the balance sheet of Israel's nuclear policy is decidedly negative. Not only did Israel's nuclear policy fail to deter Arab attacks in 1973 and 1991, but it has been unrelated or only marginally related to the Arab decisions to make peace with it. Moreover, Israel's nuclear policy has had a set of adverse side effects, the magnitude of which is only now becoming clear in light of developments during the last decade in the Middle East. If these arguments are plausible, then Israel should seriously reconsider its nuclear policy and explore using its nuclear leverage to bring about a regional agreement for a weapons of mass destruction free zone (WMDFZ) in the Middle East.

I begin the analysis by providing a brief overview of the evolution of the Israeli nuclear project and the policy of nuclear ambiguity.[1] Second, I present in turn each of the major arguments suggesting the continued success of Israel's nuclear policy. I present the evidence upon which these arguments are based and show why this evidence is tautological, nonexistent, weak, or only marginally linked to the facts. Third, I examine two significant side effects of this policy: its effect on the Middle East arms race and its antidemocratic implications. Fourth, in light of this analysis, I account for the problems in Israel's nuclear policy in terms of inherent logical and practical pitfalls. Finally, I derive policy implications for Israel's deterrence and arms control policy.

2. THE STRATEGIC FOUNDATIONS OF ISRAEL'S NUCLEAR POLICY

There exist quite a few accounts of Israel's nuclear policy. These address the origins and evolution of the Israeli nuclear option, its perception by other states in and outside the Middle East, and the underlying logic of the political use of these weapons, primarily as the ultimate deterrent. Here I discuss briefly some of the key elements of this policy, which provide a window into its foundations in the 1950s and its evolution over time.[2]

Following the Sinai War of 1956, the French government agreed to supply Israel with a nuclear reactor and natural uranium. The reactor was built secretly near the city of Dimona in southern Israel. Initial details of its existence were revealed in 1961, when the Israeli government announced that the facility would focus on nonmilitary nuclear research. Meanwhile, Israeli policymakers debated the pros and cons of developing a nuclear weapons program. Heading the pro–nuclear weapons group were David Ben-Gurion, Moshe Dayan, and Shimon Peres. Leading opponents included Ministers Yigal Allon and Israel Gallili, as well as members of the IDF general staff such as COS Zvi Zur and Yitzhak Rabin, then head of the operations branch. The timing of Israel's decision to develop nuclear weapons is unclear, but indications suggest that it was in late 1962 or early 1963 (Evron 1974).

The drive for a nuclear option originated with a doomsday scenario of Israeli policymakers in the 1950s. This scenario consisted of an amalgamation of three processes taking place at about the same time: (1) the formation of a unified Arab coalition bent on launching an all-out war against the Jewish state; (2) the pooling and mobilization of the full array of human and material resources of members of the coalition for this war; and (3) the mobilization of international support (including that of the Soviet Union) for this coalition, coupled with the international isolation of Israel (Cohen 1998, 11–14; Bar-Zohar 1987, 1550–53; Yaniv 1995, 13–19; Allon 1968, 13–65).

In the aftermath of the Sinai War of 1956, some of the elements of the doomsday scenario appeared not too far fetched. First, the perceived adverse shift of the strategic balance following the 1955 Egyptian-Soviet weapons deal raised the prospect of a drastic Israeli inferiority in terms of relative capabilities in the future. Second, the Soviet nuclear threat against Israel, France, and the United Kingdom during the war, and the pressure put on Israel and its allies by the United States, suggested that international isolation might be replayed during the most critical phases of a future Arab-Israeli crisis. Third, Nasser managed to convert his defeat in the Sinai War to his political advantage, presenting it as a victory against imperialism. Consequently, he emerged out of the war as the champion of Pan-Arabism. This suggested a potential inter-Arab trend toward a unified Arab coalition led by a radical anti-Israeli leader.

So, paradoxically, following a brilliant military campaign, during which Israel had occupied a territory three times its size in less than a week, handing a humiliating defeat to the Egyptian army, the threat perception of its leading strategists increased rather than decreased. The nuclear option was seen as an ultimate insurance policy against the possible materialization of this doomsday scenario. The conception of a "Samson Option" is not entirely accurate. The nuclear option was never seen as a mechanism of collective destruction of both Israel and its foes if the latter would succeed in their schemes. Rather, it was perceived as the ultimate deterrent against such an eventuality. It was designed to render the realization of a practical scheme to annihilate the Jewish state akin to national suicide by the Arab states.

There is no evidence suggesting that the founding fathers of Israel's nuclear policy envisioned nuclear weapons as an element in the war-fighting arsenal of the state, one that would increase its ability to win wars. However, the evolution of Israel's nuclear policy was at odds with conventional wisdom on deterrence. It may well have been at odds with the ultimate deterrence conception of people such as Ben-Gurion. In fact, there is evidence suggesting that some decision makers (e.g., Shimon Peres) have allowed the expansion of research and development of nuclear capabilities that are of an offensive rather than deterrent nature. In deterrence theory, one may wish to cast some shadow of uncertainty on the circumstances under which the deterrent threat will be put into action. One may wish to leave questions regarding the timing, location, or scope of the retaliatory strike deliberately vague.[3] Yet, in order for a deterrence threat to be minimally credible, the capability of carrying out the threat cannot be left in doubt. The challenger must know that the defender possesses the capability to carry out the threat. This is why both superpowers never made excessive efforts to conceal their nuclear tests or spent a great deal of effort to conceal the key features (e.g., range, accuracy, and yield) of their principal weapons and delivery systems.

In contrast, since its inception, the Israeli nuclear project has been shrouded in secrecy. Israel has never officially admitted its possession of nuclear weapons. Its decision makers have clung to the slogan "We shall not be the first to introduce nuclear weapons to the Middle East."[4] Israel has never openly tested a nuclear device, although rumors abound of a 1979 secret nuclear test in the South Atlantic Ocean.[5] Following a few brief visits by American scientists to the Dimona nuclear facility in the 1960s, which turned out to be highly ineffective, no foreign national was ever allowed into this or other facilities in which research, development, production, or storage of nuclear devices was suspected. Needless to say, these facilities are highly classified, and few Israelis are made *Shutafey Sod* (partners to secret) on these matters. Although scholarly discussion about Israel's nuclear policy was permitted by the military censorship, it was always treated as an academic discourse rather than a doctrinal or technological one. When real facts regarding Israel's nuclear capabilities were leaked, Israeli authorities acted decisively against the perpetrators of such leaks.[6]

On the other hand, Israeli authorities, through statements and actions, allowed it to be known that Israel possessed both nuclear weapons and a variety of delivery systems capable of carrying these weapons. First, in a number of semiofficial statements and seemingly unintended leaks, various people involved with Israel's nuclear project in the past have more or less explicitly admitted that Israel possesses effective nuclear weapons.[7]

Second, some actions and inactions of Israeli authorities can be interpreted as indirect admission of the possession of nuclear weapons. Israel is one of the four nonsignatories to the Non-Proliferation Treaty (NPT).[8] It did not sign the NPT in 1969 and persisted in its refusal to join the NPT regime during the 1995 renewal conference. Third, Israel allowed semiofficial publication of tests of its missile systems, most notably the Jericho I and II missiles, which are widely believed to possess the capability of carrying nuclear warheads over distances of up to fifteen hundred kilometers.[9]

Fourth, legal and political actions of Israeli authorities (such as the kidnapping, trial, and solitary confinement of Mordechai Vanunu and the restrictions on his movement and his freedom of speech after his release from jail in 2004) have actually served to unveil some of the ambiguity surrounding the nuclear option. These measures implied admission that Vanunu's revelations were fundamentally true. Fifth, in the course of the negotiations in the Arms Control and Regional Security (ACRS) working group, established following the 1991 Madrid Conference, Israel turned down persistent Egyptian demands for disclosing details of its nuclear program, placing its nuclear facilities under International Atomic Energy Agency (IAEA) inspection, or inserting a clause on the establishment of a nuclear weapons free zone (NWFZ) in the Middle East in the basic document of the ACRS working group. The debate between Egypt and Israel on this matter has led to the suspension of the ACRS meetings since 1995 (Feldman 1997; Landau 2001).

Israeli policy of nuclear ambiguity consists of both concealing and revealing information of its nuclear capability, with the purpose of letting its opponents guess. Prime Minister Shimon Peres epitomized this policy by saying, "Israel has made it clear that it would not be the first to introduce nuclear weapons into the Middle East. At the moment, there is only a suspicion regarding the existence of such weapons. Why should I say that we do not possess such weapons, when they serve as a deterrent?"[10]

Thus, in contrast to the notion that the possession of deterrence capabilities cannot be kept secret if they are to serve their purpose (Morgan 2003, 17), the Israeli conception has been that not only could nuclear ambiguity foster deterrence but it actually has allowed Israel to minimize the adverse political, military, and diplomatic ramifications of nuclear monopoly in the region.

Nuclear ambiguity was not developed by design. Rather, it emerged as a necessary evil. Initially, the secrecy surrounding the development of the Dimona facility in the late 1950s and the early 1960s was due primarily to diplomatic and political constraints imposed on it by the agreement with France that provided both the know-how and the materials for the construction of the reactor. It was also necessary to protect the nuclear project from friends (e.g., the United States), foes (e.g., the Soviet Union and the Arab states), and benign third parties (e.g., the international community) who regarded nuclear proliferation outside of the superpower realm as a major risk to a fragile international system. The founding fathers of Israel's nuclear program may have also wished to minimize the domestic opposition to the project (Cohen 1998, 142–47; Hersh 1991, 59–70).

Once the Dimona reactor and its potential for producing weapon-grade plutonium were revealed in the early 1960s, the formula of nuclear ambiguity grew out of an agreement between the Israeli government and the United States. In exchange for the provision of weapon systems (such as M-48 tanks, Hawk antiaircraft missiles, and later Skyhawk fighter-bomber aircraft) and acceptance of the de facto reality of the project by the United States, the Israeli government agreed to allow limited visiting rights to American scientists to Dimona. More important, Israel agreed not to test or openly reveal its nuclear weapons once they become operational (Cohen 1998, 205–17). Thus, the logic for religiously adhering to ambiguity rests not so much on the effectiveness of a deterrent of an unannounced and untested capability but rather on political and diplomatic grounds.

This agreement between Israel and the United States was put to the first test when the United States and the Soviet Union jointly sponsored the NPT in 1968. Initially, the United States put considerable pressure on Israel to join the NPT. Yet, Israeli decision makers managed to convince the Johnson and Nixon administrations to "allow" Israel to stay out of the NPT regime in exchange for clinging to nuclear ambiguity (Cohen 1998, 293–322). Since then, the policy of nuclear ambiguity has been religiously adhered to, while the production of nuclear weapons of various types and yield and of different delivery systems has continued. According to external sources, by the mid-1990s, Israel was in possession of anywhere between one hundred and two hundred nuclear devices, some of

which include SSM warheads and some of which are allegedly submarine-launched ballistic missiles (SLBMs).[11]

3. THE PRESUMED BENEFITS OF ISRAELI NUCLEAR POLICY: ARGUMENTS, DATA, PROBLEMS

3.1. *Did Israel's Nuclear Policy Deter an All-Out Arab Attack?*

As noted, the principal argument of the proponents of Israel's nuclear
policy is that it has accomplished its primary objective: deterring an all-
out Arab attack against Israel.[12] The basic evidence in support for this
argument is the nonoccurrence of such an attack. Since the early 1960s,
when information started to surface about Israel's nuclear capability,
there has been no evidence of either a political buildup or operational
planning for such an attack. On at least two occasions several Arab states
formed ad hoc coalitions bent on attacking Israel: in May–June 1967 and
in 1973. Yet the nature of these coalitions and their operational intention was not an all-out attack. Rather, they were formed with limited territorial and political aims in mind. In fact, Israel's presumed nuclear capability is seen by several scholars as a key factor that induced the Arabs to
limit the scope of these attacks.

The vehement anti-Israeli (and at instances anti-Semitic) rhetoric of
the major Arab leaders, leading journalists, intellectuals, and others provides seemingly convincing evidence for an Arab intent to bring about
the destruction of the Jewish state (Harkabi 1972; Beres 2004). Hence,
changes in the nature of this rhetoric may provide us a useful clue regarding the possible effect that Israeli nuclear deterrence had on Arab intentions.

The pre-1967 period is marked by direct and implied references to the
goal of the complete annihilation of the state of Israel—politicide, to use
Harkabi's term. This rhetoric, although still present in the political discourse of many extremist groups in the region, is no longer part and parcel of the political discourse of most Arab regimes, even those that are
still in a legal state of war with Israel.[13] The goal of annihilation was
replaced by such goals as the reoccupation of the territories captured by
Israel in 1967, the establishment of an independent Palestinian state
alongside the state of Israel, and even the establishment of normal peaceful relations with Israel, in exchange for the return of the occupied territories.[14]

This evidence seems to suggest that Israel's nuclear policy has accomplished its principal objective. The shift in Arab strategic objectives emerged from a growing awareness of the futility of this policy. It is difficult to ascertain the direct impact of Israel's nuclear policy on general deterrence in tangible strategic terms, because the noninitiation of an all-out attack on Israel can emanate from a wide variety of reasons. But perceptual evidence is important because it is in this realm that we can trace meaningful change of intentions, and this change largely parallels developments in Israel's nuclear capabilities. By association, Israeli strategists conclude that this policy was responsible for such changes.

While the policy did not (nor was it intended to) deter a limited Arab attack on Israel (or prevent Israel from needing to resort to military force to secure its vital interests), it did impose on the Arabs a substantial modification in their war aims. Specifically, Arab war planning following the emergence of an Israeli operational nuclear capability is believed to have reverted from an all-out war strategy to a limited war strategy.

The evaluation of any nuclear strategy is difficult even when nuclear deterrence is an official policy of the state and the capability aspect of that policy is, at least partially, transparent to the opponent. Detecting deterrence failures is seemingly straightforward; yet, the verification of an effective general deterrence posture is difficult and—some scholars argue—impossible.[15] This difficulty is amplified in the Israeli case due to the ambiguous nature of its deterrence and to the paucity of information regarding the decision-making calculus and strategic planning of its principal opponents, virtually all of which are totalitarian or authoritarian political regimes that thrive on secrecy.

In order to assess the effectiveness of general deterrence, the first thing to do is not to ask why the Arabs have refrained from an all-out attack on Israel. Rather, we must examine whether such an intention existed in the first place. To do so, let us examine the three elements of Ben-Gurion's doomsday scenario against available evidence on Arab behavior and intentions. If these elements had a sound empirical base, then we may proceed to the question of the effectiveness of Israeli general nuclear deterrence posture. If, however, there are fundamental flaws in the underlying strategic logic of Israel's deterrence policy, then perhaps this policy may have been superfluous in the first place.

A fundamental assumption underlying any deterrence policy concerns the presence of a real threat to some aspect of a state's national security. Such a threat consists of one or more observable enemies, with a hostile intent and an actual capability to carry it out. This combination of a motivation to change a given status quo and a capability to do so suggests to the defender that, unless something is done to alter the calculus of the challenger, the latter will embark on a forceful effort to alter the status quo (Morgan 2003, 2; Maoz 1990b, 66–67). This threat forms the rationale for any policy of deterrence. There is ample evidence that Israel's principal decision makers perceived a clear and present threat to Israel's existence. The basic evidence used by Ben-Gurion and his associates to define the magnitude of the potential threat was fourfold: (1) the recent history of the conflict, which consisted of an all-out attempt to unmake the new state of Israel in 1948 and the numerous infiltrations into Israel from Egypt and Jordan prior to the 1956 war; (2) the vehemently anti-Israeli rhetoric of the political, military, social, and economic elites in the entire Arab world, which established the intent; (3) the fundamental demographic and territorial asymmetries between Israel and its Arab neighbors; and (4) the fact that Israel confronted at least three, and as many as seven, states simultaneously and had to take all of the capabilities of these states into account when figuring out the balance of forces (Cohen 1998, 9–14; Yaniv 1987a, 12–19; 1995, 14–21; Evron 1994, 5–10; Hersh 1991, 22–23; Feldman 1997, 95–96).

Thus, Israeli decision makers' perceptions seemed to have provided a sound rationale for a nuclear insurance policy. The problem was that Israeli analysts, in their evaluation of the performance of Israeli nuclear deterrence, treated this perception as an objective reality, thus accepting it as a factual foundation to their assessments (e.g., Yaniv 1987a; Shimshoni 1988; Mearsheimer 1983; Ben-Horin and Posen 1981). Instead of performing an independent strategic analysis based on classical principles of threat assessment, Israeli analysts completely bought into the political rhetoric of the advocates of the nuclear policy.

From a strategic perspective, in order for the doomsday scenario to have a factual foundation, evidence was required of two related processes: a political process of multilateral cooperation among the Arab states and a sustained military mobilization effort by their defense establishments. First, in order to carry out a coordinated multifront attack, Arab states should have engaged in a process of interstate coordination and coalition formation. Such a process would have enabled several Arab states to coordinate their political and military policies, to pool resources, and to develop a joint policy not only vis-à-vis Israel but also vis-à-vis the international community to provide a diplomatic backing for such an attack.

Second, in order to initiate a successful all-out war, the Arab states would have had to invest substantial human and material resources in preparing for it. Such an investment would indicate an intention to convert the overwhelming demographic potential of the Arab states into a powerful military force. Inspection of inter-Arab politics and of the military policy of the key players in the Arab world strongly suggests that none of these two processes was evident during the second half of the 1950s and the first half of the 1960s, the period in which the critical decisions on the nuclear project had been made.

The Sinai War provides ample evidence against the notion that the Arabs had a coordinated Israel policy. Syrian and Jordanian forces did not fire a single shot during the blatant and unprovoked Israeli attack against Egypt (Maoz and Mor 2002a, 182; M. Maoz 1995, 52–53; Seale 1986, 262). Nor did any of the Arab states offer or provide meaningful assistance to the Egyptians during the war.

Following the war, Nasser did embark on a radical pan-Arab policy, aimed at creating a unified Arab camp, but his efforts were directed mainly at toppling the conservative regimes in Jordan and Iraq, thereby invoking opposition from most conservative Arab states.[16] The 1958–61 United Arab Republic (UAR) union between Egypt and Syria, as well as the radical uprising in Iraq and the efforts to overthrow King Hussein in Jordan, could indeed serve as an indication that Nasser's pan-Arab policy was gaining widespread support in the region. However, by the beginning of 1962, with the outbreak of the civil war in Yemen, it became transparently clear that the notion of a coordinated Arab policy was a facade (Kerr 1971, 27–43; Sela 1998, 41–54). The Yemeni civil war split the Arab world right down the middle. Over fifty thousand Egyptian troops were deployed in Yemen, supporting the radical regime of South Yemen against the North Yemeni monarchists and the Saudis and occasionally clashing with Jordanian forces (Maoz and Mor 2002b). The political split in the Arab world was never more significant than during this period.

During the May–June 1967 crisis it appeared that a process of Arab unity emerged out of the blue, as all Arab states rallied to support Nasser's campaign against Israel. The Iraqi decision to dispatch troops into Jordan and King Hussein's decision to create a unified Egyptian-Jordanian command suggested that such a coalition could form overnight. Here, too, the actual evidence suggests that, while the facade of unity was there, the actual commitment to act was a different story altogether. In fact, both the Syrians and the Jordanians did their absolute minimum to help the Egyptians during the war (Maoz 1990b, 209–12; Seale 1998, 137–40; Kam 1974). Arab policy in the post-1967 era is also characterized more by divergence than by a coordinated policy vis-à-vis Israel. Egypt showed interest in a separate deal that would allow it to renew its control over the

Sinai Peninsula, while Syria led the rejectionist front (Meital 1997, 185–94; Sela 1998, 97–132).[17]

Not only do we lack meaningful evidence of a coordinated Israel policy among the Arab states, but the existing evidence suggests that during the critical period of 1957–67, as Israel was developing a nuclear potential, inter-Arab relations were characterized by political and military discord. The Israel issue played a divisive rather than a uniting role.

When Israel made the decision to develop nuclear weapons, the actual investment in military manpower and hardware by the key Arab states was marginal, to say the least. Egypt—Israel's key opponent and, following the 1952 Free Officers' coup, a military regime reliant on the armed forces for its political survival—had an army of about ninety-five thousand soldiers in 1957, which accounted for less than half of 1 percent of its population of about 24 million. Its defense spending for that year was $224 million, about 6 percent of its GDP. Syria, the other major threat to Israel, had an armed force of sixty thousand and a defense spending of about $39 million (about 2.8 percent of its GDP). The figures for other states with the potential of posing an existential threat to the Jewish state were lower. Thus, the actual effort spent by these states on military affairs was inconsistent with the Israeli threat perception (see table 8.1).

Evidence of Arab weakness is also illuminated in the writings of key Arab military and political writers during that period and in the speeches

TABLE 8.1. Material and Human Defense Burdens, Average Annual Figures for Selected Subperiods: A Comparison between Israel and Its Two Principal Rivals

Years	Average Defense Burden (%)			Average Human Burden (%)			Average Dollar-per-Soldier Spending		
	Israel	Egypt	Syria	Israel	Egypt	Syria	Israel	Egypt	Syria
1950–56	4.5	4.8	3.7	6.4	0.03	0.8	270	1,601	1,160
1957–67	6.0	7.1	2.6	3.5	0.06	1.2	1,875	1,929	1,135
1968–73	14.9	14.2	5.2	3.5	0.09	1.3	9,554	5,172	1,980
1974–79	18.3	12.7	16.6	5.6	0.09	2.4	13,785	10,519	3,995
1980–86	17.2	3.9	16.3	5.1	0.09	2.8	23,144	7,027	9,880
1987–2001	10.4	3.9	8.9	4.0	0.08	2.9	27,576	7,067	10,522

Sources: Project on the Quantitative History of the Arab-Israeli Conflict and the Peace Process, Tel-Aviv University. Data available at http://psfaculty.ucdavis.edu/zmaoz/quanthist.html. Also Correlates of War 2004; Brom and Shapir 2000; Feldman and Shapir 2004; Stockholm International Peace Research Institute 2004, Heston, Summers, and Aten 2002.

Notes: Material burden: defense spending as percent of GDP.

Human burden: military personnel as percent of population. For Israel, military personnel consist of personnel in active duty (conscripts and professional personnel, as well as weighted proportion of reserve forces on active duty at any given date during the year). For Egypt and Syria, numbers refer to standing army only.

Dollar-per-soldier figures = defense expenditures/military personnel.

of Nasser himself. Mohammed Hassanin Heikal, Nasser's confidant, wrote in *Al Ahram* (September 25, 1964) that Nasser believed that a successful Arab strike against Israel required three preconditions: the concentration of superior military force, Arab unity, and the diplomatic isolation of Israel. Nasser himself admitted on several occasions during the 1960s that the first condition was far from being fulfilled and that anyone trying to provoke a war against Israel prematurely would betray the Arab cause (Mor 1993, 116–19; Sela 1998, 69–70; Nutting 1972, 367–68; Riad 1981, 1–17). So, instead of organizing a concentrated Arab military effort to put together a superior military capability that would enable them to carry out the kind of attack they had been talking about, most Arab states were trying to catch up to Israel's growing conventional and nonconventional power.

As noted, the third element in Ben-Gurion's doomsday scenario was an international configuration wherein Israel would find itself completely isolated. The Tripartite Declaration of 1950 made it difficult for all states in the region to acquire modern weapon systems. In the fall of 1955 there was a brief moment of fear and desperation in Israel, following the Egyptian-Soviet weapons deal. However, by the spring of 1956 and even more so after the Sinai campaign, this fear was by and large removed. Israel was getting more than its fair share in military hardware from France, the quality and quantity of weapon systems matching and even surpassing the type of systems that the Egyptians were receiving from the Soviet Union (see chap. 2).

Moreover, following the 1957 withdrawal from the Sinai, Israeli decision makers believed they had a firm American commitment to intervene directly should Egypt attempt again to blockade the Tiran Straits (Brecher 1975, 378–79). Negotiations with the United States on direct and indirect (through Germany) arms transfers were under way as the nuclear project was taking shape and form (Ben-Zvi 1998, 59–129). Thus, while one could argue that Israel's perception of international isolation had been a realistic prospect in the mid-1950s, by the late 1950s this was no longer the case.

Paradoxically, then, just when the nuclear project was taking a military turn, the gravity of the problem that it was supposed to address had significantly receded. Israel's strategic and international position continued to improve, while the threat of an Arab coalition bent on destroying the Jewish state was becoming less realistic. Most important, the conventional military balance began to tilt heavily in Israel's favor.

Thus, it appears that the firmly held Israeli beliefs about the ultimate intentions of the Arabs were not grounded in empirical reality. There is no evidence to suggest that the Arab rhetoric about the annihilation of the Jewish state was anything more than a pipe dream. The data on Arab military hardware and human and financial defense burdens indicate that at no time since 1948 did the Arabs possess a military or political capability that enabled them to accomplish this mission. All this evidence suggests that, to a large extent, the Israeli nuclear project was superfluous at best and—as I argue later—dangerous in terms of its effect on regional politics.

However, since the principal goal of the nuclear project was deterrence, it is important to examine how this policy has fared when put to the test. I now examine how Israeli nuclear deterrence performed in specific crises.

3.2. Performance of Israeli Nuclear Deterrence in Specific Crises

Israel has been involved in four wars since the inception of the nuclear project in the late 1950s. Two of these wars (the 1969–70 War of Attrition and the 1973 Yom Kippur War) were initiated by Arab states; the remaining two (the 1967 Six Day War and the 1982 Lebanon War) were initiated by Israel. The notion that Israel's nuclear deterrence played an important role in limiting the scope of Arab attacks is based on several arguments. First, the military scope of the wars initiated by the Arab states was limited. In both cases, Arab leaders hoped to create a military situation that would force the superpowers to pressure Israel into political and territorial concessions.[18] Thus, even in the Yom Kippur War, where a deliberate attack was carefully planned and coordinated by two Arab states, the military aims were limited and specific (Aronson 1984; Levite and Landau 1994, 42–43). Even when the first stage of the Yom Kippur War went better than expected for the Arabs, they did not possess operational plans for expanding the territorial scope of the war (see chap. 5).

In order to evaluate the argument regarding the effects of nuclear deterrence on the limited nature of Arab attacks, let us examine each of the major crises in more detail. While we have discussed most of these cases in previous chapters, the present discussion focuses on the role of nuclear weapons in shaping the scope, nature, and outcome of these crises.

Israeli nuclear weapons have been armed three times since the inception of the nuclear project. First, in May 1967 the project went into crash mode, producing two fairly crude devices that were armed by June 4 (Cohen 1998, 259–76). Second, Israel armed its nuclear weapons twice during the Yom Kippur War. The first time was on October 9, 1973, following the failure of the Israeli counterattack along the Suez Canal. The nuclear weapons were rearmed following reports of a Soviet ship carrying nuclear weapons that was approaching Egypt on October 22 (Hersh 1991, 225–39; A. Cohen 2000, 104–24; 2005, 2003; Aronson, with Brosh, 1992, 139–49). Third, Israeli nuclear weapons were armed immediately prior to, and stayed armed during, the entire Gulf War of 1991 (Eisenberg 1992, 307). If these reports are accurate, then clearly Israel engaged in specific nuclear deterrence at least three times. Let us examine each of these three cases, acknowledging the relatively speculative nature of the analysis due to the lack of supporting documentary material.

3.2.1. The Six Day War Crisis

The series of provocative actions by Nasser and the inflammatory anti-Israeli rhetoric in the Arab world increased substantially Israeli threat perception. There was a large gap, however, between the magnitude of threat perception experienced by key political leaders and the nature of the threat experienced by the Israeli military elite. Quite a few politicians perceived the Arab mobilization as posing a major existential threat.[19] This concern was magnified by reports about reconnaissance flights of Egyptian jets over the Dimona reactor, which prompted a speculation that Egypt planned to attack it in the near future (Oren 2002, 133; Brecher, with Geist, 1980, 230–31). Most military commanders, however, viewed the threat posed by Egyptian troops primarily as a challenge to Israeli deterrence.[20]

Be that as it may, it is implausible that the crash preparation for the arming of nuclear devices was not accompanied by a—possibly secret—threat to Nasser that an all-out Egyptian attack might provoke nuclear retaliation.[21] We do not know if or when such a threat was delivered, but the arming of nuclear devices would have been meaningless unless this fact were somehow communicated to the opponent.[22] Assuming this was the case, it is clear that the threat failed to accomplish its goal. The Egyptians escalated both their political and rhetorical threats despite this "nuclear activity."[23]

Nasser, apparently, was not too impressed with the Israeli threats. Whether this was a result of his being overtaken by his own rhetoric, as some analysts suggest, or whether it was a calculated risk of diplomatic brinkmanship, as others suggest, is immaterial from our perspective.[24] The point is that Egyptian forces kept digging in the Sinai and Egyptian threats intensified despite the Israeli threats. Ultimately, it was Israel that was forced to carry out its own threats through the initiation of a conventional war.

By now, the Six Day War is widely regarded as an inadvertent war, a "war that neither side wanted, and both tried to avoid" (Maoz 1990b, 123–30; Stein 1991a; Parker 1993, 3–98). Yet, from an Israeli perspective, the key strategic objective of the war was to rehabilitate its deterrence posture, which had been demolished by the Arab moves. The added nuclear dimension in the deterrence equation, though having played a possibly minor role, cannot be ignored.

3.2.2. The Nuclear Dimension of the Yom Kippur War

In 1973, the coordinated Egyptian-Syrian attack caught Israel completely by surprise. The magnitude of the imminent military defeat—especially along the southern front—was not made clear, however, before the failure of the Israeli counteroffensive on October 8. At the same time, Syrian forward units reached the edge of the Golan Height overlooking northern Israel (Herzog 1975, 122; Maoz 1990b, 187). From an Israeli point of view, the situation seemed critical. A number of ministers began urging the government to accept a proposal for a cease-fire in place. The purpose of arming Israel's nuclear warheads on October 8 is not entirely clear. One account suggests that the aim of this move was to coerce Washington into resupplying Israel with the weapons and munitions it needed, through an accelerated airlift (Hersh 1991, 225–39).[25] But this is a fairly heroic logical leap; the arming of nuclear warheads would have been meaningless unless information of this fact was transferred to the Egyptians and Syrians. Even if this information had not been communicated directly, Soviet intelligence satellites would have picked up some of these activities, and officials in Moscow would have then passed them along to the Egyptians (Cohen 2005).

This did not prevent the Egyptians from going out of their antitank and antiaircraft shield on October 14, launching a massive armored attack along the front. Nor did such threats deter the Syrians from firing FRUG missiles at Israel's air force base in Ramat David, hitting also civilian targets. Here, too, the effort at deterring the Arabs through the arming of nuclear weapons failed. Ultimately, Israel's response was conventional (bombing of the Syrian Defense Ministry in Damascus), and it turned out to be quite effective. But nuclear deterrence did not do what it was supposed to do.

As the Middle East crisis flared up following the violation of the cease-fire by the Israelis on October 22, the Soviet Union threatened to send troops in order to help the Egyptians, who had been routed in the Suez City area. At that point, the Israelis reportedly rearmed their nuclear warheads (Hersh 1991, 232–34; Aronson, with Brosh, 1992, 148–49).[26] However, U.S. pressure on Israel, on the one hand, and the placement of U.S. nuclear forces on alert, on the other, helped defuse the crisis, and the cease-fire was reinstated. Here, too, the arming of nuclear missiles was more an act of panic than a calculated effort at deterrence. The nature of the deterrent threat was unclear. However, this act apparently failed to impress either the Soviets, the Egyptians, or the Americans. Once again, deterrence seemed to have failed.

3.2.3. The Gulf Crisis of 1990–91

During the 1991 Gulf War, Iraq launched no less than forty-four ballistic missiles at Israel, but it refrained from launching missiles with chemical warheads, although it had the capability of doing so. The series of threats issued by Israeli decision makers during the crisis preceding the war, as well as the reiteration of such threats by American policymakers (e.g., Secretary of Defense Richard Cheney), are considered to have proved effective in preventing a nonconventional missile attack during the war.

The Gulf War presents arguably the most critical test of Israel's nuclear deterrence. On April 2, 1990, Iraqi president Saddam Hussein made a speech in which he threatened to hit Israel with binary chemical weapons. From that point on, Israeli decision makers through a number of channels issued a series of more or less explicit threats that Israel would retaliate with massive force and destructive consequences on any attempt by Iraq to hit Israel. There was a debate within the Israeli intelligence community regarding the nature of the Iraqi threat, especially whether it involved the risk of missiles carrying chemical warheads. Yet there was no question that Iraq possessed SSMs capable of hitting Israeli population centers (Arens 1995, 146–235).

Most observers agree that the launching of conventional missiles on Israel represents a deterrence failure. On the other hand, most observers claim that the fact that Saddam Hussein refrained from firing chemical missiles on Israel attests to a spectacular success of Israeli nuclear deterrence. Eisenberg (1992, 307) writes: "Top-ranking Israelis repeatedly warned that any Iraqi attack, regardless of scope, would provoke an immediate and devastating response." Steinberg (2000, 57) notes, "Israeli strategy did not prevent the conventionally armed Scud missile attack, marking the first time since 1948 that Israeli cities had been subject to attack. . . . For Israel this was a failure of deterrence, in a narrow sense, but not one that exacted an intolerable price or endangered national survival." Baram's (1992, 399) view reflects the near consensual evaluation regarding the performance of Israeli deterrence during the Gulf War: "Once the allied air force had attacked Iraq, the latter could not be deterred from launching a conventional attack on Israel. But Saddam stopped short of using nonconventional weapons, and thus, while Israel's conventional deterrence suffered a certain setback, its nonconventional deterrence remained intact."

Between Saddam's first threat of April 1990 and the outbreak of the Gulf War on January 20, 1991, Israeli political and military leaders pledged the use of extremely destructive power if Israel were hit by Iraqi missiles.[27] In the two previous crises, the relationship between the arming of Israeli nuclear weapons and a specific deterrent threat is ambiguous. The actual delivery of messages or the nature of the threat implied in them is questionable. Moreover, the secret nature of the act of arming nuclear warheads allowed Israel to back down from the implied threat without too much reputational damage. The Gulf War case, however, represents a colossal deterrence failure. In contrast to the conventional wisdom that this deterrence failure was strictly "conventional," I demonstrate here that it was Israeli nuclear strategy that failed.

There are several reasons for viewing this case as an unmistakable failure of nuclear deterrence. First, deterrent threats were explicit and public. There were also possibly a number of secret communications directly to Iraqi officials regarding a massive Israeli response to an Iraqi attack (Cohen 2005; Eisenberg 1992, 307n8). Second, the violation of the status quo by Iraq was fundamental and persistent: It launched missiles aimed at the centers of military and economic power in Israel, as well as its population centers.

Third, Israel had no effective defense against the missiles. The fact that there were no fatalities does not diminish the failure of deterrence. At the time, nobody could tell for sure where the next missile would hit, what kind of payload it would carry, and what would be the human and material damage caused by it. From Israel's point of view, every additional missile hitting it was another nail in the coffin of nuclear deterrence. The purpose of the Israeli threats prior to the Gulf War was not to minimize casualties but to prevent the launching of missiles in the first place. Saddam's decision to defy these threats constitutes a violation of the deterrent threat not because he restricted the strikes to missiles with conventional warheads but rather because he relied upon Israel's credibility—namely, its reputation for carrying out its threats— hoping for an Israeli response, in order to break up the international coalition.

Fourth, the recognition of the possibility—indeed the likelihood—of a nonconventional attack on Israel is one of the best indications of the government's de facto admission of the failure of nuclear deterrence during the Gulf War. The supportive evidence is compelling. Even before the first missile hit, statements by Israeli decision makers diminished the significance of the Iraqi missile threat, even the threat of chemical weapons.[28] This may have been a defensive avoidance mechanism justifying the possibility of Israeli inaction in the face of such attack. In reality, it indicates a belief that nuclear deterrence would fail, despite the explicit Israeli threats of massive retaliation.

Fifth, in anticipation of a gas attack, the government instructed Israelis to move into specially prepared rooms (usually in their houses or apartments) in which the windows and doors had been covered earlier with plastic sheets and taped for minimal outside ventilation. This precaution (in addition to keeping gas masks and atropine injections within reach) was the most effective passive defense measure that civilians could take against a gas attack. Such measures would have been useless against conventional warheads—and indeed could have been dangerous for Israelis who had been told to take cover in these rooms. Thus the call to take protective measures implied only one thing: the government believed that a chemical attack was imminent.[29]

After the Gulf War, Israel spent considerable financial, technological, and human effort on the development and acquisition of a wide array of offensive and defensive measures to deal with the threat of SSMs. These measures include the establishment of the Home Front Command (HFC) within the IDF, headed by a major general (and equivalent in status to the three regional commands of the IDF). The HFC was placed in charge of all activities and capabilities concerned with conventional and nonconventional missile attacks on population centers. Since its inception, the HFC has conducted hundreds of joint maneuvers with civilian authorities, simulating the response of the system to large-scale missile attacks.[30] The establishment of the HFC suggests a completely new attitude of Israeli decision makers toward home-front defense following the Gulf War and a clear indication of the belief that deterrence in general and nuclear deterrence in particular are not sufficiently effective against attacks on the Israeli rear.

Likewise, the Israeli security establishment developed—at an astronomical cost—one of the few and most sophisticated missile defense systems that exist anywhere in the world, the Arrow missile system. In parallel, Israel has invested in a wide array of offensive measures for dealing with the SSM threat. The IAF acquired the F-15I long-range attack aircraft and spent considerable doctrinal, technological, and operational efforts on offensive tactics aimed at destroying missile launchers. All these measures—the development of which accelerated considerably after the 1991 Gulf War—indicate that Israeli decision makers learned a clear lesson from that war: nuclear deterrence cannot be relied upon in the future.[31]

Some observers might argue that these are the kind of measures that any responsible government must take to protect its citizens against a grave threat, even if the likelihood of a state carrying out such a threat seems very low. Yet similar conditions had existed in the Middle East in the mid-1970s, when Arab countries in possession of SSMs (including Egypt) were still in a state of war with Israel. Earlier, Egypt had used chemical weapons during the Yemeni civil war. Later, in the 1980s, Iraq employed similar weapons during the Iran-Iraq War. In the latter conflict, Iraq also fired hundreds of conventional missiles at the Iranian capital, Tehran. Thus, even though Arab states had both the capability and the will to use nonconventional weapons and ballistic missiles for some time, only after the Gulf War did Israel begin to invest in an aggressive missile defense program.

There are two common explanations for this shift. The first is that until the Gulf War Israeli intelligence had been unaware of the gravity of the Arab missile threat (Nakdimon 1995; 2001; Arens 1995, 106). The second is that Israel's prevailing assumption was that its nuclear deterrent negated the need for defensive measures against Arab missile and chemical weapons capability. There is no direct evidence to support the latter explanation, although the Israeli threats against Iraq during the 1990–91 Gulf War may serve as indirect evidence of Israeli decision makers' confidence in the effectiveness of nuclear deterrence.[32]

The failure of Israeli deterrence during the Gulf War can also be inferred from the strategic emphasis of Syria and Egypt on the acquisition and development of SSMs in the 1990s. In contrast to the gradual decay of the conventional forces of the Syrian army (with about 50 percent of its tank force in storage and the growing obsolescence of its air force and antiaircraft defense), Syria tripled its missile force in the 1990s.[33] The Syrian shift to offensive missile capability and chemical weapon development suggests that it inferred that Israel was sensitive to attacks on its population centers. The focus on chemical warheads also suggests a first-strike doctrine emphasizing surprise attack. This is so because chemical weapons are not effective against a population equipped with defensive measures. Over that period, Egypt had also increased its SSM capability by over 50 percent. The shift in the strategic emphasis of Israel's most capable neighbors into the field of offensive missile and chemical weapon capability suggests that these armies identified the Israeli rear as a psychological—and perhaps political— soft spot. The failure of Israeli deterrence—nuclear or conventional—during the Gulf War was probably the key impetus for the military planning and development in Syria and Egypt in the 1990s.

It appears, therefore, that each time Israel actually invoked its nuclear policy in a context of an international crisis or war, its implied or explicit threats failed to achieve their intended aim. The fact that Israel did not use its nuclear capability in the face of defiance of its threats raises serious questions regarding its ability to generate effective deterrence for anything less than an existential threat—that is, in situations where the activation of the threat is already too late. It is ironic to point out that the severity of Arab attacks on Israel following its assumption of nuclear capability was much higher than before Israel became an undeclared nuclear weapon state. The total number of Israeli casualties during the Yom Kippur War approached three thousand—second only to the death toll during the War of Independence. In both the Yom Kippur War and the Gulf War, Israel's enemies did what they had not dared to do in the past: fire ballistic missiles at Israel's population centers. Just how these facts could be interpreted as consistent with a successful deterrence posture is a question that requires a more convincing answer than those provided by most Israeli strategists thus far.

3.3. Did the Israeli Nuclear Policy Limit the Scope of Arab Attacks?[34]

Proponents of Israel's nuclear policy typically minimize or discount the nuclear aspect of deterrence failure in the crises we just discussed. The blame for the Arab attacks or for escalation is placed on the conventional component of deterrence. The nuclear aspect is considered to have been instrumental in limiting the attacks or the escalation. The 1967 case is not relevant to this argument, but both the 1973 war and the Gulf War are treated as at least partial successes. In both cases, Israeli nuclear capability and policy served, according to this argument, to limit the scope and nature of Arab attack.

In 1973, the argument goes, the Egyptians and Syrians decided to launch a limited attack because they feared that a more ambitious attack—in terms of its territorial scope and targets— would provoke an Israeli nuclear strike. Specifically, Egypt refrained from occupying the entire Sinai Peninsula and the Syrians refrained from including northern Galilee in their plan of attack. Both states are said to have refrained from launching air strikes at Israeli population centers (Aronson, with Brosh, 1992, 131–37, 143). In 1991, Iraq chose not to fire chemical warheads although it had the capability of doing so. Again, the reason for this self-imposed limitation is considered to be the fear of nuclear retaliation (Eisenberg 1992; Steinberg 2000; Baram 1992). In order to assess the validity of these arguments, it is necessary to examine the decision-making process of the challengers and to inspect whether and to what extent Israeli nuclear policy had an impact on the decisions of its opponents.

The evidence we have on these two cases is uneven. The Egyptian-Syrian decision process prior to the 1973 war is one of the more (retrospectively) documented and thus transparent cases of Arab decision making regarding the Arab-Israeli conflict. In contrast, we have virtually no direct documentation of the Iraqi decision-making process on the Kuwait issue in general and of the decision to attack Israel in particular. Therefore, much of what can be said about this case is tentative and should be treated with appropriate caution.

3.3.1. The Yom Kippur War

As we saw in chapter 5, the Egyptian NSC meeting of October 24, 1972, pretty much laid out the general strategy for war against Israel. We have both verbatim transcripts and secondary documentation of this meeting (Gamassy 1993, 149–52; Shazly 1980, 176–81; Heikal 1975, 183–84; Sadat 1977, 234–36; M. Maoz 1995, 122–23; Bar Joseph 2001, 121–26). In that meeting, Sadat explained to the general staff that the principal aim of the war was political: to break the diplomatic deadlock in Israeli-Egyptian relations that had been in place since 1970. The idea was to use a war as a vehicle for jump-starting a renewed peace process, designed to regain the Sinai.

This meeting focused on the operational contours of the proposed war. At no time during the discussion—according to the transcripts available to us—did the Israeli nuclear capability come up as a factor. On the other hand, Israeli conventional capability was mentioned repeatedly as a constraint on the Egyptian ability to achieve military success. The scope of both the Egyptian and the Syrian attack was constrained by two principal factors: the political objective of the war and Israeli conventional capability. The nuclear factor was not instrumental in limiting the scope of the war. There is no evidence that it played an explicit role in the Egyptian decision-making process.

Aronson (with Brosh, 1992, 143) argues that the Syrian army refrained from taking the bridges connecting the Golan Height to northern Israel and that the Syrian armor stopped short of descending to Israel proper in the first days of the war due to the threat of Israel's nuclear retaliation. He does not provide sources for this claim, however. Yet, Seale's (1988, 194–200) biography of Asad—which relies upon a number of interviews with Asad himself—discusses at length the Syrian calculus of war but mentions nothing about the nuclear issue. From Asad's perspective, too, the principal objective of the war was to recapture the Golan Height, which Israel had occupied in 1967. This objective—more than anything else—defined the operational contours of the war. Moreover, as we saw in chapter 6, Syria had no operational plans for occupying the Galilee (cf. Pollack 2002, 481). Even this limited operational objective was conditioned by Asad's belief that Egypt would bear the major burden of the IDF's conventional power because he had thought that the Egyptian plan called for the occupation of the entire Sinai Peninsula (Seale 1988, 197).

In both Egypt and Syria, the strategic concern of the military planners was not related to the Israeli nuclear capability at all. Rather—as we saw in chapter 6—the key problems of the Arab military planners was how to overcome the overwhelming Israeli superiority in the air and in mobile armored warfare. The solutions they found for this problem required an extremely limited attack. It was necessary to keep the main armored and infantry forces under the shield of the SAM batteries and the antitank missiles. Clearly, the fact that Israel possessed nuclear weapons was irrelevant from this perspective.

3.3.2. The Gulf War

The paucity of direct evidence on the Iraqi decision-making process prior to and during the Gulf War makes it difficult to provide a definite assessment of the role of Israel's nuclear deterrence in limiting the Iraqi attack in 1991. As noted, most Israeli scholars believe that Iraq refrained from firing chemical warheads at Israel during the Gulf War for fear of nuclear retaliation (Feldman 1991; Eisenberg 1992; Steinberg 2000). Baram (1992, 399) argues: "If, as pointed out by the Iraqi sources, it is Israel's nuclear force that has for so long 'paralyzed the Arab will [to eliminate

Israel],' then there is no reason why, until the Arabs themselves have similar weapons that it should not continue to paralyze it."

Yet, we do know that (a) Iraq launched forty-four missiles, some of which were directed at the Dimona reactor but none of which got even close to it,[35] and (b) Iraq had chemical warheads but refrained from using them against either Israel or Saudi Arabia. The latter fact forms the basis of the argument regarding the effectiveness of Israeli nuclear deterrence during that war. Another point concerns an explicit threat made by Secretary of Defense Cheney during the war, who stated in a television interview (on January 2, 1991) that Israel would retaliate with nuclear weapons if hit by chemical warheads.[36]

This argument suffers from several logical and factual flaws. First, Israeli statements in 1990 threatened massive retaliation against *any* kind of attack. The contention that Israeli nuclear threats limited the scope of the Iraqi assault assumes that Israeli decision makers made an explicit distinction between a conventional missile attack and a chemical attack. The evidence does not support this assumption. As shown earlier, most statements suggest that Israel would respond regardless of the nature of the Iraqi attack. This applies to Israel's secretly communicated threats as well. It is unreasonable to suppose that Israel would have made such a distinction between its retaliation in case of a conventional missile attack and its retaliation in case of a chemical attack. Such a distinction in Israel's deterrence threats would have de facto legitimized Iraq's firing of conventional warheads.

Second, this explanation incorrectly assumes that Israeli decision makers interpreted deterrence success or failure as hinging on the potential lethality of the Iraqi attack. This is also unsupported by the evidence. If Israeli fatalities had been significant, public and political pressure to act would have been enormous. Although Saddam Hussein could not have known just how much damage the missiles would inflict, by targeting the Scud missiles at Israel's largest population centers, he was obviously hoping for as many fatalities as possible.

Saddam's decision not to use chemical weapons against Israel may have another explanation. Following the conflict, UN Special Commission (UNSCOM) inspectors discovered that Iraq's chemical warheads were quite primitive. In addition, most of the chemical warheads carried sarin nerve gas (Arens 1995, 160; Baram 1992, 400; Steinberg 2000, 55),[37] which is generally ineffective against populations equipped with emergency gas kits such as those in the possession of the Israelis. The destructive potential of a missile packed with five hundred kilograms of

TNT (such as the al-Hussein missile) is far greater than that of a chemical warhead against a protected population. Thus, if the missiles targeted at Israel had carried chemical warheads, the most significant effect would probably have been psychological, not physical. Because Saddam's main objective in this regard appears to have been to draw Israel into the conflict by producing a large number of Israeli fatalities, his greatest chance for success was the use of conventional warheads.

To support the argument that Israeli nuclear deterrence was a causal factor in shaping Iraq's military calculus in the Gulf War, two facts must be determined: (1) that Israel—not the United States—deterred Iraq from using chemical weapons and (2) that Israel's nuclear deterrent, and not some other factor, compelled Iraq to rely solely on conventional warheads. No Israeli scholar who argues that Israeli nuclear deterrence was successful provides evidence to support either of these claims. Yet even if nuclear deterrence did prevent Iraq from using chemical (or biological) weapons, there is sufficient evidence to cast doubt on both the uniqueness of the source of deterrence (i.e., Israel, not the United States) and the uniqueness of the type of retaliation (i.e., Israel's nuclear, not conventional, capability). The key evidence against the uniqueness of the source argument is that Saddam launched SSMs at both the Israelis and the Saudis. Yet, Iraq did not use chemical (or biological) weapons either against the coalition forces or against other Arab states. Moreover, Saddam refrained from using chemical (or biological) weapons even when coalition ground forces entered Iraq and when for several days it was unclear whether these forces would stop short of Baghdad.[38] Indeed, it is more plausible that the U.S. threat of retaliation exerted the greater influence over Saddam, because, unlike Israel, the United States did not have the same constraints.[39]

Moreover, it is unclear whether a nuclear retaliatory strike would have been Israel's only option had Iraq launched chemical (or biological) weapons. In fact, given Israel's successful air strike on Iraq's Osirak nuclear reactor on June 7, 1981, the Iraqis were well aware of the broad range of military options available to the Israelis, most of which did not involve nuclear weapons.[40] In none of the writings on this issue is there evidence to suggest that Israel's nuclear threat was responsible for Iraq's decision not to employ chemical weapons. Thus the argument that Israeli nuclear deterrence proved effective in the Gulf War is not only seriously flawed in terms of its logical structure; it is also based on weak and inconsistent evidence.

The analysis of the Yom Kippur and the Gulf War serves to suggest that it was Israeli conventional capability rather than its nuclear capability that affected Arab calculations and the limitations they imposed on the scope of their attacks. Yet, there is reason to question even the effect of Israeli conventional capability on the self-imposed Arab limitations. In both cases discussed previously it is quite plausible that the Arab political objectives had a greater effect on the decision of the Arab states to limit the scope of their attacks than the limited Arab capabilities. In 1973, as well as in 1991, the Arabs were willing to run high risks in order to accomplish their political objectives. Sadat was willing to sacrifice thousands of Egyptian soldiers just to have his army set foot on the eastern bank of the Suez Canal. Saddam was willing to risk devastating aerial attacks by the United States just to have a chance at splitting the international coalition fighting against him. In both cases, the overwhelming superiority of the IDF was not enough to deter these leaders. But since they sought limited political objectives, they did not need a broader conflict. The self-imposed limitations resulted from the political goals of these attacks.

3.4. Nuclear Peace? The Effect of Israel's Nuclear Policy on the Peace Process in the Middle East

Undoubtedly, the key events in the Arab-Israeli peace process were Anwar Sadat's visit to Jerusalem in November 1977, the Camp David Accord of September 1978, and the Egyptian-Israeli peace treaty of March 27, 1979. These momentous events marked a major shift in Arab-Israeli relations. It took a while before other actors joined the peace process, but eventually Egypt's lead was followed by the Oslo Accords between Israel and the PLO in September 1993, by the Israeli-Jordanian peace treaty of July 1994, and by the first direct Israeli-Syrian negotiations since the Madrid Conference of November 1991. More recent developments include the establishment of diplomatic relations with Morocco, Tunisia, Oman, and Qatar and the negotiations between Israeli and other Arab states within the framework of the multilateral talks on economics, environment, and regional security and arms control.

These events mark a fundamental shift in Arab attitudes toward Israel, a shift that is unlikely to reverse itself despite the continued Israeli-Palestinian struggle and the fallout of the American attack on Iraq in 2003. If—as its adherents suggest—Israel's nuclear policy was a key factor in producing this shift, then its unintended side effect may have even surpassed the intended objective of deterring an all-out Arab attack.[41]

Before we examine the role of Israeli nuclear policy in inducing the Arabs to negotiate, it is important to spell out some hidden assumptions behind the argument. A hidden assumption in the argument that Israel's nuclear policy has helped to bring Arab leaders to the negotiating table is that Arab states had resisted serious negotiations with Israel until its development of a nuclear capability.

A close inspection of the diplomacy—both public and secret—of the Arab-Israeli conflict reveals a different picture. Throughout the conflict—starting in the prestate era and in the early 1950s and extending into the 1960s and 1970s—there have been a number of Arab peace initiatives that offered major opportunities to end or reduce the conflict (see chap. 10). There were many reasons why these peace initiatives never advanced very far. Not the least of these was the Israeli reluctance to take the necessary measures to convert them into actual achievements. Israeli decision makers rejected most of these initiatives either because they did not take them seriously, because they suspected the sincerity of the initiators of these initiatives or of the other side, or because accepting these proposals would have required territorial concessions that they were not willing to make.

Following the Six Day War, Israel again turned down a number of Egyptian peace overtures. This, as I argue in chapter 10, was due mostly to the fact that Israeli decision makers developed a sense of arrogance and self-confidence in the ability of Israel to either dictate better terms of peace or prosper without peace. Israeli nuclear policy may have been a factor in enhancing this sense of arrogance and intransigence among Israeli politicians in the period between 1967 and 1973, but we have no evidence of such a linkage.

With the conversion of Israel into an undeclared nuclear weapon state in 1967 another watershed event took place that changed substantially the diplomatic agenda of the Middle East. The 1967 war provided Israel with a very valuable set of bargaining chips: the territories it had occupied during the war. These territories formed the basis for a new bargaining agenda, one that is well captured by the "land for peace" formula that marks the Middle East peace process to the very day.[42]

There is also no explicit admission in any of the Arab documents, writings (research and memoirs), or media reports that Israel's nuclear status was a factor in Sadat's visit to Jerusalem or in any of the other states' decisions to enter the peace process. On the contrary, the outcome of the 1973 war created a twofold incentive for peace. First, it enabled the Egyptians to regain their honor by depicting the war as a major victory. Sadat could portray Egypt's military accomplishments as evidence of the destruction of the myth of the invincibility of the IDF and the reassertion of Egyptian self-confidence. These successes allowed Sadat to negotiate from a position of honor (Sadat 1977, 289; Meital 1997, 125–26; Gamassy 1993, 150; Heikal 1975, 208–10).

Second, and more important, the Egyptians and Syrians realized that, despite the favorable starting position, the costs of war were exorbitant. Together, the two countries lost over thirteen thousand soldiers, twenty-five hundred tanks, and five hundred planes (Dupuy 1978, 609; Cordesman 1993, 5–6; Barnett 1992, 128–52; Pollack 2002, 123–25, 130–31, 498–501, 512–14). Israeli forces advanced deep into Syrian and Egyptian territories, and had it not been for the superpower imposition of a cease-fire, a substantial part of their armed forces would have been completely destroyed. Ultimately, the leaders in Cairo and Damascus reasoned that the chances of recapturing the occupied territories by force were slim. Their only viable option—and this was something Sadat had known prior to the war—was to regain the territories through negotiations. Israeli nuclear capability was irrelevant to this calculus.[43]

Israeli security policy may have been instrumental in effecting a change in the Arab attitudes toward peace. But it was the cumulative impact of Israeli conventional deterrence, rather than Israel's nuclear capabilities, that may help account for the change in the Arab willingness to make peace. The repeated military defeats in major wars; the cumulative impact of human, material, and territorial losses inflicted by these wars and short-of-war confrontations; and the consequent image of resolve and capability conveyed by Israel over time seem to have been far more instrumental—perhaps even decisive—in such a shift (Almog 1995; Lieberman 1995; Bar Joseph 1998).

The effect of the Yom Kippur War on Israeli attitudes toward peace was probably more important than the effect that this war had on Egyptian and Syrian willingness to negotiate. Israeli leaders came to realize the limits of their military power and the costs of continued conflict. The war ended in a major military victory for Israel, but it shook the confidence of Israeli leaders and public opinion. Indeed, if the nuclear option had any impact, it is because it convinced leaders like Rabin (who had been skeptical about its effect in the first place) that nuclear deterrence was irrelevant to issues of war and peace. It is for that reason that Rabin sought interim agreements with Egypt (Inbar 1999, 119–22). Thus, what helped render the postwar peace process a continued success was the willingness of the Israeli leadership to pay the territorial price for peace as much as the Arab willingness to come to the negotiation table. Again, the nuclear policy was at best marginally relevant in this respect.

4. THE SIDE EFFECTS OF
ISRAEL'S NUCLEAR POLICY

4.1. *The Effect of Israeli Nuclear Policy on the Regional Arms Race*

A key argument of the opponents of the nuclear project has been that Israeli investment in nuclear weapons might cause one of two things. First, the nuclear project was expected to impose a heavy burden on an already strained economy. The IDF commanders who were involved in the decision-making process of the early 1960s—COS Zvi Zur and head of operations Yitzhak Rabin—and politicians such as Yigal Allon and Israel Gallili argued that ultimately this project may draw away funds that would be otherwise spent on strengthening Israel's conventional capability.[44] The opponents of the nuclear project foresaw the irrelevance of nuclear weapons for deterring or deciding small- or medium-scale attacks. Hence, they believed that the trade-off between the investment in a nuclear deterrent and the ability to maintain or foster a strong and modern conventional capability was a strong argument against this project.

Second, some opponents of the nuclear project—principally Allon and Gallili—argued that the Israeli nuclear project might ignite a dual-track arms race. It would prompt Arab states to compensate for their technological inferiority in the nuclear realm by increasing substantially their conventional capabilities. Ultimately, however, Arab states would respond to the Israeli nuclear project by developing nonconventional capabilities of their own. Thus, instead of racing the Arabs once in the conventional realm, two parallel arms race processes would emerge in the region. Israel would have no choice but to react to the Arab investment in conventional capabilities, and it would also have to deal with a non-conventional capability in the future (Cohen 1998, 148–51; Evron 1994, 5–7).[45]

The two concerns were contradictory. Indeed, history suggests that the IDF concerns were unfounded; Israeli investments in the nuclear project—as costly as they may have been—did not come at the expense of the development of a powerful conventional capability. At the same time, the prediction about a dual—conventional and unconventional—arms race did materialize. The Israeli nuclear project was instrumental both in intensifying the conventional arms race and in provoking a non-conventional arms race.

We do not have any clear breakdown of military expenditures on conventional and nonconventional capabilities in the Middle East. This imposes some restrictions on the analysis. Therefore, I start by discussing the conventional arms race in the region in terms of material and human costs.[46] Let us focus first on several quantitative aspects of the regional arms race. There are several ways to conceptualize trends in arms racing. The typical way is to examine temporal trends in defense expenditures. The assessment of national defense efforts is measured by defense burdens, that is, the proportion of the total national production (GDP) that a state spends on defense. Figure 8.1 displays the defense expenditures of the key players in the Middle East arms race. Figure 8.2 displays the dollar-per-soldier ratio as an indicator of the technological arms race.[47]

These figures suggest that the military spending of the key players in the region rose dramatically in the early 1960s, a trend that was never reversed. All three states spend today tenfold or more the amounts they had spent prior to the inception of the nuclear project. This is not direct evidence that Israeli nuclear policy was a key factor in the spiraling of defense spending, but the temporal coincidence is suggestive of a growing emphasis on military spending in the first half of the 1960s and of a significant upward trend that we observe starting in 1967. What is remarkable is that it was Israeli defense burden that increased the most since 1963.[48] Neither the self-perception of nuclear deterrence nor the major victory in the Six Day War helped alleviate the financial defense burden.

On the whole, a similar trend can be observed in terms of the size of the armed forces of these states. Israeli military personnel grew from a total of 80,000–90,000 mobilized soldiers in 1948 (Ostfeld 1994, 23–24) to a total force—standing armed forces and reserves—of 630,000, over 10 percent of the total population of Israel and roughly 16 percent of the Jewish population in 2004. The Egyptian armed forces rose from a total of about 74,000 soldiers to a total of roughly 450,000 in 2003. However, in contrast to Israel, the size of the armed forces in Egypt— the human burden of defense—has never exceeded 1 percent of the population. Likewise, Syrian armed forces grew from 20,000 to roughly 400,000 troops over the 1948–2003 period, with the growth being both absolute and relative (from 1.2 percent of the population in 1948 to 2.7 percent in 2003).

If we combine the human and material dimensions of the defense effort, we can examine how this effort shifted in terms of spending per sol-

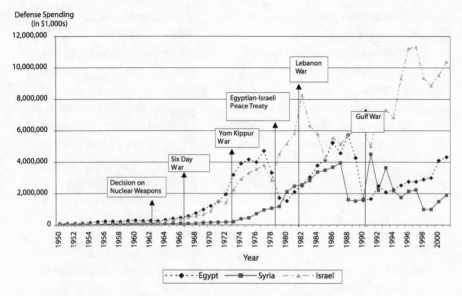

Fig. 8.1. Defense spending in Egypt, Syria, and Israel, 1950–2001

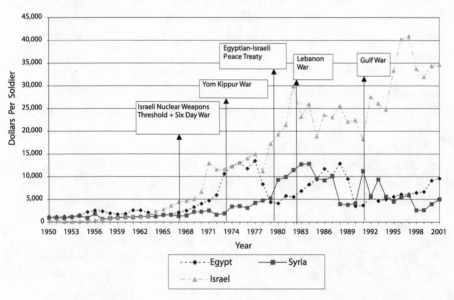

Fig. 8.2. Defense spending per soldier: Egypt, Syria, Israel, 1950–2001

dier. Higher rates of spending per soldier indicate an increased impact of high technology on the armed forces. This could imply investment in strategic technology, such as ballistic missiles, power projection capabilities, or nonconventional weapons. But it could also suggest a growing emphasis on tactical technologies, such as PGMs for tactical use; better combat platforms such as planes, tanks, artillery, and even personal tactical weapons; and support systems such as night-combat optics and small arms. Figure 8.2 suggests clearly the difference between the sharp rise in Israel's emphasis on technological superiority starting in the early 1960s compared to its principal rivals.

As we can see, all three states increased their dollar-to-soldier ratios significantly starting in 1967. However, the Israeli rate of growth in this figure was substantially higher than any of the other two states. Moreover, Egypt reduced the dollar-to-soldier ratio following the Sadat peace initiative, and Syria stabilized this ratio in the wake of the Lebanon War. Yet, Israel's spending on technological capabilities at the tactical and strategic level did not stabilize but rather grew over time. In general, defense burdens went down in most of the Middle East during the late 1980s and 1990s. There was also a relative stability in the number of major weapon systems, for example, combat aircraft, tanks, armored personnel carriers (APCs), and artillery batteries. The only area that exhibited marked growth in the region during this period was the number of ballistic missiles and nonconventional weapons. Even so, Israel's technological edge over the Arab states had widened significantly (Maoz 1996a; 1997b; Cordesman 2004).

It is difficult to directly test the magnitude and nature of the impact of Israeli nuclear policy on the Middle East arms race. Nonetheless, a suggestive statistical test can be offered as partial evidence. One of the commonly used quantitative devices in evaluation studies is interrupted time-series analysis. According to this approach, we observe the effect that a given policy intervention had on a series, based on its effect on the intercept and slope parameters of the series. From this type of analysis, we can extrapolate out the effect of a given intervention on a series (Mohr 1995, 203–24; Nachmias 1979, 58–61). I perform this test looking at the before-after differences, where the "intervention" in this case is the rough starting date of the military dimension of Israeli nuclear policy.

Table 8.2 shows the results of a set of time-series regressions of defense spending and dollar-to-soldier ratios of the three principal protagonists in the Arab-Israeli conflict. Each of these sets is based on an estimation of the following equation:

$$Y_t = \alpha + \beta_1 Y_{t-1} + \sum_{i=2}^{k} \beta_{ii} X_{it-1} + \beta_j Nuclear + \beta_h Peace + \varepsilon_t, \qquad (8.1)$$

where Y_t is the value of the dependent variable (e.g., defense expenditures of the state whose behavior is assessed) at time t. The term α is the intercept, Y_{t-1} is the value of the dependent variable in the previous year (e.g., last year's military expenditures of the focal state), the index i represents

TABLE 8.2.   The Middle East Arms Race: Time-Series Regression Analysis

State	Independent Variables	Defense Expenditures[a]	Dollar-to-Soldier Ratio[b]
Israel, 1950–2001	Lagged Israeli defense expenditures	0.825** (0.091)	0.787** (0.143)
	Lagged Egyptian defense expenditures	–0.096 (0.086)	–0.175 (0.111)
	Lagged Syrian defense expenditures	0.246* (0.142)	0.035 (0.442)
	Nuclear/nonnuclear dummy variable[c]	800,170** (347,588)	3,566** (1,369)
	Peace with Egypt dummy variable[d]	2,871 (1,793)	2,871 (1940)
Regression Statistics	N = 51	Adj. R^2 = 0.966 D-W = 1.903	Adj. R^2 = 0.976 D-W = 1.918
Egypt, 1950–2001	Lagged Israeli defense expenditures	0.126* (0.071)	0.100* (0.044)
	Lagged Egyptian defense expenditures	0.639** (0.173)	0.624** (0.162)
	Nuclear/nonnuclear dummy variable	576,607* (370,866)	1,270 (950)
	Peace with Israel dummy variable	–517,266 (540,130)	–1,874 (1,265)
Regression Statistics	N = 51	Adj. R^2 = 0.674 D-W = 1.794	Adj. R^2 = 0.681 D-W = 2.009
Syria, 1950–2001	Lagged Israeli defense expenditures	0.029 (0.051)	0.050 (0.048)
	Lagged Syrian defense expenditures	0.828** (0.109)	0.490** (0.195)
	Nuclear/nonnuclear dummy variable	123,320* (71,068)	477 (322)
	Israel-Egypt peace dummy variable	551,099** (232,747)	3,042* (1,162)
Regression Statistics	N = 51	Adj. R^2 = 0.985 D-W = 2.052	Adj. R^2 = 0.974 D-W = 2.022

Note: [a]Defense expenditures measured in 1980 constant price dollars.

[b]Dollar-to-soldier ratio is measured as military expenditures divided by military personnel, based on the calculation given in table 8.1.

[c]Nuclear/nonnuclear dummy variable, 1950–67 = 0; 1968–2001 = 1.

[d]Israel-Egypt peace: 1950–78 = 0; 1979–2001 = 1.

**$p < .01$; *$p < .05$.

All tests are single-tail, with nuclear/nonnuclear dummy expected to positively affect defense effort and peace with Egypt expected to negatively affect peace effort of Egypt and Israel and to positively affect peace effort of Syria.

a set of other states (e.g., for Israel these other states are Egypt and Syria; for Egypt and Syria the other state is Israel), and X_{it-1} is the value of the independent variable (e.g., other states' defense expenditures) for the previous year. The beta (β) terms represent the impact of a given independent variable on the dependent variable, controlling for other independent variables, and ε_t represents the (statistical) error term. The terms *Nuclear* and *Peace* represent the effects of two possible interruptions on the process. The term *Nuclear* represents the period during which Israel is said to have been in possession of nuclear weapons and is coded as 0 for the 1950–67 period and as 1 afterward. *Peace* is also a dummy variable coded as 0 over the 1950–78 period and as 1 afterward.[49]

We can see from this table that the figures do not indicate a really meaningful arms race in the sense that Israel's defense expenditures are not significantly affected by the defense expenditures of Egypt and/or Syria. Rather, the best predictor of each state's defense expenditures at a given year was the state's defense expenditures in the previous year. This indicates a bureaucratic inertia process where last year's budget is the baseline of this year's budget and budgetary changes occur only on the margins, regardless of external inputs.[50] However, if we mark 1967 as the year in which Israel became a nuclear weapon state, we can clearly see that this year affected positively the defense effort not only of Egypt and Syria but also of Israeli spending. Again, this is not conclusive evidence, since 1967 also marks the Six Day War effect on the Arab-Israeli conflict, but it does suggest that neither these events nor the peace with Egypt had any modifying effect on the Middle East arms race. What it does suggest, however, is that states responded to their own internal needs more than to the security threats represented by other states' defense spending.[51]

These results suggest the next step. At this step we can examine whether a meaningful event in the state's history had an effect on changing the pattern of defense expenditures or on its dollar-to-soldier ratio. There are several ways of isolating the effect of nuclear weapons on Israeli defense expenditures. First, we can examine whether other major events in Israel's history had an effect on the defense expenditures of Israel and its neighbors. Table 8.2 has already shown that the advent of nuclear weapons and the Six Day War had a magnifying effect on both Israel's defense expenditures and those of Syria and Egypt. We change the period dummy variable sequentially in accordance with significant turning points in the Arab-Israeli conflict. This allows us to test the effect of three other events on Israel's defense expenditures and on the dollar-per-soldier ratio: the Yom Kippur War, the Egyptian-Israeli peace treaty in 1979, and the 1982 Lebanon War.

The results of these analyses suggest that none of these events had a significant impact on the pattern of Israeli defense spending. On the other hand, when we examine the impact of the Egyptian-Israeli peace treaty on the pattern of Egypt's defense spending, we see that, up until 1979, Israeli defense spending as well as Israel's possession of nuclear weapons had a significant positive impact on both Egypt's defense spending and its dollar-to-soldier ratio. After 1979, Egypt's spending and dollar-to-soldier ratio responded mostly to its own past behavior. The goodness of fit statistics are significantly higher for the pre-1979 period than for the subsequent period. Syria's patterns are very similar to those of Egypt. The only meaningful breakdown of the period for Syria was again the Egyptian-Israeli peace treaty, which left Syria alone against Israel. Prior to this event, Syria's defense spending and its dollar-to-soldier ratio responded to past Israeli expenditures. Following the Egyptian-Israeli peace treaty, Syrian expenditures and dollar-to-soldier ratios responded to Syria's own past spending. The goodness of fit statistics are far higher for the first period compared to the second period.[52]

Another and related approach is to look at the extent to which a meaningful arms race has taken place over different periods of time. For example, we can run the basic arms race equations several times, each time changing the relevant time span. For example, we run separate tests covering the 1950–60, 1950–61, . . . , 1950–78, 1950–69, . . . , 1950–2001 periods. The equation that maximizes the fit (minimizes the root mean square error [RMSE]) is then chosen to serve as the baseline. From that point on we generate an expected series. This series allows us to develop a counterfactual history of sorts, that is, to speculate what would have been the defense expenditures of a given state had the interruption (in our case, nuclear weapons) not taken place. We can do that using defense expenditures figures, or we can perform a similar operation with military personnel figures. Figures 8.3 and 8.4 suggest the outcome of such an analysis.[53]

The results of this analysis tell an extremely suggestive story. A set of time-series regressions with varying numbers of years shows that the best arms race–related fit (and best overall fit) for the Israeli military expenditures series is for the 1950–60 period, with a RMSE of $4,300 and an R^2 of 0.995.[54] Over that period, Israel's defense expenditures were significantly affected by Egyptian defense expenditures (but not by the Syrian defense expenditures), as well as by its last year spending. If we use the year 1960 (incidentally, this is when Ben-Gurion revealed the Dimona reactor) as the baseline year, and we extrapolate from the 1950–60 period

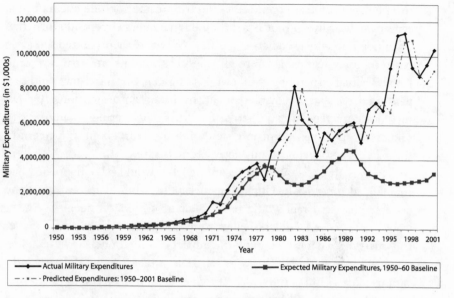

Fig. 8.3. Actual, predicted, and expected Israeli military expenditures based on the 1950–60 Arms Race

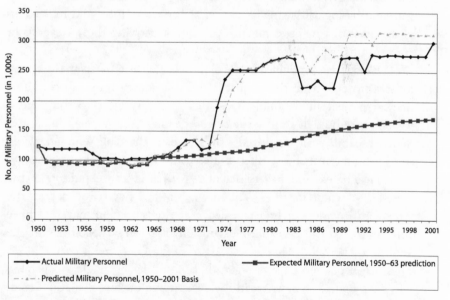

Fig. 8.4. Actual, predicted, and expected Israeli military personnel

the expected defense expenditures, on the assumption of a conventional arms race, we can see that Israel should have never expended more than $5 billion annually on defense. For the year 2001, the expected spending based on an arms race assumption is less that $3 billion, a third of what Israel is actually spending.[55] Likewise, a similar analysis of Israel's military personnel suggests that Israel should have had an armed force (which includes both regulars and active reservists) numbering about 170,000 soldiers at any given point in time during the year, about 57 percent of the soldiers who were actually activated in 2001.

There is always a question regarding what would have happened had Israel decided not to develop nuclear weapons. This analysis suggests one possible answer: Israel would have spent much less on defense. And it would have needed a much smaller army. Why is this the case? To answer this question, we must examine the impact of Israeli nuclear weapons on the qualitative nature of the Middle East arms race. One of the early indications of this kind of impact can be given by the steep rise in the dollar-to-soldier figures of all armies, but principally the Israeli figures (see table 8.1). These figures can tell us what all this extra money was spent on.

The qualitative aspect of the regional arms race requires inspection of the development of nonconventional weapons, including nuclear, chemical, and biological weapons, as well as the acquisition and indigenous development of ballistic missiles capable of carrying these weapons or conventional warheads.

The evidence available to date on other nuclear projects in the region focuses principally on the Iraqi and Iranian projects. Iraq embarked on a nuclear project in the mid-1970s, reaching very close to the nuclear weapon threshold in 1991 at the eve of the Gulf War. Virtually all of this WMD capability was destroyed, however, after the Gulf War. The widespread suspicion in the United States, Britain, and Israel was that Iraq continued to expand its arsenal of WMD after the expulsion of the UNSCOM teams in 1998. This, however, was not borne out, as the American invasion of Iraq revealed. Yet this suspicion may well have contributed to the continued expansion of Israel's capabilities in the 1999–2003 period.[56]

Israeli academic experts argue that, while Israeli nuclear capability may have figured somewhere in the background of the calculations leading to the development of a nuclear program of a military nature in Iraq, it has not been a major factor (Feldman 1997, 135; Evron 1998, 20). Rather, if there was a principal target of the Iraqi nuclear weapons, it was Iran. In the mid-1970s, Iraq had to accept a fairly humiliating agreement to its dispute with Iran over the Shatt al Arab region. Saddam had to deal first with the rapidly expanding Iranian conventional capability and later on viewed nuclear weapons as an aspect of the strategic competition with Iran.

Likewise, Iran's nuclear project, initially conceived as part of the shah's self-image of regional grandeur, was and is aimed principally at Iraq. After a dormant period in the 1980s— principally due to the effort it had put into its conventional war with Iraq—Iran revived and accelerated its nuclear program in the 1990s and during the first years of the third millennium. Israeli and American intelligence sources continuously argued that Iran was rapidly approaching toward acquisition of nuclear weapons capability, but these estimates have been changed and revised constantly (Sick 1995). Following the American-Iraqi war of 2003, the Iranian nuclear program attracted growing attention from the international community, but not much has been accomplished to curb it.[57]

More important, Iran has invested considerable resources in building long-range ballistic missiles. The Iranian missile program started with significant help from Israel (Sick 1995, 160), but after the revolution Iran turned to North Korea for help. Iranian Sheehab missiles have a range that covers all of Israel. The Israeli nuclear capability may have served as some minor motivating force, but there is no evidence to suggest that it had any meaningful effect either on the inception of the project or on the turn toward weapon-related research and development (Kam 2004). Thus, it is generally believed by Israeli experts that, even if Israel had not developed nuclear weapons, Iran and Iraq would probably be where they are at present on their project (or in the Iraqi case, even further on).

This belief, however, is inconsistent with some of the basic facts and evidence surrounding these projects. First, the timing of the Iraqi project and the fact that the strategy pursued by the Saddam regime to develop a weapon-grade nuclear capability emulated the Israeli model strongly suggest that Israel's capability had a marked effect on the Iraqi project.[58] Second, in 1977 Iraq presented a memorandum to the Arab League. This memorandum outlined the development of the Israeli nuclear project and claimed that Israel had several nuclear weapons. Other official statements by Saddam Hussein and his foreign minister, Tariq Azziz, in 1980—prior to the Israeli bombing of the Osirak reactor—also mentioned Israeli nuclear capabilities as a threat to the Arabs.[59] The Iraqi threat perception following the bombing of the Osirak reactor only intensified. To the general sense that Israeli nuclear capability posed a challenge or a threat to the Arabs was added a belief that the Israeli policy was aimed at perpetuating the Israeli nuclear monopoly in the region. And this was an unacceptable future from an Arab perspective (Levite and Landau 1994, 107, 189–90; Feldman 1997, 136).[60]

A similar argument was made by Iran. Kam argues that Israel's nuclear weapons and its technological superiority are perceived as a constant humiliation of the fundamentalist regime in Iran in particular. The Arabs, Kam argues, should not continue to allow an Israeli nuclear monopoly in the region (Kam 2004, 48–50, 198). The Begin Doctrine must have also affected Iranian approach to nuclear weapons, as is evident by recent deterrent threats by Iran's minister of defense. These threats were presumably intended to ward off an Israeli preemptive strike on Iranian nuclear installations.[61]

These points suggest that the role of the Israeli nuclear program in the overall calculations leading to the launching of nuclear weapons projects in Iraq and Iran was not at all marginal. The question is why Iran and Iraq took it upon themselves to confront the Israeli nuclear capability by a similar capability of their own, in contrast to the states bordering Israel, which are more vulnerable to such weapons. The simple answer seems to be that Iraq and Iran could afford what Egypt and Syria could not. The oil-rich states opted for the "rich man's weapons of mass destruction." The latter states could not afford the expense associated with the development of nuclear weapons, thus opting to match Israeli nuclear capability by the "poor man's weapons."[62]

In this context, let us examine the Middle East missile race. Egypt's first reaction to the information about the Israeli nuclear project was to embark upon its own missile project. Employing German scientists, Egypt attempted to build several ballistic missiles. The project was aborted partly because of an Israeli intelligence operation that scared away the German scientists and partly because of the German government's decision to prohibit German citizens from working on missile projects abroad (Black and Morris 1991, 192–201). Following the Israeli deep penetration bombings in Egypt during the War of Attrition, the Soviet Union provided Egypt and Syria with FRUG-7 and Scud-B missiles. As noted, Syria fired a number of FRUG missiles at the Israeli airbase of Ramat David during the Yom Kippur War (Herzog 1975; Dupuy 1978, 465).

Syrian and Egyptian missile development continued throughout the 1970s and 1980s, with both acquiring Scud-B and Scud-C missiles, first from the Soviet Union and then from North Korea. Egypt pursued a joint missile project with Argentina. Both Egypt and Syria embarked upon the production or improvement of the Scud missiles (Shapir 1996).

Israeli nuclear policy may not have had a dominant effect on the start-up of the Iraqi and Iranian nuclear project. However, the Israeli missile program, which is part and parcel of its nuclear policy, had a significant effect on the missile projects of Egypt and Syria, Iraq, and Iran. The pursuit of long-range missile capability by Iraq and Iran exceeds by far the geographical radius of the contiguous threat. Iraq and Iran's search for long-range missiles that are capable of carrying nonconventional warheads has quite likely been affected by the advanced missile technology—capable of carrying nuclear warheads—that has been developed by Israel since the early 1960s.

Table 8.3 provides rough estimates of the number, type, and major attributes of the SSMs possessed by the key actors in the Middle East. As can be seen, this number is over one thousand missiles, many of which are

TABLE 8.3. Ballistic Missiles in the Middle East: 2004 Estimates

State	Missile	Payload	Range	CEP[a]	Quantity	Comments
Egypt	Scud-B	985 kg	300 km	1,500m	50+	
	Scud-C	500 kg	500 km	2,000m	50+	
	Project T	985 kg	500 km	NA	90	Under development
	Vector	1,000 kg	1,000 km	NA	NA	Under development
	No Dong	1,000 kg	1,000 km	NA	24	Alleged
Iraq						None after 2003
Iran	Scud-C	500 kg	500 km	2,000m	100	
	Scud-B	985 kg	300 km	1,500m	300	
	Sheehab-3	700 kg	1,000+ km	NA	20+	Under test; nuclear warhead capable
	Sheehab-4	1,000 kg	2,000 km	NA	NA	Under development; nuclear warhead capable
Israel	Jericho 2	1,000 kg	1,500 km	NA	50	Nuclear warhead capable
	Jericho 1	500 kg	500 km	NA	50	Nuclear warhead capable
	Lance	450 kg	130 km	500m	30+	Tactical nuclear warhead capable
	Jericho 3	1,000 kg	4,800 km	NA	NA	Under development
Saudi Arabia	CSS-2	2,500 kg	2,650 km	1,500m	50	Conventional warhead only
Syria	SS-21	480 kg	70 km	30-100m	200	Tactical
	Scud-B	985 kg	300 km	1,500m	200	Chemical warhead capable
	Scud-C	500 kg	500 km	2,000m	80	Chemical warhead capable
	Scud-D	450 kg	600 km	2-3km	NA	Under development

Sources: Shapir 2004; Shoham 1998, 295–99; Lorbar 1998; Evron 1998; 5–12. See Monterey Institute of International Studies 2004; Federation of American Scientists 2004.

[a]Circular error probability is the radius of a circle in which 50% of the missiles fired at a given point are expected to hit.

capable of being, and probably are, fitted with nonconventional warheads and many of which, due to their relatively low level of accuracy, cannot serve any other purpose but strategic attacks on population centers.

The response of Egypt and Syria to the Israeli nuclear project was the development of chemical and biological weapons. Since the dismantlement of most of the Iraqi chemical and biological capabilities, Egyptian and Syrian chemical weapons projects are considered the most extensive in the Middle East.[63] Most Syrian Scud-B and Scud-C missiles are capable of carrying chemical warheads. Neither Egypt nor Syria signed the Chemical Weapons Convention (CWC) in retaliation for Israel's refusal to join the NPT. Both have signed but not ratified the Biological and Toxin Weapons Convention (BTWC).

Both the timing of the missile and chemical weapons projects in Syria and Egypt and the pursuit of long-range ballistic missile capabilities by such states as Iran and Iraq (which had actually fired them at Israel) suggest that the Israeli nuclear project was a trigger in their development and spread. The Israeli attack on the Osirak nuclear reactor in 1981 had a major impact on the Iraqi pursuit of long-range missiles capable of hitting Israel. Saddam's speech of April 2, 1990, suggests that this capability of hitting Israel was designed to issue a deterrent threat to Israel's nuclear capability. Other Arab spokesmen have reiterated the point that chemical and biological weapons represented an effort to balance the nonconventional equation vis-à-vis Israel's nuclear weapons.[64]

One could argue that a balance of terror of sorts emerged in the Middle East. Israeli nuclear capability is balanced by Syrian and Egyptian chemical and biological capabilities. The problem with the nuclear-chemical/biological equation is that it is extremely unstable. The destructive power of nuclear weapons and the fact that there is no defense against such weapons means that they can be used for deterrence purposes. This is so because the threat of nuclear retaliation is so frightening that, even if the chance of actually carrying it out is remote, it is enough to convince a would-be challenger to preserve the status quo. Chemical weapons (and possibly biological weapons) are questionable as deterrence-related weapons, however. Since there are fairly effective defenses against chemical weapon attacks, these weapons are quite ineffective as second-strike capabilities. Hence, their most effective use is as first-strike weapons, and they are best employed through a surprise attack.[65]

As noted, the traumatic experience of the missile attacks on Israel's population centers during the Gulf War accelerated Israeli antimissile defense efforts. The establishment of the HFC and the development of the Arrow antiballistic missile that became operational in 2000 are only partial measures against the threat of missile attacks. The second set of measures is offensive and is centered on an all-out effort by the IAF to develop a capability to destroy missile launchers at short, medium, and long ranges.

It is evident, from the pattern both of aircraft procurement and of doctrinal developments, that the first and almost exclusive mission of the IAF in the event of a war with one or more Arab states will be to destroy the Arab missile launchers and support systems (e.g., radars, missile silos, etc.). Knowing this, Arab states have a strong strategic incentive to shoot first. The ineffectiveness of the Israeli nuclear threats in the past suggests that such threats may be even more ineffective in the future. Given the instability of the strategic equation that was ignited by Israel's nuclear capabilities, the potential of an unwanted and unintended escalation in the event of a future crisis in the region is extremely high.

The analysis of the conventional and nonconventional arms race in the region suggests that not only did Israel's nuclear policy have a significant impact on the intensification of this arms race but also that—in some important respects—Israel may have been its chief victim. There is reason to believe that Israel faces more complex security risks in the third millennium than it did in the past; certainly it faces graver challenges than it did prior to the inception of its nuclear adventure. The nuclear program of Iran, the chemical and biological weapons in the military arsenal of all of Israel's major strategic rivals, as well as the vast proliferation of ballistic missiles put Israel at a greater peril than ever before. The removal of Iraq from the list of Israeli threats has lessened Israel's strategic problems considerably. Yet, this appears to be only a partial remedy, as the threat of the Iranian nuclear weapons program appears more ominous than ever before.

One may well argue that the development of nonconventional weapons and long-range delivery systems in the region would have taken place regardless of whether Israel developed nuclear capability. This may well be true. However, the fact is that Israel's nuclear capability had a significant effect if not on the inception of programs of nonconventional weapons in the region then on the scope of such programs and their acceleration over time.

4.2. Domestic Implications: Secrecy, Doctrine, and the Cult of Technology

The Israeli security establishment may try to seek comfort in the belief that the doctrine of nuclear ambiguity is secure, having supposedly allowed Israel to develop and maintain its nuclear posture while resisting international pressures to disarm or to inspect its nuclear facilities.[66] Israel, however, is not an ambiguous nuclear power but rather an undeclared nuclear state. Apart from ample evidence based on publicized intelligence estimates, as well as statements by Arab and Western officials, regarding the possession of nuclear weapons, the Israeli public has been overwhelmingly convinced of this fact. In a 1986 survey, 92 percent of Israelis were either certain or "pretty sure" that Israel possessed nuclear weapons (Arian 1995, 71).

By and large, the Israeli public has supported the ambiguous status of the Israeli nuclear posture, although this support has eroded over time. In 1987, 80 percent of Israelis supported nuclear ambiguity, while, in 1998, 67 percent remained in favor of ambiguity (Arian 1998, 31; 2002, 34). Israeli opinions varied, however, on scenarios that would justify the use of such weapons. For example, in the 1999 survey of the Jaffee Center for Strategic Studies (JCSS), 26 percent of Israelis opposed the use of nuclear weapons in response to a chemical or biological attack on Israel. Nearly 56 percent rejected the use of nuclear weapons even if Israel faced a desperate conventional military threat. Over 80 percent opposed the use of nuclear weapons if the Golan Height was taken by force. Over 83 percent opposed using nuclear weapons "to save many lives," and 90 percent opposed the use of nuclear weapons "instead of using the regular army" (Arian 1999, 53).[67]

These figures strongly suggest that most Israelis justify the use of nuclear weapons as a last resort—under conditions of severe and immediate threat to Israel's very survival. However, the secrecy surrounding the development and deployment of nuclear weapons—especially in light of the deliberate and unintended leaks regarding Israel's nuclear capabilities—suggests a potential disconnect between the public's perception of the purpose of Israel's nuclear weapons and their purpose as understood by the security establishment.

This potential disconnect suggests three questions. First, are the quantity and types of Israel's nuclear weapons consistent with the public image of a weapon of last resort, which in turn helps to legitimize the policy of ambiguity? Second, is there an effective political control over both doctrine and development of nuclear weapons? Third, is the public aware of the potentially destabilizing potential of offensive nuclear weapons, and would they support the development and deployment of such weapons?

According to independent sources, Israel possesses a quantity of nuclear bombs that has a significant overkill capacity. For example, to cause a total devastation of a state such as Egypt, an attack on the Aswan Dam would suffice, because it would cause a total flood of the entire Nile basin and complete devastation of all the cities along the river (e.g., Aswan, Luxor, Asyut, Bani Suwayl, Cairo, Al Minya, and Alexandria). About 80 percent of Egypt's population resides in those cities. Cairo and Alexandria alone account for 20 million Egyptians. Likewise, over two-thirds of the Syrian population is located in five cities: Damascus, Aleppo, Homs, Hama, and Latakia. Just like Egypt, Iraq's survival and economy are totally dependent on the Hidekel Dam, and over two-thirds of its population resides in three main cities: Baghdad, Mosul, and Basra. Finally, in Iran, the key cities of Tehran, Isfahan, Tabriz, Mashad, and Shiraz account for over 50 percent of the Iranian population.[68] A conservative estimate of the number of nuclear bombs that it would take to completely destroy the first- and second-tier opponents of Israel by hitting their population centers amounts to about one-third of the number of nuclear devices attributed to Israel by foreign sources. Even a credible second-strike capability would require less than half the quantity of nuclear warheads attributed to Israel. If the numbers provided by foreign intelligence estimates of about one hundred to two hundred nuclear bombs are anywhere near target, then it is the public's right to know the logic of this overkill capacity.

Foreign sources indicate the possession of tactical nuclear weapons by Israel.[69] Exactly how do these weapons fit into the professed deterrence posture of Israel's nuclear policy? Given that the Israeli public strongly opposes the use of nuclear weapons in a tactical situation, what exactly is the justification for the production of such weapons? What are the doctrinal requirements for which these weapons were produced?

The image of a "Samson Option" that is cautiously filtered by the national security establishment to the public may well be distorted. The possibility that Israel is capable of deploying its nuclear weapons for both strategic and tactical purposes was enabled by the regime of secrecy and deceit surrounding Israel's nuclear policy. Nuclear ambiguity may well imply not only an intent of "letting the Arabs guess." The policy of ambiguity may well be an instrument for maintaining high public support for Israel's nuclear policy, a support that is based on the naive belief that there exists effective political control over the production and development of nuclear weapons. Moreover, the policy of ambiguity may create a false public image that there exists a consistent linkage between the strategic deterrent role of these weapons and the quantity and types of weapons produced.

What accounts for such a discrepancy between the professed aims of the nuclear policy and the type and quantity of systems that have been produced over time? There are two possible explanations for this process. First, Arab strategists argue that Israel's nuclear policy has gone beyond deterrence, into the realm of offensive deployment. Specifically, these strategists believe that Israel's nuclear weapons are needed to support its offensive and imperial designs (Levite and Landau 1994, 24, 52–53, 56; Landau 2001, 23; Evron 1998, 18). This explanation adds another rationale to Israel's policy of nuclear ambiguity: it is presumably designed to mask not only the weapons but also the doctrine of nuclear deployment and use.

This explanation can be easily dismissed, however. The record of Israel's demonstrated willingness since 1973—regardless of the party in power—to make territorial concessions on all fronts clearly disproves this notion. Indeed, the tactical nuclear weapons attributed to Israel are not in keeping with the willingness or ability of Israel to hold on to the territories it occupied in 1967.[70]

The second explanation asserts that technological considerations and bureaucratic inertia rather than overarching strategic logic have driven research, development, and actual production of nuclear weapon systems. A coalition of scientists and weapon developers circumvented or even aligned with politicians in control of the nuclear project. The scientists set out to develop the most sophisticated weapon systems that their technological capabilities could afford, while the bureaucrats of the Nuclear Energy Commission and the Defense Ministry sought to maximize their budgets. As in other types of military-technological-industrial complexes, this coalition exaggerated the threat, "romanticized" the weapon and delivery systems, and used other ploys to create a reality that was inconsistent with or even contradicted the strategic logic of deterrence and the notion of nuclear weapons as a last resort.[71] Yet, unlike many other military-technological-industrial complexes, the Israeli nuclear coalition enjoyed an almost absolute of freedom of operation, for three reasons: (1) the secrecy of the project, (2) the almost nonexistent doctrinal discussion in political, parliamentary, and academic forums, and (3) the lack of political control and oversight.

Some of the political authorities responsible for the nuclear policy were themselves infatuated with the technological fetish. They may have been tempted by the scientists and weapon developers into supporting efforts to explore the frontiers of weapon development. Others may have been driven by political motivations.[72]

The disconnect between the public's image of Israel's nuclear capabilities and doctrine and the actual policy of the security establishment requires more elaboration than is possible here. It is evident from this analysis that the ambiguity, secrecy, and deceit that surround Israel's nuclear policy are not unique. The policy is rather another example of the security community, as a whole or in part, running way ahead (or outside) of the political system. One may argue that, by and large, the treatment of nuclear weapons was prudent and sensitive. This may be true, but it is beside the point. In a democratic political system, it is the public's right to know of the potentially destabilizing implications of such weapons, of their potentially offensive nature, and of the fact that they may be used for purposes other than deterrence, certainly other than weapons of last resort. It is important to recognize that it is not only the Israeli public that is in the dark with respect to these issues; many of Israel's legislators and opinion makers are uninformed as well. At the same time, Israel's strategic competitors may be less in the dark about these issues. If the Arab states believe that Israel possesses tactical nuclear weapons, and if they believe that Israel would use them in a difficult battlefield situation, then the incentive to strike at these weapons at the outset of the confrontation is very high. The escalatory potential of such weapons runs contrary to the professed aim of deterrence.

It may still be the case that the Israeli public and the political system would end up supporting the development and possession of tactical nuclear weapons; however, this must come after the issue is openly discussed and debated, not as a result of a bureaucratic fait accompli legitimized by secrecy and deceit and allowed to operate with little or no political control.

Because Israel's nuclear policy was not widely discussed in open political and public forums, there has been no comprehensive evaluation of its functioning. Some of the major implications of this program, such as its effect on the nonconventional arms race in the Middle East, have been almost completely ignored. Most Israeli studies of nonconventional weapons in the region depict the development and acquisition of such weapons as taking place almost independently of Israel's capabilities. The impact of Israeli nuclear capabilities on Egyptian and Syrian nonconventional weapon developments is minimized or even ignored. Such projects are seen as springing either out of such states' autonomous considerations and internal aspirations and goals or from the conventional technological gap between themselves and Israel.[73] Egyptian concerns over Israel's nuclear capabilities and their implications are regarded by some Israeli analysts as "not entirely born of the direct threat that these presumed weapons pose to Egypt." Rather, Egyptian pressure for a nuclear-free zone in the Middle East is seen to spring out of

> Egypt's interest in leading the Arab world on the nuclear issue, i.e., using the nuclear issue as a means of consolidating its leadership position in the Arab world . . . [and second] Egypt's interest in the nature of the Middle East once peace agreements have been achieved—in this future Middle East, Israel would most likely be Egypt's foremost rival for regional power, and Egypt was reluctant to reach this stage with Israel as a nuclear power. (Landau 2001, 24)

Other interpretations of Egypt's pressure on Israel on the nuclear issues typically depict Egyptian efforts as a ploy to disarm Israel to a point where Egypt could renew hostilities without the fear of nuclear retaliation. All of these notions stem from the fundamental assumption that Israeli nuclear policy was phenomenally successful and hence any effort to disarm it would severely endanger its security. The policy of ambiguity and the regime of secrecy and deceit prevent or dampen down any serious discussion of the relationship between the strategic logic of Israel's nuclear strategy and its actual capabilities.[74]

5. THE ILLOGIC OF ISRAEL'S NUCLEAR STRATEGY[75]

I have argued that, by and large, there is no evidence that Israeli nuclear policy has accomplished any of the objectives that the policy's founding fathers assigned to it. Nor has it generated any of the positive side effects attributed to it by various strategists. On the contrary, the policy's side effects in terms of both foreign and domestic politics have been negative and dangerous. Why is that the case? In this section, I identify some fundamental pitfalls underlying both the basic conception of this policy and the manner in which it was implemented. I focus on six major problems.[76]

5.1. Flawed Assumptions and Biased Expectations

As noted, the trigger to the nuclear project was a basic threat perception that relied on a number of assumptions about the potential evolution of the Arab-Israeli conflict. These assumptions were fundamentally flawed. They were flawed because they were treated by Israeli decision makers as untestable axioms rather than as testable hypotheses. They were also flawed because they were based on a noninteractive logic. Several points are relevant here.

First, the fundamental asymmetry in human, economic, and territorial resources between Israel and the Arab world was never the major issue in the strategic Arab-Israeli equation. The relevant question was whether and under what conditions this potential could be converted into an actual threat. This was an eminently testable question. Israeli decision makers had ample data for the testing of this matter both prior to the decision on the nuclear project and at any of the stages of its development. As we have seen, this potential was never converted into an actual human and material effort by any of Israel's rivals or into a practical political coalition capable of destroying the Jewish state. Nor was there any evidence of operational plans designed to convert the dream of annihilation of the state of Israel into a practical reality. The Israeli flaw was basing the threat perception entirely on Arab rhetoric and ignoring the strategic reality.

Second, the development of a capability designed to address a worst-case scenario (a general Arab coalition that mobilizes its human and material resources to attack Israel under conditions of superpower support for the Arabs and diplomatic isolation of Israel) may well have been a sound policy move. This implies perhaps creating a nuclear potential—including a human and physical infrastructure—that could be converted into actual nuclear weapons in a fairly short time. There was no reason to go beyond the nuclear threshold stage. The culmination of all of the political and military components of such a scenario could not emerge overnight. By the time an existential risk could realistically materialize, Israel could convert the nuclear potential into an actual deterrent capability. The gap between the actual nuclear capabilities attributed to Israel and the real magnitude of the threat leading to the development of nuclear weapons is as large as the gap between the Arab rhetoric and the actual effort invested in the annihilation scheme.

Third, Israeli decision makers failed to realize the interactive and spiral nature of threat perceptions due to the nuclear project. Robert Jervis has repeatedly pointed out the tendency of assuming that an opponent's intentions and plans are autonomous and independent of our behavior. At the same time, deterrence logic often asserts that the opponent will perceive deterrent threats as credible and nonthreatening (Jervis 1976, 58–84; 1985b). Because the Ben-Gurion school of thought prevailed in the nuclear debate, its assumptions about the conflict and the unidirectional nature of the threat also prevailed in subsequent strategic debates.

These assumptions generated a naive belief that, because Israel was the threatened party, its actions with respect to research and development would not be interpreted as escalatory. This was the typical party line carried by Israeli strategists and diplomats in their dealings with the United States throughout the 1960s (Cohen 1998; Aronson, with Brosh, 1992, 61–138). Thus, the Egyptian concerns about the threatening nature of the Israeli nuclear project were dismissed as part of Egyptian propaganda. Israeli decision makers failed to understand the impact of a nuclear weapons program on Arab threat perceptions.

Consequently, all Arab efforts at acquiring ballistic missiles or nonconventional capabilities were seen as part of an offensive or aggressive design, while Israeli investments in weapon systems were seen as primarily defensive. There is no better recipe for feeding a dual-track arms race than this noninteractive logic. The empirical evidence showing a divergence of Israeli defense expenditures from a strict arms race model suggests that this tendency to amplify the threat was noninteractive from the start of the nuclear project. Subsequent decisions about quantities and types of weapons were based on an increased detachment of decision makers from the interactive political reality. The implications concern not only the intensification of the nonconventional arms race in the region but also the generation of a self-fulfilling prophecy: the Middle East of today is far more dangerous to Israel's survival—in terms of the weapon systems available to its adversaries—than it was prior to the start of Israel's nuclear adventure.

5.2. Flawed Deterrence Logic

The logic of last-resort deterrence that served as the strategic foundation of the nuclear project is logically self-defeating, because it renders incredible the threat of nuclear retaliation in any other circumstances. Consequently, actual nuclear threats in circumstances that did not amount to a clear and present existential danger were not effective. The last-resort "Samson's Option" threat implied by Israel's nuclear deterrence makes it evident both to Israeli decision makers and to any would-be challenger that the first use of nuclear weapons would also be the last. If Israeli nuclear weapons were used in an actual Samson-like situation, the aftermath would not be of real relevance, because neither Israel nor its enemies would live to fight another day. But if Israeli nuclear weapons were used in a situation that was not accompanied by complete self-destruction and opponent destruction—that is, if Israel remained in existence after it had used its nuclear weapons—the international community would never allow it to keep its nuclear capability. Other international (and possibly domestic) sanctions may be so severe that the self-inflicted costs of using nuclear weapons and staying alive would significantly outweigh any political or military benefit of using them. Evidence clearly pointing out that Israel is on the brink of being annihilated is utterly paradoxical: only if Israel has been destroyed simultaneously or immediately after it has used its nuclear weapons can it justify the last-resort use of such weapons.

It is therefore of little surprise that Israeli threats and deployment of nuclear weapons in times of crisis and war have failed to impress its opponents. Israeli decision makers themselves have realized—sometimes belatedly—that their use of nuclear threats in such situations has not been really credible, hence quickly modifying the rhetoric. For example, the volume and content of Israeli threats following the Iraqi missile attacks in 1991 were significantly minor compared to the volume and content of Israeli threats during the crisis that preceded the Gulf War.

This flaw is even more apparent when one considers the credibility of nuclear threats given Israel's—qualitative and quantitative—conventional edge over its key adversaries. Since Israel possesses a wide and effective range of capabilities to respond to anything that is less than life threatening, its adversaries could, in principle, invoke any kind of challenge—as costly as it might be—basking in the knowledge that Israel would be self-deterred from using its nuclear weapons.

It is unlikely that Israel could invoke credible nuclear threats to deter a conventional or chemical missile attack, as long as such attacks do not threaten the very survival of the Jewish state. This is so even if the human and material costs may be very high in such attacks. The need to consider the real prospect that Israel would be forced to disarm after it had used its weapons "irresponsibly" may be sufficient reason to deter its decision makers from carrying out such threats.[77] Had Israel been militarily weak, and the only equalizing weapons were nuclear, such threats would have been more credible. Since Israel is powerful, both the international community and the Israeli public expect the IDF to use all other available means—and to incur the costs associated with conventional war—before it is legitimately "allowed" to use its nuclear weapons.

For that reason, the development of tactical nuclear weapons is also of very little practical value. These weapons are usable only if a decision maker becomes irrational. However, this risk is itself perceived as sufficient to induce a grave degree of threat among Arab states and to help inflame a nonconventional arms race.

5.3. *The Paradox of Ambiguity*

Israeli policy of nuclear ambiguity creates a fundamental paradox: the more successful Israel is at concealing its nuclear capability, the less credible it is, on the one hand, and the more threatening it is, on the other. Once Israel comes out of the nuclear closet, it could develop a deterrence policy that would be both more credible and less threatening. But it runs the risk of being forced to disarm.

Let us assume that Israel maintained its ambiguous nuclear status. Let us also assume that there were no unauthorized leaks of the Vanunu variety and that Arab and Soviet intelligence did not have direct access to Israel's nuclear secrets, such that all the information at the disposal of Israel's adversaries was what Israel chose to supply them with—through both clandestine and public channels. Under such conditions of "perfect ambiguity," the Arab decision makers know that Israel has the capacity to produce nuclear weapons, but they do not know (1) whether the nuclear threshold was actually crossed or, if it was, (2) how many nuclear devices Israel has, (3) of what kind, (4) and on which delivery systems such weapons were deployed. Moreover, since Israel stated that it would not be the first to introduce nuclear weapons into the region, the Arabs must also guess the circumstances under which the deterrent threat would be carried out.

"Perfect ambiguity" renders deterrence meaningless, because all of the elements of a credible threat are either vague or nonexistent. This may create a threat that "leaves everything to chance." Such a threat cannot deter because the would-be challengers do not know what would provoke retaliation, what kind of retaliation would be inflicted on them, and whether the deterrer possesses both the will and the capacity to carry out the threat.

In reality, actual ambiguity is less than perfect. Israel's adversaries have some inkling of Israel's nuclear capabilities. Yet, the lack of an explicit doctrine of deterrence in the nuclear realm[78] renders deterrence even more unstable. The disconnect between the notion of last-resort use of nuclear weapons and the possible presence of tactical and enhanced-radiation weapons raises serious questions about the kind of threats this doctrine is designed to encounter. It also casts doubt on the strictly deterrent, second-strike nature of this capability. Moreover, this kind of ambiguity may provoke Israel's adversaries to probe and erode the credibility of its deterrence at the margins, starting each time from the point where deterrence had proven defective the previous time. For example, the

Iraqis started in 1991 from the place where the Syrian ballistic missiles had stopped in 1973. If and when the circumstances of another military conflict arise, the next probe might include firing chemical weapons on Israeli targets. Because Israeli decision makers and many of its leading strategic thinkers believe that abandoning ambiguity may cause more harm than good, they may find themselves constrained even in the face of such probes.[79]

Abandoning nuclear ambiguity may serve several objectives. First, it may force Israel to spell out a clear doctrine of nuclear deterrence, including the kind of events that would trigger nuclear retaliation and the kind of retaliatory punishment one can expect if deterrence fails. Second, it could also provide for assurances against fears of the use of nuclear weapons to back or support offensive designs. Third, it may enable a more stable balance of terror, given that the process of acquisition of nuclear weapons by such Middle East states as Iran cannot be stopped in the long run. Finally, it may also have implications with respect to the willingness of Israeli decision makers to make territorial concessions in exchange for peace (Feldman 1983).[80]

At the same time, relinquishing ambiguity will force Israel to adjust its capabilities to its doctrine. Provided Israel cannot afford any other doctrine than last-resort general deterrence, it will have to provide explanations for the kind of weapons and delivery systems that are not in line with such a doctrine. Even under the most favorable scenario, international pressure would require Israel to forego all of its tactical weapons. Pressures for nuclear disarmament will quite likely mount in the context of future—bilateral and multilateral—peace negotiations. The benefit of an explicit nuclear deterrence doctrine may be increased strategic stability; but the downside is that an open nuclear posture cannot be maintained in the long run. This paradox of ambiguity will become increasingly pronounced as Iran approaches the nuclear threshold. Such a process will invariably force Israeli decision makers to reassess their nuclear posture.

5.4. *From Deterrence to Offensive Threat*

Related to the paradox of ambiguity is the difficulty of combining an ambiguous deterrence posture with reassurances. Many nuclear theorists have pointed out the importance of deterrence posture credibility with reassurances (Maoz 1990b, 96–99; Stein 1991b; Morgan 2003, 44– 65). The would-be challenger must be convinced not only of the capability and willingness of the deterrer to carry out the threat if the status quo is violated but also of the deterrer's intent not to convert a deterrent to a compellent threat.[81] Evron (1994, 188–92) points out the blurred relationship between tactical (i.e., battlefield) and strategic uses of nuclear weapons in the Middle East context. This is all the more apparent given rumors or more reliable intelligence information that Israel possesses tactical nuclear weapons. The possession of such weapons and the rationale for their development are left unspecified. Under such conditions, it is not unreasonable to speculate that the doctrine underlying these weapons is offensive.

The party line of Israeli decision makers that Israel would not be the first to introduce nuclear weapons into the region is meaningless in light of the discrepancy between the pledge and empirical reality. It is not unreasonable to expect a similar discrepancy between the ambiguous conception of last-resort use of nuclear weapons and the actual possession of tactical weapons. The reassurance aspect of deterrence cannot be made clear given the ambiguous deterrence posture. On the contrary, ambiguity generates uncertainty with respect not only to the aspects of the policy about which Israel wants to be vague but also to the aspects regarding which deterrence must be explicit. Paradoxically, this posture also creates incentives for conventional preemption (Evron 1994, 190–91). As such it evokes unnecessary threats precisely on matters about which Israel wants to be reassuring, thus inducing strategic instability. The Begin Doctrine is a good example in this context.

5.5. Between Paranoia and Arrogance

Israel's dealing with the Arab states on strategic matters seems to have all too often moved from one extreme to the other on the paranoia-arrogance continuum. The arming and deployment of Israeli nuclear weapons in crisis situations that do not risk the very existence of the state suggest a premature tendency to hit the panic button. The arrogant end of this behavior refers to the urge to preserve the Israeli monopoly of nuclear weapons in the Middle East. This is illustrated by the strike on the Osirak reactor in 1981, the Begin Doctrine that followed, and more recent threats by Israeli decision makers regarding the possibility of a preemptive strike at Iran's nuclear installations.[82] The development of weapon systems that can be construed as offensive in nature also illustrates an aspect of technological and political arrogance that is not predicated on a deterrence-related rationale.

As we saw in previous chapters, and as I will demonstrate in chapter 10, this wavering between paranoia and arrogance is not a unique trait of

Israel's nuclear policy. Yet, in this case the potential consequences are perhaps more serious than in other policy areas. Both extreme ends of this continuum may cause unintended and unwanted reactions by the targets and may prompt the targets of these behaviors to extreme measures that might defeat the very same goals of Israel's nuclear policy. Hitting the panic button when it is not necessary erodes Israel's strategic deterrence. This was the case in the 1973 arming of Israel's nuclear weapons, and it was even more pronounced following the rampant campaign of threats by Israeli politicians and generals prior to the Gulf War of 1991 and the arming of Israel's nuclear weapons during the war. The arrogance end of this continuum has a built-in potential for inadvertent escalation.

5.6. *The Lack of Self-Inspection*

Israeli decision makers may have repeated the mistakes of their predecessors in the nuclear realm due to lack of self-inspection. Despite the fairly open discussion of Israel's nuclear capabilities and threat perceptions in the academic literature and the news media, a number of key issues of this policy have been completely unexplored. With few notable exceptions, questions of doctrine were treated only sparingly and uncritically in both the scholarly and the policy discussions. The central debate focuses on the pros and cons of continued ambiguity. Issues of the effectiveness and ineffectiveness of nuclear deterrence were not given a great deal of thought. Each time deterrence failed, both academic scholars and policymakers came up with a new and different explanation of why deterrence did not really fail. The explanations of the presumed self-imposed limits on the Egyptian and Syrian attack in 1973, and the attempt to justify deterrence failure in the Gulf War by the argument that Israeli nuclear policy prevented the firing of chemical missiles at Israel, provide good examples of bolstering an empirically tenuous argument through speculation.

The rationalization of deterrence failures in the nuclear realm (in contrast to considerable self-inspection and critical writings on Israel's conventional deterrence) allowed this policy not only to persist over time but also to support an uncompromising policy on arms control in the region, which may have made Israel's strategic posture more difficult over time.

6. CONCLUSIONS AND POLICY IMPLICATIONS

As we have seen, Israel's nuclear policy is fraught with paradoxes. One particularly noteworthy paradox concerns the extent of rational debate on this policy. From the mid-1950s to the early 1960s, when Israel's nuclear option was still only an option, there was considerable debate in the Israeli policy and security communities regarding the advisability of developing a nuclear deterrent and its potential implications for the Arab-Israeli conflict. A number of prominent Israeli strategists—including Yigal Allon, Yitzhak Rabin, and possibly Ariel Sharon—opposed the investment in nuclear weapons on both financial and strategic grounds. This debate occurred when the conventional military balance was only slightly in Israel's favor. Four decades later, when Israel possesses a significant conventional edge over any possible Arab coalition—in both quantitative and qualitative terms—there is virtually no debate in Israel concerning the wisdom of maintaining its nuclear capability.

There is, however, an even more perplexing paradox. One possible reason for the decline in the substantive discussion of Israel's nuclear policy is that the Israeli policy establishment, the Israeli academic community, and the Israeli public have by and large come to consider Israel's nuclear policy as an unqualified success.[83] Nevertheless, on the eve of the 2003 U.S. attack on Iraq, the Israeli public as well as many in Israel's security community saw an Iraqi missile strike, perhaps with chemical or biological warheads, as a real possibility. So, nuclear deterrence is believed to be second to none when it comes to security, except when it is put to the test. Then there is general agreement that Israel's nuclear capability cannot deter a committed adversary.

This analysis of Israeli nuclear policy suggests several important points.

1. The notion that Israel's nuclear policy has provided an effective general deterrent is tenuous at best. There is good evidence suggesting that Israel's nuclear weapons were a superfluous deterrent against an all-out attack aimed at the destruction of the state of Israel. There is no evidence suggesting that an effective Arab coalition capable of mounting such an attack was a viable option at any time in the history of the Arab-Israeli conflict. There is no evidence that any Arab state has ever been willing or able to expend the human and material resources required for such a general attack. This study suggests that the pro-nuclear Ben-Gurion crowd overplayed the potential threat. Nuclear skeptics such as Allon, Gallili, and Rabin were more realistic in their belief that Israeli conventional capability was sufficient for dealing effectively with any threats to Israel's security. This capability has only increased with time.

2. Israeli nuclear capabilities did not limit Arab operational plans. The arming of nuclear weapons had no noticeable effect on the operational plans of Arab states at times of war. There exists no direct evidence that Israeli nuclear capability had any effect on the scope and operational nature of the Arab offensive in 1973, nor is there any evidence that it prevented the launching of ballistic missiles with chemical warheads in the Gulf War of 1991. Available evidence suggests, however, that both political objectives and Israel's conventional capabilities were prime considerations in the Egyptian, Syrian, and Iraqi calculations in these cases.

3. There is also no direct evidence linking Israel's nuclear capability to the willingness of the Arab states and the Palestinians to enter negotiations with Israel. There were numerous peace initiatives emanating from Syria and Egypt prior to the inception of the nuclear project; there were several peace initiatives emanating from the Arab states in the initial phases of this project; and there were various peace initiatives after the project reached operational status. The holdout in most of these cases was Israel rather than the Arabs. What brought about not only direct negotiations but also successful and stable agreements was the willingness of Israeli leaders to trade territories for peace. This came about to a large extent because Israeli leaders and the public came to realize (after long and traumatic experience) that neither territories nor nuclear weapons provide long-term security.

4. Israeli nuclear policy did have adverse side effects. The evidence provided here suggests that this policy was instrumental in inflaming the nonconventional and missile arms race in the Middle East. The quantitative analysis also suggests that this arms race, from the Israeli perspective, has been driven more by bureaucratic inertia than by an action-reaction process wherein Israel responded to Arab military policies and expenditures.

5. This also suggests that the Israeli nuclear project may have well been driven by technological and bureaucratic considerations rather than by a political-military deterrence doctrine. There is also reason to suspect that the political control of nuclear research, development, and production is weak. There may well exist a disconnect between the public image of Israel's last-resort nuclear posture and the actual capabilities (and perhaps even operational doctrines) in Israel's possession.

6. This kind of potentially tactical nuclear posture—to the extent that it exists—may create significant strategic instability that could lead to unintended escalation of a limited confrontation into a nonconventional exchange.

7. The regime of secrecy that supports the "ambiguous" or "undeclared" nuclear status of Israel prevents a balanced and open debate on its

nuclear policy. Most scholarly works on these issues have been uncritical and self-serving, going along with the establishment's view of the decidedly positive balance sheet of this policy and discounting calls for nuclear disarmament. Academics have willingly adopted the bureaucracy's view in attributing hidden agendas to states and individuals calling for nuclear disarmament.

8. Israel's nuclear conception and its operational posture entail a number of logical and political pitfalls and paradoxes. These paradoxes have not been properly analyzed. Nor have the internal contradictions in Israel's nuclear policy been explored. The disconnect between the "Samson Option" conception of Israel's nuclear deterrence and the actual capabilities—which are enabled by the regime of secrecy and ambiguity—carries a set of particularly destabilizing implications.

9. Even if one supports a continued nuclear deterrence posture, there can be a wide variety of ways in which this posture may be implemented. It is far from evident that the contours of the policy and the actual doctrinal and operational aspects of Israel's policy really match or optimize the goals of effective deterrence.

What are the policy implications of this analysis? Should Israel renounce nuclear weapons? The answer I suggest is yes, but for a price. Specifically, a far-sighted Israeli policy can be instrumental in building a general and credible disarmament process in the context of a regional security regime in the Middle East.[84]

It is useful to draw an analogy between Israel's nuclear policy and Israeli policy toward the occupied territories. For a long time, Israeli politicians and its public adhered to a quasi- religious belief that these territories enhanced Israel's security. Over time, however—especially following the Yom Kippur War—there has been a growing conviction that these territories do not contribute to Israel's security, they do not prevent war, and they even do not make wars less costly. More important, a growing number of Israelis have come to conclude that the occupied territories actually detract from Israel's security and corrupt its society and its value system. The attitude toward the occupied territories has shifted from one that viewed them as a security asset into one that views them as a tradable property. Starting with the Sadat peace initiative, most Israelis came to believe in the "land for peace" formula. This formula is still acceptable by a majority of Israelis, even nearly four years into the Al Aqsa Intifada (Arian 2004; 2003, 14). Even before a comprehensive peace in the region has been accomplished, it is safe to suggest that the trading of the occupied territories has increased Israel's security, its international standing, and its well-being.

Once the near-religious belief in the linkage between nuclear capability and security is broken, Israel should be willing to use its nuclear card as leverage to achieve conventional and nonconventional arms control and disarmament treaties. These agreements should be part of a comprehensive regional security regime. Not only would this regime guarantee a region free of WMDs; it should include a number of institutions facilitating the peaceful resolution of disputes, ensuring transparency, and providing security and territorial integrity guarantees to all members. This regime should be comprehensive and incorporate all states in the region—including Iraq, Iran, and possibly North African states such as Libya and Algeria, as well as the Gulf states.

Just as Israel's nuclear policy helped ignite a massive arms race in the region, it can be used as the trump card in a regional security agreement. If there is a lesson to be learned from the Arab-Israeli peace process, however, it is that Israel would be better off to initiate this kind of trade rather than being drawn into it, perhaps after these weapons have been used in combat.

PART IV

Foreign Policy:
Shadow & Open Diplomacy

— 9 —

Israeli Intervention in
Intra-Arab Affairs

I. INTRODUCTION

As noted several times in previous chapters, one of the recurrent elements of Israel's nightmare scenario involved the fear of becoming
internationally isolated. The fact that Israel was surrounded by four Arab
states and the belief (which was only partially true at best) that these
states were often aided by other Arab states made that fear all the more
salient in Israel's security calculations. The political-military leadership,
whose ideas were embodied in the basic "Iron Wall" conception, assumed
that, if Israel was to survive the protracted Arab-Israeli conflict, it had to
become both tenacious and inventive. Given the basic geographic,
demographic, and military asymmetries this conflict entailed, Israel had
to devise original strategies for surviving.

One of these strategies involved attempts at intervening in the domestic affairs of Arab states and the Palestinians. These interventions started
from the end of the 1948 war and have been pursued consistently over
the entire duration of the Arab-Israeli conflict. Some of these interventions have been of an ad hoc nature, motivated by a desire to capitalize on
opportunities that seemed to present themselves or to deal with what
seemed as imminent threats. Other interventions were long term and
involved the investment of considerable human and material resources.

While many of these episodes of direct or indirect intervention are
documented in the writings of scholars and practitioners, there has been

no effort to systematically analyze and evaluate this policy. Because the policy of covert intervention in the internal affairs of the Arab states and the Palestinians was rather persistent, as we will discover in the coming pages, it is important to assess the effectiveness of this policy and its ramifications for Israel's security and foreign policy. Accordingly, this chapter examines the following issues:

1. What were the objectives of these interventionist policies?
2. How were they carried out? To what extent were they subject to any kind of public or legislative oversight and control?
3. To what extent did they accomplish the stated (or implicit) objectives?
4. What were their short- and long-term consequences in terms of Israel's goals and relations with the Arab states? Did these policies have any noticeable effect on Israel's security and foreign policy?

This chapter reviews several operations involving direct intervention in intra-Arab affairs. Most—but not all—such operations were covert at the time, but all of them leaked out at one point or another.

Before discussing these episodes, it is instructive to define the key term of this chapter. Intervention in the internal affairs of a foreign actor is a deliberate (overt or covert) use of intelligence, military, political, or economic means, aimed at affecting the policies and/or government of a foreign (state or substate) actor by aligning with, or manipulating groups within, that actor's internal environment.

This type of process is distinguished from military or political intervention in that it does not directly involve intergovernmental interaction. Rather, the government of one state—typically through its political or military services and intelligence agencies—operates within the other actor's social and political system in a manner intended to influence the makeup or policy of the other actor.[1] Intervention, as Jentelson and Levite (1992, 5–6) point out, differs from direct use of military force along two dimensions. First, the central objective concerns the opponent's authority structure as opposed to warfare, which is moved by territorial objectives for the most part. Second, intervention entails a combination of political and military (or paramilitary) strategies, with emphasis on the former. In contrast to other studies, I focus on intervention that extends from military manipulation of actors in the target's internal setting to a broader range of manipulations. Thus, I examine patterns of economic aid and technical advice to groups within the target's domestic setting.

The Israeli policy of intervention is examined here through a comparative study of several incidents. Table 9.1 provides the list of these incidents and their characteristics.[2] Each incident is discussed in terms of the reasoning underlying Israeli policy on the eventual outcome of these processes and draws the implications for Israel's security and foreign policy. The final section contains a comparative evaluation of these policies.

2. THE "MISHAP": ISRAEL'S INTERVENTION IN EGYPTIAN POLITICS[3]

On July 23, 1952, a group of midlevel officers in the Egyptian armed forces staged a coup, overthrowing the constitutional monarch, King Farouq. This relatively bloodless coup was a "revolution from above" (Trimberger 1978), bringing to power a seemingly radical junta that adopted a revolutionary, pan-Arab, anti-Israeli rhetoric. Many of these officers were known for their anti-British attitudes; some had spent time in jail during World War II due to contacts with the approaching Nazi forces.

TABLE 9.1. Episodes of Israeli Intervention in Intra-Arab Affairs

Year(s)	Nature of Episode	Consequences
1954	Activation of an Israeli spy ring in sabotage operations in Egypt, designed to prevent the planned British evacuation of the Suez Canal	The spy ring was caught by Egyptian police; British plans for withdrawal from the canal were not altered; adverse effects on Israeli-Egyptian secret talks
1955–65	Covert support to the South in the Sudanese civil war	No noticeable effect on the outcome, eventual failure of the whole rebellion
1965–67	Covert support to the North Yemenis in the Yemen civil war	War ends in a stalemate and political settlement
1965–75	Military and economic support to the Kurdish rebellion against Iraq	Ultimate failure of the rebellion
1976	Municipal elections in the West Bank major cities, designed to defeat pro-PLO leaders and to maintain support for pro-Jordan cliques	Sweeping victories of pro-PLO leaders in most West Bank large cities
1975–2000	Alliance with the Christian Phalanges in Lebanon	Israel drawn by Christians into invasion of Lebanon, formation of Hizballah, withdrawal, security zone, decision on unilateral withdrawal
1981–1987	Formation of village leagues in the West Bank, support of religious Muslim institutions and activities designed to counterbalance the PLO influence in the West Bank	Failure, emergence of Hamas, radicalization of Palestinian politics and rise of anti-Israeli and antipeace forces

Topping this new regime's agenda was negotiating an agreement that would terminate British military control of the Suez Canal. These negotiations were seen by some elements in the Israeli security establishment as posing several major threats for Israel. In particular, these threats included the following:

1. removal of the British military buffer zone between Israel and Egypt;
2. significant improvement of Egyptian military potential;
3. American military assistance to Egypt; and
4. removal of the main obstacle for Arab countries to join in a regional defense pact (Bar Joseph 1995, 149–50).[4]

The military establishment viewed the emerging Anglo-Egyptian agreement as a strategic threat. The foreign policy community—represented by the prime minister and Foreign Minister Moshe Sharett—viewed this, however, as a problem calling for political and diplomatic assurances to compensate Israel for the deterioration in its regional position (Sheffer 1996, 654–55). Sharett did not consider Britain's prospective withdrawal as a clear and present security danger (Bar Joseph 1995, 179).

The difference in threat perception between the foreign policy elite and the security establishment was an indicator of a broader conceptual gap between the Foreign and Defense Ministries. The former, led by Moshe Sharett, believed that a political resolution of the conflict was possible and that Israel had to exhaust diplomacy before it turned to the use of force. The hard-line group—the defense minister and the IDF—believed that recent developments in the Arab world were increasingly threatening and that time was not in Israel's favor (Bar Joseph 1995, 194–95; Sheffer 1980).

Along with the perceived threats associated with an imminent Anglo-Egyptian agreement, a seeming opportunity emerged. Israeli military intelligence received information that the British army was developing an operational plan to occupy Cairo by force—under the pretext of protecting British nationals—if attacks on British forces intensified. The British concern about anti-British activities in Egypt was seen in Israel as a ray of hope. If the British grew sufficiently frustrated by the chaos along the Suez Canal and in Cairo itself, they might take military steps, thereby halting or indefinitely delaying the evacuation of the Canal Zone (Bar Joseph 1995, 176–79, 182–84).

The threat of escalation in Anglo-Egyptian relations during the first half of 1954 was sufficient to move the Egyptian security forces to quell anti-British activities in Egypt. This resulted in the renewal of Anglo-Egyptian negotiations. On July 27, 1954, an Anglo-Egyptian agreement on the transfer of the Canal Zone to Egypt was initialed by the two sides.

Over the previous two years, IDF military intelligence (AMAN) had trained a group of Egyptian Jews and prepared them as a sleeper spy ring in Cairo and Alexandria (Black and Morris 1991, 107–11). In light of the imminent Anglo-Egyptian agreement, initial preparations were made as early as March 1954 for activating the intelligence group in Egypt. The actual operational order was given in early July. The first operation of the spy ring, planting bombs in the central post office in Alexandria, was carried out on July 2, and the last operation, which brought about the exposure of the ring, took place on July 23. By early August the entire ring was exposed and arrested by the Egyptian police.[5]

The ramifications for Israeli-Egyptian relations were grave. Since 1953, secret negotiations through various channels had been conducted between Israel and the new regime in Egypt. The "mishap" created a break in these negotiations. When the negotiations resumed in October 1954, the Israeli side added a new concern: trying to dissuade the Egyptians from issuing death sentences to members of the spy ring. Most important, however, this affair may have increased Egyptian suspicion of Israel's intentions and cooled off Nasser's interest in these talks (see chap. 10).

The decision to activate Unit 131—the Israeli spy ring in Egypt—in terrorist operations aimed at derailing the Anglo-Egyptian treaty was fraught with controversy. The jury is still out on the question of whether Minister of Defense Pinhas Lavon approved this order or whether it was a strictly rogue operation initiated by the head of military intelligence, Colonel Benjamin Givli.[6] In any event, it appears that Givli was not alone in his assessment of the threats that the Anglo-British agreement posed for Israel. He may have acted on his own, believing that terrorist operations by the Israeli spy ring could possibly reverse the course of political events in Egypt. The failure of this operation and its grave implications notwithstanding, it set a precedent for other covert interventions in Arab affairs.

3. INTERVENTIONS IN SUDAN AND KURDISTAN

The Sudan and Kurdistan cases were a part of the "policy of the periphery," a conception entailing cooperation with elements in the Middle

East who could balance the anti-Israeli Arab world.[7] "The method was to break through [Israel's] regional isolation by forging links on the edges of the Middle East with non-Arab regimes that were deeply concerned, for their own reasons, by the spread of Nasserism and Communism" (Black and Morris 1991, 182).

Despite Israel's military victory in the Sinai War, Nasser managed to convert the military defeat into political capital, emerging as a regional hero who had successfully resisted an imperialist-Zionist coalition. The rise of Nasserism throughout the Middle East evoked grave concerns in Israel. The prospect of the spread of radical pan-Arab fervor into other Middle Eastern states was fueled also by a wave of subversive activity of pro-Nasserite elements in Jordan, Syria, Lebanon, and Iraq (Sela 1998; Hussein 1962; Maoz and Mor 2002a, chap. 6). The periphery policy also involved secret cooperation with the ruling elites in non-Arab states such as Turkey, Iran, and Ethiopia.

The efforts in Sudan and Kurdistan were based on a variation of the general periphery strategy theme. In the interstate aspect of the periphery strategy, the plan was to establish formal—if discreet—channels of cooperation with non-Arab governments. In the two cases examined herein, the plan was to support opposition groups in order to weaken and sabotage the ruling regimes in peripheral countries.

3.1. Sudan

The logic behind the support of the black Sudanese rebellion against the Arab ruling elite and of the Kurdish rebellion against Iraq was the simple concept of "the enemy of my enemy is my friend." Neither Iraq nor Sudan could be depicted as strict enemies of Israel, yet the support of the ruling elites in these states of the Egyptian-led anti-Israeli front persuaded the Israeli security elites that supporting the domestic oppositions in these states would benefit Israel's security.

The southern Sudanese rebellion against the government reflected both an ethnic and a religious struggle of the Muslim north against the black, mostly Christian, south. The activities of the socialist government in the south were highly oppressive and reached a peak with the expulsion of the Christian missionaries in 1963–64. Various political groups in the south organized into a paramilitary guerrilla movement named Anya Nya, which led the military struggle against the central government in Khartoum.[8]

There is little direct evidence on the scope, extent, and duration of the Israeli support given to the Anya Nya rebels in southern Sudan. However, it appears that the rebels received weapons from Israel. Israeli agents (possibly military officers) also provided training to the rebels. This support was highly classified, and it is not clear what kind of decision process produced this policy. Clearly Ben-Gurion was involved, but it is not clear whether other members of the cabinet were aware of this operation. In early 1964, some information began leaking out regarding Israeli involvement in the Sudan. At this point, the Israeli involvement seems to have either come to an end or been reduced to financial and weapons shipments only—without involvement of Israeli personnel. The limited nature of this operation had little effect on the Sudanese civil war. This war lasted for over ten years, until the central government and the rebels in Sudan reached some sort of accommodation in 1972, granting the southern region a substantial degree of autonomy (Shimoni 1977, 617–18). Fortunately for Israel, even if the Sudanese regime was aware of the Israeli aid to the rebels, it did not make an issue out of it; thus, Israeli involvement was not revealed.

3.2. Kurdistan

The Israeli-Kurdish link is far more elaborate than the Sudanese episode. The Kurdish struggle for autonomy from various occupiers goes back centuries. The Kurds are spread among four states in the Middle East: Turkey, Syria, Iran, and Iraq. At one point or another, the Kurds have rebelled against each of these states. Our concern here is with the Kurdish struggle for autonomy in Iraq, starting in World War II and ending in 1975. The leader of this struggle, Mullah Mustafa Barazani, launched a guerrilla campaign against the monarchist regime in Iraq back in 1942 (Nakdimon 1996, 43). Barazani and his people continued their struggle on the back burner for almost two decades, without a decision either way. Fighting from mountainous bases in Kurdistan, the Kurds managed to survive several attempts to crush the rebellion by various Iraqi regimes, but they were not sufficiently strong to convert this staying power into a military decision that altered their political status within the country.

Among the principal difficulties the Kurds confronted, none was more debilitating than the inability to find outside allies to their struggle. Barazani explored various avenues for securing support—first within the immediate neighbors of Iraq, Iran, and Turkey and second among the superpowers. The Iranian regime was willing to provide shelter to Barazani and his people, but not more than that. Barazani's efforts to receive shelter in the United States proved also futile. Amid these difficulties, Barazani turned to the Soviet Union. After a long march through Iran and Turkey—reminiscent of the Chinese long journey of 1927—Barazani and his people reached the Soviet Union, where they stayed and received shelter and training over a period of eleven years (1947–58).

After the 1958 coup d'etat in Iraq, Barazani returned to Iraq at the request of Abd Al-Kader Qassem. Qassem promised to recognize the Kurds' right to autonomy (Nakdimon 1996, 48). Barazani's hope that Qassem's pledge would be put into practice was soon shattered, however. The regime embarked on an effort to manipulate the Kurdish national movement through a "divide and rule" policy. In addition, a series of repressive moves against Kurdish newspapers and activists convinced Barazani that the Iraqis had no intention of establishing a Kurdish autonomous region in Iraq (Nakdimon 1996, 56–59).

By late 1959, a number of Kurdish guerrilla units started operating in the mountains of Kurdistan, launching sporadic raids against Iraqi military targets. At the same time, Barazani began exploring various avenues for purchasing weapons. By 1961, the Kurdish activities had intensified considerably, escalating to a de facto guerrilla war. By 1962, the Kurds had an army of fifteen to twenty thousand men equipped with light weapons and short-range artillery (Schmidt 1964). Despite this increased military activity, the Kurds encountered major difficulties in acquiring weapons and other supplies. They lacked professional training and medical supplies.

In 1963, Abd al-Salam Arif overthrew Qassem from power in Iraq. As in 1958, Arif tried to mobilize the Kurds by initiating talks with the Kurdish leadership. However, it soon became evident to the Kurdish negotiator, Talabani, that the Iraqis had no intention of granting the Kurds a significant measure of autonomy. At that point, the Kurds intensified their guerrilla activities and developed statelike institutions inside Kurdistan (Nakdimon 1996, 73–79; O'Balance 1973, 110–11; Bengio 1989, 22–23).

Initial Israeli-Kurdish ties were established in the late 1950s through clandestine contacts in Paris. In 1963, Badir Khan was sent by Barazani to Israel, where he met Ben-Gurion and other Israeli officials. Kahn requested communication equipment and suggested a visit by an Israeli journalist to Kurdistan. The Israelis viewed their relations with the Kurds in the context of Israeli-Iranian relations. The Iranians developed an interest in a limited but protracted Kurdish-Iraqi war (Nakdimon 1996, 80–82). Accordingly, they encouraged limited Israeli support to the Kurds, so "as to keep the flame [of rebellion] burning, but not to convert it into an uncontrollable blaze" (83). This created an extra incentive—beyond the interest in destabilizing and weakening the Iraqi state—to support the Kurds.

The first decision to provide extensive aid to the Kurds was made on April 15, 1965, in a meeting attended by Prime Minister Levi Eshkol, Foreign Minister Golda Meir, COS Yitzhak Rabin, and the head of the Mossad, Meir Amit. The first airplane with Israeli weapons reached Teheran a few days later. Several considerations brought about this decision. First, this aid fit very well into the policy of creating a "dam against Nasserism and Communism" (Nakdimon 1996, 64). By 1965, the Iraqi regime was converted into a procommunist and anti-Western regime and was seen in Israel as siding with the radical elements in the Arab world. Second, this aid also assisted Israeli-Iranian relations. The Kurdish rebellion caused the Iraqis to concentrate the greater bulk of their forces in Kurdistan, reducing the capacity of the regime to embark on adventures against Iran.[9] Third, given the 1948 experience, should a war break out between Israel and the Arab states, there was a real danger that the Iraqis would send reinforcements. Therefore, a prolonged guerrilla war in Kurdistan would take the Iraqi military capability almost completely out of the strategic equation in the Arab-Israeli conflict.

These considerations explain the unprecedented scope and extent of aid by Israel to the Kurds. Between 1965 and 1967, the Kurds received weapons ranging from small firearms and munitions to long-range artillery. Israeli military advisers trained the Kurdish forces and provided direct tactical and strategic advice to the Kurdish leaders. Also, several Israeli medical teams operated in Kurdistan. During this period, various Israeli visitors—ranging from the head of Mossad, Meir Amit, to high-ranking military officers such as Rehavam Zeevi, then head of the IDF planning division (AGAT)—visited Kurdistan (Nakdimon 1996, 100–193).

The expectation that the Kurds would help prevent Iraqi forces from being dispatched to the Israeli borders at times of crisis was tested during the May–June 1967 crisis. At the heat of the crisis, several efforts were made by the Mossad to encourage Barazani to put military pressure on Iraq so as to prevent it from dispatching forces to Jordan. Meir Amit's testimony to Nakdimon (1996, 194) is telling: "I tried to convince Mullah Mustafa to start some sort of front against the Iraqis, to put some sort of [military] pressure on the Iraqis that would prevent them from transferring forces to the front against Israel. He [Barazani] did not say no, but in practice did very little." In fairness, it must be noted that Barazani resisted approaches by the Iraqi regime to declare solidarity with the Arabs and even to expel the Israeli advisers.[10]

The 1968 coup in Iraq brought Saddam Hussein into power, still as the strongman behind the scenes. Hussein started a series of negotiations with the Kurds again promising some form of autonomy. Hussein's ambitions resided in the east and south, and the enemy was Iran. For that reason, he realized that an agreement with the Kurds might enable Iraq to move its forces to the Persian Gulf. In March 1970, Hussein and Barazani signed an agreement granting the Kurds "territorial autonomy." This agreement threatened the continued Israeli presence in Kurdistan, especially after the Iraqis began implementing various elements thereof.

However, much like previous cases of Iraqi-Kurdish rapprochement, this agreement turned out to be a disguise for a new Iraqi campaign against the Kurds. The Iraqis tried and failed to assassinate Barazani on September 29, 1971. In November 1971, the Kurds received indications of an impending Iraqi attack on the Kurdish areas. Despite a growing rift between Iran and Iraq during 1971 and 1972 (following the Iranian occupation of three islands in the Persian Gulf), the Iraqis kept putting military pressure on the Kurds via sporadic aerial attacks and occasional armored and infantry incursions. The Kurds, for their part, kept the guerrilla warfare alive. Repeated visits by key Israeli intelligence and military officers to Kurdistan and return visits by Kurdish leaders to Israel intensified this relationship. In 1972, Moshe Dayan, the Israeli defense minister, authorized the transfer to the Kurds of Soviet-made T-34 tanks and several Kurdish tank crews received training in Israel (Nakdimon 1996, 341–43).[11]

The story of the Kurdish-Israeli dialogue before the 1967 war repeated itself in 1973. At the height of the war, the representatives of the Mossad and the IDF in Kurdistan requested Barazani to intensify his military pressure on Iraq so as to prevent or slow down the dispatch of Iraqi forces to the Syrian front. These requests seem to have fallen on deaf ears. Barazani was sympathetic to Israeli requests but in practice did nothing to help. Nahum Admoni, then the head of Tevel (the major operational department in the Mossad), noted in an interview with Nakdimon (1996, 349), "We expected that [the Kurds] would do something, however minimal, to stop any Iraqi force from leaving for the front, but they let us down." The Iraqis were able to send an armored division to help the Syrians in their war effort against Israel (see chap. 5).

This did not have an adverse effect on the Israeli support for the Kurds, as these relations were based not on sympathies but rather on perceived interests. The Iraqi involvement in the Yom Kippur War as well as the growing rift between Iraq and Iran[12] intensified Israeli interest in the Kurdish guerrilla warfare. By 1974, the Kurdish forces stood at somewhere between forty and fifty thousand troops, with additional paramilitary groups roughly the same size (Nakdimon 1996, 354). Short of tanks, the Kurds had ample weapons and munitions, including medium- and short-range artillery. The Israeli involvement in training and operational planning mounted.

In April 1974, Saddam Hussein ordered a major Iraqi campaign against the Kurds. Coupled with an economic siege of the Kurdish areas and massive aerial bombardments, the Iraqis made considerable strides on the battlefield, causing floods of refugees. However, by September, the Iraqi attack was repelled, and in a series of battles, planned and overseen by Israeli officers, the Kurds were able to accomplish a major victory, causing the Iraqis over seven thousand fatalities (Nakdimon 1996, 365–71).

By the fall of 1974, however, secret Iraq-Iran talks resumed in Istanbul. The Iraqi incentive in these talks was Saddam's growing concern with the military stalemate in Kurdistan. In March 1975, Shah Reza Pahlavi of Iran and Saddam Hussein reached an agreement over the Shatt al Arab. The Iraqis made significant concessions, formally accepting Iran's occupation of the three islands in the Gulf. The Iranian quid pro quo was stopping their support of the Kurdish rebellion in Iraq. This also terminated the Israeli ability to help the Kurds, as Iran was the only route through which weapons and Israeli experts could be delivered to the Kurds. Without the Iranian-Israeli umbilical cord that provided a political, military, and economic lifeline to the Kurds, the rebellion collapsed. The Kurds accepted total Iraqi domination of the Iraqi part of Kurdistan. Barazani himself fled the country to find refuge in Tehran.

In examining the record of Israeli support for and involvement in the Kurdish rebellion, it appears that—in retrospect—the failure was twofold. First, the Israelis received very little in return. At times of need—particularly during the May–June 1967 crisis and during the 1973 Yom Kippur War—the Kurds failed to repay the enormous debt they owed Israel in real and tangible terms. Moreover, both in May 1967 and in October 1973, the Kurdish leadership refused to put military pressure on Iraq in order to prevent, to slow down, or to sabotage the dispatch of Iraqi troops to the front. At the height of the rebellion, in 1974, the Kurds forced the Iraqis to concentrate in the north three infantry divisions and one armored division. The Israeli advisers estimated the size of the Iraqi forces facing the Kurds at about eighty-five thousand troops, some six hundred tanks, and over two hundred airplanes (Nakdimon 1996, 355; Bengio 1989, 151). The fact that the Kurdish rebellion was the principal motivator of Iraqi concessions to the shah in 1975 suggests that, had Barazani wanted to do so, he would have been able to seriously hamper the Iraqi involvement in the 1967 and 1973 wars.

Second, it is quite possible that the Israeli involvement in the Kurdish rebellion, which had been an open secret since the mid-1960s, had adverse effects on the chances of the Kurds to get a decent deal from the Iraqi government. The Iraqi attitude toward Kurdish demands may well have been increasingly negative due to Israeli involvement with the Kurds. Concomitantly, the Israeli financial and military support to Barazani's forces served to intensify the Kurdish demands. The leaders of the rebellion felt that this aid made them stronger than they really were. This perception of power also increased the motivation of the Iraqi government to crush the rebellion; a victory against the Kurds would be a victory against Israeli money, advisers, and weapons.

Most important, however, Israel got entangled between two allies—the Iranians and the Kurds—who were themselves walking on a tightrope and holding a very slippery balancing rod. On the one hand, the Iranian-Kurdish alliance was based on a principle of "the enemy of my enemy is my friend." As long as the rift between Iraq and Iran continued, Iran had an interest in destabilizing Iraq. On the other hand, the Kurds in Iraq were the brothers of the Iranian Kurds, who had even fewer rights and less autonomy than their Iraqi brothers. A success of the Kurdish rebellion in Iraq would have had adverse ramifications for Iran. Once the shah decided to make peace with Iraq, the Kurds became dispensable. Israel had to decide whether to stick with its Kurdish allies or with its key oil supplier, Iran. The Kurds were abandoned.

4. THE MUNICIPAL ELECTIONS OF 1976

The growing influence and political prestige of the PLO following the 1974 speech of Arafat in the UN had important implications for politics among the Palestinians in the occupied territories. AMAN and the security service (SHABAK) reported that the moderate, pro-Jordan Palestinian leaders in the West Bank and Gaza were losing popularity fast. The support for the PLO presented a major threat to the entire clan structure of the "moderate" leadership (Gazit 1999, 167–71).

The 1972 municipal elections kept in power the pro-Jordanian leaders in most of the major cities in the West Bank and Gaza (Mishal 1986, 114). The pro-Hashemite mayors of the major West Bank cities were interested in relatively peaceful coexistence with the Israeli military government and the civilian administration. While there had been no official Israeli policy regarding the future of the occupied territories, the government's policy was consistent with the basic principles of the Allon Plan, which called for the transfer of most of the densely populated areas in the West Bank to Jordan in the context of a future peace treaty. The fact that most officials in the West Bank were on the Jordanian payroll created a fundamental dependence between the West Bank leadership and Jordan. This dependence was seen to have a moderating influence on the population.

Israeli decision makers faced a dilemma. One the one hand, the Jordanian law that governed most administrative affairs in the West Bank called for municipal elections every four years. On the other hand, the growing popularity of the PLO in the West Bank put pressure on the traditional leadership. The conservative mayors were opposed to the elections, fearing that they would be defeated by "nationalist" contenders. They tried to put pressure on the Israeli military and civilian administration.

The Israeli defense minister, Shimon Peres, believed, however, that if the elections could be handled in a way that ensured the reelection of the pro-Jordan mayors of the largest cities, this would hand a major political defeat to the PLO. AMAN and SHABAK estimated that PLO supporters would win in no more than one-third of the contested municipalities (Maoz 1985, 147). Even if the PLO did gain some support in this election, it was believed that the new mayors could be "channeled" into local management issues, which would divert them from nationalist activity (Shaliyeh 1988, 64).

This assessment was based on several factors. First, the basic idea of municipal elections was part of a larger plan developed in the Defense Ministry to grant increased municipal autonomy to local leaders. This plan was designed to dilute rising nationalistic aspirations, especially among younger Palestinians (Mishal 1986, 107–8; Shaliyeh 1988, 64; Maoz 1985, 146–47; Gazit 1999, 170–71). Second, a new legislation granting voting rights to women and to people lacking any property was believed to add to the electorate a conservative element. The idea was that women represented a traditional sector, supporting the conservative Hamula structure in the occupied territories. This new element would offset the growing support for the PLO among younger voters (Maoz 1985, 147).[13]

Finally, in order to ensure the reelection of the conservative mayors in the West Bank, the IDF deported to Lebanon some of the radical candidates who were seen as threatening to the conservative leadership. Thus, on March 23, 1976, the Israelis deported Dr. Hamzi Natsha, a candidate for mayor in Hebron, as well as Dr. Abd-al Azziz from El Bireh. "This hasty move . . . that was taken while the Israeli Supreme Court was scheduled to review the petition of the individuals expelled, invoked a new wave of students' demonstrations [in the West Bank] (and sharp protest by public figures in Israel). One could hypothesize that this move gave the final push for the ultimate victory of the nationalistic candidates in the municipal elections of April 1976" (Maoz 1985, 148).[14] Most of the West Bank cities elected nationalist mayors who openly and publicly identified with the PLO. Most traditional, pro-Jordanian mayors who had been in office since the Six Day War were ousted out of office by the very process that sought to grant them greater legitimacy.

The Israeli effort to manipulate Palestinian politics—this time done under almost complete information about the local population—backfired. The attempt to deploy a mix of democratic and oppressive tactics and to manipulate democracy in a manner consistent with Israeli goals backfired. Not only was the heavy Israeli hand felt throughout the election campaign, but in some instances—such as the expulsion of nationalistic leaders—this hand turned into a weapon directed at the one using it. The seemingly stupid, innocent, uneducated, patriarchal Palestinian population outwitted the seemingly sophisticated, experienced, highly educated Israelis, resulting in the election of pro-PLO mayors in almost all of the major cities of the West Bank.

5. THE RISE OF HAMAS

The "march of folly" in the occupied territories reached new heights with the rise to power of the Likud government in 1977. The Labor Party's policy had been aimed at blocking the PLO in order to create favorable conditions for a settlement with Jordan. In contrast, Begin was interested in blocking the PLO because he saw it as a bitter enemy for its own sake. The Likud government did not have a clear vision of the future of the West Bank. Begin was aware that an attempt to annex it would bring enormous international pressure on Israel. Yet, he was ideologically committed to Israeli control of the West Bank, and this commitment translated into his support of Jewish settlement in the area.

However, the rapidly growing Palestinian population required some sort of leadership. Begin and his new defense minister, Ezer Weizman, inherited the nationalist West Bank leadership that came to power in 1976 and had to deal with it as a democratically elected leadership. The PLO's influence in the West Bank was growing rapidly (Gazit 1999, 191–92), and there was a need to find some way to curb it. The new government adopted a two-track strategy. The new minister of agriculture, Ariel Sharon, pursued an aggressive settlement policy (Gazit 1999, 237–39). The number of Jewish settlers in the West Bank grew from less than five thousand in 1977 to over twenty-five thousand in 1983. At the same time, the Defense Ministry stepped up its efforts at finding a moderate local leadership that would be willing to cooperate with the Israelis on more than administrative matters. This effort now took two forms. One included attempts to form municipal authorities presenting an alternative to the radical mayors in the West Bank. The other strategy was to support religious groups in the Gaza Strip in order to channel the frustration of the Gaza population into welfare and religious activities rather than into nationalistic struggles against the occupation.

The attempt to cultivate an alternative leadership in the West Bank was done through the establishment of village leagues, first around the Hebron area and later on in other areas of the West Bank (Gazit 1999, 191). This process took place against the backdrop of the Israeli-Egyptian peace negotiations and the Begin autonomy plan. These developments invoked a great deal of concern among the Palestinians in the West Bank and Gaza. The Palestinian nationalists felt that yet another deal was imposed on the Palestinians without the participation of their representatives and against their will. This concern was fueled, among other things, by the aggressive settlement policy of the Likud government and its harsh treatment of the nationalist mayors (Maoz 1985, 187–93).

Israeli-Egyptian peace negotiations and the post–Camp David autonomy talks fueled growing tension in the occupied territories. This involved occasional outbreaks of civil unrest and terrorist activity against Israeli targets. The military government responded by arresting some of the local mayors and by deporting others. These policies backfired: acts of terrorism intensified and so did the frequency and severity of riots, demonstrations, rock throwing, and other acts of mass protest. The Israelis realized that they would have to bring local Palestinian leaders into the autonomy talks, but the nationalist mayors were not seen as real partners to the kind of autonomy Begin and Sharon had in mind.

The decision to turn to the conservative elements in the West Bank—headed by Mohammed Doudin, a former minister of labor and welfare in the Jordanian government—took shape during the first term of the Begin administration, under the auspices of Defense Minister Weizman. However, the implementation came only after both Dayan and Weizman had resigned from the government. Begin—now the acting defense minister—relied heavily on the advice of COS Rafael Eitan. Eitan believed that an iron fist policy would serve to crush nationalist sentiments in the occupied territories (Maoz 1985, 205–8; Shaliyeh 1988, 83–86; Tessler 1994, 552–53).

Sharon's entry into the Defense Ministry following the 1981 elections in Israel represented a major turnaround in Israel's policy toward the Palestinians in general and the PLO in particular. Sharon saw the PLO as a major threat to Israel's future in the occupied territories. The nationalist mayors and the National Guidance Council (NGC), which shaped the official policy of the Palestinians in the occupied territories (Shaliyeh 1988, 69–81), were seen as the representatives of the PLO. But, in contrast to Eitan, who believed only in military measures, Sharon realized that crushing the NGC without developing a political alternative would backfire. Thus, he decided to revive the village union, parallel to disbanding the NGC. First, he used Doudin's village union in the Hebron area as a model for establishing additional unions, based on Hamula leaders in nonurban parts of the West Bank (Gazit 1999, 206–7). Simultaneously, Sharon separated the civilian and the military administration in the occupied territories and initiated a series of deliberate political provocations designed to terminate the nationalistic hold over the key municipal councils in the West Bank (Gazit 1999, 207–11; Maoz 1985, 209).

The aims of this policy were difficult to conceal, and thus the Palestinian reaction was an unparalleled level of unified action by the PLO, the local nationalist mayors, and Jordan for the first time since the Rabat summit of 1974. The opposition to Sharon's policies took place at several levels. First, the heads of the newly established village leagues received repeated death threats. Several attempts were made on Doudin's life. On November 17, 1981, Youssuf Khatib, the head of the village union in the Ramallah area, was shot to death. The PLO claimed responsibility (Gazit 1999, 207).

Second, all of the major leaders in the occupied territories, as well as the PLO headquarters in Lebanon, called for a complete boycott of the village leagues. This call was echoed by Jordan's prime minister, Moudar Badran, in March 1982. Badran promised a death sentence to anyone who joined one of these unions. By the time Israel invaded Lebanon, two things happened in the occupied territories. The nationalist mayors were all thrown out of office by the new civil administration and replaced by Israeli officers, and the village leagues stopped functioning, existing in name only. The civilian administration, which sought to improve the standard of living of Palestinians in the West Bank, was left without Palestinian partners.

The Israeli invasion of Lebanon and the forced departure of the PLO leadership from Beirut to Tunis in 1982 had two opposite effects on the population in the occupied territories. On the one hand, the iron fist policy and the aggressive policy of settlement and land expropriations under Sharon caused considerable resentment. At the same time, the lack of a local leadership and the defeat of the PLO in Beirut caused grave disappointment with the PLO, especially among the youngest and poorest (the highest concentration of whom was in the Gaza Strip). Many of them sought refuge in religious practice. This growing religious activity was seen as a positive development by Israel's Defense Ministry, as it suggested a weakening of the PLO in the occupied territories (Kurz, with Tal, 1997, 12).

Jordan shared the Israeli concern with the PLO and Palestinian nationalism in the occupied territories. It also viewed the PLO as a threat to its status and position (Shaliyeh 1988, 143). The notion among both Israeli and Jordanian elites was that, if enough money was funneled into religious and social activities and if the younger generation turned to religious activity, there would be less interest in nationalist activity. This concept was also based on a feeling that the PLO represented a secular organization. Some of the member organizations in the PLO and the Communist Party in the West Bank were seen as having Marxist leanings. Accordingly, the support of the Muslim brotherhood and the religious and social activity in the Gaza Strip and later in the West Bank was predicated on the idea of "the enemy of my enemy is my friend" (Shaliyeh 1988, 144–62; Sayigh 1997, 629–30; Morris 2001, 563).

The radical ideology of the Islamic movement was far more anti-Israeli and antisettlement than that of the PLO, yet it was not seen as a real threat by the Israeli authorities for several reasons. First, the Islamic fundamentalists initiated relatively few terrorist activities before the outbreak of the intifada in 1987 (Kurz, with Tal, 1997, 11–12; Mishal and Sela 2000, 26; Tessler 1994, 675; Lesch and Tessler 1989, 260–62). Second, there were objective difficulties involved in dealing with this movement in military terms, because of the risk of being portrayed as anti-Islamic (Gazit 1999, 128). Third, for the first time since 1981, Israel found a common ground for cooperation with Jordan. Above all, how-

ever, the Islamic movement seemed to lack a clear organizational structure. It was seen as a loose, ill-organized movement. This was believed to
be in stark contrast to PLO-affiliated groups in the occupied territories,
which represented a major threat by virtue of their ability to convert a
political decision to military or political action on the ground.

When the intifada broke out in December 1987, the Hamas movement was formed out of the Islamic movement. Before the Israeli military
and civilian administrations understood what hit them, Hamas took over
the streets as well as the bulk of the anti-Israeli military activity, raising
the level of public protest and military activity to suicide terrorism, something that was hitherto unknown in the occupied territories. The Israelis
helped create the monster with which they have had to cope to this very
day (see chap. 7).

Israeli attempts to manipulate Palestinian politics in the occupied territories are particularly perplexing. Israel had both the power and the
information to conduct a far more sensible policy. The repeated reliance
on military and economic bullying, on the one hand, and the failure to
understand the social and political trends among the Palestinians, on the
other, cannot be explained by naïveté, stupidity, or ignorance. Common
to the considerations and factors that influenced each of these policies
was a notion that Israel could mold the Palestinian population in the
West Bank in a way that served its interests. These episodes illustrate not
only the folly of these notions but also their paradoxical implications:
each of these policies helped bring about the very same outcomes they
sought to prevent.

6. THE LEBANESE QUAGMIRE

As noted in chapter 6, Israeli politicians harbored pipe dreams of helping
establish a Christian-dominated state in Lebanon that would break the
circle of hostility of the Arab world vis-à-vis Israel.[15] During a meeting in
Ben-Gurion's office on May 16, 1955, Moshe Dayan stated,

> all it takes is to find an officer [in the Lebanese army], even a captain,
> to win his heart or buy his loyalty with money, so he should declare
> himself as the savior of the Maronite community. Then the IDF would
> enter Lebanon, will occupy the territory that is required, and will
> establish a Christian government in alliance with Israel. The area
> south of the Litany River will be completely annexed to Israel, and all
> will be well.

Sharett himself rejected this as a "crazy idea," but not because it was utterly immoral. Rather, he saw this as a completely impractical adventure. The Christians could not be relied upon to deliver their part of the bargain (Sharett 1978, 996–97).

While these ideas continued to circulate in various political circles, they had never been converted into anything remotely resembling a practical plan. Secret meetings between Israeli officials and Christian Lebanese leaders took place throughout the period of 1948–74, but no operational discussions materialized in these talks (Yaniv 1987a, 28–37; Erlich 2000). These dreams of establishing a Maronite state in Lebanon and of annexing the area south of the Litany River remained what they were—wish dreams of politicians and some military leaders in Israel. When it came to discussing these ideas in more operational terms, it became evident that the political repercussions of such a scheme were enormous. Not the least of these was the belief of many Israeli leaders that the credibility of the Christian leadership in Lebanon was questionable and that it was unlikely that the Maronites would be willing to completely disassociate themselves from the Arab world. This impression started changing in the mid-1970s.

Up until the outbreak of the Lebanese civil war in 1974, Israeli clandestine activity in Lebanon was limited to typical intelligence gathering through both electronic and human means. There were occasional secret talks between Israeli agents and Lebanese leaders, but there was no Israeli involvement in Lebanese politics. As noted in chapter 6, Lebanon was still seen as posing a relatively low threat to Israel's security.

The Syrian intervention in Lebanon was seen—despite some risks— as having net benefits for Israel. For the most part, the Syrian presence in the country helped reduce the extent of PLO activity in Lebanon. Syrian forces in Lebanon were also seen as weakening the overall capacity of Syria to wage war against Israel (Evron 1987, 160–75).

At the outbreak of the civil war, Israeli intelligence developed strong ties with the Christian militias. These ties involved typical interventionist tactics: supply of weapons, tactical advice, intelligence sharing, and so forth. In southern Lebanon a Christian paramilitary force headed by Major Sa'ad Haddad developed strong ties with the Israelis, on both official and unofficial levels (Yaniv 1987b, 61, 65). Yet, during the Rabin administration (1975–77) and the first Begin administration (1977–81), Israel's support of the Christians in Lebanon was quite limited. Once Dayan and Weizman resigned from the Begin government, the Israeli-

Christian collaboration was upgraded considerably. Begin pledged not to let the Christians down, and Bashir Gemayel took this as a cue for escalation. In April 1981, the Christians staged an attack on Zahle, operating against Syrian forces in the area. The Syrians responded by moving troops by helicopters, in violation of the "red lines" agreement of 1976.[16] Israeli planes shot down two Syrian helicopters, and the Syrians responded by introducing surface-to-air missiles (SAMs) into Lebanon, in flagrant violation of the "red lines" agreement. Israel was on the verge of escalating by launching an aerial raid designed to destroy Syrian SAM batteries but was prevented from doing so at the last moment (see chap. 6).

The Israeli-Christian alliance received an offensive turn once Ariel Sharon was appointed minister of defense in August 1981. Whereas Rabin and Weizman viewed the Christians as a minority that required limited military or humanitarian support, Sharon viewed them as pivotal players in his grand scheme of establishing a new order in Lebanon. Sharon's pressure on Bashir Gemayel resulted in the February 1982 agreement detailing the nature of military cooperation between Israel and the Phalanges in the course of the coming war. This agreement required the Phalanges to occupy the northern and western parts of the Lebanese capital and to attack the PLO headquarters located in the city. At that point, it would be possible to call for a presidential election and have Bashir Gemayel elected president of Lebanon.

As we saw in chapter 6, the plan was forged despite severe reservations of AMAN's head, Yehoshua Saguy. Saguy and his staff consistently argued that Bashir and his Phalanges were utterly unreliable and that they would betray Israel the first opportunity they had. Nevertheless, both Begin and Sharon went ahead with the plan. Up to Bashir's assassination on September 12, 1982, and the subsequent bloodbath in the Sabra and Shatilla refugee camps, this plan seemed to have worked well. This was not so much due to the cooperation of the Phalanges but rather to the bullying policies of Sharon during the war. The collapse of Sharon's grand design started first with the betrayal of the Phalanges. During the war, Bashir refused to meet his obligations to attack the PLO in west Beirut, resisting enormous pressures by Sharon and Begin to do so. Second, immediately after his election, Bashir indicated to his constituency that he had no intention of signing a peace treaty with Israel (Schiff and Yaari 1984, 233–46).

At the same time, the prospect of a Christian-dominated state in Lebanon was a large enough threat to the other ethnic groups in Lebanon to turn all of them against the Israeli forces in Lebanon. All of these groups had viewed both the PLO and the Syrians in Lebanon as a major liability, making the country's recovery from the civil war all the more difficult. The prospect of having the Palestinians and Syrians out of the country was welcomed. Thus, initially, these groups viewed Israel's invasion of Lebanon as a positive thing. However, the threat of Christian domination was perceived as more ominous than the threat of Syria or the PLO presence. As a result, without prior coordination, an anti-Christian and anti-Israeli coalition began to form in Lebanon. This coalition served to drive Israel out of Lebanon (Maoz 1989; 1990b, 239–43).

Once it became evident that the May 1983 nonaggression agreement it had signed with Lebanon was not worth the paper on which it had been printed, Israel started redeploying its troops to the south of Beirut and Sidon. In the process, the Shamir government made it very clear that it favored a strong pro-Israeli militia in southern Lebanon. This, of course, invoked considerable resentment among the Shi'ite population in the south.

Hizballah was an outgrowth of Israeli policies in southern Lebanon. Israeli attempts to impose a Christian-dominated order on southern Lebanon was an anathema to the Shi'ites (Jaber 1997, 14–19). The formation of the Hizballah was a direct reaction to this process of political manipulation. Ironically, Sharon is indirectly responsible for the formation of two of Israel's worst enemies: Hamas and Hizballah. The bitter struggle between Israel and the Hizballah, one that rages to the very day, became a constant pain in Israel's neck. This struggle has resulted in hundreds of Israeli fatalities since 1983 and in enormous economic and political costs. This is, in a nutshell, a classic example of a calculated policy that gave birth to the very same outcomes it sought to avert.

The Lebanese quagmire is perhaps the extreme of how a minor and low-key attempt to manipulate internal affairs in a neighboring state can pull the intervening actor deep into an unmanageable mess and of how disastrous this interventionist policy can turn out to be. The alliance with the Christians was ill conceived from the start; not only did the Phalanges fail to fulfill their obligation during the Lebanon War; it was preposterous to suppose that such an alliance would bring cure to this war-torn country. It was ludicrous to expect that such an alliance would work to Israel's benefit. But this episode demonstrates a broader problem of Israel's foreign and security policy, a problem that is far more fundamental than the mere tendency to think that Israel can influence other groups' or countries' domestic politics. This problem concerns a fundamental misunderstanding of Arab politics, which has been a constant malaise of Israel's national security policy.

7. CONCLUSION

Israeli attempts to manipulate Arab and Palestinian politics have been a long saga of repeated disasters. In none of the cases discussed did Israel accomplish the goals that had been at the heart of the intervention effort. At best, some of these interventions could be described as exercises in futility. A more accurate—and probably less flattering—label would be a "march of folly." The notion that clandestine actions and other mechanisms of direct and indirect political and military manipulation of the domestic system of states or organizations may help advance Israel's foreign and security policy goals has repeatedly backfired. In many cases the outcome was that the enemies that emerged as a result of this effort at political manipulation turned out to be far more ferocious and dangerous than those Israel had sought to weaken in the process of manipulation. Nevertheless, no real lessons were learned from this sad historical record.

There were quite a few other efforts to intervene in the internal affairs of the Arabs and the Palestinians. Many of these efforts lack sufficient documentation to describe, and therefore we do not have enough evidence to evaluate them. What little evidence we have about those cases suggests that they do not change the general conclusion of this chapter. In other cases, the Israeli interventions were too minor and insignificant to have an impact on the outcome. For example, prior to the Palestinian elections of February 1996 Israeli officials attempted to help the Palestinians to devise an electoral system that would benefit the PLO at the expense of Hamas. Since Hamas boycotted the election, this became irrelevant.

The Israeli attempt to isolate Arafat inside the Palestinian headquarters (the Muqata'ah) in Ramallah during much of the Al Aqsa Intifada was also an effort to reduce Arafat to irrelevance, in the hope that this would help quell the Palestinian uprising. This also had little or no effect on the intifada. Nor did it have an effect on Arafat's control of Palestinian politics and resources.

Israel has invested a great deal of thought and effort in these interventions; yet, had the Israeli security community spent a fraction of this effort analyzing its past performance, it would have saved itself considerable damage in subsequent efforts. One of the reasons for the lack of meaningful learning regarding the outcomes of these interventionist policies is that most people in the security establishment accepted Ben-Gurion's "periphery" conceptions without really examining their empirical validity. As we have seen, this was a general characteristic of other policy domains as well.

When it comes to questions of peace and war, criteria for successful or disastrous policies may readily suggest themselves (although in these cases, too, the ultimate verdict about a policy is not always universally shared by all observers). However, on matters that are inherently less dramatic, the ability to judge success or failure is more problematic. Quite a few institutions that are in charge of policy-making and policy implementation have a vested interest in preventing genuine evaluation of these policies. An independent evaluation of policy in terms of clear criteria of success and failure threatens the monopoly these institutions have over the formulation and implementation of policy.

The cases discussed in the present chapter share several elements in common.

1. Israel's efforts to manipulate intra-Arab affairs were based on a fundamental assumption, the validity of which has never been established: Israel's national security is enhanced when the Arab world is weak and divided or when Arab states become increasingly unstable domestically. Alternatively, in some cases, a state in the Arab world or periphery may be strengthened if the "right" elements come to power, and this contributes to Israeli security.[17] Thus, there is a notion that Israel has major stakes in the internal makeup and stability of Arab states or periphery states.

2. Another premise underlying these policies is the notion that Israel can effectively manipulate the domestic politics of Arab states or of different groups within these states. This assumption, too, has yet to be supported by tangible empirical evidence.

3. All those policies started as clandestine efforts, managed by various intelligence agencies. For the most part, these manipulation efforts were kept out of the public's eye. Most cases were not subject to parliamentary oversight until they emerged on the public agenda—typically after the extent of disaster became public knowledge.

4. It is incorrect to associate these operations with a particular political party in Israeli politics. They were conducted by both major parties with about the same degree of persuasion and with similar results. It is also unfair to ascribe to a given individual principal responsibility for these policies. Ben-Gurion was the founding father of the "policy of the

periphery." But this policy was applied very conservatively during his tenure of power. It was upgraded and expanded considerably by his successors. Typically, one person escalated the interventionist practices started by one's predecessor, and another person may have modified the interventionist policies of one's predecessor. However, there is a basic consistency in the pattern of intervention that cuts across parties in power and individuals in given positions.

These points suggest some general policy implications.

1. In general, policies aimed at changing internal balances within Arab states or groups within states should be considered extremely carefully, given the abysmal record of past interventionist strategies.

2. The assumptions underlying such policies must be carefully examined. The overall premise underlying the "divide and rule" approach was tenuous even at the height of the Arab-Israeli conflict; it is probably shakier at the present stage of the conflict. This applies not only to Israel's intervention policies but also to the apparently ill-conceived American attempt to restructure Iraqi politics.

3. It is crucial to establish independent mechanisms of oversight outside the network of people and institutions involved in implementing such policies. The most effective oversight is a public one, but given the clandestine nature of many of these activities, it is impossible to impose public review of such policies. A NSC that is not involved in policy implementation or a more effective Committee on Foreign and Security Affairs (CFSA) in the Knesset can serve such functions.

This chapter corroborates the overwhelming dominance of security considerations on foreign policy matters and the almost exclusive role of the military and intelligence community in these operations. Two other important foreign policy and security ventures vis-à-vis periphery states were briefly mentioned in this chapter. A few words on the Israeli-Iranian and Israeli-Turkish ties can be said here. The Israeli-Iranian ties during the 1953–79 era involved political cooperation (e.g., joint support of the Kurdish rebellion in Iraq), economic ties (Iranian supply of oil to Israel), and security cooperation. Israel helped Iran in the first stages of the Iranian missile program (Sick 1995, 160; Segev 1989, 95). Israeli intelligence also worked closely with the Iranian domestic intelligence service SAVAK. The benefit of this cooperation—especially the military and intelligence aspects thereof—with the shah's regime is not clear. The costs of this kind of cooperation became very clear, however, once the shah's regime collapsed.

The Israeli-Turkish alliance appears to vindicate virtually all other cases of failure of the "periphery policy." The ties between the two states, which were semiofficial and secret until the early 1990s, burst into the open big time after the 1991 Gulf War. The depth of military cooperation between the two states is only second to Israeli-American ties in this area. The benefits to Israel seem highly significant and obvious. However, the Israeli-Turkish ties invoke a great deal of opposition from other states that see this informal alliance as highly threatening (Aras 2000, 162). The problem here, as in the case of Iran, is that this alliance rests almost exclusively on the ties between Israel and the military elite in Ankara. As long as the military elite maintains its tight control over the political system in Turkey, this appears to be an unequivocally good deal for both states. What would happen if this reality were to change is another matter altogether.

— 10 —

Never Missing an Opportunity
to Miss an Opportunity

*The Israeli Nonpolicy of Peace
in the Middle East*

I. INTRODUCTION

"The Palestinians never missed an opportunity to miss an opportunity" was Abba Eban's astute observation. Underlying Eban's statement was a long-held Israeli notion: Israel has repeatedly stretched out its hand to peace, but this hand was left hanging for a long time; there was no real partner for peace on the other side. This notion is not just an empty slogan; it is a widely held belief by many Israeli politicians and by Israeli public opinion.[1] Eban, unfortunately, failed to look in the mirror. And he should have known better. As a leading Israeli diplomat during the 1948–74 period, he was, in one capacity or another, at the center of several missed opportunities of peace for which Israel was primarily responsible.

This chapter surveys Israeli peace policy by examining cases that can be broadly described as opportunities to make peace with one or more of its neighbors or with the Palestinians. The brief descriptions of cases serve as factual foundations for an assessment of the basic patterns that characterize this policy. In particular, this survey helps us explain the most significant aspect of this policy: the Israeli reluctant and risk-averse approach to peace.

Before we begin the review of the various junctures of possible or actual peace in Israel's history, it is important to make some methodological notes. First, a proper evaluation of Israel's peace policy requires examining both the success and failure of these policies. Looking only at failed efforts at peace would rightly create an impression that we misuse history to make a point. Israel did sign peace treaties with Egypt and Jordan, a disengagement agreement with Syria, and a number of interim agreements with the Palestinians. An assessment of Israel's peace policy must therefore focus on these cases as seeming counterpoints to the "missed opportunities" theme.

Second, we also need a clear definition of policy outcomes, so as to be able to judge whether a given case constitutes successful or failed policy. Underlying my conception of policy outcomes with regard to Israel's peace policy is the acceptance of the fundamental notion that has been restated over and over by all of Israel's diplomats: Israel wants peace and would do all it can to advance and secure peace, so long as this is real peace. In light of this notion, I define a policy outcome as a success or failure in terms of long-term peace-related achievements. Specifically, a policy is seen as successful if it brought about a fairly permanent cessation of military hostilities between Israel and the other side. Accordingly, a policy is seen as a failure if it did not lead to an agreement or if the formal or tacit agreement did not bring about cessation of hostilities.

But there is another dimension along which we can assess policy outcomes. This is the nature and extent of change in Israeli positions on various issues over time. Specifically, if Israel had abandoned at time $t + 1$ positions that it had held at time t and that had derailed a possible agreement, then the policy at time t had most likely been a failure. Analytically, this implies that, if Israel were given a chance to go back in time and change its position and if that change would have brought about a stable agreement at t that would have prevented the hostilities and other costs of conflict that took place between t and $t + 1$, then it probably would have done so. Thus, even if one could justify the policy in terms of the perceptions and considerations of Israeli policymakers at that particular historical juncture, from an outcome-based perspective, this is clearly a policy failure.

Third, the problem of counterfactuals is really important here. We can tell what happened, but we cannot tell what would have transpired had Israel followed different policies. This is a particularly troubling issue because, in some cases, the leaders who initiated peace overtures were removed from office shortly after their offers were rejected or ignored by the Israelis. In other cases, some events intervened that derailed a given peace overture, and history shifted considerably after these events. Yet, from a point of view of policy evaluation, the test is whether, given the notion that over time Israeli decision makers have modified their positions to accept terms of peace they had rejected in the past, we can make a fairly reliable judgment regarding the policy's outcome.

Finally, in examining the historical cases, we seek to explain the factors that brought about a given outcome. We will examine possible trends and commonalities across different cases and under different circumstances. We will use these factors to develop general propositions about Israel's peace policy in the final section.

The present chapter makes a number of arguments about these trends and overriding characteristics of Israel's peace policy. First, Israel's decision makers were as reluctant and risk averse when it came to making peace as they were daring and trigger happy when it came to making war. Second, the official Israeli decision makers typically did not initiate peace overtures; most of the peace initiatives in the Arab-Israeli conflict came either from the Arab world, from the international community, or from grass-roots and informal channels. Third, when Israel was willing to take risks for peace, these usually paid off. The Arabs generally showed a remarkable tendency for compliance with their treaty obligations. In quite a few cases, it was Israel—rather than the Arabs—that violated formal and informal agreements.

Fourth, Israel's peace policy is characterized by a tragic pattern. I call it the "over my dead body syndrome." This is a process whereby Israel accepted peace proposals at one point in time that it had resisted at a previous point in time, after it had paid a heavy price for its rejection policy. This syndrome quite probably continues to afflict its policy vis-à-vis the Palestinians at present.

The explanations for these policy patterns are quite complex. Some emphasize psychological barriers, others emphasize domestic political considerations, and still others emphasize structural factors. I review these explanations and argue that all provide some insight into Israel's behavior. I emphasize the structural explanation that focuses on the role of the security community in these processes and show that it played an important spoiling role in many instances. The adverse impact of the security establishment on Israel's peace policy was due to its tendency to view peace through the sights of a rifle, that is, to subjugate diplomacy to military and security considerations. The dominance of the security community in Israel's foreign policy was perhaps more instrumental than other factors in derailing, foiling, or slowing down many opportunities for peace between Israel and its neighbors.

Table 10.1 lists the cases examined in this chapter. Clearly, this list is incomplete. We do not have a complete historical record of secret initiatives of Israel, its neighbors, and outside parties due to the classification of documents in Israel and due to the paucity of information about peace-

TABLE 10.1.   Realized and Unrealized Opportunities of Peace in Israel's History, 1949–2003

Dates	Initiator of Process	Nature of Initiative	Outcome	Explanation
March–August 1949	Husni Za'im, Syria	Offer of formal Israeli-Syrian peace and settlement of Palestinian refugees in Syria	Failure	Israeli decision makers stonewalled, Za'im toppled in coup d'etat.
1948–49	King Abdullah, Transjordan	Offer of peace treaty in exchange for corridor to Mediterranean	Failure	Failure due to gaps in positions
1950	King Abdullah, Transjordan	Offer of nonaggression treaty for five years	Failure	Domestic opposition to Abdullah in Jordan
1953–54	Israel and Egypt	Offer of secret agreement allowing for Israeli shipping in the Suez Canal and reduction in tensions, with future formal peace	Failure	"Mishap" derailed policy, later Israeli reprisals rendered proposal irrelevant
1964–66	King Hussein, Jordan	Secret talks with Israeli officials, offer of de facto peace in return for Israeli recognition of Hashemite control of West Bank	Failure	Israeli launching of Samu operation in November 1966
July–November 1967	Israel	Secret offer to return Sinai to Egypt and Golan Height to Syria in exchange for contractual peace	Failure	Rejection by Egypt and Syria, retraction of offer by Israel following the Khartoum Declaration
October 1969	William Rogers, United States	Offer to exchange the Sinai for Israeli-Egyptian peace	Failure	Rejected by both Israel and Egypt
1968–88	King Hussein, Jordan	Offer to sign contractual peace in return for West Bank and Jerusalem	Failure	Rejected by Israel
1971–94	King Hussein, Israeli leaders	Modus vivendi and de facto nonaggression along Israeli-Jordanian border	Success	No concessions required of Israel; in the interest of Jordan

(continues)

TABLE 10.1.—Continued

Dates	Initiator of Process	Nature of Initiative	Outcome	Explanation
February 4, 1971	Anwar Sadat, Egypt	Offer of interim agreement along Suez Canal	Failure	Israeli rejection of terms of offer
February 17, 1971	Anwar Sadat, Egypt	Offer of contractual peace in return for Israeli withdrawal from the Sinai	Failure	Israeli rejection
October 1973– January 1974	Henry Kissinger, United States	Disengagement agreement between Israel and Egypt	Success	Outcome of Yom Kippur War, American pressure on Israel
February– May 1974	Henry Kissinger, United States	Disengagement agreement between Israel and Syria	Success	Outcome of Yom Kippur War, American pressure on Israel
March– September 1975	Henry Kissinger, United States	Interim agreement between Israel and Egypt	Success	American pressure on Israel
July 1977– March 1979	Anwar Sadat, Egypt	Israeli-Egyptian peace treaty	Success	Israeli calculations and interests, American pressure
1979–81	Anwar Sadat, Egypt	Offer of autonomy to Palestinians in West Bank and Gaza	Failure	Israeli rejection and settlement policy; suspended by Egypt
November 1984– July 1987	Shimon Peres, Israel; King Hussein, Jordan	Peres-Hussein London Agreement, possible Jordanian-Palestinian federation in West Bank and Gaza	Failure	Rejection by Likud faction in Israeli government
1991–2000	James Baker, United States	Direct negotiations between Israel and Syria leading to final peace agreement	Failure	Israeli refusal to withdraw to 1967 borders and surrender DMZs, death of Hafez Asad
1993–2000	Israeli academics, PLO officials	Oslo Accords: mutual recognition between Israel and PLO, steps toward a final status settlement	Failure	Failure of implementation, mutual violations of agreement
July 2000– January 2001	Ehud Barak, Israel	Offer of final status Israeli-Palestinian agreement	Failure	Palestinian rejection, limited Israeli offer

related issues in Arab sources. In addition, some cases simply do not have sufficient merit to be considered as significant ventures from a historical perspective. Many cases have not materialized to a point where they could be considered as sufficiently meaningful opportunities. I mention some of them in passing, but they are not part of the present study.

2. MISSED AND REALIZED OPPORTUNITIES

2.1. The Za'im Initiative, April–September 1949

Following the end of the War of Independence, a series of meetings took place between Israeli and Arab diplomats to sign armistice agreements. The Israelis viewed the armistice negotiations as a prelude to formal peace treaties. The Israeli position was that the boundaries of the War of Independence would become the final and recognized boundaries of the state of Israel. In the course of the war, Israel had made a number of territorial advances in the Sinai, in Lebanon, and in the West Bank. Several prominent Israelis suggested that Israel take advantage of its military superiority and acquire additional territories. Ben-Gurion not only rejected most of these ideas but actually ordered the withdrawal of the Israeli forces from the Sinai, the Lebanese border, and some West Bank positions. The only exception to this rule was his decision to authorize the capturing of the southern village of Um-Rashrash (later to be known as Eilat).

The Israeli position in the armistice negotiations with Syria reflected an ambivalence toward the territorial status quo along the Israeli-Syrian border. On the one hand, Israel was in possession of most of the area within the international boundary.[2] On the other hand, the Israelis thought that Syria controlled a stretch of territory to which it was not entitled. However, insisting on Syrian withdrawal from the territories it had occupied during the war might result in a Syrian demand for Israeli adherence to the 1947 partition plan. There were also "more immediate, as well as contradictory, considerations: on the one hand, a strong urge to end the war, consolidate the existence of the state, and normalize life, and on the other, a sense that there was no point in making concessions on important issues when Israel enjoyed an overwhelming advantage over a weak Syria practically devoid of Arab support" (Rabinovich 1991, 68).

Israeli position was influenced by the willingness of the United States and the UN to underwrite the Israeli-Syrian agreement by forming the Mixed Armistice Commission (MAC), composed of Syrian and Israeli officers and diplomats as well as UN officials. The MAC would manage the implementation of the agreement. In light of the international support for an armistice regime based on mutual compromise, insistence on Syrian withdrawal to the international boundaries did not seem advisable.

On March 30, 1949, a military coup d'etat led to the overthrow of the civilian government in Syria. Husni Za'im, COS of the Syrian armed forces, assumed power (Seale 1986, 44–45). While Syrian agreement to conduct armistice talks with Israel was given by former Syrian president Quwatli, it was Za'im's government that started the practical negotiations. Za'im was willing not only to honor the international commitments of his predecessor but to do much more than that.

Once the armistice negotiations started, Syrian officers approached the Israeli delegates and offered a separate Israeli-Syrian peace treaty. This treaty would include formal diplomatic relations, open boundaries, and even the formation of a joint Israeli-Syrian army. In a meeting between Za'im and James Keely, the American ambassador to Syria, on April 28, 1949, the former stated that Syria would be willing to settle between 250,000 and 300,000 Palestinian refugees inside Syria. In return, Za'im demanded that Syria be allowed control of half of Lake Kinneret and that the border between Israel and Syria north of Lake Kinneret be drawn on the Jordan River. Za'im also requested American aid as part of the peace package (Rabinovich 1991, 69–75).

What were the considerations underlying this unusual offer? Za'im's capture of power came amid fundamental dissatisfaction with, and sharp criticism of, the poor performance of the Syrian army in the War of Independence. Za'im himself had led the abortive attack on Kibbutz Deganiah in May 1948. It is quite likely that Za'im's coup d'etat was largely a "combination of Za'im's personal ambition and the dissatisfaction felt by many army officers with the civilian government" (Rathmel 1995, 25). Za'im's coup d'etat may well have been a preemptive action designed to prevent his arrest amid charges of corruption (Rathmel 1995, 26; Seale 1986, 43).

Most observers describe Za'im as erratic, opportunistic, and nonideological in his approach to politics. The Israelis were not blind to these personal idiosyncrasies. However, it seems that several considerations can help explain this generous offer to the Israelis. The Syrians were eager to gain some fishing rights in Lake Kinneret and to legitimize the acquisition of the territories that they had occupied during the War of Independence. Syria did not possess the capabilities to defend these territories. If Israel decided to alter the status quo, it would be able to do so without significant cost. As long as there was no agreement, the Syrian territorial position in the southwest was under constant threat.

Inter-Arab considerations also entered the dissatisfaction picture. Initially, the Za'im coup was viewed as having been instigated and supported by King Abdullah of Transjordan as part of the Hashemite dream of Greater Syria (Pipes 1990, 59; Rathmel 1995, 25; Rabinovich 1991, 104).

However, it soon became evident that Za'im was his own man. The overture toward Israel may have well been his way of dealing with the potential inter-Arab resentment of his new regime.

Israel's response to Za'im's initiative underwent fundamental change over the four-month period during which Za'im was in power. The initial reaction was generally negative. Some Israeli politicians viewed Za'im's initiative as a major breakthrough in Israeli-Arab relations. Yet, the key players—Ben-Gurion in particular—felt that the terms of the Syrian proposal were unacceptable. The appeal of a formal Israeli-Syrian peace treaty notwithstanding, the idea of giving up half of Lake Kinneret and legitimizing Syria's territorial infringement of the international border—even if they were merely initial bargaining overtures—was seen as a non-starter. Thus, Ben-Gurion's response was that a meeting between Za'im and himself was premature before the armistice agreement was signed (Rabinovich 1991, 69).

Several factors drove this response. First, Ben-Gurion took a hard-line position regarding Syria's possession of territories west of the international border. As Ben-Gurion stated his position, "I am quite prepared to meet Colonel Za'im in order to promote peace between the two countries, but I see no purpose in any such meeting as long as the representatives of Syria in the armistice negotiations do not declare unequivocally that their forces will withdraw to the prewar territory" (Rabinovich 1991, 72). Ben-Gurion may also have been confused by what was apparently a two-track Syrian approach to negotiations. On the one hand, Syrian officials negotiated an armistice agreement under UN auspices. Parallel to these negotiations, they offered, through both direct and indirect channels, a formal and full-fledged peace treaty.

The Israeli position was guided by two considerations. First, Ben-Gurion was dissatisfied with the territorial status quo that left Syria with occupied territories in violation of the international border. Second, he felt that Israel had the capability to impose its terms on Syria.

> [F]rom the Israeli perspective, the principle of adhering to Palestine's international borders had been established earlier when Israel withdrew from Egyptian and Lebanese territory, and so Israel felt that this principle should also be respected when Israel was at a [territorial] disadvantage. . . . [There was also] a sense of superior capabilities which gave Israel a potential to alter this status quo by force. Israel was as acutely aware as Syria was of the strategic importance of water resources, and so Syria's attempt to acquire new leverage only stiffened Israel's resolve to hold on to the established international frontier.

Thus "there was no point in making concessions on important issues when Israel enjoyed an overwhelming advantage over a weak Syria practically devoid of Arab support" (Rabinovich 1991, 68). Ben-Gurion's position was summed up by the following statement: "[T]here is no . . . need to run after peace. . . . If we run after peace, the Arabs will demand from us as the price borders or refugees or both" (Shalev 1993, 35).

Another factor that drove Ben-Gurion's response was that the Israelis thought that Syrian weakness would enable Israel to revive the comprehensive peace idea once the territorial issues were settled in the armistice talks. In fact, during May and June 1949, Ben-Gurion considered a military operation designed to push the Syrian forces back to the international border. Only the opposition of Foreign Minister Sharett prevented such an action. But Sharett was unable to prevent the suspension of the armistice talks for over a month (Sheffer 1996, 472–73; Shalev 1993, 34–36).

In May 1949, the Syrians made another, modified offer. They proposed including in the peace treaty a Syrian pledge to resettle three hundred thousand Palestinian refugees. This offer prompted the pragmatists in Israel to put pressure on Ben-Gurion to respond favorably. This new element was an extremely appealing idea to Israel. The Palestinian refugee problem had emerged as a major obstacle to the resolution of the Arab-Israeli conflict. Thus, the new Syrian offer, which included a formal stipulation by an Arab state to resettle over a third of all the Palestinian refugees of 1947–48, would become an important precedent for future agreements with other states and a potential model for Arab-Israeli reconciliation. It would have created a standard for defusing the Palestinian problem in the context of agreements between Arab states and Israel (Sheffer 1996, 472–74).

This offer changed the Israeli position. Ben-Gurion now expressed interest in meeting with Za'im to discuss the details of the new Syrian offer. This shift in Ben-Gurion's position was also a result of the Syrian acceptance of the compromise solution for the occupied territories in the armistice talks. This suggested to Ben-Gurion that the prospects of further negotiations were not as bleak as he had imagined (Rabinovich 1991, 78–79; Sheffer 1996, 473–76). In practice, however, the Israeli response was delayed until after the signing of the armistice agreement. Unfortunately, Israel's favorable response to Za'im's initiative at the end of July 1949 was too little and too late. On August 14, another military coup by Brigadier General Sammy al Hinnawi overthrew Za'im's government. Za'im and his prime minister were court-martialed and executed.

The first major peace initiative between Israel and Syria died along with its initiator.

Israel's stonewalling on Za'im's offer was due to both intragovernmental politics and international considerations. Ben-Gurion's approach was marked by a fundamental skepticism of Za'im's aims and his ability to deliver. This skepticism was also supported by a sense that—given Israel's superior military position vis-à-vis Syria—a separate Israeli-Syrian peace was not a top priority (Rabinovich 1991, 99–110; Shalev 1993, 35–36).

Had Israel been willing to adopt a more forthcoming position early on, the Za'im initiative could have paved the way for a model of refugee resettlement that Israel could use as a precedent for other agreements with Arab states with large numbers of Palestinian refugees. The whole refugee question would have taken on an entirely different form. As it turns out, the refugee issue continues to haunt Israeli peace policy to the very day.

2.2. *Israeli-Jordanian Negotiations, 1948–51*

The dialogue between the Jewish leadership and King Abdullah of Jordan started before the outbreak of the Palestine war of 1948 (Shlaim 1988; Bar Joseph 1987; Schueftan 1987). In a meeting in Naharayim (on the Jordan River) on November 17, 1947, Golda Meir reached a tacit understanding with King Abdullah, according to which Transjordan would occupy the West Bank part of Palestine and Israel would occupy the rest. Both sides would recognize the fait accompli that each side established during the war (Shlaim 2000, 30; 1988, 110–17). On the eve of the war, Golda Meir again met King Abdullah in Amman, in an effort to prevent Transjordan from joining the Arab war coalition. Abdullah, under enormous pressure from other Arab states, said he could not stay out of the war but offered to occupy peacefully the entire area of Palestine and grant the Jews autonomy in a part of it. Golda rejected this proposal out of hand. The November 1947 agreement was seemingly dead (Shlaim 1988, 205–9).

Neither Israel nor Transjordan was completely satisfied with the boundaries established in the course of the War of Independence, and both wanted to change them. However, Ben-Gurion resisted pressure from military officers to occupy the West Bank (Shlaim 2000, 38–39, 56). The de facto Transjordanian behavior during the war suggested that Abdullah remained "remarkably loyal to his original understanding with Golda Meir" (Shlaim 2000, 39).

Meetings between Israeli emissaries and Abdullah were resumed in

November 1948. Abdullah expressed an interest in an Israeli-Jordanian peace treaty in return for Israel's recognition of Jordanian annexation of the West Bank (Rabinovich 1991, 114). The Israeli leadership turned a cold shoulder to this offer. First, Ben-Gurion wanted to capture the southern part of the Negev and Eilat. This was expected to lead to a clash with the Jordanian Legion. More important, however, Ben-Gurion felt that the Jordanian regime was unstable and that an Israeli-Jordanian agreement perpetuating the territorial status quo in the West Bank would damage the prospect of an agreement with Egypt. The cost of an agreement would be the legitimization of the "ridiculous" borders in the West Bank (Rabinovich 1991, 116), thus denying from Israel future opportunities to occupy it.

By summer 1949, due to strong urging of the Foreign Ministry, Ben-Gurion gradually shifted his position on peace with Transjordan. He was still fundamentally skeptical of the possibility of such an agreement but was willing to go along with the foreign policy group that urged negotiations with Abdullah (Rabinovich 1991, 117–18). Negotiations started on November 27, 1949, with the aim of reaching a peace agreement. In preparatory meetings, King Abdullah presented extreme positions, demanding—among other things—that the Israelis cede Jaffa, Ramlah, and Lydda.

In the formal negotiations, the king modified these positions but demanded several other Israeli concessions, including Israel's withdrawal from the southern Negev, control of the Gaza Strip, and access to the Haifa port in order to connect Transjordan to the Mediterranean Sea (Rabinovich 1991, 120–21). On December 13, the Israelis agreed to offer Transjordan access to the Mediterranean, but they did not agree to yield the southern Negev. The Israelis did pose some conditions on their concessions. First, Israel would maintain free access across the corridor provided to Transjordan to the Mediterranean. Second, no army installations would be allowed within this corridor. Third, the Jordanian-British (defense) treaty would not apply to the corridor (Shlaim 2000, 63; Rabinovich 1991, 128–29; Schueftan 1987, 127). This agreement seemed a real breakthrough (Shlaim 1988, 528; Schueftan 1987, 127).

When the parties got down to the nitty-gritty—such as the width of the corridor—talks were quickly stalled. The Jordanians wanted a corridor that would be several kilometers wide. The Israelis were willing to give only a few dozen meters. The sea outlet of this corridor also became a problem. The Israelis were willing to provide the Transjordanians with a seafront of three kilometers in a dune area near Gaza. One of the Israeli negotiators, Eliyahu Sasson, "made a tactical error by observing that Jordan was not the key to peace with the Arab world. The implication was this being the case, extensive concessions to Jordan were not warranted" (Rabinovich 1991, 131–32). Abdullah tried to break the impasse by suggesting a meeting between Ben-Gurion and Rifai, the Jordanian prime minister. Ben-Gurion turned down this offer, offering instead a meeting between Sharett and Rifai. The meeting never took place. The idea of a peace treaty between the parties was dead.

Subsequent Israeli-Jordanian negotiations converged on efforts at resolving the problems of Jerusalem. In these talks different proposals were exchanged, but no progress was made. However, at a meeting in the city of Shuneh on February 17, 1950, King Abdullah shifted the focus of the discussion by making a dramatic offer to the Israelis. The offer was for a five-year nonaggression treaty based on the current territorial status quo. Committees would be established to discuss a formal peace treaty. During the interim period a joint committee would establish trade relations between the states. Jordan would be granted access to the port of Haifa. Palestinians would be allowed to return to Israel or to send a lawyer to handle their property (Rabinovich 1991, 134; Shlaim 2000, 64).

The Israeli government endorsed this agreement on February 22. The Jordanian Council of Ministers approved the agreement in principle on February 26. But the meeting between the Israeli and the Transjordanian delegations on February 28 was marred by a bitter dispute. The new Jordanian text of the proposal omitted the paragraph on trade relations between the states and termed the entire proposal as a "modification of the armistice agreement" (Shlaim 2000, 65). The Israelis responded by saying they had no intention of "signing a new edition of the armistice agreement, let alone an inferior one" (Rabinovich 1991, 138). The king himself was surprised by his own people's modifications of the original agreement, saying he was prepared to initiate a governmental crisis in Transjordan to ensure passage of this agreement. Such a crisis did indeed take place, with the resignation of the prime minister, Tawfiq Abu al-Huda. However, this crisis suggested to the king that such an agreement would confront an inordinate amount of criticism in the Arab world and in Transjordan. In the next Israeli-Jordanian meeting of March 7, the king proposed temporary suspension of negotiations. He indicated his commitment to the agreement but made it clear that the time was not ripe (Shlaim 2000, 65; Rabinovich 1991, 139–43).

In April, King Abdullah announced the annexation of the West Bank to Transjordan. Israel issued a formal protest but privately indicated its interest in continued negotiations. Such negotiations were resumed in December 1950, but now the aim of the talks was modified considerably. Instead of focusing on a nonaggression treaty, the talks centered on the implementation of the armistice agreement, with the focus on Israeli access to Mount Scopus. By that time, Ben-Gurion had become extremely skeptical of the prospects of an agreement with Jordan. He may have also started thinking of a second round of war aimed at fixing the "ridiculous" borders in the West Bank (Shlaim 2000, 66–67). The assassination of Abdullah by a Palestinian radical on July 20, 1951, ended the Israeli-Jordanian dialogue.

There are two different interpretations of this Israeli-Jordanian episode. The conservative historian interpretation is simple. Israel went out of its way to meet Abdullah's demands. It could not accept all of them, because many demands were utterly unreasonable. Yet, the Israeli government did endorse Abdullah's February 15, 1950, offer of a nonaggression pact. It was the fundamental weakness of Abdullah and the opposition to this plan in his own country and in the rest of the Arab world that put an end to this effort (Rabinovich 1991, 148–55). Revisionist historians, while supporting this explanation, argue that the notion of Abdullah's internal and inter-Arab weakness tells only part of the story. Israel had an important part to play in the failure of the negotiations throughout the period.

> Although the King's determination to move forward to a settlement with Israel never faltered, he was increasingly isolated and powerless in the quest for peace. His offer to go to Jerusalem and meet the Israeli prime minister in person provoked a stony silence. Ben Gurion, for his part, showed no imagination and no vision in his approach to Jordan. All he would agree to was minor border changes based on reciprocity, while what the king needed was a generous deal that could vindicate his stand in favor of Arab acceptance of Israel. The quest for an overall settlement was thus doomed essentially because Israel was too strong and inflexible, while Abdullah was too weak and isolated. (Shlaim 2000, 67)

It seems that Abdullah was clearly eager to make peace with Israel. Yet, at the early stages of the negotiations Israel turned a cold shoulder and perhaps missed an opportune moment, as had been the case with the Za'im initiative. At later stages, Israel presented fairly forthcoming positions, but the king's domestic and inter-Arab problems prevented him from getting the nonaggression agreement off the ground. At that point, the Israelis lost interest in an agreement with Jordan. The "Iron Wall" notion had started to settle in. Ben-Gurion shifted to the view that the Arab-Israeli conflict could be settled only when the Arabs recognized the futility of attempting to destroy Israel by force or to subdue it by diplomatic pressure. Even moderates like Sharett did not dispute these fundamental premises.

2.3. *Israeli-Egyptian Secret Negotiations, 1953–54*[3]

When the Free Officers overthrew the Egyptian monarchy in their July 1952 coup d'etat, many people in the Israeli foreign policy establishment viewed this as a positive development. Moshe Sharett, the foreign minister, was particularly optimistic, because in his view the coup "removes at least one obstacle to peace which is wounded armour propre of a headstrong monarch."[4] Even Ben-Gurion, who was always suspicious of the Arabs, viewed this as a potentially positive event. He thought that the new Egyptian nationalist leadership would place Egyptian internal development before the expansionist ambitions that had characterized Arab monarchs (Shlaim 2000, 77).

The Israelis sent a secret dispatch to General Naguib, who was the nominal leader of the Free Officers group, offering a secret meeting to discuss peace between the two states. This message received no official response, but unofficially several Egyptian diplomats who brushed shoulders with Israeli diplomats in official functions suggested that there was a possibility of a dialogue. A secret line of communication was established between Shmuel Divon, the first secretary in the Israeli embassy in Paris, and Abdel Rahman Sadeq, the Egyptian press attaché. The Israelis believed that Sadeq was an emissary of the Egyptian Revolutionary Command Council (RCC) and a close confidant of Nasser, the second in command in the formal RCC hierarchy, who emerged as the actual leader of the Free Officers group.

The first message from Nasser was that Egypt could not afford—for domestic and inter-Arab reasons—to drastically change its position on Palestine but that it would be willing to consider a gradual and unofficial improvement of relations with Israel. Egypt requested that Israel use its contacts to lobby for American economic aid to Egypt, as well as for American support to bring about a British evacuation of the Suez Canal Zone. The Israeli response consisted of several parts.

1. Israel hoped for a fundamental transformation of relations between the two countries but thought that at the very least Egypt should

observe the armistice agreement and UN Security Council resolutions on freedom of navigation through the Suez Canal and the Gulf of Aqaba.

2. Israel was willing to assist Egypt in the economic sphere by placing a $5 million order for the purchase of cotton and other products if Egypt lifted the restrictions on the passage of Israeli oil tankers through the Suez Canal and the Gulf of Aqaba.

3. Israel sympathized with Egypt's wish to see the evacuation of the British forces and was willing to support Egypt in this matter if Egypt first improved Egyptian-Israeli relations.

4. Israel repeated its suggestion of a secret high-level meeting to remove the barriers to better relations between the two countries (Shlaim 2000, 79–80).

The Egyptian response came on May 13, 1953, in a letter on RCC stationery signed by Nasser. Nasser explained that opening up an official dialogue with Israel was premature due to public opinion in Egypt and the Arab world but that Egypt would reduce its anti-Israel propaganda and would act to curb infiltrations along the border. He repeated the request of Israeli help to bring about an Anglo-Egyptian agreement of the British evacuation of the Canal Zone. This would help move Egyptian-Israeli relations forward. Nasser also promised to review the possible passage of Israeli ships in the canal and the Gulf of Aqaba, and some initial steps toward this had already been taken (Shlaim 2000, 80).

Ben-Gurion's interpretation of Nasser's response was typical of his fundamental attitude toward the Arabs. In a letter to Sharett, Ben-Gurion instructed Sharett to respond to the Egyptian letter in fairly harsh terms: "(1) We would be prepared to mobilize our political influence on behalf of the Egyptian demands in the Suez matter, but only if we receive explicit commitments of free passages through Suez and to Eilat for Israeli ships and ships going to Israel. (2) As long as peace between us and Egypt is not secured—we would oppose the giving of arms to Egypt" (Shlaim 2000, 80).

Sharett, however, modified the Israeli reply. He insisted on the Egyptian granting of free passage to Israeli ships as a precondition to any kind of Israeli action on behalf of Egypt. This terminated the first round of discussions between the two states. Divon later learned from Sadeq that the RCC decided to suspend temporarily the contacts until the Egyptian-British negotiations were concluded. By that time, even the Israeli doves became skeptical of Egyptian seriousness.

Several Israeli actions served to derail this sensitive diplomatic back channel. First, the "mishap"—the botched Israeli spy operation designed to derail the Anglo-Egyptian agreement on the British evacuation of the Canal Zone—put a major damper on Egyptian perceptions of Israeli goodwill (see chap. 9). It added another layer of grievance and suspicion to Israeli-Egyptian relations. Now much of the secret dialogue focused on Israeli attempts to free the Jewish members of the Israeli spy ring in Egypt.

Second, before the dust had settled on the "mishap"-related developments, the activists within the Israeli security establishment put enormous pressure on Sharett to try to break the Egyptian blockade on Israeli shipping in the Suez Canal. Instead of proceeding cautiously with these delicate negotiations, Sharett finally gave in to the activists and authorized a plan to challenge the Egyptian blockade by attempting to slip in an Israeli ship, the *Bat Galim*, through the Suez Canal. The Egyptians were expected to seize the ship, thereby bringing the entire matter to the UN and the international court of justice. The ship was indeed seized by the Egyptians on October 1954, but Israeli appeals to the major powers and to the UN fell on deaf ears. What this action served to accomplish was another matter to appeal to Nasser for release of the sailors and of the ship.

The Israelis reactivated the secret channel to Nasser via Sadeq in Paris. On December 21, 1954, Sharett sent a pleading dispatch to Nasser requesting leniency in the espionage trials of the Israeli spy ring (as well as the opening of the canal for Israeli shipping). Nasser's reply of December 31 was terse and enigmatic.

> I have received your letter of 21 December. I have instructed my special emissary to transmit verbal answers to the questions you have mentioned in your letters. I am glad that you realize the efforts spent from our side to bring the relations to a peaceful solution. I hope that they will be met by similar efforts from your side thus permitting us to achieve the results we are seeking for the benefit of both countries. (quoted in Rafael 1981, 39)

The verbal responses that Sadeq conveyed included several issues.

> Egypt was interested . . . in a quiet border and was taking measures to ensure this. Reciprocal steps were expected from Israel. The present state of relations between the two countries did not allow the raising of the level of the existing contacts. . . . The present envoy was authorized to remain in touch with representatives of Israel. Israel's activities against the signature of the Anglo-Egyptian treaty and in particu-

lar the revelations of the Cairo trial had deeply disturbed the atmosphere between the two states. Before any practical arrangement for
Israel's shipping through the Suez Canal could be discussed, the present tensions must be reduced. (quoted in Rafael 1981, 39)

Rafael interpreted this message to mean that Nasser was playing a
double game: trying to remove Israel's threats against Egypt while building up his image in the Arab world. What he and most other Israelis who
had been privy to the back channel exchanges missed was the fact that
Nasser was interested in keeping this channel open despite the blatant
Israeli acts of aggression against Egypt. Less than two months after
Nasser's reply to Sharett Israel launched the Gaza raid. This condemned
the efforts to reach quiet accommodation to a sudden death.[5]

Was Nasser serious or was he playing a double game, as many Israelis
thought? Clearly the Free Officers had been concerned about their relations with Israel. It is plausible to assume that Nasser's real objective was
to pacify the Israelis until he built his internal and inter-Arab base, but he
had no real intention of reaching some sort of accommodation with
Israel. Moreover, it could be said that Israeli responses were more than
forthcoming and that its demands from Egypt were quite reasonable. The
UN resolution of 1951 established Israel's right to free passage in the Suez
Canal and the Gulf of Aqaba. Egyptian blockade of these passages to
Israeli shipping was in violation of this resolution. The evasive nature of
the Egyptian response to these demands, as well as the Egyptian seizure of
the *Bat Galim*, suggested that they had no intention of complying with
this resolution. So, there may have been no real opportunity, and therefore nothing was missed. If someone had missed an opportunity, it was the
Egyptians, who failed to respond to Israeli gestures and demands. This is
the prevailing perception among Israeli diplomats and historians (e.g.,
Rafael 1981, 39; Tal 1998, 108–9).

This is a simplistic approach, however. These contacts with Nasser did
represent a major opportunity. Yet, the Israeli positions and its escalatory
behavior may well have caused this opportunity to dissipate. First, Israeli
leaders at the time did not see peace with the Arab world as a priority.[6]
More important, there was a concern that, if the dialogue with Egypt continued, the Egyptians would demand reciprocity for implementation of
the UN Security Council's resolutions, for example, about the resettlement of the refugees and the partition boundaries. This clearly was not
something that the Israeli leadership—including Sharett—was prepared
to discuss (Tal 1998, 102–3).

Second, the costs entailed in continued negotiations with Egypt were minor. It was obvious that Nasser was trying to reduce the threats emanating from Israel. As we saw in chapters 2 and 7, by that time ideas about an inevitable second round were floating freely in the security establishment. When Lavon replaced Ben-Gurion as defense minister, these ideas became more frequent and the schemes became more hair brained. The Israeli security establishment had been itching for war. The question was who would be the target of this war. So Nasser's threat perception was not all that far removed from reality. Israel may have overplayed its card by offering Egypt to use its influence with the United States and England to facilitate the Egyptian-British negotiations about the Suez Canal (Tal 1998, 102), but there was no damage in continuing the dialogue with Nasser. Israel could always refuse to discuss the post-1948 boundaries as they had been agreed upon during the armistice negotiations. Also, in the Divon-Sadeq talks, the refugee problem did not come up.

Third, Egyptian hesitation and ambivalence were not extremely conducive. Israeli diplomats had problems interpreting subtlety and prudence. Especially in the context of the Sharett–Ben-Gurion struggle over foreign and security policy, the doves in the government and Foreign Ministry needed more ammunition from the Egyptians to confront the militant war-eager camp. There was no person in authority who could interpret the domestic and inter-Arab context in which the new regime in Egypt had been operating and its sense of threat perception and insecurity. There was nobody in the Israeli foreign and security establishment who could correctly interpret the effect of Israeli policies on Egypt. Seen in this light, the absence of a clearer commitment by Egypt to advance relations with Israel and to consider some practical gestures played into the hands of the hawks.

Most damaging, however, were Israeli actions—in particular, the Gaza raid of February 1955. These actions closed the window of opportunity. Nasser was willing to continue communicating with the Israelis even after the "mishap" and even after he learned of Israeli duplicity with regard to the Anglo-Egyptian agreement on the Suez Canal. Naturally, the Israeli shock at the death sentences given to two members of the Jewish spy ring was magnified by the fact that Sadeq had expressed his belief that the courts would show leniency toward them. But this clearly was not the key objective of the secret channel discussions. More disturbing was the fact that one branch of the Israeli government acted in direct contravention of the acts of another branch of the government.

In retrospect, this seems also to have been a failed opportunity because, from that point on, the relations between the two countries embarked on a collision course that escalated up until the end of the War of Attrition in 1970. There was one brief attempt at arranging a secret meeting in Cairo between Meir Amit, the head of the Mossad, and General Amer in 1966, but the Israeli government turned down this offer because it feared that it was a ploy to capture Amit (Haber 1987, 64–65; Shlaim 2000, 225–26). But, to the extent that we know, given the classification of documents from the early 1960s on, no significant diplomatic contacts between the two states took place for at least fifteen years and two wars later. On the contrary, there is good reason to believe that Israeli policy and actions played an important part in the radicalization of Egyptian foreign policy. So in this respect, too, the botched dialogue with the young regime in Egypt can be seen in retrospect as a missed opportunity.

2.4. Initial Contacts with King Hussein, 1963–66

Many facets of Israeli-Jordanian relations were revealed only recently, following the 1994 peace treaty between these two states. Various press reports told about secret meetings between King Hussein and various Israeli leaders over the years. Probably the first of these many secret meetings was in September 1963. King Hussein met Dr. Yaacov Herzog, the director general of the prime minister's office, in the house of the king's Jewish physician in London. Hussein's objective was to "develop in an appropriately discrete manner avenues of cooperation directed at the final settlement" (Zak 1996, 41–42; Shlaim 2000, 227).

As noted in chapter 7, this period was marked by mutual Israeli and Jordanian restraint with respect to border issues, so there were no specific outstanding issues between the states. The second meeting took place in Paris in 1965; this time Israel was represented by its foreign minister, Golda Meir. This was a cordial meeting that was not supposed to produce any specific agreement. Rather, it was "a meeting of breaking the ice, of getting to know one another. . . . There wasn't very much that happened, just an agreement to keep in touch whenever possible" (quoted in Shlaim 2000, 227). But this meeting did pave the way to security cooperation between the intelligence communities of both states. Also, and quite symbolically, both states agreed to abide by the Johnston proposal for water sharing.[7] This was significant especially in the context of the Arab summit's resolution to divert the Jordan River's headways, in response to the Israeli Kinneret-Negev project.

There were probably other meetings between lower-level Israeli and Jordanian officials over the period prior to the November 13 Israeli raid on the village of Samu, though no documentary evidence of such meetings is available to date. What we do know is that the Israeli raid of Samu' had a devastating effect on King Hussein. As he indicated to Avi Shlaim, "Why did the Israelis attack instead of trying to figure out a way of dealing with the threats in a different way, in a joint way? So it was a shock" (Shlaim 2000, 233). From that point to December 1967, no meetings took place between the two states.

Both the raid and the lack of contact between the states during the critical period of November 1966 to June 1967 may well account for King Hussein's behavior during the May-June crisis of 1967. The Samu raid ignited widespread Palestinian demonstrations in the West Bank. Hussein must have felt cheated by the Israelis. The Israelis had expressed a strong interest in the survival and territorial integrity of a Hashemite Jordan (Shlaim 2000, 227; Zak 1996, 12). Yet the Samu raid indicated just the opposite. There is reason to believe—and this is certainly something that happened during the 1973 war—that, had there been prior communication between the two states, Hussein would not have intervened in the 1967 war.

This is yet another tragic demonstration of how goodwill on the diplomatic level was destroyed by adventuristic and miscalculated military action and how short-term and narrow military considerations derailed an important channel of communications between Israeli and Arab leaders.

2.5. *Israel's Postwar Peace Proposal*

Israel's proposal of June 19, 1967, is one of the few examples of a real Israeli peace initiative. Unfortunately, it was also a short-lived one. One of the least known facts in Israel is that the Israeli government actually offered to trade the Sinai Peninsula and the Golan Height for peace with Egypt and Syria, respectively. Less known is the fact that Menachem Begin and the GAHAL Party (succeeded by the ruling Likud Party) were full and willing participants in this initiative. In the first government deliberation on postwar foreign policy that took place on June 16 and 19, there was a consensus that the war created new opportunities for peace with the Arabs. Israel had territories that it could trade for peace. No longer did Israel need to defend its 1948 borders amid Arab and international demands that it return to the partition plan of 1947. Israel's new position was that, if the Arabs agreed to direct negotiations and to peace in the 1948 borders, Israel would and should be willing to abide.

There was agreement in the government that the "land for peace" principle applied fully to the Sinai and the Golan. No such consensus existed with respect to the West Bank, however. All the GAHAL ministers and some Mapai and Ahdut Ha'Avodah ministers thought that the West Bank, due to its religious significance to the Jews, was a special case that required further deliberation. Moreover, all were in agreement that Jerusalem must be united under Israeli sovereignty. On June 19, the government adopted the following resolution:

> Israel proposes the conclusion of a peace agreement with Egypt based on the international border and the security needs of Israel. Israel security needs include: (1) guarantee of freedom of navigation in the Straits of Tiran and the Gulf of Aqaba; (2) guarantee of freedom of navigation in the Suez Canal; (3) guarantee of over flight rights in the Straits of Tiran and the Gulf of Aqaba; and (4) the demilitarization of the Sinai Peninsula.
>
> Israel proposes the conclusion of a peace agreement with Syria based on the international border and the security needs of Israel. These security needs include: (1) demilitarization of the Golan Height, and absolute guarantee of noninterference with the flow of water from the sources of the Jordan River to Israel. (quoted in Dayan 1976, 490–92; Shlaim 2000, 253; M. Maoz 1995, 102)[8]

The Israeli government forwarded this proposal to the United States. In Foreign Minister Eban's words, "Here was Israel, on the morrow of her victory, offering to renounce most of her gains in return for the simple condition of a permanent peace. This was the most dramatic initiative ever taken by an Israeli government before or since 1967, and it had a visibly strong impact on the United States" (Eban 1977, 436). Dean Rusk, the U.S. secretary of state, returned to Eban several days later, informing him that Egypt and Syria had rejected the Israeli proposal out of hand. Their demand was for an unconditional Israeli withdrawal from the occupied territories.

Shlaim (2000, 254) notes that immediately after the decision was made ministers who had subscribed to it started having second thoughts, and as early as July 1967 plans for settling Israelis on the Golan Height were drawn in various government ministries. He argues that "the decision of 19 June became a dead letter even before its formal cancellation in October [1967]." Yet, the final straw that ended the Israeli initiative was the Khartoum Declaration of September 2, 1967. This declaration contained three nays regarding Arab-Israeli relations: no recognition of

Israel, no direct negotiations with it, and no peace treaty with it. These three nays were interpreted by the Israeli political elite as a total Arab refusal to consider peaceful coexistence with Israel, with or without the occupied territories. In the context of this declaration, offering the Arabs a return of the territories for peace seemed an empty and self-defeating gesture. On October 17, the government reversed its peace policy. The new decision, approved by the Knesset on October 30, stated that, in light of the three nays of Khartoum, "Israel will maintain the situation fixed by the cease-fire agreements and reinforce its position by taking into account its security and development needs" (Pedatzur 1996, 113).

The government itself made a secret decision to base Israel's demands in peace negotiations on the notion of "secure and defensible borders." This implied that Israel was committed now to require territorial amendments of an unspecified nature (Pedatzur 1996, 113). In the UN, meanwhile, the United States, Great Britain, France, and the Soviet Union began drafting a resolution with regard to the fundamental principles of a political solution to the Arab-Israeli conflict. UN Security Council Resolution 242 of November 22, 1967, called for Israeli withdrawal from territories occupied in June 1967 in return for recognition of, and respect for, the right of every state in the region to "live in peace within secure and recognized boundaries, free from threats or acts of force."[9]

Israel refrained from accepting this resolution publicly to prevent a breakup of the national unity government. Unofficially, however, the Israeli foreign minister informed the United States that Israel was willing to accept the English version of this resolution. This did not contradict the government's decision of October 30. The official acceptance of this resolution by Israel came only in August 1970 (and after the GAHAL Party left the government).

Israel flatly rejected the Rogers peace proposal of December 1969, even though this plan was based on Resolution 242 and on the original bargaining position of the Eshkol government. Israeli decision makers failed to realize that the plan was one that Israel could live with in the long run. When we examine subsequent U.S. proposals for Arab-Israeli peace, the Rogers Plan looks like a really good deal even from the perspective of today's hawks. It does entail the return to the 1967 boundaries, but it does not discuss all fronts. It does discuss the need to address the Palestinian problem, but it treats it as a refugee problem rather than a national problem. The fact that this proposal was also flatly rejected by the Egyptians helped bail Israel out of trouble with the United States. But in the long run, not only has Israel accepted most of the terms of this proposal; it has been willing to accept far worse proposals in terms of the value system of the very same politicians and diplomats (e.g., Rabin) who had rejected it.

More important than the change in government policy and the retraction of its initiative of June 19, 1967, was the conversion of the concept of "defensible borders" into a sacred principle by subsequent Israeli governments and by its security community. The very same people who had been willing to trade the Golan Height and the Sinai Peninsula for peace prior to the Khartoum Declaration were now strenuously opposed to the return to the international boundaries on grounds of security. What kind of changes in strategic doctrine, weapons technology, or actual military capabilities in the region between June 19 and October 30, 1967, led people like Moshe Dayan and Yigal Allon to cling to the territories on security grounds at the end of the period, when they had been willing to prefer peace to territorial expansion at the beginning of the period? What kind of strategic logic gave birth to the famous Dayan statement, "we prefer Sharm a-Sheikh without peace to peace without Sharm a-Sheikh"?

In retrospect the answer is quite simple. The key determinant of the new Israeli concept of "secure and defensible borders" was domestic politics. Once the Arabs turned down the generous Israeli offer, this new position seemed an expedient policy domestically. The spirit of elation and arrogance that engulfed Israeli public opinion after the Six Day War was accompanied by the formation of popular movements such as "the Land of Israel movement," which was composed of important literary and intellectual personalities from across the political spectrum. More important, pressures were already mounting on the government to allow settlements in the occupied territories. These pressures did not come from fringe political groups but rather from important elements within the Labor movement (Mapai and Ahdut Ha'avodah) (Pedatzur 1996, 160–75).

It is important to note that the IDF, in contrast to other occasions where it had been dominant in political and diplomatic decisions, was not a key player. In fact, just prior to the 1967 war, Rabin as COS approved a plan presented to him by Abraham Tamir, then a colonel in the Operations Division of the IDF. This plan stated, among other things, that "As a general proposition, the State of Israel could progress and achieve its national goals within the territory obtained by the 1949 armistice lines (the so-called 'green line')" (Tamir 1988, 170). The politicians were those who began drawing maps that accorded major military significance to territorial depth. Allon and Dayan presented competing conceptions of the lines of defense in the West Bank. The Allon Plan called for the annexation of the Jordan Valley and the Gush Etzion area. The Palestinians would be granted autonomy over the hilly area of the West Bank where most of the Palestinian population lived. Dayan's plan called for Israeli control of four "fists" on the mountain ridge of the West Bank. These fists would be composed of major army bases surrounded by civilian settlements. These fists would be connected to the green line by four major highways under Israeli control (Shlaim 2000, 256–58; Gazit 1999, 144–48, 329ff; Brecher 1975, 460–62).

Many politicians felt that reaping the fruits of victory in 1967 by territorial aggrandizement made good political sense—especially given Arab refusal to negotiate. Putting a security garment on this territorial expansion was even a better idea. The next step—settling some of these territories—came only naturally, given the Labor movement's notion that the boundaries of the Jewish state would be determined by its settlements. This security doctrine—elevated to a religious belief—combined with the settlement policy became a major obstacle to peace because it tied the hands of the very politicians who had been willing to trade the territories for peace.

2.6. De Facto Peace and Negotiations with Jordan, 1967–76

With regard to the West Bank, Israeli politicians were divided into at least three camps. The first one called for the annexation of the West Bank to Israel, for both religious and security reasons. The second called for a solution of the Palestinian problem in the West Bank. Most of the politicians in a position of power in 1967 who supported this solution thought of a plan whereby Israel would maintain security control over the West Bank but would allow some degree of autonomy to the Palestinian population (Shlaim 2000, 255–58; Morris 2001, 330–34). The third school of thought called for the solution of the West Bank in the context of an agreement with Jordan. This implied negotiating with King Hussein an exchange of territory for peace. Both Dayan and Allon initially supported the Palestinian autonomy option, as it provided Israel with most control over the West Bank. However, discussions between Israeli politicians and Palestinian leaders in the West Bank and Gaza convinced the Israeli politicians that this was a nonstarter. The Palestinians "listened politely to Israel's suggestions of limited autonomy, but they wanted real independence, which was not being offered" (Shlaim 2000, 261).

Annexation of the West Bank seemed also unfeasible and undesirable. There were eight hundred thousand Palestinians in the West Bank and four hundred thousand in Gaza. Annexing the West Bank alone would create (together with the Arab minority in Israel proper) a minority of 35 percent Arabs in the expanded state. When Golda Meir expressed concern about the demographic problem due to continued Israeli occupation of the West Bank, Eshkol responded: "You like the dowry, but you don't like the bride" (Shlaim 2000, 255). It was also obvious that Israel would confront an inordinate amount of international pressure if it annexed the West Bank. The international reaction to the Israeli decision of June 28, 1967, to annex east Jerusalem suggested that the annexation of the West Bank would be a diplomatic disaster.

Thus, the so-called Jordanian Option became by default the focus of Israeli policy vis-à-vis the West Bank. In December 1967, Abba Eban met King Hussein in London and hinted that Israel might be willing to withdraw from the bulk of the West Bank in exchange for a peace treaty with Jordan. Israel wanted, however, to keep east Jerusalem and parts of the Jordan Valley. The contours of the Allon Plan were not given precisely, but the logic of the plan was presented to the king. Allon himself presented his plan to the king in a meeting on September 28, 1968. The king flatly rejected this proposal. Hussein's response was "all or nothing." He responded that if Israel wanted a formal peace treaty with Jordan, it must return all of the West Bank, including east Jerusalem (Shlaim 2000, 263–64).

These Israeli offers to Hussein were repeated several times in the course of the period of 1967–87 and were repeatedly rejected by Hussein. Up to 1987, Hussein's position remained unchanged. No progress was made toward a formal agreement. But from a different perspective, these contacts were a huge success. The Israelis believed that the continued involvement of Jordan in West Bank economics and politics prevented the rise of the PLO as a major force in the West Bank. More important, these discussions yielded a peaceful modus vivendi between Israel and Jordan. During the period of 1967–70, there were frequent clashes between Israeli and Jordanian forces, with numerous Israeli raids into Jordan against Palestinian terrorist bases. But the Israelis were aware that the king was in a fragile political position and therefore walked on a tightrope in their military operations. Once the king decided to end the state-within-a-state reality imposed by the Palestinians in September 1970, this modus vivendi was converted into a de facto state of peace between the two states.

A key bonus of the dialogue with Hussein was the intelligence cooperation between the two states. Over time both states' intelligence services shared a great deal of information about Arab states and about the Palestinians. Perhaps the most important episode in this context was the September 25, 1973, meeting between King Hussein and Golda Meir. During this meeting, the king warned Israel of an impending Egyptian-Syrian attack (Zak 1996, 130–31; Bar Joseph 2001, 243–45). The Israelis and Golda Meir in particular, both suspicious of hidden agendas and untrusting, dismissed this information.[10] The result is well known.

During the early hours of October 6, 1973, when the Israeli government was deliberating how to respond to the information about the impending attack, it sent a secret message to Hussein: stay out of the war. This time Hussein did not fall for the Egyptian and Syrian promises of a quick and easy victory. He informed Israel that he would refrain from any escalatory move on the border with Israel. He did, however, feel that Jordan needed to show solidarity with the Arab war effort. He therefore sent an armored brigade to the Syrian front. This brigade saw very limited action in the war and returned to Jordan as soon as the cease-fire agreement was signed on October 24. Yet, the basic mistrust by the Israelis of the Jordanian pledge not to take part in the war was such that, for the first two weeks of the war, Israel maintained a sizable force along the border with Jordan in anticipation of some Jordanian attack (Zak 1996, 46–47, 131–38).

In 1974 the Arab summit in Rabat resolved that the PLO was the only formal representative of the Palestinian people, thus implying that it had the first claim to the West Bank and Gaza. Hussein complied with the resolution. Informally, however, he continued to pay the salaries of the public officials in the West Bank. The border between the two states was relatively quiet, and the few exceptions of attempts by Palestinians to infiltrate Israeli from the Jordanian border were foiled by the Jordanian army or by the Israelis.

This modus vivendi worked for several reasons. The first and most important one was that Hussein did not condition it on Israeli territorial concessions. Second, the Israelis were concerned about the rise of nationalist forces in the West Bank. The ties between Jordan and the West Bank seemingly served to check the PLO's influence over West Bank politics. As we saw in chapter 9, this perception was false, but even in the mid-1980s quite a few politicians—especially from the Labor Party—still believed that Jordan exerted significant influence in the West Bank. Third, Jordan was seen by some Israelis—especially people like Ariel Sharon—as a substitute for a Palestinian state; having it controlled by a moderate pro-Western regime was an important strategic asset. From an

Israeli perspective this arrangement was extremely convenient. It was in Klieman's (1986) terms an "unpeaceful coexistence" that was as stable as any formal agreement Israel had signed with Arab states.

2.7. Sadat's Initiative of an Interim Agreement, 1971

On February 4, 1971, in a speech to the People's Assembly of Egypt, Anwar Sadat announced that he was offering to negotiate an interim settlement with Israel. In this settlement, Israel was to withdraw its forces thirty to forty kilometers east of the Suez Canal (to the Mitla and Gidi mountain passes in the Sinai). A symbolic force of Egyptian police was to cross the canal. Egypt would open the canal, and there would be a de facto disengagement of forces. Sadat wanted Israel to acknowledge that this would be the first stage in a longer process leading to an ultimate Israeli withdrawal to the international border.[11]

Sadat did not offer Israel any concession in terms of recognition, nonaggression, or any form of positive relations between Egypt and Israel. However, on February 17, 1971, Egypt forwarded its official response to the questions that had been posed to it by the UN special envoy to the Middle East, Gunnar Jarring. Egyptian foreign minister Mahmoud Riad's letter to Jarring stated that Egypt would be willing to "enter into a peace agreement with Israel containing all the . . . obligations as provided for in Security Council Resolution 242" (Riad 1981, 188; Yaacobi 1990a, 177–78), once Israel withdrew from the Sinai.

The combined significance of the Egyptian offers could not be overstated. In contrast to many previous episodes of semipeace initiatives, the credibility of which was questionable, these were official and authoritative Egyptian commitments. This was the first time that the Egyptians openly and formally offered a graduated process of settling their dispute with Israel. At the end of the road was what the Israelis had been, presumably, praying for over the past twenty-three years: a full-fledged peace treaty. Had Israel been offered such a deal prior to 1967, it would have taken it with both hands because it implied a formal acceptance of and peace with a Jewish state in the Middle East by the strongest and most important Arab state. In 1971, however, the price tag for this deal appeared excessively high to the Israeli decision makers.

These momentous events seemed to have little or no effect on the Israeli government. The overall mood in the government toward Sadat's offer was negative (Yaacobi 1990a, 79–81). The initial Israeli response was to ignore this proposal altogether. In her February 9 speech in the Knesset, Golda Meir adopted a typical self-righteous attitude, lashing at

Sadat's lack of flexibility and claiming that Sadat's unconditional agreement to renew the cease-fire agreement for a period of thirty days was tantamount to the resumption of hostilities. She then pointed out that Israel had no objection, in principle, to negotiating on a reopening of the Suez Canal but wanted this negotiation to be well coordinated with the United States.

The Israeli response to Jarring's queries of February 8 regarding the conditions under which Israel would be willing to withdraw from the occupied territories reflected this arrogant attitude. The government stated that, in exchange for contractual peace treaties with the Arab states, Israel would be willing to withdraw from territories occupied in 1967 but would not withdraw to the 1967 lines. Rather, it would demand territorial changes so that it could possess "secure and defensible borders" (Gazit 1983, 77–92).

The U.S. State Department—especially Secretary of State William Rogers—viewed Sadat's initiative as a major opportunity. This was not only the first step in a process that could lead to a full-fledged peace treaty between the two most bitter enemies in the Middle East; it could serve American interests in the Middle East to mediate such a process. Accordingly, Rogers and Undersecretary for Near Eastern and South Asian Affairs Joseph Sisco started a process of shuttle diplomacy between Cairo and Jerusalem. The Rogers-Sisco team identified the key Israeli concern: acceptance of the idea of an interim settlement would commit Israel to a final settlement that entailed full withdrawal from the Sinai. In order to placate this fear, Sisco presented to Rabin on March 6 a proposal he had drafted. The Sisco proposal basically reiterated the terms of the interim agreement, but with respect to the linkage issue it states,

> Egypt and Israel agree to increase their efforts to accomplish, under the auspices of Ambassador Jarring, the overall agreement according to UN Resolution 242, and this interim agreement will be considered a first step toward this goal.[12]

Rogers and Sisco's enthusiasm about the Sadat initiative notwithstanding, they were up against two formidable enemies: Golda Meir in Israel and Henry Kissinger, the U.S. national security adviser, in Washington. Each of these politicians—for different reasons—viewed the interim agreement with utter skepticism and invested a great deal of time and effort to derail it. Ironically, the potential allies of this initiative in Israel—people such as Moshe Dayan and Abba Eban—were either too weak politically or not sufficiently motivated to confront the resolve and political power of Golda Meir and her hawkish colleagues in the Israeli government. In addition, President Nixon was also not willing to put pressure on the Israeli government to be more forthcoming.

In two separate sessions, on March 22 and 28, the Israeli government discussed the response to the Sisco memorandum. Two factions emerged. The soft-line faction included Abba Eban, the foreign minister; Pinchas Sapir, the finance minister; and the ministers from the Mapam and Liberal parties. This coalition advocated using the Sisco memorandum as a basis for negotiation and inserting in it minor modifications. These ministers argued that there was no harm in withdrawing forty kilometers. In fact, from a military perspective this may well have been preferable, as it would form a demilitarized buffer zone between the armies and would reduce tensions due to the high concentration of forces of both states along the Suez Canal. The opening of the Suez Canal would reduce the risk of war. The possibility of opening the canal to Israeli shipping would be a major achievement. Finally, the interim agreement was a positive shift from fighting to a negotiated process. Egyptian compliance with this agreement could serve as a test for future negotiations (Yaacobi 1990a, 110–17; Eban 1977, 469–70; Gazit 1983, 85–87).

The hawkish coalition was not against the idea of an interim settlement. Most of its members saw the political advantages of a political agreement with Egypt. They believed, however, that this agreement opened up a slippery slope to full withdrawal from the Sinai. First, key elements of Sisco's memorandum implied an Israeli precommitment to a process of withdrawal. Moreover, accepting the American memorandum would open the door to future American pressures on Israel to withdraw from the occupied territories. With the Rogers Plan of 1969 fresh in their mind, this was seen as another effort by the State Department to impose a settlement on Israel against her best judgment.

Second, the terms of the agreement appeared to them politically and militarily unacceptable. The extent of the withdrawal from the Canal Zone seemed excessive in return for too little political concessions by Egypt. Even the possibility of allowing Israeli shipping to cross the Suez Canal was not a sufficient incentive for such a large withdrawal. Moreover, the hawkish coalition believed that the Suez Canal presented a formidable obstacle to a possible Egyptian ground attack, so withdrawing from it meant a major military concession.

Third, the notion of having even a token Egyptian police force present east of the Suez was an anathema to members of this coalition. This would represent a major diplomatic victory for Egypt. Sadat would be able to get through diplomacy that which Nasser was unable to accomplish in one thousand days of the War of Attrition. Moreover, these people were fundamentally distrustful of the Egyptians in general and of Sadat in particular. The point of departure for them was that the Egyptians were bent to violate the agreement. A substantial Israeli withdrawal coupled with permission to Egypt to place police forces east of the canal would create a major opportunity to cheat and put Egyptian military forces past the canal barrier under the guise of an agreement. This would tie Israel's hand as it did when the Egyptians moved their SAM missiles to the canal area after the cease-fire agreement of August 1970 (Gazit 1983, 86; Yaacobi 1990a, 113–14; 1990b).

Moshe Dayan's heart and half of his mind were with the soft-liners. Dayan, as we have seen, was never happy with the idea of the IDF sitting on the Suez Canal. He always felt that this elevated the Egyptian sense of grievance and frustration to a very dangerous point. Moreover, he felt that creating a DMZ between the two armies and positioning the forward IDF units at the Sinai passes did not do any strategic damage (Yaacobi 1990a, 110–11). However, Dayan was not willing to come out against Golda Meir, who appeared vehemently opposed to a large-scale withdrawal. During the government meeting of March 28, Eban passed a note to Dayan asking him to cooperate in support of acceptance (with modifications) of the Sisco memorandum. Dayan responded: "If Golda does not support my position, I do not support my position either" (Eban 1977, 470).

Dayan's decision to refrain from pressing his views made for an easy victory of the hard-line coalition. On April 15, Israel sent a counterproposal to the United States. This response was strictly in line with the hard-line conception. It did not specify the line of Israeli withdrawal, it opposed the stationing of any Egyptian military or police forces east of the canal, and it completely fudged the issue of the agreement being a part of a process leading to further withdrawals.[13]

In the United States, a bureaucratic turf struggle had been going on between William Rogers and Henry Kissinger. Kissinger's attitude toward the idea of an interim agreement was skeptical. He stated (1979, 1281):

> Disengagement had no chance of success as long as it had to be negotiated together with an overall settlement. And if there was no chance of success, I saw no reason for us to involve ourselves. Our ace in the hole was that if we played our cards right, we could produce tangible progress in diplomacy while the Soviets could promise only help in war. But for this strategy to work we had to be effectual; we could not waste our pres-

tige on futile maneuvers. To succeed, an interim agreement therefore had to be separated from the comprehensive settlement; if they were linked, we would merely dissipate our influence by chasing a mirage that had all the difficulties of the comprehensive schemes it purported to replace and that we were no more able to produce.

Both Kissinger and Rogers sensed that the Israeli reply to Sisco was a nonstarter (Kissinger 1979, 1282; Rabin 1979, 378–79). They agreed that, if this process were to bear fruit, the United States would have to put a great deal of pressure on Israel. Yet, whereas Rogers thought that putting pressure on Israel would benefit the United States, Kissinger felt that it would harm U.S. interests.

Nevertheless, in response to Rogers's request, President Nixon approved a shuttle mission of Rogers and Sisco to the Middle East to try to move the parties from their positions to a point that would make an interim agreement feasible. Having visited Cairo in late March, Rogers and Sisco arrived in Jerusalem. In their meeting with Golda Meir and some members of her kitchen cabinet, they were presented the same Israeli positions as in the April 15 response. However, following this meeting Dayan requested a private meeting with the U.S. emissaries. In this meeting, he offered an opening, suggesting that Israel would withdraw to the Mitla-Gidi line in the Sinai in return for the Egyptian signature of a nonbelligerency treaty (Dayan 1976, 527).

This message was music to the Americans' ears, but it was not Golda's view. Kissinger (1979, 1283) pointed out that "Rogers' trip had no result except to get Dayan in some trouble at home when the differences between his government's position and his own became publicly known." After another round of meetings in Cairo, where some progress was achieved in terms of getting modifications in the Egyptian positions, and in Jerusalem, where he got nothing, Sisco had to admit failure (Sisco 1990; Kissinger 1979, 1284).

Throughout 1971 and 1972 U.S. efforts at mediation between Egypt and Israel continued, but the general sense was that the interim agreement was dead in the water (Quandt 2001, 94–96; Yaacobi 1990a, 157–72).[14] In June 1972, Sadat—profoundly dissatisfied with the reaction to his initiative—issued a directive to his minister of war to prepare plans for a war. The timer to the Yom Kippur War started clicking.

That this was a missed opportunity of major proportions is not a new idea. Gad Yaacobi, a close confidant of Dayan and Peres and the deputy minister of transportation in 1972, freely admits (1990a, 173–75; 1990b) that an interim agreement may well have averted the Yom Kippur War. There are also significant indications from Egyptian sources (e.g., Sadat 1977; Riad 1981, 209–10) that Sadat was committed to a settlement. His subsequent decision to initiate a war was largely influenced by the outcome of the negotiations over the interim agreement. But the most important evidence of the Israeli failure in this case comes from the wisdom of hindsight. Israel agreed to a far worse deal in January 1974 after the traumatic Yom Kippur War. It was willing to accept more than a token Egyptian force east of the canal. This force was military and well armed. The canal was not opened until November 1975, after an additional Israeli withdrawal to the east side of the passes. Israel could have accepted more in an interim agreement than it did after it lost three thousand soldiers and spent over $10 billion (Dupuy 1978; Barnett 1992, 185–209).

It could be argued that, in fact, Israel had avoided a major calamity in turning down the interim agreement in 1971. If the Yom Kippur War had started after the Egyptians had already positioned troops in the eastern part of the canal, they would have been able to accomplish an even greater achievement than they actually did in the war, because they would not have had to cross the canal barrier. In retrospect, and given the strategic contours of the Yom Kippur War, however, just the opposite was the case. The Egyptians agreed to have a token force east of the canal in the context of an agreement. Not only would moving large forces across the canal have constituted a clear violation of the agreement; it would have sent a clear signal of offensive intentions. The Egyptians would have exceeded their SAM shield and would have exposed their infantry and armor to the Israeli offensive. Even if they were able to accomplish surprise, the ability of the Israeli forces to defend the passes was far better than the Israeli ability to hold on to the Maozim during the Yom Kippur War. Finally, the fact that this issue did not play an important role in the Israeli calculations during the 1974 and 1975 interim agreements with Egypt—agreements that came after Israel had experienced a surprise attack on the Suez Canal—seems to suggest that it should have not been a major consideration in 1971.

How can we explain the Israeli failure to seize this opportunity? Four principal reasons account for this fiasco. First and foremost, Israeli political and military elite misread Sadat. Second, Israeli politicians did not believe that the deal they had been offered was good enough to justify territorial concessions. Third, Israeli domestic politics were a fundamental obstacle. Fourth, the bureaucratic struggle in the Nixon administration and the failure of the president to back up a more critical stand toward Israel, as Secretary of State Rogers had hoped, doomed this initiative to failure.

Israeli perceptions of Sadat were formed through a series of intelligence reports issued by AMAN under the glorified reign of Aharon Yariv. As we saw in previous chapters, Yariv's AMAN had already made a series of strategic errors in reading Arab intentions in the past. Yet, rather than drawing lessons from these strategic mistakes, the government continued to have an extremely high regard for Yariv. When Sadat came to power in October 1970, AMAN did not give him more than half a year in office. AMAN regarded Sadat as an interim caretaker who would soon be replaced by more powerful people like Ali Sabri, the secretary-general of the Arab Socialist Union (ASU), Egypt's ruling party. Sadat was also thought to be erratic and spineless. He was seen to have no meaningful conception regarding Egypt's foreign and domestic policy.

Thus, AMAN's discounting of the significance of the Sadat interim agreement idea and the Egyptian reply to Jarring's questions helped cultivate Golda's perception of the interim agreement as an Egyptian ploy to start a war from favorable conditions. Nobody in AMAN or in the government paid attention to the inherent contradiction in the Israeli interpretation of the Egyptian position: If the Egyptians wanted to start a war after they had been allowed to cross the canal under the cover of an interim agreement, why would they insist on a clear and time-bound linkage of the interim agreement to the final agreement, in which they had already stated their commitment to make contractual peace with Israel?

Even after Sadat purged the so-called centers of power—Ali Sabri and his procommunist group in the ASU that had threatened his position—in early May 1971, AMAN did not change its assessment of the likelihood of Sadat's political survival. Sadat's continuing contact with the United States did not help impress AMAN of the sincerity of the interim agreement initiative. On the other hand, when Egypt and the Soviet Union signed the Treaty of Friendship on May 27, 1971—which had absolutely no practical meaning since the Soviets were already heavily involved in the supply and training of the Egyptian army—Yariv appeared before the Israeli government on June 8, 1971, stating that it was the most far-reaching agreement between any noncommunist state and the Soviet Union (Yaacobi 1990a, 139). Consequently, when Sisco discussed in Jerusalem the Egyptian responses to the American proposal, he spent most of his time talking with the Israelis about the implications of the Egyptian-Soviet treaty on the region rather than about the Sadat initiative (Sisco 1990; Atherton 1990). The Israelis furnished him with intelligence reports that the Soviets had been stepping up their involvement in Egypt as a result of the treaty. Obviously, the Israelis demanded from the United States an additional forty Phantom F-4 jets to counter this increased threat.[15]

The Israeli position was also boosted by the existence of a real anti-concessions opposition. The GAHAL right-wing party repeatedly attacked the government's negotiation position. When Dayan's remarks to Sisco and Rogers expressing support for a modified version of the Sisco memorandum leaked out to the press, the opposition raised hell with the government, accusing it of appeasement. This also came in handy in dealing with the United States. The "moderate" opposition to the government's position was—of course—in the coalition, so it was unwilling to rock the boat over the agreement.

The picture could have been changed dramatically had the United States decided to put pressure on Israel. This was not to be, however. Kissinger was hostile to the notion of an interim agreement. He viewed it as a device for strengthening Soviet influence in the region, and the Egyptian-Soviet treaty supported this assessment. A May 31 memo from Kissinger to the president suggested that

> [t]he Egyptian Army is dependent on Soviet support. In turn, Sadat is at the moment dependent on his military for his base of power, having purged the party and the bureaucracy. Rather than strengthening Sadat's flexibility with respect to negotiating the Canal settlement, the treaty could give the Soviet Union a veto over the future negotiations. Thus, whatever the outcome of the negotiations . . . recent events may have enhanced Soviet long-term influence. Certainly the Soviets are committed to engage themselves as never before in case of resumption of hostilities. (Kissinger 1979, 1284)

This position was a killer of Rogers's hope that he could get presidential pressure on Israel to modify its position. Indeed, after the Egyptians had indicated in their reply to the Sisco memorandum that there was room for flexibility and that their attitude to the ideas raised in this memorandum was positive, Kissinger managed to delay the Sisco Mideast mission by over a month, thus indicating to the Israelis that there would be no adverse diplomatic backlash to their April 18 uncompromising position.

The tragedy is that key players on all sides of this process were convinced that an interim agreement could be a transformative event, and they had been genuinely interested in achieving it. However, the three visionary players—Sadat, Rogers, and Dayan—were not enough to make this work. They confronted tremendous opposition at home, beyond the usual difference of views of negotiation counterparts. What could have been the first step in a peace process that would have averted the Yom Kippur War turned out to be a chief motivating factor for the Egyptian decision to initiate the war.

2.8. The Post–Yom Kippur Disengagement Agreements and the 1975 Sinai Interim Agreement

Following the Yom Kippur War, Israel signed three agreements with Egypt and Syria over the course of one and a half years. These agreements share several features in common. First, they were all signed in the shadow—and as a direct result—of the Yom Kippur War. Second, they were all negotiated via the energetic mediation of the U.S. secretary of state, Henry Kissinger. Third, they were all part of a careful American negotiation strategy, termed the step-by-step diplomacy (Touval 1982). This strategy envisioned a set of partial agreements extending over a long period of time as a prelude to comprehensive peace agreements. Fourth, they were all accomplished only after substantial American pressure on a reluctant Israeli government, in some cases involving tangible sanctions. Fifth, they were all successful. All parties to the agreements exhibited exemplary commitment to and compliance with the agreements over time. The two Sinai agreements between Israel and Egypt paved the way for the 1979 peace treaty between the two states. The Israeli-Syrian agreement in the Golan was an island of stability in the otherwise extremely hostile relationship between these two states. Both sides complied with its provisions even when they were engaged in a bitter shooting war in Lebanon. In that sense, these agreements helped establish the credibility and sustainability of the "land for peace" principle that lay at the heart of UN Resolutions 242 and 338.

Once the Yom Kippur War ended, Kissinger began to apply the strategy of mediation he started developing when the war broke out. His principal goal was to break the tension between Israel and Egypt by separating the two armies. The positioning of the Israeli and Egyptian armies entailed a high risk of renewed hostilities. More important, Kissinger was interested in getting a foot into the Egyptian door in order to convince Sadat that he would be better off turning to the United States than continuing his military and political reliance on the Soviet Union (Kissinger 1982, 634–35).

For Israel, the most pressing matter was to bring about an exchange of prisoners and to stabilize the cease-fire lines. As long as the risk of renewed hostilities was high, Israel had to keep sizable military forces on hand. Thus, the IDF continued to be overextended, and most of the reserve forces were left mobilized. This put a choke on the economy. The Israeli society was still in shock, given the large number of casualties and the inconclusive outcome of the war. However, the government found itself in a bind. To accept a territorial status quo that left Egyptian forces on the eastern bank of the Suez Canal would mean to admit some degree of political defeat. To reject this demand would leave Israel in a tenuous military and political position. But Israel felt it had considerable leverage over the Egyptians: the Third Egyptian Army was completely encircled by Israeli forces and needed urgent supplies.

For the Egyptians, the top priority was to provide supplies to the encircled Third Egyptian Army. But Sadat, who still believed he had won the war, wanted a settlement that would acknowledge this fact. Specifically, he wanted an agreement that would remove the Israeli forces from the West Bank of the Suez Canal but would also allow Egypt to keep its on the eastern side of the canal.

Kissinger's strategy focused on decoupling the immediate crisis around the Third Egyptian Army and the Israeli prisoners of war (POWs) from the more complex problem of a disengagement agreement. He urged the sides to start talks between representatives of the two armed forces on a limited military arrangement that would focus on the pressing issues of POWs and supplies to the encircled Third Egyptian Army.

On October 29, 1973, the first meeting between the Israeli representative, Major General (Res.) Aharon Yariv, and the Egyptian representative, Lieutenant General Abd el Ghani Gamassy, took place on the 101st kilometer of the Cairo-Suez road. Within thirteen days, and with the active urging of Kissinger while shuttling between Jerusalem and Cairo, an initial agreement was reached on the provision of supplies to the encircled Third Egyptian Army, on exchanging POWs, and on beginning talks about disengagement of the armed forces of the two states.[16] This provided both the Israeli government and Sadat some breathing room.

However, the road to a political agreement that would end the war was a rocky one. First, Israel faced elections on December 31. The government was reluctant to enter into any agreement that might entail significant concessions before the elections (Golan 1976, 130–31;

Kissinger 1982, 751–52). Second, Sadat was still suspicious of the Israelis and Americans and feared that they might deprive Egypt of the fruits of what he perceived as a major military victory. Third, Sadat had considerable problems with Asad, who was still unwilling to recognize the gravity of the Syrian military situation (Seale 1988, 220–21; Sadat 1977, 202–3; Fahmy 1983, 56–59).

In order to keep the political momentum alive while the parties dealt with their internal and inter-Arab difficulties, Kissinger offered an international conference in Geneva, under the auspices of the UN, the United States, and the Soviet Union. This conference would serve as the first leg of the bilateral negotiations. Israel, Egypt, and Jordan accepted, while Syria refused to participate. The conference met on December 21, 1973, and was limited to a plenary meeting of foreign ministers. After the formal speeches were given, the conference adjourned, and the bilateral talks continued at the 101st kilometer. The Israeli election resulted in a decline in the electoral power of the Labor Party but still left the incumbent government in power. This allowed for the negotiations to resume in full force.

Kissinger returned to the Middle East in early January and embarked on a series of shuttle meetings with the Egyptian and Israeli leaderships. The Israelis were reluctant to give up pre–October 1973 territory. The deal that Kissinger offered was a far worse deal than the one the Israelis had turned down in 1971. Moreover, there was no Egyptian political quid pro quo, such as an offer to open the canal for shipping or nonbelligerence.

Kissinger, however, was determined to get an agreement. There was no need for American threats; the Israelis understood the trade-offs. Israel was completely dependent on the United States for supply and replenishment of the equipment and ammunitions spent during the war. In contrast to the Rogers-Sisco missions in 1971, this time there was no bureaucratic struggle in the Nixon administration: the secretary of state and the national security adviser were the same person. Moreover, the president was—for all practical purposes—out of circulation due to the Watergate crisis. Kissinger also employed a number of negotiation tactics, such as threats, promises, and misrepresentations of positions. The Israeli government was far from happy with the deal it had been offered but saw little choice but to agree.

The Egyptian-Israeli disengagement agreement[17] of January 18, 1974, entailed an Israeli withdrawal to about twenty kilometers east of the Suez Canal. The area evacuated by Israel was to be divided into two roughly equal parts, one part held by a limited contingent of Egyptian troops and the other part by UN forces. This implied an Israeli admission of some partial Egyptian achievement during the war (Golan 1976, 170–75). The Israeli achievement in this agreement was the military disengagement and the creation of a UN buffer zone between the armies. This represented some form of deterrent to a resumption of hostilities.

This was a primarily military agreement, but its last paragraph stated that this agreement was the first step toward comprehensive peace negotiations. The fact that it was negotiated directly between two official representatives of the parties was also meaningful. The agreement established the position of Kissinger as a mutually acceptable mediator (Kissinger 1982, 844–45; Golan 1976, 170–75).[18] Yet, compared to the Sisco memorandum of April 1971, this agreement consisted of all the elements that the Israeli government had deemed unacceptable in 1971 and had an added element of a substantial Egyptian military force east of the Suez Canal.

Kissinger's next task was to negotiate a similar agreement between Israel and Syria. From a Syrian perspective, the agreement was seen as a first step toward reacquisition of the Golan Height. As such, a return to the Purple Line (the cease-fire line of June 11, 1967) was unacceptable. Asad was better off without an agreement than with one that would suggest to everybody that Syria got nothing out of the war. Moreover, Asad and the Syrian press publicly criticized Sadat for having signed a separate agreement with Israel, stating that "Egypt is leaving the battle. . . . Israeli troops opposite [Egypt] will now be moved to the Golan" (Seale 1988, 238). At the same time Asad realized that even the meager achievement of the Egyptians—the fact that they maintained control of a narrow strip of land east of the Suez Canal—allowed Sadat to show his own public that he got some territorial gain out of the war. Asad could not afford to accept less than Sadat (Seale 1988, 239).

Asad held two cards in his hand. One was a list, and indeed the lives, of over fifty Israeli POWs in Syria. The other was the ability to conduct a war of attrition that would spill additional blood of a powerful but psychologically exhausted Israel. So while this was a risky long-term strategy, in the short term this could lead to some, at least symbolic, Israeli concessions. Asad's profound dissatisfaction with the postwar status quo combined with a lack of capability to change it dictated cooperation with Kissinger. His strategy of attrition and of tough negotiation was designed to ensure a symbolic territorial victory. By that time, however, Asad knew that Syria was on its own. If negotiations failed he would have

Israeli forces within forty kilometers of Damascus. Thus, not reaching an agreement was clearly inferior to some kind of political agreement.

The Israeli government was faced by a multitude of problems when substantive negotiations with Syria started. On the one hand, there was strong domestic pressure to obtain the list of Israeli POWs in Syrian hands. The war of attrition that was being waged in the north also put a heavy burden on the government. But above all, the growing domestic criticism and the rise of a popular movement calling for the resignation of Dayan and of Golda put strong pressure on the government. Objectively, the Israeli government felt that Israel had considerable leverage on Syria due to the threat of Israeli forces on Damascus. Israeli decision makers were confident that, if a war broke out, they would be able to move deep into Syrian territory. However, Dayan and Golda had neither the political will nor the domestic support for a military option.

The fact that the American secretary of state was willing to conduct a prolonged shuttle diplomacy between Jerusalem and Damascus at the height of a major crisis in American politics implied that failure to reach an agreement would have extremely adverse consequences. Kissinger was very adept at describing for the parties the ramifications of stalemate. For the Israelis he portrayed a gloomy scenario that included a flare-up of the war, with Egypt, Iraq, and Jordan joining in; a renewed Arab oil embargo; major pressure on Israel by the Europeans and others to return to the 1967 borders; the return of the Soviet Union to the Middle East; and so forth. Even the United States would not be able to bail Israel out under such circumstances (Golan 1976, 154–55; Aronson 1978, 240). To Asad, Kissinger stressed the precarious military situation and the prospect that a resumption of large-scale hostilities could bring Israel to the gates of Damascus in a matter of days.

On April 11, 1974, under considerable public pressure, Golda Meir resigned, thereby bringing about the downfall of the government established after the general elections of December 1973. The Labor Party became engaged in a process of selecting a new candidate for prime minister, and the competition narrowed down to a choice between Shimon Peres and Yitzhak Rabin, who had ended his term as Israeli ambassador to the United States just before the war. Rabin narrowly defeated Peres in the internal party election and was in the process of forming a new coalition. However, the Golda government continued to handle negotiations with Syria as a caretaker cabinet.

Israel's position was focused on three issues. One was that any agreement should bring about the exchange of POWs, but before the agreement was signed, Israel should get the list of POWs in Syria and Syria should allow Red Cross representatives to visit with the Israeli POWs. Second, Israel did not insist on maintaining control of the Mazra'at Beit-Ja'an salient captured during the war but was unwilling to withdraw from any part of the Golan Height, as the Syrians demanded. Third, Israel wished for this agreement to create a buffer zone—to be managed by an international force—between the Israeli and Syrian forces (Golan 1976, 183–84; Dayan 1976, 572; Aronson 1978, 240–42).

During the negotiations it became clear that Israel would not be able to reach an agreement with Syria on the basis of the Purple Line. Yet, if Syria were handed a symbolic territorial accomplishment, it would be willing to give in to the other two points in the Israeli position. With the help of Kissinger's clarifications and veiled threats, Israel felt that giving up the city of Qunaytra was not such a major concession. The agreement was thus at hand.

The domestic and international circumstances under which Israel negotiated with Syria were such that Israel was willing to come to terms with a symbolic withdrawal from land occupied during the 1967 war without getting any political recognition. There was growing pressure in Israel to get back the POWs. Also, the maintenance of the Mazra'at Beit-Ja'an salient required a large IDF contingent. The IDF had been over-stretched by then and was in dire need of regrouping after the war.

The same international constraints that had operated on the Meir government in its negotiations with the Egyptians were at work here as well. Kissinger did not have illusions about changing Syrian pro-Soviet orientation, but he did view this agreement as important from the point of view of broader U.S. interests in the Middle East (Kissinger 1982, 1033–36; Spiegel 1985, 276–78). He made it clear to the Israelis that he had staked his and the United States' reputation on this agreement. Turning down the deal would have costly international ramifications for Israel. Thus, reluctantly, the Israelis signed the agreement.

This agreement stipulated the withdrawal of Israeli forces to the pre–October 1973 Purple Line, with one exception. The city of Qunaytra and a small area around it were handed over to the Syrians. Israeli and Syrian forces were separated by an area covering the entire Golan Height from north to south, ranging from one to three kilometers in width. In this area, a new UN force—the United Nations Disengagement Observer Force (UNDOF)—was established to monitor the agreement. Israel and Syria exchanged POWs. The agreement did not stipulate—as in the Egyptian case—that it would be a first stage in a peace process between the two states. This agreement was more favorable to Israel, even in symbolic terms, than had been the Israeli-Egyptian disengagement agreement. Nevertheless, it confronted considerable criticism from the right-wing parties in Israel. Yet, since the Meir government was on its way out, the criticism subsided rather quickly.

Once the new Israeli government under Rabin was in place, Kissinger started exploring possibilities for a second stage of Egyptian-Israeli negotiations.[19] Kissinger continued to maintain that it was premature to go for a full-fledged peace agreement because the positions of the parties were too far apart. He also realized that domestic politics prevented major diplomatic breakthroughs (Quandt 2001, 137–39).

Kissinger renewed his shuttle diplomacy in March 1975. He hoped to conclude a second agreement by the end of the month, but it soon became evident that this was not to be. The initial expectations of the two adversaries had been too far apart to make this possible.

> Sadat wanted this step to be treated as another military disengagement, with only minimal political overtones. He felt he could not afford to be seen in the Arab world as having withdrawn from the conflict with Israel. . . . Israel hoped to split Egypt from Syria and thus reduce the prospect of a combined Arab offensive such as had occurred in October 1973. To do so would require that Egypt make substantial political concessions as the price of further Israeli withdrawal. (Quandt 2001, 160)

After several trips between Cairo and Jerusalem, Kissinger concluded that the talks had reached an impasse. At the heart of the dispute was Israeli insistence on maintaining control over an intelligence installation at Um Khasheeba and Sadat's insistence on a nonuse of force formula as the political cover of the agreement, in contrast to Israel's demand that this be labeled a nonbelligerence agreement (Sheehan 1976, 155–62; Quandt 2001, 160; Rabin 1979, 458). On March 21, Kissinger announced the suspension of his mission, indirectly putting the blame squarely at Israel's doorstep (Golan 1976, 241–42; Spiegel 1985, 294–95; Sheehan 1976, 165). This was followed by a presidential decision on a "reassessment of U.S. policy," which entailed a de facto suspension of American weapon shipments to Israel.

Israel responded by using its ties to the United States to influence the administration into reconsidering its reassessment policy. But the real breakthrough came from Egypt. In June 1975 Sadat signaled that he was genuinely interested in getting this agreement signed by unilaterally opening the Suez Canal for shipping and by indicating that he would be willing to allow foreign ships coming from and going to Israel to pass in the canal. This was seen as an important gesture. Israel responded by reducing the size of its forces in the western part of the Sinai (Rabin 1979, 466; Spiegel 1985, 297; Fahmy 1983, 163).

This exercise in reciprocal gestures paved the way for yet another round of shuttles by Kissinger in late August. After some difficulties and major anti-American and anti-Kissinger demonstrations in Israel, the Sinai II interim agreement was signed on September 1, 1975. The agreement entailed Israeli withdrawal from yet another portion of the Sinai, to east of the Mitla and Gidi passes in northern and central Sinai, and some withdrawal from the Suez Bay area. Moreover, Israel agreed to abandon its intelligence installation in Um Khasheeba, but Egypt allowed the installation of an American observation station that could be used by Israel. Also, Israel allowed Egypt access to the oil fields along the eastern shore of the Suez Bay in Abu Rhodeys. More important, this represented the first political agreement that stated that both parties needed to denounce the threat or use of force as an instrument of diplomacy.[20] This was short of what the Israelis wanted—nonbelligerency—but more than what some Egyptians had been willing to give. Egyptian foreign minister Ismail Fahmy refused to sign the agreement because he felt Egypt had made too many political concessions for too little Israeli withdrawal (Fahmy 1983, 165–66).

In this case, more than in the case of the two disengagement agreements of 1974, American pressure on Israel proved effective. Israel was pushed into this agreement by massive U.S. pressure. The Israeli government was divided over the agreement. Rabin and his foreign minister, Yigal Allon, were in favor of it. Shimon Peres—reflecting the IDF's position—was reserved about it. Peres felt that giving up Um Khasheeba and the Mitla and Gidi passes would put Israel in a precarious strategic position should hostilities be resumed. However, he too understood that resisting the United States on this matter would be even more costly. Even Rabin and Allon did not support the agreement for its own sake. Rather, it was a trade-off between the perceived domestic and security risks associated with an agreement and a major rift with the United States. Since the latter matter weighted heavier with Israeli decision makers at that time, this led them to support the interim agreement.

The United States helped Israel sign the agreement by offering significant inducements. First, the United States agreed to station its own troops in the buffer zone between the Israeli and Egyptian forces, as well as to place American personnel at the Um Khasheeba early warning installation. Second, the United States agreed to resume the weapon shipments to Israel, offering it advanced F-15 jets. Third, and most important, the United States agreed that it would not recognize the PLO or negotiate with it as long as the PLO continued to reject UN Resolution 242 and did not renounce terrorism. The shaky Rabin government could present this to the Israeli public as a major political accomplishment.

What are the lessons of these three processes of negotiations? First and foremost, in all three cases, the Israeli government was a reluctant partner to an agreement. It took strong inducements and some sanctions by the United States to make the Israelis accept these agreements. Second, as in previous cases, the IDF intelligence was extremely suspicious of the opponents' intentions, examining the proposed positions of Egypt and Syria from a point of departure that they had been interested in improving their territorial position so that they could violate the agreement in the future. The IDF was reluctant to give up territorial assets, despite the fact that it faced fundamental manpower difficulties.

Third, it is evident that the Israelis accepted the agreement more to avoid a political rift with the United States than to improve the Israeli strategic and political situation. Fourth, while there were demonstrations against each and every one of these proposed agreements, Israeli public opinion overwhelmingly supported these agreements once they had been signed. This implies that the obsessive fear of Israeli politicians of a seemingly uncompromising public was also unfounded.

In retrospect it is evident that the decisions made by the Meir and Rabin governments to sign these agreements proved adaptive over the long haul. It is also evident that most of the Israeli fears and suspicions were totally unfounded. The Egyptians and Syrians complied with the letter and spirit of these agreements. The agreements with Egypt were instrumental in advancing the prospect of an Israeli-Egyptian peace treaty because they caused a strategic reorientation of Egyptian foreign and economic policy to the west and a complete disassociation from the Soviet Union. They also established U.S. influence in Egypt and in particular built a rapport of trust and mutual understanding with Sadat. Sadat was able to use the political capital he made out of the Yom Kippur War—despite significant opposition to these agreements among his own advisers—to launch peace initiatives. This epitomizes the Jewish idiom *Mitoch shelo lishmo, ba lishmo*—"What is being done not for its own sake is converted to something for its own sake."

2.9. The Sadat Peace Initiative and
the Egyptian-Israeli Peace Treaty

The election of Jimmy Carter to the presidency of the United States offered both risks and opportunities to the peace process (Spiegel 1985, 315–18). Carter was inexperienced in the intricacies of Middle East policy. In contrast to Kissinger and his associates, Joseph Sisco and Roy Atherthon, who had many years of Mideast diplomacy under their belt, Cyrus Vance and Zbigniew Brzezinski, Carter's principal foreign policy advisers, had little exposure to the Mideast picture,[21] and what little exposure they had was based on their criticism of the Ford-Kissinger Mideast policy (Brzezinski, Duchêne, and Saeki 1975, 3–17). In the winter and spring months of 1977, Carter initiated a series of meetings with the leaders of Egypt, Jordan, and Israel to explore their positions toward the peace process. Not surprising, the most difficult meetings were between Carter and Rabin in March 1977.[22] By that time, Carter knew that Rabin was running for reelection in Israel. In these meetings, Carter suggested shifting the peace process agenda from a bilateral step-by-step approach to a comprehensive peace approach, via a renewed Geneva Conference. The idea was to use this conference as a springboard for a set of simultaneous bilateral negotiation processes. It was evident that the Carter administration was on the "Brookings Path," urging an Israeli withdrawal to the 1967 boundaries (Quandt 1986, 34–38; Rabin 1979, 507–19).[23]

In May, the first change of power in Israeli politics took place when the Likud Party, headed by Menachem Begin, replaced the Labor government. Begin, an avowed hard-liner, seemingly opposed to Israeli territorial concessions, made a number of speeches that seemed to be consistent with his hard-line and uncompromising image. However, at the same time, he also made a number of political moves that indicated his interest in peace. One of those was the appointment of Moshe Dayan as foreign minister. In one of his first trips abroad, Begin met with Romanian president Nikolai Ceausescu. The latter reported to Sadat that Begin was serious about peace with Egypt. More important, Begin made the impression of someone who could deliver his pledges (Sadat 1977, 233; Israeli 1985, 223–24).

Sadat had initially been willing to go along with the Carter plan to reconvene the Geneva Conference. However, he soon became convinced that this road was bound to nowhere, because the Arabs could not get their act together. Sadat's testimony on this matter is telling: "It is a pity, really, because we could have achieved something this year [toward peace], but unfortunately, it is the Arab position which is hindering it, not the Super Powers. . . . Because of party maneuvers in Syria, it appears they are not ready; one day they say they are ready and the other day they refuse to go [to Geneva]. It is always a double-face policy."[24]

Arab haggling over procedural aspects of the Geneva Conference led Sadat to a secret track to Israel. Following a secret visit to Morocco on September 4, 1977, Moshe Dayan was invited by King Hassan of Morocco to return to another meeting. This time, on September 16, the other guest in the meeting was Dr. Hassan Touhamy, the deputy prime minister of Egypt and a close confidant of Sadat. Touhamy indicated that Sadat was interested in direct negotiations with Israel and that he would be willing to meet Begin if the latter agreed to the principle of full withdrawal (Dayan 1981, 44–45). Touhamy made it clear that, in return for full Israeli withdrawal and for Israel's acceptance of a Palestinian homeland (linked to Jordan), Egypt would be willing to sign a full-fledged peace agreement and would agree to any guarantees Israel would require.

Dayan did not make any commitment other than to say he would convey Touhamy's message to Begin. The parties agreed to schedule another meeting after the leaders considered the various positions and proposals. However, at that point, the key moves were made in Washington and Moscow. On October 1, a joint statement coauthored by Cyrus Vance, the American secretary of state, and Andre Gromyko, the Soviet foreign minister, called for convening the Geneva Conference with Palestinian representation and accepted the "legitimate rights of the Palestinian people."[25]

This joint statement drew fire from both the American Jewish community and the U.S. Congress. It invoked direct opposition from Israel. Sadat realized that the road to Geneva was probably blocked. Even if some formula were found to convene the conference, the prospects of this general gathering producing real progress were slim. In particular, Sadat was extremely upset at the U.S.-Soviet joint communiqué because it implied for him bringing the Soviets back to Middle East peacemaking. This was a major mistake. The only viable alternative was to launch a direct process vis-à-vis Israel.

The question was then how to get this process off the ground. Here, too, Sadat faced two options. The first was to continue through the secret Moroccan channel. The other was to go public. Sadat, with his usual flair for drama, chose the second option. On November 9, 1977, in a speech to the Egyptian National Assembly, he announced that he would be willing to go to the end of the world—even to Jerusalem—and talk to every-body—even directly to the Israeli people—in order to convince them that he wanted peace. Israeli reaction did not take too long. Within forty-eight hours, Begin sent an invitation to Sadat to visit Jerusalem.

On November 17, 1977, Sadat's plane landed at Ben-Gurion Airport. On the next day, Sadat delivered a historic speech to the Knesset. In his speech, Sadat pledged to accept Israel's right to exist and committed him-self to a political settlement of the conflict, precluding the use of force as a viable option. However, Sadat's prescription of the solution was one that the Israelis found difficult to digest: full withdrawal from all the ter-ritories occupied in 1967 and the formation of the Palestinian state in the West Bank and Gaza.[26]

Sadat viewed this as a major gesture that required a strong Israeli response. In his mind—and that came out clearly in his speech to the Knesset—the proper Israeli response should have been to accept his demand. He foresaw a quick negotiation process based on the agenda he proposed, since he had already complied with Israel's demands of recog-nition and peace by virtue of his trip to Jerusalem (Sadat 1977, 237–38). However, the result of the trip was an agreement on the format of nego-tiations. Specifically, it was agreed that direct negotiations would start immediately along two parallel tracks. There would be two negotiating teams; the political negotiations would be conducted in Israel and the military negotiations in Egypt (Sadat 1977, 237; Dayan 1981, 85).

These negotiations quickly ran into considerable difficulties. The Egyptians demanded a total Israeli withdrawal from the Sinai and major Israeli concessions on the Palestinian issue, including an Israeli accep-tance of a Palestinian state and a commitment to withdraw from the West Bank and Gaza. The Israelis were reluctant to give up three airfields they had constructed in the Sinai and the settlements that had been con-structed in the Rafah area (between Rafah and El Arish). On the Pales-tinian issue, the Israeli proposal consisted of a plan to provide the Pales-tinians with limited autonomy to conduct some key areas of their internal affairs (e.g., health and education). However, Israel insisted on maintain-ing military and political control over the West Bank and Gaza.

Several crises characterized the negotiations. On December 25, another summit meeting took place in the city of Ismailya on the West Bank of the Suez Canal. This meeting, while not ending in an explicit breakdown, nevertheless did not produce any progress.[27] The first meet-ing of the Political Committee in Jerusalem on January 17, 1978, was a disaster. In his opening statement, Menachem Begin called the head of

the Egyptian delegation, Mohammed Ibrahim Kamel, "my young friend."
Using a diplomatic pretext of being insulted, the Egyptians left Jerusalem
the next day.

Other meetings between Weizman and Sadat in Cairo (February
1978) and between Dayan and Sadat in Leeds Castle (July 17, 1978)
failed to produce any meaningful progress. The military negotiations were
another story, however (Tamir 1988, 21–29). As time went by and no
real progress was accomplished, President Carter and his Middle East
team started expressing growing concern with the stalemate. The domestic and inter-Arab risks that Sadat was facing were enormous. As Carter
(1982, 315–16) quotes from his diary:

> Sadat is meeting with the radical Arabs to try to repair his fences with
> them, which is not a good omen (July 27, 1978). . . . [T]he situation is
> getting into an extreme state, and I'm concerned that Sadat might
> precipitate a conflict in October, as he has hinted several times. The
> Arabs are really pushing Sadat and, [so as] not to stay vulnerable in
> the long run, I think he is wanting either to come back to them or to
> some resolution of the question (July 31, 1978).

Over the month of July, the American team, which consisted of
Carter, Vance, Brzezinski, and William Quandt, devised a bold and risky
plan that was meant to break the deadlock: bring both leaders with a
small team of advisers to a summit meeting at Camp David. During this
meeting, the parties would strive to reach an agreement. By proposing
this plan, the administration staked its reputation on a successful outcome, but it also demonstrated to both parties how committed it was to
an agreement between Egypt and Israel (Quandt 2001, 197; 1986, 201–6;
Telhami 1990, 139–41; Touval 1982, 298–300). Somewhat to the surprise of Carter, both leaders accepted the Camp David invitation, and so,
on September 5, 1978, the Camp David conference started.

The conference was a fascinating exercise in diplomacy and mediation. Not surprising, it has generated a considerable number of accounts
on its intricacies, ups and downs, and outcome.[28] A detailed account of
this conference is beyond the scope of this study. However, two issues can
be briefly explored: first, the problems at stake and how they were
resolved; and second, the role of the participants in securing the successful outcome of the summit. There were three principal points of disagreement that separated the parties at the start of this conference: first, the
linkage between the Israeli-Egyptian peace treaty and the Palestinian
problem; second, the manner in which Jordan and the Palestinians were

to be associated with future negotiations; and third, the question of Israeli withdrawal from the settlements in the Rafah area and the Sinai airfields.

The Israelis opted for a separate Israeli-Egyptian agreement with little or no linkage to the Palestinian issue. Sadat sought a firm commitment of Israeli withdrawal from the West Bank and Gaza in the course of negotiations with Jordan and the Palestinians. The resolution of the issue was to conclude a full-fledged peace agreement between Israel and Egypt but to include in it an annex stipulating its linkage to the Palestinian issue. Specifically, talks on Palestinian autonomy were to start as soon as the bilateral peace treaty was concluded, and Israel was to refrain from building settlements in the West Bank and the Gaza Strip during these negotiations.

The question of the Sinai airfields was resolved due to an American pledge to replace these airfields by building three air bases for Israel in the Negev. The stickier problem concerned the Israeli settlements in the Rafah area. This was a difficult problem for Begin for two reasons. First, he felt it would be the most difficult domestic political problem to overcome (Benziman 1981; Weizman 1981, 344–45; Quandt 1986, 236–37). Second, dismantling Israeli settlements in Israeli occupied territories could become a precedent for future agreements in the Golan and the West Bank.

The solution to this problem was to have Begin promise to put this issue before the Israeli Knesset and to have it determine the fate of the settlements. It was evident that Begin would put his weight behind a resolution calling for the dismantlement of the settlements and so would other members of his government.[29]

Other sticky issues, principally the issue of Jerusalem and the question of the Israeli policy of building settlements in the West Bank, were left open for future negotiations or were framed in deliberately vague terms to allow the other aspects of the agreement to be concluded. Thus, thirteen days after the Camp David conference started, on September 17, 1978, a joint press conference took place in Washington in which Presidents Carter and Sadat and Prime Minister Begin presented the accords.[30]

Soon after the conference ended, however, the latent disagreements between the parties broke out into the open. In his effort to mobilize support for the agreement, Begin revealed that his promise to refrain from building new settlements in the West Bank was supposed to cover the subsequent three months, during which the final Israeli-Egyptian peace treaty was to be concluded. Egypt and the United States interpreted the Israeli position on this issue in Camp David to imply that Israel would refrain from building new settlements as long as the West Bank autonomy talks were in progress (Dayan 1981, 151–56; Carter 1982, 406–10).

It soon became evident that the negotiations over the final Israeli-Egyptian peace treaty were more difficult than expected. The devil was, indeed, in the details, especially since so many issues had been left open or had been framed in vague terms during the Camp David conference. The Camp David Accords allowed for a three-month period for the negotiation of a peace treaty. However, the reality was more complex. The Israelis and the Egyptians rediscovered the suspicion and mistrust that had characterized their pre–Camp David relations. One of the new issues that arose during the negotiations was the question of the relation of the Egyptian-Israeli agreement to other agreements that Egypt had. In particular, the Israelis demanded that the Israeli-Egyptian peace treaty take precedence over the defense pacts that Egypt had with other Arab states—most notably with Syria. The Egyptians contended that acceptance of this principle would amount to giving a blank check to an Israeli attack on Syria (which indeed turned out to be the case in 1982). In addition, the Egyptians wanted to link progress on the implementation of the Israeli-Egyptian agreement—specifically, the opening of diplomatic relations and economic ties—to progress on the Palestinian autonomy talks (Dayan 1981, 178–79; Quandt 1986, 297–311).

At that point, President Carter decided to intervene directly. On a brief shuttle trip to Jerusalem and Cairo, again mixing pressures and pledges and bridging the remaining differences through a series of letters to the parties, Carter managed to get the final agreement. On March 27, 1979, nearly four months after the previously agreed deadline for an agreement, Menachem Begin and Anwar Sadat signed the first Arab-Israeli peace treaty on the White House lawn in Washington.

Sadat's initiative was an opportunity that could not be missed. From an Israeli perspective there were four fundamental issues at stake. First, this was an opportunity to get their most powerful enemy out of the Arab-Israeli conflict and at a strategic price that was extremely profitable. By the time the parties convened in Camp David, the terms of the military agreement had already been drafted in Cairo by the military delegations of the two sides. The two sides agreed that the Sinai would be demilitarized, that Egypt would hold only one brigade in the Sinai, and that the military parameters of the agreement would be monitored by an international force. This put a two-hundred-kilometer buffer between the Egyptian and the Israeli armies—a better early warning system could hardly be devised. Getting Egypt out of the conflict implied that Israel could reduce its defense burden, which by that time approached 23 percent of the GDP. Without Egypt, any Arab military effort against Israel was a significantly less threatening prospect.

Second, and this had been Begin's vision, Egypt could be extracted from the conflict without making significant sacrifices on the Palestinian issue. It was clear that some lip service to Palestinian autonomy had to be paid for the agreement to be signed, but this was a small price to pay for keeping Israeli control of the West Bank while the world stood by and watched Israel strengthen its hold over this area by establishing further settlements. The Sinai–West Bank trade-off appealed to Begin enormously. He was even willing to sacrifice the Rafah settlements for this purpose. It was the principal reason why Sharon strongly supported the Egyptian-Israeli peace treaty and was willing to dismantle the Rafah settlements using force in the spring of 1982, when this part of the agreement was to be implemented.

Third, this agreement was a major opportunity to consolidate relations with the United States. By inviting the parties to the summit at Camp David, President Carter staked his reputation on the success of this conference. Playing hard to get was a useful tactic in order to extract concessions from the United States in exchange for "painful concessions" in the Sinai. Israel ended up with a $1.8 billion annual military aid package and an additional $1 billion annual economic aid package.

Fourth, Sadat had staked his personal and political future on direct negotiations with Israel. His major concession had been made even before Israel made a single concession—recognition of Israel and a pledge of "no more war" in front of the Israeli Knesset and the entire international community. This is what Maoz and Felsenthal (1987) call a "self-binding commitment." Turning down the agreement would have jeopardized not only Sadat's life and political career but any chance that another Arab leader would be willing to come forth with some form of peace proposal in the future. The diplomatic cost would have been huge.

In addition, there was also a significant domestic political cost to consider. In 1977 a new peace organization, Peace Now, was established in Israel urging the government to respond favorably to the Sadat initiative. Just before his departure to Camp David, Begin witnessed one of the largest demonstrations in Israel, with over one hundred thousand demonstrators urging him to reach an agreement with Egypt. Failure to do so would have cost the Begin government a great deal of public support. More important, Begin knew that he could count on the Labor opposition in the Knesset to support a peace agreement that entailed territorial concessions, but he would have to engage in a fierce parliamentary struggle if he failed to reach an agreement. The downside domestically was that Begin could confront significant opposition in his own party. However, getting Sharon on board was a big asset from the intraparty perspective.

Finally, it is important to note that the people surrounding Begin had an important role in the outcome of the negotiations. Begin himself was highly reserved on many items of the agreement, even though he obviously saw the key advantages of such an accord. At the same time, Begin's closest advisers—Moshe Dayan and Ezer Weizman—were strong supporters of an agreement. They understood—possibly better than Begin himself—the strategic significance of such an agreement. They also understood the kind of person they were dealing with on the Egyptian side. Dayan, as we have seen, detected back in 1971 the seriousness of Sadat and his ability to understand strategic realities on a global and regional scale. He had also orchestrated the first disengagement agreement in Egypt in 1974. He felt that this was a unique opportunity because Israel was facing a man of vision and a person who could be trusted on the other side of the agreement. Both he and Weizman established a good rapport with Sadat and felt that, if Israel did not reach agreement with Sadat, the prospects of future agreement with anyone in Egypt would be extremely slim. These two advisers—as well as other less senior advisers, such as General Abraham (Abrasha) Tamir and Attorney General Aharon Barak—were able to influence Begin into overcoming his fears and hesitations and signing the agreement.

2.10. The Autonomy Scam, 1979–81

In the Camp David Accords, a modified plan for temporary Palestinian autonomy was inserted as part of the "Framework for Peace in the Middle East" annex of the agreement. A committee composed of Israeli, Egyptian, Jordanian, and elected Palestinian representatives was formed to "decide by agreement on the modalities of admission of persons displaced from the West Bank and Gaza in 1967, together with necessary measures to prevent disruption and disorder. Other matters of common concern may also be dealt with by this committee" (Camp David 1978).

Immediately following the joint press conference that ended the Camp David summit, the scam of the "Framework" agreement started getting clear. Upon his return to Israel, Begin announced that his agreement on a freeze on Israeli settlements referred only to the three-month period scheduled for finalization of the Egyptian-Israeli peace treaty, not—as the Americans and Egyptians interpreted the "Framework" agreement—the entire five-year period of temporary self-rule for the Palestinians (Shlaim 2000, 379; Quandt 2001, 207–8). The Americans in particular viewed Begin's public statements about the "Framework" agreement as blocking the possibility of Jordan joining the autonomy talks and of a Saudi approval of the agreement (Quandt 2001, 208). Yet, despite their disapproval of the Israeli interpretation of the settlement issues, neither the Americans nor the Egyptians were willing to allow this to derail the Egyptian-Israeli peace treaty. So both sides swallowed their pride and decided to take this issue up at the first round of autonomy negotiations (Quandt 2001, 209, 211, 230–34).

Begin's conception of Palestinian autonomy was minimalist. In early May 1979, he spelled out his conception in a document he submitted to the Israeli government. He suggested that the Israeli residents of the West Bank and Gaza and issues of land and water be left under the jurisdiction of the Israeli military government. The Palestinians would be granted autonomy only over people, and their institutions would deal with education, culture, and limited economic matters. Israel would maintain principal responsibility for security, foreign policy, and management of key resources in the West Bank and Gaza. Most important, Begin maintained that at the end of the interim autonomy period (five years after the conclusion of the negotiations) Israel would claim its right to sovereignty over the West Bank (Dayan, 1981, 304; Weizman 1981, 383–84; Quandt 2001, 237–38).

Taking advantage of the Iranian crisis and of the fact that 1980 was an election year in the United States, Begin sought to put the autonomy talks on the back burner. He had some unexpected allies. King Hussein and the Palestinians refused to participate in the autonomy talks. This rendered the Egyptian and American position relatively weak. Moreover, President Carter, preoccupied with other matters and also profoundly exhausted by the Egyptian-Israeli peace process, delegated the handling of the autonomy talks to secondary players (Robert Strauss and Sol Linowitz; see Quandt 2001, 238–39). To add insult to injury, Begin appointed Interior Minister Joseph Burg of the National Religious Party (NRP) to head the Israeli negotiation team. Not only was this a slap in Moshe Dayan's face; it was a clear indication that Begin had no intention of having the autonomy talks lead anywhere. And, to accentuate his refusal to freeze the settlements, Begin allowed Minister of Agriculture Ariel Sharon to establish a series of settlements in the West Bank. In the process, he managed to alienate his two senior ministers, Moshe Dayan and Ezer Weizman. Both resigned in protest of Begin's new hard-line policy. Weizman describes this shift in Begin's approach:

> Alarmed by the peace treaty they had just concluded, Begin and his supporters had eroded their achievement by provocative settlement programs and unnecessary land confiscations, trumpeting verbal challenges to the world as they withdrew into their mental ghetto. . . . [No] sooner had the treaty been signed than Begin gave up promoting the peace process. Instead of forging ahead, leading Israel to a new era, he withdrew into his pipe dreams. At the same time he began to treat this peace we had struggled for as something banal, almost despicable. (Weizman 1981, 384)

Dayan's recounting of this process is more understated than Weizman, but his conclusion was the same (Dayan 1981, 313): Begin intended to convert the autonomy negotiations into a dead letter. He had offered a plan for Palestinian autonomy but was subverting it in word and deed. While Dayan and Weizman thought that this would endanger the Egyptian-Israeli peace treaty, this was not the case. The terms of the treaty required that Israel complete its withdrawal from the Sinai within three years. This implied that the last Israeli troops would leave the Sinai by the end of March 1982. The Egyptians had to clench their teeth and continue the process so Israel would complete its withdrawal from the Sinai. The negotiations dragged through the middle of 1981 but accomplished nothing.

Sadat, however, continued to make efforts to move negotiations forward. He met with Begin several days before the Israeli attack on the Iraqi nuclear reactor and again in August 1981. These meetings took place in the face of repeated Israeli insults to Egypt. Sadat viewed the Israeli attack on the Iraqi nuclear reactor as a slap in the face (Shlaim 2000, 388). The new Israeli government that Begin introduced to the Knesset in August 1981 had in its plan statements about the "inalienable right of the Jewish people to the entire land of Israel." Nevertheless, Sadat met Begin again on August 26 in Alexandria and restated his commitment to peace. After Sadat's assassination on October 6, 1981, the autonomy talks indeed became a dead letter.

There are three possible explanations of Israeli behavior regarding Palestinian autonomy. The first is that Israel—especially Begin—had a different interpretation of the "Framework" agreement from that of the Americans and the Egyptians. Begin simply insisted on the implementation of his own version of what had been agreed on at Camp David. The

Egyptians and the Americans were unable to deliver the Jordanians and the Palestinians to the autonomy talks, and in the absence of partners to the autonomy, Israel was not obliged to make any concessions. The domestic and international circumstances—the Iran hostage crisis, the American presidential elections, and the refusal of Jordan and the Palestinians to participate—rendered the firm Israeli stand more sustainable. But Begin did not violate the Israeli commitments to the Camp David Accords. The best evidence for this argument is that Israel implemented to the last letter its obligations under the Egyptian-Israeli peace treaty, as painful as these actions were to Israel.

In addition, even if Begin wanted to be more flexible in the talks, he realized that he had reached the end of his domestic political rope. Only a minority of his own party members had supported the Camp David Accords. The signature of the Egypt-Israeli peace treaty led to a breakup of a group of Likud members and the formation of the extremist Revival Party. Some of Begin's coalition partners were also very unhappy with the agreement, in particular with the "Framework" aspect. Moreover, during the period of 1979–81, the economic crisis in Israel was exacerbated. Inflation rose to new heights, and the support for the Begin government was eroding rapidly. Flexibility under these circumstances appeared to be extremely costly in terms of domestic politics.

The second interpretation is that Begin himself had reached the end of the concessions he was willing to make for peace with Egypt. Weizman's and Dayan's perception of Begin's hardening was not that of people from the opposition. Rather, both were close confidants, who had walked with him a long way during the peace process with Egypt. What both men saw was that Begin was a changed person after Camp David. The six-month road from the Camp David Accords to the actual peace treaty was fraught with tensions within the Israeli government. Both Weizman (1981, 332) and Dayan (1981, 303) mention their deteriorating relations with their colleagues in the government, as well as with Begin himself. Benziman (1981, 168–228) argues that even at Camp David Begin was pressured into concessions he would not have willingly made by a group of advisers who surrounded him—or, rather, put him under siege. Coming out of Camp David, Begin realized how much he had deviated from his own vision of the concessions that could be made for peace. But once he had signed an agreement, he could not afford to back out. But he could prevent further concessions on the issues that were closest to his heart. Thus, even if that would force a head-on collision with the president of the United States, he would not budge on settlements and on the Israeli claim to the West Bank following the interim autonomy period.

Begin was also adamant in his refusal to allow the Palestinians any control over resources that would prevent Israel from asserting its sovereignty in the West Bank when the time came. His aggressive settlement policy was used not only to demonstrate his resolve to the Americans and the Egyptians but also to purge his government from the two key players who had pushed him into the Camp David agreement.

The third, and possibly most plausible, interpretation of the Israeli autonomy is embedded in the notion of a "scam." This interpretation asserts that Begin's strategy was to get Egypt out of the conflict in order to assert Israeli control over the West Bank and Gaza Strip. The "Framework" agreement was necessary in order to buy Egypt into a separate peace with Israel. To accomplish that goal, Begin was willing to make substantial concessions in the Israeli-Egyptian peace treaty, and he followed the implementation of this part of the agreement to the letter. However, he also understood that this part of the agreement rendered Egypt dependent upon Israel for at least three years. During those years Israel could consolidate its hold over the West Bank. And this could be accomplished if Israel gave nothing away in the autonomy talks with Egypt. From this perspective the plan worked. But the price would be paid later on.

The scam explanation is supported by Begin's behavior during the Egyptian-Israeli peace negotiations. First, Begin launched the autonomy campaign in December 1977 during his visit to Washington to counter Sadat's demand for an independent Palestinian state in the West Bank and Gaza. Throughout this process, Begin's presentation of his ideas of an autonomy were consistent. Begin never agreed to provide the Palestinians control over any meaningful resources such as water or land.

Second, throughout the negotiations, Begin tried to keep the notion of autonomy deliberately vague. He was aware that, once his more specific conception of autonomy was revealed, it would probably kill the Egyptian-Israeli deal. Even his close advisers—such as Dayan and Weizman—were deceived by what he had in mind. During the Camp David negotiations, Begin refused to budge on virtually anything that concerned the "Framework" agreement. He insisted on Israel's right after the five-year interim period of Palestinian self-rule to claim its sovereignty over Judea and Samaria; and he insisted (in his two letters to Carter of September 17 and 18, 1978) on limiting the freeze of settlement activity to the three-month period scheduled for the finalization of the Egyptian-

Israeli treaty. He stuck by this interpretation, despite the fact that Carter returned his letters to him twice (Quandt 2001, 202–3). Moreover, during the deliberations in the Israeli government on October 26, Begin in fact initiated a settlement-related corollary to the decision to approve the Camp David Accords. This decision called for "thickening" (or expanding) the existing settlements in the West Bank (Quandt 2001, 215).

Most important, however, the notion that Begin was "pushed" into the Camp David Accords by his advisers is simply inconsistent with both Begin's personality and the narrative of the Camp David negotiations. Begin consistently proved to be the most extreme member of his delegation, insisting on seemingly innocent terms such as "autonomy" as opposed to "self-rule," on the labeling of the West Bank as "Judea and Samaria" in the Hebrew text, and on the use of the phrase "undivided Jerusalem." Dayan (1981, 153–54) provides an interesting description of Begin's handling of the negotiations at Camp David:

> No one disputed Begin's right, as Prime Minister and head of our delegation, to be the final and authorized arbiter of Israel's position on all matters under review. But none of us was disposed to accept, as if they were the Sinai Tablets, those of his views which seemed to me extreme and unreasonable. [O]n those occasions when I disagreed with him and questioned his proposals, he got angry, and would dismiss any suggestion that did not appeal to him as likely to cause inestimable harm to Israel.

A similar view is offered by Weizman (1981, 371–72):

> Menachem Begin faced the dilemma of his lifetime. He was in growing disagreement with the leading members of his own delegation. He was under enormous pressure from the Americans. Equally urgent was his own desire to go down in history as the man who had brought peace to Israel. But all these constraints, which favored his making necessary concessions, were in conflict with the ingrained philosophy he had followed throughout his life.
>
> For many long and nerve-wrecking hours, it appeared that Begin's ideology would outweigh dictates of immediate reality. Israel's prime minister refused to make the concessions everyone demanded of him—particularly because Sadat refused to budge on issues such as his insistence that the final communiqué agree to the "nonacquisition of territory by force."

Most observers were impressed with the internal conflict of Menachem Begin. They were impressed by the fact that he did eventually give in on such matters as the Rafah settlements, despite his ideology. Yet, they missed the fact that in the Camp David Accords Begin managed to accomplish an important feat in terms of his strategy: to have the Egyptian-Israeli peace treaty precede the negotiations on Palestinian autonomy. This sequence allowed three important achievements in terms of Begin's scam. First, it secured a separate peace before the size of the gap between Egypt and Israel was revealed. Second, because of this separate peace, it reduced the likelihood of Jordanian and Palestinian participation in the autonomy talks, a key weapon in Begin's negotiating strategy. Third, it created an Egyptian dependence on a prolonged process of Israeli withdrawal that ensured Egyptian willingness to swallow quite a few frogs handed them by the Israelis during the autonomy talks, such as accelerated settlement activity in the West Bank.

The scam seemed to have worked, as far as Begin was concerned. The Egyptian-Israeli peace treaty withstood both Israeli intransigence in the autonomy talks and more severe blows, such as the Osirak attack of July 1981 and the Lebanon War of June 1982. The long-term outcome, however, was far less adaptive in terms of Begin's scheme. And the costs down the road to Israel were excessively high.

2.11. *The Hussein-Peres Agreement of 1987*

The elections of 1984 created a de facto draw between the two largest political parties in Israel. Labor had more seats than Likud, but the balance of blocs was equal. Shimon Peres, the leader of the Labor Party, and Yitzhak Shamir, Begin's successor as the leader of the Likud Party, had no alternative but to form a national unity government. It was agreed that the premiership would rotate between the two. Peres would serve as prime minister for the first two years and Shamir for the last two.

Peres faced a number of major challenges. First and foremost, he wanted to get Israel out of Lebanon. Second, the economy was in shambles, with inflation rates running as high as 500 percent annually. Third, he wanted to move forward Arab-Israeli relations that had suffered severe setbacks since the Egyptian-Israeli agreement. Peres's view was that the most promising avenue of Arab-Israeli diplomacy was a renewed dialogue with Jordan on the West Bank. His first year in office was devoted mostly to the two first challenges.

During this year, however, Peres's director general, General (Res.) Abraham Tamir, put together a team of experts representing both the security community and the academic community that engaged in a broad review of the basic processes in the Middle East. Tamir's memo that summarized this process recommended an aggressive peace diplomacy aimed at an Israeli-Jordanian agreement (Shlaim 2000, 432). On July 19, 1985, Peres met with King Hussein for the first time since 1977. The two leaders continued to meet on a regular basis over the next two years. In these meetings, Peres and Hussein, along with Yitzhak Rabin on the Israeli side and Prime Minister Zaid al-Rifa'i on the Jordanian side, entered into a series of negotiations designed to prepare a framework for formal and open negotiations between Israel and a Jordanian-Palestinian delegation on the future of the West Bank.

The negotiations were not about an agreement between the two states but about the process and structure of formal negotiations to be taken in the future. In effect these negotiations were what bargaining theorists call "prenegotiation" (Stein 1989). The United States was brought into the picture, and Richard Murphy, assistant secretary of state for Near Eastern and south Asian affairs, offered a number of formulas that helped resolve differences between Israel and Jordan.

There were two issues that formed the center of discussion during the first year of deliberations. The first was the structure of the international conference, and the second was the question of PLO participation in the joint Jordanian-Palestinian delegation. Hussein was bound by the 1982 resolution of the Arab summit at Fez that any future negotiations with Israel must be conducted through an international conference. Yet, at the same time he did not want the conference to constrain Jordan's freedom of maneuver. Peres, like most Israeli politicians, had been reluctant to negotiate within a conference framework because this kind of setting was seen as an "all against one" forum that would press Israel into inordinate concessions. Any Israeli refusal would brand Israel as the spoiler.

The solution to this problem was relatively simple. Murphy proposed a formula that entailed a ceremonial international conference. After its conclusion, negotiations would be conducted in bilateral settings. The Jordanian-Palestinian delegation would conduct separate negotiations with Israel.

The other issue was more difficult to resolve, however. Here, Hussein was bound by the 1974 Rabat resolution that designated the PLO as the sole representative of the Palestinians. More important, on February 11, 1985, Hussein and Arafat reached an agreement on a Jordanian-Palestinian confederation and on a joint Jordanian-PLO delegation to negotiate with Israel. Accordingly, Hussein wanted the Palestinian part of the Jordanian-Palestinian delegation to be composed of PLO members (Zak 1996, 199–200). Peres strongly objected to this requirement, not so much because he was opposed to this but because he knew that allowing PLO representatives in this delegation would result in the breakup of the national unity government in Israel. Moreover, President Reagan was strongly opposed to any PLO participation in the talks prior to its acceptance of Resolutions 242 and 338 and to abandoning terrorism, in accordance with the 1975 Kissinger pledge to Rabin (Quandt 2001, 265; Zak 1996, 264).

Fortunately for Peres, the Jordan-PLO agreement broke down within a year. The PLO refused to recognize Resolutions 242 and 338, and as long as that was the case, it was evident that no progress could be made vis-à-vis Israel and the United States with the PLO in the bargain. On February 19, 1986, Hussein announced the Jordanian-PLO agreement dead. Now, the major obstacle for an agreement was seemingly removed. However, while the pace of secret negotiations with Hussein was stepped up (Shlaim 2000, 437–38; Zak 1996, 264–66; Garfinkle 1992, 128–35), no agreement was reached in 1986. Thus, in accordance with the rotation plan, in October 1986, Peres was replaced by Shamir in the premiership. Peres became foreign minister, and Rabin stayed on as defense minister.

This delay in the agreement turned out to be critical. Peres and Hussein continued to negotiate, but now Shamir "was as indefatigable in suppressing diplomatic initiatives as Peres was in promoting them" (Shlaim 2000, 443). Shamir was thoroughly opposed to an international conference—ceremonial or otherwise—because any kind of negotiation would require Israel to make territorial concessions. He could rely upon the United States, which was also not too enthusiastic about this idea, because the Soviets would serve as cosponsors (Quandt 2001, 269–71).

In a last desperate effort to make some progress on the Jordanian track, Peres initiated another meeting with King Hussein in London, on April 11, 1987. The details of this meeting have been discussed by the Israeli participants (Peres 1995, 205–12; Ben Porat 1996, 89–94; Shlaim 2000, 443–45). The meeting produced a joint Israeli document, known as the London Agreement, that contained several principles.

1. A UN-sponsored international conference would take place, with all five permanent members of the Security Council and the participants of the Arab-Israeli conflict, to negotiate peace agreements between Israel and its neighbors and to "respond to the legitimate rights of the Palestinian people."
2. This conference would invite the parties to negotiate specific agreements in bilateral committees.

3. The international conference would not have any power to impose solutions on the parties. Agreements would be reached only through bilateral negotiations between Israel and its neighbors.

4. The Palestinian issue would be negotiated between an Israeli delegation and a joint Jordanian-Palestinian delegation.

5. Participation in this conference would be based on acceptance of UN Resolutions 242 and 338 and the renunciation of violence and terrorism.

6. The agreement would depend upon its approval by the governments of Israel and Jordan and would be presented as an American proposal (so as not to reduce the likelihood of its acceptance by other Arab states).[31]

In terms of Israel's national interests, this was a pathbreaking agreement for several reasons. First, it was the first bilateral agreement with Jordan and the first follow-up agreement after the Egyptian-Israeli peace treaty. Second, it effectively excluded the PLO from the negotiations as long as it continued to reject UN Resolutions 242 and 338 and did not renounce terrorism. Third, it revived the concept of a Jordanian solution to the Palestinian problem rather than an independent Palestinian state. Fourth, it presented a practically bilateral model for negotiations that was preferred by Israel. Fifth, Israeli-Jordanian negotiations would proceed even if other Arab states rejected this agreement. In other words, if the UN convened an international conference, it was assumed that Egypt would accept. But Egyptian-Israeli relations had already been resolved, so there was nothing to negotiate with Egypt. However, if Syria and the Palestinians rejected the conference, Israeli-Jordanian negotiations would still take place. Finally, Hussein indicated his commitment to economic and political involvement in West Bank matters, so that, even if the substantive negotiations dragged on for a long time, Jordanian economic and political activity in the West Bank (and possibly Gaza) would be stepped up and maintained throughout the process.

This is not how Shamir and his colleagues of the Likud Party saw the agreement, however. Shamir turned down an offer by U.S. secretary of state George Shultz to visit the region and advance the London Agreement in a series of meetings with regional leaders. He indicated his strong opposition to the agreement from the moment he received it.[32] Shamir felt that the only way to progress was through the renewal of the autonomy negotiations, which had been suspended in 1981. He also made it clear that he was prepared to dismantle the national unity government over this issue. On May 6, Peres presented the agreement at the cabinet meeting. In the ensuing debate it became evident that, if a vote were taken, there would be a tie between the Labor supporters of the agreement and the Likud opponents. In this case, the Likud would prevail.

Peres faced a major dilemma. He could break up the national unity government. But if he resigned, he ran the risk that the London Agreement would be leaked out, even if he presented his resignation as the result of the Likud's refusal to agree to the so-called Shultz initiative. This would violate his promise to Hussein to keep the circumstances leading to the Shultz proposal secret. This might result in Hussein backing out of the deal. Moreover, there was a significant chance that Shamir would be able to form a narrow coalition, thus ending up taking all the credit for the achievements of the first two years of the national unity government in economic affairs and for the withdrawal from Lebanon. Or he could stay and try to push for other avenues of negotiations from within. Reluctantly, Peres chose the latter option and stayed in the government.

Shamir was able to arrange a meeting with Hussein in London. The meeting took place on July 18, 1987. Shamir offered Hussein to continue with the autonomy talks, but Hussein turned this down. Following this meeting, Hussein concluded that, as long as Shamir was in power, there was no real chance of progress in the negotiation (Shlaim 2000, 448–49; Shultz 1993, 942–43). The London Agreement was dead in the water.

In order to understand how big an opportunity this agreement had been, it is important to consider what followed the subversion of this agreement by the Shamir gang. In December 1987 the intifada broke out, embroiling Israel in a wave of terrorism and violence that lasted for four years. On July 31, 1988, King Hussein announced that Jordan was severing all economic and administrative ties with the West Bank and that it was up to the Palestinians and their representatives to decide the future of the West Bank, either through direct negotiations with the Israelis or through whatever other means they deemed preferable. This put the tombstone over the grave of the Jordanian option.

In November 1988, the Palestinian National Council (PNC) accepted all UN resolutions on the Arab-Israeli conflict, starting with Resolution 181 of November 29, 1947, calling for the partition of Palestine, and continuing with Resolutions 242 and 338. The PNC also recognized Israel and called for a two-state solution to the Palestinian problem. The PNC also renounced terrorism as a means to achieve the two-state solution goal (Morris 2001, 605–6; Tessler 1994, 721–22; Shlaim 2000, 466). This paved the way for the opening of an American-Palestinian dialogue, the last political act of the Reagan administration before being replaced by George Bush (Quandt 2001, 282–85). From that point on, the PLO became the principal partner to negotiations on the Palestinian issue. To put a clincher on this issue, Shamir himself agreed—albeit reluctantly—to participate in the same international conference in 1991 that he had rejected back in 1987, after nearly four years of violence and bloodshed.

There is no question as to who killed the London Agreement. There is also little doubt as to the reasons for that. Shamir felt that any agreement on negotiations meant also an a priori Israeli agreement for territorial concessions in the West Bank. Moreover, if the Syrians accepted the UN offer to participate in the conference, this would oblige Israel to make territorial concessions on the Golan Height as well. Since he was opposed to any notion of territorial concessions (he had abstained in the vote on the Egyptian-Israeli treaty in 1978 and 1979), anything that remotely smelled of this word was immediately dismissed. Of course, Shamir did not anticipate the intifada, but even if he did he would not have agreed to proceed on the basis of the London Agreement. The structure of the national unity government in Israel and the fact that none of the Likud ministers was willing to break rank with his party on this matter prevented this agreement from being implemented.

Peres made a strategic political mistake by not resigning and bringing down the national unity government. Even if Shamir succeeded in forming a narrow coalition, Peres could have attacked this government on its antipeace policy. He could have blamed the Likud for the outbreak of the intifada, and—in retrospect—the chances of Labor winning the 1988 elections would have been higher than actually was the case. Peres decided to break up the national unity coalition in 1990 over a minor issue, and he did not benefit from it personally. In 1992 he was defeated by Rabin in the Labor primaries. Rabin ended up reaping many of the fruits of Peres's political prudence, not the least of which was the Israeli-Jordanian peace treaty of 1994.

2.12. The Politics of the Madrid Conference, 1991

The elections of October 1988 produced again a near tie between the two large parties. The Likud Party had a slight advantage and could have formed a narrow coalition with the right-wing parties, but Shamir preferred to renew the national unity government. This time, however, no rotation was offered. Shamir was to stay at the prime minister's post for the duration of this government. While Peres continued to serve as foreign minister and Rabin continued as defense minister, Shamir took de facto leadership over foreign affairs and over peace policy. This implied stagnation.

In January 1989, a new administration came into office in Washington. James Baker, the new secretary of state under President George Bush, spent considerable time trying to work out some formula for negotiations, but the Likud coalition blocked every effort that would allow the PLO even some symbolic or indirect representation in the talks. Negotiations with Syria were not even on the Israeli agenda.

By May 1990, the national unity government collapsed, and the Likud Party formed a narrow coalition that relied on extreme right-wing support. The prospects of peace seemed bleak. The intifada was raging, and relief was nowhere in sight. But neither were there serious prospects for escalation on the Golan or in Lebanon. Shamir's government could not be more pleased with the strategic status quo along its boundaries.

But the threats to regional stability emerged from elsewhere in the Middle East. On August 1, 1990, Iraqi forces invaded Kuwait and within two days occupied the tiny oil-rich state. The United States—fearing a follow-up Iraqi attack on Saudi Arabia—placed its rapid deployment forces in the Saudi kingdom and demanded an unconditional Iraqi withdrawal from Kuwait. The ensuing five-month crisis involved attempts both to resolve the crisis diplomatically and to build a large international coalition that would force the Iraqis out of Kuwait. This coalition was led by the United States and involved several European states, as well as Arab countries such as Saudi Arabia, Egypt, and Syria. Most of these states committed troops to the emerging war effort.

The Gulf War broke out on January 19, 1991, and lasted forty-four days. It resulted in an unequivocal victory of the coalition. Iraq was driven out of Kuwait, and strict measures of surrender were imposed upon it, including a requirement to disarm its WMDs. The Iraqi threat to Israel and to others in the region was removed. The U.S. presence in the region was enhanced.

But the key result of the Gulf War from an Arab-Israeli point of view was the new U.S. initiative to convene a Middle East peace conference in order to open the gates for direct Arab-Israeli peace talks. The initiative was a direct consequence of the Bush administration's wish to capitalize on global and regional transformations and on the results of the Gulf War to start an ambitious process of conflict resolution in the Arab-Israeli context.

The starting point of this initiative was an assumption by Bush and

Baker that the previous efforts of U.S. mediators to launch a limited set of Israeli-Palestinian talks had exhausted themselves. In addition, two key players in these mediation efforts—Jordan and the PLO—were out of grace with the United States due to their support of Iraq during the war. Yet the new opportunities that had arisen after the war allowed for a bold expansion of the circle of Middle East participants in the process. The expectations of success were low, as Baker pointed out in a memo to the president: "I don't have high expectations [regarding the possibility of convening a regional peace conference], but there are some new realities that make progress possible and we owe it to ourselves and everyone else to make the effort" (Baker, with Defrank, 1995, 443). Israel and Syria were seen as key participants and the hardest nuts that needed to be cracked. But the Jordanian-Palestinian delegation was also a significant obstacle. The issue there, as ever, was the identity of the Palestinian participants and their ties to the PLO.

Initially, both Israel and Syria turned a cold shoulder to Baker's idea of an international conference. Israel objected to just about anything in the proposed framework. It opposed UN sponsorship, Soviet participation and cochairmanship, the basic formula for the conference, the proposed Palestinian representation, the location of the conference, and various procedural issues that were strictly technical.[33] The idea of direct talks with the Syrians was appealing, but the catch was that territorial issues would soon emerge. Shamir was unwilling to allow that to happen. Of particular concern to Shamir was the notion that an international conference would pit all Arab states, the Palestinians, the United States, and the Soviet Union against Israel. Israel would find itself completely isolated. This was the same paranoia that moved Shamir's opposition to the London Agreement. Shamir used to say, "The sea is the same sea, and the Arabs are the same Arabs." And Shamir was the same Shamir.

The dilemma in 1991 was different from the dilemma of 1987. In 1987 the United States was not enamored with the notion of an international conference. In 1991 the idea of an international conference emanated from the United States. Israel's problem this time was that it could not afford to reject a U.S. initiative to launch a peace conference and thereby be depicted as rejectionist and inflexible. Such a rejection would endanger Israeli-American relations, at a time when Israel was trying to reap the fruits of its policy of restraint during the war, including the U.S. loan guarantees and the absorption of a huge wave of immigration of Jews from the Soviet Union. Baker was aware of this dilemma and tried to exploit it in his discussions with Shamir: "'What I am asking you to do is give me enough procedural flexibility to make this work. . . . If this doesn't work, at least put us in a position where together we can leave this dead cat on the Arab doorstep'. . . . From the beginning, it was the leverage I had" (Baker, with Defrank, 1995, 450).

Baker became increasingly frustrated and agitated by Israeli procedural haggling. Yet the idea of putting the blame for failure to convene the conference at Asad's doorstep sounded increasingly attractive to Shamir. Gradually, the Israeli reservations diminished to a point where the Israelis felt they could agree to the principle of a ceremonial conference, gambling that the other side—particularly Asad—would refuse to attend such a conference.

Baker adopted a similar approach with Asad. Asad's initial position was that an international conference should (1) be under joint U.S.-USSR-UN sponsorship, (2) be continuous, and (3) have guaranteed results. The latter of the three points was a typical Syrian approach, as we will soon see. Any one of these demands appeared initially sufficient to kill the idea. However, over a series of grueling meetings with Baker,[34] Asad gradually modified his demands as well. Here, too, Baker used the "dead cat at the Israeli doorstep" strategy as a major bargaining chip. In addition, the major argument was that this was the only way to induce the Israelis into a possible withdrawal from the Golan Height (Baker, with Defrank, 1995, 456–57).

Either due to the parties' reassessment of their own interests or—more likely—due to the fear of bearing responsibility for the failure of the conference and the expectation that the opponent's intransigence would be the cause of failure, both Israel and Syria gradually removed their reservations. Both were surprised when finally a formula was found to convene the conference in Madrid. On October 30, 1991, the Madrid Conference convened, under the joint chairmanship of the United States, with President Bush present, and the Soviet Union, with Secretary-General Gorbachev present. The participants in the conference included Egypt, Jordan, Israel, Lebanon, the Palestinians (as part of the Jordanian delegation), and Syria.

As noted, the form and structure of the Madrid Conference were virtually identical to the one Shamir had rejected four years and one intifada earlier. The differences between the conference envisioned in the London Agreement and the Madrid Conference were—in terms of Shamir's own value system—clearly in favor of the former. Once the bilateral negotiations started, it immediately became evident that—while the Palestinians in the joint Jordanian-Palestinian delegation were not officially affiliated with the PLO—they consulted with Arafat and the PLO on every move they made. The PLO, so to speak, was sitting in the room behind the negotiators and whispering in the Palestinian delegates' ears. Moreover, in 1987 Syria was almost certain to reject an international conference. In 1991 it was in, and pressing for an Israeli withdrawal from, the Golan Height.

Clearly, Shamir was dragged kicking and screaming to the Madrid Conference. He was aware of that and therefore sought to render the bilateral negotiations meaningless. His directive to the Israeli negotiators was to engage in meaningless rhetoric and to concede nothing (Shlaim 2000, 492; M. Maoz 1995, 217–18; Rabinovich 1998, 40–43). It is unclear what the long-term vision of this strategy was, and it is not clear that there was a clear Israeli strategy other than consistent stonewalling. But it was a typical Shamir approach. Fortunately, this approach was defeated in the May 1992 election. A new government came to power that turned Israeli peace policy around.

2.13. Israeli-Syrian Negotiations, 1992–2000

One of Rabin's first decisions upon assuming office was to change the negotiation strategy vis-à-vis Syria. This change assumed two forms. First, Rabin shuffled the Israeli delegation to the Washington talks with Syria, replacing the hard-line head of the delegation, Yossi Ben-Aharon, with the more moderate Middle East history professor Itamar Rabinovich, who was also appointed ambassador to the United States. Second, and more important, Rabin adopted a new formula on the territorial issue. During the first meeting of the new Israeli delegation with the Syrians on August 24, 1992, Rabinovich declared, "Israel accepts the UN Resolution 242 on all of its aspects and sees it as applying to the Golan Height." The obvious interpretation of this was that Israel accepts the "land for peace" principle to apply to the Golan Height (Rabinovich 1998, 81).

This change seems to have improved the tone and substance of negotiations significantly. The initial Syrian reaction was to extract more specific information from the Israelis regarding the implications of this statement, but ultimately the Syrian delegation presented for the first time a draft declaration of principles. This draft posed some major difficulties for the Israelis because it suggested that this negotiation process would be protracted and difficult (Rabinovich 1988, 87). However, the atmosphere of the negotiations changed markedly. Both parties were engaged in the process in a sincere effort to move it forward (Mu'alem 1997).

Israel's key dilemmas were domestic. The Rabin government faced a powerful right-wing opposition that continuously criticized the government. Perceived deterioration in the personal safety of Israeli citizens due to repeated terrorist attacks, as well as an increase in the casualty rate in southern Lebanon, drew sharp criticism. More important, the coalitional basis of the government was shaky. There was considerable conflict between the two extreme elements in the coalition: the left-wing Meretz Party and the ultra-orthodox religious party Shas, the voters of which were considerably more hard-line than its leadership.

Rabin believed that he would not be able to proceed simultaneously on all fronts because movement implied Israeli concessions, and excessive concessions were a hard sell under any circumstances, let alone by a left-wing government. Rabin had to select which track would receive priority. His own inclination was to try the Syrian track. Rabin was concerned about the adverse implications of a stalemate on the Israeli-Syrian front for Israel's strategic situation. In particular, he was aware that Syria had been amassing high numbers of SSMs. It also had an accelerated chemical weapons program, with the SSMs capable of carrying chemical warheads. This implied that Syria posed the most serious challenge to Israel's security. If this threat could be defused through a peace treaty, he would markedly improve Israel's basic security (Inbar 1999, 144–45).

As the negotiations in Washington progressed during 1993, Rabin became increasingly convinced that no major breakthrough could be achieved unless Israel provided Syria with some indication that a deal on the entire Golan Height was possible. However, he wanted to make sure that—if Israel were to make a commitment to withdraw from the Golan Height—its major security concerns and its demands for full peace would be met by Asad. Thus, on August 3, 1993, in a meeting with Warren Christopher, the new U.S. secretary of state, and Dennis Ross, the senior adviser for Middle East policy, Rabin made a major policy departure. He instructed the two American diplomats to inquire with Asad whether Syria would be willing to accept Israel's security and peace requirements if Israel were to commit itself to *full* withdrawal from the Golan Height (Rabinovich 1998, 104–6; Ross 2004, 111).

Asad's response was typically cautious. He responded favorably to Rabin's unilateral gesture. He was also willing to respond positively to some of the conditions mentioned by Rabin. But on the major questions Rabin posed, the responses were either vague or negative. These included questions on the pace of withdrawal, on the Syrian willingness to offer aspects of peace during early stages of the Israeli withdrawal, and on security issues (Rabinovich 1998, 141–42; Ross 2004, 111–14). More important, Asad posed a key question of clarification to Rabin: What did Israel mean by "full withdrawal"? Did it mean a willingness to withdraw to the international boundary, or did it mean a readiness to withdraw to the June 4, 1967, border? Clearly, Israel's response to this question would have a major impact on Syria's willingness to make concessions on other issues.

Rabin was deeply disappointed by Asad's reply. He felt that he had handed Asad a major instrument for a real breakthrough in the negotiations and in return got the same old qualified response. Rabin was also disappointed with the American negotiators. He felt that they had not been sufficiently assertive and active at a crucial point in the negotiations (Baker Institute 1998). The major conclusion derived by Rabin from this exchange was that the Israeli-Syrian track was not going to move forward considerably. Hence he gave a green light to the Israeli negotiators in Oslo to conclude a deal with the PLO. On September 13, 1993, the Oslo Accords were signed on the White House lawn.

From August 1993 to November 1995, Israeli-Syrian negotiations dragged on slowly, seemingly making little progress. In practice, the parties were making substantial headway toward an agreement (Sagie 1998, 220–33; Ross 2004, 145–63). Several road marks are worth noting along this rocky road. First, on July 19, 1994, Rabin finally responded to Asad's query regarding the operational definition of the "full withdrawal" concept. He instructed Warren Christopher to convey to Asad that his (Christopher's) impression was that Rabin meant withdrawal to the June 4, 1967, lines (Rabinovich 1998, 189–90; Ross 2004, 147–48).

Second, the discussions of security arrangements were stepped up considerably. On December 1994 the Israeli COS, Ehud Barak, and the Syrian COS, Hikmat Shihabi, met in Washington to discuss these security arrangements. While there were still major disagreements on various issues on the security aspects of the agreement, considerable progress was made. In particular, the Syrians modified their requirement for *reciprocal and equal* security arrangements to *reciprocal* security arrangements.[35]

Third, the U.S. negotiators drafted a nonpaper entitled "Aims and Principles of Israeli-Syrian Security Arrangements" (Ben 1997; Ross 2004, 153–61). This document was circulated to the parties and served as a working draft but did not have any official status. At any rate, the mere drafting of this nonpaper suggested that some principles seemed to have been agreed upon between the principals.

A second meeting of the COSs of both states took place in July 1995;

this time the Israeli COS was Amnon Lipkin-Shahak. During this meeting, reportedly, major issues were resolved, though the gaps were still considerable. Other issues at stake, including problems of water sharing, were discussed seriously with considerable progress (Sagie 1998, 272; Ross 2004, 159–61).

Rabin's assassination on November 4, 1995, brought Shimon Peres—the former foreign minister—to the prime minister's office. Rabin may not have fully briefed Peres of the Israeli concessions during the negotiations (Rabinovich 1998, 19–21; Azoulay-Katz 1996, 17–27). Nonetheless, Peres was willing to reaffirm Rabin's conditional pledges on the withdrawal issue (Ross 2004, 212–13). However, Peres's agenda in the negotiations was different. Whereas Rabin placed prime emphasis on security issues, Peres's emphasis was on economic cooperation (Savir 1998, 307–9). Peres also wanted the Israeli-Syrian process to open the gates to a full normalization of Israeli-Arab relations. This change of approach required a change of personnel. Peres replaced Rabinovich with Uri Savir, the director general of the prime minister's office, although Rabinovich remained a member of the Israeli delegation.

The Syrian delegation, while responding favorably to some aspects of the new Israeli approach to peace, was hesitant to move along this dimension. One aspect in particular stood in the background. Rabin had publicly pledged to hold a referendum if and when Israel and Syria reached an agreement. This posed a considerable risk for Asad because of the possibility that the Israeli public would reject a deal wherein Syria made major public concessions. As a result, Asad repeatedly turned down Israeli requests for face-to-face meetings between the heads of state.[36]

The Israeli-Syrian meetings that took place at the Wye Plantation in Maryland during the first months of 1996 came to a halt as a result of the Israeli prime minister's decision to call for early elections. More important, the escalation along the Israeli-Lebanese border during March–April 1996 culminated in Israel's Operation Grapes of Wrath (see chap. 7). The Israeli elections of May 29 1996, brought a major change of government. Peres was replaced by hard-liner Benjamin Netanyahu from the Likud Party. The Netanyahu coalition included a number of defectors from the Labor Party who were strongly opposed to Rabin's conciliatory policy on the Golan issue. Netanyahu, while publicly committed to negotiations with Syria, changed Israeli policy considerably. In contrast to the Israeli-Palestinian track, where the new government was bound by prior formal agreements, in the Israeli-Syrian case, no binding document existed. Thus, the Israeli position was that negotiations should be resumed without any preconditions. Each side could lay on the table its demands. And the Israeli demand would be full peace but no withdrawal (Netanyahu 2000).

The Syrians demanded that the new Israeli government reaffirm the Rabin and Peres pledge of full withdrawal in the context of a peace treaty. From the Syrian perspective, this pledge had been the official Israeli position and the new government was bound by it (Mu'alem 1997). From the Israeli perspective, this pledge had been conditional on Syrian acceptance of Israeli demands on security and normalization.

During Netanyahu's reign, no public negotiations were conducted between Israel and Syria. Yet, Netanyahu did engage in secret diplomacy, which deviated considerably from his public stand. Using the services of a close American friend, the multimillionaire Ron Lauder, who shuttled between Damascus and Jerusalem, Netanyahu let Asad know that he would be willing to consider substantial territorial concessions in exchange for peace with Syria. However, when Asad demanded that specific details of the proposed extent of Israeli withdrawal be shown on a map, Netanyahu backed out of the negotiations (Ross 2004, 511–12). It was Ariel Sharon's veto that brought the contacts between Netanyahu and Asad to a premature end (Edelist 2003, 127–29; Schiff 1999; Ben 2000a, 2000b).

Ehud Barak's victory in the 1999 elections gave his policy a special sense of public legitimacy. This, at least, was his personal perception. In practice, however, he was dependent on a coalition government composed of ideologically diverse parties. Barak also faced a priority dilemma similar to that of Rabin in 1992–93. Like Rabin, he chose to go with the Syrian track first, largely at the expense of the Palestinians. This made sense to him not only in terms of what he thought was the more tractable process but also given his preelection pledge to get Israel out of Lebanon within a year. Accordingly, he started sending unofficial feelers, exploring a renewal of formal negotiations from the point where the secret negotiations between Asad and Netanyahu had been left off. His intention was to reach a quick settlement with Syria based on the Rabin "deposit" or "pocket." Barak confided in President Clinton and informed him of his wish to start out with the Syrian option (Drucker 2002, 65; Edelist 2003, 134–39).

Asad responded well to the change in Israeli policy. Uri Sagie, the new head of the Israeli negotiation team with Syria, met with the legal counsel of the Syrian Foreign Ministry in Geneva. President Clinton began communicating directly with Asad over the phone. Asad wanted assurances of an Israeli commitment to full withdrawal from the Golan Height before resuming the formal negotiations, but Barak was not willing to do so for domestic reasons. He did, however, allow leaking the details of the secret Netanyahu-Asad negotiations to the press (Schiff 1999; Ben 2000a). After considerable persuasion by Clinton, Asad agreed to resume formal negotiations without getting a commitment from Israel to full withdrawal from the Golan (Drucker 2002, 69). Most surprising, Asad decided to send to the meeting in Shepherdstown, Maryland, none other than his foreign minister, Farouk a-Shar'a. On the Israeli side, Barak himself decided to head the Israeli delegation.

Prior to his departure to the meeting with a-Shar'a, Barak ran secret public opinion polls to test the extent to which the Israeli public would be willing to support an agreement entailing complete Israeli withdrawal from the Golan Height. The results suggested that there was no majority support for such an agreement. Barak was aware that this posed a major problem: both Rabin and he had pledged that any agreement that entailed Israeli withdrawal from the Golan Height would be brought to a national referendum. By the time Barak arrived in Shepherdstown he had already decided that he was not going to take the plunge to an agreement (Drucker 2002, 84–85).

The Shepherdstown talks produced significant progress in terms of Syrian movement toward Israeli demands. The Syrians agreed to the principle of DMZs on the Golan Height and to areas of reduced force concentrations beyond the Golan (based on similar areas in the Galilee—the Israeli area bordering the Golan Height). They also accepted the Israeli formula of "full peace," which included the exchange of diplomatic missions and open borders. Finally, the Syrians also agreed to the continued operation of the early warning station on Mount Hermon by foreign crews and under Syrian control. What the Syrians wanted in return was a public statement by Barak to the effect that Israel would be willing to withdraw to the June 4, 1967, lines. Barak refused to make this statement. His persistent message that he would honor Rabin's "pledge" or "deposit" did not satisfy the Syrian foreign minister (Drucker 2002, 91–92; Edelist 2003, 214–32; Ross 2004, 549–68).

Most disturbing, from a Syrian perspective, was the fact that the American document that served as the basis for the negotiations (the single negotiating text, or SNT) and that entailed many of the Syrian concessions was leaked to the Israeli press and was published in the Israeli daily Ha'aretz. The Syrians, both in response to the leak and due to their frustration with the results of the Shepherdstown summit, decided to suspend further negotiations.

President Clinton made a last effort to bring about an agreement. On March 27, 2000, he met with Hafez Asad in Geneva. He had obtained Barak's permission to offer Asad a full Israeli withdrawal from the Golan Height, except for an area of about fifty meters wide and two kilometers long on the northeast shore of Lake Kinneret. This was designed to ensure Israel complete control of the lake. Asad flatly rejected this proposal. He would not discuss any other element of Israeli-Syrian peace before he had an Israeli commitment to full and complete withdrawal to the June 4, 1967, borders (*Mideast Mirror* 2000; Ross 2004, 583–87). The failure of the Clinton-Asad summit came as a blow to Israel, but there was hope that this was just a temporary setback and that the Syrians would return to the negotiation table shortly. This was not to be. Hafez Asad died on June 10. His son, Bashar, who replaced him, spent the first few months in office establishing his control over the embattled Syrian state. In September 2000, the Al Aqsa Intifada erupted. The peace process with Syria was dead in the water.

Martin Indyk, the American ambassador to Israel at the time and also a scholar of Middle East politics, had been a key player in Israeli-Syrian negotiations. In an interview to the Israeli daily *Yediot Aharonot*, he observed: "in April 2000, when Barak was ready [to concede the June 4 boundaries], Asad did not have enough time. He had to perform the last act of his life and he chose to ensure his succession by his son in Syria. This [peace dialogue between Barak and Asad] was like two ships passing each other at night. Had Barak signed [the June 4 pledge] when it had been possible, the Middle East would have been different."[37]

There is no question that the Syrians were extremely inflexible in the negotiations. But the Israeli negotiation tactic of inching back to the June 4, 1967, boundaries was probably the principal reason for the failure of the negotiations. Rabin had already made this pledge in 1994, and the Syrians regarded it as an irrevocable Israeli commitment. This is not how subsequent Israeli leaders thought. Each time a new leader came to power in Israel—and the Syrians negotiated with three different Israeli prime ministers after Rabin—the Syrians confronted a new and more conservative Israeli position on the Golan. This appeared as a zigzag policy to Asad, who had little confidence in the Israelis to begin with. The Israeli leaders' fear of a hostile public opinion, accompanied by intragovernmental politics, prevented successive Israeli prime ministers from uttering the sacred words "full withdrawal." From a Syrian perspective, they had made all the concessions to the Israelis and had received nothing in return. It would be another three tension-filled years in Israeli-Syrian relations before another Syrian offer to negotiate would come, only to be met with a cold Israeli shoulder.

2.14. The Birth, Short Life, and Sudden Death of the Israeli-Palestinian Peace, 1993–2003

Many Israelis regarded the PLO as a terrorist organization of the worst kind. Yassir Arafat was depicted as the successor of the infamous Haj Amin al Husseini, the Jerusalem Mufti who led the Arab revolt against the British in 1936, who collaborated with the Nazis, and who led the Palestinian resistance to the 1947 UN partition resolution. Many Israeli leaders pledged never to talk to the PLO. In 1990, the Knesset passed a law prohibiting Israeli citizens from talking to PLO representatives. Arafat himself had been the target of several Israeli assassination attempts.

The Rabin government stepped up negotiations with the Jordanian-Palestinian delegation in Washington in late 1992. But the negotiations were extremely slow. The absence of PLO representatives in the negotiations was highly disruptive, as the Palestinian delegates had to consult with the PLO leadership in Tunis at every step. More important, the subjects of the talks were of little substantive interest to the PLO. The Palestinians were in the negotiations in order not to disrupt the Madrid process, but unless some dramatic change were to take place, these negotiations were not going anywhere. Arafat himself was weary of the Washington negotiations, worried that these would signal his own personal downfall and that of the PLO in general (Sayigh 1997, 655).

By 1992 a significant shift took place within the PLO perspective. Due to both a financial crisis and deteriorating political status within the occupied territories, the leadership of the PLO in Tunis was willing to reassess its all-or-nothing approach toward the issue of a Palestinian state. The notion of a process wherein the PLO assumed a greater degree of autonomy in the occupied territories and built an infrastructure for a future Palestinian state became increasingly appealing to Arafat, especially considering the alternatives (Sayigh 1997, 655–56; Kimmerling and Migdal 2003, 317–30).

Left-wing Israeli politicians had held secret meetings with PLO representatives since the late 1960s. This was considered by many Israelis as acts of treason, but none of these politicians was arrested and charged with anything illegal.[38] The Palestinian attitude to those encounters had been less tolerant, however. Two of the key Palestinian leaders who had met with the Israelis on a regular basis, Said al-Hamami and Isam al-Sartawi, were assassinated by the Abu Nidal faction (Sayigh 1997, 425, 558). Nevertheless, these meetings continued, and the Israelis even reported occasionally to the prime minister in power of the contents of these talks. Such meetings intensified in the early 1990s (Beilin 1997, 29–48).

Following the 1992 election, and through the mediation of Norwegian diplomats, a group of Israelis affiliated with the Labor Party started meeting with PLO representatives in Oslo. These meetings were orchestrated in Israel behind screen by Yossi Beilin, the deputy minister of foreign affairs. The Palestinian delegation was headed by Ahmad Queriya (Abu Ala), Arafat's financial adviser. These talks were conducted under a heavy veil of secrecy, due to the Israeli law prohibiting meetings with PLO representatives and due to the fact that Rabin was reluctant to allow for any process to proceed outside the formal Washington talks (Beilin 1997, 75–85; Sayigh 1997, 655–56).

In early February 1993, a tentative agreement was reached by the two delegations in Oslo. At that point, Beilin decided to inform his superiors of the secret Oslo track (Beilin 1997, 87–89). Rabin did not approve these talks but also did not veto them. He appeared skeptical about their practicality but allowed them to continue. By May 1993, the talks reached a critical stage. The parties had a tentative agreement, but this agreement would have been meaningless if it was not approved by the Israeli authorities. Rabin authorized the participation of Uri Savir, the director general of the Foreign Ministry (Beilin 1997, 100–102; Savir 1998, 5–9). As the talks progressed, the makeup of the Israeli delegation was upgraded. By August, the draft agreement was nearly ready. At about the same time, Rabin's disappointment with the Syrian track became a significant factor in the Israeli calculus (Rabinovich 1998, 106–7), and the Syrian response to Rabin's full withdrawal pledge convinced Rabin to give the green light to making the Oslo agreement official.

On September 13, 1993, Israel and the PLO signed the historic mutual recognition agreement, known as the Oslo Accords.[39] These accords included several elements. First, they included an exchange of letters between Israel and the PLO of mutual recognition. Second, the declaration of principles established the framework for the subsequent peace process between the Israelis and the Palestinians. Third, this framework was to extend over a five-year period, labeled as the interim self-government period. Three years into the interim process, the parties were to start negotiations on a permanent status agreement. Fourth, and most important, the logic of this agreement was cumulative and gradual. The two sides pledged to start a process leading to a full-fledged peace agreement. Implementation of this process would be gradual. The purpose was to create a system of mutual dependence and growing level of trust between Israel and the Palestinians.

This framework was based on several basic principles. First, it launched a gradual process of Palestinian autonomy, led by the PLO. The Palestinians were to assume full domestic autonomy over designated areas—starting with Gaza and Jericho. The PLO pledged to do everything in its power to curb terrorism, among other things through the establishment of security organs in the areas under its control. The Palestinians also pledged to develop political institutions for the management of the autonomous areas. These territories were to be managed by a so-called Palestinian Interim Self-Governing Authority.

Israel was to help the Palestinians, through economic and political measures. The Israelis were supposed to gradually withdraw from population centers in the West Bank and Gaza. The overall security for the occupied territories was left in Israel's hands. It was understood that neither side would take unilateral steps that altered the status of the territories and prejudiced the final status negotiations.

A key objective of this process from an Israeli point of view was to prepare Israeli public opinion to accept both a partner and a process that ran contrary to everything that it had been fed by previous governments (Shlaim 2000, 520–21; Morris 2001, 621). The hope was that implementation of this agreement would make the Israeli public willing to swallow the concept of a Palestinian state, because it would increase the level of personal security in Israel. The public indeed responded with reserved support for the Oslo agreement (Arian 2003, 24–25). A narrow majority of Israelis supported the agreement, but their support fluctuated considerably with time.

The need to change public opinion, as well as to change the established maxims of key politicians such as Rabin and other Labor Party hawks, rendered the Oslo process highly volatile. The key criterion for the success of the process was the reduction of Palestinian terrorism. This is how the Israeli politicians tried to sell the process to the public. From the Palestinian perspective, the key test of the Oslo process was threefold: reduction of Israeli presence in the occupied territories, freezing of settlement activity, and economic and political development in the territories freed of Israeli control.

However, this was not to be. Just as in Israel there were many vocal opponents to Israeli-Palestinian peace, there were quite a few Palestinian opponents to the process. Extremists on both sides tried their best to undermine the process. On the Palestinian side, the Islamic organizations of Hamas and the Islamic Jihad embarked on a campaign of suicide bombings designed, among other things, to bring about harsh Israeli response in the form of repeated closures and heightened military activity, thus turning Palestinian public opinion against the peace process. The new strategy adopted by these organizations to derail the peace process was a wave of suicide bombings that started in 1993 and continues to the very day. There were also a few incidents of Israeli terrorist actions against Palestinians, the most notable of which was the massacre of thirty-six Palestinians by a Jewish extremist on February 25, 1994, in Hebron.

Despite these incidents, which caused occasional disruptions in the negotiations, the peace process continued. On May 4, 1994, Rabin and Arafat signed in Cairo the implementation agreement of the Gaza and Jericho transfer. Arafat entered Gaza on July 1. The transfer of authority and the establishment of Palestinian autonomy in these cities continued slowly due—in large measure—to frequent disruptions caused by Israeli closures and other sanctions in response to terrorist attacks. The second phase of the Oslo process entailed the transfer of authority over all of the largely populated cities in the West Bank and the Gaza Strip. Negotiations on this aspect of the agreement lasted nearly a year. On September 29, 1995, the so-called Oslo II Accord was signed in Washington by Rabin and Arafat. This accord was approved in the Knesset by a narrow majority (sixty-one to fifty-nine).

The Oslo Accords had an important set of side effects. First and foremost, they opened the gates of much of the Arab world for ties with Israel. Tunisia and Morocco established formal diplomatic relations with Israel, and the Gulf states and Israel exchanged economic interests offices. Most important, the Oslo Accords finally removed the inhibitions that King Hussein had on open ties with Israel. Once Hussein had severed Jordan's ties with the West Bank, there was little at stake in this process and a considerable amount of mutual gain. After nearly a year of secret negotiations, Israel and Jordan signed a formal peace treaty on October 26, 1994. This accord formalized nearly three decades of secret ties between the two states and almost two and a half decades of de facto peaceful relations.

The Arab League lifted the boycott over Israeli goods. While Saudi Arabia, Libya, and Syria refused to trade with Israel, directly or indirectly, others started to develop limited economic ties with it. Considerable economic and political interaction between Israel and various Arab states took place within the Barcelona framework of the European Community that tried to establish a practical dialogue among the countries bordering the Mediterranean.

Throughout the entire period, Rabin's government had been under relentless political attacks by the right-wing parties (the so-called nationalist camp). Frequent demonstrations, constant heckling in his Knesset and other public speeches, and finally a series of threats on his life did not deter Rabin and Peres from continuing implementation of the process. In his speech to the Knesset prior to the vote on the Oslo II Accord, Rabin outlined his vision of the final status settlement with the Palestinians. This vision was very narrow, consisting of Israeli military presence along the Jordan Valley and the establishment of a Palestinian entity that was less than a state (Shlaim 2000, 528; Beilin 1997, 203–4). This sounded like an extremely disappointing vision from a Palestinian perspective, but it also suggested a strong commitment to persist in the Oslo process (Beilin 1997, 204).

The peace process received its most severe blow since its inception with the assassination of Yitzhak Rabin on November 4, 1995, by an Israeli ultra-nationalist. Shimon Peres succeeded Rabin and pledged to continue his legacy. However, Peres's first few months in office were marked by a wave of suicide bombings in Jerusalem and Tel Aviv that left sixty-four Israelis dead and hundreds wounded. These suicide bombings came in revenge for the Israeli killing of two leading Palestinian terrorists: Fathi Shikaki, the leader of the Islamic Jihad who was assassinated in Malta by Mossad people in September 1995, and Yihya Ayash, who was assassinated by SHABAK in February 1996. These suicide bombings eroded a substantial lead that Peres had in the polls. In the May 1996 elections, Peres was narrowly defeated by Netanyahu and the Likud Party.

Netanyahu, who was personally opposed to the Oslo Accords, nevertheless felt bound by the decisions of previous Israeli governments. Hence, despite a major clash with the Palestinians in September 1996, he went on to implement the redeployment of the IDF in Hebron, which was a leftover issue in the Oslo II Accords. Surprisingly, the Palestinian security forces—now with clear directives from Arafat—went on to clamp down on the Hamas and Islamic Jihad militants in the occupied territories. This brought about a significant reduction in the number of terrorist attacks in the 1997–2000 period. In 1998, under the auspices of President Clinton, Netanyahu and Arafat negotiated a limited agreement on a "third phase" of the interim agreement, which involved the transfer of about 13 percent of the sparsely populated territories of the West Bank to the Palestinians. Netanyahu, however, failed to implement this agreement, arguing that the Palestinians had not fulfilled their pledge to disarm and arrest Hamas activists.

The Oslo Accords were due to expire within five years of their signing. The talks on final status opened up ceremonially in May 1996. These were not resumed under Netanyahu's administration. The Palestinians threatened to issue a unilateral proclamation of the formation of an independent Palestinian state. Israel threatened that, if this happened, it would annex all the areas under its jurisdiction (areas B and C in the Oslo II map, which constituted about 65 percent of the West Bank). President Clinton, alarmed by the prospect, paid a visit to the region and addressed the Palestinian National Council meeting. He requested them to put off the unilateral declaration of state and pledged to work with Israel and the PLO to get the final status negotiations started (Ross 2004, 483–90).

The 1999 elections brought Ehud Barak to power, and the pendulum of moods was on the rise again. Barak met with Arafat and promised to carry out the third-stage withdrawal that had been agreed upon during the Wye Plantation talks in 1998. However, he used a terrorist attack to postpone delivery of the territories to the Palestinians. In his meeting with Arafat in Sharm a-Sheikh on September 4, 1999, Barak agreed to speed up the final status talks. Several tracks had been pursued. A formal track was established in which an Israeli delegation headed by Oded Eran, an experienced diplomat and a former Israeli ambassador to Jordan, met with a Palestinian delegation headed by Yassir Abed Rabo, Arafat's adviser. The Israelis started making concrete proposals to the Palestinians. The first Israeli offer to the Palestinians was to establish a Palestinian state over 55–60 percent of the West Bank. The Palestinians flatly rejected the offer (Sher 2003, 67–68). Negotiations on the official track continued slowly without any meaningful progress, largely due to Barak's decision to focus on the Syrian track first and slow down the final status negotiations.

A second track engaged the Israeli minister of internal security, Shlomo Ben-Ami (a former history professor at Tel Aviv University), and the minister of tourism, Amnon Lipkin-Shahak (a former COS of the IDF), with two key Palestinian figures, Ahmed Queriya (Abu Ala) and Mahmoud Abbas (Abu Mazen). This track involved general discussions on various aspects of the final status agreement, again without much progress (Sher 2003, 73). By that time, the Syrian track was at a dead end, following the Geneva summit. Barak decided to speed up the final status negotiations with the Palestinians. He appointed Gilead Sher, a close personal friend, together with Ben Ami to engage in secret negotiations in Jerusalem and Stockholm with Hassan Azfur and Abu Ala. The key aim of the secret track was to reach a framework peace agreement, much like the Camp David Accords of 1978, and to negotiate the detailed peace treaty later on. The meeting in Stockholm produced no progress. The Palestinians responded negatively to the Ben Ami-Sher offer of 76 percent of the territory in the West Bank and demanded to discuss the matters of refugees and Jerusalem, something that the Israelis were not ready to discuss at that point (Sher 2003, 90–91).

The negotiations were conducted under the threat of a unilateral Palestinian declaration of a Palestinian state in September 2000. The deliberate slowing down of the final status negotiations with the Palestinians in the second half of 1999 and the first quarter of 2000 turned out to be a major mistake. The Palestinian frustration with the pace of negotiations and the upcoming American presidential elections put considerable time pressure on the Israelis. By the spring of 2000, Barak's coalition government started to shrink. More important, public opinion polls suggested a significant erosion in the support for Barak's foreign and domestic policy. His own performance ratings were down significantly (Edelist 2003, 294).

To signal what might be the ramifications of a failure to reach an Israeli-Palestinian final status agreement, the Palestinians announced two "days of rage" on May 19–20, during which large-scale demonstrations and confrontations with the IDF forces took place throughout the occupied territories. The IDF activated for the first time attack helicopters to fire at Palestinians, also a demonstration of the shape of things to come without an agreement. Israel's political reaction, however, was to recall its delegation from Stockholm and to discontinue the third-stage redeployment process that Barak had promised Arafat in December 1999 (Sher 2003, 97; Edelist 2003, 306–10).

Barak had to sum up his first year as prime minister as a year of disappointments, and he started to realize that his time was running out. His idea for extracting the negotiations from the impasse they were headed to was to suggest that President Clinton convene a summit conference in order to try to reach a framework agreement between Barak and Arafat.

In his meeting in Lisbon with President Clinton in early June, Barak made this proposal. The American negotiation team was not enamored with the proposal (Ross 2004, 622–23). They felt that such a conference was premature, given the wide gaps between the parties. More important, by that time, Barak and his advisers had developed a conception that the Israeli public would be willing to buy the concessions required in the context of a final status agreement with the Palestinians only if it involved an "end of conflict" clause. This clause, in which the Palestinians would commit to having no further claims to Israel, would allow Barak to depict the agreement as a final agreement, one that provides complete closure of the Israeli-Palestinian conflict (Sher 2003, 99–100; Edelist 2003, 324).

Despite the reservations regarding a hastily organized summit among members of the American team (Agha and Malley 2001; Ross 2001; Shikaki 2004, 3), President Clinton decided to yield to Barak's pressure and invited the parties to a summit meeting at Camp David on July 10. The preliminary discussions between the Israelis and the Palestinians were ineffective. There was a sense of frustration among the Palestinians even before the summit started. Arafat felt that he had been pushed into the summit against his will. As Agha and Malley (2001) put it:

> Camp David seemed to Arafat to encapsulate his worst nightmares. It was high-wire summitry, designed to increase the pressure on the Palestinians to reach a quick agreement while heightening the political and symbolic costs if they did not. And it clearly was a Clinton/Barak idea both in concept and timing, and for that reason alone highly suspect. That the US issued the invitations despite Israel's refusal to carry out its earlier commitments and despite Arafat's plea for additional time to prepare only reinforced in his mind the sense of a US-Israeli conspiracy.

Thus, Arafat went into this summit with a heavy heart and deep suspicion of a hidden agenda underlying the very idea of the summit. His suspicions were confirmed once Barak laid out the Israeli offer. There are quite a few versions of the nature of the Israeli offers at Camp David (Sher 2003, 151–233; Edelist 2003, 338–94; Drucker 2002, 189–250; Agha and Malley 2001, 2002; Ross 2001; Morris 2001; Shikaki 2004; Ross 2004, 650–711). The official Israeli version is that Barak offered the Palestinians a state extending over 91 percent of the West Bank and the entire Gaza Strip, control over the Arab quarter of east Jerusalem, shared management of the Holy Basin, and exchange of territory in the Negev (Haluza Dunes) as compensation for the territory to be annexed by Israel.

Israel, according to this interpretation of Barak's offer, would annex an area that encompasses roughly 80 percent of the settler population in the West Bank and would maintain control over the Jewish quarter of the Old City in Jerusalem, as well as all of the Jewish neighborhoods of Jerusalem that had been built outside the 1967 borders. The Palestinian state that was to be established according to Barak's proposal would be demilitarized, with only police and internal security forces. The refugee problem would be settled within the Palestinian state. Israel would contribute to an international fund designed to settle the refugees either within the Palestinian state or within the Arab states if they so choose.

From an Israeli perspective, this proposal was seen as an extremely—even excessively—generous offer. As Agha and Malley (2001), in their criticism of Israeli and American strategies at Camp David, put it:

> If there is one issue that Israelis agree on, it is that Barak broke every conceivable taboo and went as far as any Israeli prime minister had gone or could go. Coming into office on a pledge to retain Jerusalem as Israel's "eternal and undivided capital," he ended up appearing to agree to Palestinian sovereignty—first over some, then over all, of the Arab sectors of East Jerusalem. Originally adamant in rejecting the argument that Israel should swap some of the occupied West Bank territory for land within its 1967 borders, he finally came around to that view. After initially speaking of a Palestinian state covering roughly 80 percent of the West Bank, he gradually moved up to the low 90s before acquiescing to the mid-90s range.

The Palestinians, according to this Israeli view, not only rejected the generous Israeli and American proposals; they made not even one concrete counterproposal throughout the summit (Morris 2002; Ross 2001, 9; Shavit 2001, 14).

From the Palestinian perspective, however, Barak's and Clinton's proposals were seen as almost insulting (Pressman 2003, 15–17; Shikaki 2004, 13; Agha and Malley 2001). For them, Barak's offer was not only demeaning in terms of the territorial size of the Palestinian state (92 percent of the West Bank, including 1 percent land swap); it also offered to cut the West Bank into three cantons separated by Israeli enclaves of settlements and roads (Pressman 2003, 17). Moreover, the Palestinians did not get a tangible Israeli offer on the matter of the refugees (Pressman 2003, 31; Agha and Malley 2001, 2002). The Palestinians did not put in a specific counterproposal but—in fact—made a number of important concessions in their responses to the American and Israeli proposals.

They agreed that "Israel could annex some settlement blocs. . . . They also agreed that Israel could annex Israeli/Jewish neighborhoods established in East Jerusalem since 1967. . . . Palestinians accepted the principle of [land] swaps as compensation for West Bank territory to be annexed by Israel. They also discussed Israeli security measures, agreeing on the stationing of an international force in the Jordan Valley. . . . Furthermore, the Palestinians at Camp David and Taba had their own maps of proposed land divisions of the West Bank" (Pressman 2003, 23). They also agreed to the principle of de facto demilitarization of the Palestinian state, which was—from an Israeli security perspective—perhaps the single most important concession that they could get.

The failure of the Camp David summit, as traumatic as it appeared, would not have been as devastating and confidence shattering as it actually turned out to be had Israel and the United States framed the outcome of the conference in different terms. Had Barak and Clinton presented it as a mere temporary setback, as they had presented the breakdown of the Israeli-Syrian negotiations in March, the psychological and political damage caused by the breakdown of this summit would have been reduced considerably. But Barak's domestic political situation was desperate, and he needed an urgent vindication for the "unforgivable" proposals he had made at Camp David. Thus, he put the entire blame for the failure of the summit on Yassir Arafat. And he successfully mobilized President Clinton to do the same. In his statement following the Camp David summit, President Clinton credited Barak for his generous and courageous concessions: "Prime Minister Barak showed particular courage, vision, and an understanding of the historical importance of this moment."[40] By implication, Arafat failed this historic test. In an interview to the Israeli public television, Clinton actually made a comparison between Arafat and Barak that was completely one-sided in favor of the latter.

Barak compounded this by claiming that the basic intention of his entire peace strategy was to go as far as possible in order to examine whether Israel had a true partner for peace on the other side. The purpose had been to "unmask Arafat" (Pundak 2001, 39; Pressman 2003, 11). Barak argued that Arafat had never intended to make a final peace with Israel (Shavit 2001, 15; Morris 2002, 42; Ross 2004, 13, 796–97). His entire strategy had been based on getting more land from the Israelis in a series of interim agreements. But when push came to shove, he revealed his true form. This strategy of blaming Arafat for everything did little to help Barak domestically, but it went a long way in confirming the pre-summit Palestinian suspicion that the Camp David summit had been an Israeli plot all along. The Americans had either been willing partners in this plot or had naively fallen into the carefully laid Israeli plan (Sontag 2001; Shikaki 2004).

Yet, despite the profound disappointment in the outcome of the Camp David summit, neither the Israelis nor the Palestinians gave up hope to reach an agreement. Gilead Sher met with Saeb Erekat in early August in Jerusalem. Shlomo Ben-Ami, now doubling as minister of internal security and foreign minister, joined these talks (Sher 2003, 249). The Palestinians continued to offer modifications to the Israeli and American proposals, in contrast to the arguments of Barak and Ben-Ami (Sher 2003, 249–59). These two teams were then joined by a small American team that included Dennis Ross, Martin Indyk, and Dan Kurzer, the American ambassador to Egypt. In early September, these meetings continued in New York. Saeb Erekat was joined by Mohammed Dahlan, the head of one of the Palestinian security organizations in Gaza (Sher 2003, 260–72). While the Palestinians came with additional proposals, the Israelis maintained their old positions of maintaining control of parts of the Jordan Valley, annexing excessively large settlement blocs to Israel, using Palestinian airspace for the IAF, and controlling the holy places in Jerusalem (Sher 2003, 273).

On September 21, Sher and Erekat agreed to put in writing some principles for managing the Old City of Jerusalem as an "open city." On September 25, Barak and Arafat met in Barak's house in Kochav Yair. Both agreed to continue the secret talks in Washington under the auspices of U.S. Secretary of State Madeline Albright (Sher 2003, 281–82). At that point it became apparent that the Americans were preparing a framework proposal of their own that attempted to reconcile the key differences between the Israelis and the Palestinians.

While the two delegations were negotiating in Washington, Barak allowed Ariel Sharon, the leader of the opposition, to stage a provocative visit of the Temple Mount. The Palestinians responded on September 28 with widespread demonstrations that quickly turned violent and engulfed the occupied territories. The Al Aqsa Intifada broke out in full force. Nevertheless, negotiations did not stop despite the outbreak of violence. But the intifada sealed Barak's political faith; the negotiations with the Palestinians were becoming an academic exercise. Everybody understood that time was running out. Clinton was on his way out, and Barak had no coalition. Sooner or later he would have to call for elections.

In order to save his coalition, Barak faced a dilemma: either call the

Likud Party into a national unity government or try to bring the ultra-orthodox Shas Party back in. The former option would almost certainly kill any chance for negotiation with the Palestinians. The second one had the drawback that it would still be a shaky coalition in which Barak would have to yield a great deal to Shas on religious affairs. In addition, the credibility of a long-term Shas commitment to a peace-oriented coalition was shaky. Most of their voters were far more hawkish than the leadership of the party (Drucker 2002, 348–52). As many predicted, this coalition did not last long. On November 28, 2000, Barak announced in the Knesset his intention to call for election for the prime minister's office. From then on, he was a lame duck prime minister.

On December 23, President Clinton provided the parties with a set of parameters that represented the American views of the key principles of a final status agreement between the Israelis and the Palestinians. These parameters suggested a transfer to the Palestinian state of 94–96 percent of the West Bank and an additional 1–3 percent of territory in a land swap. Israel's presence in some key areas of the Jordan Valley would be allowed for thirty-six months, and Israel would be allowed to hold some monitoring stations in the West Bank with Palestinian liaison. The control of the holy places in Jerusalem would be determined functionally, with shared sovereignty. A bridging formula for the issue of the refugees was offered in which the Israelis would recognize the suffering caused to the Palestinians and a joint commission would implement UN Resolution 194 on the right of return. But the solution had to be based on the notion of a two-state principle as the overall solution concept of the Israeli-Palestinian conflict. The parties would sign a statement ending the conflict (Sher 2003, 360–63; Ross 2004, 748–53).[41]

Both the Israelis and the Palestinians accepted the Clinton parameters in principle. But each side had a long list of reservations.[42] Nevertheless, the Clinton plan prompted the parties to try one last effort at negotiations before the Israeli elections. On January 21 Israeli and Palestinian delegations met for a last-minute effort in Taba, some fifteen kilometers south of Eilat. The Israelis came to the meeting knowing that their effort was based on shaky legal principles and that it would probably not be binding if a new government came to power in Israel. The Palestinians knew the same thing. Moreover, while the parties were still negotiating in Taba, the violence in the occupied territories continued in full force. A number of attacks causing Israeli fatalities resulted in temporary breaks in the negotiations. During the negotiations, the Israelis gradually modified their position, reducing the size of the territory to be annexed to

Israel from 8 percent, proposed at Camp David, to 3 percent. Israel also modified its demands on security-related matters and on Jerusalem. The key change in the Israeli position was on the right of return. The Israeli position allowed a limited number of refugees to return to Israel as part of family unifications. This was a symbolic application of the right-of-return principle.

The political circumstances did not allow for an agreement. The Palestinians knew that Barak would not be able to deliver an agreement; thus, they were not going to sign anything that would commit them to concessions that would not be binding if Sharon were elected as prime minister. Nevertheless, both sides agreed that the Taba talks produced considerable progress. There were gaps on most issues under contention, but these gaps were considerably smaller than they had ever been before. Indeed, in the joint Israeli-Palestinian statement of January 27, 2001, that concluded the Taba Conference, the parties stated:

> The sides declare that they have never been closer to reaching an agreement and it is thus our shared belief that the remaining gaps could be bridged with the resumption of negotiations following the Israeli elections.[43]

But the die was cast. Barak lost the elections by a wide margin. Sharon came to power. With it came the death of the Israeli-Palestinian peace process that had started more than seven years earlier in Oslo.

What were the reasons for the failure of this process of peacemaking and reconciliation between the Israelis and the Palestinians? Where and why did this process go awry? Was it misconceived from the outset? Some Israelis claim that the original sin was the recognition of the PLO, which had been and remained a terrorist organization rather than a national liberation movement. Was the process itself a reasonable path to peace, but its implementation was problematic? Or was only the last stage—the final status negotiations—the one that derailed the entire process because the gaps on the key issues—territories, Jerusalem, the refugees—were too wide to bridge in such a short time? Finally, who is to blame for the failure? The Palestinians, the Israelis, or the Americans?[44]

These are difficult questions, and the answers vary considerably, depending on who does this evaluation. The official Israeli version is simple: the Israelis set out on a process of peace and reconciliation during which they consistently gave the Palestinians additional control over their lives, their fate, and their security. Throughout the process, the Palestinians reneged on their promises and cheated. They refused to disarm the militant organizations within and outside the PLO. They established a "revolving door policy" wherein they captured terrorists only to release them several days later. They continued and even intensified their campaign of terror against Israelis. Between September 13, 1993, and September 28, 2000, 242 Israelis (179 civilians and 63 security personnel) were killed and over 1,000 Israelis were wounded in terrorist attacks under the cover of a peace process. Despite these repeated terrorist attacks—in direct violation of the Palestinian pledge to curb terrorism—Israel continued to carry out its commitments by withdrawing from additional territories. Moreover, Israel continued to negotiate with the Palestinians further agreements entailing additional Israeli concessions. The final straw was, of course, the rejection of the extremely (or even outrageously) generous Israeli offers at Camp David. This proved to many Israelis, some of whom had been ardent supporters of the peace process (such as Shlomo Ben Ami and Ehud Barak), that the Palestinians—especially Yassir Arafat—were still bent on the destruction of Israel (Morris 2002; Shavit 2001; Sher 2003, 416).

All the factual aspects of the official Israeli explanation of the process are true. But this is only a small part of the whole story. It ignores completely the Israeli measures that were equally responsible for derailing the peace process. In fact, the peace process was doomed to fail much before the outbreak of the intifada, and Israel and the Palestinians share equal responsibility for the failure. A brief assessment of the reasons for failure seems appropriate at this point.

Both sides failed to fulfill their obligations to the peace process throughout the period of September 1993 to September 2000. The Palestinian Authority (PA) failed to effectively curb terrorism. It seems that this was due not to the weakness of the PA but to a belief that a dose of terrorism was a credible threat of the shape of things to come if the process failed. This was the Palestinians' basic weapon of compellence. When Arafat was interested in lowering the flames of violence, the Palestinian security forces proved quite effective. The Palestinians never fully addressed the Israeli expectation of reduced violence as a key fruit of peace. Moreover, Arafat was not willing to disarm the militant Islamic organizations. That proved a fatal problem, because once the Israelis destroyed the security infrastructure that Arafat had built under the PA, the Hamas and the Islamic Jihad became the driving force of the Al Aqsa Intifada.[45]

The PA failed also in developing a functioning set of political institutions with widespread legitimacy. The economic system they developed was profoundly corrupt and self-serving. They mishandled the funds they had received from the Organization of Economic Cooperation and Development (OECD) states and from the Arab states and the tax refunds they had received from the Israelis. The central PA leaders were, quite probably, deeply involved in this corruption (World Bank 2003, 39).[46] The economic performance of the PA had been abysmal. The per capita GDP in the occupied territories had declined by over 11 percent since 1993. The PA failed to generate a working economic infrastructure for the Palestinians, and the continued reliance on the employment of Palestinians in Israel continued their dependence on Israel and thus their dissatisfaction with Israeli closures and the substitution of the Palestinian workforce in Israel by foreign workers from Africa, Asia, or Eastern Europe (World Bank 2004, 3–9).

Finally, the Palestinians—Arafat in particular—made numerous political mistakes. Many of these mistakes increased suspicion among Israelis of his true intentions in the process. His speeches to Palestinians throughout the process were in many respects contradictory to the image of moderation and cooperation he had tried to project when discussing the process with foreign diplomats or his Israeli counterparts. He did not make a noticeable effort to curb anti-Israeli incitement in the occupied territories, also believing that this would come in handy if the peace process failed. Most important, he presented uncompromising positions at Camp David and afterward and attempted to use the Al Aqsa Intifada to extract concessions from the Israelis. Ultimately, this has backfired. The Palestinian condition at present is far worse than it was in 2000 from any conceivable perspective.

Having said that, the Israeli responsibility for the failure of the Oslo Accords is—at the very least—as profound as that of the Palestinians. Since this is an evaluation of Israeli policy, we need to examine in some detail Israeli behavior since the Oslo Accords. First and foremost, Israel has violated the spirit and text of the Oslo Accords by fundamentally changing the status quo through a widespread settlement policy. Figure 10.1 provides data on Israeli settlement policy in the occupied territories since the occupation of the West Bank and Gaza in 1967. As can be seen from the table, in 1993 there were about 110,000 settlers in the occupied territories. In 2001 there were 195,000. (Note that the number of settlers increased by 18 percent during the Al Aqsa Intifada.)[47] This was an increase of 73 percent under the guise of an agreement wherein Israel committed itself not to change the territorial status quo. This violation was not the doing of one but rather of four different Israeli governments

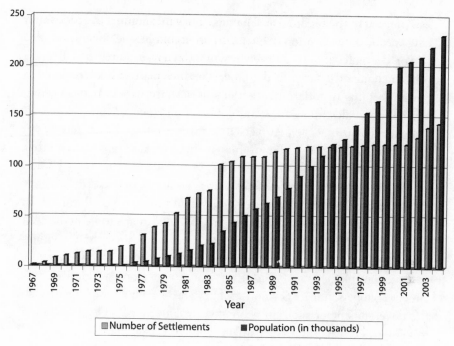

Fig. 10.1. Settlements in the occupied territories, 1967–2003

since 1993, and it could not be seen by the longest stretch of the imagi-
nation as a retaliation to Palestinian violations of the Oslo Accords. The
increase in settlement activity was simply a failure of the various Israeli
governments to stand up to domestic pressure of a vocal and militant
minority that had little support in Israeli public opinion.

More important, however, the settlement policy was self-defeating,
because it made the task of peace more difficult domestically. It was clear
from the outset of the Oslo process that settlements would have to be dismantled as part of the final status agreement. By building more settlements and authorizing new construction in the existing ones, the Israeli
governments effectively engaged in a self-defeating process that would tie
their hands in the final status agreements. The October 1995 agreement
between Yossi Beilin and Abu Mazen established a principle that, in the
final status settlement, Israel would keep 80 percent of the settler population in fifty West Bank settlements.[48] If this principle were applied on the
basis of the 1995 settler population, it would have implied the relocation
of twenty-six thousand settlers in the West Bank and another five thou-

sand settlers in the Gaza Strip. The same principle applied in 2000 would have meant the relocation of over forty thousand people.

For the Palestinians, the settlement activity suggested a deliberate plan to change the facts on the ground and to make matters difficult in the final status negotiations. Settlement activity, more than anything else, eroded Palestinian elite and public confidence in the Oslo track. The fact that this settlement activity continued both under Labor governments and under the Netanyahu government suggested to them that there was no real Israeli intention of going back to the 1967 border. Moreover, in all negotiations, Israeli representatives stressed the fact that an attempt to dismantle all settlements would result in a civil war. Thus, while the Israelis were demanding from the Palestinians to launch a civil war in order to disarm Hamas and to curb terrorism, they were not willing to risk a civil war in Israel to reach peace (Khalidi 2002; Pundak 2001).

Israel has blamed the PA for the failure to develop a viable Palestinian economy and for its corruption. However, Israeli actions have made the development of such an economy virtually impossible. In 1993, a total of ninety thousand Palestinians worked in Israel. These accounted for roughly 27 percent of the Palestinian workforce. By 1996 this number went down to thirty thousand workers—about 5 percent of the Palestinian workforce (World Bank 1999, 5–6). This figure increased to an average daily employment rate of between fifty thousand and sixty thousand workers over the period of 1997–2000 (Bulmer 2001, 2). A key factor in the Palestinian reliance on Israeli sources of income was the Israeli policy of border closures as a collective punishment measure following terrorist attacks. Over the period of 1993–96, the number of closure days per year averaged sixty days. This is a total of two months without income not only to many Palestinian workers in Israel but to tens of thousands of Palestinians who traded with Israel, as the closure prevented Palestinian exports into Israel and Israeli imports into the West Bank and Gaza (World Bank 2002, 22).

Israel used also a variety of economic retaliation measures to put pressure on the PA to curb terrorism. Among these measures were the withholding of taxes of Palestinian workers in Israel that were supposed to go to the PA for payment to the PA employees; the freezing of Palestinian ties with the Arab world, by blocking exports to Jordan and Egypt during closure periods; and other collective punishments such as roadblocks and slowdowns of movement of people and goods from the West Bank to Gaza and vice versa. All these measures had an adverse effect on the Palestinian economy. But, more important, these measures had a confidence-destroying impact on the more liberal sectors of the Palestinian business community. Joint ventures and industrial parks, which had been established in the Erez area and in the West Bank, were also affected by closures. In short, Israeli actions had probably more adverse effect on the Palestinian economy than did the inefficiency and corruption of the PA (Arnon and Wienbladt 2001, F299–300).

Israel also continued its policy of disproportionate reprisals directed at the Palestinian population. Thus instead of seeing a reduction of Israeli military presence as a result of the redeployment agreements, the Palestinians saw substantial military presence that was nearly as intrusive as it had been prior to the Oslo Accords.

These Israeli practices eroded the confidence of the Palestinian public in the Oslo Accords. However, what was more disturbing from the leadership's perspective was the Israeli habit of reneging on aspects of the implementation of the various agreements that had been reached along the way. Both the Israelis and the Palestinians started the process with significant reservations about its logic and structure. Rabin said that the Oslo Accords were "full of holes like Swiss cheese." From the Palestinian perspective the risk entailed in agreeing to a gradual process of moving toward a state entailed a risk that the process would be stopped short of the goal. The way Arafat and the PLO leadership tried to sell the process to their public was to suggest several immediate benefits and a continuous momentum of self-rule and self-determination. The immediate benefits were the recognition of the PLO and the return of the PLO leadership to the occupied territory. The long-term benefits included the gradual diminishment of Israeli control of the occupied territories, economic progress, and improved position when the time came for final status negotiations. It was assumed that, if Israel was not willing to meet Palestinian conditions for a final status settlement, during the ensuing period of stalemate, the PA would have control over a vast majority of the Palestinians in the occupied territories (Kimmerling and Migdal 2003, 358–61; Rabani 2001, 72–73).

From a Palestinian perspective, a pattern was developed in which "Israel first refuses to implement its own commitments, then seeks and obtains their dilution in a new agreement, subsequently engages in systematic prevarication, and finally demands additional negotiations, leading to yet a further diluted agreement" (Rabani 2001, 71). This was the case with the Hebron redeployment, which was supposed to be part of the 1995 Oslo II Accord and was renegotiated by Netanyahu. This was the case with the third redeployment, which was again supposed to be part of the Oslo II Accord and was renegotiated by Netanyahu and Arafat in the Wye Plantation conference in 1998. Netanyahu never implemented this agreement, and Barak renegotiated part of it in the 1999 Sharm a-Sheikh summit, also failing to implement the transfer of Abu Deis and Azaria to the Palestinians.

The fate of the final status negotiation was no different. The formal talks were due to start in May 1996. Yet serious final status negotiations did not start before March 2000. The Palestinians saw repeated Israeli violations of the agreement and—realizing their basic political weakness—had to give in to this pattern of behavior. But this had eroded their confidence in the Israeli willingness to reach a viable and honorable final status agreement. They were offended by Barak's strategy of delay. Barak repeatedly tried to renege on the Israeli commitment to a 13 percent redeployment by arguing that there was no point in implementing it because final status talks were getting under way. At the same time he put the final status talks on the back burner while investing most of his energy on the Israeli-Syrian track.[49]

There is little surprise, therefore, that the idea of a final big summit at Camp David that would settle everything at once was very troubling to Arafat. The Israeli offers prior to that summit were totally unacceptable to the Palestinians, and Arafat suspected that at Camp David these proposals would get the blessing of President Clinton. To a large extent, these suspicions were verified by the Barak proposals at Camp David. It had been quite clear from these proposals that Barak opted for a 8–9 percent annexation of West Bank territories in exchange for an end-of-conflict commitment from the Palestinians. The all-or-nothing approach and the asymmetrical scheme where the Palestinians were required to make substantial concessions and the Israelis got the end-of-conflict pledge were not acceptable and could not be acceptable even if there were no basic Palestinian suspicion of the Israelis in general and of Barak in particular. Despite the failure of Camp David, and despite his depiction as intransigent by Clinton and Barak, Arafat was willing to continue negotiations. The Palestinians did offer that Israel move to carry out the third redeployment agreement and that negotiations would continue. During the period between July and September, both sides made significant progress. But the missed opportunity at Camp David cast a heavy shadow on these talks. Barak's crippled political position was also a significant liability.

Most important, many observers of the process (Agha and Malley 2001; Pundak 2001; Shikaki 2004) suggest that the lack of a fallback negotiation strategy by both Israel and the PLO was a debilitating factor. This focus on "all or nothing" suggested that, if the "all" option failed, the recourse would be violence. This had been both the Palestinian and Israeli expectation. The initial Israeli reaction to the Palestinian popular uprising following the Sharon visit on the Temple Mount was excessively harsh and aimed at crippling the PA. This contributed to the escalation of the intifada and to its conversion into a wave of guerrilla warfare and widespread terrorism (Khalidi 2002).

The Barak government, like its predecessors since Oslo, continued to tie its hands with the settlements. It was unwilling to recognize the illegality of these settlements and was not willing to come to terms with the need to dismantle a substantial proportion of the settlements. On the other hand, the Palestinians were willing to accept Israel's annexation of blocs of settlements, but they were never given adequate compensation for what they believed was acceptance of Israeli colonialism. Moreover, throughout the negotiations, Israel imposed on the Palestinians fairly ridiculous military constraints that were meaningless in terms of strategy (such as early warning stations or control of certain areas of the Jordan Valley). These demands were imposed by narrow-minded military officers, and the politicians bought into them without questions.[50] The upshot was that these demands helped poison the atmosphere throughout the negotiations and contributed to their failure.

3. EXPLANATION OF THE NONPOLICY OF PEACE

A historian looking at the Arab-Israeli conflict a hundred years from now will probably wonder why it took so long to resolve it, given that reasonable solutions to the conflict existed since its inception as a set of interstate conflicts. Compared to other contemporary conflicts, the Arab-Israeli conflict attracted disproportionate amounts of attention from the international community. In practice, however, it was probably less severe and probably more soluble than many other conflicts. The survey of missed opportunities for peace suggests that the conflict could have been much shorter and less severe than it turned out to be. Most agreements that were implemented eventually by the parties to the conflict had been feasible to them much prior to their actual realization. These agreements could have been achieved at a significantly lower cost to all parties involved, as well as to many innocent bystanders who ended up as collateral damage victims of this conflict.

It must be stated at the outset that, to a large extent, the analysis offered subsequently of the underlying problems of Israel's peace policy is one sided and biased. The Arabs were afflicted by the same reluctance, short-sightedness, and "over my dead body" syndrome as were the Israelis. They were impaired by psychological fears and ideological rigidity as were the Israelis. Consider the Egyptian refusal to make formal peace with Israel prior to 1967. While Nasser may have sought secret channels to reach some sort of modus vivendi with Israel in the 1950s, he was not willing to negotiate with Israel in the open, nor was he willing to concede minimal Israeli requests such as freedom of navigation in the Suez Canal. Egypt understood that its claim to the Negev would be a nonstarter for negotiations. Ultimately, after Egypt lost the Sinai in the Six Day War and thousands of more Egyptian soldiers in the War of Attrition and the Yom Kippur War, it signed a peace treaty with Israel on terms that could have been clearly accomplished at least twenty years earlier.

Consider Jordanian reluctance to make peace with Israel. King Abdullah and later on King Hussein could have reached a peace treaty with Israel that would have maintained their control over and annexation of the West Bank. Israel would have gladly supported the Hashemite regime in case of threats from Syria or Egypt. Jordan ended up losing the West Bank in 1967, but if Hussein were willing to sign a peace treaty between 1967 and 1977 (when the Labor Party with the Jordanian option was still in power in Israel), he would probably have received at least what the Israelis ended up offering the Palestinians at Taba in January 2001. The peace treaty that King Hussein ended up signing with Israel in 1994 could have been signed much earlier on the same terms.

Abba Eban's characterization of the Palestinians is as valid today as it was when he made the observation about their phenomenal skill at missing opportunities. The chances that the Palestinians will get as generous a deal as they had gotten from Barak at Taba—at least in the foreseeable future—are extremely slim. Yezid Sayigh's (2001) analysis of the intifada is very insightful; the tragedy that befell the Palestinian people in September 2000 is probably as profound as the Naqba (the catastrophe of 1948). And it is largely their own doing, because they could have quelled or prevented the violence and resumed negotiations in the hope of improving on the deal offered to them at Camp David.

Consider Syria. The best that Syria can hope for in the context of a peace agreement with Israel is getting back the Golan Height. It could have accomplished that in 1967, again in 1994, and again in 2000. It could have signed peace with Israel (perhaps without some of the DMZs) before 1967, thereby saving thousands of Syrian lives lost in the 1967, 1973, and possibly the 1982 wars.

The upshot of all this is that the Arab-Israeli conflict is a tragedy of errors, and these errors are not the fault of one side only; clearly they are not only Israeli errors. The tragedy of errors in this conflict deserves a more thorough and balanced study than can be offered here. It is quite possible that the mistakes that the Arab states made in pursuing the conflict against Israel were far more costly than those made by Israel. I will explore this further in chapter 13. But this is not a study of the Arab-Israeli conflict per se; it is an attempt to evaluate Israel's security and foreign policy. My aim is to derive lessons from Israel's past behavior in order to offer avenues to improving and changing these policies in a manner that would help overcome some of the mistakes Israel has made in the past, hence the focus on Israeli responsibility for these "missed opportunities" for peace.

Several conclusions stem from the historical and analytical survey of Israel's diplomacy of peace over the years. These are the basic aspects of the policy that I will try to explain in this section.

1. Israel was a reluctant partner to peace. It played a central spoiler role in many of the cases that presented opportunity for negotiation. This applied to both preliminary stages that entailed no concessions on its part and more advanced stages where a major transformation of Israel's relations with its Arab neighbors and/or the Palestinians could be achieved at the price of Israeli concessions.

2. Most cases that ended up in agreements were not initiated by an official Israeli policy. Rather, they were initiated either by the Arab side, by a third party (e.g., the United States), or by private individuals (e.g., Oslo). Israeli peace policy was mostly reactive, not proactive. This is in sharp contrast to Israel's proactive (or hyperactive) approach to the use of military force. Israeli diplomacy very often relied on the "waiting for a phone call from the Arabs" attitude.

3. Several peace initiatives failed due to Israeli military or intelligence operations that derailed diplomatic efforts. These include negotiations with Nasser in 1953–54 and the tacit understandings with Hussein in the 1960s. Israeli military and settlement activity in the occupied territories in the 1990s contributed to the failure of the Oslo process.

4. Over the years, but especially since the Six Day War, Israel built myths of security based on territory. These myths were not born out of serious strategic analyses. Nor was there a discussion that attempted to

integrate security considerations and foreign policy and democracy issues. Rather, the territorial idol was due to a political competition among and within political parties. This myth of territorial security was accompanied by another myth transported from the prestate era: that Israeli settlements would determine the state's final borders. Taken together, these myths became a self-perpetuating part of the Israeli public discourse on the fate of the occupied territories. They also created practical constraints on decision making, which placed significant limits on Israeli responsiveness to expressions of peace from the Arab side.

5. A key characteristic of Israel's peace policy over the years was the "over my dead body" syndrome (Maoz 1996b). This syndrome concerns a tendency to establish artificial "red lines" in negotiations that have no real strategic or political significance. Some of these red lines were drawn as a bargaining ploy; others were drawn because politicians believed them to be strategically crucial at the time. The problem was that insistence on these red lines blocked agreements and helped cause wars. Yet, following such wars and conflicts, the Israeli government was willing to concede these red lines. It turns out that, in most of these cases where previous red lines turned blue, the agreements they enabled held up. But this happened only after considerable human and material costs were expended. This syndrome afflicted all Israeli governments, and it suggests that in retrospect Israel could have better served its interests by insisting on Arab measures of quid pro quo rather than trying to impose unrealistic political and military measures that turned out to be not as significant in the final analysis.

6. The Israeli approach to political agreements with the Arabs—especially following the Six Day War—was characterized by a gradualist conception. This conception favored limited and gradual accords over comprehensive agreements. This approach was embedded in a deep suspicion that, whenever an Arab leader was willing to negotiate a political settlement, this was actually a ploy designed to deprive Israel of important strategic assets and to renew the military pressure on it when Israel became weaker. Gradualism was supposed to test the water and minimize Israeli concessions, while maintaining a momentum for peace. In general, this policy had some successes—most notably the post–Yom Kippur War disengagement agreements with Egypt and Syria. In other cases, the gradualist approach was less successful. The key examples are the secret negotiations with Jordan and the Oslo process. In these cases, gradualism may well have been a liability. Israel could arguably have gotten better agreements if it had adopted a final treaty approach, even if implementation would have been gradual.

7.   Israel's reluctant peacemaking was based on a number of flawed axioms. These axioms were refuted time and again by historical developments, but this did not bother Israeli political and military elites. A chief axiom was that Israel could not afford to make simultaneous agreements with several Arab states. Related to it was the notion that a multilateral peace conference was bound to result in excessive pressure on Israel to make concessions. As a result, Israel's peace policy was based on the notion that a divided Arab world offered better opportunities (for both war and peace). Israel's peace policy attempted to drive a wedge between and among Arab states, no matter who was involved. These axioms impaired progress toward peace. When Israel was pressured into changing its approach to multilateral diplomacy, it generally benefited from this shift.

8.   For the most part, Israel's neighbors had a fairly good record of compliance with signed agreements. In cases where agreements were subject to violations, Israel was as responsible for violations as was the other side. When Israel did plunge and made concessions for peace, and when it kept its side of the bargain, the other side did too. The peace agreements that Israel signed with Egypt and Jordan, the interim agreements it signed with the Syrians, and the secret understandings it established with Jordan prior to the 1994 peace treaty manifest a positive record of compliance and helped establish stability along the relevant fronts. In retrospect it could be said that Israeli concessions in the context of these agreements paid off. The lack of "warm peace" between Israel and Egypt and Israel and Jordan is a symptom of the failure to solve the Palestinian problem, but it does not represent a strategic problem. Cold peace is a typical Middle East practice even among Arab states.

The discrepancy between the Israeli official claim that "there is no one in the Arab world that is willing to take our outstretched hand to peace" and the actual Israeli reluctance to make peace is quite puzzling. To explain these findings we must examine a mix of psychological, political, and bureaucratic factors. Many of these factors were mentioned in passing earlier in this chapter. Here I offer a more analytic discussion of the elements that seem to be instrumental in accounting for the reluctant Israeli peace policy.

3.1. *The Psychology of Reluctant Peacemaking*

Two basic and contradictory beliefs permeated Israeli thinking about peace. The first is grounded in a profound sense of paranoia. I label this the "siege mentality." The second is what Yehoshafat Harkabi, a former head of military intelligence and a professor of international politics at the Hebrew University, calls the "policy of arrogance." A brief exposition of these beliefs is central to the understanding of Israel's peace policy.

The siege mentality is best expressed in Ben-Gurion's notion of a small state surrounded by far larger enemies that must develop and prosper under conditions of existential threat. The profound hostility of the Arabs to Israel creates a permanent motivation for war. Therefore, any verbal or behavioral expression that fits this image of the Arabs should be seen as a genuine expression of intent. On the other hand, any verbal or behavioral gesture that contradicts this image of hostility and destructive potential should be viewed with suspicion. If the Arab offer of peace comes with an attached price tag, it should be viewed even more skeptically, because it may well be part of a plan to weaken Israel even further by depriving it of strategic assets.

An interesting feature of the siege mentality is a tendency to define Israel's interests not in their own terms, that is, what is good for Israel, but rather as derivatives of Arab interests. If something is seen as good for the Arabs, then by implication it must be bad for Israel. So Israel does not need to define or redefine its interests in terms of its inherent goals and preferences. Rather, it can define them as the inverse of the Arab demands. If the Arabs require territorial concessions for peace, then they must regard the territory Israel possesses as significant assets. Consequently, Israel must insist on holding on to the territories not because it needs them for security or other purposes but because the Arabs want them. Even if a given territory has no strategic value per se, and even if the Israelis are aware of that, giving it up would be interpreted by the Arabs as a sign of weakness. This would only boost their resolve and determination to destroy Israel even further.[51]

The siege mentality is not directed only at the Arabs. It is also an underlying characteristic of the Israeli perception of the international system as a whole. The notion of a "people that dwells alone" is an acute expression of the belief that Israel cannot completely rely on anybody in the international system. Adversaries are always there and do not change ("the sea is the same sea and the Arabs are the same Arabs," as Yitzhak Shamir used to say). Allies are only temporary and—for the most part—cannot be trusted to come to Israel's aid when push comes to shove. Even the most friendly states have their own interests, which very often require maintaining good relations with the Arab world. Thus, peace proposals of third parties must also be taken with suspicion and skepticism. Israel needs the Western world for weapons, markets, and political support in international organizations. But ultimately it can only rely on itself for its security. International organizations cannot be trusted because they have let Israel down in the past (e.g., the UN force in Egypt prior to the Six Day War and the UNIFIL forces in Lebanon).[52] Any peace initiative originating from or involving an international organization such as the UN is typically considered pro-Arab and thus rejected out of hand. This was the case with the Jarring mission in 1971 and the repeated Israeli rejection of UN-sponsored conferences since 1974.

Ben-Gurion's doomsday scenario that provoked Israel's nuclear program had a diplomatic equivalent. Israel's approach to multilateral peace diplomacy envisioned a process wherein the Arab states would form a coherent diplomatic front that would present to the outside world a seemingly "reasonable" position. Engaging Israel as a bloc, the Arabs would effectively isolate Israel in the world community, swaying U.S. policy to their side as well. This would impose on Israel enormous diplomatic pressure for excessive territorial concessions that would endanger its security. For that reason, Israel should resist any multilateral forums on diplomatic and security-related matters. Rather, peace negotiations are best conducted in bilateral settings, where each Arab state (or the Palestinians) followed their own national interests and could be more open minded when it came to Israel's security needs. Moreover, Israeli politicians typically perceived multilateral settings as driven by the most extreme common denominator of the Arab positions. The fear of an Arab-Western diplomatic collusion against Israel was at the heart of the longtime Israeli opposition to resolution of the conflict through multilateral diplomacy.

Michael Handel (1995, 542), hardly a revisionist historian, labels this the "ghetto mentality." He points out the relationship between this deeply embedded paranoia and the preference for military solutions over political and diplomatic ones.

> This not unexpected turn of events [an automatic anti-Israel majority in the UN General Assembly, Arab control of oil, and increasing Arab international influence] fueled the Israeli search for self-reliance, if not withdrawal, fostering a ghetto mentality that precluded an emphasis on the political and diplomatic dimensions of strategy.

The policy of arrogance entails an expectation that, when the Arabs are sufficiently weak, they would be willing to settle on Israel's terms.

This idea is succinctly expressed by Mordechai (Motta) Gur, a former COS and deputy minister of defense under Yitzhak Rabin, in his analysis of the lessons Israel has drawn from the War of Attrition.

> Did only one conclusion follow from it [our victory in the War of Attrition]—to sit and do nothing? . . . [W]e are strong and if the Arabs want peace, they have to come to us on their knees and accept our terms? This was the great political and strategic mistake—the reliance on force as the almost exclusive factor in the formulation of policy. (Gur 1987)[53]

An important concept in the policy of arrogance is the notion of "peace for peace" as an alternative to the "land for peace" concept. This concept implies that Israel's capability can serve not only as a deterrent but also as a compellent. The demonstration and actual use of Israel's military power is meant to convince the Arabs that peace is not only a valuable commodity to Israel; it is even more valuable for them. Once the Arabs become convinced of that, they can afford to live with what they have and would come to terms with Israel's occupation of Arab territory (Shamir 1994, 258–62; Netanyahu 2000, 321–52). This approach is also inherent in the treatment of Israel's nuclear policy by hawkish politicians and strategists. For that reason, it does not make sense to allow for other states in the Middle East to acquire nuclear weapons. Nuclear deterrence must be asymmetrical. Israel deters but cannot be deterred by other Arab states, because mutual assured destruction would generate a strategic stalemate that might kill the "peace for peace" concept.

The two strands of the Israeli conception of peace—the siege mentality and the policy of arrogance—seem to contradict each other. To an outside observer this may be so, but for most Israelis, these strands imply similar things. Israeli politicians believe that, if the Arabs are strong, Israeli moderation would spell weakness, thereby encouraging the Arabs to attack Israel. When the Arabs are weak, there is no reason to make concessions. Let the Arabs come to the table on Israel's terms. Moshe Sharett described two general approaches that characterized Israeli peace policy.

> One approach holds that the Arabs understand only a language of force. Israel is so small and so isolated, and it may be so weak (based on the criteria of territory, population, and potential) that if it does not double its actual power by a very high factor of demonstrable [military] activity, it will face bleak consequences. The state of Israel must demonstrate every so often that it is strong and able and willing to use

force. . . . With regard to peace this approach maintains that it is, in any event, a dubious or very remote issue. If peace comes, it will come only when they [the Arabs] are persuaded that this state cannot be defeated. . . . [T]he problem of peace should therefore not serve as a constraining consideration when the question of a large-scale demonstration of force is contemplated in order to solve an immediate security problem. . . . [T]he fire is there anyway. . . .

What does the other approach say? The issue of peace must not be absent from our considerations, even for one moment. [But] it is not merely a matter of political consideration; in the long term it is a crucial security consideration. [And so] without belittling the importance of the immediate security consideration, we must always include the issue of peace in our comprehensive view of things; we must moderate our reactions. (Sharett 1958, 8–10)[54]

The first approach summarizes the duality of the siege mentality and the policy of arrogance quite well. The second approach, certainly more moderate and forthcoming, nevertheless lists peace as just another factor that may supplement the security calculus that is still dominated by the logic of demonstrating force to instill an image of invincibility. It does not claim that peace is a priority; rather, it is one of several priorities. Nor does it claim that peace-related considerations should supersede security considerations; rather, they should supplement them. Thus, even the more moderate approach accepts many of the basic premises of the "Iron Wall" conception.

The upshot of this duality is a fundamental risk aversiveness when it comes to peace and, in sharp contrast, a risk-seeking behavior that characterizes Israeli tendency to use force. The peace-related risk aversiveness accounts for a number of trends in Israeli peace policy. First, it accounts for the lack of peace-related initiatives for fear that they would entail concessions. Second, it explains the a priori suspicion of Arab or foreign initiatives. Third, it involves setting up artificially high red lines that cannot be really defended. The policy of arrogance also explains the relative lack of Israeli peace initiatives (except those cases where the outstretched hand to peace implied having the Arabs accept the status quo). It also accounts for the outright rejection of a number of peace initiatives of Arab leaders and third parties that entailed Israeli concessions.

3.2. *The Political Sociology of Peacemaking*

Israeli decision makers were concerned with building a new model of an Israeli citizen. The diaspora Jew image was that of a submissive and withdrawn person, soft spoken and acquiescent, one who tried to get by pleasing the goyim but who ultimately got crushed by them. In contrast, the "Israeli" model was symbolized by the term *Sabra*—a nickname for Israeli-born children who, like the Mediterranean cactus, have a prickly outside but are sweet and tasty on the inside. The image of the Sabra was to be one of a resolute person, a person who stands up for his or her rights, who is willing to fight for them and to die for them if necessary. This person is tough toward enemies. At the same time, this person is warm, friendly, and utterly loyal to other members of the group. Moderation and accommodation were not part of this image (Almog 1997; Golani 2002, 61–93).

Building a society on principles of self-defense dictated a social and national posture in which security was the first and most important value. The IDF was to play the role of the principal melting pot for this new model of Sabra. Israel faced a huge influx of immigrants who had to be absorbed quickly and who had to accept fairly harsh standards of living during the first years of the state. Moreover, to support the newly established state, Israel had to rely on significant amounts of financial support from the world Jewry—mostly the American Jewry. Solving Israel's external problems by signing peace treaties with the Arab world would not make as convincing a case for contributions from American Jews as would a case consisting of both defense-related and immigrant absorption–related needs.

The militarization of the Israeli society served also the economic and social needs of the political elites of the time. Revisionist historians and sociologists argue that magnification of security threats in the early statehood period served the political and economic goals of the Ashkenazi incumbent elite amid large waves of Jewish immigration, mostly from the Arab world (Ben-Eliezer 1998, 207–29; 2003, 31–34). Political settlements with Arab states would have implied the readmission of at least some Palestinian refugees and the return of some of their possessions and lands that had been confiscated by the government. Distributing the lands and property of exiled Palestinians to newly arrived immigrants seemed like a good deal. A peace agreement could have spoiled this process (Levy 1997, 62).

There is no question that peace was a value in the newly established state of Israel, which had just emerged victorious from a war of national liberation (Segev 1984). However, peace was not the principal value. Ben-Gurion, in a meeting with senior foreign and security policy officials on October 1, 1952, listed his order of priorities of Israeli policy.

But at the same time we have to remember that there are limits to our desire for peace with the Arabs. This is one of our vital interests, but it is not the first and all-determining interest. First and foremost, we have to see to Israel's needs, whether or not this brings improvement in our relations with the Arabs. The second factor in our existence is American Jewry and its relationship with us (and the state of America since these Jews live in it). The third thing—[is] peace with the Arabs. This is the order of priorities.[55]

The building of a new Israeli model of citizen-soldier moved peace even further down the list of national priorities. Ben-Gurion did not elaborate on his first priority: "seeing to Israel's needs." However, in other places, he made this far more clear. The Israeli model of activism that was applied decisively in the first eight years of Israel's independence was much more in line with the conception of "Israel's basic needs" than was the Israeli conception of concessions for peace. Clearly, Israel would have been far more forthcoming if the Arabs had accepted the "peace for peace" formula. But even when Za'im offered a deal that was almost better than a "peace for peace" concept, Ben-Gurion was reluctant to accept it, discounting the opportunities entailed in this offer due to the demands for Israeli concessions. It is difficult to explain Ben-Gurion's attitude unless we see it in terms of a larger scheme in which peace was not a top priority.

The sociology of peace is also reflected in the Ben-Gurion–Sharett debate. This debate entailed significant substantive differences, but as students of these two politicians have observed (e.g., Sheffer 1996, 909–18; 1988; Bialer 1971; Brecher 1972, 251–90), the differences in substantive positions were not all that great. The subtle differences—the differences in terms of the sources of these positions—were more significant. Sharett felt that Israel must be more connected to the outside world. It must ultimately rely on external support—military, economic, diplomatic, and moral—to survive in the long run. In a manner of speaking, Sharett's view of the asymmetry between Israel and the Arab world was more bleak than that of Ben-Gurion. His view was more consistent than that of Ben-Gurion as well. Sharett believed that Israel's long-term survival could not be assured unless it was supported by key powers in the international system. Ben-Gurion also recognized the constraints imposed on Israel by the great powers and therefore viewed major power support for war-related ventures as a necessary condition to war initiation.

But Ben-Gurion did not believe that a conciliatory policy was necessary to gain major power support, nor did he believe that such a conciliatory policy would improve Israel's relations with a major power to a point that Israel could rely on military help in time of need. Thus, the external drive to make peace was not as important for Ben-Gurion as it was for Sharett. Ben-Gurion envisioned the IDF to have a key role in the process of state building (Yaniv 1993). If the IDF was indeed to serve as a "melting pot," an environment that converts newcomers from all over the world into a new model Israeli citizen-soldier, it had to be an effective organization (Ben-Eliezer 1998, 210–12). To be such an organization, it had to have considerable combat experience. This experience would come from the exercise of force in limited military operations. But if agreements were signed with the Arab states, Israel could neither afford nor justify a large army. Thus the dilemma could be resolved by putting peace aside in favor of a military posture.

In the wake of the Sinai War, the Ben-Gurion conception emerged as victorious. It did not face a significant ideological challenge from the left wing of the political spectrum. Nobody was there to suggest that it may have been this choice of the militant route in the early 1950s that actually intensified the political—if not military—conflict with the Arab world. The Ben-Gurion legacy for the operational echelon of the Defense Ministry and the IDF was the same ethos of the Israeli soldier that was built gradually during the period of the reprisal raids in the early 1950s and was fortified during the Sinai War.

The Six Day War brought this ethos to new heights. But the war also created a new territorial reality and defined a new type of political discourse. Now the status quo ante bellum that had been perceived as a viable—even desirable—political solution before the war was no longer acceptable. The notion of defensible borders was now meshed with religious aspirations toward the holy places of Judaism in the West Bank. This religious element drew into the foreign and security discourse new political elements that—up to the Six Day War—had been willingly absent from the security dimension (Levy 2003, 133–35). The tacit deal between Ben-Gurion and the religious parties during the first two decades of Israel's independence had been one whereby these parties were in charge of the secular-religious status quo that had been established in 1948. In exchange, they supported the foreign and security policy, which was handled by the Mapai (and later the Labor) Party. The religious ministers in the government were among the most moderate and least militant elements in the Israeli government up to and immediately following the Six Day War.

The religious parties gradually emerged as a key player in the security game. They took over the settlement movement in the occupied territories—especially in the West Bank—and started bargaining with the leading secular parties on foreign and security matters. The traditional division of labor was disrupted, and it was disrupted in a one-sided manner. The religious parties supported expansionist policies, and they were also not willing to budge on state religion matters. The growing political instability in Israeli politics forced the ruling party (the first one to do so was the Likud Party under Begin in 1977) to bring in not only the moderate NRP but also the ultra-orthodox Agudat Israel and later on the Shas Party. The latter have reversed numerous liberal legislations.

More important, however, was the practical aspect of the disruption of the religious-secular arrangement, namely, the domination of the settlement movement by religious elements. Once religious ideology became a major drive in the settlement policy, an unspoken alliance was formed between annexationist elements in the Labor Party and the Likud Party, on the one hand, and national-religious groups such as Gush Emunim, on the other. This alliance was an instrumental factor in shaping the settlement policies of both governments. Likud-led governments were willing participants in this movement because—for a very long time—they believed that this policy served both ideological and security goals. Labor-led governments were too weak to resist this trend even when there were no national-religious elements in the coalition.

Taken together, these processes defined the Israeli intransigence with respect to the occupied territories over the 1967–73 era. The shock wave that the Yom Kippur War sent through Israeli political and social circles had polarizing effects on Israeli society (Barzilai 1996). On the one hand, the war did help drive home to some Israeli elites the notion that reliance on force as a means of ensuring control over the territories was bound to be extremely costly. The war also caused a dent in the invincible image of the Israeli Sabra. A growing number of Israelis, especially the secular western elites who had been the backbone of the pre-1973 Israeli militarism, began to treat the occupied territories as a liability rather than an asset and to view them as tradable commodities rather than as valued real estate.

On the other hand, the war increased the commitment of the religious and right wing to preserve the occupied territories, especially those in the

West Bank. This polarization of Israeli society on security and foreign affairs was not only a difference in political positions shared by political elites; it now went down to the mass public. By then, the difficulty of the government to deal with the settlement issue had already tied the government's hands and prevented any movement in the 1970s toward a settlement with Jordan. By the late 1960s and more so by the mid-1970s, Israeli voting patterns, where religious observance and socioeconomic status were negatively related to votes for Labor and leftist parties, had been engraved into the Israeli political system (Shamir and Arian 1999). The rise of the Likud Party to power in 1977 had a significant impact on Israeli settlement policy. Over the period of 1977–85 the settler population increased by an annual average of 35 percent. This increase declined to slightly over 12 percent per year over the period of 1986–92 (with the years 1990–92 showing higher than average rates of growth).

By the time the Oslo agreement was signed, the settler population in the occupied territories had reached 110,000—not including the new Jewish neighborhoods surrounding Jerusalem. This was seen by Israeli politicians as an insurmountable political hurdle. The Israeli goal—even of politicians who recognized the strategic folly of these settlements—now became arranging for a political settlement that would keep a large portion of these settlers within Israeli sovereignty.

The sociology and politics of Israeli diplomacy suggest that Israeli politicians were sometimes willing participants in a game where they willingly tied their hands in golden handcuffs that limited their diplomatic flexibility. In other cases, Israeli politicians were not aware of the adverse consequences of their policies until it was too late. In 2003, Ariel Sharon, the grand wazir of Israel's settlement policy, became aware of the utter folly of Israeli settlements in Gaza as well as in many parts of the West Bank. After three years of combat against the Palestinians the Israeli prime minister started talking about the corrupting effects of the occupation, about the demographic implications of continued Israeli presence in densely populated Palestinian territories, and about the need to make painful territorial concessions for peace. But by that time he had to deal with a population of 230,000 settlers, including 7,000 settlers in the Gaza Strip. The notion of unilateral Israeli withdrawal from the Gaza Strip—including dismantlement of the Jewish settlements there—emerged only after 950 Israelis had been killed and thousands more wounded defending those settlements. His enemies turned out to be not only the usual suspects—the right-wing politicians in his own party and the national religious and right-wing parties; the IDF itself now realized that unilateral withdrawal might amount to an admission of failure of its policies.

The sociology and politics of Israeli diplomacy provide a powerful explanation for the "over my dead body" syndrome. It explains how self-imposed barriers were constructed, and it also accounts for the late willingness to eradicate them when the price of their maintenance turned out to be excessive. This explanation also accounts for the Israeli violations of some agreements (e.g., Oslo) in order to pacify the settler population. The political sociology of Israeli policy also explains the convoluted Israeli proposals to the Palestinians at Camp David. Israeli politicians have actually shot themselves in the foot by trying to accommodate the extreme right. Rather than develop a coherent strategic argument that portrays the occupied territories as a strategic liability and the settlements in those territories as military, political, and social folly, they created for themselves a seemingly insurmountable political and social obstacle to peace.

3.3. *The Strategic Foundations of Intransigence*

An interesting question arising from this survey of Israel's ventures in peace diplomacy is this: What were the positions of the security community in peace-related deliberations? On what side of the fence were the generals in uniform when a trade of seemingly important security assets had to be made in exchange for peace-related benefits? Given the prominence of military considerations in Israel's peace diplomacy, the positions and assessments of key IDF officers in such deliberations would have played an important role in shaping the final outcome.

The quick and short response to this question is that the security community most often was sitting on the fence in peace-related deliberations. In many cases the generals did not take a clear position either in favor of a moderate policy or against it. In other cases they simply converted the policies of the civilian leaders into military plans. This applies to cases where these political plans were of a conciliatory nature or reflected an uncompromising position. This implies a seemingly proper role of the military echelon in political decision making: the military offers professional views and assessments, but it is not really engaged in influencing political decisions. A deeper probe into Israel's peace diplomacy suggests, however, that the military's role was more subtle than it appears at first blush. In most of the cases discussed here, the military was instrumental in mounting numerous obstacles and constraining the more moderate politicians.

The military's invisible obstacles to a more forthcoming peace policy were expressed in several ways over the years. First, the military's pressure on a proactive approach to reprisals and its strategic approach of escalation dominance in those operations often put a damper on diplomatic efforts. Under Sharett's reign, Dayan's IDF, with the help of Defense Minister Lavon, engaged in numerous military operations, some of them (such as the "mishap") unauthorized, that derailed peace efforts with Egypt. The Samu operation of November 1966 may have been instrumental in shattering the de facto peace between Israel and Jordan over the previous decade.

Second, in many cases, the intelligence assessments of Arab intentions were suspicious and skeptical toward peace overtures emanating from the Arab world. This was the case with Sadat's offer of an interim settlement along the Suez Canal in 1971 and with regard to Egypt's response to Jarring's questions in February 1971. This was the case with Sadat's offer to visit Jerusalem in November 1977, and this has generally been the IDF's intelligence attitude toward the Palestinians and Arafat. The IDF intelligence assessment of the consequences of an Israeli withdrawal from southern Lebanon also suggests a motivated bias against a unilateralist policy that would bring greater peace to Israel.

There were a number of exceptions, however, to this generally pessimistic and suspicious treatment of peace overtures from the Arab world. The intelligence community typically treated King Hussein of Jordan as a reliable partner to peace. The deputy head of the Mossad, Ephraim Halevi, was instrumental in the secret negotiations that led to the Israeli-Jordanian peace treaty of 1994. IDF intelligence under the leadership of Uri Sagie took very seriously Asad's strategic shift toward negotiations with Israel, claiming (in contrast to the Mossad's continued negative attitude) that Asad's shift was genuine and that he intended to make peace with Israel for the right price (Sagie 1998). On other occasions some senior IDF officers had actually challenged the intelligence's skeptical view of Sadat (Tamir 1988, 20–21).

Third, and most important, the IDF almost always developed maximalist plans for Israeli deployment in the context of peace agreements. It always relied on significant margins of safety of a territorial nature and intelligence-related requirements. These margins imposed significant constraints on decision makers in terms of their responses to peace proposals from the Arab world and the Palestinians. Some examples illustrate this point. Tamir (1988, 18–21) tells of Begin's proposal for peace with Egypt in December 1977, submitted to the Egyptians in the Ismailiya summit. This proposal was fairly minimalist, as it offered to keep Israeli settlements in the Rafah area, to maintain Israel's airfields and intelligence-monitoring station in the Sinai under Israeli control, and to propose a long-term withdrawal from the Sinai. Even so, this proposal was seen by the IDF as overly generous from a military point of view. IDF COS Mordechai (Motta) Gur drafted a proposal of his own, where Israel's final line of withdrawal would be an imaginary line connecting the city of El Arish in the north of the Sinai to the southern tip of the Sinai at Ras Muhammad. Had this proposal been accepted by the government, this probably would have put an end to the Israeli-Egyptian negotiations.

The IDF's proposals for a territorial settlement along the West Bank consistently demanded that the IDF control the Jordan Valley as a buffer against possible invasion from Jordan. Beyond the strategic folly of such a buffer, Israeli sovereignty along the Jordan Valley would have been unacceptable both to Jordan and to the Palestinians. The control of the Jordan Valley by the IDF was built in to Allon's proposal and became an axiom of Israel's security. All the plans drawn by the IDF in the context of peace negotiations involving the West Bank had this as a built-in imperative.

A similar conception guided the IDF's logic with regard to a possible peace treaty with Syria. The intelligence-monitoring station on Mount Hermon, labeled by an Israeli soldier of the Golani brigade as "the eyes of the State of Israel," was seen as an irreplaceable security asset, and it therefore had to stay under Israeli control. The IDF also felt that a military presence on the Golan Height was a military imperative (Shalev 1994; Bar Lev 1999). Whenever requested to define the military requirements of a possible agreement with Syria, the IDF opted for territorial control rather than for security arrangements of a nonterritorial nature. A similar approach characterized the IDF's attitude toward the implementation of agreements with the Palestinians. Throughout the Oslo process, the IDF insisted on continued presence in the occupied territories for security purposes, and it may well have been this presence that served to deepen the Palestinian suspicions of Israel's motives in these agreements or their frustrations with the truncated manner of the IDF's implementation of the Oslo Accords. These considerations also affected the contours of the Barak proposals at Camp David, which offered the Palestinians an impossible territorial settlement (Roy 2002, 11–14; Rabani 2001, 71–72; Pundak 2001, 34–35).

When politicians took these so-called security needs seriously, the IDF's proposals always served to put a damper on political moderation. It was only when politicians were able and willing to go beyond the narrow-minded military proposals that peace became possible. Alternatively, when the IDF was led by open-minded generals—and this did not happen very often—the IDF's positions in such negotiations were constructive.

The interesting aspect of civil-military relations in peace-related ventures has to do with the shift in the perspective of former military generals turned politicians with respect to military inputs in negotiations. Quite a few generals who had been extremely intransigent and risk averse regarding peace-related issues when wearing uniforms became significantly more flexible when they shed their uniforms and became civilian politicians. People such as Moshe Dayan, Yitzhak Rabin, Haim Bar-Lev, Ezer Weizman, Mordechai Gur, Ehud Barak, and Amnon Lipkin-Shahak are examples of this breed of generals. These people evolved into politicians who were able to see a broader picture and to understand strategy in terms that went beyond the strictly territorial parameters that had characterized their thinking when in uniform. Yet, even then, their perspectives were in many cases confined to a risk-avoiding approach when it came to security calculations. Other generals turned politicians never shed their narrow military focus in their latter careers. Rafael Eitan, Dan Shomron, Avigdor Kahalani, and Shaul Mofaz remained equally narrow minded and hostile to peace in their capacity as political leaders as they had been as military officers (Peri 2003). Up until 2003 Ariel Sharon was similar to the latter group. The recent changes in Sharon's philosophy seem to suggest that he may have moderated his views considerably, but the jury on that is still out.

The duality of the military approach toward peace and war is best illustrated in the military's preference for gradual and limited settlements, backed up by considerable military review of the events on the ground (which was done typically by the IDF staff, which had the only capacity to monitor these things). This was in sharp contrast to the focus of the military on quick and decisive military strikes when it came to crisis escalation. The IDF, if given a choice, was always in favor of partial, graduated implementation of agreements rather than full-blown deals. This was a prudent attitude in most cases, and it proved to be supported by many of the agreements Israel signed with its former enemies. However, the application of this approach as a blanket strategy clearly backfired in the Lebanon case, as well as in the case of the Oslo process.

4. CONCLUSION

Israel's peace diplomacy is a sharp contrast to its use of force strategy. If one could characterize Israel's military strategy under the phrase "he who dares—wins," then Israel's diplomacy is best characterized by the notion of "better safe than sorry." This reluctant peace policy was due to several factors: (1) the domination of military considerations and military bureaucracies in diplomatic matters, (2) the impact of psychological paranoia combined with a seemingly contradictory sense of arrogance, (3) the establishment of socially and politically self-imposed barriers to peace, and (4) the need to develop a new ethos of security as part of the state-building process. The costs of this policy have been enormous. They seem to have well outweighed any benefits that Israel's reluctance to make peace may have served. This reluctance will continue to haunt Israeli policy unless the fundamental factors that guide Israel's diplomacy undergo fundamental change. These factors may well endanger even the significant peace-related achievements that were made over time.

PART V

Causes and Implications of the Mismanagement of National Security & Foreign Policy

$$— \ 11 \ —$$

The Structure and Process
of National Security and
Foreign Policy in Israel

I. INTRODUCTION

This study has identified a number of serious problems of a continuing and persistent nature in the ways Israel designed and carried out its security and foreign policy. These problems are recurrent over time and across policy areas. In each of the preceding chapters I attempted to account for the underlying causes of the policy problems I identified. I examined different explanations that have appeared in the analytical and historical literature and evaluated their plausibility. In quite a few cases I offered alternatives to prevailing explanations of Israeli policies and behaviors. In some cases my explanations were the only ones offered simply because there have been few or no systematic studies of such issues as Israeli clandestine interventions in intra-Arab affairs and Israel's peace diplomacy. As I stated in chapter 1, the explanations were neither simple nor elegant. In many cases I argued that the actual policies were due to a multitude of factors and processes and could not be explained by one or even a few overarching causes.

Nevertheless, throughout the book I have argued repeatedly that policy-making in Israel has always been and continues to be dominated by a centralized, self-serving, and self-perpetuating security community. The structure of this community and the way it affects policy, relative to other bodies in the Israeli political and bureaucratic system, seems to be an overriding factor that has affected Israel's policies over time and across issues. In this chapter I explore the linkages between the structure of the Israeli foreign and security community and policy outcomes. I argue that the ways in which the Israeli security community is organized account for its deficient behavior in a wide array of policy areas. Moreover, the lack of proper oversight on this community accounts for the continuous policy failures and for the fact that there have been so many self-perpetuating follies over the years.

Clearly, structure is not everything. Nor is it completely deterministic in terms of its effects on policy. When making public policy, people, their ideas, and their personalities matter. The interpersonal relationships among people have a major impact on policy-making and policy implementation. Opportunities and challenges in the nation's external environment and the state's basic attributes define to a large extent the parameters within which the state operates. Internal political, economic, and social processes that operate parallel to the formal and informal policy networks have an important bearing on the process and outcome of the policy. All these factors may vary from one issue to another, from one point in time to another, and from one policy problem to another.

The structure of the security and foreign policy communities is but a filter through which external and internal inputs are converted into perceptions of problems that need to be resolved and into solutions that are available for their resolution (Brecher 1972, 117–33). But it is a very effective filter nevertheless, and therefore it deserves close attention. A significant number of studies on Israeli security and foreign policy have analyzed the external and internal settings of Israel's foreign and security doctrine. However, there is relatively little analysis of the structures within such policies are made. Brecher's (1972) monumental work is perhaps the single most important study of the structure of Israel's foreign policy setting. It does pay considerable attention to the analysis of the military establishment, but its focus is on the foreign policy system. As we will see, one of the key problems of Israel's policy-making architecture is that its foreign policy system was always weak and subordinate to the security community. International and foreign policy considerations were, for the most part, secondary to security considerations and military objectives. Several studies that focus on civil-military relations (e.g., Perlmutter 1969; Ben Meir 1995; S. Cohen 2000, 2003; Levy 2003) note the problematic nature of these relationships. But their discussion of the structural aspects of these relations is very general and not directly tied to fundamental policy issues.

The structure of the foreign and security system concerns the institutions that are engaged in making policy and the web of relationship among them. Clearly, the number of such institutions is vast and the relationships among all these institutions are extremely complex. Moreover, there are multiple relationships between organizations that bear formal responsibility for making and carrying out security and foreign policy and other social institutions. In many areas, the boundaries between national security institutions and other institutions are blurred. For example, since 1967 the IDF has been engaged in police operations in the occupied territories. The IDF was and still is engaged in societal functions such as settlement, education, and disaster relief. Thus, a comprehensive analysis of the security and foreign affairs community would require a separate volume.

This chapter seeks to fill this relative void in the literature in a limited manner. It is not designed to be a description of the foreign and security bureaucracy. Rather, it discusses how this structure accounts for the findings of this study. The key themes of the present chapter are as follows:

1. Israeli policy-making on national security and foreign affairs is characterized by an overwhelming preponderance of the security community. This preponderance is due both to the strength and effectiveness of the IDF and other security-related institutions (e.g., the secret services) and to the weakness and ineffectiveness of the foreign policy and diplomatic community.

2. The dominance of the security community is enhanced by the lack of a civilian institution that provides decision makers or legislators with staff-related infrastructure. Existing civilian institutions such as the National Security Council (NSC) or the Ministry of Foreign Affairs's Department of Policy Research and Planning (DPRP) do not come even close to fulfilling this function.

3. The infiltration of the security community into the policy community is helped by the significant infusion of former senior military officers into the political arena. Many former generals captured the highest posts in the policy community. This infiltration of former generals into policy areas had some interesting implications for policy—some of them quite surprising— but in general it helped sustain the dominance of security considerations over other considerations and the dominance of the security establishment over the foreign policy establishment in the policy-making process.

4. The legislature has consistently failed to oversee and limit the dominance of the IDF and the security community in foreign and security affairs. Although it is constitutionally entrusted with the task of overseeing and criticizing government operations, the Knesset has neither the tools nor the political will to do so. Despite repeated efforts to fulfill this task, the Knesset Committee on Foreign and Security Affairs (CFSA) and its subcommittees have failed to impact the security community in any significant way.

5. Despite an admirable record of liberal ruling on matters of individual rights and liberties, the Supreme Court and the judiciary generally have displayed a basic deference to the positions of the security community. This pattern consists of repeated rulings in favor of the security community on petitions concerning the behavior of the IDF or the government vis-à-vis the occupied territories. It also concerns violations of basic human rights of Israelis who were charged with or convicted of violations of security and secrecy laws.

6. The implications of the dominant influence of the security community in policy-making are fairly fundamental. Above and beyond the whims and preferences of individual politicians, the complex and polarized structure of the party system, and the substantive issues that have been discussed in this study, the structure of the policy-making system provides a strategic and comprehensive explanation for the wide-ranging array of findings in this book. Specifically,

(a) this structure accounts for the trigger-happy and risk-taking management of violent conflicts;

(b) it accounts for the converse pattern of risk-shunning behavior in the management of peace diplomacy;

(c) it accounts for quite a few harebrained schemes of manipulating the domestic system of other states and actors in the region;

(d) it accounts for the ability to run a covert and unsupervised nuclear program that is driven by technocrats rather than by strategists and political leaders; and

(e) it accounts for the ability of the security community to cover up strategic mistakes and to prevent a critical evaluation of its actions and policies.

I examine four elements of this structure that are fundamental to the understanding of the policy-making process over a wide array of issues: (1) the intelligence community; (2) the military bureaucracy; (3) the political setting, in particular the government and the Knesset; and (4) the judiciary and the civilian settings, which are supposed to oversee, control, and criticize the bureaucracy.[1] In the last section of this chapter, I connect the structure of the policy-making system to its social and political environment.

2. THE INTELLIGENCE COMMUNITY

Three principal organizations have traditionally been responsible for collecting, analyzing, and interpreting information that affect Israel's security and foreign policy: the military intelligence branch of the IDF (AMAN, to use the Hebrew acronym), the Institute for Intelligence and Special Operations (Mossad), and the General Secret Service (GSS, or SHABAK). The Foreign Ministry, through its network of embassies and consulates around the world, is an important source of intelligence and information—most of it unclassified. The role of the Foreign Ministry was institutionally expanded following the Yom Kippur intelligence fiasco.[2]

AMAN reports to the COS of the IDF and, through him, to the minister of defense. Mossad and SHABAK are part of the office of the prime minister and report to him or her directly. The DPRP reports to the foreign minister. There exists a coordinating committee, called the Committee of the Heads of Intelligence Services (VARASH, to use the Hebrew acronym), that is responsible for interagency coordination.

AMAN is by far the largest and best-funded intelligence agency. Its tasks include collection, analysis, and assessment of intelligence from all over the world, but its principal focus is on the Arab world and the non-Arab Middle East. AMAN's collection of resources includes human intelligence (HumInt), principally spies and informants; signal intelligence (SigInt), principally surveillance of communication and computer traffic; and visual intelligence (VisInt), principally satellite and aerial photography. It also feeds on field intelligence coming from IDF observation posts along Israeli borders through the intelligence staff departments in the various regional commands of the IDF. Data coming from AMAN's own resources, from the other intelligence agencies, as well as from public sources go through a first phase of screening and analysis within the various professional "desks" and then move to the research division. The research division is in charge of issuing the intelligence reports on a regular basis (daily, weekly, monthly, and annually) to the policy community. AMAN is in charge of the national intelligence estimate (NIE). Its principal task is to provide early warning of war preparations and of an impending war. However, in the early 1990s it was also put in charge of peace-related estimates, and it was heavily involved in establishing intelligence estimates on all aspects of the peace process during the 1990s (Sagie 1998, 234–35; Gazit 2003, 23).

The Mossad was involved primarily in espionage and connections with foreign intelligence services and organizations around the world, including the Arab world and the "periphery." It was the principal agency in charge of special operations abroad. These included the assassination, capture, and hijacking of Nazi war criminals; the assassination and intimidation of scientists who aided the Arab states in weapons development; the assassination of PLO operatives inside and outside of the Middle East; and so forth (Black and Morris 1991; Melman and Raviv 1989). As a result of the recommendations of the Agranat inquiry commission in 1974, the Mossad established its own research branch in an effort to increase the pluralism of intelligence estimates and to remove the monopoly of AMAN on this aspect of intelligence work (Gazit 2003, 15–16).

SHABAK's traditional areas of responsibility prior to the Six Day War included (1) engaging in counterespionage, (2) detecting and interrogating subversive activity among the Arab population in Israel, (3) detecting and interrogating subversive activity among the Jewish population in Israel, and (4) protecting the prime minister and a few other political functionaries—much like the U.S. Secret Service. Following the Six Day War, SHABAK was entrusted with two additional tasks. First, it was put in charge of intelligence operations—both intelligence collection and some special operations—in the occupied territories. Second, it was entrusted with securing Israeli institutions and airlines abroad. Because it now had to deal with intelligence regarding the occupied territories, SHABAK formed its own research branch, but this was a fairly small operation. AMAN's research branch had maintained its principal responsibility for estimating Palestinian intentions.

There were quite a few debates and conflicts among intelligence services. These consisted of conflicts over the execution of special operations, the use and activation of sources, and differences in interpretation of intelligence. The major and persistent conflict was on areas of responsibility, namely, around the question of "who is in charge of what." For the most part this was a typical bureaucratic turf war. In other instances, however, the conflicts were due to ambiguous or nonexistent definitions of boundaries. This competition notwithstanding, there was a fair degree of cooperation and coordination among the services over the years. The domination of AMAN over NIEs was established in government decisions and regulations and was supported by a disproportionate allocation of resources to its various organs.

Shlomo Gazit, a former head of AMAN, notes (2003, 10):

> Operational successes—that have received international acclaim—as well as the stunning victory of the IDF in the Six Day War . . . built the reputation of the intelligence community as a body which nothing escapes it. This reputation was not only the perception among the general public, but was also prevalent among the officer corps of the IDF, among the political leadership of the state, and—unfortunately—among intelligence people themselves.
>
> Under these circumstances, when the Egyptian-Syrian surprise attack of October 6, . . . 1973 occurred, the shock was particularly great. Therefore . . . there was an urgent need to understand and explain what happened, and a strong urge to search for, and take measures that would prevent the recurrence of another intelligence failure of this sort.

The image of an omniscient intelligence community could not be further from the truth even before the Yom Kippur surprise attack. It is true that the Mossad staged some impressive operations in the 1950s and 1960s, such as the capture of Adolph Eichman, the sabotage of the Egyptian SSM program, and the forging of intelligence ties and political or military cooperation with periphery groups and states. Yet, these operations had little to do with the provision of accurate intelligence estimates to policymakers. AMAN had its share of major failures prior to the Six Day War, and these were exacerbated in the 1969–73 period. Even the Yom Kippur fiasco was not sufficiently severe to shake the intelligence community from its tendency for overconfidence and its propensity to make strategic errors. I discuss very briefly some of the key intelligence failures in Israel's history and analyze their causes and implications as an introduction for a broader evaluation of the problems of national intelligence making in Israel.

2.1. *Intelligence Failures in Israel's History*

In a separate study (Maoz 2004d) I develop and examine a broad analytic framework of intelligence failures. A classification of intelligence failures is offered, which provides—among other things—a better understanding

of the causes and implications of faulty intelligence. I discuss each of the
Israeli intelligence failures within the different categories provided in the
other study. These failures are listed chronologically.

The "mishap." The key cause of the "mishap" was a faulty intelligence assessment of a "false alarm" type, namely, the forecasting of an
imminent danger to a state's security that was not really happening. In
this case, IDF intelligence warned that the Anglo-Egyptian agreement for
the removal of the British troops from the Suez Canal would expose Israel
to direct threat by Egyptian forces. The consequence of this prediction
was the unauthorized activation of the Jewish spy ring in Egypt that led to
the "mishap" of 1954. The "mishap" is discussed in chapter 9.

The Soviet-Egyptian weapons deal of 1955. This was a combination of
two types of intelligence failures. First, it was a case of false alarm. IDF
intelligence interpreted this weapons deal as commensurate with Egyptian offensive intentions, suggesting that Egypt was bent on using these
weapons to attack Israel in the future. The actual Egyptian intent was primarily defensive. Second, this was a case of incorrect estimate of capabilities. IDF intelligence considerably inflated the Egyptian capabilities, presenting the postagreement balance of forces as having fundamentally
shifted in favor of the Egyptians. This could not have been further from
the truth, especially after the Israeli-French weapons deal of June 1956. I
discuss this event in chapter 2.

The Rotem crisis. (Bar Joseph 1996). This was a tactical surprise that
could have been converted into a strategic surprise. IDF intelligence was
slow to detect the insertion of Egyptian troops into the Sinai in February
1960—in violation of the tacit demilitarization agreement of 1957. Fortunately for Israel, Nasser had no intention of attacking it, and the prudent management of the crisis by both Egypt and Israel led to its peaceful
resolution.

The 1967 surprise. This case concerns the failure of AMAN to
understand the threat perception of Syria and Egypt as a result of Israeli
actions and threats in 1966 and 1967. Accordingly, AMAN failed to
anticipate the insertion of Egyptian troops into the Sinai on May 15,
1967. This falls under the category of misinterpretation of opponent's
behavior. The case is briefly discussed in chapter 3.

The failure to anticipate Soviet involvement in the War of Attrition.
AMAN underestimated Soviet willingness to involve Soviet troops in
the fighting. This was also a misinterpretation of the opponent's behavior. This case is discussed in chapter 4.

The 1971 Sadat peace initiative. AMAN discounted both the capacity of the Sadat regime to survive and—more important—the seriousness and significance of the dual aspects of the Sadat peace initiative: the response to the Jarring questions that indicated Egyptian readiness to enter into a full peace treaty with Israel in exchange for the Sinai and the initiative for an interim agreement along the Suez Canal. This was also a misinterpretation of the opponent's behavior. This initiative is discussed in chapter 10.

The 1973 Yom Kippur surprise. This surprise had two components. The first and extensively researched component was the failure to antici-pate the Egyptian-Syrian attack on October 6. This component falls under the category of surprise attacks. The second, less studied but more fundamental, surprise consisted of the failure to understand the oppo-nent's military doctrine, technology, and their combination in the Yom Kippur War. The surprise is discussed in chapter 5.

The 1976 municipal elections in the West Bank. SHABAK, the mili-tary and civilian administrations, and AMAN supported the notion that municipal elections in the main cities of the West Bank would result in the election of moderate pro-Jordanian mayors and would erode the sup-port for the PLO. This falls under the category of failure to understand long-term political processes. These elections are discussed in chapter 9.

The 1977 Sadat initiative. AMAN failed to detect the change in Sadat's approach to a peace treaty through direct negotiations with Israel. More important, it interpreted Sadat's offer to visit Jerusalem as a decep-tive move, under whose cover Egypt was said to launch a surprise attack against Israel. This was a case of false alarm. It is discussed in chapter 10.[3]

The 1985–2000 Lebanon quagmire. This failure was twofold. First, AMAN failed to anticipate the rise of Shi'ite opposition to the IDF in the security zone prior to the decision to stay in a security zone in 1985. Sec-ond, AMAN and Mossad failed to understand the goals and modus operandi of Hizballah, repeatedly claiming that Hizballah would attack Israeli settlements if the IDF withdrew from southern Lebanon. Both cases fall under the category of failure to understand long-term political processes. They are discussed extensively in chapter 6.

The 1987 intifada. The scope, severity, and duration of the first intifada came as a shock and surprise to AMAN and SHABAK.[4] This was also a failure to understand long-term political processes. It is dis-cussed in chapter 7.

Iraqi WMD capabilities in 1990–91. AMAN and Mossad were aware of the Iraqi chemical weapons program, as well as of the Iraqi nuclear weapons program. They also had a fairly good knowledge of Iraqi SSM capability. They had not been aware of the extent of the Iraqi advances in nuclear technology, nor were they aware of the extent of the Iraqi biological weapons program. These were revealed only by the UNSCOM inspections following the Gulf War of 1991 and by the defection of Hussein Kamel, Saddam Hussein's son in-law, to Jordan in 1993.[5]

Iraqi WMD capabilities in 2003.   AMAN overestimated Iraqi missile, chemical, and biological capabilities on the eve of the Iraq War in 2003. As a result, Israel spent over $1 billion in resupplying gas masks and equipment for defense against chemical weapons. There is also evidence suggesting that AMAN provided American and British intelligence with inaccurate information regarding Iraqi WMD capabilities, which had been deliberately doctored to boost the position of the two major powers vis-à-vis the international community in the diplomatic campaign to arrange for a multilateral war coalition.[6]

The Israeli intelligence community also had a number of important successes. For example, in the early 1990s, AMAN under General Uri Sagie predicted correctly that Hafez Asad would make a strategic commitment to peace with Israel in return for regaining the Golan Height. We have also mentioned AMAN's accurate forecast about the unreliability of the Christians and the adverse consequences of an alliance with them for the planned invasion of Lebanon in 1982. Finally, AMAN and SHABAK accurately predicted the outbreak of a Palestinian intifada if the final status Israeli-Palestinian talks failed to yield an agreement. In each of these cases, however, external observers—including quite a few academics who had not been privy to classified information—made similar forecasts on the basis of strictly unclassified information.

An analysis of these intelligence failures, as well as the intelligence coups—successful predictions of the intentions and capabilities of opponents despite efforts at deception by the opponent—shows that they were due to a fairly small number of factors. First, without exception, all cases of intelligence failure were due to faulty analysis of available information; they were never due to missing information. The information available to the intelligence community when it made accurate forecasts was not significantly more precise, unambiguous, or specific than in the cases of intelligence failures. In both intelligence failures and intelligence coups, significant items of information were missing, data contained numerous ambiguities, and indicators were consistent with a number of different—even diametrically opposed—hypotheses about adversaries' intentions or capabilities.

Second, in most intelligence failures, preconceived theories dominated critical inspection of data. On the other hand, intelligence coups were of two types. One type consisted of situations where the underlying theories of leading intelligence specialists were in line with the more indicative data. In other words, the theories were "correct" and the data just corroborated them. The other and more significant case was the one in which intelligence analysts were willing to critically reexamine their theories in light of data that challenged preexisting beliefs. In other words, when intelligence analysts were willing to engage in a critical dialogue in which multiple hypotheses about the opponent's intentions and capabilities were contrasted with actual indicators in a critical manner (Ben Israel 1999), shifts in prior estimates led to accurate forecasts.

Third, some of the more significant intelligence failures resulted from the failure of subordinates to press their views—which turned out to be ex post facto correct—with their superiors. These cases consisted of the reluctance of senior intelligence officers to insist on warning political leaders when their immediate superiors held opposing views. Such was the tragic case of Yehoshua Saguy before and during the early stages of the Lebanon War (see chap. 6). At lower levels, senior intelligence analysts failed to go over the heads of their superiors in the intelligence community and challenge their superiors' forecasts to the COS. This was the case on the eve of the Yom Kippur War in 1973. Several intelligence analysts—including the head of the Syrian "desk" in AMAN and the head of the 8200 SigInt unit—strongly believed that the Egyptians and Syrians had been planning a surprise attack, but their views were dismissed by their superiors in AMAN (Ben Porat 1991; Bar Joseph 2001).

Fourth, a special category of intelligence failures raises the suspicion that the intelligence community—or at least significant parts thereof—tailored intelligence estimates to what they believed were the political preference of superiors within the defense establishment or in the political arena. The intelligence estimates of AMAN in 1954 and in 1955–56 and those in 1971 regarding Sadat's peace initiative may well be cases in point. A similar problem of intelligence failure concerns the tendency to cover up past errors by generating consistently flawed forecasts despite contradictory evidence. The intelligence forecasts about the Hizballah's expected behavior following Israeli withdrawal from the security zone in southern Lebanon is a case in point (see chap. 6).

Finally, a major source of intelligence failures was the lack of net assessment—intelligence assessments based on an interactive analysis of the effect of one's own policy on an opponent's intentions and capabilities. As opposed to SHABAK, which deals with subversive Jewish activity—the mandate of both AMAN and the Mossad prevents them from analyzing the effects of Israeli behavior on the intentions and capabilities of the Arab states. For that reason, there is a natural tendency—as well as an epistemological inclination—to view the opponent's behavior as driven primarily by inherent needs and intentions rather than as a logical response to Israel's behavior. The failure to understand the impact of Israeli policy on Arab behavior was at the heart of the failure of the intelligence community to forecast correctly the first escalatory phase in the May–June 1967 crisis. It was also at the heart of the failure to foresee the emergence of Hamas in the occupied territories and of Hizballah in Lebanon. It was the root of the failure to predict the outbreak of the first intifada, and it was an underlying cause of the Yom Kippur intelligence failure.

Contrary to conventional wisdom, pluralism in the intelligence community is no safeguard against intelligence failure. In some of the most pernicious intelligence failures in Israel's history there were divergent views among different branches of the intelligence community. The same applies to some of the most outstanding cases of intelligence success. Likewise, there were both cases of intelligence failure as well as cases of intelligence successes that were characterized by consensus among different intelligence services as well as within each of these services.

This less than luminous record of performance of the intelligence community accounts in part for quite a few poor policy choices in Israel's history. Both military commanders and political decision makers received inaccurate or irrelevant information or failed to receive relevant and indicative data about their external environment. In some cases—Weizman and Begin's override of AMAN's warning of Sadat's visit to Jerusalem is an example—decision makers made prudent and adaptive decisions despite faulty intelligence forecasts.

While I cannot offer a comprehensive explanation of these failures, it is clear that one central characteristic of these failures was some degree of rigidity in the analysis of available information. This rigidity has both structural-bureaucratic and sociological causes. I discuss these causes in the next two sections.

2.2. Structural Stagnation and Efforts at Reform in the Intelligence Community

The dominance of military and security considerations over other dimensions of policy is facilitated, to a large extent, by the near monopoly that the intelligence community possesses over the information available to decision makers. It is therefore important to understand how the structure and process of intelligence serve to create the key patterns of Israeli security and foreign policy that were discussed in the previous chapter.

Over the years, there have been several attempts to reform the intelligence community in Israel. Most of these entailed proposals of reshaping and reforming specific intelligence agencies, redefining the areas of responsibility of each, and designing new institutions that connect the intelligence and the policy communities (such as a special adviser for intelligence to the prime minister, the creation of the NSC, and so forth).[7] However, the bottom line of these reforms is very simple: *plus ça change, plus c'est la meme chose*—"the more things change, the more they remain the same." AMAN preserved its position of primacy vis-à-vis the other intelligence services with respect to virtually all matters of intelligence, with the exception of the Palestinians. Regarding the Palestinians, SHABAK's research branch became increasingly influential but still not dominant. The heads of AMAN were successful at resisting various efforts to change the balance of power among different intelligence agencies. They also managed to render ineffective any new position and institution that was supposed to mediate between AMAN and the key decision makers—such as the special adviser for intelligence to the prime minister or the NSC. AMAN also resisted any significant internal changes in its methods of intelligence assessment beyond some cosmetic alterations.[8]

The AMAN research branch deals not only with military affairs and with the Arab world; it consistently furnishes assessments of political and diplomatic affairs concerning the international system as a whole. It assesses on a regular basis U.S. policy and positions on both Middle Eastern and global affairs. During the cold war it was the principal source for assessing Soviet intentions and behavior in the Middle East and elsewhere. AMAN also deals with long-term and large-scale regional processes such as the effect of fundamentalist movements on the stability of Middle East regimes, as well as with economic issues such as oil prices. The head of AMAN and the head of the research department are regular participants in cabinet meetings; they appear before the cabinet much more often than does the director general of the Foreign Ministry, even when not just strictly security issues are discussed.

Mossad has remained mostly an intelligence-gathering and espionage agency. Its research unit has little impact on actual decision-making processes, except in cases where decision makers have felt more comfortable with Mossad's assessments than with those of AMAN. However, during the decade of 1991–2002, there was a gradual erosion in the ability of Mossad to influence decision makers, due to the focus on the peace process and to the fact that AMAN got increasingly involved in peace-related issues. There was also a sharp decline in Mossad's operational capabilities and quite a large number of operational fiascoes (e.g., attempts to plant listening devices in the Iran mission in Geneva, the capture of two Mossad agents in Cyprus, and the bungled assassination attempt of Khaled Mash'al in Jordan). The research branch of Mossad has a fraction of the manpower and technology of its AMAN counterpart (although Mossad people are better trained academically than AMAN's research branch officers). Their research tasks are more long term and general than those of AMAN, and they are not exposed to as much classified (especially electronic intelligence [ElInt]) material as are AMAN researchers.

The Foreign Ministry's DPRP has been marginalized even within its own ministry. It is manned by diplomats between tours of duty and has only a small staff of professional researchers. Most foreign ministers have not paid much attention to this department or to its reports. The availability of classified information to DPRP is extremely limited, and its members are outside the intelligence loop on most issues. They serve more as suppliers of intelligence assessments and less as recipients of intelligence reports. The director general of the Foreign Ministry is not a participant of the VARASH coordination process.

In light of this situation, it appears that AMAN's near monopoly over national intelligence estimates has not eroded despite its numerous and fairly fundamental errors of judgment. In the course of fifty-six years of history, only three intelligence chiefs were removed from office, and only one of them—Eliyahu Zeira—due to a failure of estimate. The other two— Benjamin Givli and Yehoshua Saguy—were removed for reasons other than faulty intelligence estimates.[9] The accountability of the intelligence community given fairly grave errors of judgment seems to have been minimal at best.

As long as this monopoly is preserved, political leaders will continue to depend on AMAN for information that is crucial for decision making. More important, many political leaders have been unequipped to deal with raw intelligence material and thus have depended on the analysis and interpretation of this material by intelligence analysts. This implies that a military institution that reports to the COS and the defense minister is in charge of both the collection and interpretation of intelligence for political decision makers. The head of AMAN and the head of the research department are appointed by the COS, and their promotion and advancement depend on him. The mandate for NIEs for peace and war is therefore bureaucratically subordinate to the interests of the IDF. The professionalism of AMAN researchers notwithstanding, there is a built-in tension between the interests of the IDF and AMAN's capacity and willingness to furnish estimates that may directly challenge those interests.

2.3. *The Sociology of the Intelligence Community*

The sociology of the intelligence community—with or without the dominance of AMAN—is also an important determinant of the inherent bias in intelligence analyses. Gazit (2003, 47) points out that only four out of the fifteen individuals who have served as heads of AMAN had prior intelligence background. The other came from the cadre of field commanders. This is only the tip of the iceberg, however. The environment of AMAN is one that fosters antipluralism of the worst kind. The screening and recruitment procedures of intelligence officers are extremely selective prior to the conscription of young kids to the IDF. However, many of these people go to Unit 8200, which is in charge of SigInt. Those who go to the research branch have also been identified as possessing high analytic skills. Yet their academic training consists of predominantly two principal competencies: mastery of Arabic (and/or Farsi) and knowledge of Middle East history. A vast majority of the officers in the research branch are graduates of the Departments of Middle East History in the major research universities in Israel. Only a small minority is trained in social science disciplines, and even a smaller fraction of officers in the research branch of AMAN are trained in modern social science—including training in statistical methods and mathematical modeling.[10]

There are several important implications of this kind of sociology. First, there is no question that mastery of Middle Eastern languages is a key asset for intelligence work that focuses primarily on the Middle East. Nor is there any doubt that mastery of the history of the states and actors that AMAN research officers are required to follow is an important skill for their work. At the same time, lack of a proper academic background in the politics, economics, and social processes is a severe liability of such researchers. Second, social sciences—their significant limitations notwithstanding—emphasize structural and behavioral aspects of the kind of processes that AMAN people are required to assess on a regular basis. Without proper theoretical and empirical background, the work of

AMAN researchers is based mostly on the analysis and interpretations of written texts. When texts provide unambiguous evidence of intended behavior, this is of course not a liability. However, the modal pattern of intelligence work entails dealing with multiple, often contradictory texts. More important, some of the most important headways in terms of analysis and interpretation of contradictory data have been made in the social sciences. There was and still exists a constant resistance in the intelligence community in general, and in AMAN in particular, to the introduction of social scientific methodologies, from social psychology to game theory, into intelligence analysis. The principal method of intelligence assessment still remains a "seat of the pants" intuitive analysis of intelligence data.

In light of this fairly primitive approach to intelligence, it is not surprising that AMAN has not done all that well over the years. Where AMAN truly has succeeded is in its bureaucratic struggle with other intelligence bodies and in ingenious cover-ups of its fiascos that prevented any serious effort at accountability and structural reform. A recent example of the shielding of AMAN from true accountability is the effort by the subcommittee on intelligence services (SCSS) of the Knesset's CFSA to investigate AMAN's intelligence failure prior to the Iraq War of 2003. The subcommittee's report (Steinitz 2004a) contains sharp criticism of the intelligence community and of the IDF's behavior during the war that falls into the realm of false alarms. The reaction of the COS was to dismiss the subcommittee's report as being at odds with reality. It is unlikely that any of the recommendations of this subcommittee will be implemented by the government or by the IDF. It is unlikely—as we will see in the next sections—that the Knesset will impose these reforms on the executive branch, the way the U.S. Congress forced the Bush administration to reform U.S. intelligence according to the 9/11 commission's recommendations.

Since there existed no body with the resources and information to challenge AMAN's monopoly in the civilian government bureaucracy, there was almost never a real competition between AMAN and the other branches of the intelligence community. Moreover, the research departments of the other intelligence services are staffed largely by retired AMAN officers, thus sharing the same academic and organizational background as their AMAN counterparts.

Up until 1998 Israel lacked a civilian NSC. When the NSC was established by a government decree in 1998, it immediately confronted strong opposition from the IDF—especially from AMAN—and the NSC personnel were barred from access to intelligence data. Most national security advisers who have headed the NSC since 1998 have come from the IDF or the Mossad,[11] and even when these people tried to engage in an effort to develop a mechanism for net assessment, they confronted fierce opposition from the IDF. The IDF also used its influence to block long-term policy planning through the application of simulations by the NSC.

Since situational assessments are essential for the diagnosis of problems by civilian decision makers, AMAN has very powerful control over the most sensitive type of information that the decision makers receive. The way in which information is relayed and—more important— in which it is framed in the intelligence reports has a strong effect on decision makers. With a fairly poor record of performance over the course of Israel's history, it is no wonder therefore that policy-making in a wide array of issues is laden with problems and deficiencies. Concomitantly, such intelligence estimates are likely to be clouded by military considerations, due to the inherent loyalties of the intelligence to its principal customers—the IDF. Gazit (2003, 54) cites a statement by Ehud Barak in the 1980s, while serving as head of AMAN: "There is a looming danger that the direct link [of AMAN] to the military system would give birth to a bias—even a subconscious one—to assign the military-technical side of reality a larger part of the situational picture than other elements."

The linkage between intelligence estimates whose sources were a military bureaucracy and some of the principal findings of this study is quite transparent. A trigger-happy policy on national security affairs and a risk-averse peace policy were both based on such intelligence reports. The lack of independent sources of information—especially in the earlier period—created an almost exclusive reliance on military intelligence. As long as the near monopoly of AMAN on the information and assessments reaching the policymakers is maintained, and despite the image of growing pluralism in the intelligence community, the domination of military considerations over political ones will continue to characterize Israeli foreign and security affairs.

3. THE MILITARY BUREAUCRACY

Intelligence provides one of the key inputs for national security decision making. But intelligence alone does not determine the outcomes of this policy. This is especially so when policy is not a one-shot decision but rather a more long-term series of commitments. In such situations, other factors become increasingly important. Constraints on the ability of the system to carry out certain courses of action, the personal and institutional preferences of the decision makers, and feedback mechanisms have a significant impact on the policy itself. For example, Israel's nuclear policy may have been sensitive to intelligence assessments of long-term trends in the Arab world at the inception of this policy. But as this policy progressed it may have taken a course that was affected by factors other than specific intelligence reports on the capabilities and intentions of Israel's enemies. The same applies to other aspects of Israel's R&D in weapons systems.

Long-term policies are also governed by "decision regimes," that is, by a set of procedures, norms, and conventions that determine—over a fairly long period of time—how decisions are made as well as the substantive content of those decisions (Kuperman 1999). In these situations—for example, response to guerrilla or terrorist attacks—specific intelligence is still significant, but the characteristics of the decision regime tend to have a greater impact on the general orientation of the cabinet. The menu of options available to the cabinet may be determined by factors other than specific intelligence.

The impact of the military bureaucracy on political decision making has been evident throughout the book. It was expressed in the overwhelming dominance of security and military considerations over diplomatic and political considerations in matters of war and peace alike. It was largely responsible—though not exclusively so—for the risk-seeking behavior of decision makers during security crises and for their reluctance and risk avoidance in the face of opportunities to make peace. It was apparent in the attempts to manipulate internal political processes within Arab states and between Arab states. It was apparent in the nearly autonomous development of Israel's nuclear policy—which bore no relationship to Israel's security needs and little attention to the escalatory and destabilizing implications of this program for regional security. It was apparent in the lack of self-inspection, given consistently failing policies in Lebanon and the two intifadas. And it was evident in the lack of accountability of military and intelligence bureaucrats in light of repeated strategic failures.

Three key factors explain the primacy of the military and security bureaucracy in the making of Israel's foreign and security policy: (1) the effectiveness of the military bureaucracy compared to the total lack of comparable staff bodies in the civilian establishment, (2) the involvement of retired military officers in politics, and (3) the almost blind respect to the IDF by civilian decision makers.

3.1. *Military Efficiency and Civilian Void in Foreign and Security Affairs*

The IDF possesses the only institutionalized staff that is capable of preparing the groundwork for well-organized decision making in foreign and security affairs. There exists no civilian institution—let alone a civilian institution of similar efficiency and scope—that can counter the IDF's ability to present a situational picture, lay out policy alternatives, analyze the costs and benefits associated with each alternative, and identify constraints. This is not to suggest that other bodies, such as the Ministry of Foreign Affairs, are incapable of doing similar staff work on foreign policy. The fact is that over the course of Israel's history—with the possible exception of Sharett's tenure as foreign minister—this ministry simply did not compete with the IDF. The only comparable bureaucracy in terms of staff-related resources and efficiency is the Finance Ministry. But most of the confrontations between the Finance and the Defense Ministries have taken place outside of the cabinet or the Knesset committees. Consequently, complex decisions on foreign and security affairs tend to be dominated by papers and analyses presented by the IDF and other Defense Ministry bodies. Decision makers who have no access to the military must rely on their own intuition, knowledge, and experience. It is very seldom that the government is presented with well-prepared options that are based on systematic staff work that does not originate from the military or the security bureaucracy.

The clearest expression of this huge imbalance of decision-making tools on military versus nonmilitary considerations concerns processes of crisis management. Several examples illustrate this point. In 1956, after a small circle of politicians and military officers prepared the diplomatic and political groundwork for the Sinai invasion, Ben-Gurion brought the information about the impending unprovoked attack on Egypt to the cabinet. The cabinet was confronted with a well-laid plan that included collusion with France and Britain, a military plan of attack on the Egyptian army in the Sinai, and no real vision of what would happen or what should happen after the war. No alternatives were presented. The status quo was implied, but the framing of an ominous strategic future if this attack was not carried out made this status quo quite unappealing. Nobody challenged the flawed presentation of the balance of power provided by Dayan. Nobody was there to question what might be the reaction of the United States and the Soviet Union to this attack, and nobody was able to uncover the hidden agenda of attempting to over-throw Nasser by outside aggression.

A similar situation prevailed in the 1967 crisis. The IDF (following a colossal intelligence failure to predict the Egyptian entry into the Sinai) was the only body that provided a threat assessment. There was no alter-native threat assessment—political, economic, or diplomatic—in the cabinet. Contrary to the IDF's recommendation, however, the moderate ministers in the cabinet were able to give diplomacy a chance, but this was due more to the fact that Prime Minister Eshkol and some key minis-ters urged prudence even after Nasser closed the Tiran Straits. Still, the pressure of the IDF, aided by the full mobilization of reserves, slowly eroded the moderates' capacity to resist the military option. During the war itself, nobody countered effectively the IDF's demand to occupy the West Bank. While Dayan was saying in the cabinet that the response to Jordanian provocations should be limited to silencing the sources of Jor-danian fire, he gave directives to the IDF to launch an offensive in the Jenin and Jerusalem areas (Brecher, with Geist, 1980, 265; Oren 2000, 190–91). As noted in chapter 3, the pressure of the commander of the northern command, David Elazar, finally convinced Dayan to authorize the occupation of the Golan Height. No real debate in the government—supported by an assessment of the implications of this move after Egypt, Jordan, and Syria had agreed to a cease-fire—was offered by anybody in the cabinet.

The most obvious example of military domination of crisis manage-ment is the case of the Lebanon War. Starting with the missile crisis of April 1981 and ending with the Sabra and Shatilla massacre, Sharon and Eitan were the key players in the government decision-making process, with absolute monopoly over the definition of the situation, the delin-eation of options, and the recommendation of a preferred course of action. No alternative body was able or willing to come up with a com-peting analysis, different courses of action, or—most important—alter-nate policy recommendations.

The case of limited use of force over the years is based on a very simi-lar pattern. Suffice it to provide an example from the management of the Al Aqsa Intifada. Since the rise of Sharon to power in February 2001, the Israeli Foreign Ministry did not provide a single alternative to the policy of limited use of force. It faithfully fulfilled the role assigned to it by Ben-Gurion: the Defense Ministry makes policy; the Foreign Ministry explains it. The only solutions that have been offered over the course of three years of struggle with the Palestinians have been military. Most cabinet meetings during the intifada consisted of the IDF presenting operational plans and the cabinet approving the less extreme of those presented. Israel had multiple strategies for fighting wars and limited engagements—because the IDF had a large arsenal of contingency plans. But it had few strategies for peace, not because politicians lacked ideas but because there was no coherent process of staff work that could serve as an alternative to the military. It was only when the military itself admitted that it could not decide the intifada by military means that the notion of unilateral withdrawal from the Gaza Strip emerged as a viable policy. The emergence of this policy—as well as the establishment of the security barrier (the defensive wall) in the West Bank as a result of grassroots pressure on the government—is clear evidence of the bankruptcy of military solutions to the intifada.

Over the years, a large number of people have criticized the asymmetric balance of power between the security administration and the foreign policy administration. Almost anybody who studied government decision-making processes pointed out the relative void of staff work on foreign affairs, in particular when foreign and security interests were not compatible. Various scholars and practitioners had repeatedly recommended the establishment of a NSC serving the prime minister and the cabinet. However, most prime ministers and defense ministers resisted this idea. There were various efforts to establish a NSC. Ariel Sharon, serving as defense minister, established a Unit for National Security (UNS) in the Defense Department. This unit, led by Major General Abraham Tamir, functioned as a staff support for the defense minister. It was disbanded when Sharon was replaced by Moshe Arens as defense minister.

Yitzhak Shamir also formed a small national security team (NST) when he became prime minister in 1988. This team—headed by Yitzhak Ravid—proved marginal in foreign and security policy-making and never posed a bureaucratic threat to the IDF establishment. It was barred from any information that had operational implications, and its access to the prime minister was limited. A similar fate befell the NST appointed by Rabin in 1992, and it was disbanded shortly after its establishment. In 1998, the cabinet decided to form a full-fledged NSC. This decision became possible only after Defense Minister Yitzhak Mordechai, who had been opposed to the idea, resigned from the government. The NSC was stationed in Ramat Hasharon and received a small budget and staff. All of the NSAs came from the IDF or the Defense Ministry, and most of the members of the NSC small staff also came from the defense establishment. Since 1998, a protracted bureaucratic war has been waged between the NSC and the IDF. The winner of each encounter—without exception—was the IDF. Although it was part of the prime minister's office, the NSC never had the kind of access to decision makers as had the IDF and the other bodies of the defense community. Its papers and plans often went unread and unnoticed. A succession of directors of the NSC resigned, citing lack of attention and influence on national decisions. The personal and organizational structure of the NSC and the lack of support from the prime ministers doomed it to marginalization from the outset.

More important, the cabinet never established a coherent interagency structure of staff work for decision making. Since the IDF and the Defense Ministry were always concerned about losing their influence, they successfully blocked any effort at interagency cooperation through integrative forums on matters of security and foreign policy. The NSC was never able to accomplish the role of integrating foreign- and security-related work, because it never received the kind of cooperation required for such a task from other government ministries. No prime minister was willing to prevail over the bureaucratic turf wars to mandate such a task by the NSC and to compel the various ministries to cooperate in inter-agency integration.

Most Israeli prime ministers felt comfortable working with a small staff of close advisers in the prime minister's quarters. This staff had frequent access to the prime minister. Next to this staff, they held a small circle of advisers—coming mostly from the IDF and the intelligence community. Very often, prime ministers would rely on military or intelligence people (or even people outside the bureaucratic circle) to perform sensitive diplomatic missions. For example, on the eve of the Six Day War—and following several futile attempts by Foreign Minister Abba Eban to secure some sort of American commitment to open the Tiran Straits—Eshkol sent Meir Amit, head of the Mossad, to secure American support for an Israeli preemptive strike against Egypt. Golda Meir's meeting with King Hussein on September 22, 1973, was attended by several intelligence people. Yitzhak Rabin used Ephraim Halevi, the deputy head of Mossad, to handle the negotiations with King Hussein on an Israeli-Jordanian peace treaty. Benjamin Netanyahu, Ehud Barak, and Ariel Sharon relied on close advisers who came from completely outside the bureaucracy to handle sensitive negotiations. Netanyahu used American millionaire Ron Lauder to negotiate with Hafez Asad. Barak employed Gilead Sher for sensitive negotiations with the Palestinians. Sharon used his son

Omry and his COS, Dov Weisglass, to handle negotiations with the Palestinians and with the American administration.

There were some significant exceptions, however. The principal example, of course, concerns the Oslo negotiations, which led to the September 13, 1993, agreement between Israel and the PLO. Most of the Israeli-Palestinian negotiations over the 1993–96 period were handled by the Foreign Ministry under Shimon Peres. Military officers did participate in these talks and were instrumental in guiding the security-related aspects of these negotiations, but overall responsibility was handed to the Foreign Ministry. Nevertheless, even when Foreign Ministry officials were involved in sensitive negotiations, they often went over the head of their superiors, reporting directly to the prime minister (with the foreign minister very often out of the loop). Yitzhak Rabin, serving as ambassador to the United States under Abba Eban, reported directly to Golda Meir. Itamar Rabinovich, serving in the same capacity, had a direct line to Yitzhak Rabin, often going around Shimon Peres—especially with regard to negotiations with Syria. David Levy, who served as foreign minister under Shamir and Barak, was often bypassed by ambassadors, who reported directly to the prime minister. But these exceptions only serve to highlight the common tendency of prime ministers to rely on informal civilian networks in diplomatic affairs and to rely exclusively on the security community in general and the IDF in particular for more systematic staff work.

3.2. Military Officers Turned Politicians

Over its fifty-six-year history, Israel has had twelve different prime ministers and thirteen different defense ministers. Three of the prime ministers and seven of the defense ministers were former generals. A significant number of government ministers have also been retired generals. Nine out of the seventeen officers who served as COSs of the IDF subsequently served as cabinet ministers. At least twenty other officers at the rank of brigadier general or higher have served as ministers in the various cabinets. Quite a few senior officers have served as Knesset members. The surprising thing about this trend is that it accelerated rather than declined as time went by (Peri 2003, 125–27; Shelah 2003, 63–65). The structure of military careers in Israel is such that most senior officers retire in their late forties and early fifties, so that they have a long time for a second career. Many of them have turned to politics and have been warmly greeted by civilian politicians for reasons that will be discussed in the next section (Peri 1983, 101–29). Here, however, we focus on the impact of retired military officers turned politicians on the structure of decision making on foreign and security affairs.

It is difficult to establish a clear pattern of the kind of positions that retired military officers who entered politics have taken on foreign, security, or social matters. Some sociologists argue that the large number of generals turned politicians is an indicator of the militarization of Israeli society (Ben-Eliezer 1997; 2000, 242–49; Kimmerling 1993). We will elaborate on this argument in the next section, but for now it is important to note that—generally speaking—retired generals and colonels were spread all over the left-right political spectrum. There is no clear ideological characterization of the retired officers. On the face of it, they appeared to have been no more nationalistic or liberal than the average civilian politicians. A survey conducted by Peri (1983) among senior military officers found their views to be highly correlated with the views of the general population on foreign and security affairs.

There is, however, an interesting—and perhaps surprising—pattern concerning former generals who were upgraded to major decision-making posts in security and foreign affairs: most of them—with few notable exceptions—tended to become moderate relative to their previous beliefs and behavior while in uniform. Moreover, in many cases they were even more moderate than politicians who came from a civilian background. Two of the three generals turned prime ministers—Yitzhak Rabin and Ehud Barak—moderated their positions on national security affairs and on peace policies compared to their positions in their military or even compared to their previous political incarnations. During his first term in the prime minister's office, Rabin negotiated the September 1975 interim agreement with Egypt. In his second term as prime minister, Rabin pledged to withdraw from the Golan Height in return for peace and security arrangements with Syria. He enabled the Oslo process and approved the Oslo II treaty with the Palestinians three months before he was assassinated.[12]

Ehud Barak had been very much opposed to the Oslo treaty when he was COS. He had argued that the process entailed in the framework agreement had major "security-related loopholes" (Barak 2003, 33). He had also been opposed to unilateral withdrawal from Lebanon as COS and had played an important role in the intelligence failure concerning southern Lebanon as head of AMAN in the 1980s. Yet, upon becoming prime minister, he initiated the unilateral withdrawal from Lebanon, renewed Rabin's pledge for withdrawal from the Golan Height (with some minor exceptions), and—most important—made what had been considered by many Israelis as far-reaching or even excessive concessions to the Palestinians in an effort to reach a final status agreement.

The pattern of moderation of views applies to generals turned defense ministers as well. Moshe Dayan and Ezer Weizman—who had been branded loose cannons as generals in uniform— became fairly prudent politicians. Dayan was one of the more moderate members of the Meir government in the late 1960s and early 1970s. As foreign minister in Begin's government, aided by Ezer Weizman as the defense minister, he was one of the staunch supporters of concessions to Egypt in order to bring about a peace treaty. Both Dayan and Weizman resigned from the government when Begin and Sharon's settlement policy threatened to derail the autonomy talks with the Egyptians in 1981. Weizman, who served as minister of science and technology under the national unity government from 1988 to 1990, met with PLO representatives in clear violation of government policy, nearly getting himself dismissed by Shamir. Two other generals turned defense ministers (Yitzhak Mordechai and Benjamin Ben-Eliezer) did not distinguish themselves either way and generally supported the positions of the incumbent prime minister.

There were, however, notable exceptions to this rule of moderation in political office of former generals. Ariel Sharon is, of course, a principal example of a person whose views and actions did not change upon his transition from general to politician. He engaged in a rampant campaign of settlement building as minister of agriculture. He led the country head-on into a disastrous war in Lebanon, displaying the same patterns of deceit and insubordination as he did as a general in the IDF. As prime minister he escalated the struggle against the Palestinians, avoiding any kind of political negotiations. He turned down an offer of Bashar Asad to renew negotiations with Syria in the fall of 2003 and during 2004.

There are, however, signs that even Sharon had succumbed to the moderating influence of national leadership. After three years of intifada, he began to gradually grasp the adverse effects of the prolonged occupation on Israeli society and on national security. His 2004 unilateral disengagement plan from the Gaza Strip—including a plan to dismantle all Jewish settlements in the area—may well be a result of this awakening. His defense minister, Shaul Mofaz, was a close ally of Sharon both in the military escalation during Operation Defensive Shield in 2002 and in the disengagement plan.

The militarization of Israeli national security and foreign policy does not appear to have had significant substantive implications. It could be reasonably argued that, had the Israeli political system been less overloaded by former senior officers, it would not have fluctuated differently across substantive policies as it actually did. Yet there are two other dimensions through which the military background of some decision makers affects decision making on security and foreign affairs. First, the procedures and methodology of decision making reflect the military background of political decision makers. Second, the military background of policymakers has a cultural impact on their behavior and—more important—on their substantive positions.

Generals turned politicians have long been socialized to rely on the IDF's staff work for most decision-related tasks, such as diagnosis of problems, outline of policy options (especially those that entail military actions), estimates regarding possible outcomes of specific options, and implementation. Therefore, they have tended to rely heavily on the services of the military establishment for planning and decision making. This reliance on the IDF and the defense establishment has preserved the dominance of these bodies in national security decision making.

It is difficult to gauge the cultural impact of the military background of decision makers. There is little hard evidence of this impact. The substantive positions of generals turned politicians on major policy issues were—for the most part—no different than those of their fellow civilians. Yet, it is fair to suggest that their positions with respect to the military- and security- related dimensions of specific decisions were significantly affected by their military background. This could have been a good thing in many cases, because they were in a position to smell all kinds of rats fed to them by the IDF. Their civilian counterparts lacked the expertise to do so in many cases. More important, IDF officers who presented plans to political decision makers had to be more detailed and precise when the politicians were former military officers. However, when former generals focused only on the operational dimensions of the problem at hand, their military background channeled them into a narrow view of the problem, typically through the barrel of the gun.

There are many examples of this tendency. Ezer Weizman—serving as minister of transportation in the national unity government during the War of Attrition—applied constant pressure for deep penetration bombings against Egypt, discounting the escalatory potential of such raids. He found a strong ally in Rabin, who served as ambassador to the United States. Rabin's expulsion of the four hundred suspected Hamas activists to Lebanon in December 1992, following the kidnapping of an IDF soldier by Hamas terrorists, ignored the political ramifications of this act. Rabin and Barak's management of the implementation process of Oslo was based on narrow security considerations rather than on the need to establish trust with the Palestinians. Barak's, Sharon's, Ben-Eliezer's, and Mofaz's handling of the Al Aqsa Intifada was strongly affected by their military background, focusing primarily on offensive military strategies and the use of high-end technology to battle a low-intensity war.

The combination of the dominant role of the IDF and the weakness of the foreign policy establishment in decision making on foreign and security affairs often converts policy discussions into debates on operational aspects of the decision. The socialization and background of military officers turned politicians prime them very often to focus on the operational parameters of the military options. If those do not look extremely bad, then the military responses to policy challenges receive priority over the nonmilitary ones. This priming focus on operational issues on most security matters is offset only by weighty diplomatic, political, and economic factors. However, very often the cabinet is not offered the relevant information and/or arguments that are needed to offset military considerations. Maoz and Mor (2002a, chaps. 6–7), who studied twenty-three different decisions in the course of the Egyptian-Israeli conflict over the 1948–79 period and thirty-three decisions in the course of the Israeli-Syrian rivalry over the 1948–98 period, note the consistent dominance of military- and security-related considerations over political ones. A more detailed study of Israeli decisions over the 1970–74 period (Maoz 1997a) shows again this tendency.[13]

3.3. *The Public Image of the IDF*

The trust and respect of the IDF among virtually all levels of Israeli society is perhaps the single most important resource that the IDF possesses with respect to political decision making. This kind of respect is shared by both the general public and civilian politicians with a great deal of experience As Arian (2003, 37) points out, "the IDF has long been associated [by the Israeli public] with Israeli might, pride, and independence, and the army is often described as a major agency for integration and socialization for immigrants." Roughly one-third of the Israeli public rates the IDF as more efficient than other institutions (Arian 2003, 2001). The Israeli public has generally been more agreeable to raising taxes in order to fund defense spending than have virtually all other democratic states (Arian 1995, 64–65), and this figure has increased over the four years of the Al Aqsa Intifada to a high of 36 percent (Arian 2003, 22).

This image of efficiency, apolitical nature, and professionalism of the IDF has eroded over the years, but it has remained high, certainly higher than that of many other Israeli institutions. It has been bolstered by the high number of military officers turned politicians, who have—despite their varied political positions on substantive issues—worked to maintain respect for the IDF inside and outside of other political institutions. Contrary to the perception that the positions of other institutions are marred by partisan and personal agendas, the IDF's views, whatever they are, are typically seen as purely professional. For that reason, the views and assessments of the IDF tend to count more than those of other institutions. As we will see subsequently, even institutions that command an overwhelming respect by the Israeli public— such as the Supreme Court—tend to treat the IDF's positions and actions with a great deal of respect and deference.

For that reason, many political decision makers with no military experience have tended to allow the IDF considerable freedom of maneuver in both financial and operational matters. Eshkol and Begin let the IDF have its way in terms of the military budget. During the Eshkol era, Israel's defense spending increased by 288 percent and the defense burden increased from 4 percent of the GDP to 9 percent. During Begin's era (1977–83) defense spending increased by 66 percent and the defense burden rose from 18 percent to 25 percent of the GDP. Shamir's era is characterized for the most part by significant budgetary restraint, probably due to the fact that Rabin served as his defense minister for four of the six years of Shamir's tenure.

As noted in chapter 3, Eshkol allowed the IDF a wide latitude in the management of the border war with the Syrians in the mid-1960s. Begin gave the IDF a free hand in the process of escalating hostilities with the Syrians and the PLO in Lebanon during 1981. Sharett, on the other hand, tried to limit the freedom of action of the IDF as far as reprisals were concerned, but he was frequently manipulated and outmaneuvered by Minister of Defense Lavon and by COS Dayan.

Curiously, decision makers with a strong security background and military officers who became leading decision makers tended to be more critical of the IDF's proposals or budget appropriations than were decision makers without prior military background. Ben-Gurion forced Yigael Yadin, the third COS, to resign due to fundamental differences of opinion regarding the IDF budget (Yaniv 1987b, 113–14). We noted in chapter 8 the debate between Yitzhak Rabin and Defense Minister Peres on the defense budget and the spending on the nuclear program in 1975 and 1976. Rabin and Barak also reduced the defense budget, with Rabin fixing it at a declining burden concept (as an increasingly smaller percentage of the GDP over time).[14] However, when it came to consideration of military operations, the government—whether it was led by a person with a security background or without it—was more permissive than constraining. It must be noted, however, that the military leaders understood their limitations and therefore only rarely came to the cabinet with outrageous plans for military operations. Because the plans the IDF brought for government approval always seemed reasonable—striking a delicate balance between engaging in extremely escalatory acts and doing nothing—the government tended to approve these plans in most cases. In the absence of well-defined policy or diplomatic alternatives, "reasonable" military action often seemed the right response to security challenges. As we saw in chapter 7, even Sharett was pulled into this trap.

All in all, the impact of the security community—especially the IDF—on national security and foreign affairs is probably unrivaled in democratic states. It stems not only from the organizational and logistical power of that community but from the weakness of other, equally relevant, communities that must contribute to decision making in these matters. This impact rests also on sociological grounds—the deep penetration of military officers to all strands of policy-making and the respect and deference that former officers tend to command from their colleagues. This structural effect is compounded by the lack of significant control and oversight on the security community by the legislature, the judiciary, and informal watchdogs such as the Israeli media and various public institutions. I now turn to a discussion of these communities.

4. THE MYTH OF LEGISLATIVE OVERSIGHT

The Knesset is probably one of the most factionalized parliaments in the democratic world. With anywhere from ten to fifteen parties represented in it at any given time, one would imagine that it must exercise effective oversight functions over the operations of the executive branch and its various organizations. All governments in Israel's history have consistently faced significant challenges from the opposition—including a number of successful no-confidence votes that unseated incumbents several times. In light of this political history, it is stunning to learn how little oversight has actually been exercised by the sovereign branch of government in Israel over the executive in general and on national security and foreign policy in particular.

The relevant forums for parliamentary oversight of government operations are the plenary sessions of the Knesset and the CFSA. The former forum suffers from certain drawbacks because of its public sessions. However, the CFSA meets in closed sessions and has the power to convene any person carrying out an official role to answer questions and address the committee. More important, the Knesset is permitted by law to form parliamentary commissions of inquiry (PCIs) on any matter it deems necessary. Such PCIs must include members of the opposition parties, so that it would be impossible to use such commissions as a lip service to the public in order to fudge tough issues that may arise in the process of inquiry. The CFSA can also form special subcommittees to deal with more specific subjects. While there have been numerous leaks from the CFSA plenary, the proceedings of its specialized subcommittees have been strictly classified. There have been few leaks from these subcommittees. Indeed, over the years, the CFSA has operated two significant subcommittees: the Subcommittee on Secret Services (SCSS), which is supposed to oversee the functioning of the Israeli intelligence services, and the Subcommittee on the Security Doctrine (SCSD), which examines various aspects of the Israeli security conception and the structure of the IDF and the security community as a whole.

As noted previously in section 2 on the intelligence community, the SCSS formed ad hoc inquiry commissions for the investigation of specific intelligence fiascos. Two notable investigations in this area include the investigation of the foiled assassination attempt of Khaled Mash'al in Jordan in 1997 by Mossad and the inquiry commission on the intelligence failure in Iraq in 2003.

While CFSA has considerable formal responsibilities for overseeing the security community by law, the reality of this practice is quite different. First, like all other civilian institutions dealing with security and foreign affairs, the CFSA lacks a professional staff that is capable of briefing and supporting the members of the Knesset (MKs) on the committee in a manner that would allow the latter to conduct serious inspection of the security community. Therefore, the CFSA relies exclusively on the information it receives from this community and has no independent means of verifying or cross-checking this information. Second, because of repeated leaks from the CFSA plenary, many military and security people who appear before the committee limit their presentations and responses to unclassified issues. Third, the composition of the CFSA in general and of the SCSD and SCSS in particular is such that no significant alternative voice could be heard in such forums.

While the most extreme right-wing radicals are allowed to be members of these forums, extreme left-wing MKs—especially Arabs—are barred from these committees. More important, membership in the most exclusive subcommittees is restricted to the old boys' network that makes the IDF and intelligence bureaucrats comfortable. The formal excuse is security clearance. In practice, most members of these subcommittees tend to be former members of the security community. In many cases, opposition party members of these subcommittees are past policymakers in the executive or aspire to future executive positions. The same old boys' network that affects decision making in the cabinet seems to control the CFSA subcommittees.

This is part of the reason why former chairs of CFSA who invested a great deal of time and effort in both the plenary and subcommittees have admitted that CFSA has little impact on policy and has done very little to actually investigate or oversee the security community. "The CFSA today has no real significance," notes Dan Meridor, a former chair of CFSA and a long-standing chair of SCSD. "It looks like another session of *Popolitics*" [a popular television talk show] (Allon 1994). The treatment of the two critical reports of SCSS on the intelligence community in the Mash'al and the Iraq cases by the security community corroborates this impression.

The SCSD put considerable work in the late 1980s and early 1990s into a study designed to revise and update Israel's security doctrine. Starting with a subcommittee headed by Benjamin Begin (Menachem Begin's son), who was later succeeded by Dan Meridor, the SCSD interviewed a large number of people in the security establishment, including most members of the general staff under Dan Shomron and Ehud Barak. It issued a classified paper in the early 1990s, but it is not clear whether this paper had any significant impact on the actual structure or doctrine of the IDF or the security community in general. In the first few years of the third millennium, the SCSD renewed its work under the chairmanship of Yuval Steinitz, focusing on matters of second nuclear strike capability and submarine launched ballistic missiles (SLBMs). Without going into the details of these reports, it is clear that the SCSD could not develop a thorough assessment of Israel's defense policy. The subcommittee lacked the staff support and data for a more thorough analysis and evaluation of the enormous array of topics that would be required to analyze and integrate in a comprehensive study of Israel's security conception.[15]

In 1997, Minister of Defense Yitzhak Mordechai launched a large-scale project designed to reassess Israel's national security policy. This project consisted of a number of teams, each focusing on a different aspect of Israel's security policy. In contrast to the SCSD effort, the Defense

Ministry's effort was far more comprehensive and entailed considerable staff work—due to the fact that this was an effort mandated by the Defense Ministry and was done in close cooperation with the IDF and the intelligence community. One of the unusual characteristics of this effort was that it involved academics from different disciplines, some with non-conventional views of security and strategy. The more "sensitive" issues, including various R&D projects and the nuclear issue, were discussed, however, by internal teams consisting of *Shutafey Sod*—"partners to secret"—people with the highest level of security clearance (Barzilai 1998). The report itself was completed in 2000 and submitted by the head of the NSC, David Ivry (who had been the director general and the coordinator of the process in Mordechai's Defense Ministry), to Ehud Barak, who was doubling as defense minister and prime minister. According to one account (Barzilai 1999), that document was shelved by Barak. It is not entirely clear what happened to the Steinitz SCSD report and whether it had any impact. Steinitz himself admitted quite frankly that his committee was staging an uphill battle to render the CFSA an effective tool for oversight of the security establishment in a manner that actually asserted the Knesset's sovereignty rather than as a "House of Lords," as this committee had been described by IDF generals (Steinitz 2004b).

The CFSA and its subcommittees have, in theory, considerable constitutional powers of oversight on the security community. In practice, however, this committee serves as window dressing to almost every policy—whether successful or unsuccessful. Consequently, very often the reports of independent inquiry commissions that follow major policy fiascos are far more influential in terms of inducing personal, organizational, and policy change in the security community than is the constitutional body in charge of political oversight and evaluation of this community.

5. THE INJUDICIOUS JUDICIARY

The Israeli judiciary is typically considered a highly liberal institution. It is regarded as one of the most prestigious Israeli institutions by the Israeli public (Kretzmer 2002, 12–13; Barzilai, Yuchtman-Yaar, and Segal 1994, 177–81). More important, over the last decade or so, the Supreme Court—especially, but not exclusively, under Chief Justice Aharon Barak—has engaged in a so-called constitutional revolution. This revolution entailed the lobbying for the legislation of two basic laws on human rights: Basic Law: Human Dignity and Liberty and Basic Law: Freedom of Occupation (Levitzky 2001). It also entailed the liberal interpretation of these laws, even when this interpretation entailed issues that were at the center of social controversy. Kretzmer (2002, 13) argues that the Supreme Court—acting as a High Court of Justice (HCJ)— enacted what amounted to a "judicial bill of rights."[16] This bill of rights rests on the following theory:

> Basic rights of the individual are an essential feature of every democratic regime. . . . Even before any of these rights were defined in Basic Laws, the Court looked to accepted standards in other democratic countries and in international documents to define which rights were to be recognized. Over the years, the Court has referred to a long list of recognized rights that includes freedom of speech, the right to equality, freedom of association, the right to bodily integrity, and freedom of religion.

In many critical cases, when this liberal interpretation of individual rights and liberties clashed with the position of the authorities, the Supreme Court was not deterred from ruling against the authorities. Nor was it reluctant to intervene and render justiciable matters that were at the heart of controversies such as conflicts between religious laws and basic civil or individual rights. This represents a seemingly courageous position of the judiciary and a real check on executive powers, especially given the weakness of the legislative branch in terms of overseeing and balancing executive power.

Yet, on matters of national security in general and on matters concerning the human dignity, freedom, civil, and property rights of Palestinians under occupation in particular, the Supreme Court has "rationalized virtually all controversial actions of Israeli authorities, especially those most problematic under principles of international humanitarian law" (Kretzmer 2002, 187). In his telling study of the Supreme Court's rulings on matters concerning the occupied territories—including matters of changing the status of the occupied territories, deportations, establishment of settlements and land confiscations, detention of suspects without trial, house demolitions, and other forms of collective punishments—Kretzmer (2002) shows that the Supreme Court consistently engaged in convoluted interpretation of international law or even outright legitimization of violations of the Geneva Conventions and the Hague Regulations, which cover the international norms of occupation. More important, on these matters, the Supreme Court has demonstrated significant reluctance to challenge the military authorities' actions. In many cases, it has declined to rule in petitions against the IDF and the military government in the occupied territories on the grounds of unjusticiability. In other cases, it has simply turned down petitioners' arguments in favor of the arguments of the authorities, based on a fairly convoluted logic that even mainstream legal scholars in Israel found puzzling, to say the least.

One may argue that, on matters concerning international law and the occupied territories, such judgments are not all that surprising. Specifically, the Palestinians under occupation are not Israeli citizens. The mere fact that the court is willing to deal with their petitions is a sign of liberalism and independence of the judiciary, as well as a constant challenge to the authorities. As Yitzhak Rabin pointed out when he justified transfer of weapons and law-and-order privileges to the PA in Gaza: "I hope that we will find a partner which will be responsible in Gaza for the internal Palestinian problems. It will deal with Gaza without the problems of the High Court of Justice, without the problems of B'tselem and without the problems raised by all kinds of sensitive souls and all kinds of mothers and fathers."[17] So, even though the Supreme Court seemed reluctant to challenge the decision of the military government and the IDF in the occupied territories, it created a perception that it is willing and able to review and even limit the actions of the executive branch. This image, in and of itself, may have constrained the IDF from taking even more radical actions vis-à-vis the Palestinian population.

If this were the only security-related matter wherein the Supreme Court seemed to overwhelmingly favor the executive's policies, then this image of liberalism would have been somehow vindicated. However, this deference to the positions of the executive and the favorable legitimization of many of its acts in virtually all matters concerning security affairs seems to have been the norm rather than the exception in the HCJ's rulings.

The treatment of Israelis who were accused and found guilty of treason and espionage by the courts was far harsher than the treatment of the worst Israeli criminals, even first-degree murderers. Prior to the trial, the security authorities often denied these people basic rights, such as access to an attorney or attorneys' rights to examine the evidence against their clients. The HCJ allowed their detention prior to trial under complete isolation. The argument of the SHABAK and the prosecution was typically that providing these suspects with any basic rights— which are standard for "ordinary" criminals—would jeopardize Israeli security. The evidence typically brought by the prosecution in such cases was testimonies by members of the security services that this would indeed be the case. Almost invariably, the courts ruled in favor of the prosecution's demand for limitations on the right of the accused or convicted person.

There are quite a few cases that fit this pattern. Two of them are very relevant because both concern Israel's nuclear policy. Mordechai Vanunu, a past employee of the Dimona nuclear reactor, took pictures of the internal structure of the reactor and then provided an extensive interview to the British newspaper *Sunday Times* in 1986 (Barnaby 1989). Vanunu was lured by a Mossad agent to go to Italy, where he was kidnapped by Mossad agents and brought back to stand trial in Israel. Prior to and during the trial, his attorney was under severe restrictions in terms of meetings with Vanunu and in terms of access to documentary evidence. Vanunu was sentenced to eighteen years in prison, eleven of which he served in solitary confinement. No parole or deduction of one-third of the prison term due to good behavior was considered. Upon his release on April 21, 2004, he was placed under severe restrictions. He was not allowed to leave Israel and was barred from any newspaper interview. His movements are still closely monitored. Vanunu may have been released from jail only to be put under de facto house arrest after he had fully served his prison term. The courts approved these draconian measures without hesitation.

Brigadier General Yitzhak Yaacov served as head of the Department of Weapons and Technological Development of the Ministry of Defense (MAFAT, to use its Hebrew acronym) in the mid-1960s. He retired from the IDF in 1975 and started a successful business career in the United States. In the mid-1990s he decided to publicize his memoirs, possibly including the role he had played in the Israeli nuclear project. He granted an interview to an Israeli journalist that contained much of the things he had done over the years in the IDF. In 2001, several months after celebrating his seventy-fifth birthday, he was arrested and put in solitary confinement. His lawyer was barred any contact with him for weeks. Neither was he allowed visits of members of his family. He was initially charged with severe espionage. The Tel Aviv district court denied several petitions by his attorney to improve his terms of imprisonment. Only after several months in solitary confinement did the Supreme Court order that he be placed in a hospice and be given permission to see his wife and meet his attorney on a regular basis. Throughout the trial period, his attorneys were barred from vital evidence and information. After more than a year and a half, the district court cleared Yaacov of the espionage

charges but found him guilty of providing secret information to unauthorized persons. He was sentenced to two years in prison but was released
immediately after the trial.[18]

The picture that emerges in the case of the judiciary is very similar to
what we have seen regarding the other branches of government. The
security community has an enormous amount of power vis-à-vis the other
branches of government. The judiciary serves in many cases as a legit-
imizer of acts of the security establishment that either are illegal from the
perspective of international law or entail fundamental violations of civil
rights. In other cases, it is willing to give up its judicial discretion in favor
of what it considers to be the security needs of the state— needs that are
defined exclusively by the security establishment. In the process, the judiciary frequently sacrifices the very same principles of civil and individual
rights on which it prides itself in other domains.

The judiciary may face a real dilemma when it comes to matters of
national security. These matters constitute the essence of the Israeli consensus. Even the most controversial actions of the IDF and the military
government in the occupied territories have been always justified on
grounds of national security. A frontal clash between the HCJ and the
security community may threaten the autonomy and independence of the
judiciary on other matters of civil rights, because of so-called HCJ-
detouring legislation, that is, legislation that would limit the ability of the
HJC to interpret legislation. Moreover, many of the acts of the security
community rely on the Defence Emergency Regulations (DER) that
Israel adapted from the British Mandate Law (Hofnung 1996, 47–61). Up
to 1992, there was no other legislation that could counterbalance the
DER. The legislation in 1992 of the two basic laws, Basic Law: Human
Dignity and Liberty and Basic Law: Freedom of Occupation, would have
provided the HCJ at least some vehicle for limiting the application of the
emergency regulations. This did not happen, however. The judiciary
maintained the pattern of succumbing to virtually every whim of the
security community.

These realities provide both an explanation and a rationale of the deference of the judiciary to the executive on security-related affairs. Kretzmer (2002, 78, 218n12) brings the traditional defense of the HCJ justices
amid charges of its antirights policies with regard to security affairs. The
HCJ faces a real dilemma when ruling against the government on matters
of settlements—especially given a Likud government that views settlement in the occupied territories as a national priority. Supreme Court justices believe that the independence of the Supreme Court is under con-

stant threat from a hostile legislature. There have been numerous protests—especially by the ultra-orthodox parties—against liberal rulings of the HCJ on religious matters. The prospect that the Knesset would establish a constitutional court above the HCJ where justices would be political appointees is an ominous threat. Challenging the government and the Knesset by issuing controversial rulings on security affairs would provoke these branches to limit the independence of the judiciary. The "judicial revolution" or "constitutional revolution"—the liberalization of rulings on civil rights—would be doomed to failure. The strategy of the judiciary has therefore been to minimize as far as possible the likelihood of head- on collisions with the executive on matters of national security. The idea has been to cause some limited harm in order to prevent greater harm. But this is an unacceptable compromise, because it constitutes the defense of all judiciaries that legitimized human rights violations in truncated democracies such as South Africa, Rhodesia, or the United States in the nineteenth century under the slavery regime. Human rights, democracy, and the rule of law paid the price of this compromise. None of these judiciaries has registered its name in history as a progressive institution that promoted justice. Rather, these judiciaries have gone down in history as full partners in systems entailing flagrant violations of civil and individual rights and the systematic abuse of justice.

In the case of the courts, too, the sociology of strength and weakness has an important effect on HJC rulings on security matters. The first generation of Supreme Court justices came from European background. Virtually all of the Supreme Court justices over the 1948–70 period had been educated in Europe, and almost none of them had held public office before being selected to the bench in the Supreme Court. In contrast, most of the post-1970 justices have been educated in preindependence Palestine or in Israel. Many of the leading justices of the new generation have had no previous judicial experience. The two most recent chief justices, Meir Shamgar and Aharon Barak, served as attorney generals, defending the government in many cases of potential violations of human, civil rights, or international law before being appointed to the Supreme Court. Shamgar also spent a seven-year stint as IDF advocate general. The next chief justice who is designated to replace Barak in 2006, Dorit Beinish, as well as two recent appointees to the Supreme Court, Elyakim Rubinstein and Edna Arbel, served as chief advocates and attorney generals (Kretzmer 2002, 9–10). The dissonance there cannot be more pronounced. Supreme Court justices must rule on petitions that are extremely similar if not identical to those that they defended as public officials or IDF advocates. This creates an anomaly that is abundantly transparent in the Supreme Court's record of rulings on matters concerning national security.

6. CONCLUSIONS AND IMPLICATIONS

I noted at the beginning of this chapter that the structure of the national security and foreign policy bureaucracy is not the only explanation of the patterns of behavior and policy-making we have identified in this book. Yet, the principal aspects of the structure of the security and foreign affairs community stand as an overarching meta-explanation that underlies the specific explanations of these issues. The idiosyncrasies of individual decision makers; the substantive challenges that Israel has faced; the contentious, competitive, and diversified nature of its political system; and the inherent tension between the demands of security and other societal needs could not have led to such systematic patterns of behavior had it not been for the special characteristics of policy-making on security and foreign affairs.

Sociologists and historians (e.g., Levy 2003, 1997; Ben-Eliezer 2003, 1998, 1997; Kimmerling 1993; Golani 2002; Almog 1997) emphasize the sociological and cultural aspects of the militarization of Israeli society. Yaniv (1993) notes the fact that the IDF had been assigned a large number of social duties, thus affecting in terms of its organizational culture other aspects of Israeli society. There also appears to be a close network of relationships among former military officers who enter public policy or the private sector. This is unavoidable in a small, closely knit society in which most people perform military service. Yet, the militarization of Israeli society takes on a structural form as well. The dominance of the IDF and the security community in policy-making on national security and affairs highlights new dimensions of Israeli militarism.

First, it highlights the effectiveness and political skill of the security administration. These skills are not always in the areas of responsibility of the security community. Rather, they are demonstrated in the capacity of this community to disguise failures as successes, to cover up for mistakes, and—most important—to closely guard its imperialist capacity to affect policy and prevent others from challenging it.

Second, it highlights the pathetic weakness and near irrelevance of other institutions that are supposed to be an integral part of policy-making on national security and foreign policy. It also highlights the lack of will, limited foresight, or utter incompetence of political decision makers who are incapable of supporting the very same institutions that are likely to set them free of the complete dependence on the security community in their decision making. Repeated voices from the academic community calling for the formation or real empowerment of a civilian NSC fell on deaf ears. Repeated efforts by academics and policy experts to form a professional staff around the prime minister's office were defeated in turf wars. The IDF proved itself far more competent and resourceful in these turf wars than in its management of high-intensity and low-intensity conflicts (LICs).

Third, this aspect of structural militarization—or rather securitization—of policy-making on national security and foreign affairs highlights the total lack of oversight and control of the IDF and the security community by the civilian community. It shows how the legislature and the judiciary completely bow to the security community on virtually any aspect of its involvement in shaping policy. After nearly forty years of occupation, during which the IDF engaged in numerous instances of killings of civilians, land confiscations, collective punishments, deportations, and house demolitions, there still exists no external body that is capable of investigating the IDF's actions. The entire web of institutions that forms a democratic government accepts this as an act of God. Consider the HCJ's ruling on a petition by the Israeli Human Rights Organization and other organizations following the Israeli massive destruction in Rafah during April 2004. This petition called for an inquiry into alleged atrocities that left fifty-eight people—most of them civilians—dead and resulted in the demolition of 183 houses.[19] After accepting the explanation of the commander of IDF forces regarding the measures the IDF had taken to ensure the safety and well-being of the Palestinians in Rafah, the justices turned down the request of the petitioners to open an inquiry of the IDF's behavior in Rafah.

> The investigation of this tragic event has not yet been completed. All the material will be passed on to the IDF Judge-Advocate General. Under these circumstances, there is no call, at this stage, for any action on our part. Petitioners must wait for the findings of the investigation and the decision of the Judge-Advocate General. It may be assumed that lessons will be drawn, and if there is a need for a change in the instructions that are given to the troops, this will be implemented. At this stage, in the absence of facts, we can only repeat the obvious: the army must employ all possible caution in order to avoid harming a civilian population, even one that is protesting against it. (HCJ 4764/04, 23–24)

Repeated efforts by well-intended politicians to empower the Knesset CFSA in a manner that would effectively both oversee the intelligence community and examine the IDF's proposed budget ended in complete failure.

The interface between the sociological account of Israeli militarization and the bureaucratic and structural discussion in this chapter concerns the involvement of former military officers in politics. This involvement is deep and wide; not only does it nurture a culture of dominance of military considerations in foreign and security affairs, but it also is effective in shielding the IDF from criticism and oversight by civilian institutions.

It must be said to the credit of the security community in general and the IDF in particular that they know very well how to walk along the fine line that separates influence and even domination from a strictly military regime (Ben-Eliezer 1997; Ben Meir 1995, 169–77). With few exceptions of deception and insubordination of the military leadership, the IDF accepted civilian authority almost without question. Even in major crises in civil-military relations—such as the May–June 1967 crisis, several incidents during the 1996–99 Netanyahu era, and the Barak directive for withdrawal from Lebanon in 2000—IDF commanders fulfilled the directives of the political echelon. The IDF followed political directives even when its commanders had been clearly unhappy with them. The IDF also knows how to exert influence in subtle and unobtrusive ways rather than in direct and bullying ones. It also knows which battles to wage and which to avoid altogether, and it knows how to lose a political battle in order to win the war. This is a source of strength of the IDF rather than weakness in terms of its political standing, because it preserves its image as a military in the service of the state rather than one in which the state is servicing the IDF.

The implications of this structure are quite profound. First, there may be significant political differences among parties and among different politicians on major matters of foreign and security policy. Yet, the elites of the leading political parties are sprinkled (and sometimes saturated) by people with a military background who come from the same social and organizational culture. Even beyond these elites, the IDF and the security community have come to command such respect and trust by civilians that the views and recommendations of the IDF are very seldom challenged. Moreover, the common cultural and organizational background of generals turned politicians forms a "securitized" political culture wherein military considerations tend to weigh heavier than diplomatic, economic, or even domestic political considerations. Some issues—for example, the nuclear policy—have become consensual without proper inspection of what it means to possess nuclear weapons in the absence of political oversight. The fact that the IDF's policies in the occupied territories and the measures it has used to deal with Palestinian resistance of all forms has not changed across different governments suggests that a basic consensus regarding these matters prevails over the wide gap that exists across parties regarding the merits and the future of the occupation.

Second, we noted the contradiction between the risk-seeking and trigger-happy management of conflict and the risk-avoiding and reluctant approach to peace. This is not due to the fact that all Israeli decision makers were intransigent and hard-liners. On the contrary, many of them were quite moderate. The willingness of many political leaders from both the left and the right wings of the political arena to make territorial concessions for peace attests to this fact. However, the structure in which a security community is a prominent actor in both peace and war decisions and in which other institutions tend to be weak or subordinate to the security bureaucracy provides a powerful explanation for this paradox. Military options tend to come naturally whenever a security challenge arises. On the other hand, this community is likely to look for loopholes and pitfalls of a military nature in every opening for peace that requires concessions. The interpretation of the intentions of adversaries is largely based on the intelligence assessments furnished by the same community. Given the background and dominant culture of the intelligence community, these intentions are likely to be viewed with suspicion and mistrust regardless of the true intentions of the adversary. When Anwar Sadat spoke of the psychological barrier that accounted for 80 percent of the failure to reach Arab-Israeli peace he may well have included the institutional as well as the popular aspect of this psychology.

More important, even in the course of peace negotiations, the security community is likely to come up with sometimes the most ridiculous arguments regarding military necessities that have a major deal-breaking potential. Examples of this tendency include the IDF's insistence on the Sinai airfields in the 1977–79 negotiations with Egypt, the stubborn clinging to a demand to maintain control of the Hermon early warning station in the negotiations with the Syrians, and the demand for military control of the Jordan Valley and overflight rights in the negotiations with the Palestinians. Ironically, many people in the policy-making circle who must weigh these military "requirements" against political, social, and economic considerations often come from the very same security com-

munity. This does not make matters easier. Even when the principal decision makers are civilians, they tend to accept the necessity of these
"requirements" at face value because they do not have an authoritative
forum that can furnish alternative perspectives on these matters.

Third, the tendency to deal with political problems through covert
operations—mainly by attempting to manipulate domestic political
processes and institutions in enemy states—is mostly an undertaking of
the security community. The mere notion that Israel can affect British
decisions to withdraw from the Suez Canal, help defeat the Muslim
regime in Sudan, help establish an autonomous Kurdish state in Iraq, create a new order in Lebanon, and manipulate Palestinian politics through
military measures seems preposterous even to a diplomatic intern. The
fact that Israel repeated such operations over and over, even when these
efforts consistently failed or backfired, is best explained by the structural
domination of the security establishment on policy. The same applies to
the ludicrous notion that one can crush a struggle for national liberation
by assassinating the leaders of militant organizations. The only area
where the security community has been helpful and instrumental in
improving Israel's regional standing was when it engaged in covert diplomacy and forged secret ties with states such as Turkey, Morocco, Tunisia,
and Jordan (and more recently with states such as Malaysia, Indonesia,
and Pakistan). In these cases, straightforward diplomatic practice—
backed by the ability of the security community to provide incentives to
the foreign country (such as weapons and security cooperation)—is what
made such deals stick and survive for a long time.

Finally, throughout the book I have noted that policies that consistently failed or consistently backfired were never fully inspected and evaluated in a thorough manner. This was the case with regard to the aver-
sion to drawing lessons from Israel's wars—the successful as well as the
less successful ones. This was the case with regard to the lack of thorough
analysis and evaluation of Israel's strategies of LIC. This was the case with
respect to inspecting Israel's covert operations designed to manipulate
events and processes in Arab states or among the Palestinians. And this
was the case with the unsubstantiated claims regarding the accomplishments of Israel's nuclear policy. The security community managed to
effectively block criticism even in the face of repeated failures.

When a process of evaluation and inquiry outside of the security community did take place—such as the case of the Agranat, Kahan, and
Shamgar inquiry commissions—it was partial and truncated. More
important, most recommendations of these commissions—especially

those that required structural reforms in the security community—were never implemented or were implemented in a partial and flawed manner.

As long as the key structural features of the national security and foreign policy-making process remain the same, the fundamental flaws and problems in the substantive policies are likely to persist. Israel's national decision-making architecture must change, and this change is not too difficult to accomplish. A reform consists of several principal features.

First, the NSC must be expanded and be made a principal instrument for staff work for the cabinet in general and for the prime minister in particular. Its key function is not to compete with the intelligence community on intelligence assessment but rather to engage in policy analysis, to prepare and develop options for short-range policy problems, to engage in analysis of long-term plans and policies, and to perform studies for decision makers on matters of national policy in all areas that concern national security and foreign affairs. The NSC should also develop, maintain, and activate a crisis management center of an interagency nature and be made responsible for handling staff work during foreign and security crises.

Second, the intelligence assessment function must be taken out of the hands of AMAN and handed over to a civilian organization—perhaps within the NSC. This organization should be delegated all of the research and assessments functions of AMAN. It should be staffed by a wide range of experts, including a substantial body of people with modern social scientific skills. Its purpose should be to analyze and evaluate intelligence data from a wide array of classified and unclassified sources and to engage in net assessment processes that entail an understanding of the interaction between Israel's policies and those of its friends and foes.

Third, the Foreign Ministry should further develop its own strategic staff capacity, focusing on both short- and long-term planning of Israel's foreign policy and diplomacy. It should be converted from a ministry that engages primarily in public relations (Hasbarah, in Hebrew), and is not very good at it, to an effective arm that implements Israel's diplomacy. In the early 1950s, under the leadership of Moshe Sharett and to a lesser extent under Golda Meir, the Foreign Ministry—with far fewer resources—was much more active than it is today. The activity of the Foreign Ministry and its impact on Israel's policy-making should be increased by involving the foreign policy bureaucracy more deeply in the new national security architecture. This could be done by rotating foreign policy analysts and diplomats in the intelligence organization and the NSC and by involving strategic experts from the NSC and the intelligence organization in diplomatic missions. This cannot happen unless future ministers of foreign affairs are willing to upgrade the staff planning and research functions of their own ministries rather than act as beggars at the doorstep of the military security community.

Fourth, the Knesset has two of the most effective tools of structural reforms: legislation and budget appropriations. It must be willing to use them more effectively. Because structural reforms are by nature nonpartisan, forming a forum that would examine ways to improve the CFSA's ability to oversee the security community and back it up by appropriate legislation should become a major priority. A key feature of the CFSA's ability to become a meaningful forum for such tasks is establishing an effective support staff for this committee and for its subcommittees. This staff should be completely independent of the staff and the functions of the organizations belonging to the executive branch so as to form impartial assessments and evaluations of the operations of the security community. This staff should also have an economic and operations research capacity so as to be able to study and offer alternatives to budget appropriations recommended by the government and to supervise the cost-effectiveness of the operations of the security community and the defense industry from an economic as well as a strategic perspective. The supervisory capacity of the CFSA and its permanent and ad hoc subcommittees must be backed up by legislation so as to provide it with an ability to require documentation and testimonies under oath from people and institutions in the security community.

It is not evident that there are any legislative changes that can and should be made to ensure a more critical judicial policy by the Supreme Court. Perhaps the only meaningful legislative action would be to abolish the DER, but this is not likely to happen. Even if this does not happen, a more activist interpretation of the contradiction between the Basic Law: Human Dignity and Liberty and the DER is required with respect to defining the limits of the government to declare a state of emergency.[20] This activist interpretation cannot come as long as the conservative culture of the Supreme Court with respect to security affairs continues to prevail. One can only speculate that, if civilian control and oversight over the security community is tightened in the Knesset, it is more likely that the HCJ will become increasingly liberal in terms of imposing limits on the exclusive ability of the government to maintain a permanent state of emergency.

It is not immediately evident that any structural reforms—let alone sweeping ones of the nature discussed previously—will necessarily improve policy-making. Yet, there is a good chance that they will make policy-making more analytic and more systematic. These reforms will not weaken the power of the executive. In some respect they will even strengthen its capacity to make decisions and to develop long-term plans. They will undoubtedly place greater restrictions on the security community and render it more accountable for its actions than it had been in the past. And if that alone is accomplished, it would amount to a major revolution in, and upgrade of, Israeli democracy.

— 12 —

Principal Findings and Lessons

1. INTRODUCTION

This study's purpose was not to document history but rather to evaluate policy. I examined various episodes in Israel's history—principally the major wars in which it was involved—as well as long-term policy issues—such as the limited use of force, nuclear policy, peace diplomacy, and covert interventions. Several common findings emerge from this investigation. The following section outlines the most significant ones. The last section draws some policy recommendations on the basis of these findings. These findings and recommendations serve as a basis for the outline of some future scenarios in chapter 14.

2. PRINCIPAL FINDINGS

1. *Several of the principal assumptions on which Israel's national security doctrine was built are based on flawed empirical foundations. Despite the fundamental flaws in these assumptions the security and foreign policy elite in Israel never revised the basic building blocks of its doctrines.*

Israel's security and foreign policy has rested since its inception on the premise that it was under a constant and severe existential threat: that the Arab states and the Palestinians were bent on the destruction of the Jewish state. The perceived severity and magnitude of this threat were due to two fundamental sets of evidence. Arab rhetoric indicated the intent to carry out this threat. It suggested—as Harkabi (1972) points out—the totalism of the Arab aims. The material and human asymmetry between Israel and the Arab world indicated that the Arabs had the potential capabilities for annihilating the state of Israel.

This threat perception was shared by Israeli practitioners and by many scholars who studied Israel's politics and society in general and its security and foreign policy in particular. There is no question that this was and to some extent still is a genuine perception at both the elite and mass levels.[1] But what is the validity of these perceptions?

Because this book is not about Arab intentions and policies, we cannot go into a detailed analysis of the extent to which Israel's threat perception matched the actual intentions and policies of the Arab states and of the Palestinians. I did discuss previously, however, three important aspects of Arab intentions and policies. First, the analysis of official and unofficial writings and speeches of Arab leaders, opinion makers, and others suggests very clearly that Arab rhetoric was extremely hostile and still tends to be so. It was and still is considerably anti-Israeli and anti-Semitic. So there is more than a grain of truth to the Israeli threat perception. Yet, from the late 1960s on, there has been an increasing trend in Arab rhetoric that suggests a willingness to accept the state of Israel and to live in peace with it. There has also been a growing wave of self-criticism in parts of the Arab world and among the Palestinians regarding the adverse effects that the Arab-Israeli conflict has had on the Arab world. This trend, which for the lack of a better term I will label "Arab liberalism," is more than offset by the growing radicalism among Islamic groups that is both anti-Western and anti-Semitic. But Arab liberalism is a new trend; the link of Arab-Israeli peace to progress and democracy in the Arab world is a new brand of liberalism, one that did not exist before.[2]

Second, there is a huge gap between the hostility to Israel in Arab rhetoric and the actual efforts invested in fighting it. In fact, for a long time there may well have been an inverse correlation between rhetoric and effort in the Arab-Israeli conflict: those states and groups that made the most noise did the least action. Moreover, the states that suffered the most casualties in the conflict were—for the most part—the first to engage in de facto or de jure peace with Israel. And given the stability of the Egyptian-Israeli and Jordanian-Israeli peace agreements, and even the Syrian-Israeli disengagement agreement in the Golan Height, it is fair to say that the existential threat from the immediate circle of enemies was removed to a considerable degree.

Third, at no time—including during the 1948 War of Independence—did the Arab world invest in the kind of human and material resources that would have been required to carry out a military or economic campaign capable of bringing about the destruction of Israel. Only a very small proportion of the population in the Arab states serves in the armed forces. Only a relatively small proportion of the GDP in most Arab states goes to military expenditures. Moreover, most of the states in the region—even those that had suffered greatly from Israeli military actions and the occupation of their territories—did not engage in developing WMDs that would allow them to destroy Israel. As we saw in chapter 8, most programs aimed at developing WMDs and delivery systems in the Arab world emerged largely in response to Israel's nuclear policy. In each and every war—including the 1948 War of Independence—Israel enjoyed an overwhelming superiority in terms of both quantitative and qualitative capabilities to the Arab forces that actually confronted it. Israel was never the David in this conflict, and the Arabs never played the role of Goliath. As we shall see in chapter 13, the qualitative and quantitative edge that Israel enjoys over any plausible Arab coalition is substantial and is widening as time goes by.

As we saw in chapter 8, the notion of an all-encompassing Arab coalition was always a myth rather than an empirical reality. Even when there seemed to be an Arab effort to pool resources in order to attack Israel—in 1948, in 1967, and in 1973—the instances of deceit and the failure to fulfill actual pledges by various Arab states to others were far more numerous and far more severe than the cases of mutual help and joint efforts by several Arab states dedicated to the purpose of fighting Israel. The Palestinian issue may have captured much of that Arab rhetoric. But the actual effort that the Arab states invested in defending and supporting the Palestinians or in actually helping them realize their dreams (whatever these may have been) was minimal. Both in peace and in war, the Arab states were far more likely to betray and deceive each other than to act in concert.

Another foundational assumption of Israel's security policy was the debilitating constraints of Israel's geographic features on its war-fighting strategy. The upshot—which applied to a large extent to Israel's geography prior to 1967—was that Israel could not afford to fight defensive wars due to its small size and narrow "waist." This idea was an important incentive for the "second round" rhetoric in the early 1950s, for the Sinai campaign, and for the preemptive strike in 1967. While this axiom had some plausibility in the 1950s and 1960s, it certainly was not true after 1967. The opposite assumption shared by many Israeli strategists after the Six-Day War—that territorial depth would give Israel strategic breathing space—also does not hold water. First, the War of Attrition and the Yom Kippur War suggest that the territories were not much help; in many ways they became a trap. Second, technology—especially Revolution in Military Affairs (RMA)-related technologies such as precision-guided munitions (PGMs)—enables a defensive strategy that is capable of stopping large enemy formations much before they reach the battlefield. Third, contrary to Israeli strategic thinking, the possession of territories damaged Israeli conventional deterrence because it increased Arab motivation to challenge it (Maoz 1990b, 90–96) and because it imposed constraints on Israel's ability to use offensive force in a preemptive manner, as evidenced by the Israeli decision to refrain from a preemptive strike on October 6, 1973. Finally, Israel's geography may well be a diplomatic asset. It legitimizes the demand for security arrangements in the context of peace agreements, such as the demilitarization of border areas, international buffer forces, and reduced force zones in adjacent areas. These security arrangements not only increase Israel's security—possibly more than territorial depth and so-called defensible borders—but also serve as confidence and security building measures (CSBMs), which reduce the risk of inadvertent war. And as we have seen in the study of the origins of the Six Day War, inadvertent wars can happen.

It is particularly important to examine the "Iron Wall" axiom. Jabotinsky's conception of an Iron Wall—a Spartan state living on its sword—that would ultimately convince the Arabs to make peace became an implicit foundation of Israel's security conception. Did Israeli security benefit from following this logic? This study argues that it did not. On the contrary, Israel's success in fighting wars did not result in a greater degree of acceptance by its enemies. Its greatest military victory only served to increase Arab motivation to fight. Rather, it was only when Israel's leaders reached the conclusion that the sword cannot "devour forever"—to use Dayan's phrase—and realized the need for concessions that Israel got its peace. Technological and military superiority did not save Israeli society from paying a high price due to Palestinian terrorism and Hizballah guerrilla warfare. It was only its unilateral withdrawal from Lebanon that cut its losses in that unfortunate war (also driven by the Iron Wall conception). And it may well be that its decision to build a wall around the West Bank and Gaza—which is an actual admission of defeat of military strategy in the Al Aqsa Intifada—will serve to cut down on its casualties in this unfortunate and prolonged fiasco.

Because many of the basic axioms of Israel's security conception appear to be flawed, quite a few of the principles of Israel's strategic doctrine discussed in chapter 1 are in need of revision. This need stems both from discrepancies between the abstract principles and their practical implementation and from basic problems with the principles themselves. I discuss briefly how the major principles of Israel's security doctrine match with the findings of the present study.

2. *Quite a few of the basic principles of Israel's security doctrine either have not been applied in accordance with the doctrine or have not been adhered to at all. Consequently, it is imperative to reassess these principles and to revise at least some of them.*

I review here very briefly each of the basic principles of Israel's security doctrine, discuss their inherent theoretical problems or the problems related to their application, and suggest ways in which they should be reassessed and revised.

1. *The principle of qualitative edge.* This principle was and remains one of the few valid principles of Israel's security doctrine. It accounted to a large extent for Israel's overwhelming military superiority since 1948. At the same time, the qualitative technological and human superiority had its limits and sometimes (e.g., in the Yom Kippur War) was also a source of complacency and entrapment. Israel's qualitative edge was not an important factor in its LIC-related performance and in its struggle against terrorism. Israel needs to increase the weight of motivation and resolve in the assessment of qualitative components of military power. Qualitative technological superiority cannot be deployed to compensate for low morale and wars of choice.

2. *A nation at arms.* This principle was followed rather closely by the architects of Israel's security policy over its entire history. As we will see in chapter 13, it had some important benefits in terms of nation-building processes. Yet, as I have pointed out in several places throughout the book, the mobilization of Israeli society carried a heavy cost. It served to prevent real treatment of some fundamental social problems in Israeli society. And over the long run, it had an indirect effect on Israel's economic, technological, and social performance relative to the Western industrialized world, which serves as Israel's reference group in these areas. Some observers of Israel's security have advocated (e.g., Shelah 2003; S. Cohen 2003) a consideration of a new mobilization scheme—a professional standing army and a ready reserve system that is mobilized on a regular basis only for training purposes and is activated in acute emergencies. These observers also recommend a general conscription system, which includes the ultra-orthodox religious and the Israeli-Arab commu-

nities, in addition to people who have physical liabilities that exclude them from military service. The idea is that those who are not drafted into military service can engage in social projects (e.g., social and community work). These ideas merit close consideration, given that the IDF was never a melting pot of Israelis but rather served as a significant factor enhancing and sustaining social stratification and increasing rather than reducing social and economic inequalities.

3. *The principle of strategic defensive and operational offensive.* This principle was nice in theory but was not applied in any systematic manner. In practice—as we saw in parts II–IV of the book—Israel was not really a status quo state. Almost from its inception it sought to alter the territorial, political, and strategic environment in which it lived. We have not discussed the War of Independence but during the period of November 1947–January 1949, Israel acted to create a fait accompli that would alter fundamentally the very same partition resolution it had accepted.[3] It initiated two aggressive wars that were designed to change the political structure of its region through regime change. It engaged in multiple covert ventures designed to affect domestic political processes in Arab states and the Palestinians. And it relied on escalation dominance strategies both in its LIC-related warfare and in its high-intensity wars. Paradoxically, the only area where Israel was strategically defensive was its peace diplomacy. In this field it seldom launched peace initiatives, generally displaying risk-averse behavior. This principle requires fundamental reassessment not only due to its weak empirical foundations but also due to its questionable strategic value.

4. *Short wars aimed at quick military decision.* This is a nice principle in theory, except that it does not work in practice. Israel can determine sometimes when a war will start, especially if it is the initiator of this war. It can almost never determine, however, when a war will end. Even when it reaches a conventional military decision, the adversary can shift to a different strategy. The only war in which this principle seems to apply was the Sinai War. The quick victory in the Six Day War soon turned into the three-year War of Attrition. In the Yom Kippur War, after Henry Kissinger talked Israeli decision makers out of a cease-fire in place, Israel actually sought to prolong the war in order to complete its military operations against the Egyptians and Syrians. The Lebanon War illustrates more than any other case the inapplicability of the short war principle. The Al Aqsa Intifada corroborates this finding. In fact, Israeli society has shown a surprising degree of resilience and staying power even when the wars were not consensual and even when they were seen by

most of the public as "wars of choice." Israel's strategic history suggests, as a matter of fact, an entirely different principle: the wider the territorial margins of Israel, the higher the need to fight long wars.

5. *Major power support for war.* Israel has generally adhered to this principle, but its operational interpretation in specific cases has been rather loose. In the Sinai War, this entailed a contractual treaty with two declining colonial powers, but Israel failed to secure the support of the United States, and this turned out to be a crucial flaw in the plan. In the Six Day War Israel worked hard at obtaining U.S. support for a first strike, but all it got was some vague statement. Nevertheless, this consultation proved useful because the United States ended up backing up Israel's actions. In the War of Attrition Israel escalated despite U.S. reservations and had to reluctantly accept the American-initiated cease-fire proposal. In 1973, U.S. opposition to a preemptive strike served to kill this option. This proved to be a crucial decision, as it was instrumental in securing U.S. diplomatic and military support during the war and immediately following it (to the point of a declaration of a nuclear alert by the United States on October 23–24). In Lebanon Israel again invested a great deal of effort in attempting to secure U.S. support and got some equivocal statement. However, during the war it acted in total defiance of American demands. Surprisingly, it was not punished for this. In the Gulf War of 1991, American opposition to an Israeli strike on Iraq was the principal factor that determined Israeli restraint. And Israel benefited from this in the long run. During the Al Aqsa Intifada, the relations between the two states fluctuated between tension and close cooperation. In general, however, both states saw eye to eye on most political and military issues, and Israel did make an effort to coordinate with the Unites States the principal moves. Of all the basic principles of Israel's security doctrine, this was by far the most useful and beneficial one.

6. *Autonomy of action before alliance.* This principle is difficult to evaluate because reality forced Israel to adhere to it; it did not have much of an option. Israel was never offered a long-term defense alliance with anybody. At best it engaged in secret collaboration (e.g., the Sinai War) or in less than full-fledged strategic collaboration (e.g., the Memorandum of Agreement [MOA] with the United States since 1981). In the few instances where Israel acted autonomously and in defiance of friends of allies, the diplomatic results were mixed. In some areas, however, Israel may consider rethinking this principle. This may apply to Israel's future reliance on nuclear weapons for security instead of a binding defense pact.

7. Cumulative deterrence. The performance of Israel's cumulative deterrence concept is mixed at best. Almog (2004, 1995), Bar Joseph (1998), and Lieberman (1995) may be correct in arguing that cumulative deterrence was effective in reducing Arab propensity to attack Israel. Cumulative deterrence may have even played a role in bringing the Arab states to the negotiation table. That said, however, cumulative deterrence did not free Israel from the need to make territorial concessions to ensure peace. Nor was it effective against guerrilla and terrorist attacks. When Israel relied exclusively on cumulative deterrence, it ended up engaging in additional wars and conflicts. It was only when its deterrence policy was supplemented by political flexibility that deterrence had its maximal effect.

8. The Samson Option. This principle was followed closely by Israeli decision makers starting in the early 1960s, and the policy remained largely unchanged. As I argued in chapter 8, this policy brought more harm than good. I elaborate on this later, but the implication is that Israel would be better off reconsidering the substitution of nuclear deterrence by regional security structures that entail WMD disarmament.

9. Settlements determine borders. Israel followed this policy consistently and systematically. But this policy did not do much good. Israel had to dismantle its settlements in the Rafah area following the Camp David Accords of 1978; it had to give up Taba following the international arbitration of 1985. In both cases it benefited from doing so. Moreover, the intention of Ariel Sharon, the architect of Israel's settlement policy since the late 1970s, to dismantle the Israeli settlements in the Gaza Strip suggests that it is politics and diplomacy that determined and will continue to determine Israel's final boundaries, not its settlement policy. There is one thing to be said, however, for this principle. The Palestinian acceptance at Camp David in 2000 and in Taba in 2001 of the principle that Israel would annex its blocs of Jewish settlements in the West Bank does support this principle to a limited extent. Whether this acceptance is translated into a viable political agreement between Israel and the Palestinians and whether this agreement would hold remain to be seen.

Many of these arguments about the validity and adaptiveness of the basic tenets of Israel's security doctrine and its foreign policy posture will be elaborated upon in the following findings. I turn now to more general points that emerge from the analysis in the various chapters of the book.

3. *Israel's approach to the use of force was risk acceptant and trigger happy. Most of Israel's wars were either due to its aggressive designs, due to miscalculations in conflict management strategies, or avoidable. Its limited force strategies were largely ineffective.*

The notion that Israel's wars were wars of self-defense and that its limited military actions were primarily "retaliatory" in nature rests on shaky foundations. Many Israeli politicians and institutional historians have tried to sell the world and the Israeli public for decades the conception that Israel's military actions were primarily actions of self-defense. Some Israeli strategists have supported this notion by arguing that Israeli strategic posture was politically defensive (i.e., status quo oriented) but militarily offensive (e.g., Yaniv 1987a, 1995; Tal 2000; Levite 1989). The second part of this observation is generally true; the first part is not. The central conclusion of the first part of this book is that most of Israel's wars were the result of deliberate aggressive designs or flawed conflict management strategies. At least one war (the Yom Kippur War) could have been avoided by judicious diplomacy. Israel's war experience is a story of folly, recklessness, and self-made traps. None of the wars—with the possible exception of the 1948 War of Independence—was what Israelis call *Milhemet Ein Brerah* ("war of necessity"). They were all wars of choice or wars of folly.

Israel has often used LIC as a vehicle for escalating its conflict with the Arab states, thus paving the way for major military showdowns. The distinguishing feature of Israel's limited force strategy (as well as its strategy of high-intensity conflict) has been escalation dominance. Even when the chief objective of the limited military actions was to avoid escalation, the escalation dominance principle dominated military action. This logic of escalation dominance got Israel into significant trouble in the mid-1960s, causing a slippery slope that led to the Six Day War. In the same vein, the policy of assassinations during the Al Aqsa Intifada provoked escalation of violence and led to the Israeli reoccupation of the West Bank and repeated incursions into the Gaza Strip.

On the whole, Israeli approach to the use of force was risk acceptant. Israel's decision makers tended to overwhelmingly and systematically rely on the use of force as a favorite solution to both military and political challenges. This culture of trigger happiness characterized all of Israel's governments, regardless of period and of the person or party in power. The effectiveness of this tool has been limited at best (Bar Joseph 2004, 149–52). None of Israel's major military encounters—those in which it won overwhelmingly, those in which its victory was a pyrrhic one (e.g., the Yom Kippur War), or those in which it lost (e.g., the Lebanon War and the Al Aqsa Intifada)—led to a political outcome that made Israel more secure than it had been before their outbreak. Israel's limited use of force strategies—by and large—proved ineffective, and some of them even backfired to produce unwanted outcomes. Israel's national security was improved not by the use of force but by the willingness to give diplomacy a chance as a substitute for the use of military strategies.

4. *Israel's nuclear policy did not accomplish any of its direct goals or the positive side effects attributed to it by Israeli strategists. On the contrary, the policy had significant adverse side effects. It was instrumental in fomenting a nonconventional arms race in the region, and it created an antidemocratic regime of secrecy and deceit lacking any significant civilian oversight.*

Israel's nuclear policy—both its nuclear weapons program and its policy of ambiguity—is considered by many to be the pinnacle of success of Israel's national security policy. Zeev Schiff), the renowned Israeli military commentator, sums up some of the key points in the following argument (2001, 247):

> If I had to recommend someone for the Israel Award [the most prestigious award in Israel] for security conception, I would have awarded it to whoever invented . . . the conception of nuclear ambiguity. Since we have considerable experience extending over decades that indicates clearly the success of this conception and that it had a positive effect on our enemies. And it was effective from a deterrence perspective, and it proved effective in terms of our relations with the United States, the administration, the Congress, and American public opinion. And I will also add that it also had a positive effect on the IDF, in the sense that the overall calculations of the IDF did not create a situation in which someone in the General Staff thought that it is possible to reduce the conventional capability of the IDF only because the entire world says and thinks that Israel had nuclear capability. This is an unequivocal success in terms of all of the above points.

My findings challenge this widespread belief. Israel's nuclear policy had little or no effect on the Arab design to destroy the state of Israel simply because this design did not go beyond the realm of pipe dreams in terms of allocation of resources or inter-Arab military and diplomatic coordination. On the contrary, each time Israel armed its nuclear weapons in an effort to deter an Arab attack or to limit escalation, it consistently failed in effecting a desirable outcome. Moreover, the argument of Israeli strategists that its nuclear policy was instrumental in limiting Arab operational objectives or in bringing them to the negotiation table is not supported by empirical evidence. The limitation of Arab operational objectives was induced by limited political objectives and by conventional deterrence. The key influence that Israel exerted on Arab's decision to make peace was a perception of moderation in Israel rather than a perception of capability.

Israel's ambiguous nuclear doctrine rests on shaky theoretical and logical foundations. It cannot be logically construed as a last-resort general deterrence policy. It has built-in destabilizing features in that it can be easily interpreted as an offensive strategy in which tactical nuclear weapons might be used in conventional war situations. Concomitantly, this policy has generated over the years two significant adverse side effects. First, it was instrumental in fomenting a nonconventional arms race in the region, encouraging some states to develop nuclear weapons while pushing others into developing the "poor man's WMD"—chemical, biological, and ballistic missile capabilities. Second, the policy of ambiguity formed a regime of secrecy and deceit that allowed the technocrats in the defense industry—with the help of eager politicians—to develop capabilities that were not in line with the principal goals of general deterrence and may have even accelerated nonconventional arms races in the region. This nuclear regime operates strictly outside the bounds of the control and oversight of political institutions and public debates. Schiff's statement contains an inherent contradiction that accentuates a key problem of Israel's nuclear policy: it did not diminish the need to develop a strong conventional capability because Israel's nuclear weapons did not lower the likelihood of conventional military challenges (and may even have increased it).

5. *Israel's peace policy has been as reluctant and risk averse as its military policy has been daring and risk acceptant. Israel has almost never initiated any significant peace effort. It was as responsible for the failure of peace-related efforts as were the Arab states or the Palestinians. When this pattern of hesitation, reluctance, and fear was broken and Israel made a sincere effort at peace, this generally paid off. Israel's security and international standing after major peace agreements have improved dramatically compared to the prepeace periods.*

Israel's spokespersons often claim that Israel has always outstretched her hand for peace, only to be greeted by hostility, animosity, and rejection. The facts suggest that Israel was the spoiler of peace on numerous occasions. A comprehensive analysis of Israel's peace policy shows that Israel has been at least as responsible for missing opportunities for peace as have its adversaries. Israel has almost never initiated a peace plan, and it has been a reluctant partner to the peace initiatives originating in the Arab world and elsewhere. In many cases, Israel put deliberate or unintended obstacles in the path of peace. Its decision makers were reluctant to make the concessions required to have peace initiatives materialize. They were often slow to respond to the other side's overtures and have often raised petty objections and obstacles that have derailed serious efforts at transforming the conflict.

On those rare occasions when Israel made daring efforts to render peace negotiations successful, it usually benefited. The returns of Israel's reluctant peace policy were far more beneficial than the returns of Israel's daring military policies. The history of Israel's peace policy strongly refutes the myth of clinging to occupied territory as a measure of security. Most of the cases wherein Israel was willing to apply the "land for peace" principle helped stabilize and improve Israel's security. Even the limited and problematic experiment of the application of the "land for peace" principle toward the Palestinians suggests that it had the potential of transforming and stabilizing Israeli-Palestinian relations.

Israel's reactive and reluctant peace policy was embedded in deep psychological problems that plagued its political leadership and its society. It was also affected by structural and political problems and by strategic myths that were never evaluated in terms of their actual performance. These factors continue to operate and constitute formidable barriers to peace. Unless they can be overcome, Israel will continue to live by its sword.

6. *Israel's overt and covert ventures designed to manipulate domestic politics within the Arab States or among the Palestinians have not only failed miserably; in many cases these ventures have backfired to the point of forming or empowering enemies that were far worse, more determined, and more dangerous than those they were designed to remove.*

Israeli efforts to manipulate domestic political processes within Arab states were based on the notion of "the enemy of my enemy is my friend." This notion proved tenuous time and again. In some cases, the enemy of the enemy turned out to be an even fiercer enemy. More important, even if this notion had been true, it was true until the enemy of the enemy stayed enemies with the enemy. Politics in the Middle East not only can lead to strange bedfellows but may also lead to frequent changes in rivalries. Israel spent enormous resources to cultivate actors and groups in the region that had been engaged in conflict with Israel's enemies. Even if such alliances worked for a while, they usually turned out to be short term and one sided. When push came to shove, Israel's allies in the Arab world frequently betrayed or reneged on their alliance commitments. In some cases (e.g., Lebanon) the allies dragged Israel into war; in others (e.g., the Sudanese rebels, the Lebanese Phalanges, and the Kurds), they failed to meet their commitments when this alliance was put to test. In other cases (e.g., the pro-Jordan forces in the West Bank, the village leagues, and the shah in Iran), Israel bet on the losing horse, often provoking and strengthening the opponents of Israel's allies. Despite repeated failures and counterproductive outcomes of the policy of intervention in intra-Arab affairs, Israel continued to attempt such efforts in the PA during the intifada.

7. *The fundamental problems in Israel's security and foreign policy are due to many reasons. But perhaps the most important structural cause of these problems concerns the domination of Israel's national security and foreign policy by a centralized, narrow-minded, self-serving, and self-perpetuating security community. The most successful feature of this community is that it has managed to resist virtually every effort to reform it or to reduce its impact on both security and nonsecurity (e.g., diplomacy) matters. It has also succeeded in concealing numerous blunders and continuous policy failures or in diverting attention from the ineffectiveness of many of the policies it supported. The cabinet, the parliament, the judiciary, and the civilian bodies that are authorized to conduct policy planning and policy evaluation (e.g., the NSC, the Foreign Ministry, the Knesset CFSA) lack the ability and the will to properly oversee policy in these areas.*

The structure of the Israeli system of policy-making on national security and foreign affairs is sociologically, organizationally, and culturally centralized. This system is dominated by the security community. The IDF possesses a nearly complete monopoly over intelligence analysis and assessment both on military and on political affairs. The security community—more specifically, the IDF—is the only body in Israel with the staff and organization to conduct both short-term and long-term policy planning and crisis management. The Foreign Ministry's principal task is to explain policy—even foreign policy—rather than to participate in making it. Other civilian bodies—such as the NSC—have little or no impact on policy planning and policy-making. The consistent absence of political oversight of these bodies by the political system is even more perplexing. The Knesset CFSA has failed to fulfill its primary responsibility for over five decades. It serves as a window dressing for almost every policy of the community and the government. The judiciary has consistently cir-cumvented both international law and virtually any basic standard of human rights and civil liberties in rulings that legitimized the security community's violations of human rights in the occupied territories. It also denied basic human rights to Israelis who were charged with security-related crimes. As such, the judiciary—the HCJ in particular—has served as a partner in crime to the policy establishment.

The sociology of the part of the political system that deals with national security affairs helps perpetuate the domination of the old boys' network on the making and evaluation of policy in these matters. The extensive involvement of former military officers in policy-making and in the legislature hampers independent analysis and evaluation of these policies. These former generals also serve as accomplices in the efforts of the security community to create high barriers for civilian organizations that could limit the monopoly of the existing institutions on shaping pol-icy. Officers in uniform and former officers in the cabinet and in the Knesset form a tight-knit group despite the diverse views of its members on key policy issues. This group tends to consistently assign priority to security considerations over other considerations in the making of policy.

A similar sociology characterizes the judiciary. The background of many Supreme Court justices involves long experience in shaping judi-cial guidelines in the IDF and the government. Many of them served in the IDF and in the government as attorney generals and prosecutors, defending the executive's policy on national security matters. This cre-ates a closed system of self-perpetuating values and ideas that are immune to criticism and oversight. Unless fundamental changes take place in this structure, the adverse patterns and follies that we have observed through-out this book are likely to persist in the future.

8. *The psychology of war, peace, and national security of Israel is character-ized by a seeming contradiction: frequent fluctuation between a siege men-tality and an attitude of arrogance. This fluctuation from one extreme—characterized by deep paranoia—to another—characterized by contempt and condescension of others—has served to underlie a wide array of policies and behaviors in Israel's history. A more thorough understanding of this phenomenon is needed.*

This book is not a study in the political psychology of national secu-rity. Yet, it is impossible to avoid some observations about the psychological factors that seem to have affected various aspects of Israel's national security and foreign policy. Similar perceptions of fear and arrogance have emerged in the study of peace and war decisions, policies of covert intervention, the policy of nuclear weapons development, and the arming of nuclear weapons in times of crisis. These perceptions characterize the writings and speeches of most Israeli leaders. They also characterize public perceptions (Arian 1995). The siege mentality has been at the root of Israel's trigger happiness and the pursuit of escalation dominance in the use of force. It shaped the doomsday scenario that gave birth to the notion that nuclear weapons can serve as an ultimate insurance policy. And it also served as the underlying logic of various efforts at affecting the domestic politics of Arab states (e.g., the "mishap" of 1954). The feeling of arrogance was a direct outgrowth of successful Israeli performance on the battlefield, which cultivated notions that the Arabs would come to the negotiation table on Israel's terms because they were too weak to induce Israel to make concessions. Such perceptions of paranoia, on the one hand, and a sense of arrogance, on the other, are not uncommon in enduring rivalries. However, what seems to be rather unusual in the Israeli case are the extreme and rapid shifts from one to the other.

Clearly, these elite and public perceptions were genuine to a large extent. There is, however, reason to believe that quite a few Israeli politicians have manipulated the shift from one type of belief to another to advance both their perception of national goals and their narrow political interests. A thorough and detailed study of the political psychology of Israel's national security and foreign policy is urgently needed. If we are to help Israel alter its fundamental behavior, it needs to be put on the couch; the psychological problems of both its leaders and its public opinion need to be identified in order to be cured. Having another Anwar Sadat serve as Israel's national psychiatrist by coming to Jerusalem is not likely to happen. It is not clear that it is advisable either. It is incumbent upon Israelis to face up to their fears and superiority complexes and to deal with them.

3. AN ALTERNATIVE SECURITY POSTURE

The notion that Israel has no short-term way of affecting regional developments has long characterized Israeli thinking. On the one hand, Israel's strategic and political ideology was based on the notion that its staying power and deterrence policy will ultimately determine its acceptance into the region. Its diplomacy, however, was assumed to have little effect on the fundamental attitudes of the Arab states. Thus its military strategy was generally proactive and relied on initiatives and on excessive force. Its diplomacy was generally reactive and hesitant. The notion of an "Iron Wall" is still a fundamental maxim in Israeli thinking.

On the other hand, Israel did try to manipulate regional developments through its policy of the periphery. Its semisecret ties with Iran in the 1950–79 period and with Turkey in the 1960–90 period (and the open relations with Turkey afterward) represent one aspect of this proactive regional diplomacy. The cases of intervention in intra-Arab affairs that I discussed in chapter 9 represent another facet of this kind of diplomacy. When there was a sense in the early 1990s that many states in the region were finally willing to accept Israel into the region, Israeli diplomacy was converted almost instantly into a proactive regional cooperation mode. This was guided by Peres's vision of a new Middle East. And it invoked a great deal of suspicion and resistance in the Arab world long before the Oslo process collapsed. Many argued that it was not so much the pushy Israeli diplomacy that provoked this reaction. Rather, any major regional arrangement in which Israel was a major player challenged the national identity notions of other regional actors, such as Egypt (Landau 2001; Landau and Malz 2003; Krause 2003). This is mentioned as an important reason for the failure of the multilateral talks, especially in the ACRS context.

Israel must abandon the assumption that only steadfastness and deterrence on its side would affect the Arab attitudes toward peace. A deterrent posture is effective only if it is accompanied by reassurances, and even then it may fail. In order to reach a fundamental transformation of the relations in the region, Israel needs to examine the possibility that true cooperative gestures have long-term impact on Israel's environment no less—and perhaps more—than deterrent or compellent moves. Israel was able to effect large-scale regional developments not by trying to manipulate the domestic setup or international orientations of actors in the Middle East but rather by changing its relations with regional actors in an overt and explicit manner. Israel's deterrence may have had a cumulative effect on Sadat's decision to visit Jerusalem, but it was only the Israeli willingness to withdraw from the Sinai and to offer concessions on the Palestinian issue that sealed the peace treaty. Once the peace with Egypt was signed, it has been primarily the redefinition of Egyptian interests that has held it stable.

The Israeli-Egyptian peace treaty had a watershed effect on regional developments. The isolation of Egypt in the Arab world over the

1979–88 period turned into a general acceptance of Sadat's strategy by all Arab states. The Oslo Accords and the Israeli-Jordanian peace treaty converted regional politics into a far more cooperative mode than they had been in the past—even in an inter-Arab context. Israel may have little effect on the political and social liberties within Arab states, but Arab states are not oblivious to the relationship between democracy, economic liberalization, and development that Israel signifies.

Israel's peace diplomacy may have a major impact on the turn of events in the Middle East. As long as the conflict with the Palestinians continues, and as long as the relations with Syria and Lebanon are fundamentally hostile—even if not violent—the impact of liberal forces on states in the region is apt to be marginal. On the other hand, the impact of radical forces is likely to increase. Even if most governments in the region have shown a great deal of prudence and levelheadedness in terms of foreign policy, the need to pay lip service to the radical forces has limited their willingness and ability to engage in joint problem solving of regional problems.

But even if Israel changes its policies vis-à-vis the Palestinians and Syria, the militarization of the region is unlikely to change if it does not make serious efforts at reaching comprehensive arms reduction agreements. I tried to show in chapter 8 that such agreements would be in Israel's best strategic interests. An aggressive arms reduction initiative—especially in the realm of WMDs—by Israel would have tremendous impact on regional armaments, and it would go a long way toward establishing confidence in the region. This kind of process may well help spill over to other issue areas such as economics, environmental affairs, and civil society and regional institutions.

Israel's long-term security posture can continue to rely on some of the fundamental elements that have characterized it in the past. In particular are the following elements:

1. A strong, mobile standing army that relies on RMA technologies in all four dimensions (air, sea, ground, information). The size of the standing army may be reduced due to changes in missions once the policing duties due to the occupation are no longer part of the duties of the IDF.
2. An active reserve force that could be quickly mobilized during national emergencies. Such a force should be kept ready by annual training of its units. Its principal peacetime mission should be train-

ing, and its units should be used for border guarding missions only under limited circumstances to relieve standing army units.

3. A versatile doctrine that relies on both offensive and defensive postures, as well as training processes and weapons systems that allow quick shifts from one mode of combat to another.

4. A long-range force projection capacity with air, naval, and ground forces for threats beyond the contiguous borders.

5. An effective intelligence using a wide range of sources and methods for information collection and dissemination.

These elements of the security posture can be accomplished through a significantly reduced budget and a significantly smaller standing army. On the other hand, other elements of the current security posture require fundamental change.

1. Significantly enhanced political control of the security establishment by the government, the Knesset, the judiciary, and civilian bureaucracies. The institutions that are constitutionally responsible for overseeing the security establishment should be assigned a significantly more active role. Knesset CFSA needs support staff of professionals who will aid committee members in performing their oversight functions. Legislation allowing the CFSA and its subcommittees more "teeth" in questioning security officials may also enhance its capacity to perform its oversight duties.

2. Intelligence collection needs to be separated from intelligence analysis. The analysis and net assessment functions of intelligence should be taken out of AMAN and handed over to a civilian institution such as the NSC or a specially designed national intelligence council. This civilian administration should have the capability to engage in long-range research and forecasts, as well as in ad hoc and current intelligence assessment. It should have the capability to conduct analyses of general issues that affect national behavior and international processes such as economic patterns, technological patterns, and social and political issues. The personnel of this institution should be diversified in terms of its training and should be exposed to considerably more disciplines and methodologies—specifically social scientific ones.

3. Israel should return to a strictly conventional doctrine and posture and offer to trade its nuclear weapons for an effective regional security

regime that includes both institutions for conflict resolution and conflict management and effective monitoring structures and organizations that could verify compliance with the arms control and disarmament treaties.

4. Israel needs to increasingly rely on a professional army with longer career horizons for both noncommissioned and commissioned officers. This will increase the professionalism of the standing army and will reduce the burden of pensions and grants to IDF retirees who then go on to second civilian careers. It will also reduce the involvement of retired generals in politics.

5. Israel needs to revise and rejuvenate its LIC doctrine and practices. It must increasingly rely on a strategy that combines defensive measures with preventive and offensive ones. While Israel's defensive and preventive (through a combination of good field intelligence—both HumInt and ElInt) measures were relatively effective, its offensive strategies were, in general, counterproductive. Israel must rely increasingly on mobile LIC warfare conducted by small units with an ability to identify targets and hit or capture perpetrators. Israel's LIC strategy must emphasize minimum levels of collateral damage and civilian casualties. Israel must abandon its reliance on collective punishment and blanket escalation, as well as its tendency to rely on static military outposts, roadblocks, and barracks in occupied territories.

6. Israel must reduce its spending on defense industries. Defense industries need to be economically viable organizations with minimum government support. Government spending on the defense industries must be restricted to R&D projects that are essential for continued technological edge as long as regional security arrangements are not up and running. Defense industries need to be streamlined or become economically viable through trade. Since arms trade is likely to decline, some of these industries will have to be transformed to high-tech civilian production.

7. Israel should seriously consider entering into a defense pact with the United States, but not at the expense of an effective regional security regime. If states in the region are willing to move toward the establishment of regional institutions—especially in the security realm—Israel's security needs will be better served by an effective regional security system. However, if such an alliance does not contradict regional security arrangements, or if regional security structures do not appear to emerge, Israel's security may be better served by an alliance

with the United States than by continued possession and development of nuclear weapons.

Each of these elements of Israel's future security posture needs to be evaluated first and foremost in terms of its own interests. But the guiding principle is that Israel's national interests are not incompatible with a stable and cooperative Middle East. The old notion that a divided and factionalized Arab world serves Israel's security has long been refuted by history. A divided Arab world can quickly converge into a unified front if Israel misbehaves, as was the case on the eve of the Six Day War. A unified Arab world can be open minded and receptive toward Israel, as was the case in much of the 1990s. Israeli strategists need to reassess the basic tenets of Israel's security conception and revise many of them. If they do, and if Israel's national security posture changes and so does its diplomatic activity, its overall level of security will improve, and its proclivity for solving problems through repeated use of force will decline substantially. These changes will also have broader regional implications, as I will argue in chapter 14.

— 13 —

If So Bad, Why So Good?

*Explaining the Paradox of the
Israeli Success Story*

1. INTRODUCTION

In this chapter I deal with a fundamental paradox that emerges out of this study. Specifically, how can we explain the seemingly phenomenal success story of the Jewish state despite the tale of follies, problems, and fiascos exposed in the present study? I first discuss the paradox of Israel's success. I then attempt to explain it. In the concluding section, I derive some policy implications of this paradox.

2. THE PARADOX OF THE ISRAELI SUCCESS STORY

This study portrays Israel as a militarized, trigger-happy state that has made diplomacy a subordinate and inferior priority to military strategy. Israel may have had objective security problems, but it has also blown them out of proportion and quite possibly aggravated these problems by its own actions. This study shows that, in most areas of its national security and foreign policy, Israel's policies were not all that successful, to say the least. A society of this sort—one that was armed to its teeth, engaged in never-ending conflict, and persisted in carrying out bad policies exacting high human and material cost—could not survive for a long time. Yet, Israel has not only survived, it has—generally speaking—prospered and developed despite the excessive human and material resources it has expended on security affairs and despite what appear to be self-destructing national and security policies. A few facts will demonstrate the nature and enormity of the Israeli paradox.

The social, political, economic, and military development of Israel over its fifty-six-year period is astounding. Born into a war that led to the mobilization of the entire society, Israel has grown from a population of 650,000 in 1948 to 6.5 million in 2004. In its first five years only, Israeli population grew by more than 1 million and then tripled itself within fifteen years. Most of Israel's population during the first two decades was made up of new immigrants, many of them Holocaust survivors from Europe as well as Jews from Arab countries in Asia and Africa. These immigrants lacked a common language, a common culture, a tradition of service in the military, and a commitment to sacrifice for the sake of accomplishing collective social goals. Most of the new immigrants were not familiar with the specifics of Zionist ideology. They came to Israel as refugees because they had nowhere else to go or because they followed their families who had emigrated there earlier. They were thrown at once into a society that differed dramatically from their societies of origin. Many of the new immigrants came without any financial resources. All of them had to be provided with housing, employment, and basic means of subsistence. They had to be taught the language and provided with basic services and welfare; their children required education, health services, and—in many cases—social care.

At the same time, the resources available to the newly established political and social authorities were extremely limited. The state had no natural resources or other sources of income. It could only rely on its own production capacity. The prestate economy was very limited, largely based on agricultural products and small services. Exports were extremely limited, such that export-related revenues could not be relied upon. The amount of foreign aid was also quite small in the first decade of independence. The major sources of foreign aid were the contributions of Jewish communities abroad and the reparations agreement with Germany. These could cover only a minuscule portion of what the new state needed to absorb immigrants, to deal with its security needs, and to develop its economy and society.

Given these adverse initial conditions, it is remarkable how well Israel has managed to deal with its internal and external challenges over the years. I list a number of key aspects of the Israeli "miracle" to highlight the extent of these achievements. In order to discuss the Israeli paradox in more general terms, I compare Israeli performance on social, economic, political, and military issues to the performance of its key rivals in the Arab-Israeli conflict.

2.1. National Security and Military Capabilities

Israel started out with an armed force of roughly 85,000 people in 1948. During the War of Independence Israel's mobilization ratio (the number of people in the armed forces to the total Jewish population) was roughly 12 percent. This ratio was maintained throughout the period. In 2004, the IDF's nominal military personnel (conscripts and reservists) amounted to 631,000 men and women.[1] Israel's strategic reference group—the group of states that forms the basis for Israel's threat assessment and force-building designs—traditionally (up to 2003) consisted of Egypt, Syria, Jordan, one-third of the Iraqi army (which could be dispatched to the front in case of war with Israel), and one-tenth of the Saudi army. If we examine the ratio of the IDF personnel to that of the reference group, then Israeli military personnel averaged anywhere between one to seven and one to four during the 1948–2004 period. Over the more recent period (1980–2004) this ratio underwent considerable fluctuations. Most of the confrontation states maintained a fairly stable size of military personnel. Iraq, however, more than doubled its military personnel over the 1980–88 period, reaching an armed force of 1 million men. This armed force was sliced in half after Iraq's defeat in the Gulf War. The subsequent defeat and de facto dissolution of the Iraqi military in the 2003 U.S-Iraq War further improved the personnel ratio.

Israel's defense burden (military expenditures to GDP) fluctuated significantly over the period, from a low of 3 percent in 1953 to a high of over 25 percent following the Yom Kippur War and again in 1986. Since the mid-1980s, there has been a constant decline in the Israeli defense burden, reaching a low of 9.8 percent of the GDP in 2000. This figure has increased since the outbreak of the Al Aqsa Intifada and now stands roughly at 10 percent of the GDP. In comparison to its strategic reference group, Israel spends roughly 20 percent more than its entire reference group put together. If we exclude the Saudi factor from this equation,[2] then the ratio of Israel's defense spending to that of Egypt, Iraq, Syria, and Jordan is over 1.5 to 1 in favor of Israel.

In terms of major battle systems, Israel's air combat aircraft fleet is roughly 50 percent the size of the combined air forces of its strategic reference group. The Israeli fleet of main battle tanks is roughly 58 percent the size of the tank force of its strategic reference group. However, these numbers are quite misleading because the quality of the military hardware in the IDF is several times higher than that of its competitors. Gordon (2003) compared the power of the IAF to that of its strategic reference group, taking into account both the number of aircraft and the overall quality of air power, including munitions, infrastructure, manpower, and C⁴I (command, control, communications, computers, and intelligence) systems. This study suggests that the ratio of the IAF's offensive power to that of its strategic reference group is roughly 1.4 to 1. In terms of defensive power this ratio declines slightly to 1.3 to 1 but is still significantly in favor of Israel. Although no comparable analysis for the navies, the armored corps, and the infantry forces exists, it appears that the weighted relative power on these dimensions is similar to the figures concerning the comparative strength of the air forces. If we combine all these factors—taking into account the economic base of military capabilities—then we can get a fairly good assessment of the relative capabilities of the major protagonists in the Middle East over time. This assessment is given in figure 13.1.

Where Israel's relative disadvantage is clearly present is in terms of population ratios. When this ratio is removed from the figure, then Israeli capabilities are higher than that of the most threatening coalition of states in Israel's strategic reference group. So Israel has been able to overcome its inferiority and to surpass the capabilities of its opponents. Even under the most adverse conditions, it is unlikely that Israel would confront simultaneously the entire strength of the coalition, composed of Egypt, Jordan (with whom Israel has formal peace treaties), Syria, an Iraqi contingent, and a Saudi contingent. This represents a worst-case but low probability scenario. It appears therefore that Israel has managed its military capabilities quite well, again dispelling the notion of the Israeli David facing the Arab Goliath.[3]

More important, the qualitative edge in weapons system, C⁴I technologies, logistics, maintenance, and manpower that Israel possesses over the Arab states more than compensates for whatever inferiorities exist in terms of manpower and platforms. In a conventional war involving large formations, these advantages are likely to offset the quantitative disadvantages in terms of platforms that Israel may be subject to, given a surprise attack (Cordesman 2002, 157–63). This is accentuated by the fact that Israel has been one of the leaders in the Revolution in Military Affairs (RMA), which entails reliance on high-end technologies, precision-guided munitions, space-based intelligence, and sophisticated C⁴I systems (Maoz 2004c).

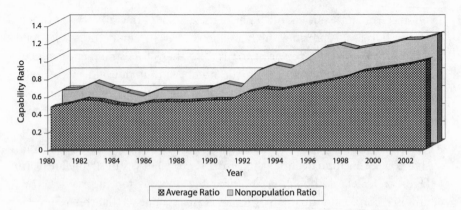

Fig. 13.1. Capability Ratio: Israel/confrontation states, 1980–2003. Capability ratios are calculated as a mean of population ratios, military expenditures ratios, military personnel ratios, main battle tank ratios, and SSMs, weighted by a quality factor. Quality factors are based on Gordon 2003. (Data from Maoz 1996a; QHAIC 2004 [see chap. 2, n5].)

2.2. Economic Performance

Figure 13.2 shows the evolution of Israel's economic growth relative to that of the key Arab states. Figure 13.3 shows changes in per capita GDP over time. These data clearly suggest the extremely robust performance of the Israeli economy compared to the economies of its Arab neighbors. Israel's economic performance is in an entirely different dimension compared to the economies of any of its Arab neighbors. When controlling for the size of the various economies, in terms of per capita GDP, Israel's economic performance is significantly better than all of its neighbors put together.

Not only is the overall growth of the Israeli economy remarkable. What also is notable is the structure of the Israeli economy compared to that of its neighbors. Israeli economy started as a predominantly agricultural economy. For years the major export goods of Israel were agricultural, mainly oranges. The Israeli industrial output increased over the years, but its increase was largely linear. The major nonagricultural export commodity was processed diamonds.

After the economic reform of 1985, which helped curb inflation, a major transformation took place in the Israeli economy. An increasingly large portion of the Israeli output was based on the export of high-tech products, including sophisticated medical equipment, agricultural equipment, and computer hardware and software. The Israeli economy was

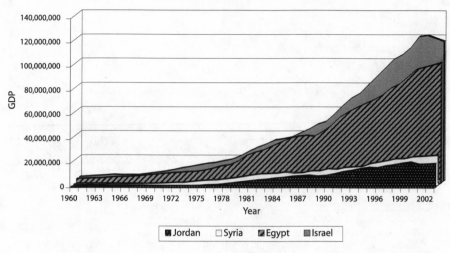

Fig. 13.2. Economic performance of Arab-Israeli protagonists, 1960–2003

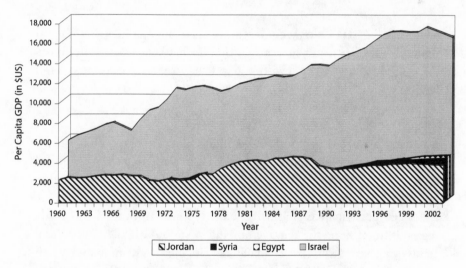

Fig. 13.3. Per capita GDP in the Middle East. (Data from Heston, Summers, and Aten 2002.)

transformed from a semi-industrial, largely centralized, and state-controlled economy to an open market economy and became increasingly incorporated into a globalized international economy. This transformation is apparent in the exponential takeoff of Israeli trade patterns. Israel's total trade started exceeding that of Egypt (a state ten times the Israeli population), and in the late 1980s Israeli trade with the world surpassed the trade of its two major (former) adversaries by a significant

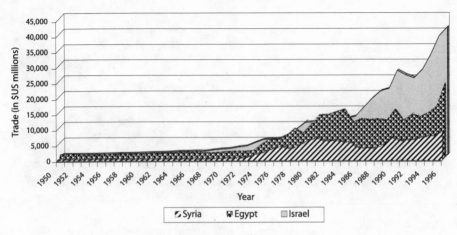

Fig. 13.4. Patterns of total trade of Middle East states, 1950–96. (Data from IMF Direction of Trade, courtesy Barbieri, Keshik, and Pollins 2003.)

amount. The 1993 Oslo Accords sparked again a major increase in Israeli trade levels as both new export and import markets—especially in east Asia—opened up for the Jewish state.[4] These trade patterns are given in figure 13.4.

2.3. Social and Political Performance

Israeli society in the third millennium is a typical OECD society (although it is not a member of the OECD) in terms of most social development indicators. In contrast, virtually all of the societies of its neighbors can be characterized as developing societies. One way to compare the social performance of Israeli society to those of other states in the region is to examine the relative ranking of various Middle East states in terms of a combined index of human development. The human development index, or HDI (UNDP 2003), juxtaposes several social and economic indictors to develop an integrated standard of living index. States have been ranked on this index since 1975. Table 13.1 provides a listing of the ten top-ranked states on the HDI, as well as the ranking of all states in the Middle East. I added to this table a statistic indicating the percentage of the GDP invested in R&D. This is derived from the UNESCO Institute for Statistics Web site (UNESCO 2004).

The table provides illuminating information regarding Israel's level of social development. Israel is ranked 22nd out of 191 countries in terms of its HDI. The next highest country in the Middle East is Bahrain, ranked 37th, and next to it is a set of oil-rich states. Since this index is heavily

TABLE 13.1. Human Development Ranking of States in the Middle East, 2001

HDI Rank	State	Life Expectancy	Adult Literacy Rate	Gross Enrollment Ratio	GDP per Capita	Life Expectancy Index	Education Index	GDP Index	R&D Expenditure % of GDP	Human Development Index (HDI)
1	Norway	78.7	99.9	98	29,620	0.90	0.99	0.95	1.6	0.944
2	Iceland	79.6	99.9	91	29,990	0.91	0.96	0.95	3.04	0.942
3	Sweden	79.9	99.9	113	24,180	0.91	0.99	0.92	4.61	0.941
4	Australia	79.0	99.9	114	25,370	0.90	0.99	0.92	1.53	0.939
5	Netherlands	78.2	99.9	99	27,190	0.89	0.99	0.94	1.95	0.938
6	Belgium	78.5	99.9	107	25,520	0.89	0.99	0.92	0.55	0.937
7	United States	76.9	99.9	94	34,320	0.86	0.97	0.97	2.8	0.937
8	Canada	79.2	99.9	94	27,130	0.90	0.97	0.94	1.85	0.937
9	Japan	81.3	99.9	83	25,130	0.94	0.94	0.92	3.09	0.932
10	Switzerland	79.0	99.9	88	28,100	0.90	0.95	0.94	2.64	0.932
22	**Israel**	**78.9**	**95.1**	**90**	**19,790**	**0.90**	**0.93**	**0.88**	**4.96**	**0.905**
37	Bahrain	73.7	87.9	81	16,060	0.81	0.86	0.85	—	0.839
44	Qatar	71.8	81.7	81	19,844	0.78	0.82	0.88	—	0.826
48	United Arab Emirates	74.4	76.7	67	20,530	0.82	0.73	0.89	—	0.816
73	Saudi Arabia	71.9	77.1	58	13,330	0.78	0.71	0.82	—	0.769
79	Oman	72.2	73.0	58	12,040	0.79	0.68	0.80	—	0.755
83	Lebanon	73.3	86.5	76	4,170	0.80	0.83	0.62	—	0.752
90	Jordan	70.6	90.3	77	3,870	0.76	0.86	0.61	—	0.743
91	Tunisia	72.5	72.1	76	6,390	0.79	0.73	0.69	0.45	0.740
96	Turkey	70.1	85.5	60	5,890	0.75	0.77	0.68	0.64	0.734
98	Occupied Palestinian Territory	72.1	89.2	77	—	0.97	0.85	0.56	—	0.731
106	Iran, Islamic Rep. of	69.8	77.1	64	6,000	0.75	0.73	0.68	—	0.719
107	Algeria	69.2	67.8	71	6,090	0.74	0.69	0.69	—	0.704
110	Syrian Arab Republic	71.5	75.3	59	3,280	0.77	0.70	0.58	0.18	0.685
120	Egypt	68.3	56.1	76	3,520	0.72	0.63	0.59	0.19	0.648
126	Morocco	68.1	49.8	51	3,600	0.72	0.50	0.60	—	0.606
138	Sudan	55.4	58.8	34	1,970	0.51	0.51	0.50	—	0.503
148	Yemen	59.4	47.7	52	790	0.57	0.49	0.34	—	0.470

Source: UNDP 2003. Specific indices are explained in the source.

dependent on per capita GDP figures, HDI indices of the Gulf states are much higher than if the index were based on technology. Israel's present and former rivals—Egypt, Syria, Jordan, Lebanon, and even Iran and Iraq (not in the current versions of the HDI but appearing in previous versions)—are ranked considerably lower on virtually all indices that make up the HDI. The differences are stark, not only considering the human and material resource base of many of these states but even more so considering the fact that many states in the region have fairly homogenous societies and had longer time to develop than Israel.

The Israeli system of education is a highly advanced system. Israel is consistently ranked as one of the top five to ten states in terms of the number of scientific publications per capita. Some of its academic departments are ranked in the top centile of research departments in the world, and many others are ranked in the upper quartile of academic departments. Its technological status is indicated by the production of high-end defense-related technologies such as communication and intelligence satellites; all kinds of late-generation precision-guided munitions (PGMs), including air-to-air, air-to-ground, sea-launched, and land-based ballistic missiles; and a variety of communication technologies. It is also indicated by the large number of R&D sites in Israel of high-tech companies—such as Intel, IBM, Microsoft, and various biomedical and pharmaceutical companies. Israeli scientific achievements were recognized by the granting of Nobel Prizes to four Israeli (or former Israeli) scientists: two in economics and two in medicine.[5]

Israel is the only democratic state in the Middle East—at least with respect to the Jewish population in Israel. The Arab population residing within the green line has nominal full citizen rights, although it is widely agreed that there exists significant economic and social discrimination of this population. Israeli citizens enjoy full civil—personal and collective—liberties, such as the ability to elect and be elected as representatives in free and competitive elections, freedoms of expression, and freedoms of association. Israel is not only a nominal democracy; it is a vibrant, politically active society. Quite a few political analysts would describe Israeli democracy as hyperactive, characterized by a significant level of political instability. This is indicated by the fact that over its fifty-six years of independence, Israel has been governed by no less than thirty different governments—each government averaging twenty months in office. However, despite the high political volatility, Israel's democracy was never under a serious threat. This is quite remarkable in a region wherein almost each state has undergone at least one regime change during the 1948–2004 period (and those that did not simply survived quite a few coup attempts). Despite the social and economic discrimination against Israeli Arabs, the political liberties and economic opportunities of Israeli Arabs far exceed those of their brothers residing in Arab states and in the Palestinian territories.

The key question that emerges from this survey of national security and foreign policy is therefore not explaining why so many structural problems have persisted for so long. Rather, it is to explain why Israel did so well despite so many problems in its national security and foreign policy. The findings of this book seem to be inconsistent with the facts about Israeli economic, political, and social development. The militarization of policy and society, the frequent and excessive use of force, the repeated failures in overt and covert diplomacy, the rampant and uncontrolled escalation of nuclear weapons programs under a veil of secrecy, and the dominant role of the IDF and the security community in policy-making should have worn down the Israeli society, eroded its democratic character, imposed an impossible toll on its economy, and polarized it to a point of civil war. The story of incompetence and follies outlined in this book does not add up to the success story of Israel in terms of military capabilities, economic development, and social and political openness.

An explanation of this puzzle is required if the book's themes are to be taken seriously. Either I have completely missed the key thrust of Israel's policies, criticizing them rather than praising them, or I have overstated the severity and magnitude of the problems I have identified in these policy areas, depicting minor problems as major calamities. Clearly, many of the themes I have emphasized in the previous chapters challenge the conventional wisdom of most Israeli academic students of these matters. They certainly challenge the institutional conventional wisdom that pervades most of the policy issues discussed herein. It behooves me, therefore, to account for this seeming paradox.

I offer three complementary explanations of this paradox of Israeli success and folly. The first explanation focuses on the relative performance of Israeli policies compared to those of its Arab adversaries. The second explanation focuses on the relationship between protracted conflict management and nation building. The third explanation does not challenge the presence of the paradox. Rather, it argues that this paradox has for a long time diminished in importance; there is a longstanding connection between the problems of security and foreign policy and gradual deterioration of Israeli society. This continued social, economic, and political decline may evolve in one of two ways. First, Israel might continue to muddle through by following the same problematic foreign and security policies, and these might convert the seeming success story into a social, political, and economic disaster. Alternatively, Israel might change course radically, thereby reversing the adverse social, economic, and political trends that have plagued the country—in one way or another—since the occupation of the territories in the Six Day War.

3. WITH SUCH ENEMIES, WE CAN AFFORD A FEW FAILURES

David Ben-Gurion often stated that, while the Arabs could afford to lose dozens of wars, Israel could not afford to lose even one. The fact of the matter is that—given the nature of its adversaries and the character of their political, economic, and social systems—Israel could afford to make quite a few mistakes, even lose several military encounters. In fact, Israel's key problem may well have been winning in too many encounters and not losing some. Israel's military success and its social, political, and economic achievements appear to be monumental compared to other states in the Middle East. Yet, when this performance is compared to other states that emerged from the ashes at roughly the same time as Israel was born, it is a quite modest one.

We noted that the Arab states never exerted a concentrated social, political, and military effort in converting the dream of destroying the state of Israel into reality. The rhetoric of genocide and politicide was not backed up by anything close to the kind of resources and diplomatic coordination that was required for realizing this dream. Most Israeli politicians and scholars accepted the fundamental asymmetry in resources as a constant in the strategic equation of the Arab-Israeli conflict. Yet nearly nobody bothered to ask why—if the Arab states were so committed to the destruction of the Jewish state—they refrained from investing the resources required for such a "project." One may argue that Israel's nuclear capability rendered the realization of this dream an act of national suicide. This may be true, but as we saw in chapter 8, the Arab military effort prior to the acquisition of nuclear weapons by Israel had been much lower than it was after Israel acquired nuclear weapons. So this cannot be the reason.

Had the Arabs indeed invested their entire human and material potential in fighting Israel, they could have exhausted the Jewish state socially and economically without firing a single shot. Had Egypt mobilized an army that was proportionate to the size of the Israeli army (a standing army of 3.4 percent of its population and a rapidly mobilizable reserve force consisting of 9 percent of the population) it would have had a standing army of 2.7 million conscripts and a reserve force of over 5 million. Syria's proportionate armed forces would be over 2 million. Even without moving their armies to the border area, just keeping them equipped and in good shape in terms of military preparedness would have imposed on Israel an impossible burden. If both Egypt and Syria had simultaneously raised their military spending to Israel's levels, Israel would have had to return to the level of defense spending of roughly 25 percent of its GDP, barely maintaining a qualitative superiority—with the margin of advantage much lower than the one it currently has. While Israel could sustain this kind of effort for a short time, it would not be possible to sustain this level of human and material effort for a long time. Certainly, if the Arab states had raised their defense spending to levels above 10 percent of their GDP in the early 1950s and 1960s, Israel would have found itself in an unsustainable economic and social situation.

Even if the human and material military burdens of the Arab states were to stay at their current levels, the Arabs could put together an incredible economic and social challenge to Israel simply by forming a military coalition that pooled their resources in an effective and rational manner. Saudi Arabia, for example, spends $22 billion on defense annually, more than twice the Israeli defense budget. It has fairly free access to American and Western European weapons markets. Had it decided to put its military hardware and financial resources at the disposal of this Arab coalition, Israel would have been under extremely precarious strategic conditions. Again, no shots have to be fired in order to erode Israel's capacity to meet these challenges. Finally, consider an effective implementation of the Arab boycott on Israel and on companies trading with it and couple it by a threat to deny or limit the exports of oil to Israel's main trading partners. If the oil-rich Arab states had been willing to suffer the economic costs of such a threat, Israel's trade with the outside world would have significantly declined. Since Israel imports much of its basic needs in food, energy, and industrial inputs, it would not have been able to survive economically.

Thus, there exist several scenarios—none of them far fetched if we follow the logic of Israeli politicians and strategists—in which Israel loses the big war without having a single shot fired at it. But the Arab states never came close to materializing the elements of these scenarios. Why? One of the—quite reasonable—answers to this question is simply that they never had the intention of destroying Israel. Clearly, the numerous peace overtures by Syrian and Egyptian leaders in the early 1950s and the secret meetings between King Abdullah and King Hussein with the Israeli leaders throughout the 1947–94 era suggest as much. The extremely hostile rhetoric was strictly for domestic and inter-Arab consumption; it was a weapon in the struggle for leadership in the Arab world. It was also an instrument for diverting domestic attention from the economic, social, and political problems of the regimes. Right from the start, the Arab leaders knew that destroying Israel was an unrealistic dream. At the same time, they could not afford to change the anti-Israel rhetoric from an extremely hostile one to a peaceful one; many of those who tried paid with their lives. This hostile rhetoric turned into a double-edged sword (Rubin 2002, 193–226).

In light of this situation, the discrepancy between words and deeds in Arab politics portrays a different picture from the one arising from Israeli doomsday scenarios. Starting in the preindependence period, Israel faced a strategic reality that was dramatically different from what its leaders had perceived and—more important—from what they had the Israeli public believe. In this sense, the Israeli leadership was as responsible for misrepresenting the gravity of the conflict to its society as were Arab leaders with regard to their own societies. There was one monumental difference, however, between the employment of hostile perception and rhetoric by Israeli leaders and Arab leaders. The Israeli leadership used the magnified threat perception to effectively mobilize its society for political, economic, and social development. The Arab leadership, almost without exception, used hatred and hostility toward Israel to deepen and perpetuate the state of backwardness, underdevelopment, and political stagnation that characterized the Arab Middle East since the withdrawal of France and Britain in the late 1940s. And it is this difference that helps account for the ability of Israel to develop an effective political, economic, and social system despite the continued state of conflict. I will focus on how this state of conflict helped Israel succeed in its domestic endeavors in the next section. Here I discuss the Arab failure that makes the Israeli success story appear so remarkable.

Arab societies in the 1930s and 1940s had been as underdeveloped as most Asian societies. Both types of societies had been under colonial rule. Both were plagued by problems of poverty, economic underdevelopment, and lack of human and social infrastructure for integration into a modern world. When the colonial powers retreated from states such as India, Pakistan, Korea, Singapore, Indonesia, the Philippines, Thailand, and Vietnam and when the Chinese civil war ended in the retreat of the Kuomintang to Formosa (Taiwan), they left just as much scorched terrain as they had left in the Middle East. And just as the Arab states had an arch-enemy in the form of Israel, most Asian states had a potential or actual enemy that was just as formidable. However, quite a few Asian states overcame the external threat or continued to live with it in a way that did not hamper either their economic development or their political free-doms. Other states, however, used their conflict to do the same things that the Arab states did, stagnating the society and the economy under an authoritarian political system. The case of the two Koreas and the two Chinas is highly illustrative of these points. Both sets of states were divided by either postwar arrangements or civil war. Both parts of the divided society started out under authoritarian or totalitarian rule. In both cases one element of the divided state system prospered and changed into a democratic government under the shadow of conflict, while the other continued to stagnate and deteriorate, using the conflict with the adversary as a lame excuse for the sorry state of affairs of the society, the economy, and the coercive regime.

The Arab world was long plagued by a strong tendency of the elites—both the political and intellectual—to put the blame for their internal problems on others. First these were the colonial powers, the British and the French, then they were the Zionists, and now it is the Americans who are responsible for everything that is wrong in the Arab world. The Mid-dle East is second only to Africa in terms of economic underdevelopment, and it is far less democratic than all of the other regions of the world.[6] The Arab-Israeli conflict is not a cause of this unfortunate state of affairs, but it is constantly used as an excuse—along with the story about the damaging impact of foreign imperialism and influence. Let us consider these linkages in terms of economics, political stability, and social development.

Henry and Springborg (2001) point out that the key determinant of economic development and underdevelopment in the Middle East is political structure. The political system had a major effect on the devel-opment and underdevelopment of economics in the region. This is true for Israel, and it is even a more valid characterization of the Arab states. Most Middle East and North African (MENA) states have had underde-veloped economies that either were largely agricultural and striving toward autarky (low levels of trade relative to their GDP) or were closed by seemingly socialist governments that tried to control traditional economies. The flow of capital and foreign direct investment into most MENA states has been rather slow. The oil exporting states have had economies that rely almost exclusively on foreign trade for both revenues and the import of most basic commodities (including a considerable portion of their labor). For many Middle Eastern states this economic structure was required to support the kind of regimes in power. Some states in the region, such as Algeria and Iraq, are labeled by Henry and Springborg (2001, 20) as "bunker states." The regimes in these states "rule primarily by coercion—from their metaphorical or, in some cases, actual bunkers— because the state lacks autonomy from social formations." States such as Egypt and Syria are labeled as "bully states." They are "largely autonomous from social forces, whether traditional or modern, and have relatively strong administrations though they, too, depend principally on military/security forces." In both bunker and bully states, the influx of capital and foreign direct investment poses a grave threat to the stability of their regimes.

In the oil exporting states and the more traditional monarchies, revenues are largely invested outside the country. Much of the labor—principally more the skilled labor force—is foreign. Here, too, private enterprise and the rise of an entrepreneurial middle class are largely restricted by the regime. The regimes failed to capitalize on the oil boom in the 1970s and 1980s. They increased their import dependence during this era, and the decline in oil prices in the late 1980s and the 1990s forced them to increase borrowing in order to prevent risks to internal stability due to economic recession (Hinnebusch 2003, 45–51).

Even during the "golden era" of the Oslo Accords and the multilateral track in the 1990s, Arab leaders and intellectuals regarded with suspicion and mistrust notions of a "new Middle East" (Peres 1993) in which peace would bring enormous economic and social dividends to states in the region. The leading perception among Arab elites was that Israel would use this notion of the new Middle East to substitute its military domination by economic domination of the region. Peace was seen by many to carry more threats than promise. As Rubin points out (2002, 215), the Arabs did not want to renew the state of war, but they did not want to convert the region into an open economic system in which both information and trade flow freely. This would have threatened the stability of the authoritarian and traditional regimes in the region. Full peace would mean the end of authoritarianism in the region.

But the threat to the Arab regimes was not only from the emergence of a liberal middle class that would opt for democracy. A more immediate and severe threat was that of radical Islam. Islamic groups took upon themselves the championing of anti-Israeli rhetoric in an effort to mobilize opposition to the willingness of the incumbent regimes to make peace with Israel—even if that peace had been a cold one. This opposition forced the Arab rulers to attempt to walk a fine line between their strategic interests that dictated peace and stability in the region and a need to calm down what appeared to be a militant opposition to normalization with the Jewish state. Here the threat to the regimes of a stable and open regional economic system was that radical Islamic groups would rise to power under the guise of democracy. Most Arab states, therefore, retreated again into the authoritarian bunker, using anti-Israeli rhetoric as a diversion device.

Even those states that signed peace agreements with Israel have not been able to transform their societies. Egypt has significantly reduced its defense spending and—since Sadat's *Intifah* (opening or economic liberalization) of 1974—has reduced governmental controls of economic activity and has liberalized trade. This policy has dramatically increased its trade interdependence. However, the more structural aspects of economic transformation—privatization of government-controlled economic enterprises, investment in industrial development, education, and political liberalization—that are necessary for economic development did not happen (Richards and Waterbury 1996, 391–97; Barnett 1992, 128–52; Henry and Springborg 2001, 143–48). Jordan's defense spending was never a major impediment to its economic development, because it was not as high as in other Arab states. However, here, too, the economy was fundamentally stagnant and the regime—faced by threats from Islamic groups and Palestinian opponents—focused on efforts to maintain domestic stability and failed to liberalize (Henry and Springborg 2002, 191–92).

Most leading opponents of Israel are authoritarian regimes that have relied on the military as a major source of regime legitimacy. Egypt has not faced a significant challenge to its regime since 1952, but all of its leaders came from the Free Officers group that staged the 1952 coup. The current president, Hosni Mubarak, is a former commander of the Egyptian air force. In Syria, Hafez Asad was also a commander of the air force, and his son Bashar's orientation involved military service. Nevertheless, none of the Arab states managed to convert its military into an effective war-fighting machine. Pollack's (2002) comprehensive study of the Arab war experience shows a continuously abysmal record of military performance in conventional war. He dismisses arguments that poor Arab military conduct was due to cowardice of soldiers and commanders, to poor unit cohesion, and to poor logistics as unconvincing explanations. Rather, he argues that the key factors that account for the poor battlefield performance of the Arab military consist primarily of poor tactical leadership, poor information management, poor weapons handling, and poor maintenance. Secondary factors that emerged repeatedly in the cases he studied consist of poor generalship, poor morale, and inadequate training.

The abysmal record of performance of the Arabs in war was general. This is evident equally from Arab-Israeli wars as from numerous inter-Arab military confrontations. This record must be understood not only in terms of traditional military history and military strategy. It must be examined in the broader context of the ambivalent role of the military in politics in authoritarian societies in general and in the Arab world in particular. The political role of the top military echelon and its preoccupation with domestic political processes have affected the military's professionalism. The fear that mid-level officers and professional noncommissioned personnel would become a source of rebellion and unrest has always served as a deterrent against developing a modern, professional officer corps in the Arab armies. There were also considerable constraints on the advancement of professional officers who were not from the "right" ethnic group, sect, or tribal origin (Zisser 2002; De Atkine 2002; Rubin 2002, 140–47; Maoz 2003b, 27–28).

Seen in this light, the relative success of Israel appears enormous in light of the tendency of most Arab regimes to use the Arab-Israeli conflict as a justification for the state of underdevelopment and authoritarianism of their societies. Israel's neighbors did so poorly because they used the conflict to perpetuate and deepen the poor human and social conditions that had existed long before the establishment of the state of Israel. Even if they had wanted to invest significant resources in managing the conflict effectively, they were both socially and economically unequipped to do so. Syria, which had embarked on a policy of strategic parity with Israel in the 1980s, discovered very quickly that this was much above its economic capacity (Maoz and Mor 2002a, 196–97). When the Soviets stopped providing Syria with generous credits, demanding instead hard cash for their military hardware, Syria was forced to suspend most of the planned imports. Consequently, the Syrian military faces significant problems due to the obsolescence and decay of its military equipment.

Those Arab regimes that made peace with Israel failed to cash in on the peace dividends. These regimes failed to induce economic cooperation with Israel. In light of these tendencies, it is of little surprise that Israel has been able to do so well economically, politically, and socially. It has never faced a significant economic challenge from the Arab states. Such a challenge would have made diversifying resources for both military security and economic and social projects practically impossible. It was the folly and incompetence of the surrounding Arab regimes that allowed Israel to engage both in ambitious military adventures and in significant economic development. Whether it did so efficiently and sensibly is something we will discuss in section 5.

4. SECURITY AS A GROWTH AND DEVELOPMENT INCENTIVE

In stark contrast to the tendency of Arab states to use the Arab-Israeli conflict as a vehicle for sustaining corrupt, inefficient regimes and underdeveloped societies, Israel was able to use the conflict to do just the opposite. In fact, one of the key puzzles in examining Israel's national security policies concerns the failure of the security community to realize that the actual threat to Israel was far less severe and acute than they had led the public to believe. A plausible explanation is not that the security community failed to realize that the external threat was hardly an existential one but that it actually inflated and manipulated the threat perception of Israelis in order to advance social and economic development processes.

As noted in chapter 7, the IDF during the early 1950s was a fairly ineffective body. Many of the senior commanders of the War of Independence had left the army and returned to their civilian professions. Many of the new recruits were new immigrants, barely conversant in Hebrew and with little motivation to risk their lives for their new country. Fortunately for Israel, the opposing armies were even more ineffective and did not present much of a challenge to the IDF. There was a concern in the political leadership that the IDF's fighting capacity might erode if this trend continued. One aspect of that concern had to do with the decline of the motivation to serve in the IDF, mostly among the more educated people who could qualify for command positions.

At the same time, Ben-Gurion and his associates were preoccupied with the social and economic problems that the country faced with the huge waves of immigration and the economic constraints of a rapidly changing society. Ben-Gurion did not hesitate to enter into a head-on collision with the IDF leadership over cutting the defense budget, up to the point of accepting the resignation of COS Yigael Yadin. So, while the IDF required additional resources to prepare for the next round of war, the government had to invest increased resources into state building and social projects.

The national dilemma was an important source of concern, but Ben-

Gurion and his associates were also astute political animals. They knew that the new immigrants were also new voters and that those voters could bring about the overthrow of the ruling socialist elite. They had to be socialized not only into embracing a new culture but also into supporting a political elite that required them to make major sacrifices. At the same time, the ruling Mapai elite were neither ideologically nor politically willing to abandon their power bases in the various elements of the labor movement—the Kibbutzim and Moshavim and the lower middle class in the central cities.

A society of immigrants, whose social composition changed on an almost daily basis, had also to be unified around a set of symbols that would make people identify with and be willing to sacrifice personal comfort and values. The only common set of values of the new immigrants and the indigenous population was Judaism. But Judaism implied religiosity, and inserting religious values into politics was not something the ruling elites were willing to accept. So an alternative was required. The IDF became the organizing symbol of statehood, nationalism, and Israelism and an alternative to Judaism as a mobilizing instrument. Israeli militarism, as it developed in the early 1950s and intensified in the 1960s and 1970s, was first and foremost symbolic. But the use of a siege mentality as a social motivator took not only a symbolic form; it also had important practical aspects. Four significant strategies were employed to develop militarism as a social motivator and as a state-building force. These strategies were (1) building a fully mobilized society through a system of general conscription and a large reserve force; (2) maintaining the conflict on a back burner, thus cultivating a permanent siege mentality; (3) using the IDF as an instrument of political legitimacy by creating a stratified military force; and (4) engaging the IDF in social and state-building projects. I discuss briefly each of these strategies.

Ben-Gurion felt that building a society united around its armed forces served two purposes. First, it provided a solution to the fundamental security problem that he believed Israel was facing. Second, it provided a symbol that could unite the nation and guide its nation-building process. It could provide a new definition of citizenship—one that stipulates both the obligations and privileges of Israeli citizens. Accordingly, the idea of a combination of a fully mobilized conscript army and a ready reserve army was formed (Ostfeld 1994, 780–81). The compulsory mobilization to the conscript army created armed forces whose size was determined principally by the cohort of Israelis reaching the age of eighteen and a small contingent of newly arrived immigrants below the age of twenty-four. The draft for men was general and almost without exception. Only Israeli Arabs, people with severe medical problems, and a handful of ultra-orthodox youngsters studying in Yeshivas were exempt from compulsory army service. Women were also subject to compulsory draft, but for them it was more selective. Married women, women who declared they were religious, and even women who declared pacifism were exempt. Male recruits were drafted for a period of thirty months initially, and this was increased to thirty-six months after the 1967 war. Women were drafted for eighteen months initially, and later on this was increased to twenty months. The army was run by a relatively small cadre of commissioned and noncommissioned officers who made military service a long-term career.

In addition to the conscript army, a large reserve force was established. This force consisted of all males between the ages of twenty-one and fifty who had been discharged from the conscript army. These men were organized into distinct reserve formations (e.g., divisions and brigades) in the ground forces that were commanded both by reserve officers and by career professional officers. In the air force and navy—which were largely based on both conscripts and career soldiers—reservists complemented the regular units without forming new ones. In nonemergency years, reservists were mobilized every year for varying periods ranging from a few weeks to forty-five days. When a state of emergency was declared, the defense minister could authorize the drafting of some or all of the reserve units.

This mode of service created a situation where almost all males between the ages of eighteen and fifty served in the IDF. Service was seen as an important element of social status in general, and the nature and length of military service was seen as a source of social and political capital (Levy 2003). The political elite and the IDF were particularly adept at developing a strong connection between contribution to the army and contribution to the society at large. No matter what a person did in his or her civilian life, if he or she did not serve in the armed forces, an important element of citizenship and patriotism was missing from his or her social image. Because everybody served in the IDF, and because most healthy adults had to spend at least some time each year in military service, it was important to make this service meaningful. The reserve duties consisted of two principal elements: training and operational activity (which included guarding the borders prior to the Six Day War and policing the occupied territories after the Six Day War). The IDF became a key element in the national identity of Israelis. Therefore, the prolonged compulsory service and the requirement of constant service in reserve duty had to be justified. Following a policy that would reduce tensions and would render that kind of service superfluous was not seen as a good move in terms of the nation-building process.

Ben-Gurion used to say that Israel could not afford to raise two flags simultaneously: the security and social welfare flag could not be made equally important. Security meant survival; therefore, it had to come first; social issues had to be sacrificed for the sake of national security. Justifying the national order of priorities in which people had to make social and economic sacrifice to guarantee security implied that Israel needed a certain level of security-related tension to allow for those social sacrifices. The siege mentality that Ben-Gurion propagated may have been a genuine perception. It was also a very useful social mobilizer. And it may have also been an important aspect of the ruling party's strategy for maintaining its political power. Finally, inflating the security threat emerged as an extremely effective strategy for raising funds from Jews all over the world. Ben-Gurion's statement on October 1, 1952 (see chap. 10, p. 487), that peace with the Arabs was not the top priority should be seen in this light.

With some notable exceptions—for example, the Sinai War and the Lebanon War—most Israeli leaders did not seek to deliberately escalate the conflict in order to advance nation-building projects or to divert attention from domestic problems. Nevertheless, keeping the conflict on a back burner did serve the goal of domestic cohesion. In a system as pluralistic and polarized as the Israeli society, the Arab threat was perhaps the only unifying factor that kept the Israeli polity stable, especially during the first two decades. The cultivation of the siege mentality by the elites worked quite well in this respect. It helped play down fundamental gaps between the social and economic elites, mostly of Ashkenazi origin, as well as the labor movement, which was concentrated in the Kibbutzim and Moshavim. It helped calm down the fundamental conflict between religious movements and a secular state. And it helped justify systematic discrimination against Israeli Arabs.

As long as the widespread belief that Israel was engaged in a long-term existential struggle persisted, the Israeli public—in spite of its deep social and religions divisions—pulled together to advance national goals. But this belief began to gradually shatter, especially following the Lebanon War. The peace with Egypt and the Oslo Accords reduced the Israeli threat perception. This was coupled with a growing polarization with regard to the future of the occupied territories. The implications of this reduced threat perception were significant changes in the attitude of

Israelis to the IDF and to the centrality of military service as a foundation of full citizenship (Levy 2003, 193–235).

There also seems to have been a significant change in the stratifying role of the IDF in Israeli society. As Levy (2003) argues, over the 1950–82 period, the IDF was structured such that its top command posts were overwhelmingly controlled by members of the social elite: males, Ashkenazis, Kibbutz, and Moshav members or officers who came from the upper middle class in the urban centers. Its lower ranks—including most of the noncommissioned officer positions and the service-related positions in the various units—were manned by people from an Asian-African origin and people from the lower and lower middle classes. For the officers who had made the military a long-term career, the IDF served as a springboard to a second career in the political, public, and business sectors after their retirement. Those who served as noncommissioned officers or simple conscripts went out to the civilian world to stay in the social classes from which they had emerged. The image of the IDF as a melting pot and as a vehicle for social mobility was really a facade (S. Cohen 1997, 89–100).

Social, economic, and political changes in Israel during the 1970s and the 1980s reduced the motivation of the traditional elites to use the IDF as a mechanism for maintaining their status in Israeli society. This was accompanied by a fundamental change in the attitude of those elites to the mobilizing role of the Arab-Israeli conflict; many of them began to see the conflict as an impediment to economic and social development and shifted to supporting a political solution to the conflict. This reduced their motivation to serve in the IDF. New social groups began to fill the vacuum that was formed by the reduced propensity of the traditional elites to serve. These social groups consisted of national religious groups who were committed to the vision of maintaining control over the occupied territories and consequently to the persistence of the conflict. Israelis of Asian-African origin and new immigrants from the former Soviet Union also started to regard the IDF as a mechanism for social mobility. The traditional elites shifted to other strategies for preserving their social and economic status. The Al Aqsa Intifada may have changed this trend but not significantly so. The movement for conscientious objection to service in Lebanon in the early 1980s, the support to the Four Mothers group from past military officers, and the conscientious objection to serve in the occupied territories during the Al Aqsa Intifada were composed almost exclusively of people belonging to the traditional elites (Linn 1996; Levy 2003, 424–26).

In a society where one out of every twenty people is in uniform at any given point in time, it is difficult not to have significant contact between the civilian and military sphere. This contact was constantly nurtured, however, through a variety of social projects that the IDF had taken upon itself over the years in order to increase its involvement in nation building. Lissak (1993, 59) calls this phenomenon "role expansion." He argues that this role expansion "includes such diverse activities as education, civilian vocational training, organizing national ceremonies, managing industrial plants, accepting responsibility for planning of national security, and the like." In the early 1950s, during the large waves of immigration, the IDF helped civilian authorities in building temporary camps for new immigrants. It then engaged in using women soldiers as tutors of children and Hebrew teachers for new immigrants in newly established towns and settlements. Initially, the IDF did not draft illiterates but gradually took upon itself to teach them to read and write as part of their military service. More important, the IDF engaged in a wide variety of support plans for recruits who had personal, family, or financial problems, by providing them with special terms of service. During a substantial period after the Six Day War, the IDF organized a female-based unit that helped the police in personal security-related duties, such as patrolling public places and inspecting suspicious people (Allon 1980).

After the establishment of the Home Front Command following the 1991 Gulf War, the IDF became increasingly involved in a number of civilian projects that were designed to deal not only with the possible implications of missile attacks on population centers but also with general natural and man-made disasters. Special IDF units participate in disaster relief—both in Israel and abroad. The IDF sent medical teams to Rwanda in 1994 and to Turkey after the major earthquake of 2000 and has helped recover people from collapsed buildings in Israel over the years.

Many of these projects were eventually terminated, primarily due to budgetary constraints but also because they had served their social purpose in depicting the IDF as a socially responsible organization. But these programs helped build the image of the IDF as part and parcel of the nation-building process. They helped disguise Israeli militarism as social responsibility. The prevailing perception that the IDF knows how to run major projects more efficiently than civilian organizations rendered this involvement of the IDF in noncombat- and nondefense-related projects almost natural. This "natural" social involvement prevented a thorough analysis of the adverse implications of this process, such as the weakening of social institutions. The declining prestige of the IDF over the last decade, therefore, was not accompanied by a simultaneous increase in the status of social institutions dealing with immigrant assimilation, social projects, education, and so forth (we will examine some of these trends in the next section).

Taken together, these four strategies of employing militarism as a nation-building force allowed Israel to do what the Arab states have failed to do: to use the conflict as a vehicle for social, economic, and political development. The reliance on militarism as a major mobilizing force in a heterogeneous and rapidly changing society was enabled within a democratic political structure rather than a praetorian regime (Lissak 1993). Yet this democratic structure was pluralistic with respect to everything except the dominant role of the IDF, the civilian security establishment, and national security considerations in the making of policy. This arrangement wherein the conflict played a mobilizing role and the IDF served a wide variety of functions beyond its security mission had the potential for creating some major social tensions. For example, the universal conscription law had the potential of antagonizing the religious—especially the ultra-orthodox—community. The IDF and the political elites were careful to smooth out this conflict by going for selective mobilization. Male conscientious objectors did not fare that well, however. Their rights were denied both by the IDF and by the Supreme Court. There were, as we have seen, quite a few civil-military clashes, but these were not so severe as to threaten the dominance of the IDF, and therefore militarism and democracy seemed to have survived the potential tension between them.

5. THE POLITICAL ECONOMY OF MILITARISM

Israel may have done extremely well in terms of economic, political, and social development when compared to its Arab neighbors. But has it done as well when compared to other reference groups? We may consider two alternative reference groups to compare to Israel's patterns of development amid conflict. One is the OECD, which is currently composed of thirty developed countries. The comparison to these countries is somewhat problematic, as most of them did not face a situation of acute threat over the 1949–2004 period (although many of them have been involved in quite a few militarized disputes and wars). Nevertheless, such a comparison makes sense because the OECD is a reference group that serves as an important standard of comparison for many Israelis. The second group consists of the Asian Tigers—Singapore, Taiwan, and South Korea. While none of these states has been directly involved in any war since 1953, all three Asian Tigers face severe threats from immediate neighbors. These potential enemies are generally thought to be far more powerful than the Asian Tigers.

Helpman (1998) argues that Israel's economic growth rates over the 1960–92 period were above the world's average, but Israel was not exceptional compared to states at the same level of development. Most of Israel's growth was due to the increase in the number of working hours in the Israeli economy. Thus, "[economic] growth was based largely on 'sweat and tears'" (32). Helpman concludes that Israel possesses a major potential for growth that has yet to be exploited. A more comprehensive study—focusing on a longer period—offers a bleaker view of Israel's growth. Ben David (2003) compares Israeli growth rates to a select group of sixteen OECD states. I added Singapore to this list, using the Penn World Table 6.1 data (Heston, Summers, and Aten 2002). Ben David points out that series on comparative growth rates should take into account the break point in growth cycles. Each state has experienced a break point in its pattern of economic growth. In order to allow for a fair and standardized comparison, growth rates must be compared before and after those individual break points. For Israel, Ben David (2003, 30) identifies the year 1973 as the break point in its economic growth cycle. The comparative data on growth rates is presented in figure 13.5.

As can be clearly seen, Israel experienced one of the highest rates of growth of this group of states prior to 1973 but the lowest growth rate in the post–break point era. The contrast to the Asian Tigers is particularly stark. Had Israel continued at the growth rate it had prior to 1973, it would have overtaken the U.S. per capita GDP by 1990. Instead, Israel's per capita GDP declined from 56.3 percent of the U.S. per capita GDP in 1972 to 52.1 percent in 2003. This happened in spite of the fact that defense expenditures in Israel declined over the period from 25 percent to 10 percent of the GDP. Ben David points out that, while the average growth rates of the G-7 states over the 1973–99 period averaged 2 percent, Israel's growth rates averaged only 1.5 percent. More important, since Israel experienced negative growth in each year of the 2001–3 period, and current forecasts suggest only 1 percent growth for 2004, the long-term average is likely to be even lower.

These low growth rates have been accompanied by a significant growth in income inequality. In terms of gross income, the Gini index, which measures income inequality, has increased from 43 percent in 1978

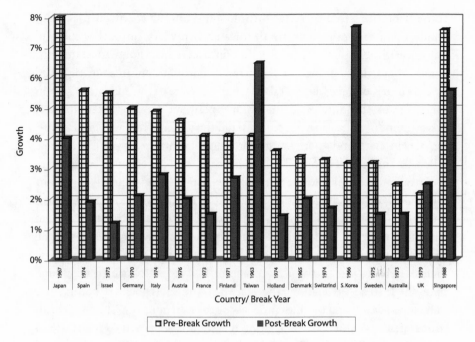

Fig. 13.5. Rates of growth of selected OECD and Tiger states compared to Israel. (From Ben David 2003, 32. Used by permission.)

to 52 percent in 2000. In terms of net income (after transfer payments and direct taxes), the Gini index increased from 32 percent to 36 percent over the same period. The difference between inequality based on gross income and inequality based on net income is covered mostly by a quantum jump in welfare and social support of households over the same period (from 6.8 percent of the GDP in 1980 to 11 percent of the GDP in 2000) (Ben David 2003, 38). Without transfer payments, over 34 percent of the Israeli households would have been below the poverty line in 2000, compared to 28 percent of the households in 1979. After transfer payments, the percentages in both periods are similar (17 percent and 16 percent, respectively). Again, the gap was bridged by a huge increase in welfare spending.

Ben David analyzes some of the key causes of this abysmal record of economic performance. He shows a significant deterioration in the quality of mathematics and science education in Israel. Israeli fourth grade and eighth grade children were at the top of the OECD states in terms of standardized test scores in the early 1960s. Israel's math test score average ranked first and was twenty-five points higher than the OECD average. In

1995, Israel was ranked twenty-third of the OECD countries for fourth graders and was ranked thirtieth for eighth graders (in both 1995 and 1999), with its test score below the OECD average. Ben David demonstrates that this is not merely due to reduced investment in education. On the contrary, comparing the relative performance of the education system in terms of the difference in ranking between public (and national) investment in education per student and the ranking of fourth and eighth graders in math and science test scores, Israel ranks in twenty-sixth place (Ben David 2003, 62–65). This means that the educational productivity per student in Israel is lower than average. Israel spends roughly 8 percent of its GDP on education (the budget of the Ministry of Education is second only to that of the Ministry of Defense). However, while educational spending went up, performance went down. Ben David concludes: "The Israeli educational system lost its eminence in the teaching of the basic fields of study, just as the Israeli market lost its eminence in economic growth. Instead of leading, the state (of Israel) is located behind the developed world and behind some less developed countries, in terms of all three areas on which the educational system is supposed to focus: (low) achievements, (significant) gaps in achievements within the state, and (high) education expenditures" (Ben David 2003, 69).[7]

This deteriorating quality of elementary education in Israel and the growing selectivity of the intermediate education system is a major factor in producing another adverse trend in Israel: growing structural unemployment. The level of participation in the labor force by males between the ages of fifteen and sixty-four declined from 80 percent in 1955 to 61 percent in 2000. This was compensated by a growing level of female employment, from 27 percent to 48 percent over the same period. The overall participation in the labor force for both sexes has remained fairly stable over the period, but this is in contrast with the general trend in the developed countries. In 1997, Israel was ranked seventeenth out of twenty-two OECD countries in terms of the percentage of nonparticipants in the labor force for both sexes.[8] More disturbing, however, is the fact that certain populations are almost completely excluded from the labor force. Almost 80 percent of all ultra-orthodox males between the ages of fifteen and sixty-four are unemployed.[9] Roughly 35 percent of Israeli Arab males are out of the labor force, and roughly 78 percent of female Israeli Arabs are unemployed (Ben David 2003, 77). This structural unemployment has become an intergenerational phenomenon, with second and even third generations of these populations being excluded from the labor force. Ben David shows a strong inverse relationship between education and unemployment (83). The level of unemployment among Israelis with twelve or fewer years of formal education is 61 percent; the level of unemployment for those with more than twelve years of education is 23 percent. Ben David concludes that "the combination of growing gaps in gross income inequality in Israel and widening gaps in per capita income between Israel and the advanced western states is due—among other things—to the fact that an increasingly lower percentage of the Israeli population possesses the level of education and competence that fit a modern competitive market" (87).

A key factor in growth-generating processes is the widening of infrastructure for productive activities. One of these kinds of infrastructure is road and transportation-related infrastructure. Again, an international comparison shows that Israel is ranked at the top among OECD countries in terms of road density (kilometers traveled divided by road area). Israel has invested about 6.3 percent less than the average investment of OECD states in road construction and maintenance. The implication of the eroding road infrastructure is significant. Israel is ranked first among OECD states in terms of both travel density and the number of traffic accident casualties per ten thousand people (Ben David 2003, 99). Ben David points out that "[these] data indicate a loss of 1.5 points of the optimal growth rate of the state, as a result of under investment in transportation infrastructure. . . . A calculation that takes into account the compound effect of the decline in the rate of growth indicates a lost product of 11.5 times compared to the overall investment in transportation infrastructure" (100).

Does the prolonged burden of the conflict account for the relative decline in Israel's economic and educational performance relative to the advanced industrial world? The answer is yes and no. Clearly, the general trend since the mid-1980s has been a decline in both financial and human defense burdens. At the same time, there has been a dramatic growth in social expenditures. So, contrary to the conventional wisdom, the defense-welfare trade-off does not appear to be responsible for this relative decline. It appears that the government became increasingly inefficient in turning its social spending into productive economic and human development outcomes.

More important, the military infrastructure has been a significant element of Israel's economy for a long time, and it has been responsible for a significant increase in Israel's qualitative edge compared to the Arab world, as well as for a significant proportion of employment of Israelis (Mintz 1984, 111). Israel's weapons exports have increased significantly since 1973 (Klieman 1985).[10] Israel has struck numerous weapons and weapons upgrade deals with quite a few states and is selling visual intelligence data to states such as Turkey and (possibly) Jordan. So it appears that the military-industrial complex has experienced dramatic increases in its exporting capacity, thus contributing rather than detracting from Israel's growth potential. This is more apparent than real, however. The global trend of significant cuts in defense spending since the late 1980s has also affected the Israeli defense industry. A parallel trend characterized the relative decline in defense burdens in Israel during the same period. Reduced defense budgets resulted in reduced purchases by the IDF from local industries—from nearly 10 percent of the GDP in 1984 to 4.2 percent in 1998 (Tov 1998, 48; Lifschitz 1995). It also resulted in reduced purchases of traditional production by outside industries. Whereas in the past Israel could sell its obsolete military equipment to developing countries, now it had to convert its defense industry to compete with the high-tech industries in Western Europe and the United States. The opening of the weapons markets for former Soviet weapon industries made it also very difficult for the defense industry to be competitive. On the other hand, exporting high-end technologies was problematic from a political and diplomatic perspectives. Many of the technologies developed were either secret or subject to restrictions by the United States. The overall defense-related exports went down from $1.8 billion in 1987 to $1.1 billion in 1998 (Tov 1998, 184). The defense industries began losing significantly, and the government—convinced that it had to maintain an indigenous base of domestic arms production—spent increasingly larger sums of money to sustain them (Tov 1998, 170–90; Lifschitz 2003, 238–44).[11]

However, it appears that the burden of the conflict has materialized in three important factors that affect Israel's relative economic and social decline. These include (1) the economic, political, and social burden of the occupied territories; (2) the militarization of politics and the continued centrality of national security affairs in Israel's social and political discourse; and (3) the alternative cost of defense.

The occupied territories were initially a major source of economic growth. They allowed rapid expansion of the Israeli economy that was much more substantial than the increase in defense spending over the 1968–73 period. They allowed for increased productivity in traditional branches of the Israeli economy by bringing in a cheap and productive labor force of Palestinians from the occupied territories (Shalev 1992, 58–59, 270–71). The occupied territories also brought in cheap agricultural products and expanded the Israeli markets for various goods and services. This accounts in part for the relatively rapid growth rates during the 1968–73 period, in contrast to the economic contraction during the 1965–67 period (see figure 13.3). Following the Yom Kippur War, however, the defense burden increased up to 25 percent of the GDP. After 1977, there was also a sharp increase in the establishment of settlements and road infrastructure in the occupied territories. The territories began to be a major burden because the investment per settler was about five times the investment per citizen in Israel proper. At about the same time, there was a significant rise in inflation and unemployment that slowed down the economy for the next five years. Unemployment rates went above 5 percent in 1979 and never looked back (Ben David 2003, 34). The Lebanon War again led to an increase in defense burdens. By that time, structural unemployment began to set in with the rise in the reliance on Palestinian labor and the growth of welfare spending by the government to deal with the problem (Ben David 2003, 38). The economic effects of the first intifada have again contributed to the relative slowdown in growth rates.

Beyond the disruptions caused by the closures imposed on the Palestinian population, the investment in inefficient road infrastructure and in profitable construction in the occupied territories came at the expense of investment in infrastructure within Israel proper. The investment in the settlements in the occupied territories increased with the growth in settler population. The growing pressure from the settler population forced excessive investment in both physical and human infrastructure. Social services, security-related expenses, and subsidized construction were all significantly higher in the occupied territories than in Israel proper. The B'Tselem organization (2002, 82–85) shows that the self-generated income per capita in West Bank settlements (due to local taxes) was 66 percent of the rate of self-generated income by municipalities in Israel. On the other hand, government spending per capita on West Bank settlements was 210 percent of the rate of per capita government spending in Israel proper.[12]

The occupation was a central cause of political polarization in Israel, and this polarization has dominated Israeli politics for the last thirty-seven years. Whereas the major parties moved closer to each other in terms of their social and economic positions (Barzilai 1996, 205–11; Shafir and Peled 2001, 239–45), they drifted back and forth in terms of foreign policy positions. These fluctuations dominated the political discourse and competition between the two largest parties. Even during the periods of the national unity governments (1967–70, 1984–90 2001–2), most of the governments' energy and interparty competition centered on security affairs. Without an ability to generate a long-term and rational economic policy, the government was not able to generate a sustained growth policy. There were two significant exceptions to these processes. One was the "package deal"—the economic policy of Shimon Peres from Labor and Yitzhak Moda'l from Likud—in 1984. This policy pulled Israel out of a deep inflation, and despite the relative slowdown in economic growth in the two-year period following the plan, the structural transformation of the Israeli economy enabled relatively rapid growth rates in the first half of the 1990s. The second exception was the significant growth in domestic investment in both education and physical infrastructure during the second Rabin and Peres governments (1992–96). This investment—despite the government's public statements to this effect—did not come at the expense of investment in the occupied territories. Rather, it came at the price of growing budget deficits, but it did show a growing concern of the government to Israel's domestic problems that were not security related. However, this changed again with the rise to power of the Netanyahu government and was not reversed during the subsequent governments (even that of Barak).[13]

The opportunity costs of defense spending and defense investments are enormous. We saw in chapter 8 that, had Israel followed a classic arms race model, it should have spent less than 50 percent of what it actually spent on defense. The difference could have been converted either into investment in civilian projects or into a reduction in taxes. In 1997, Israel's Finance Ministry reported that the tax burden was 40.8 percent of the GDP.[14] This gradually increased over the period 1973–2004 as the government revenues from taxes declined due to growing unemployment. An interesting aspect of the militarization of the Israeli society over the period concerns the fact that an increasingly larger portion of the defense budget is devoted to salary and compensation (e.g., pension payments). Since the rise in IDF salaries is generally proportionate to the rise in salaries in the public sector, the growing share of personnel pay in the military budget is due to the accumulation of high pensions by retired IDF personnel. These pensions are substantially higher than those of the nonmilitary public sector. Coupled with substantial discharge endowments for retirees, these payments have become a significant burden on the military budget. Because the IDF is committed to relatively short careers (about 85 percent of all professional service personnel retire by the age of forty), this has become a major factor in the growth of the defense budget. Changes in the pension terms and discharge allowance for IDF retirees would have freed significant resources.

The indirect effect of the continued state of conflict—especially but not exclusively since the Six Day War—on the Israeli economy and society is therefore a significant factor in explaining the relative decline of the Israeli economy compared to that of the advanced Western world.

6. CONCLUSION

How was Israel able to do so well despite its involvement in a protracted conflict that extracted a great deal of energy from its society? This chapter provided a threefold answer to this question.

1. Israel did well compared to its adversaries because the latter used the conflict as a device for perpetuating and even deepening economic underdevelopment. They used the conflict as an excuse for totalitarian and authoritarian regimes. And, unfortunately, they were successful in mobilizing their intellectuals in that task (Ajami 1998). Even when some of Israel's adversaries attempted to liberalize their economic and political systems following peace agreements, they failed to do so due to both structural economic and political decay.

2. On the other hand, the Israeli leadership quite successfully employed militarization as a nation-building device. It used the conflict as a tool for social mobilization, for cultural assimilation, and for diversion of public attention from fundamental social and political problems in the Israeli society. The IDF was a key player in Israeli society and in the political system. Militarism and the conflict played an important role in deepening and sustaining social, economic, and political stratifications in Israel. They allowed maintaining a delicate relationship between the security establishment and the democratic regime.

3. Israel has done well economically and politically compared to its adversaries, but it is losing significant grounds in comparison to the developed states. It is doing particularly poorly in comparison to states that emerged at about the same time in Asia. Its growth rates have been the slowest among all OECD states over the period of 1974–2004. Its labor force is shrinking compared to those of OECD states. Its primary and secondary educational systems are in constant decline compared to most developing societies. Its physical infrastructure is also in constant decline. The Arab-Israeli conflict and defense spending, while not directly responsible for this comparative decline, have had a significant indirect impact on these trends.

The last point suggests important implications for Israel's future. If the conflict continues and if the structure of the Israeli political system—in particular the dominant role of the security establishment in Israeli politics and economics—does not undergo dramatic change, there is a good chance that this relative decline will deepen in the future. There are several possible scenarios that follow from the present study. These are the subject of the last chapter.

— 14 —

Paths to the Future

Scenarios and Prescriptions

I. INTRODUCTION

A study of this sort cannot be concluded without discussing the impli-cations of its key findings. One question arising out of the discussion of the problems in Israel's security and foreign policy is, What next? For example, what happens if the trends we have detailed in the present study continue uninterrupted? How can these trends change by forces beyond Israel's control? How can they be changed if Israelis are willing to learn from their mistakes, not to repeat them but to correct them? This chapter concludes the study by delineating four possible futures in the Middle East. These scenarios are not mutually exclusive. Elements from one sce-nario may be present in another. Nor are these scenarios exhaustive; there are other scenarios or combinations of the various scenarios that are as plausible as the ones I discuss here. Readers should regard these sce-narios more as frameworks for analyzing and prescribing policies than as forecasts of alternative futures.

The purpose of introducing these scenarios is threefold. First, I exam-ine various extrapolations of the general trends and issues I discussed in the previous chapters. Second, I wish to examine how alternative Israeli behaviors and organization of its foreign and security policy may affect each of these scenarios and how Israel's situation might be affected by these scenarios. Third, I wish to use these scenarios to provide some pol-icy prescriptions for Israel. Accordingly, this chapter is organized as follows. In sections 2–5, I outline the scenarios. I also examine how Israeli national security and foreign policy may affect the emergence of the specific scenario and how it may be affected by the elements entailed in it. Section 6 discusses ways in which fundamental reforms in Israeli policy may help determine the relative likelihood of the various scenarios, increasing the prospects of desired scenarios and reducing the probability of undesired ones. I conclude this book by examining some issues that have not been adequately covered and by offering paths to future research.

A methodological note is in order before we go into a discussion of the various scenarios. The starting point of each scenario is the near present. The basic circumstances are the following:

1. Israel has contractual peace agreements with Egypt and Jordan. These treaties, while marking a fairly cold peace, are nevertheless stable and have withstood several tests, such as the Lebanon War and four years of the Al Aqsa Intifada (Maoz 2004c).

2. Israeli-Syrian relations are tense. There is no open warfare, but peace negotiations have not resumed. Israel accuses Syria of supporting Hizballah and harboring Palestinian terrorist organizations. Syria is engaged in fierce anti-Israel rhetoric.

3. There are infrequent—and limited—clashes between Israel and Hizballah, mostly due to Israeli overflights in Lebanon. Occasionally, Hizballah fires at Israeli positions in the disputed Shab'ah area and Israel responds by shelling Hizballah positions in southern Lebanon, but the confrontation is mostly limited to a war of words.

4. The Israeli-Palestinian conflict—the Al Aqsa Intifada—is still ongoing without any sign of negotiations between the parties.

5. The United States continues to be the dominant superpower in world politics, but there are several political challenges to its Middle East policy from the international community, including from some of its closest allies.

6. The United States is deeply involved in Iraq, continuing to suffer casualties due to insurgency emanating from various factions within the country.

7. The threat of global terrorism continues to impose considerable constraints on the relations between the United States and various Middle East states, such as Syria, Iran, and the Palestinians.

8. Israel and the United States suspect that Iran is pursuing a nuclear

weapons program in defiance of the IAEA and the international community. Diplomatically, however, Iran denies these charges but plays a cat and mouse game with IAEA regarding the second protocol of the NPT, which allows surprise inspections of nuclear sites.

9. The Israeli government and security community are unchanged. The security community continues to dominate policy-making, while other elements of the bureaucracy and the political system continue to play a minor role in the process. The Israeli public is still divided on the question of the occupied territories but generally supports government policy with respect to the management of the intifada. Elements in the Israeli political system and the general public that offer a political solution are seen as a small and marginal minority in Israel.

Each of the scenarios evolves from these characteristics of the present reality. In each case, I discuss a possible evolutionary—or revolutionary—path leading from these characteristics to some future reality, keeping in mind it is only one of the possible paths to the future. These scenarios depict a general picture of the Middle East political, military, and economic layouts. Quite a few factors are left out, thus the description of each scenario is necessarily incomplete.

2. THE REGIONAL ESCALATION SCENARIO

What would happen if Ben-Gurion's doomsday scenario came true? As noted, this scenario had three central elements: (a) a cohesive and general coalition of most Arab states that (b) would mobilize all of its human and material resources for the single task of staging an all-out attack on Israel and (c) time this attack at a point where Israel finds itself completely isolated in the international arena. The regional escalation scenario describes such a process in more detail. I discuss the conditions that are required for it to materialize and analyze its implications for Israel's national security and foreign policy.

Taking the present environment as the baseline for this scenario, there are several paths that may lead from the present to the regional escalation scenario. One concerns the escalation and expansion of the Israeli-Palestinian conflict to a more regional conflagration. The second path concerns a confrontation between Israel and Iran that draws in other Arab states. The third path concerns a general radicalization of the Middle East due to the collapse of the moderate regimes in Egypt, Jordan, and Saudi Arabia, as well as the collapse of the more radical but still prudent regime in Syria and the collapse of the Pax Americana in Iraq. I focus on the third path as the lead from the present to the future scenario of regional escalation but will tie it to the other paths as well.

A wave of radical Islamic revolutions engulfs the Middle East over a period of several years. Political revolutions and coups—in some cases with the aid of radical elements within the military forces of various states—result in the overthrow of the regimes in Egypt, Saudi Arabia, Jordan, Syria, and Lebanon. The PA collapses, and the Hamas takes over the struggle against Israel in the occupied territories. The interim Iraqi government collapses after the withdrawal of U.S. and British troops from the country, and radical Islamic forces—possibly Shi'a dominated—take over power in Iraq. The new governments form the Islamic Organization of Middle East States, the first resolution of which is to form a military alliance under a joint command. The principal aim of this alliance is to develop an effective Arab force whose key mission is the staging of an all-out attack aimed at destroying the state of Israel. The Islamic republics of Egypt and Jordan abrogate their peace treaties with Israel, and the Palestinians declare all agreements with the Jewish state null and void.

In order to expedite the process of preparation for war, the new Islamic organization announces a series of steps. First, all Arab states commit to raising their defense spending to levels of 10–15 percent of their respective GDPs and to increasing the size of their armed forces, so that they can put together a combined military force of 2.5 million soldiers. The collapse of the Saudi regime puts at the disposal of the joint Islamic command a large number of high-end military technologies that had been sold to Saudi Arabia by the United States.

Second, Iran steps up its nuclear program, withdrawing from the NPT. It announces that its nuclear weapons program, once completed, would provide a nuclear umbrella to any Islamic state that is subject to an attack by the Jewish entity. Other Islamic states also withdraw from the NPT in protest of the international community's failure to impose nuclear disarmament on the Jewish state. Although none of these states starts nuclear weapons programs, and although Iran is not willing to share its know-how and its technologies with other Islamic regimes, it does sell Egypt and Syria some of its long-range Sheehab missiles. The Syrians and the Egyptians adjust these missiles to carry chemical and biological warheads.

Third, the Islamic organization decides to renew and tighten the economic boycott on Israel. It announces that any country or any company trading with the Jewish entity not only would be subject to a trade boycott by the Islamic states but would also be subject to an oil embargo. It puts considerable pressure on the Turkish government—still under the control of secular parties and the Turkish military—to disband all military and commercial ties with Israel. The Turkish government gives in to this demand.

In the face of the threat from the Islamic organization, the European Union (EU) suspends the EU-Israel Association Agreement.[1] The EU's justification for this action is the continued Israeli occupation of the territories. The United States, on the other hand, does not budge to the Islamic pressure and finds itself subject to an oil embargo. Oil prices in the United States increase significantly, leading to growing public pressure on the administration to cut its military and economic aid to Israel as long as it clings to the occupied territories. Previous talks between Israel and the United States on military coordination as part of the Memorandum of Agreement (MOA) on security and technology cooperation are suspended subject to a review by the administration. The Israeli government gets a strong signal from Washington that the United States would not be able to support Israel politically, economically, and militarily in the case of a preventive war or a strike at Iran's nuclear facilities.

Inside Palestine the civil war is still raging. The Palestinians continue to stage suicide bombings in Israel as well as attacks on Israeli settlements and on IDF positions in the occupied territories. Israel continues its policy of targeted assassinations and launches large-scale raids on various Palestinian population centers to uncover terrorist cells, weapons, and munitions hideouts. The IDF continues its policy of making life difficult for the Palestinian population in the hope that it will exert pressure on Hamas to curb its attacks on Israeli targets. Numerous efforts on the part of the international community to resume negotiations have failed. As more governments in the region are replaced by Islamic regimes, the prospect of a negotiated settlement between the Israelis and the Palestinians becomes bleak. Accordingly, Israel completes construction of the separation wall around the West Bank, but both sides keep hitting each other occasionally.

Granted, this kind of scenario may appear extremely dangerous from an Israeli perspective, but it also requires a combination of an inordinate number of structural changes in the region. This may well render it highly unlikely. The issue is not, however, the likelihood of this scenario. Rather, it is the kind of challenges that this scenario poses for Israel's security. Any responsible Israeli decision maker needs to consider such a scenario not as an imminent and likely future but as a high-threat evolutionary process that Israel might face. What does this scenario imply for

Israel's security? How could Israel cope with this kind of ominous set of processes? To what extent could it rely on its nuclear weapons as a deterrent? Could Israel deal with this kind of situation on its own? Would it be able to thwart the military and political threats by conventional means or through the use of diplomacy?

The long-time Israeli belief has been that its actions and policies may have little or no effect on the emergence of such a scenario. The nuclear policy was designed to deter the conversion of the Arab economic and military potential into an actual attack. If Israel disarmed its nuclear weapons—as I suggested it should—it would not possess such a deterrent (Beres 2004). Clearly, Israel's military and political position would be very precarious if the elements of this scenario came together.

Three major strategic avenues are available to Israel to counter this scenario. The first is deterrence. In prescribing a nuclear disarmament policy in chapter 8, I did not suggest that Israel dismantle its nuclear weapons unilaterally and without proper guarantees. Rather, I suggested that Israel initiate or encourage a regional regime that includes—in addition to political and economic institutions—conventional and WMD arms reduction programs. As long as such a regime does not emerge or if it is not effective, Israel would be justified to maintain its nuclear arsenal. If the escalation scenario materializes before such a disarmament regime was established, Israel would probably possess its nuclear arsenal and could attempt to deter such an attack by reverting to an open and explicit nuclear posture. Indeed, quite a few people—including former prime minister Benjamin Netanyahu—have urged an overt nuclear posture should Iran cross the nuclear weapons threshold. If the escalation scenario evolves after the WMD-free zone regime had been established in the Middle East, and Israel had started or completed dismantling its nuclear arsenal as part of this regime, Israel has both the technology and the human and physical infrastructure not only to rearm itself but to do it faster and at higher quantities and sophistication than Iran or any other of its adversaries.

The key problem of an Arab nuclear attack on Israel is that any such attack on Israel's population centers not only would inflict tremendous losses to the Jewish population but would quite likely obliterate most of the Palestinian population in the occupied territories. Nuclear fallout may well affect Jordan, Syria, and Lebanon. For an Arab or Islamic state to use nuclear weapons as a first strike option is possibly as irrational as it would be for Israel to use such weapons against Jordan, the Palestinians, and possibly even Syria.

Second, Israel could try to use preventive or preemptive war to thwart this kind of existential threat. Israel has already shown that, if it feels that its back is against the wall and if it has exhausted its diplomatic options, it can defend itself even at a significant diplomatic cost. The evolution of the escalation scenario is necessarily a long and drawn-out process. Converting an Arab decision to put together a large conventional army would take time. Israel could use its qualitative and quantitative edge to attack before the balance of power shifted to its disadvantage. It could strike at its immediate neighbors, or it could attack Iranian nuclear installations, as quite a few Israeli military and political leaders indicated that it should do if all diplomatic measures were exhausted.

Third, and I believe most important and practical, Israel could use diplomacy in order to generate powerful international pressure on the Islamic organizations and/or on individual Arab states to stop their war-related preparations. Israel would under such circumstances alert the West to the danger that the new Islamic configuration in the region poses to the free flow of oil and to regional stability. Alternatively, Israel could threaten unilateral action if the international community does not actively intervene to stop the Islamic war plan. The emergence of an Islamic regime in the Middle East poses not only a threat to Israel; it entails major threats to the West in general and to the United States in particular. Israel can rely increasingly on American actions to thwart at least some of the more threatening elements of such a scenario. Forging a security alliance with the United States would make much sense from both Israeli and American perspectives under such circumstances.

Nevertheless, this scenario has important and extremely costly implications for Israel. First and foremost, it would force Israel to return to a posture of maximal militarization. This implies significant growth in defense spending and higher rates of mobilization and readiness. Second, this implies growing social tensions and a worsening of the domestic conditions in such areas as welfare, education, and economic development. It will also bring about growing tensions between the Jewish and Arab population in Israel. At the same time, it may actually reduce political and social factionalism and tensions within the Jewish public.

The real Israeli challenge, however, is not how to respond to this scenario once it materializes but rather how to prevent this scenario from materializing in the first place. Contrary to the Israeli perception, this study suggests that what Israel says and does has a tremendous impact on the region. Israel's actions at present and in the near future have as much or greater an impact on the probability of this scenario as do the actions of any other regional or extraregional actor. If Israel continues to turn down peace initiatives and follows the logic of escalation dominance and risk-seeking security policy, it elevates the chances of the escalation scenario. If it is willing to take calculated risks for peace, it may reduce the probability of this scenario.

3. THE CONFLICT UNENDING SCENARIO

The conflict unending scenario is essentially a straightforward—more of the same—extrapolation from the state of affairs that has characterized Israeli reality since the outbreak of the Al Aqsa Intifada in 2000. The conflict with the Palestinians continues in a fairly uninterrupted manner. Palestinian attacks on Israeli civilians, on settlers, and on the IDF continue on a fairly regular basis. Israel continues to build the separation wall, but attacks on Israeli targets persist. Israeli casualties continue to mount, albeit at a lower level.

The IDF engages in occasional incursions into Palestinian population centers in the West Bank and Gaza and continues with the policy of targeted assassinations. Palestinian casualties continue to pile up. The Palestinian leadership continues to vacillate between encouragement of terrorism and negotiations, and Abu Mazen's intention to bring about a cease-fire of all the Palestinian organizations and reach some agreement with Israel fails to materialize due both to defiance by Hamas and to Israeli actions in the occupied territories.

Things are generally quiet along the Israeli-Lebanese border, but once in a while Israel and the Hizballah exchange fire. Israeli-Hizballah clashes do not escalate to population centers, but the war of threats between the two sides continues. Israel continues to hold Syria responsible for Hizballah's activity and threatens reprisals against Syrian targets in Lebanon. The cold war between Israel and Syria continues. Syria strengthens its ties with Iran, and there are speculations that Iran would supply Syria with SSMs.

Relations between Israel and Egypt and between Israel and Jordan are tense despite formal peace. The détente between Israel and the rest of the Arab world has been suspended. The Arab boycott, although not officially renewed, has some impact on Israel's trade partners. Several orders of goods and services by some Asian states and Turkey have been suspended.

Iran continues work on its nuclear weapons program, while—at the same time—continuing its stalling game with the international community and IAEA. It also continues its Sheehab missile program. Sheehab IV, with a possible range of two thousand kilometers, has been tested successfully. The threat of an Israeli strike at Iranian missile installations is confronted by threats that Iran would use extreme measures to defend itself.

The risk of crises and of possibly limited wars is ever present. Fear of escalation of the Israeli-Palestinian conflict due to a megahit in Israel that results in numerous casualties is the key concern. Another concern has to do with a flare-up of Israeli-Lebanese-Syrian conflict due to an escalation of a local clash in the north. There is growing concern that any such flare-up would result in the entry of Egyptian or Jordanian troops into battle with Israel. Finally, the threat of an Israeli-Iranian conflict looms larger as the Iranian nuclear program goes forward. There is a growing concern by all actors in the region—as well as by the EU, the United States, and east Asia—about the prospects of (intended or unintended) escalation of hostilities in the region. Yet international efforts at resolving the conflict are unsuccessful.

This scenario is a familiar sight to anybody who reads newspapers and watches the news. There is not much that the parties need to do in order to make this scenario happen; all they need to do is to follow the same policies they have been pursuing since September 2000. The implications of this scenario for Israel are quite severe, however. Specifically, the general patterns of social, political, economic, and military deterioration will probably persist and even intensify.

From a military perspective, even after the collapse of the Saddam regime in Iraq, a large-scale conventional war is still a realistic prospect, as there is no basic transformation of relations with Syria and the Arab world. Thus the IDF is compelled to maintain a fairly high state of readiness of both its standing army and its reserve force. The problem, as has been the case over the four-year period between September 2000 and 2004, is that the standing army is stretched thin in policing the occupied territories. The IDF's ability to conduct large-scale maneuvers is rather limited. Financial constraints due to the deteriorating economic situation further limit the IDF's ability to mobilize reserve units for training purposes. The morale of the IDF is also going downhill, as indicated by the growing number of conscientious objectors to service in the occupied territories and by "latent" objection indicated by increasingly lower rates of reservists, many of whom opt out of service for medical and other reasons. Reports of declining motivation to serve in the IDF are prevalent.

Economic slowdown continues. Israel returns to positive growth with gradual improvement in the world economy, but growth rates remain very low (1–2 percent). Unemployment also declines at the margin but remains around 10 percent. The global rise in oil prices places heavier burdens on the already stretched economy. Pressures both for high military spending and for welfare services impose a growing deficit in the budget. The government's economic policies fail to induce greater growth and economic stability. Public dissatisfaction with the government's economic policy will probably not be converted into support of the opposition because the latter lacks a charismatic leadership and a grass-roots organization that is capable of capitalizing on the abysmal government performance.

Tensions between religious and secular groups and between Israeli Arabs and Jews continue to characterize social and political relations in Israel. The tense security situation and the stagnating economy prevent the launching of meaningful social policies that would help reduce these tensions.

This scenario is one wherein Israel continues to muddle through without any major changes in its situation. Its policy is guided by the belief that there is no partner to peace on the other side and that Israel's policies have little impact on the Palestinians and on the Arab world. Israel continues to do much better than the Arab states and certainly fares much better than the Palestinians in terms of economic and social progress. At the same time, the economic, social, and educational gap between Israel and the Western world continues to widen. Israel continues to be the most developed state in the Middle East, but it will gradually become a developing society with a stagnating economy, a multitude of social and political problems, and a security burden that will become increasingly harder to bear.

Clearly, a concentrated effort at changing the state of conflict is a major precondition for transforming these trends. But this is not the only change that is required. Perhaps it is not even the first one. As noted, a transformation in the orientation of managing the state, from a military and security orientation to one that is primarily civilian, is perhaps the most important precondition. Only such a perspective will be able to change national priorities. Conflict resolution strategies are likely to follow.

4. THE LIMITED PEACE SCENARIO

War weariness, leadership change, or gradual awareness of the futility of the continued state of conflict brings Israeli and Palestinian leaders to the negotiation table. Unable to resolve all of the outstanding issues—especially the problem of the right of return of Palestinian refugees and the status of Jerusalem—Israel and the Palestinians reach a limited agreement. The Palestinian state is formed within interim borders (along the lines of the Taba understandings). The Palestinians agree to a demilitarized state and to a unified police and security apparatus that disarms all factions of their weapons. Israel and Palestine sign a nonbelligerence agreement wherein both pledge to resolve the outstanding issues through negotiations and not to resort to violence in order to settle their dispute. The status of Jerusalem and the right of return will be determined in future negotiations over a period of up to five years. If still unresolved at that time, they will be subject to international arbitration.

Under a threat of violent breakup, Hamas and Islamic Jihad grudgingly accept a truce for a period of five years in order to allow negotiations on the outstanding issues to progress and in order to enter the political process as separate parties. The Palestinians hold competitive elections to the new Parliament. Fatah wins a majority of the seats in the Parliament and forms a coalition government with other factions of the PLO. Hamas is excluded from the government but holds 25 percent of the seats in the Parliament.

Israel and Syria also sign a peace agreement. Israel withdraws from the Golan Height to the 1967 border. The territory on the northeast part of Lake Kinneret is still in dispute, and negotiations on its status continue. If not resolved within five years, this matter will also be handed to international arbitration. The Golan Height is demilitarized, and both sides agree to limited force deployment along a twenty-kilometer zone bordering the Golan Height from east and west. Israel and Syria open embassies in each of the respective capitals, and a formal agreement on tourism and trade is signed, but the understanding is that the implementation of this agreement will be delayed for a number of years so that both sides can prepare their publics for the new peace reality. Since Israel has already withdrawn from Lebanon, a formal peace treaty is now signed between the two states based on the international border. The principles regarding the implementation of tourism and trade between the countries are the same as in the Israeli-Syrian agreement.

Following the Israeli-Palestinian, Israeli-Syrian, and Israeli-Lebanese agreement, many Arab states gradually establish diplomatic relations with Israel. However, because of the uncertainty that still surrounds Israeli-Palestinian relations due to unresolved issues, the process of reconciliation is slow and tentative. Israel is given to understand that the improved relations with the Arab world may well change if Israeli-Palestinian negotiations fail. Nevertheless, a dramatic change in the Arab-Israeli conflict has taken place, and the prospect of a final agreement that will end all parties' claims has become a realistic prospect.

This scenario may appear a sharp and—to many observers—fairly unrealistic departure from the reality of 2004. However, under the right conditions, it may not be far fetched. A leadership change in Israel and in the PA may bring about a change in atmosphere and a renewed level of trust that is necessary to return to the Israeli-Palestinian peace process. Yet, it is not realism that we wish to examine here but rather the requirements for making this scenario happen and the implications for Israel if it does.

Two or more of the four following sets of conditions must happen for this scenario to become realistic. First, a leadership change in Israel must happen that would bring to power a moderate coalition that is willing to return to the Clinton parameters and encourage change among the Palestinians by some significant gestures, including a pullout of IDF forces from the population centers, the dismantlement of all illegal settlements that have been established since 2000, and continued evacuation of the Gaza Strip (including dismantlement of the Jewish settlements there). Such a leadership must also return to Rabin's and Barak's pledges to withdraw from the Golan Height in return for peace and security arrangements with Syria.

Second, the leadership change that took place on the Palestinian side after Arafat's death must be effective in asserting centralized control over the various guerrilla and terrorist groups. Abu Mazen must be willing and able to do that which Arafat was not. The leader must be willing to strike an agreement with all militant Palestinian organizations to lay down their arms and stop the armed resistance. Alternatively, if such an agreement cannot be implemented, he (or his successor) must act to forcefully disarm all militant organizations. This leader must be willing to enter into negotiations with Israel on a less than final agreement that would leave some symbolic issues for further negotiations in order to realize the establishment of a Palestinian state in near final borders.

Third, the international community—the United States in particular—must be willing to apply carrots and sticks to get both parties out of their entrenched positions. It must be able to put pressure on Israel to dismantle settlements and reassure the Palestinians that it is indeed willing to make territorial concessions for peace. It must also put pressure on the Palestinians to disarm their militant organization and to abandon terrorism if they ever hope to get their own state. At the same time, both sides must be given meaningful economic and diplomatic incentives to move toward peace. These incentives may include economic aid for the Palestinians, associate membership in the EU for Israel, a security package from the United States in return for the Golan Height, and even possibly an upgrade of the U.S.-Israeli strategic cooperation agreements to the level of a defense pact. The international community must be willing to underwrite the Israeli-Palestinian, Israeli-Syrian, and Israeli-Lebanese agreement and to provide the parties with guarantees against unilateral violations of these agreements.

Fourth, the Arab world—in particular the leading states such as Egypt and Saudi Arabia—must be willing to take a more proactive and balanced role that would consist of positive inducements to Israel, the Palestinians, and Syria in order to encourage their movement toward peace. In particular, elements of the Saudi initiative that involve recognition and opening toward Israel may be offered as gestures in the hope of reciprocated Israeli gestures toward the Palestinians. Offers of mediation between Israel and Syria may also be made. The strongest pressure must be put on the Palestinians in order to facilitate the changes that must take place in the policy of the PA for progress to occur. Here, Egypt and Syria may offer both carrots and sticks, threatening to disassociate themselves from the Palestinians if they are not willing to make the necessary changes and promising substantial financial and political support if the Palestinians make those changes.

The implications of this scenario for Israel are largely positive. They entail a real hope for a termination of the state of conflict with the Palestinians, increased security due to the peace agreements with Syria and Lebanon, and new economic opportunities due to the renewal and opening of new relations with Arab states. In time, the evolution of this scenario would allow Israel to reduce its defense spending and to increase its trade with the Arab world and other Muslim states in Asia. Israel would probably be the key winner of the peace dividend in this kind of scenario because the economic adjustment it would be able to make in order to benefit from peace would be minimal and the gains from reduced defense spending and increased trade would be maximal. This would also provide Israel with an opportunity to deal with the social and economic problems we discussed in the previous chapter. Whether Israel can capitalize on this opportunity and change its economic and social policies in a manner that deals with the continued deterioration in its relative economic, educational, and social standing vis-à-vis the developed states is quite uncertain. However, it is more likely that the reduction of Israel's security challenges would divert resources and national attention to dealing with these problems.

This scenario offers also a significant prospect of improvement in the economic, political, and social conditions of the Palestinians as well as those in Syria. Here, too, the question remains whether these nations would capitalize on these opportunities to tackle the sorry state of their economies, their societies, and their political systems.

The significant opportunities of a brighter future for the Israelis, the Palestinians, the Syrians, and the Lebanese in this scenario are limited, however, if we consider broader trends in the region. The Middle East is marred by structural problems that are not the making of a specific set of states and their policies but the result of decades of neglect and mismanagement of national and international matters. Many of these problems are collective problems, problems that were not made by single national policies and cannot be fixed unless a concentrated effort is made by all members of the region. This scenario is labeled a limited peace scenario precisely because it does not include a concentrated regional effort at dealing with some of the fundamental problems in the region. Hence, states may deal with their own economic, social, and political problems more effectively than in the past, but the regional problems may overtake these local successes and convert them into long-term disasters. I develop this idea at the end of the next section, which brings together all scenarios in an attempt to extrapolate some of the possible regional futures in an integrative and comparative manner.

5. THE REGIONAL PEACE SCENARIO

The regional peace scenario encompasses all elements of the previous scenarios and expands upon them in a manner that looks at a possible coming together of the principal actors in the region. A comprehensive process of regional, bilateral, and domestic change takes place in the Middle East. A stable government is established in Iraq that unites the country and engages in effective negotiations with its neighbors that resolve all outstanding disputes and grievances. This leads to the resolution of most or all outstanding international conflicts in the region, starting with a comprehensive Arab-Israeli peace and continuing to the resolution of such conflicts as Israel-Iran, Israel-Iraq, Iran-Iraq, Syria-Turkey, and Iraq-Kuwait/Gulf states.

In addition, both regional actors and extraregional actors engage in a sustained process of collective problem solving aimed at confronting the strategic, economic, political, social, and environmental problems of the region as a whole. These collective negotiations aim also at establishing a set of regional institutions designed to foster cooperation and coordination on a regional scale. A regional security organization is established that includes subsidiary organizations for regional disarmament. An economic development and trade organization and a regional bank are also established. Finally, this process of collective negotiation produces institutions for democratization and political reform. The international community helps this process by providing economic incentives and advice, but the decision making and institution-building process are primarily intraregional.

This regional cooperation process leads to a significant reduction in the level of armaments and military spending in the region, fosters economic growth, and curbs adverse processes such as unchecked population growth and depletion of regional resources. This process is a follow-up on the multilateral process that started in Madrid but is now taken far more seriously than the process that characterized Middle East dialogues in the early 1990s. Once the key conflicts in the region are settled, all regional actors will be more willing to participate in regional cooperation ventures. In order to characterize possible trends in regional dynamics, I present the implications of alternative regional scenarios for various elements of regional development.

I start with population dynamics. Figure 14.1 presents alternative scenarios of population dynamics in the religion. The extrapolation scenario shows expected population growth in the region if states do not invest in family planning measures. This rate of population growth is based on the assumption that population growth rates in the region will continue at the average rates of the preceding two decades. This is a conservative assumption because growth rates are based both on birth rates and on an increasing life expectancy—a factor that was not taken into account here. At these rates, the Middle East population will nearly double by the year 2030. Population dynamics in the region have always been a major concern to Israel because the growth rates of the Jewish population are far lower than those of the Arab populations both within Palestine and in the region at large. But these growth rates are also an important concern to the other states in the region because they swallow up economic growth. If we assume that effective population control policies are introduced, and population growth rates slow down by an average of 10 percent per year (the modified growth scenario in fig. 13.1), the growth of

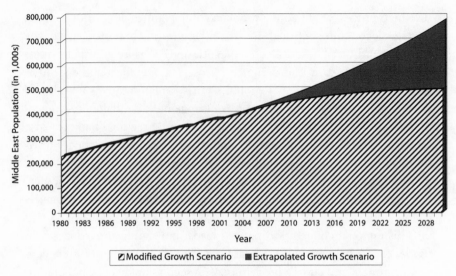

Fig. 14.1. Population dynamics in the Middle East. (Data from Correlates of War project, at http://cow2.la.psu.edu/. Also from Singer, Bremer, and Stuckey 1972; Singer 1987.)

the Middle East population will be slowed by as much as 60 percent compared to the natural extrapolation scenario.

Population dynamics are a collective regional problem for several reasons. First, family planning policies in a region dominated by Islam are a religious matter. Any government policy that does not fit Islamic laws and norms is likely to fail. It is important to have the religious Islamic leadership on board in order to effect population policies. Second, uneven population growth rates are likely to be a source of social and political pressure. Fundamental economic inequalities that are already quite deep in the region are likely to widen if those states that experience most rapid growth rates do not curb them. Third, high population growth rates not only nullify economic growth but also impose severe demands for basic infrastructure. Because these growth rates are often accompanied by rapid urbanization processes, the prospects of economic decay in population centers due to deteriorating infrastructure are particularly high. Both economic inequalities and declining urbanization are a fertile ground for processes of internal and international instability.

Figure 14.2 provides data on per capita GDP on a regional basis, thus illustrating economic trends in the Middle East under different scenarios. Data from 1980–2004 are average GDP per capita figures for the Middle East. Here, too, if the future patterns of economic growth emulate the

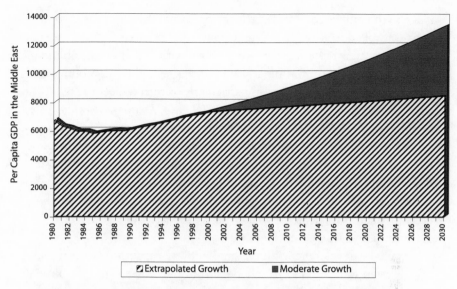

Fig. 14.2. Economic growth in the Middle East: alternative scenarios. (Data for the 1980–2000 period are from Heston, Summers, and Aten 2002.)

average rates of growth of the 1980–2004 period, the overall regional growth rate will be barely 10 percent over the next twenty-five years. A regional peace may lead to the introduction of effective economic policies—coupled by restrained population growth rates—through trade agreements, joint ventures, and direct foreign investment. If we assume that these policies induce moderate growth rates averaging 2 percent per year (again, a fairly conservative estimate), then by the year 2030, the regional level of income may well double compared to what it is today. This will make for a dramatic shift in the standards of living in the Middle East.

One caveat about the moderate GDP growth scenario under an umbrella of regional economic cooperation must be emphasized. It is important that policies that are designed to induce economic growth in the region do not at the same time widen regional income inequalities within and among states. The Gini coefficient for the region's GDP for 2000 is 0.56, which is an excessive level of income inequality. Therefore, any economic policy that does not attempt to reduce international levels of income inequality may face considerable problems due to significant deprivation of the poor states in the region. These feelings may either derail economic policies or spill over to military conflict.

Perhaps the most important contribution that a regional regime may make to the individual states in the region and to the region as a whole is arms control and disarmament agreements. As I pointed out in chapter 8, Israel—especially following peace treaties with all of its neighbors— would benefit from initiating and supporting regional arms control and disarmament agreements. This is particularly so with respect to creating a weapons of mass destruction free zone (WMDFZ) in the Middle East, because such a regime—endowed with effective measures of verification—would greatly reduce threat perceptions in an already tense region. Conventional arms control that entails the reduction in the sizes of standing armies and that puts caps on weapon systems would also reduce a great deal of burden from regional economies. To illustrate these benefits, figure 14.3 depicts two alternative scenarios of regional developments in terms of defense expenditures.

If we take developments in regional military capabilities over the last decade as an indication of the shape of things to come—and certainly if we consider the regional escalation or the conflict unending scenarios— then the extrapolated area marks a reasonable and possibly conservative estimate of the region's defense expenditures. These would reach $120 billion by 2030, which is more than 20 percent higher than the region's defense spending during the 1991 Gulf War. With a stagnating GDP, regional expenditures are likely to become a powerful burden on the regional economies and—even without overt international conflict— might generate patterns of regional instability.

I do not discuss different weapon systems, but clearly the current arms race in WMDs stands in fairly stark contrast to the remarkable stability in major conventional battle platforms. As more states in the region try to introduce RMA-related technologies as an integral part of their arsenals (Maoz 2004b), these costs may well increase. If, however, regional actors manage to reach agreements that allow them to reduce defense spending by 1 percent for the first decade and then increase the drop in spending by an additional 1 percent each decade, decline in military spending would be substantial. Again, this is a conservative assessment of the effect of regional arms control agreements on defense spending, but the result is a substantial drop in levels of armaments in the region.

Finally, if regional policies that encourage democratization and civil liberty are to develop in the context of a regional regime, this may change considerably the rather authoritarian makeup of the Middle East. Figure 14.4 lists the average regime score in the Middle East compared to the world's average regime score. As we can see from this figure, the world has become increasingly democratized, crossing the zero democracy-autoc-

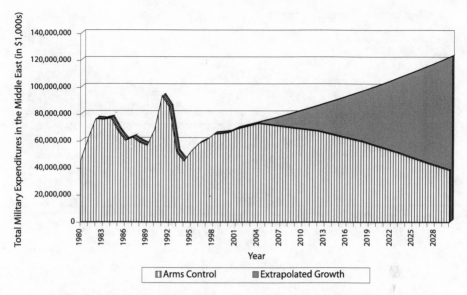

Fig. 14.3. Middle East defense expenditures. (Data from Correlates of War project, at http://cow2.la.psu.edu/. Also from Singer, Bremer, and Stuckey 1972; Singer 1987.)

racy threshold in 1990 and never looking back. The regime structure of Middle East states, however, is still predominantly authoritarian. In figure 14.4, I posit two possible evolutions of the Middle East regime structures (assuming that worldwide democratization continues at the average rate of the last two decades). The first scenario, labeled as the Middle East average, assumes that the rate of democratization in the region continues at the average rate of political change over the 1990–2002 period. This suggests that, by the year 2030, the Middle East would still be predominantly authoritarian. A conservative projection of the effect of regional regimes on the rates of democratization in the Middle East assumes that the region would democratize at a 5 percent annual rate of change. If this happens, as depicted by the extrapolation scenario in figure 14.4, the region would still be authoritarian by 2030, but much less so than in the current rate of political change in the Middle East.

The key to this scenario is a fundamental change in the approach of regional actors to issues of conflict management and regional problem solving. Looking at these requirements from the present state of affairs in the region, the regional peace scenario may appear remote and unlikely. It is not necessarily so, however. The seeds of regional cooperation were

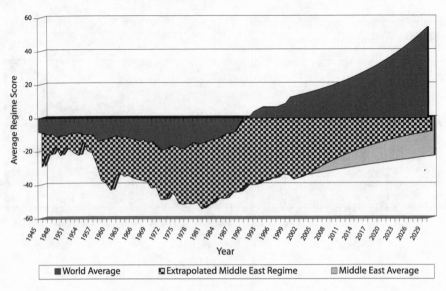

Fig. 14.4. Average regime score in the Middle East, 1945–2002. (Data from
Polity IV project, at http://www.cidcm.umd.edu/inscr/polity/.)

sown during the multilateral process of the 1990s (Maoz 2003b). It is true
that both domestic and regional forces worked against the efforts to establish a more cooperative system in the Middle East (Spiegel 2003; Krause
2003; Heller 2003). Yet, many of these forces are strongly tied to a
conflict system in the region that consists—in addition to the Arab-
Israeli rivalry—of rivalries among Arab states or between Arab and non-
Arab states in the region. The removal of those rivalries may open the
door to a greater degree of cooperation in the region. Liberalization
processes in some of the Arab states that have taken place on a back
burner over the last two decades may also contribute to this trend (Solingen 1998, 165–215).

Israel may help make this scenario happen by allaying the concerns of
its regional partners of an intent to replace its military domination by
economic and technological domination. The seemingly pushy attitude
Israel has taken in the multilateral negotiations—driven by Shimon
Peres's vision of a new Middle East (Peres 1993)—has rendered many
political leaders and intellectuals in the Arab world weary of the notion
of a regional order. A key element in a more modest and forthcoming
Israeli approach is a willingness to pursue a more proactive arms control
policy, especially in the nuclear realm. But clearly, what is required to
make this kind of scenario happen is the willingness of the political and

intellectual elites in the Arab world to open up to new ideas about social and political development concerning their responsibilities and concerning the need and necessity of collective action in order to address the fundamental problems of the Middle East.

What happens in the future will be determined by many actors and many factors. It is impossible to predict with any degree of accuracy the factors determining which particular scenario would be realized, how we may move from the present reality into some future one, and when. As this book has suggested, Israel's actions and inactions have a regional ripple effect, even though Israel is far from being a regional hegemon. A reevaluation and restructuring of Israel's security and foreign policy postures may therefore be an instrumental aspect of the kind of scenario that will characterize the Middle East in the future.

6. PATHS FOR FUTURE RESEARCH

This has been a fairly comprehensive study of Israel's national security and foreign policy. But, comprehensive as it may have been, there are still quite a few issues that I have not discussed at all. Still other issues were treated only in passing. Next I offer several ideas for research on Israeli security and foreign policy. Some of these issues were not covered here; others are spin-offs of some of the points made in the present study.

1. *The evolution of Israeli thinking on national security.* The voluminous literature on national security in Israel does not contain a systematic study of both different strands of thought on these subjects and changes in Israeli security conceptions over time. There is no systematic study of Ben-Gurion's thinking on security matters, although there are several biographies of Ben-Gurion (e.g., Tevet 1985, 1987, 1976) and quite a few studies of aspects of his thinking (e.g., Shalom 2002; Aronson 1999; Ostfeld 1994); there is no systematic analysis—let alone a critical one—of his thinking on security matters. Only one study exists of Rabin's strategic perspective (Inbar 1999), and it is more a survey of Rabin's ideas than a critical analysis of his thought. Treatises by political leaders such as Allon (1968) and Netanyahu (2000) or by military thinkers (e.g., Tal 2000) are also partial, subjective, and exceptionally uncritical. A comprehensive, analytical study of people and ideas in Israel's national security making would shed considerable light on the evolution of this thinking over time and may provide a more insightful base for evaluating and criticizing this thinking.

2. *The political economy of Israeli security.* There exist some texts dealing with this subject (principally, Lifschitz 2003; Tov 1998), but these texts are extremely conventional, written by people who came from the Finance Ministry (Lifschitz) or from the Defense Ministry (Tov). Analytic accounts of the economy of Israel's national security or specific aspects thereof (Berglas 1986; Ward and Mintz 1989; Mintz 1984) are partial and outdated. There are no systematic analytical studies of the politics and social aspects of defense spending or the relationship between defense spending and economic growth in Israel. There are no detailed data-based analyses of Israel's defense industries and their place in Israel's economy. Nor are there analyses of the economic costs of conflict and war. I touched upon some of these issues in passing. but they deserve a better and more systematic treatment.

3. *The effects of the conflict on Israeli society.* Israeli sociologists and political scientists have done a fairly good job at examining various aspects of the interface between security and society. The works of Kimmerling (1985); Ben-Eliezer (2003, 1998); Levy (1997, 2003); Barzilai (1996); Arian (1995); S. Cohen (2003); Lissak (1993) and others highlight important facets of these relationships. They also provide a fairly wide range of perspectives of this interface between militarism and social development. Other studies (e.g., Perlmutter 1969; Ben Meir 1995) discuss a more narrow aspect of civil-military relations—the interface between military and political decision making. What we miss, however, is a more comprehensive assessment of the positive and negative impact of the protracted Arab-Israeli conflict on Israeli society. The paradox I discussed in chapter 13 offers a starting point for such a study, but I have barely scratched the surface on these matters. More systematic knowledge is required.

4. *Update on Israel's foreign policy and on foreign policy decisions.* Michael Brecher's monumental works on the Israeli foreign policy system (1972), on decisions in Israel's foreign policy making (1975), and on its crisis decision making (with Geist, 1980) are among the most outstanding studies of foreign policy of any country in the modern era. However, they end in 1973. More updated reviews of Israel's foreign relations (e.g., Klieman 1990) are more of a general survey of Israel's foreign relations. Since then, we have had no systematic attempt to trace Israeli decision-making patterns. Some analyses I have conducted in the past (Maoz 1981, 1997a; Maoz and Astorino 1992a, 1992b; Maoz and Mor 2002a) offer additional cases but in fairly general terms. An update of foreign policy patterns and decision-making processes covering the more current

periods is badly needed. In particular, we need more systematic analyses of decision-making patterns of the type offered by Kuperman (1999) that go beyond the issue of limited force operations.

5. *Israel's peace diplomacy.* Chapter 10 is an episode-based analysis of this issue. However, neither is it comprehensive nor does it delve deeply into any of these episodes. Moreover, since the perspective I adopt in this chapter is evaluative, it does not try to see the peace diplomacy from the eyes of the decision makers involved in the process. A more analytic account of the twists and turns of Israel's peace diplomacy would be an important contribution to the understanding of Israel's behavior. In particular, what is needed in this context is a study of the psychology of peace and war both at the level of elites who participated in these events and at the mass level.

6. *The interaction between Israel's behavior and the behavior of its adversaries.* The books on the Arab-Israeli conflict can fill a medium-size university library. Nevertheless, I know of no systematic and comprehensive study that examines the interaction between Israel's behavior and the behavior of the Arab states. Maoz and Mor 2002a (chaps. 6–7) is the only effort to do that over time and across two rivalries. In order to understand and to be able to project into the future, we need a more thorough understanding of the extent and manner to which Israel and the Arab states have affected each other through their perceptions and their verbal and physical actions.

7. *The psychology of Israel's security and foreign policy.* I noted the tendency of Israeli decision makers—and possibly of the mass public—to move between an extreme characterized by deep paranoia and a perception of arrogance and superiority. I also argued that the fluctuation between a siege mentality and a policy of arrogance has been an important factor affecting both Israel's military strategy and its peace diplomacy. A more systematic look into elite and mass perceptions over time in terms of psychological theories is warranted. Arian (1995) presents an important work in this context, but it tends to emphasize the siege mentality and focuses only on public opinion. It is impossible to accomplish a deep understanding of the trends in Israel's security and foreign policy behavior without examining the psychological factors that have driven these trends over time.

It is impossible to conclude this study without dealing with the question of the practical impact of studies of this sort on policy-making. To what extent could any academic study be influential in affecting changes in the structure and content of policy? I have examined quite a few issues and have made quite a few—possibly controversial—observations and recommendations. Even if we assume—which is quite a leap of faith—that enough people would agree with the insights offered by this study, would they consider changing course or structures? The history of academic impact on the organization, structure, and outcomes of the Israeli security community is quite bleak. We saw in chapter 11 that even government-appointed inquiry commissions—such as the Agranat commission—have a very limited effect on actual changes in that community. So why bother?

I believe that studies of this sort have a long-term effect in two ways. First, if people read and think about these matters—even when they are students at universities and are still away from the centers of power—some ideas sink in and stay. When these young people advance, their ideas may advance with them. Knowledge is the basis for reasoned and structured change. Second, quite a few changes in Israeli political structures—for better and for worse—were born in the ivory tower of Israeli academia. The movement for (and later against) the direct elections of the prime minister originated in academic circles. More important, ideas that flow outside the gates of academic institutions to the society may effect grass-roots action. In this case, my hope is that this study helps people think more deeply and critically about issues that have always been considered to be the sine qua non of Israeli society and politics. We have seen that grass-roots movements can have enormous power, and in many cases this power can work to change things in a manner that even the most powerful security establishment cannot resist. If this book contributes to such thinking, this would be my major return on the investment entailed in writing it.

Afterword: The Second Lebanon Fiasco and the Never-Ending Intifada

1. THE SECOND LEBANON WAR, JULY–AUGUST 2006

On July 12, 2006, a well-planned attack of the Hizballah on an IDF convoy inside northern Israel resulted in the killing of three Israeli soldiers and the kidnapping of an additional two. A unit that attempted to chase the kidnappers ran into another ambush, and the clash resulted in an additional five Israeli fatalities and a destroyed tank (Vinograd 2007, 66). Israel's response was quick and harsh. The IAF launched a massive attack at Lebanese infrastructural targets in the Beirut area, targeting power stations, bridges, and buildings in Beirut that had been suspected to be Hizballah communications centers (Shelah and Limor 2007, 61; Harel and Issacharoff 2008, 172–73). Thus started the Second Lebanon War, a war that lasted 34 days, resulting in 1,500 Lebanese and 159 Israeli fatalities. More important, during this period, Hizballah fired 3,990 Katyusha rockets at Israeli population centers, some of them hitting as far as the city of Hadera, 120 kilometers south of the Israel-Lebanon border. During the war, a third of Israel's population and about the same proportion of Lebanon's population fled their houses and became refugees in their own country. The economy of both societies was badly damaged by the fighting.[1]

After a month of intense fighting, the UN Security Council issued Resolution 1701, which called for a cease-fire and the pullout of Israeli troops from South Lebanon. This resolution expanded the mandate and the size of UNIFIL in South Lebanon and called on the Lebanese government to send the Lebanese army to South Lebanon and disarm the Hizballah. The situation in the ensuing two years in that border area can be best characterized as a tense stalemate, with both sides actively preparing for yet another round of fighting but neither breaking the cease-fire agreement.

The Israeli public offered almost unequivocal support to the government at the outbreak of the war, but as the war prolonged and as the Katyushas kept dropping, support dwindled. Polls run during the war showed that as much as 97 percent of the Israeli public saw the war as justified on July 19—a week into the war. This level of support had gone down to 72 percent by August 13—the day the war ended. On the other hand, the public's evaluation of the government's performance fluctuated from 80 percent support at the start of the war to less than 40 percent on August 13. A similar trend characterized the approval ratings of Prime Minister Olmert (from 78 percent approval at the start of the war to 42 percent approval at the end of the war) and of Defense Minister Peretz (from 65 percent approval at the start of the war to 37 percent at the end of the war) (Shavit et al. 2006). Public perceptions of the outcome of the war suggest that only 26 percent of the public viewed the outcome of the war as an Israeli victory, 21 percent perceived it as a Hizballah victory, and another 35 percent interpreted the outcome as favoring neither of the parties.

Despite claims by Israeli politicians about significant accomplishments, the war was a fiasco. This outcome is stunning given the deluxe nature of the war. Israel enjoyed an overwhelming advantage in capabilities. The government enjoyed widespread public support. From a foreign policy perspective, Israel operated—perhaps for the first time in its military history—without internationally imposed time constraints. The Bush administration provided it with what amounted to a blank check to continue its military operations for as long as it needed, fending off diplomatic attempts by the international community to put an end to the conflict. The administration's hope was that Israel would destroy the Hizballah and deliver a political blow to Iran and Syria, Hizballah's supporters. This would indirectly help the United States in its war in Iraq and in its broader war on terror (Harel and Issacharoff 2008, 205–8; Shelah and Limor 2007, 88). Nobody in the Arab world lifted a finger to help the Lebanese, beyond mild condemnation of Israel's actions. Never had Israel enjoyed such favorable international conditions for the conduct of its military operations. UN Resolution 1701 created a potentially stable situation in southern Lebanon, but the stability of this situation was based entirely on Hizballah's willingness to cooperate; neither UNIFIL nor the Lebanese government had any meaningful means of enforcing the cease-fire if Hizballah had been intent on breaking it.

The objective of the Israeli strategy in Lebanon—as COS Dan Halutz put it on July 12—was to fundamentally "change the 'situation.' The purpose of this change is deterrence . . . [to] change the rules of the game, or to change the reality along [the Israeli-Lebanese] border" (Vinograd 2007, 70).[2] In fact, neither of these objectives was accomplished. The aerial strikes and the ground attacks did great damage to the civilian infrastructure of Lebanon, causing numerous civilian fatalities. But they had little effect on Hizballah's rocket-launching capacity or on its overall capabilities (Cordesman 2006; Makovsky and White 2006; Perthes 2007, 115– 19). In the summer of 2008, Hizballah's capabilities have vastly surpassed those it possessed in 2006 (*Defense and Foreign Affairs* 2007). The defective performance of the IDF throughout the war served only to erode Israel's cumulative deterrence. Hizballah was able to claim victory over the most powerful army in the Middle East, emerging as a hero and a model for all anti-Israel and anti-Western forces in the Middle East (Norton 2007, 475–91; Salem 2008, 15–24; Telhami 2007, 21–26).[3] As these lines are written, Israel has completed yet another humiliating prisoner exchange deal with Hizballah. It freed several Lebanese captured during the Second Lebanon War as well as Samir Kuntar, a Lebanese terrorist who had participated in the killing of an Israeli family in Nahariya in 1978 and had been in an Israeli jail since that time. In exchange the Israelis received the bodies of the two soldiers that had been kidnapped (and apparently killed) by Hizballah on July 12. Nothing illuminates the absurdity of this war more clearly than this prisoner exchange.

Israel and the United States had a strong interest in strengthening the moderate Lebanese government, headed by Fouad Seniora, vis-à-vis the Hizballah and pro-Syrian factions in the Lebanese political system. The war, in fact, has accomplished the opposite. Hizballah and its pro-Syrian allies have worked to destabilize the Lebanese government since the end of the war. This has had no significant effect on the operation of the government, but the prospect of renewed civil violence in Lebanon—which had been lessened considerably since the mid-1990s and even more so since the withdrawal of the Syrian troops in 2005—has again become real (Salem 2008, 15–24).

Acting under public pressure, the Israeli government was forced to appoint an inquiry commission to investigate the political and military conduct of the war. The commission issued its interim report—focusing on the first week of the war—in April 2007 (Vinograd 2007) and its final report—focusing on the subsequent stages of the war—in January 2008 (Vinograd 2008). The interim report was profoundly critical of the political conduct of the war. Although it did not criticize the decision to go to war, it severely criticized the decision-making process in the cabinet. The report also noted the absurd fact that when the government decided on massive air attacks on civilian and infrastructural targets in Lebanon it was not aware that this would actually amount to an act of war. The IDF was the principal target of the Vinograd Inquiry Commission's final report.

The political and military management of the war corroborate the key findings of the first edition of *Defending the Holy Land*. Several specific aspects of these findings are highlighted by this war. First, this was another war of choice. The decision to go to war was hasty, ill-conceived, and subject to multiple miscalculations. It is important to contrast the Israeli decision of July 12, 2006, to the decision-making process of the Israeli government in May–June 1967 in order to understand the magnitude of folly and shortsightedness that characterized the former. In May 1967, the Egyptians amassed their troops in the Sinai Peninsula, closed the Straits of Tiran to Israeli shipping, and sent reconnaissance flights over the Dimona nuclear reactor, and the entire Arab world mobilized for a war aimed at the annihilation of Israel. Even under these dire circumstances, it took the Israeli government three weeks before it decided to launch a preemptive war. During these weeks the government withstood tremendous pressure from the IDF generals and from various parts of the political system and sought to exhaust all diplomatic avenues to defuse this crisis. In July 2006, it took the Israeli government a few hours to decide on war. The Olmert cabinet failed to consider diplomatic options and did not adequately analyze the political and military implications of the war. The Israelis were well aware of Hizballah's capabilities, and yet the cabinet disregarded the impact of its decision to attack civilian targets in Lebanon on Hizballah's ability to hit Israeli population centers. It neglected to consider the implications of a failure of its military strategy for the credibility of Israel's deterrence, especially the possibility that an unsuccessful military campaign may erode its deterrence more than a diplomatic strategy of crisis management.

As I argued in chapter 11, the IDF had a virtual monopoly over the assessment of the situation, over the advocacy of policy—or rather military—options, and over the execution of most of the policy's aspects. The civilian ministers—including people who had been skeptical about the wisdom of a military response to Hizballah—ended up rubber-stamping the IDF's recommendations throughout the war.[4] The decision making throughout the war is a classical case of groupthink (Janis 1982). People who may have had misgivings, or even those who voiced them during cabinet meetings, ended up voting with the prime minister, who usually followed the military's recommendations without much questioning.

Tragically, this war accentuated the traditional role of Israel's Foreign Ministry: explaining military policy rather than shaping foreign policy. In this case, the Foreign Ministry seemingly got lucky in that the Bush administration supported Israeli policies at the UN and handled for it most of the international negotiations. Even so, the Foreign Ministry failed in offering a real diplomatic alternative to the military policy. Its attempts to explain the massive use of force against civilians appeared feeble at best and hypocritical for the most part.

The military strategy was itself dominated by what I had characterized as the "cult of technology" (295, 344–45), namely, a belief that it is possible to compel an opponent to fulfill one's will merely by the use of airpower and PGMs. The bureaucratic inertia that characterized Israeli LIC strategy in the 1990s and the years of the Al Aqsa Intifada dominated the thinking of the IDF in the summer of 2006. The fact that the chief of staff, Dan Halutz, was a former pilot and IAF commander made the reliance on this strategy almost predetermined. Despite its obvious failing in the Lebanon War, the cult of technology continued to dominate Israel's strategic conception even after Halutz was forced to resign as a result of this war (Maoz 2007, 319–49).

The war created a huge shock wave in Israel. There were multiple calls for the resignation of Olmert, Peretz, and Halutz. In fact, only the latter two resigned;[5] Olmert showed remarkable resilience, remaining in power because of the fear that, if the government fell, it would be replaced by a resurgent Likud Party headed by Benjamin Netanyahu. In the IDF, most of the key commanders either were fired during or immediately after the war or were soon replaced by Gabi Ashkenazi, Halutz's successor. The Vinograd Inquiry Commission found serious pitfalls and problems in the functioning of individual decision makers—principally Olmert, Peretz, and Halutz—as well as in the functioning of the government as a whole. The final report focused primarily on major problems in the functioning of the IDF on its various elements. It also issued a number of fairly fundamental institutional recommendations that were designed to increase civilian oversight over the IDF. The commission recommended upgrading the NSC to the point of forming a major interdepartmental political-military staff to support the decision-making process in the government. It proposed the creation of a crisis management center and advocated greater involvement of the Foreign Ministry staff in decision making that entails international implications. The report also contains tactical, legal, and communications-related recommendations for the IDF.

The commission did not challenge, however, the basic premises of the political conceptions and the military strategy during the war. Nor did it challenge the logical and moral foundations of the strategy of compellence through deliberate destruction of civilian targets during the war. The shakeup of the IDF after the war—as will become clear in the next section—was cosmetic and personal in nature. The foundations of the military strategy did not change; neither did the outcome of the continued application of fundamentally flawed methods of dealing with low-intensity conflicts.

Unfortunately, none of the key recommendations of the Vinograd Inquiry Commission nor many other recommendations by independent experts, journalists, and academics—most of whom had actually supported the war at the outset—were implemented two years after the war ended. The conduct of the Intifada attests to the fact that the process of muddling through has survived even this devastating war.

2. THE AL AQSA INTIFADA

Several events and processes may have suggested a winding down of the Al Aqsa Intifada during 2005. First, Arafat's death on November 11, 2004, led to the election of the moderate Mahmoud Abbas (Abu Mazen) as president of the Palestinian Authority in January 2005. Second, the Israeli decision to withdraw its troops from, and dismantle the Jewish settlements in, the Gaza Strip seems to have ended Israeli occupation of that turbulent area. Third, there was a noticeable downward trend in violence: Palestinian fatalities dropped to 320 (from 812 in 2004), and Israeli fatalities dropped to 45 (down from 107 in 2004). The volume of violent interactions also declined sharply: Palestinian suicide bombing attempts went down from 134 in 2004 to 22 in 2005 (7 of which "succeeded" in 2005 as opposed to 15 in 2004); Israeli targeted assassinations went down from a high of 137 in 2004 to 46 in 2005.[6] Most important, however, negotiations between Israel and the Palestinians resumed, and there appeared to be some diplomatic progress made toward a sort of modus vivendi as a prelude to substantive diplomacy aimed at a more fundamental resolution of this conflict.

These hopes were premature, however. The Hamas victory in the Palestinian parliamentary elections of February 2006 created a two-headed Hydra in the Palestinian authority: a Fatah president and a Hamas-led government. The Israeli government shelved the disengagement plan in the West Bank that had been developed by Sharon and used as the centerpiece of Olmert's election campaign in 2006. The West Bank settlements continued the slow but steady process of expansion. Only one of the two dozen or so new (and illegal) settlements and outposts established in the West Bank by the Jewish settler movements was dismantled by the IDF. Israel's hope that the withdrawal from Gaza would reduce the pressure off the IDF in the south proved premature. The Palestinians started firing primitive rockets—called Kassams—at Israeli settlements along the Israel–Gaza Strip border. The city of Sderot was a favorite target of the Palestinians.

Israel's responses to the Kassam attacks were generally restrained, principally because these attacks resulted in little damage and inflicted very few casualties. However, the IDF continued advocating limited attacks on Gaza, including hitting infrastructures and limiting the power supply to this region. This recommendation was rejected by Olmert due to concern about U.S. reaction. However, on June 25, a Palestinian group attacked an Israeli outpost near Kerem Shalom and kidnapped an Israeli soldier, Gilead Shalit. Israel reacted with the first large-scale incursion into the Gaza Strip since the withdrawal (Shelah and Limor 2007, 46–49). Israel's harsh response to the kidnapping of its two soldiers less than three weeks later can be seen in the context of the Shalit kidnapping.

During the Second Lebanon War, Israel stepped up its military operations in the Gaza Strip and the West Bank. Over the course of 2006, 656 Palestinians were killed, nearly half of them children and most of them during the second half of this year. The number of Palestinian fatalities in 2007 was 327 (as opposed to 6 Israeli fatalities that year). From January to March 2008, 297 Palestinians and 6 Israelis were killed. Israel returned to the policy of targeted assassinations—killing 86 Palestinians in 2006, 137 in 2007, and 100 between January and March 2008. The ratio of Palestinian to Israeli fatalities went up from 2.4 Palestinians killed for every Israeli in 2002 to over 59.6 Palestinians killed for every Israeli in 2006; the ratio was 37 to 1 in 2007. However, the number of Palestinian rocket attacks from the Gaza Strip has increased from 222 in 2005 to 861 in 2006 and 896 in 2007.

The internal struggle in the Palestinian Authority intensified. A number of Egyptian attempts to mediate between the Abbas-led Fatah and the Hamas government led by Ismail Haniya resulted in a continued stalemate. The Israelis refused to deal with Hamas and to provide any legitimacy to a Hamas government. This position was backed by the Bush administration in the United States. The tension between Hamas and Fatah was bound to escalate. In May 2007, a series of clashes broke out in the Gaza Strip between Hamas and Fatah. Within two weeks, the Hamas troops routed out the Fatah, destroying their headquarters and forcing the remaining Fatah activists into hiding or into an escape to the West Bank. Over 150 Palestinians died in these clashes. This created an abnormal situation: a Hamas-controlled Gaza Strip and a Fatah-controlled West Bank.

Israel tightened its blockade of the Gaza Strip, threatening to cut off electricity and in fact reducing the oil, medical, and food supplies to the Gaza Strip. Olmert met Abbas several times, the most important meeting taking place in Annapolis, Maryland, under the auspices of President Bush. In this meeting both leaders pledged to resume final status negotiations. But both leaders were crippled domestically: Abbas controlling only the West Bank, and even there quite tenuously, and Olmert at an unprecedented low level of domestic support. Neither leader could assert the kind of authority that was required to reach an agreement, let alone to implement one.

In this case, too, Israeli policy was driven primarily by military considerations. Diplomacy did take place, but nothing meaningful could be achieved, given the lack of domestic support for the leaders on both sides. The continued mistrust due to constant breaches of any understanding that was accomplished in negotiations did not help either. The lack of centralized control over the Palestinian organizations and the division of authority due to the Hamas-Fatah conflict prevented any meaningful lull in the attempted attacks on Israeli targets. On the Israeli side, the continued activity of the IDF in both the Gaza Strip—where this activity was at least partly justified as retaliation for and prevention of rocket attacks—and the West Bank—where there were virtually no Palestinian provocations—continued to erode Palestinian trust in any kind of progress toward peace.

Here, too, the trends and processes I identified in the first edition of the book and in other published work since (Maoz 2006; 2007) seem to stand. Israeli offensive strategies have failed to accomplish any meaningful reduction in Palestinian violence. Its reliance on various forms of collective punishment has typically backfired. The factors that accounted for the reduction of Palestinian violence against Israel were the separation wall and the constant improvement in intelligence that allowed the security forces to foil a vast majority of the attempted suicide bombings.[7] These defensive and preventive measures pushed the Palestinian organizations to shift the focus of their activity from suicide bombings to rocket launching. This shift is one for which the IDF still has no appropriate response. Neither repeated incursions into the Gaza Strip nor the renewal of targeted assassinations nor collective punishments in the form of a de facto blockade on basic supplies to the Gaza Strip have reduced the number of rocket attacks on Israeli cities. That said, however, the effectiveness of these rocket attacks in terms of Israeli casualties or economic damage has been marginal at best.

The continued Israeli refusal to deal with Hamas in any direct way is probably the key factor that prevents some sort of permanent cease-fire that can pave the way to serious negotiations about a final status settlement. Indirectly, this feeds into the Fatah-Hamas conflict. The difficulty of the Palestinians to resolve their domestic leadership crisis provides an opportunity for the Israelis to continue meddling in the internal affairs of the Palestinians. As I showed in chapter 9, this strategy had failed in the past; it has backfired again in the last two years. Nevertheless, the Israeli security community persistently refuses to learn from its past mistakes. In the future, Israel may not only have to deal with Hamas, but it would consider Hamas as the more moderate faction, which needs to be salvaged from more radical Palestinian organizations. The "over my dead body" syndrome I discussed in chapter 10 seems to be operative here as well.

The management of the Intifada reflects the same trends as previous Israeli approaches to low-intensity conflicts. Military strategy dominates politics, putting diplomacy to work at explaining and justifying the use of force. The initial military reaction to any kind of security challenge is offensive, and the emphasis is on disproportionate (and even indiscriminate) use of force. Since there is no effective Palestinian government, the aim of the strategy is to put pressure on the population in the vain hope that it would pressure insurgents to stop their attacks. Only after this fails, Israel resorts to other—typically more effective—military measures. Diplomacy is used only as a last resort, often when it is too late. Here, too, despite the overwhelming quantitative and qualitative edge Israel enjoys in terms of military capabilities, it could not decide the Intifada via military means alone. Ultimately, the Intifada would end through political settlement. Who would be the Palestinian partner in this settlement, how long would it take to accomplish, and how much blood will be spilled on both sides before it is signed are open questions.

3. THE NUCLEAR SPECTER

Perhaps the most serious security concern cited by Israeli politicians over the last two years is the prospect of Iranian nuclear weapons. Iran has continued its nuclear program despite warnings and sanctions by the UN Security Council. Israeli politicians and most members of its security community are convinced that Iran is actively developing a nuclear weapons program. In November 2007, a U.S. national intelligence estimate claimed with "high confidence [that] in fall 2003 Tehran halted its nuclear weapons program." It also asserted with "moderate confidence [that] Tehran had not restarted its nuclear weapons program as of mid-2007" (National Intelligence Council 2007). However, Israeli decision makers rejected this estimate. The campaign of Israeli-Iranian threats and counterthreats continued. Several Israeli leaders—including Olmert himself—repeatedly stated that Israel would not allow Iran to develop nuclear weapons. Others went even further. On April 10, 2008, Benjamin Ben Eliezer, minister of infrastructure and a former defense minister, stated that Israel would destroy Iran if it attacked.[8]

However, the most important development in this area was an Israeli air raid on September 6, 2007, in which it destroyed a suspected nuclear facility in northeast Syria. Israel did not officially admit that it had carried out this attack, yet details of the raid were leaked to the media.[9] According to these reports, the facility had been a nuclear reactor that had been supplied to Syria by North Korea and was constructed secretly for the purpose of producing nuclear weapons. This claim was supported by U.S. intelligence in late April 2008. U.S. intelligence released pictures of the facility, claiming it to be a North Korean–type nuclear reactor.[10] Syria continuously denied these allegations, claiming that the evidence was doctored and that this was a military base but not a nuclear reactor.

These processes and events suggest several points about Israel's nuclear policy. Most of these points further highlight arguments made in chapter 8.

1. Israel's insistence on nuclear monopoly in the region—following the Begin Doctrine—continues. However, the pressures and limitations of this policy have been accentuated over the last two years and are likely to increase in the future. Other states in the region—including

Egypt, Saudi Arabia, and the Gulf states—have indicated their intention to develop a nuclear weapons program should Iran continue to do the same.

2. Israel regards the Iranian nuclear program as an existential threat. There are serious questions regarding whether Israel can or will strike Iran's installations at some point. But the attack on the Syrian facility indicates that the will is there. The consequences of an attack on Iran might be far more severe than the attack on Syria.

3. The contradictions of Israel's nuclear policy are more evident than they have been in the past, even though Israeli politicians and experts refuse to acknowledge them. Specifically, Israel's nuclear weapons program is aimed at deterrence, but whenever Israel confronts a deterrence challenge, it turns out that its leaders do not really trust the deterrence capacity of these weapons. Israel's nuclear weapons did not deter against limited wars—they did not deter Iraq from launching missiles at its population centers, nor did they deter the Hizballah from launching thousands of rockets on northern Israel for thirty-four days. They are irrelevant in the case of LIC and in fact contribute to the paradox of Israeli power vis-à-vis the Hizballah and the Palestinians. The need to resort to force in order to destroy suspected nuclear installations implies deterrence failure. It also implies that Israel does not believe that any kind of mutual assured destruction situation can or should exist in the Middle East.

4. Finally, the last two years have shown again that Israel's policy provides other states in the region a powerful incentive to develop their own nuclear programs. Israel will not be able to preserve the very same monopoly over the long term. It will also not be able to prevent other states in the region from developing or acquiring nuclear weapons by bombing their installations. Ultimately, Israel would have to face the real dilemma—a choice between a nuclearized Middle East and a region free of WMDs. By continuing to insist on a requirement of nuclear monopoly, Israel is accelerating the prospect of a nuclearized Middle East. It still has the option of helping realize a regime of arms control and WMD disarmament in the region. Unfortunately, now, as two years ago, virtually nobody in its security community and only a handful of intellectuals and academics see the last option as worth pursuing.

Notes

CHAPTER 1

1. For the standard definition of MIDs see Gochman and Maoz 1984, 586.

2. In contrast, in the United States—the only global power in the third millennium—only one out of every thirty-five Americans of relevant age is in uniform and only one out of thirty-two dollars that Americans produce goes to defense.

3. The reader may consult almost any of the major works on Israel's history, national security, and foreign policy for a more elaborate discussion of these ideas (e.g., Tal 2000; Yaniv 1987a, 1995; Levite 1989; Brecher 1972; Kober 1995; Handel 1995; Cohen, Eisentadt, and Bacevich 1998). The concise and lucid exposition of the foundational logic of Jabotinsky and Ben-Gurion in Shlaim 2000 (11–22), focusing on the "Iron Wall" concept, is particularly useful here.

4. For a discussion of types of deterrence see Morgan 2003 (8–26, 80–115). General deterrence refers to the use of threats to prevent an all-out attack on the state. Specific deterrence concerns the attempt to prevent—through the threat of military retaliation—the violation of specific aspects of the status quo that do not necessitate an all-out attack by the enemy.

5. The methodological and theoretical problems with the analysis of counterfactuals in international politics are too elaborate to consider here. For statements on these issues as they relate to world politics, see Fearon 1991; Tetlock and Belkin 1996; Lebow 2000.

CHAPTER 2

1. Brecher (1975, 253) notes that, in an interview he held with Ben-Gurion in 1971, the former prime minister and defense minister mentioned that the two main objectives of the campaign were ending the Fedayeen infiltrations and opening the Tiran Straits to Israeli shipping.

2. The elements of this weapons deal are listed in a number of sources, with considerable cross-source discrepancies. What is important here is the perception of Israeli decision makers. In this context, the most relevant list is given in Bar-On 1991

(12–13). The list includes 90–100 Mig-15 fighter planes, 48 Ilyushin jet bombers, 170 T-34 tanks and 60 Stalin heavy tanks, 200 BTR armored personnel carriers (APCs), over 570 cannons of various sizes and ranges, 2 destroyers, and 6 submarines. The deal also called for the replacement of all light weapons in the Egyptian armed forces with Soviet-made rifles and undisclosed amounts of ammunition and bombs.

3. Sources for the Israeli threat perception arising from the Egyptian-Soviet weapons deal include Bar-On 1991, 15–32, 35–42; 1992, 13–39; Brecher 1975, 243–54; Ben-Gurion 1959, 33–60, 95–110, 192–218; Dayan 1959, 9–23; and Toren 1990, 180–95. Brecher's work provides a rigorous analysis of these perceptions and their policy implications in terms of advocacy of military and/or political options by various decision makers.

4. Golani (1997, 16) mentions also the intent to derail an inter-Arab coalition aimed at attacking Israel, the formation of which appeared imminent to Israeli decision makers in 1955–56, but this is not well supported by other sources.

5. All the quantitative data in this book are based on the project entitled "Quantitative History of the Arab-Israeli Conflict" (QHAIC), unless alternative sources are specified. The data are available at the project's Web site at http://psfaculty.ucdavis .edu/zmaoz/quanthist.html. Data were collected by Zeev Maoz and Ranan Kuperman (Kuperman 2001). The number of casualties in this figure includes both Israeli civilians killed due to infiltrations by irregulars and Israelis (civilians and soldiers) killed by shelling and military operations by Arab states. For similar figures see Morris 1993, 99–102; and Tevet 1971, 430–32.

6. These data show that between 1949 and 1956 a total of 756 Israelis were killed and 1,230 were wounded. This is equivalent to a rate of 756,000 dead and 1,230,000 wounded if this had taken place in the United States at roughly the same time.

7. Morris (1993, 64–67) recounts several incidents wherein alleged Egyptian intelligence officers tried to recruit Palestinians in the West Bank to conduct infiltrations. Also, he mentions several incidents wherein intelligence-gathering operations by Bedouins and Egyptian agents resulted in Israeli deaths. However, there is no conclusive evidence that prior to February 28, 1955, an Egyptian policy existed to encourage or instigate infiltrations. On the other hand, there exists ample political evidence—mainly contacts between Egyptian political figures and American or British ones—suggesting that the regime was opposed to such infiltrations. See Morris 1993, 83–94. In addition, Israeli intelligence infiltrations into the Gaza Strip and the Sinai were a common undertaking during this era.

8. Evron (1986, 26–32) provides documents of the Egyptian military intelligence discussing the planning of infiltrations and intelligence operations into Israel. These documents are dated to 1956. The indications of Egyptian involvement in infiltration prior to 1955 are less clear.

9. See Golani 1994; 1997, 30–35; Morris 1993, 340–50; Sheffer 1996, 784–88.

10. Sayed-Ahmed (1989, 107–8) argues that the Gaza raid increased the domestic and inter-Arab threats to Nasser's regime, as it weakened his position vis-à-vis the Egyptian army, on the one hand, and against his inter-Arab rival, Nuri al-Said of Iraq, on the other. Hahn (1991, 188–90) also argues that the raid propelled Nasser to neutralism and an anti-Western sentiment and eventually helped push him into the Soviet fold. Oren (1994) takes the position that the Gaza raid accelerated Egypt's search for weapons, which had been under way since the Free Officers' Coup in 1952, and its shift toward the Soviet Union, but it had no substantive effect on the reorientation of Egypt. Nevertheless, he cites American documents based on transcripts of discussions between American diplomats (Henry Beyroad) and Nasser, noting that Nasser claimed he was

not prepared to suffer any more humiliations from either the Israelis or from Nuri Sa'id (42). Morris (1993, 343–50) argues most explicitly that the raid was a watershed in Israeli-Egyptian relations. Not only did it kill any diplomatic efforts under way, but also it actually moved Egypt to a position of outright hostility toward Israel, motivating it to acquire modern weapons to defend itself against a clear and present Israeli threat. See also Evron's (1986, 179–89) interview with Professor Shimon Shamir.

11. Peres (1995, 105) reports that, according to the Vermers agreement of June 22, 1956, between Israel and France, Israel was scheduled to receive seventy-two Mystère jets, two hundred AMX tanks, and large quantities of ammunition. The deal totaled $100 million. While it was not stated explicitly, this would have been the first leg of a longer strategic relationship. More important, by July 26, after Nasser had nationalized the Suez Canal, France promised Israel a steady supply of arms in the future.

12. Israel received additional weapons—especially more tanks and APCs—in October 1956 as part of the preparations for a joint French-British-Israeli operation. But such weapons would have arrived—probably not much later—irrespective of an agreement regarding the joint operation. See Sachar 1981, 102–3; Tsur 1968, 159–60, 166.

13. Bar-On (1992, 56–58) mentions discussions starting in 1953 of a doctrine of "offensive defense." This doctrine called for a preemptive strike by the IAF on the Egyptian forces in order to minimize the risk of an Arab aerial attack on Israeli population centers. The key problem was to come up with the proper political pretext for such a strike.

14. It is unlikely that Ben-Gurion would have authorized such a deep penetration strike. Even in the context of a coordinated attack with France and Great Britain, Ben-Gurion was concerned by the possibility that the Egyptian air force would strike at Israel's main population centers. Thus, he demanded that the French and British air forces destroy Egyptian airplanes on the ground. He also asked for French pilots and planes to provide air defense over Israel's air space (Dupuy 1978, 142; Golani 1997, 363–90; Bar-On 1992, 280, 283, 287–88). The IAF's principal tasks during the campaign were to defend Israeli air space and to provide tactical support to the Israeli ground forces in the Sinai. This was in contrast to the IAF's wish to define its principal task as the destruction of the Egyptian air force. See Dayan 1967, 58, 61–62.

15. The international relations literature on war distinguishes between underlying and immediate causes of war. Underlying causes are fundamental and structural processes that are remote in time and context from the issues at stake and include the circumstances of the war's outbreak. Immediate causes are events and issues that are directly related to the context in which the war breaks out. See Levy 1989a and 1998 for a discussion of this distinction.

16. Again, the Ben-Gurion conception failed to recognize the responsibility of Israel, by virtue of such actions as expulsions of Bedouins and other refugees who attempted to return to their abandoned villages, the Hulla draining project, and incursions into demilitarized zones (DMZs). See Morris 1993, 148–84; 1990, 237–53; Shalev 1994; M. Maoz 1995.

17. Statement attributed by Moshe Sharett to Lieutenant Colonel Matti Peled in late 1953. Quote cited by Morris (1993, 12) from Moshe Sharett's personal diary, 1:80–81. Generally speaking, the top echelon of the IDF was a persistent pressure group in favor of initiating or creating circumstances leading to the initiation of a second round. See Dayan 1976, 122.

18. One could argue that the Sinai Peninsula was a desirable strategic asset, but there is no evidence to support the notion that ideas regarding a war with Egypt relied on territorial aspirations in the Sinai.

19. Most Israeli analysts (e.g., Yaniv 1995, 109–11; 1987a, 60–61; Shimshoni 1988, 103–9) interpreted Dayan's approach to the policy of reprisals as an instrument of deterrence. The key sources for this interpretation are Dayan 1955 and 1959. While there may have been a deterrence element in Dayan's approach to retaliation, it soon became evident that it was neither the only element nor—especially after 1955—a major one.

20. Italics are mine.

21. Lieutenant General E. L. M Burns was the commander of the United Nations Truce Supervision Organization (UNTSO), the UN force charged with supervising the implementation of the armistice agreements.

22. Morris (1993, 293) calls it a policy of gradual escalation. The Hebrew term is *Mediniyut Ha'dirdur*.

23. From a French point of view, Nasser was a major threat due to his assistance to the Algerian rebel movement. See Nutting 1972, 147–48; Tsur 1968, 224–25.

24. On this controversy see Sheffer 1996, 680–711, 841–58; 1988; 1980; Bar-Simantov 1988; Bialer 1971; Brecher 1972, 251–90.

25. On the various changes in the planning of Operation Musketeer, see Gorst 2000; Golani 1997, 297–316; Sellers 1990; Martin 1990.

26. See, for example, James 1990; Amery 1991; Gorst 2000; Hourani 1989.

27. The Suez Group, an informal British group of members of Parliament and other officials, was "concerned with maintaining the British Commonwealth as a military and political entity." This group had some contacts with Egyptians, such as former prime minister Nahas Pasha and exiled military and political figures associated with the ancien regime. These were, presumably, ready to assume power once the Nasser regime fell. However, we have no direct evidence suggesting that there were any official plans to place them in power. Also, nobody bothered to check, even if Nasser's regime were replaced by Nahas Pasha and his associates, to what extent they had any meaningful support inside Egypt. See Amery 1991, 121; Lucas 2000, 120–21.

28. See, for example, Ikle 1971; Pillar 1983, 5–10; Goemans 2000. The recent U.S. occupation of Iraq is another case in point.

29. The IDF and the IAF did not share Ben-Gurion's concern, although Dayan did go along with Ben-Gurion's requests of the French and British at Sèvres (Dayan 1976, 242–43).

30. See Yaniv 1995, 123; Brecher 1972, 261–69; Bar-Zohar 1977, 1211–13.

31. Several of the French and British writers on Operation Musketeer (e.g., Amery 1991; James 1990; Martin 1991; Kyle 1989) mention also the domestic political loopholes, such as a failure to secure parliamentary support.

CHAPTER 3

1. Brecher (1975, 326) provides unemployment figures of between forty thousand and one hundred thousand and a decline in immigration rates from an average of sixty-five thousand in the previous decade to twelve thousand in 1966–67.

2. Stein (1991a) and Parker (1993) provide probably the most persuasive accounts based on the adverse effects of deterrence attempts. Yaniv (1987a, 115–23) as well as Safran (1969) argue that the Israeli initial irresolute response to the Egyptian troop insertion into the Sinai actually demonstrates a failure to deter the Egyptians, which caused the subsequent escalatory moves by Egypt.

3. Maoz (1990b, 123–30) and Mor (1991; 1993, 107–52) explore this explanation.

4. Interview to *Ba'Mahane*, the IDF weekly magazine, September 9, 1966. Cited in Oren 2002, 30.

5. Brecher, with Geist, (1980, 46) cites an address delivered by Rabin on September 21, 1967, in which he stated that in the first phase of the crisis "the Egyptians wanted to deter Israel, to demonstrate the deterrence of Israel before Syria, and not to initiate or create conditions that would lead to war."

6. The Soviet ambassador to Tel-Aviv, Chuvakhin, refused an invitation by Eshkol to visit the northern border to see with his own eyes that there were no such troop concentrations (Parker 1993, 17–18; Oren 2002, 59; Brecher, with Geist, 1980, 46–47).

7. Parker (1993, 3–35) examines the relative plausibility of various explanations of Soviet behavior, using both Egyptian and Soviet/Russian sources. He concludes that it is difficult to precisely identify the sources of the Soviet intelligence failure and argues that a mixture of explanations may well account for the seemingly puzzling Soviet behavior. These explanations include the possibility that Soviet intelligence received some wind that the Israelis—while not actually concentrating troops along the border—were planning a major strike against Syria. Yet, he dismisses a deliberate Soviet scheme to heat things up in order to bail out the Syrian regime or to boost Nasser's image in the Arab world.

8. Schelling (1966, 44–45) uses this term to describe the logic of crisis management in a nuclear context.

9. This view is pressed by Nasser's biographers (Lacouture 1973; Nutting 1972), as well as by Kimche and Bawly (1968). For a review of this thesis, see Mor 1993, 124.

10. Probably the most detailed account of this thesis is given by Parker (1993, 76–98) and Oren (2002, 82–85, 92–97, 119–21, 158–64).

11. Kimche and Bawly (1968, 95–96) argue that Nasser's decision to close the Tiran Straits was influenced by Eshkol's May 22 moderate speech in the Knesset. Parker (1993, 72), however, dismisses this explanation on the ground that Nasser's decision to close the straits was made before Eshkol's Knesset speech. But it is possible that the generally conciliatory line of statements by Israeli politicians after the withdrawal of the United Nations Emergency Force (UNEF) may well have contributed to his willingness to gamble (Mor 1991).

12. Eventually, as we have seen, Soviet pressure on Egypt led to the suspension of Operation Dawn. The Soviets warned Nasser of the possibility of U.S. intervention. They also indicated that they would not be able to help Egypt if it attacked first (Oren 2002, 119–21). Nasser's initial support of Amer's Operation Dawn suggests that he felt that the Egyptian army could successfully engage the IDF.

13. Oren (2002, 128) describes a debate that took place on June 2 between Muhammad Sadiq, the chief of military intelligence, and Muhammad Sidqi, the air force commander. Sadiq demanded that the air force redeploy its planes stationed in the forward fields in the Sinai because they were vulnerable to an Israeli first strike. Sidqi objected. Sidqi pressed for a first strike by the Egyptian air force and claimed that, if the Israelis struck first, the Egyptian air force would lose between 15 and 20 percent of its planes. However, in response to Nasser's question of how much damage the remaining jets could inflict on the IAF, Sidqi's answer was, "sixty or 70 percent."

14. In retrospect, Badran and other members of the Egyptian delegation to Moscow report that they had received ample political support and some quite explicit private assurances—especially from Marshal Grechkov, the minister of defense—but not an explicit pledge of direct military intervention. However, at the time it was quite rea-

sonable to interpret Soviet public statements and private assurances as a possibility of Soviet military intervention. See Parker 1993, 30–33; Oren 2002, 116–19.

15. This program collapsed after the Israeli Mossad frightened away most of the German scientists and after the German government put pressure on the scientists to stop their work for Egypt. See Black and Morris 1991, 195–201; Melman and Raviv 1989, 122–25.

16. Levite and Landau (1994, 41–42) claim that Egypt's behavior in the May–June 1967 crisis can be accounted for by its wish to preempt the Israeli nuclear capability by destroying the Dimona reactor. Although an aerial attack on Dimona was an integral element of Operation Dawn and although it was almost launched on May 28, there is no direct evidence to suggest that the nuclear project conditioned Nasser's behavior in the crisis toward preemption.

17. After the November 1965 election, which actually strengthened Eshkol's electoral position vis-à-vis Ben-Gurion's RAFI faction, the latter accused Eshkol of two security blunders. The "little blunder" referred to the Mossad's involvement in the assassination of Mohammad Ben-Barka, a Moroccan opposition leader, by Morocco's secret service (Black and Morris 1996, 202–5). The second "major blunder" concerned Eshkol's agreement to allow visits by American scientists to the Dimona reactor (Aronson, with Brosh, 1992, 106).

18. Rabin himself had also been affiliated with Ahdut Ha'avodah. His promotion was delayed because he had defied an order by Ben-Gurion prohibiting IDF officers from participating in a Palmach rally in 1949. Rabin mentions this as a constant source of friction between himself and Ben-Gurion (Rabin 1979, 109–10, 148–49).

19. The first edition was published in 1960, but drafts of the new edition were circulating in the media during 1965 and 1966.

20. This is possibly Major General Aharon Yariv, head of military intelligence (Oren 2002, 52).

21. Ben Meir (1995, 128–29) cites the civil-military crisis during May as one of the most severe clashes between politicians and generals in Israel's history.

22. Dayan claimed that the pressure of the Kibbutzim on the government to occupy the Golan Height had little to do with the Syrian harassments prior to the war and more to do with their "hunger" for the fertile land of the Golan Height (Tal 1997).

23. We did not discuss here the American role in the crisis, which—many claim—also acted to increase miscalculation and misperception. See, for example, Parker 1993, 99–122; Sharabi 1970.

CHAPTER 4

1. See Schueftan 1989, 37–62, 97–109; Bar-Simantov 1980, 43–69; Gawrych 2000, 106–9; Gamassy 1993, 97–98; Stein 1985, 38–41.

2. See Gawrych 2000, 100; Rabin 1979, 209; Korn 1992, 95–96.

3. Much of this is based on Muhammad Fawzi's memoirs in his book *The Three-Year War, 1967–1970*, cited extensively in Schueftan 1989. See also Gamassy 1993, 97–99.

4. Schueftan (1989, 133) argues that this incident was possibly initiated by Israel as a signal that it would respond decisively to any Egyptian attempt to infiltrate across the canal.

5. Israeli swimming in the canal and the habit of hurling curses across it continued. The October incident involved Egyptian artillery fire on a group of soldiers who

were playing soccer in the open (Schueftan 1989, 133; Parker 1993, 129–30; Garwych 2000, 103).

6. See Brecher 1975, 460–62, for different political versions of prescribed territorial solutions for the occupied territories, including the Sinai. Brecher argues that an "oral law" had developed in the national unity government regarding the territories. This oral law stated that a final peace agreement with Egypt required Israeli control over Sharm a-Sheikh, with a territorial corridor linking it to Eilat.

7. As a young paratroop lieutenant, I commanded one of these fortresses—code-named Carmela and later Botzer—for a period of five months from January to June 1972.

8. The English translation is in Bar-Simantov 1980, 69.

9. See Maoz 1990c on the manipulation of policy decisions by the framing of the decision problem.

10. On the negotiations leading up to the U.S. proposal, known as the Rogers Plan, see Korn 1992, 14–161; and Quandt 1977, 83–89. On the reactions to the plan in Egypt, see Riad 1981, 109–12; Meital 1997, 66–67; and Schueftan 1989, 217–19. On the Israeli response, see Brecher 1975, 480–86; Margalit 1971; Yaacobi 1990a, 9–12. Also see chapter 10.

11. For a list of targets and damage reports, see Gawrych 2000, 114–16; Korn 1992, 178–89; Schueftan 1989, 247–51.

12. Golda Meir argued in an interview (*Ha'aretz*, July 24, 1970) that the "responsible factors," that is, the intelligence community, believed that the likelihood of Soviet intervention was low. See also Korn 1992, 173–74, 177.

13. This is a reference to Golda Meir.

14. Weizman (1975, 269) reports that the IAF lost nineteen planes during the initial attack on the Egyptian air fields. Dupuy (1978, 333) reports that total IAF losses in the Six Day War were forty planes.

15. Schueftan (1989, 439) notes that Israeli sources report the downing of only 19 planes during the War of Attrition. Egyptian sources report the shooting down of 190 Israeli planes during the same period. However, Schiff (1970) mentions that June and July saw the downing of at least twice the number of IAF planes reported by Schueftan.

16. See also the assessment of the war by Schueftan (1989, 395–411) in terms of the Egyptian objectives. While Schueftan does not claim that Egypt lost the war, he does argue that it failed to accomplish its principal objectives and was, in fact, compelled to accept the cease-fire. Perhaps the most sober Israeli assessment of the outcome of the War of Attrition is Bar-Simantov 1980, 192–200.

CHAPTER 5

1. A partial list includes scholarly studies (e.g., Ben-Zvi 1976; Shlaim 1976; Levite 1983; Kam 1987; Brecher, with Geist, 1980; Lanir 1983; Klein 1976; Bar Joseph 2001); journalistic accounts (e.g., Ben Porat et al. 1974; Nakdimon 1982), and memoirs of people who have been directly or indirectly involved in the events (e.g., Ben Porat 1991; Zeira 1993; Braun 1992; Dayan 1976; Meir 1975; Eban 1977; Bartov 1978, vol. 2).

2. The COS, Lieutenant General Elazar, was found responsible for "lack of adequate preparation of the IDF for the war." Elazar and his supporters have fought this verdict to the day that he died in 1976. (See especially Bartov 1978, 2:354–57.) Not much

evidence was given by the inquiry commission to back up this claim, but it appears to be the key problem of the war, as will be discussed later.

3. Lanir (1983, 49–52) also discusses the inability of the IDF to understand the use of the SAM shield, as well as its inability to comprehend the quantum leap in the ability of the Syrian and Egyptian forces to conduct night warfare as fundamental surprises.

4. The October 8 counteroffensive was an attack by two armored divisions (commanded by Generals Adan and Mandler), with a third division (under the command of Ariel Sharon) as a strategic reserve. The attack failed miserably, causing the IDF enormous damage in tanks and hurting the morale of its commanders and soldiers. See Bartov 1978, 2:79–113; Adan 1980, 117–64; Van Creveld 1987.

5. The battle on the Golan Height (Dupuy 1978; Herzog 1975; Bartov 1978, vol. 2; Kahalani 1984) was fought under extremely difficult conditions. Nevertheless, by October 9, the Israeli counteroffensive pushed the Syrians back, destroying over six hundred tanks (half of their total losses in the war [Dupuy 1978, 609]). This suggests that the standing forces as well as the IAF did most of the stopping job.

6. Pollack (2002, 101) argues that "the phase one offensive [the crossing of the canal] was planned down to the last detail; every contingency was examined, all equipment and capabilities needed for its success were procured, and all of Egypt's training and exercises were geared toward executing this mission. The other phases—the breakout to the passes and the reoccupation of the eastern Sinai—were completely ignored; planning never progressed beyond the vaguest outlines, and Egyptian forces never trained to execute them."

7. Moshe Maoz (1995, 130) argues that there was apparently a plan to occupy the city of Nazareth. This does not seem credible. First, there is no evidence of such planning. Second, the distance from the 1967 Israeli-Syrian border to Nazareth is about fifty kilometers, substantially larger than the entire width of the Golan Height. It also involves a difficult climb from the Lake Kinneret/Jordan Valley area to the Nazareth area. Third, there are a large number of more "attractive" targets between Lake Kinneret or the Jordan River and Nazareth.

8. Riad (1981, 243) claims that the general command expected twenty thousand fatalities in the crossing effort.

9. As is typically the case in the reconstruction of events that could have been disastrous in retrospect, the Israeli versions of the cease-fire options are different, depending on the kind of source one is consulting. Braun (1992, 161–64) claims that COS Elazar was in favor of a cease-fire in place. Bartov (1978, 2:187–89) argues that it had been Dayan's idea. Dayan (1976) almost does not discuss this issue but notes that on October 12 he went to Golda Meir and offered to resign (620).

10. During the period of October 9–14, the IDF operated on two contradictory assumptions. One was that a cease-fire would be accomplished within days. The key goal was therefore to strive for significant territorial gains in the Syrian front—perhaps reaching the outskirts of Damascus (Braun 1992, 153–56). On the Egyptian front, Israel must be prepared to accept the loss of the Suez Canal. Second, should the cease-fire resolution be delayed, the IDF would plan a major offensive in the Canal Zone, including a crossing to the western bank of the canal.

11. Hafez Ismail's memoirs, quoted in Gamassy 1993, 272. See also Pollack 2002, 101, 101n143).

12. One part of the contrasting Egyptian versions concerns the "tactical pause" of October 9–14. Shazly (1980, 245–47) argues that he strongly opposed any offensive move toward the passes, let alone an immediate offensive following the Israeli abortive counteroffensive of October 8. This is corroborated by Gamassy (1993, 266–68). Both

military commanders agree that Ahmad Ismail, the minister of war, was in favor of a tactical pause but that he did start pressuring the generals to begin planning for an attack on October 14. This is confirmed in an interview given by Ismail to Heikal on November 18, 1973 (cited in Gamassy 1993, 270). See also Heikal 1975, 230; Pollack 2002, 113–14.

13. Shazly (1980, 246–47) reports that, on October 12, when the Egyptian field commanders were given orders to prepare for an offensive toward the passes, one of them—Saad Mamoun, the commander of the Second Egyptian Army—offered his resignation, claiming that he could not carry out this command.

14. Curiously, Sadat ignores this whole episode in his memoirs. He mentions the period of October 7–18 only in the context of his negotiations with the United States (through the British ambassador) and with the Russians, but he does not talk about the decision to launch the October 14 offensive.

15. The numbers in Dupuy 1978 (609) indicate a far lower ratio of about five to one, however.

16. The Merkava project was started in 1970, chiefly the result of the failure to materialize an arms deal with the United Kingdom on the purchase of Chiftain tanks. Yet, the project was stepped up considerably and received a major priority following the Yom Kippur War. The first Merkava tanks came off the production line in 1979. See http://www.idf.il/merkava4/hebrew/index.stm (in Hebrew). See also Tal 2000; Cordesman 2002, 73–77.

17. Many in the INF attributed this sinking to another successful hit by the Egyptians. The submarine was discovered thirty years later south of Crete, and it was determined that it sank due to mechanical malfunction.

CHAPTER 6

1. See, for example, Maoz 1986 for an analysis of the Sabra and Shatilla decision and Maoz 1990c for the decisions prior to and during the outbreak of the war.

2. Sharon urged the government to interpret the cease-fire agreement with the PLO as encompassing all PLO actions against Israeli targets inside or outside the Middle East in order to provide a diplomatic pretext for breaking the cease-fire agreement (Sharon 1989, 432).

3. Sharon, who had served as the antiterrorism adviser to Yitzhak Rabin, opposed the 1976 Israeli-Syrian agreement (Sharon 1989, 423).

4. A slightly different articulation of these objectives exists in Sharon's directive to the IDF in October 1981 (Benziman 1985, 231; Schiff and Yaari 1984, 42–43; Evron 1987, 115). Sharon's own interpretation of the goals of the plan was—of course—limited to the military objectives of the war, with an emphasis on "neutralizing the Syrians through threatening maneuvers while attempting to avoid real fighting with them" (Sharon 1989, 436).

5. Yaniv (1987b, 100–107) offers an excellent analysis of the "calculus" of the invasion.

6. Evron bases this view on a number of newspaper interviews with Sharon during the first month of the Lebanon War. See also Feldman and Rechnitz-Kijner 1984.

7. Schiff and Yaari (1984, 43) point out that, following the expulsion of the PLO from Lebanon, "the PLO leadership . . . would be forced into a 'gilded cage' in Damascus and lose any vestige of independence, whereupon its influence over the West Bank would promptly wither, allowing moderate local Palestinians to step forward and conduct negotiations with Israel over a constitution of autonomy for the inhabitants of the

occupied territories—by Israel's rules, of course. Sharon explained to his aides that, in his estimation, a successful operation in Lebanon would ensure unchallenged Israeli superiority [in the occupied territories] for thirty years to come, during which time Israel would be free to establish fait accomplis in its best interests." See also Rabil 2003, 65; Naor 1986, 29–30; 1993, 267–68.

8. Some observers suggest that Begin's conception of the war was dramatically different from that of Sharon. According to this view, Begin viewed the war as a large-scale operation designed to clean southern Lebanon of the PLO (but not necessarily to occupy Beirut or to engage the Syrians) and to establish a buffer zone of roughly forty kilometers between the Israeli border and any kind of armed force inside Lebanon. (See Naor 1993, 250; Yaniv 1987b, 100–101). This is inconsistent, however, with Begin's behavior in the eight-month period prior to the war or during the war itself. I elaborate on this issue later.

9. The Christians opposed an Israeli landing in Junieh, because it would reveal the extent of their complicity in the Israeli invasion (Schiff and Yaari 1984, 52).

10. Sharon had been convinced that this time the government would approve the attack. The IDF had already been alerted to consider May 17 as the D-day for the attack (Schiff and Yaari 1984, 55).

11. Major General David Ivry, the commander of the IAF, had severe reservations about the attack on the Syrian SAM batteries. Therefore, Sharon did not bring him to the cabinet meeting of June 9. Instead he brought with him Brigadier General Amos Amir (Schiff and Yaari 1984, 164; Naor 1986, 70–71). Naor also points out that many of the ministers thought that the authorization to attack the Syrian SAMs called for a surgical air strike. They were not aware that Sharon's plan called for a follow-up ground attack and that what they had, in fact, authorized was the "formal" opening of a second front against the Syrian army.

12. Schiff and Yaari's (1984) Hebrew version provides a more detailed account of the Sharon-Gemayel meeting of September 12. In this version they argue that the two leaders had reached a detailed understanding of the political steps toward a normalization process between Israel and Lebanon. Schiff and Yaari provide excerpts from the notes taken during this meeting.

13. Quoted from Sharon's memo prepared for his testimony to the Kahan inquiry commission. Cited in the Hebrew version of Schiff and Yaari 1984.

14. This is evident from Sharon's memo to the Kahan commission, but there is no evidence to substantiate these figures about the PLO guerrillas, nor is there supporting evidence of that fact in the testimonies of the key intelligence officials to the Kahan commission.

15. Polls published in late June 1982 show that 77.6 percent of the Jewish population in Israel unconditionally supported the invasion of Lebanon. Another 15 percent provided conditional support. In November 1982, 49.2 percent of the Israelis said that they support the war even knowing how it had turned out, while 77.7 percent still viewed the war as justified. See the AP report of November 19, 1982, in http://web.lexis-nexis.com/universe/document?_m=b6c32d514127ff6a37fdf7a7ffb790 6b&_docnum=5&wchp=dGLbVtb-zSkVb&_md5=cd1cf99b6cbb047e26532a6b09ed 5a9e.

16. Merom's (2003, 178) figures do not include several cases of attacks (e.g., the attack on the IDF headquarters in Sidon in April 1983 that initially was thought to have been due to a gas explosion). For different figures see Pappe 2003, 348.

17. Barak (2003, 32) mentions that when Rabin discussed the three-stage withdrawal plan from Lebanon he had recommended that Israel establish not one but three

local forces: a Christian, a Shi'ite Muslim, and a Sunni Muslim force. Rabin rejected this proposal. It is impossible to tell what would have happened if this proposal were adopted, but the composition of the SLA became a source of conflict in the south, thus increasing SLA's dependence on Israel.

18. One of the few critics of Israeli strategy in Lebanon, Wald (1987) suggests that the IDF's performance during the first stage of the war was cumbersome and inefficient and that this is in fact indicative of the failure of the IDF strategy in the second part of the war.

19. These difficulties reached such a level that by the later 1990s the IDF started replacing troops in southern Lebanon by helicopter transport.

20. Two prominent cases in this vein are worth mentioning. The first was a special forces operation in Ansariyah on September 5, 1997, in which the IDF naval commando force was ambushed by the Hizballah, resulting in the death of twelve Israelis. The second involved the roadside bombing of an Israeli convoy on February 28, 1999, in which the IDF commander of the liaison unit to Lebanon, Brigadier General Erez Gerstein, was killed.

21. See http://www.moqawama.tv/page2/f_mopera.htm. The Web site is constantly changing, and it may be difficult to obtain the statistics later on. An Excel file with the Hizballah data set is available from the author upon request. Data for 1999 and 2000 are skimpy. Possibly the most reliable element of these data concerns the number of so-called martyrs, Hizballah fighters killed in action.

22. Eliot Cohen, one of the key scholars of the Revolution in Military Affairs (RMA), cautions against the indiscriminate deployment of RMA-related capabilities in guerrilla settings. He argues that the RMA does not render guerrilla and terrorism obsolete. On the contrary, states relying on RMA technologies may confront increased incidence of LIC where such technologies are inapplicable (E. Cohen 1997, 51).

23. Such an approach is embodied in Merom's (2003, 33–47) argument that in order to win in LICs states must be willing to apply brute force to the point of complete annihilation of the opposition and its supporting population.

24. Brom 1999 is an example of a conformist analysis of Israel's policy in southern Lebanon.

25. See the Knesset Web site at http://www.knesset.gov.il/divrey/qform.asp. There are actually thirty-six cases where the term *Lebanon* is mentioned in the title of an agenda item. However, these remaining twenty-one do not cover matters of policy. The agenda or protocols of the Knesset Committee on Foreign and Security Affairs (CFSA) are not available on the Web site. It is quite possible that there were more discussions of the Lebanon issue in that committee, but there is no indication that any of these discussions led to policy decisions.

26. Another bright light in this process is that the "Four Mothers" show that a group employing nonviolent legitimate strategies of public protest can be effective in the long run. This is a sharp contrast to the violent and often illegal strategies used by right-wing movements such as "Gush Emunim" and the various organizations affiliated with it.

CHAPTER 7

Data for this chapter are based on the events data set in the Quantitative History of the Arab-Israeli Conflict (QHAIC) and Peace Process Project, available at http://psfac ulty.ucdavis.edu/zmaoz/quanthist.html. In addition, data on Israeli-Hizballah clashes in Lebanon were provided by Ranan Kuperman of the University of Haifa.

1. See http://cow2.la.psu.edu/ (downloadable data set).

2. This is a translation of the title of the Hebrew version of Dayan 1981.

3. Prime Minister Yitzhak Rabin was the first Israeli official who admitted openly (in 1994) that terrorism—hitherto seen as a minor challenge—had became a strategic threat, in terms of its effect on Israeli public opinion and the society. See Inbar 1999, 142.

4. To the best of my knowledge, there is no complete account of Israel's experience with LIC. Several sources cover elements of this strategy. Morris 1993 provides a detailed history of the period from 1948 to 1956. Tal 1998 and Golan 2000 review the same period from a more mainstream institutional perspective. Shimshoni 1988 discusses the same period (as well as the 1967–70 period) in the context of conventional deterrence theory. The most analytic and comprehensive account of Israel's reprisals policy is Kuperman 1999, which focuses on the decision-making processes governing Israeli reprisals over time. Blechman 1972 provides a quantitative evaluation of the period from 1949 to 1970. There exist, as of yet, no good historical and/or analytic sources on the warfare in Lebanon during the 1982–2000 period. Nor do we have good analytic and/or historical sources on Israel's antiterrorism policy and on Israel's management of problems of popular unrest and civil disobedience (although there are studies of the first intifada of 1987–92; see, e.g., Schiff and Yaari 1990; Peretz 1990; Shalev 1990). Obviously, nothing exists to date on the Al Aqsa Intifada.

5. IDF operations document, quoted and translated by Morris (1993, 185).

6. Tessler (1994, 403) notes that about a quarter of the prewar population of the West Bank (some 350,000 people) fled into Jordan during and immediately following the Six Day War.

7. This may have been due to the belief by key Israeli policymakers that it would be possible to reach an agreement with Jordan on the exchange of the West Bank for peace (see, e.g., Gazit 1999, 30).

8. See Astorino-Courtois 1998; Astorino 1994; Dowty 1984; Maoz and Mor 2002a, 2002b.

9. For good reviews of the Israeli-Lebanese relations, the Palestinian and Syrian operations in Lebanon, and the domestic politics of the country, see Dawisha 1980; Rabinovich 1984; Yaniv 1987b, 27–90; Evron 1987; Weinberger 1986.

10. The "Grapes of Wrath Understandings" is available at http://www.knesset .gov.il/process/docs/grapes_eng.htm and http://www.mideastinfo.com/documents/ grapesofwrath.htm.

11. Zeev Maoz, "IDF Intelligence and the Withdrawal from Lebanon," Ha'aretz. February 21, 2000.

12. For example, Yaacov Amidror, "There Is Control and There Are Lessons," Ha'aretz, March 23, 2000. Major General Amidror had served as head of the research branch of the IDF intelligence and at the time of the writing of that article served as the commandant of the National Defense College of the IDF.

13. See also Drucker 2002; Edelist 2003.

14. Gazit is actually referring to political—rather than legal—constraints imposed on the GSS investigation of the Jewish underground. The law does not restrict the application of the DER to Arabs but not to Jews. It was the government that imposed these restrictions on the GSS. The more intrusive practices of dealing with extremist Jewish organizations were instituted only after the Rabin assassination of 1995, but even then the DER are invoked only infrequently and selectively with respect to Jews and almost indiscriminately with respect to Arabs. See Hofnung 1996; Kretzmer 2002.

15. See figure 7.2. The figures of Israeli fatalities during the period also include an average of twenty-three Israeli soldiers killed in southern Lebanon, so the trend is even more pronounced than the figure suggests.

16. Data cover the period of September 28, 2000, to August 1, 2004.

17. Data on the intifada are based on several sources: IDF 2003; B'Tselem 2002; Palestinian National Authority 2003.

18. See Bush 2002.

19. Consider, for example, the bungled Mossad attempt to assassinate Khaled Mash'al, the Hamas leader, in Jordan in the fall of 1997, which caused a crisis in Israeli-Jordanian relations.

20. See Alon 1980 for a discussion of antiterrorism policy in the 1980s. Unfortunately, there exist no scholarly studies of Israel's antiterrorist policies for later periods. One exception is Gordon 2002, which provides more of a prescriptive discussion than an analytical one.

21. English translation in Morris 1993, 176.

22. Quoted in Yaniv 1995, 157.

23. For example, the major texts on these matters (e.g., Yaniv 1995, 1987a; Tal 1997; Wald 1992) do not discuss this matter. Almog (1995) and Lieberman (1995) attribute this change to the growing Arab perception of the Israeli ability in terms of cumulative deterrence but do not examine the impact of war on Israeli strategy and diplomacy.

24. Specific deterrence is typically a threat of retaliation if the challenger violates a specific aspect of the status quo, short of an all-out attack on the defender. Compellence refers to a policy of sustained, yet limited use of force designed to induce the opponent to discontinue some actions it has been carrying out prior to and during the exercise of force by the compeller. Alternatively, a policy of compellence may be designed to force an opponent into doing something it has not been doing and that the compeller wants carried out. See Schelling 1966; George and Simmons 1994; and George 1991. George and Simmons (1994, 7–11) offer the most explicit typology of coercive actions and contrast these to various forms of deterrence.

25. Quoted in Morris 1993, 177. Text in brackets are Morris's clarifications.

26. Transcripts of a discussion in the Israeli Ministry of Foreign Affairs, February 2, 1953, Quoted in Tal 1998, 68.

27. Tal (1998, 213–19) challenges Bar-On's (1992, 1991) thesis that Ben-Gurion knew about and even encouraged the policy of deterioration but admits that there is no primary documentation of private conversations between Dayan and Ben-Gurion to substantiate his thesis.

28. According to the data of the Correlates of War project, Israel's population grew from 717,000 at the end of 1948 to 1,650,000 in 1953, an increase of 130 percent in five years. Other estimates are even higher (e.g., Friedlander and Goldschider 1979, 31).

29. Ehud Barak commanded the IDF force that raided the PFLP headquarters in Beirut in April 1973 (Operation Spring Youth). Amnon Lipkin had led the Naj Hamadi raid in 1967 and had been the head of military intelligence, under whose command Sayeret Matkal is believed to have staged the assassination of Abu Jihad in Tunis in 1988 (Melman and Raviv 1989, 26–33). According to Abu Jihad's wife, this operation had been videotaped, presumably for "future training and morale boosting" (32).

30. Quoted in Melman and Raviv 1989, 34.

CHAPTER 8

A considerably abridged version of this chapter was published in *International Security* (Maoz 2003a).

1. Cohen and Frankel (1990) make a distinction between opaque and ambiguous nuclear postures, labeling the Israeli posture *opaque*. I prefer the use of the term *ambiguous*, as do most students of Israel's nuclear policy.

2. This is a rather short review of the evolution of the Israeli nuclear policy. For more detailed accounts see Cohen 1998; Aronson, with Brosh, 1992; Evron 1994, 1974; Hersh 1991; Farr 1999.

3. This is "the threat that leaves something to chance." See Schelling 1960, 187–203.

4. The first to have introduced this slogan was probably Levy Eshkol, who replaced Ben-Gurion as prime minister; it appears in a "Memorandum of Understanding" signed on March 10, 1965, between Israel and the United States (Cohen 1998, 207).

5. On September 22 1979, a VELLA satellite detected two bright flashes in the South Atlantic. Various sources, including South Africa's foreign minister, Aziz Pahed (in an interview to the Israeli daily *Ha'aretz*, April 21, 1997), argued that this was a test—conducted in cooperation with South Africa—of two low-grade Israeli nuclear devices.

6. The three best-known cases in this regard are the kidnapping (by Mossad) and sentencing of Mordechai Vanunu, a former employee in the Dimona nuclear reactor who leaked details of nuclear weapons production in Dimona to the London daily *The Sunday Times* (October 5, 1986); the attempt to arrest and indict the historian Avner Cohen, who was suspected of circumventing censorship procedures while publishing his book, *Israel and the Bomb*; and the arrest and sentencing in 2001 of Brigadier General (Reserve) Yitzhak Yaacov (Yatza), who had served as the head of the Department of Weapons and Technological Development (MAFAT) in the Defense Ministry during the critical era of the movement from nuclear potential to actual nuclear production in the 1960s and 1970s.

7. A partial list of examples includes the following: (1) The president of Israel, Ephraim Katzir, a leading biophysicist and a key player in the reorganization of the Israeli nuclear project in the 1960s (Cohen 1998, 21–22), stated on December 1, 1974, that "Israel now has nuclear potential" (*Ma'ariv*, December 2, 1974). (2) In 1976, Moshe Dayan stated in an interview to Israeli Radio that he believed that Israel must have the option—the knowledge and operational capability—to produce nuclear weapons (excerpts of this interview in *Yediot Aharonot*, November 17, 1976). (3) During the spring, summer, and fall of 1990, various officials—responding to threatening statements made by Saddam Hussein—issued a number of statements about the potential destructiveness of Israeli retaliatory capability (see some examples in Alper 1992). (4) In a meeting with the committee of the senior editors of the Israeli news media on December 25, 1995, Prime Minister Shimon Peres stated: "Give me peace and I will give up our nukes" (*Ma'ariv*, December 26, 1995). (5) In a documentary program on Israel's national television channel on November 4, 2001 (entitled "A Bomb in the Basement"), Shimon Peres documented in detail the history of the Israeli project in the 1950s, discussing nuclear diplomacy in a fairly revealing fashion (text of documentary available on file).

8. The other states are India, Pakistan, and (as of 2003) North Korea.

9. For a discussion of the diplomacy surrounding the Jericho I missiles that had

originally been developed with the Marcel Dessault industries in France, see Aronson, with Brosh, 1992, 91–106; Cohen 1998, 232, 379n7.

10. Quoted in *Maariv*, December 26, 1995.

11. Sources on the nature, quantities, and delivery systems of the Israeli nuclear arsenal include official intelligence estimates of the Russian Federation (presented by then head of military intelligence, Yevgeny Primakov, on April 19, 1995). See Aluf Ben, "Soviet Intelligence Reveals Israel's Nuclear Capability," *Ha'aretz*, April 20, 1995, and semiofficial estimates by private organizations and nongovernmental organizations (NGOs) (e.g., *Jane's Intelligence Review*, September 1997, and the Web site of the Federation of American Scientists [FAS] on nuclear weapons, http://www.fas.org/nuke/guide/index.html; a number of data resources on these issues can be found at http://first.sipri.org/).

12. There is a debate in the literature about whether nuclear ambiguity was an essential component of this success or whether Israeli deterrence could have been better served by an overt nuclear policy. See, for example, Feldman 1983 for an argument against ambiguity and Evron 1994 for a proambiguity argument. Aronson (with Brosh, 1992) is probably one of the most ardent supporters of this view. (See also interviews with Feldman and Aronson in Bob Levin, with Milan J. Kubic, "Should Israel Build a Nuclear Bomb?" *Newsweek*, May 4, 1981, 42. With the notable exception of Yair Evron's work (e.g., 1994, 35–80) virtually nobody challenges the notion that Israeli nuclear policy did prove an effective deterrent.

13. Compare Harkabi's (1972) discussion of Arab rhetoric of the 1950s and 1960s to his subsequent discussion of Arab rhetoric in the post–Six Day War period (Harkabi 1975).

14. The most recent and dramatic shift in this regard is the March 28, 2002, decision of the Arab League in the Beirut Summit to adopt the Saudi Arabian initiative. This resolution states that—in return for full Israeli withdrawal to the June 4, 1967, lines and the establishment of a Palestinian state—the Arab states will (a) consider the Arab-Israeli conflict ended, enter into a peace agreement with Israel, and provide security for all the states of the region; and (b) establish normal relations with Israel in the context of this comprehensive peace. See McFarquhar 2002. The most comprehensive account of the impact of Israel's nuclear image on Arab perceptions is Levite and Landau 1994. These authors suggest that Israel's nuclear image had a major impact on Arab strategic perceptions, though from their account it is unclear whether this impact was toward the modification of their strategic goals or toward an increase in their threat perception.

15. See Morgan 2003, 2; George and Smoke 1989; Jervis 1989; and Lebow and Stein 1989; but see the dissenting view in Achen and Snidal 1989.

16. On inter-Arab politics during this era, see Podeh 1995; Kerr 1971; Seale 1986; Nutting 1972, 196–293; Sela 1998, 41–54.

17. For a discussion of the extent of Arab disagreement regarding the settlement with Israel following the Six Day War, see Farid 1994, 51–67, 109–22. During the 1990s, the overriding fear of both the Syrians and the Palestinians was that they would be "betrayed" by each other's signing of a separate deal with the Israelis. See Ross 2004.

18. On Nasser's objectives during the War of Attrition, see Whetten 1974, 141; Bar-Simantov 1980, 43–71; Schueftan 1989, 39–147; Stein 1985, 38–49. Sadat's strategy prior to the Yom Kippur War is discussed in Shazly 1980, 172–81; Sadat 1977, 234–37; Israeli 1985, 29; Meital 1997, 111–12.

19. For a general and analytic discussion of Israeli threat perception during the crisis, see Brecher 1975, 331–55.

20. The Egyptian army in the Sinai was positioned in a defensive posture, and the Israelis knew that (see chap. 3). See also Rabin 1979, 157–58; Dayan 1976, 322–23, 331; Weizman 1975, 260. For an analytical perspective of this aspect see Yaniv 1987a, 115–23.

21. Cohen (1998, 266–76) argues that, in the final analysis, no nuclear deterrent threat was issued, principally because Israeli decision makers weighted the adverse implications of such a threat—revealing the nuclear potential—to outweigh the strategic benefits. However, he also admits that, "if the possession of nuclear weapons is the criterion by which a state is judged to be a nuclear-weapon state, then by May of 1967, Israel was a nuclear weapon state." It is unclear therefore what the purpose was of the acceleration of the project, unless it was to provide Israel with a credible deterrent at the heat of the crisis.

22. Peres (1995, 145) writes about his role during the crisis period: "My contribution during that dramatic period was something I still cannot write about openly, for reasons of state security. After Dayan was appointed defense minister, I submitted to him a certain proposal that in my opinion then—and in my opinion today, nearly three decades later—would have deterred the Arabs and prevented the war. My proposal, which Yigael Yadin knew about and supported, was considered—and rejected." It is fairly clear that Peres was proposing the communication of an explicit nuclear threat to Nasser. While it may have been rejected by the political leaders at the time, it is not inconceivable that heightened activity in Dimona was detected by the Egyptians and that the possibility that a nuclear device existed by then was considered by Nasser and his military aides.

23. In fact, there is reason to suspect that the drive of Amer for the staging of Operation Dawn on May 28—which was narrowly averted due to Soviet pressure—may have been a response to the crash preparations in the Dimona nuclear reactor. See Oren 2000, 92–97, 118–21.

24. On the first perspective see Nutting 1972, 395–417; Lebow 1981, 242–44. The second perspective is best demonstrated in Mor 1993 and 1991. See also chapter 3.

25. Aronson (with Brosh, 1992, 139–49) argues that this was an act of panic. Dayan's critics after the war claimed that he had planned to use nuclear weapons on Damascus should the Syrians descend from the Golan Height into the Galilee. Aronson (332–33n23) argues that the nuclear threat was instrumental in bringing about the American airlift to Israel on October 14.

26. Bar Joseph (1982, 216) argues that the arming of Israel's nuclear weapons may have provoked the Soviets into sending a military supply vessel carrying nuclear warheads to Port Said on October 25, 1973. Yet, "if the Soviets did bring these arms in reaction to an Israeli nuclear alert, they disproved the conceptions of Dayan's pro-nuclear group. This demonstrated that even under the threat of an Israeli 'bomb in the basement,' the Arab side could ignore the threat, embark upon a war, and even receive nuclear guarantees from the Soviet Union."

27. A number of representative statements follow: Yitzhak Rabin, then minister of defense (Ha'aretz, April 6, 1990): "We shall retaliate using weapons that are a thousand times more effective. We have a significantly more decisive response [to Iraq's binary chemical weapons]." Yuval Ne'eman, minister of science and technology and one of the key players in the Israeli nuclear project, in a radio interview ("The Voice of Israel") and in the International Herald Tribune, July 28, 1990: "In my opinion, we have an excellent response [to the Iraqi threat], and this is to threaten Saddam Hussein with the same weapons [that he threatens us with]." Moshe Arens, who replaced Rabin as minis-

ter of defense, in his testimony at the Knesset CFSA on August 15, 1990 (quoted in *Jerusalem Post*, August 16): "Israel will launch a massive aerial strike [on Iraq, if the latter attacked Israel]." Yitzhak Shamir, Israeli prime minister, in a speech before the U.S. bonds delegation (quoted in *Yediot Aharonot*, August 24, 1990): "Whoever tries to challenge us, will pay a terrible price." Shamir again (*Yediot Aharonot*, September 27, 1990): "If Israel is attacked it will retaliate with ferocious power." Ariel Sharon, minister of housing (*Yediot Aharonot*, January 10, 1991): "To Saddam Hussein, I would say 'Do not attack Israel because Israel will retaliate in the most decisive and immediate manner.'" Ehud Olmert, minister of health (*Yediot Aharonot*, January 10, 1991): "If Israel is attacked directly, then we will retaliate in such a manner that Saddam would never forget." Lieutenant General Dan Shomron, IDF COS (*Ha'aretz*, January 13, 1991): "It is imperative that Saddam does not make a mistake here, and that he takes into account a ferocious Israeli response if he attacks or tries to attack us." Additional quotes regarding Israeli pledges to respond to Iraqi attacks are given in Feldman 1991; Mendelsohn 2003; 1999, 120–55.

28. For example, in a December 24, 1990, television interview, Arens stated: "We have no way of intercepting incoming missiles . . . but the physical damage such missiles would cause is limited." Quoted in *Ha'aretz*, December 25, 1990. Prime Minister Shamir stated that, even if chemical weapons were used against Israel, "this is not an existential threat" (*Ha'aretz*, January 10, 1991; cited in Mendelsohn 1999, 144–45).

29. See, for example, the instructions provided in the IDF Home Front Command's (HFC) Web site for protective measures in the face of a conventional attack and/or a chemical attack. Note that these instructions have been unified following the Gulf War, including specific engineering instructions regarding the construction of safe rooms in individual apartments or collective shelters in apartment and office buildings. See http://www.idf.il/hebrew/organization/homefront/index1.stm.

30. Official information about the HFC, its organizational structure, it functions, and its operational doctrine can be obtained at http://www1.idf.il/OREF/site/he/main.asp. An English version is under construction in August 2004.

31. Another dimension of Israeli strategic effort aimed at the proliferation of WMDs in the Middle East also collapsed during the 1980s. Following the Israeli attack on the Iraqi nuclear reactor in Osirak (June 7, 1981), Israel adopted the so-called Begin Doctrine, which stated that "under no circumstances would [Israel] allow the enemy to develop weapons of mass destruction against our nation" (Feldman 1997, 109). Virtually all of Israel's enemies have developed or are in the process of developing WMDs and long-range SSMs.

32. Until the Gulf War, Israel confronted strategic challenges such as Arab SSMs or nonconventional weapons primarily with offensive measures (e.g., developing the Jericho missile, producing nuclear weapons, and investing in the IAF). The increasing emphasis on defensive measures and the bolstering of home front infrastructure since the Gulf War suggest a growing belief among some Israelis that deterrence is no longer the iron-clad guarantee against attack that they once thought it was. One of the leading proponents of this shift was Yitzhak Rabin, who drew two principal conclusions from the Gulf War: (1) Israel needed to develop a wide array of defensive and offensive weapons to counter the proliferation of missiles in the region, because deterrence was not enough, and (2) the most effective way to increase Israeli security was to sign peace treaties with as many Arab states as possible. See Inbar 1999, 119–22.

33. On Egyptian and Syrian emphasis on missile forces in relation to their conventional armed forces, see Gilboa 1996; Shapir 1996; and Cordesman 2004, 1996.

34. This section corroborates the arguments made in Evron 1994, 62–75, 202–14. The analyses here and in Evron are fairly similar, though I expand on a number of issues that are not covered by Evron.

35. The number of missiles reported to have been fired at Israel during the Gulf War varies between the official Israeli version of thirty-nine missiles and a number of forty-four missiles reported by foreign sources. Part of the difference may be due to unreported missiles by Israeli sources due to the intended targets of those missiles. Muhamedou (1998, 159) claims that Iraq fired six missiles at the Dimona reactor in retribution for the Israeli 1981 attack on the Osirak reactor.

36. Cheney interview with Wolf Blitzer on CNN's "Evans and Novak Program." This argument was made principally by Feldman (1991, 273–74).

37. For the numbers and types of warheads uncovered after the Gulf War, see UNSCOM, "Comprehensive Review on Iraq," January 25, 1999, available at http://cns .miis.edu/research/iraq/ucreport/index.htm. Annex C of the review acknowledged that far less was known about Iraq's biological weapons capabilities. In addition, the UNSCOM teams were unable to verify most of the Iraqi reports or to develop independent assessments of Iraq's bioweapons capabilities. The discrepancies between the Iraqi reports and UNSCOM verification statements are especially significant in this area. The reports found no evidence, however, that Iraq had conducted field tests of its bio-missiles. Clearly, the lack of any evidence of WMDs following the 2003 American-Iraqi war suggests that no such weapons remained after their post-1991 dismantlement by UNSCOM teams.

38. On the course of the Gulf War, see Friedman and Karsh 1993; Hiro 1992; Pollack 2002.

39. An important source of confusion is Richard Cheney's January 2, 1991, statement (in the CNN interview with Wolf Blitzer) that Israel would retaliate to a chemical weapons attack with nuclear weapons. This also ignores, however, the more obvious threats by the United States that it would retaliate with brute force if Iraq used chemical weapons against anybody, not just Israel. It is more likely that Saddam knew that U.S. stakes in the conflict would increase tenfold if he used such weapons.

40. Evron (1994, 211–12) argues that technological and operational problems, rather than Israeli threats of nuclear retaliation, prevented Saddam from using chemical weapons. Khadduri and Ghareeb (1997, 171) make a similar case: "The Scud missiles, however, are known for being highly inaccurate and quite an ineffective weapon . . . nor do they contain very powerful warheads; indeed, in one case it was found that an Iraqi warhead was made of cement." Evron suggests that Saddam saw Iraq's chemical weapons more as a deterrent against threats to his regime than as an offensive option.

41. Aronson (with Brosh, 1992, 160–64) argues that Sadat not only was convinced of the futility of pursuing the unrealistic goal of the destruction of Israel but, moreover, was concerned with the possibly destructive implication of a future war in the Middle East.

42. The centrality of this agenda is best illustrated by the fact that all peace negotiations following the 1967 war were based on UN Resolutions 242 and (after the 1973 war) 338, which guarantee the right of all states in the region to live in peace and secure borders. Egypt and Jordan as early as 1969 and (subsequently) Syria (after 1973) accepted these resolutions. This clearly suggests that these states were willing to make this territories-peace trade-off when Israel's nuclear capability was still in the stage of "a bomb in the basement."

43. Aronson (with Brosh, 1992, 162–63) mentions Egyptian demands during the Israeli-Egyptian peace negotiations that Israel join the NPT. He also mentions (163)

that the failure to accomplish the latter objective as part of the actual treaty formed the basis for criticism of Sadat's initiative by prominent Egyptian diplomats (e.g., Ismail Fahmy) and generals (e.g., Sa'ad Shazly). However, the fact remains that Sadat did sign a peace treaty with Israel and that this treaty survived quite a few crises, despite Israel's continued refusal to join the NPT regime.

44. Hersh (1991, 65) also mentions Eshkol and Sapir on the sides of the financial opposition to the nuclear project. Peres claimed that he had raised all the money that was needed to build the Dimona reactor—$40 million—from American Jews. However, conservative estimates of the construction and development costs of the Dimona reactor were in the "hundreds of millions" by the mid-1960s. More important, the operating costs of the reactor are in the dozens of billions.

45. Hersh (1991, 67) lists also Ariel Sharon on the side of this particular opposition to the nuclear project.

46. There are various estimates of the portion of the Israeli defense expenditures that cover the direct and indirect costs of the nuclear project. Hersh (1991, 136) argues that the Dimona project accounted for about 10 percent of Israel's military expenditures in the 1960s. Cohen (1998, 367–68n66) mentions an estimate by Amos de Shalit, one of the key players in the project, that the cost of Dimona was about $175 million. Hersh argues that the cost of the Dimona reactor was about $500 million. Given that we must include the cost of development and maintenance of delivery systems and the training of specialized military and engineering personnel in the overall cost of the nuclear project, it is reasonable to suggest that the nuclear project accounts for about 10–15 percent of Israel's defense expenditures.

47. Figures are U.S. dollars in 1990 constant prices. Estimates of defense expenditures for all of the Middle East states are inaccurate. For Israel, most of the nuclear-related expenditures are either hidden or placed in civilian budget headlines (Lifschitz 2003, 49). There might also be significant misreporting by the Arab states.

48. Evron (1974) and Cohen (1998, 149–50) mention a secret meeting probably in Dimona toward the second half of 1962, where the key decisions on the nuclear weapon project were taken.

49. This denotes the pre– and post–Israeli-Egyptian peace periods, respectively.

50. The classic work in this area is Wildavsky 1974.

51. A similar set of tests was run on defense burdens, that is, on a dependent variable measured as military expenditures as a proportion of GDP. Results were almost identical to those reported in table 8.2.

52. Numerical results are not provided here for the sake of brevity.

53. This analysis is reported here for Israel only, but it was also conducted for Egypt and Syria. In the Egyptian case, the best-fitting arms race equation covers the 1950–73 period, with an R^2 of 0.996 and an RMSE of $33,040. If Egypt had continued the trend for that period, it would have required a defense budget of over $20 billion by 2001. For Syria, the best fit is accomplished for the period of 1967–90 (R^2 of 0.993 and RMSE of $21,000). Had Syria continued this trend, its 2001 military expenditures would have been roughly $5 billion.

54. This means that, on average, the predicted military expenditures for Israel in a given year diverged from the actual expenditures by only $4,300 and that the analysis accounts for 99.5 percent of the variance in Israel's military expenditures. A similar analysis was conducted on material defense burdens (defense spending over GDP) and on dollar-to-soldier ratios, with nearly identical results.

55. The *predicted* figures are the values predicted by the overall 1950–2001 equation, which, as noted, does not indicate a strategic arms race on Israel's side.

56. On the Iraqi nuclear project, see Snyder 1983; Hamza, with Stein, 2000; Baghat 2003; and Cordesman 1994, 103–11.

57. On the Iranian project, see Kam 2004; Sick 1995; and Cordesman 1999; 1994, 258–73.

58. See Hamza, with Stein, 2000, 62–66. Hamza, a senior figure in the Iraqi nuclear project who escaped to the United States in 1994, mentions a conversation between himself and the two directors of the Iraqi Atomic Energy Authority sometime in 1972 or 1973 that gave birth to the Atomic Energy Authority's plan to develop a nuclear weapons program. The starting point of this discussion was Jaber 1971. He also suggests that this discussion was probably launched by a directive from Saddam Hussein. Also, Hamza clearly suggests that the general plan of acquiring a small reactor from France followed closely the model established by the Israelis (see especially 69, 108–9).

59. See Levite and Landau 1994, 107; Evron 1994, 198. These authors argue that Iraq used the Israeli nuclear threat as moral and political rationale for its own nuclear program.

60. See also Shazly 1986, 46–47.

61. See statement by Iran's minister of defense, Ali Shamakani, on February 5, 2002, in the *Jerusalem Post*, February 6, 2002.

62. The Libyan nuclear project was shrouded in secrecy, and thus it is not clear what exactly motivated Mu'ammar Ghaddafi to pursue nuclear weapons. It is not likely that the Israeli nuclear policy was a major factor in this project, but there is no evidence either way.

63. See Shoham 2001, 32–40; 2000. See also the Center for Nonproliferation Studies at the Monterey Institute of International Studies at http://cns.miis.edu/research/wmdme/index.htm.

64. For example, in a joint press conference with Egyptian president Hosni Mubarak, on May 1, 1997, Hafez Asad, the Syrian president, stated in response to a question about Syrian chemical weapons program: "Those who possess nuclear weapons have no right to criticize the others for possessing any other type of weapons, and if they want disarmament, then let us start with the nuclear weapons" (reported by Deutsche Presse Agentur, May 1, 1997). In a *Sunday Times* story on July 25, 1999, Uzi Manahaimi reports, based on Israeli military sources, of a Syrian offer of an agreement to exchange Israeli nuclear disarmament for Syrian chemical and biological disarmament. On the Egyptian and Syrian conception of a balance of mutual deterrence based on the nuclear-chemical/biological equation, see Evron 1998, 12–15, 16–17.

65. Shoham (2001, 82) provides a table with estimated probabilities that different states would use chemical and biological weapons under different scenarios. For example, Iraq and Iran are said to be willing to use chemical or biological weapons as a first-strike option with a probability range of 0.3–0.6; Syria is expected to use these weapons in a first strike with a probability range of 0.2–0.4; and Egypt's probability of a chemical or biological first strike ranges from 0.1–0.3. All this assumes that these countries operate under a nuclear umbrella—presumably of Iran and Iraq. There is no evidence to support these estimates. Moreover, Shoham does not discuss the logic of employing such weapons in the context of a first or retaliatory strike.

66. In a television program entitled "A Bomb in the Basement" (November 11, 2001), Shimon Peres stated: "Had Israel performed a nuclear test, it would have invited tremendous [international] pressure. You know, there is some pleasure in the [nuclear] ambiguity, just as there is deterrence in the ambiguity. We have chosen ambiguity—deterrence towards the Arabs, and pleasure towards friends."

67. For a distribution of such opinions over the 1986–93 period, see Arian 1995,

72–73. In the 2002 survey only 16.75 percent favored nuclear retaliation to a possible chemical or biological missile attack by Iraq.

68. See country notes in the U.S. State Department Web site: http://www.state .gov/r/pa/bgn/.

69. Some have even mentioned the possession of low-yield neutron bombs, that is, "dirty" bombs that cause significant numbers of human casualties but little damage to property. See Hersh 1991, 199–200; Farr 1999.

70. In fact, several scholars as well as left-wing politicians strongly support Israel's nuclear posture as a means of ensuring the peace once the occupied territories are returned. See Feldman 1983, 237–43. See also the statement by Shimon Peres in a press conference on July 13, 1998, in which he said that Israel "built a nuclear option not in order to have a Hiroshima but an Oslo" (cited in Barletta and Ellington 1998, 1).

71. The secrecy surrounding the project makes it difficult to provide evidence for this explanation. However, some indirect evidence can be provided from available sources. Mardor's (1981) book is a good example of this kind of process. Mardor, who has served as the director general of the Israeli Weapons Development Authority (RAFAEL in Hebrew), enumerates a large number of "initiatives from below" in the realm of sophisticated weapons systems. Cohen (1998, 223–35) and Hersh (1991, 216–18) also detail a number of bureaucratic struggles and initiatives during various years that suggest that weapons development related to minitiaturization of weapons and diversification of delivery systems was not necessarily in line with the deterrence logic.

72. Again, some indirect hints can be given regarding this issue. Rabin (1979, 526) recounts an episode in 1976 when Peres attempted to boost the defense budget by using a letter by the COS stating that the IDF should not be held responsible for any fiasco that might happen if the defense budget were cut. Peres (1995, 149), on his part, responded that "every defense minister fights for higher budget" by warning the cabinet of the dangers of scrimping on defense. Again, it is not clear which precise elements of the defense budget were in contention, but it is not inconceivable that nuclear weapon production and delivery systems were among the items in dispute.

73. For example, Feldman 1997; Shoham 2001. An exception is Evron (1998, 1994), who considers Israeli nuclear weapons as part of the threat perception of both Egypt and Syria.

74. There are other domestic implications of the opaque nature of Israel's nuclear status, including moral, legal, medical, environmental, and democratic issues. These will not be discussed here. Cohen 2005 is a very good source on these matters.

75. I adapted this heading title from Jervis 1985a.

76. Evron 1994, 215–76, is the most detailed and balanced analysis of Israeli security dilemmas in the nuclear realm.

77. Arian (2002, 34) asked Israelis how Israel should react if Iraq launched at it chemical or biological missiles. Only 17 percent advocated nuclear retaliation, while 46 percent advocated retaliation with similar weapons, 16 percent advocated conventional retaliation, and 22 percent suggested letting the United States handle the matter. These figures again indicate an extremely strong public belief that nuclear weapons should be used only as a last resort in an imminent event of total annihilation and nothing less.

78. In contrast to the lack of writing about Israel's nuclear doctrine, there is ample work on Israeli conventional deterrence doctrines. See Yaniv 1987b, 1995; Shimshoni 1988; Tal 2000; Handel 1973, 1995; Ben-Horin and Posen 1981; Inbar 1998. The most widely used semiofficial source is Allon 1968.

79. For example, Zeev Schiff suggests that continued ambiguity may provoke an

Iranian ambiguous nuclear posture. This would create an extremely unstable regional reality. See Schiff, "How Long Can Nuclear Ambiguity Last?" *Ha'aretz*, August 24, 2000. See the FAS Web site at http://www.fas.org/news/israel/000824-israel.htm.

80. See also the arguments for and against ambiguity in Evron 1994, 255–59. Evron is in favor of continued ambiguity but prefers nuclear disarmament to nuclear proliferation in the Middle East (272).

81. On the distinction between deterrence and compellence, see Schelling 1966, 69–78; Maoz 1990b, 67–68; and George and Simmons 1994.

82. For example, the statement by Major General Uzi Dayan, head of the planning division of the IDF, on December 30, 1994 (*Agence France Presse*, December 30, 1994) and threats by then Israeli COS Shaul Mofaz on March 4, 2002, regarding the ability of Israel to hit Iran if the latter developed nuclear capability. See *Ha'aretz*, March 5, 2002. More recent reports include a commentary by Arnaud de Borchgrave on July 2, 2004 (cited in United Press International Lexis Nexis edition), and an article by Uzi Manahaimi and Peter Conradi in London's *Sunday Times* (July 18, 2004) about preparations in Israel for a strike against Iranian nuclear installations.

83. In a survey conducted in the spring of 2002, the Israeli daily *Yediot Aharonot* asked readers to rank order the fifty most successful decisions in Israel's history. The decision to build the Dimona reactor came first, with a large margin from the second most successful decision.

84. Only a few members of Israel's security community have called for reconsideration of Israel's approach to disarmament. See, for example, Shmuel Gordon, "The Iranian Threat," *Yediot Aharonot*, May 28, 2002, available at http://www.ynet.co.il/articles/1,7340,L-1914319,00.html; Oded Balaban, "A Recipe to Regional Conflagration," *Ha'aretz*, June 6, 2002, 82; and Pa'il 1998.

CHAPTER 9

A previous and abridged version of this chapter was published elsewhere (Maoz 2001). I wish to thank Avi Ben-Zvi and Aharon Klieman for their perceptive comments on previous drafts.

1. There are numerous, and somewhat different, definitions of the term *intervention*. Space constraints preclude a more elaborate discussion of the concept. For reviews of the various definitional issues involved, see Jentelson and Levite 1992, 5–11; and Vertzberger 1998, 3–7.

2. The list is far from comprehensive. There were several other instances of intervention efforts, including the exchange of ideas about Israel's assistance with launch plots in Syria in 1957–58 (M. Maoz 1995, 45–46); participation of Israeli agents in the kidnapping and assassination of the Moroccan opposition leader, Mehdi Ben-Barka, in 1965 (Black and Morris 1991, 202–5); and provision of information regarding Algerian Front Liberation Nationale leaders to the French secret service in 1956 (Black and Morris 1991, 172–73). However, these were brief and relatively insignificant episodes. Two significant Israeli support policies to Muslim non-Arab states—Israeli-Iranian relations during the shah's regime and Israeli-Turkish relations—are not included here because they entail direct government-to-government ties.

3. Bar Joseph (1995, 149) translates the Hebrew phrase *Esek Bish*, which was the code name of this affair in the censored Israeli press at the time, as "unfortunate affair." I prefer to use the term "the mishap." See Sheffer 1996, 750.

4. Cited from an official estimate by the chief of military intelligence on June 16, 1954.

5. The only ring member not arrested was the Israeli operator of the spy ring, Avri El-Ad, who escaped from Egypt in early August. El-Ad came under suspicion of being turned into a double agent by the Egyptian secret service (Bar Joseph 1995, 194–201).

6. Bar Joseph (1995, 210) argues that "Givli's Egyptian operation of 1954 is a clear-cut case of the crudest type of interference in the conduct of national foreign policy by an intelligence organization. . . . Givli's attempt to decide the fate of Israel looks especially grave, furthermore, when one considers what type that foreign policy was." This is an exaggeration, however, because the operation was not designed to affect Israel's fate but rather to intervene in others' domestic affairs. Bar Joseph does provide, however, a sober estimate of the damage this operation caused to Israeli-Egyptian relations.

7. Another case in this class of interventions was revealed recently (*Ha'aretz,* February 20, 2000, 1) by former head of the Mossad Shabtai Shavit. This involved the supply of military equipment and military advisers to the royalist forces in the Yemen civil war (1962–67), mostly during the 1965–67 period. This assistance was based on an effort to help thwart Egyptian forces in the civil war. This episode will not be discussed herein due to lack of information. Nevertheless, it clearly had little or no effect on the process or outcome of that war. Nor did it prevent the Egyptians from pulling out their troops as soon as the May–June 1967 crisis broke out.

8. On the rebellion in Sudan, see Shimoni 1977, 612–618; and O'Balance 2000.

9. The shah advocated a "low flame" policy because the number of Kurds in Iran (4 million) was double the number of Kurds in Iraq (2 million). A successful rebellion in Iraq would have invoked similar claims for autonomy by the Iranian Kurds (Bengio 1989).

10. In contrast to other cases of covert intervention, the Israelis made relatively little effort to hide their involvement in the Kurdish rebellion. Although the Israeli advisers stationed in Kurdistan had to wear local uniforms and avoid speaking in Hebrew, there were numerous reports of Israeli aid to the Kurds in the Arab and international press. Israeli weapons were captured by the Iraqis, and Kurdish prisoners revealed details of this aid. Barazani's visit to Israel in 1968 involved a number of public receptions, including a meeting with the Israeli newspaper editors (Nakdimon 1996, 221–28).

11. In practice, logistical and other problems prevented the actual delivery of these tanks to the Kurds.

12. The Israeli intelligence community was not aware of the secret Iranian-Iraqi talks to resolve their conflict (Nakdimon 1996, 348).

13. The number of eligible voters in 1976 was over eighty-eight thousand, as opposed to thirty-one thousand in 1972 (Mishal 1986, 110; Maoz 1985, 149).

14. For detailed analyses of the election results, see Mishal 1986, 114–18; and Maoz 1985, 149–52.

15. I discuss the Lebanon War in chapter 6. In this section I focus only on the Israeli-Christian-Shi'ite triangle.

16. On this crisis, see Yaniv 1987b, 85–90; Seale 1988, 368–70; Evron 1987; and Maoz and Mor 2002a, 192–93; 2002b, 41–44.

17. This applies to Jordan since the early 1950s and to Egypt after the 1979 peace treaty. This was also the logic of the vision of a Christian-dominated state in Lebanon leading to the 1982 invasion.

CHAPTER 10

1. See Arian 2003, 24–25, for an analysis of long-term Israeli public perceptions of Arab intentions.

2. The international boundary was demarcated by the British and French in 1923. See Shalev 1994.

3. On earlier peace efforts vis-à-vis Egypt, see Rabinovich 1991, 168–208.

4. Quoted in Shlaim 2000, 77.

5. Haim Handwerker (2002) reports of secret documents of the German Ministry of Foreign Affairs that discuss an attempt by Nasser in April 1953 to use German mediation to explore the conditions under which Israel would be willing to sign a peace treaty with Egypt. According to Wolfgang Schwanitz, a German historian who was given these documents, this initiative did not advance very far both because the Israelis did not respond to the German review of Nasser's queries and because Germany, who was just about to be granted formal independence by the occupying powers, was reluctant to engage in secret diplomacy with Egypt that might upset the British.

6. Shlaim 2000, 78. See also Ben-Gurion's quote of October 1, 1952 (chap. 10, p. 487).

7. Eric Johnston was a representative of President Eisenhower who developed a plan for water sharing between Israel and its neighbors (Jordan, Syria, and Lebanon), patterned after the Tennessee Valley Authority. The Johnston Plan was published in 1954, and after a debate in the Israeli cabinet (wherein Lavon and the IDF opposed the agreement), it was adopted by Israel. Syria and Jordan did not sign the agreement but tacitly abided by it (Shlaim 2000, 109–10).

8. This was a secret decision. The government did not relay it even to the COS. Yitzhak Rabin learned of this decision only after becoming ambassador to Washington (Shlaim 2000, 254).

9. This was the English version of Resolution 242. The French version called for Israeli withdrawal from the territories it had occupied in June 1967, and, by implication, it demanded Israeli return to the international borders.

10. The transcripts of the meeting were delivered to the military intelligence. Zeira (1993, 96) claims that, despite the severity of the warning, Golda Meir did not delve further into specifics in her discussion with Hussein. Thus the transcripts contained a general warning without any dates or specific details. Golda and the military officers who participated in this meeting were surprised to hear this warning but did not consider it to indicate a clear and present danger (Zak 1996, 143–44n87; Braun 1992, 40; Bar Joseph 2001, 245–46).

11. The full text of the Sadat speech is given in Israeli 1979, 30–32.

12. The full text of Sisco's proposal is given in Yaacobi 1990a, 180–81. The text was confirmed by Joseph Sisco in an interview with Zeev Maoz and Allison Astorino (Sisco 1990).

13. The text of the Israeli response is given in Yaacobi 1990a, 180–81.

14. Israeli (1985, 67) quotes a statement by Sadat in August 1971 claiming that the Israeli-Egyptian agreement had only a 1 percent chance of success.

15. It is interesting to note that Dayan—who had an obsessive fear of Soviet involvement—did not share this perception of Egypt and Sadat. In meetings with RAFI Party members, Dayan insisted that Sadat had an interest in an agreement because he was aware of the consequences of war. It was not inconceivable that Sadat was really interested in normalization of the relations with Israel but needed a substantial diplomatic victory to strengthen his position inside Egypt. In any event, Israel could afford to "throw Sadat a hook he could hold on to" and should do more than sit back and have Sadat meet its terms (Yaacobi 1990a, 148). However, Dayan was not willing to press his views in the cabinet. Indeed, Sisco noted that Dayan, in his talks with the Israeli delegation, refused to make any comment (Sisco 1990). This suggested to Sisco that

Dayan's position was as a political outlier and he did not have any chance to sway the government. Sisco failed to elicit any new Israeli proposal (Atherton 1990).

16. For the text of this agreement, see Dayan 1976, 675; Kissinger 1982, 641; Fahmy 1983, 55.

17. The text of the agreement is given in Dayan 1976, 702–3; and Kissinger 1982, 1250–51. Kissinger (1982, 839) provides a map of the agreement.

18. Fahmy (1983, 79–80) argues that the agreement was strictly military and that Egypt successfully purged it from any political implications. He questions the letters exchanged between Golda Meir and Sadat toward the final phases of the negotiations. These letters are cited in Kissinger 1982, 836, 844.

19. In fact, Kissinger's initial inclination had been to attempt some disengagement agreement between Israel and Jordan, but he realized very quickly that this was not feasible at the time (Quandt 2001, 157–59; Spiegel 1985, 283–84).

20. The text of the agreement is given in Sheehan 1976, 245–57; deliberately selected articles are given in Fahmy 1983, 166. A map of the lines of redeployment is given in Rabin 1979, 489.

21. Both Brzezinski and William Quandt, who became the National Security Council staff member in charge of Mideast policy, had published the policy paper, which many saw as the fundamental philosophy of the Carter administration (Brookings Institution 1975). Various members of this group have written separate articles advocating the abandonment of the step-by-step approach and the move to a more comprehensive peace strategy that would entail major territorial concessions on Israel's part. See Ball 1977; Brzezinski 1975; Hoffmann 1975; Ullman 1975.

22. Rabin himself recounted his impression of the difficult nature of the meeting in a discussion with me during a meeting in his office in February 1993. He said that it was the most difficult encounter he had had with an American president either as an ambassador or as prime minister.

23. Immediately after his meeting with Rabin, while Rabin was still in the United States conducting meetings with the Jewish leadership, Carter made a speech supporting the Palestinian rights for self-determination and for a "homeland" (Spiegel 1985, 332).

24. Sadat interview to the *Times* of London, June 4, 1976. Cited in Israeli 1979, 1285–86.

25. The full text of the statement is given in Vance 1983, 463–64.

26. The text of Sadat's speech is given in Sadat 1977, 255–63; and Quandt 1986, 345–55.

27. See the principal elements of the Israeli proposal in Ismailiya in Tamir 1988, 18–19.

28. A sample includes the memoirs of the American and Israeli participants (e.g., Carter 1982, 319–403; Vance 1983, 219–31; Quandt 1986, 206–58; Dayan 1981, 132–66; Weizman 1981, 313–47; Tamir 1988, 31–51) and more analytical studies of journalists and scholars (e.g., Benziman 1981; Haber, Schiff, and Yaari 1979; Telhami 1990; Touval 1982; Quandt 2001, 197–203; 1986, 168–258; Stein 1999).

29. Various sources (Weizman 1981, 342; Benziman 1981, 198–99) report of a telephone conversation between Begin and Sharon, then the minister of agriculture, in which the latter promised to support a resolution calling for the dismantlement of the Sinai settlements.

30. The text of the Camp David Accord of September 17, 1978, is available online from the Israeli Foreign Ministry Web site (see Camp David 1978).

31. For the full text of the agreement, see Peres 1995, 361–62.

32. The account of the Israeli political process surrounding the agreement is given in Peres 1995, 308–12; and Shamir 1994, 168–72. See also Shlaim 2000, 445–49. For American accounts of this affair, see Shultz 1993, 426–62; and Quandt 2001, 270–73.

33. A typical example of this kind of procedural haggling is vividly cited by Baker (with Defrank, 1995). In a letter from Shamir to Baker, dated April 15, 1991, Shamir raises a point about the name for the conference: "Since the regional meeting will not be the forum for peace negotiations . . . it makes no sense to call it a *peace conference* (449, italics added). See also Shamir 1994, 227.

34. Baker coined these meetings "bladder diplomacy" due to their length and continuous nature (Baker, with Defrank, 1995, 454).

35. This referred specifically to issues of DMZs and reduced forces zones along the two sides of the border. In practice a ten-to-six formula was developed, suggesting that for each ten kilometers of demilitarization on the Syrian side, there would be six kilometers of demilitarization on the Israeli side. See Ben 1997.

36. Asad also saw the Israeli sensitivity to domestic public opinion as a device to pressure him into concessions (Ross 2004, 144–45).

37. Quoted in Drucker 2002, 98. See also Edelist 2003, 280. This is also Ross's (2004, 588) view.

38. See a report on some of these meetings in Avnery 1986.

39. The full text of the 1993 Oslo Accords, as well as subsequent Israeli-Palestinian agreements, can be found at the Israeli Ministry of Foreign Affairs Web site at http://www.mfa.gov.il/mfa/go.asp?MFAH00q00.

40. See statement of July 25, 2000, by President Clinton, available at http://www.yale.edu/lawweb/avalon/mideast/mid027.htm.

41. The minutes of the meeting where Clinton presented his parameters can be found online at http://www.peacelobby.org/clinton_parameters.htm.

42. For the Israeli reservations, see Sher 2003, 372–74.

43. Joint Israeli-Palestinian statement, January 27, 2011, available at http://www.mfa.gov.il/mfa/go.asp?MFAH0j700.

44. There exist some good evaluations of the Oslo process. Among them are Kimmerling and Migdal 2003, 315–97; Sayigh 2001; Khalidi 2002; Hirshfeld 2000; Pundak 2001.

45. The same applies to the Tanzim and to Force 17 of the Fatah, which never fully succumbed to Arafat's authority.

46. Data cited from the World Bank report are corroborated by the survey of July 27–29, 2000, by Professor Khalil Shikaki of the Palestinian Center for Policy and Survey Research at Birzeit University in Ramallah (formerly at A Najah University in Nablus). This poll shows that in July 2000, prior to the outbreak of the Al Aqsa Intifada, 76 percent of the Palestinians believed that the PA was plagued by widespread corruption. This shows a growing disaffection with the PA's economic policies. Data are available online at http://www.pcpsr.org/survey/index.html.

47. Sources for this figure are B'Tselem 2002; and Foundation for Middle East Peace 2004.

48. On the Beilin-Abu-Mazen dialogue and the general principles of the agreement, see Beilin 1997, 195–213. This agreement served as a basis for subsequent negotiations during the Barak era. See Sher 2003; and Edelist 2003, 302.

49. See Haim Ramon's statement on this matter, quoted in Pundak 2001, 36.

50. Despite the prevalent Israeli conception that control of the Jordan Valley is essential for Israel's security (e.g., the Allon Plan), Israeli military presence in the Jordan Valley is a strategic burden rather than a strategic asset. A limited military force in

the topographically inferior Jordan Valley will be sandwiched between two topographically superior areas controlled by potential enemies. It would be easily seized in the event of war and would force the IDF to try desperate rescue operations rather than focus on primary missions. Since the history of Israeli-Jordanian relations since 1970 is essentially peaceful and since it is in Israel's interest to maintain the independence and territorial integrity of Jordan, such a force would have no stabilizing effect. Moreover, Israel could cover via electronic and aerial intelligence most of the area. If these stations are manned by foreign personnel, their reliability is reduced considerably, as Israel would be reluctant to place highly sensitive intelligence equipment in such stations.

51. There are numerous illustrations of this conception, but two central ones drive this point home. One illustration was the insistence of Israel not to dismantle any settlement in the occupied territories prior to the signing of the final status agreement with the Palestinians. This forced Israel to maintain an inordinate number of troops to defend remote settlements in the West Bank and the Gaza Strip. Related to that is the tremendous resistance in the right half of the Israeli political spectrum to Sharon's 2004 proposal to dismantle the Gaza settlements. The major argument is that it would be seen as a sign of defeat by the Palestinians and would only increase their appetite.

52. Of course, nobody talks about the cases of successful international involvement, for example, the Multilateral Force and Observers (MFO) in the Sinai since 1980 and the United Nations Disengagement Observer Force (UNDOF) on the Golan Height since 1974.

53. Translated and quoted in Shlaim 2000, 297.

54. Translated into English in Rabinovich 1991, 32. Brackets in original.

55. Quote derived from "Documents on Israel's Foreign Policy 1948–1953." Cited in Shlaim 2000, 78. Source given there is Raphael 1981, 36, but this quote is not found in the source.

CHAPTER 11

1. A fifth element in this structure is the technological community that is involved in the research, development, and production of military hardware. I do not discuss it here because it is discussed in part in chapter 8 and because its impact on national security decision making is not as crucial in other, nonnuclear matters as the other communities covered in the analysis of Israel's nuclear policy.

2. The IAF and the INF have their own intelligence bodies, but these deal principally with field and doctrinal intelligence of a strictly military nature. They report to the heads of the respective services.

3. Shlomo Gazit, the head of AMAN during the 1974–78 period, admits frankly the first aspect of this failure but does not mention the latter part of the flawed estimate (2003, 40).

4. Schiff and Yaari (1990, 34) note that "toward the end of 1986 Military Intelligence did, in fact, forecast that serious disturbances could be expected in the territories in the coming year. But beyond making the prediction, it did not press the matter at all by raising it for deliberation by the government."

5. An unpublished manuscript by Israeli journalist Shlomo Nakdimon (Nakdimon 1995) claims that the Israeli intelligence community was completely misinformed of Iraqi WMD capabilities over the entire decade following the destruction of the Osirak nuclear reactor.

6. There are several other candidates of intelligence failure—such as the failure to predict King Hussein's decision to disengage from the West Bank in 1988 and the PLO's

subsequent recognition of Resolutions 242 and 338. There is also a failure to assess the impact of Israel's nuclear capability on the arms race in the Middle East (see chap. 8). I do not discuss these cases because there is no clear evidence on the nature and underlying causes of intelligence failure. Gazit (2003, 40–42) lists a number of other intelligence failures of a more limited nature. Also see Bar Joseph (2004, 139–40) for a similar discussion of the problems in Israel's intelligence assessments.

7. Gazit (2003, 12–23) provides a concise history of the twists and turns in those efforts at reforming the intelligence community in Israel's history. Later on (23–28) he discusses internal reforms in the research branch of AMAN following the Yom Kippur fiasco.

8. Gazit (2003, 25–28) discusses an array of changes introduced in AMAN following the Agranat Commission report. The most significant methodological changes include the establishment of a control unit within the research branch whose function it is to serve as a "devil's advocate" in intelligence analysis, as well as the development of an annual "postmortem" analysis that matches AMAN's annual intelligence estimate with the actual developments for that year and attempts to analyze the prediction errors and their reasons. However, as long as both functions are performed by people who had been brought up in the system and whose promotion depends on the people whom they are supposed to criticize, these functions cannot be effective. And as we have seen, given the continued record of mediocre performance of AMAN, they apparently have not been effective.

9. Givli was removed due to a seemingly unauthorized activation of the Jewish spy ring in Egypt in 1954 (Givli himself argued that he received authorization from Defense Minister Lavon [Bar Joseph 1995]). Saguy was removed for his failure to press his suspicions to the government regarding a possible massacre by the Christians in the Sabra and Shatilla refugee camps. See chapter 6. Another head of AMAN—Yehoshafat Harkabi—was dismissed due to an unauthorized activation of a mobilization drill in 1958 that created widespread panic in Egypt.

10. The Knessett subcommittee that investigated the performance of the intelligence community during the 2003 Iraq war recommended the development of a special set of programs for training intelligence analysts in collaboration with the academic institutions in Israel and/or the establishment of a special intelligence academy (Steinitz 2004a, 63–64).

11. One of them, Major General Uzi Dayan, had served as national security adviser while still in uniform as an active military officer "on loan" from the IDF to the prime minister's office. Another source of competition existed between the national security adviser and the military secretary of the prime minister (who had been a major general since 1994), who served as the liaison between the IDF and the prime minister.

12. On the shift in Rabin's thought with respect to these and other issues, see Inbar 1999.

13. Ben-Eliezer (2000, 245) argues that generals affect political decisions by "the nurturing of an 'understanding' between [the military] and the [political system]. This understanding is based on a common mentality, . . . on social ties, and on a similar vision of reality. . . . The parachuting of generals to politics, from an institutional perspective, was a path that confirmed and advanced the notion of the nexus between the army and the society or political system, and the cultural insight about a common denominator according to which it is legitimate for the army to have political impact on matters of peace and war, all this—of course—in a manner that does not endanger the political leadership and the formal democratic arrangements of Israel."

14. Curiously enough, the IDF was not opposed to this concept because during this time (the early and mid-1990s), Israel experienced significant growth rates, so that its actual raw allocations did not decline significantly (Tov 1998, 122–25). There are, generally speaking, few studies of the politics of Israeli defense spending. The most important studies are Ward and Mintz 1989; Lifschitz 2003; and Tov 1998.

15. Some elements of ideas that emerged in these discussions, however, have appeared in a number of lectures and presentations (e.g., Ben Israel 2001; Steinitz 2004b, 2002).

16. The Supreme Court, acting as a HCJ, deals with the petitions of private individuals or organizations against state authorities.

17. Cited in Kretzmer 2002, 2.

18. A similar case where the courts and parole committees have completely capitulated to the whims of the security establishment was that of Brigadier General Rami Dotan, who was found guilty of embezzlement and theft from the IAF, where he had served as head of the acquisitions department. Dotan was sentenced to ten years in prison, and when his time for parole came up, the entire IAF administration put pressure on the parole committee to deny him parole. Dotan served the full term in prison. Most convicted murderers in Israel are released from prison after having served two-thirds of their jail sentence.

19. The ruling was handed down on May 30, 2004. An English transcript of the ruling of the HCJ is available at http://62.90.71.124/eng/verdict/framesetSrch.html.

20. Article 12 of the "Basic Law: Human Dignity and Liberty" states: "This Basic Law cannot be varied, suspended, or made subject to conditions by emergency regulations; notwithstanding, when a state of emergency exists, by virtue of a declaration under section 9 of the Law and Administration Ordinance, 5708–1948, emergency regulations may be enacted by virtue of said section to deny or restrict rights under this Basic Law, provided the denial or restriction shall be for a proper purpose and for a period and extent no greater than is required." See the text of the basic law at the Knesset Web site, http://www.knesset.gov.il/laws/special/eng/basic3_eng.htm. This article is designed to resolve this contradiction and to place it under criteria of worthy causes and proportionality. However, since Israel has been legally under a state of emergency since its inception, the basic law is in effect subordinate to the DER. Kretzmer (2002, 155) states that, "In recent cases, after the enactment of . . . the Basic Law: Human Dignity and Liberty, the [High Court of Justice] has conceded that even if it may not invalidate regulation 119 [of the DER, dealing with forfeiture and demolition of houses], the regulation must be interpreted and applied according to the principles of the Basic Law. This means that measures offending protected rights must be used for a worthy purpose and must meet the proportionality test. However, the Court has held that deterrence is a worthy purpose."

CHAPTER 12

1. Recent data on trends in threat perception among the Israelis, as envisaged in perception of Arab intentions, are given in Arian 2003, 24. It shows that the average support for the claim that Arab intentions were to destroy the state of Israel was well over 50 percent and reached 68 percent in 2003.

2. I discuss this trend later on. One example of some ideas provided in the rhetoric of Arab liberalism is given in Rubin 2002, 207–9. A major resource for some of the most significant current writings—both conservative and liberal—in the Arab media can be

found at the Middle East Media Research Institute (MEMRI) Web site, http://www.memri.org.il.

3. Good sources on that include Shlaim 1988; 2000, 28–41; and Morris 2004.

CHAPTER 13

1. In calculating the standing order of battle at any given point in time when the entire reserve force is not mobilized, we assume that roughly one-twelfth of the reserve force serves at any given time in addition to the order of battle of the standing army, which stands currently (in 2004) at 186,500 men and women, or roughly 3.8 percent of the Jewish population, so that at any given point in time roughly between 4 and 5 percent of the Jewish population is in the IDF. During emergency, as noted, this figure can rise to 12 percent within seventy-two hours.

2. Saudi Arabia spends roughly $22 billion on defense (more than twice the Israeli defense spending), so that 10 percent of this budget is a significant addition to the capabilities of Israel's strategic reference group.

3. We include in this picture $1.8 billion that Israel has received each year since 1979 from the United States in the form of military aid, of which $1 billion is allocated to procurement of equipment from the United States.

4. On more general characteristics that distinguish the Israeli economy from those of the Middle East and North African (MENA) countries, see Henry and Springborg 2001.

5. This is in addition to a Nobel Prize for Literature and the Nobel Peace Prize to Menachem Begin, Yitzhak Rabin, and Shimon Peres.

6. The per capita GDP of the Middle East in 2001 was roughly $5,000. This compares with a per capita GDP of $6,600 in Eastern Europe, a per capita GDP of $2,730 in south Asia, and a GDP of $1,831 for sub-Saharan Africa (UNDP 2003, 241). However, the Middle East per capita GDP is inflated due to oil revenues, and the Asian GDP is driven down by largely populated states such as India and Indonesia. Karatnycky (2002, 10) notes that most of the Arab states are ranked as "non-free" by Freedom House ratings and that only three states in the region—except Israel, which is rated "free"—are rated as "partly free" in the Freedom House survey. These are Turkey, Jordan, and Kuwait. The Polity IV data set (Marshall and Jaggers 2004) lists only Israel and Turkey as democracies and Iran's democracy score as larger than its autocracy score.

7. A report in 2003 by the OECD (2003) shows a significant deterioration in Israeli educational standing. Israel is ranked thirtieth in terms of reading literacy, thirty-first in terms of math skills, and thirty-third in scientific literacy for children at the age of fifteen.

8. Higher ranks indicate lower rates of nonparticipation in the labor force (Ben David 2003, 76).

9. There are no figures for female unemployment for this population, but it is safe to assume that it is close to 100 percent.

10. According to Hagelin, Bromely, and Wezman (2004) Israel is ranked twelfth in the world in terms of arms sales, which amounted to over $1 billion over the 1998–2003 period.

11. Helpman's (1998, 30–31) discusses the rapid growth in Israel's R&D investment during the 1980s and 1990s and argues that this growth in R&D accounts for 17 percent in the growth in productivity over the period 1970–90. However, it is unclear whether this investment included investment in military R&D as well. If so, then per-

haps the growth in R&D could have been greater if a greater proportion had been invested in civilian R&D.

12. If Arab municipalities in Israel are excluded, then the difference between government spending in the West Bank and in Jewish municipalities in Israel is roughly 170 percent.

13. For an earlier analysis of the social, political, and economic effects of the occupied territories on Israel, see Maoz 1990b, 267–72.

14. See http://www.mof.gov.il/revenue_e/state1/98217_04a.htm.

CHAPTER 14

1. The EU-Israel Association Agreement was signed in 1995 and entered into effect in 2000. It consists of a free-trade area and scientific cooperation agreement and entails a political dialogue between the sides. See http://europa.eu.int/comm/exter nal_relations/israel/intro/index.htm.

AFTERWORD

1. Ben Israel (2007, 41) provides additional data on the extent of Israeli use of air power and ground forces. He suggests that the IAF carried out 11,897 sorties, more than it carried out during any other war in Israel's history. He also argues that Israel's use of PGMs during this war was more extensive than any other time in Israel's history and was second only to the U.S. attack on Iraq in 2003 (49).

2. In his statement in the Knesset, Prime Minister Olmert defined the goals of the war as such: "And in Lebanon, we will insist on compliance with the terms stipulated long ago by the international community, as unequivocally expressed only yesterday in the resolution of the 8 leading countries of the world: The return of the hostages, Ehud (Udi) Goldwasser and Eldad Regev; A complete cease fire; Deployment of the Lebanese army in all of Southern Lebanon; Expulsion of Hizballah from the area, and fulfillment of United Nations Resolution 1559." See http://www.knesset.gov.il/docs/eng/olmert speech2006_eng.htm (accessed April 9, 2008).

3. This is so despite the fact that Hassan Nasrallah, Hizballah's leader, admitted in an interview shortly after the war that, had he known that Israel's reaction would be as harsh as it was, he would probably not have authorized the kidnapping operation. Telhami's study—based on a broad survey of Lebanese public opinion—shows that overall support for Hizballah has increased but that the perception of Hizballah and of the outcome of the war varies by ethnic group. Shi'ites predominantly supported Hizballah and viewed the war as a success, while most other groups' attitudes toward Hizballah became increasingly negative. In general, Telhami suggests that the war had overall polarizing effects on Lebanon, thus eroding its political stability. Salem (2008, 23) reaches a similar conclusion about the polarizing effects of the war.

4. See, for example, Peres's testimony before the Vinograd Inquiry Commission. Peres stated that he had argued on July 12 that "military pressure on Lebanon would not yield meaningful results due to the weakness of the Lebanese government. . . . the military response seems shortsighted, routine, and expected. In his view, a more productive course of action would entail pressure by France and the United States on the Lebanese government. He asked the chief of staff, 'We need to think two steps ahead. Suppose we do this [bomb Lebanon], they would respond, then what next?'" Transcript of July 12 cabinet meeting, quoted in Vinograd 2007, 78. Yet, he ended up supporting the military attack on Lebanon. Other ministers noted also the dominant position of the IDF's rec-

ommendations throughout the war. See also Vinograd 2007, 76–82; Shelah and Limor 2007, 55–60; Harel and Issacharoff 2008, 170–76.

5. More accurately, Peretz was voted out of his job due to internal elections in the Labor Party that brought Ehud Barak back as party leader. Consequently, Barak was nominated to replace Peretz in the Defense Ministry in June 2007.

6. Data sources for these figures include Btselem 2008; ITIC 2008; PHRMG 2007.

7. The rate of successful to attempted suicide bombings went down from 64 percent in 2001 and 34 percent in 2002 to less than 6 percent (4 successful suicide bombings out of 71 attempts) in 2006 and less than 4 percent in 2007.

8. Barak Ravid and Youval Azoulay, "Ben Eliezer: If Iran Attacks Israel, We Will Destroy It," *Haaretz*, April 11, 2008.

9. Olmert himself hinted to it several times, as did Netanyahu, who said he had been consulted about this matter prior to the air raid.

10. David E. Sanger, "Bush Administration Releases Images to Bolster Its Claims about Syrian Reactor," *New York Times*, April 25, 2008.

Glossary

ACRS	Arms Control and Regional Security. One of the regional working groups established as a result of the Madrid Conference in 1991.
AGAT	The planning branch of the IDF (Hebrew acronym)
AMAN	Israeli military intelligence. The principal intelligence agency in Israel (Hebrew acronym).
APC	armored personnel carrier
ASU	Arab Socialist Union. The ruling party in Egypt since the 1952 coup.
BTWC	Biological and Toxin Weapons Convention. The 1975 convention on the prohibition of the development, production, and stockpiling of bacteriological (biological) and toxin weapons and on their destruction.
CSBM	confidence and security building measures
C^{4}I	command, control, communications, computers, and intelligence. The synergic "brain" of any modern military force.
CFSA	Committee on Foreign and Security Affairs (in the Knesset)
COS	chief of staff of the IDF
CWC	Chemical Weapons Convention. The 1997 treaty prohibiting the production, stockpiling, and usage of chemical weapons.
DER	Defence Emergency Regulations. Emergency measures established in 1945 by the British mandate to deal with Jewish and Arab terrorists that allow imprisonment without trial, expulsions, and house demolitions. These regulations were adapted by the state of Israel and are still in force.
DMZ	demilitarized zone (in the Israeli-Syrian border pre-1967)
DPRP	Department of Policy Research and Planning. The research and intelligence division of the Israeli Ministry of Foreign Affairs.
ElInt	electronic intelligence. Includes signal intelligence, communications intelligence, and visual intelligence.
EU	European Union

FAS	Federation of American Scientists
GDP	gross domestic product
GSS	General Secret Service (see SHABAK)
HCJ	High Court of Justice. The Supreme Court forums that rule on petitions of private individuals and groups against the state's authorities.
HDI	human development index. An index that measures national standards of living, based on a number of economic, demographic, and social indicators.
HFC	Home Front Command. A military branch devoted to dealing with missile threats on population centers in Israel.
HumInt	human intelligence. Based on information provided by humans (spies, informants, etc.)
IAEA	International Atomic Energy Agency
IAF	Israeli Air Force
IDF	Israeli Defense Forces
INF	Israeli Naval Force
JCSS	Jaffee Center for Strategic Studies. A strategic think tank located at Tel Aviv University in Israel.
LAMDAN	the Israeli Air Force Intelligence Branch
LIC	low-intensity conflict
MAC	Mixed Armistice Commission. An international body that included Israeli and Syrian representative that acted in the early 1950s to consider complaints by the parties regarding the violation of the armistice agreement.
MAFAT	Department of Weapons and Technological Development. Part of Israel's Defense Ministry (Hebrew acronym).
MEMRI	Middle East Media Research Institute. An Israeli research institute specializing in translation of media reports and articles from the Arab media.
MENA	Middle East and North Africa. The collection of states that designates the modern Middle East.
MFO	Multilateral Force and Observers in the Sinai. A multilateral force overseeing the implementation of the Egyptian-Israeli peace agreement in the Sinai.
MID	militarized interstate dispute. A set of militarized incidents between or among states involving the threat, display, or use of force in short intervals. These incidents are government sanctioned and government directed (Gochman and Maoz 1984, 586).
MK	member of the Knesset
MOA	Memorandum of Agreement. A document of strategic cooperation between Israel and the United States First signed on November 30, 1981, and renewed several times since then.
NGC	National Guidance Council. A council of Palestinian leaders in the occupied territories that operated in the late 1970s and early 1980s.
NGO	nongovernmental organizations
NIE	national intelligence estimate. An annual intelligence report listing the strategic challenges opportunities confronting Israel's security.

NPT Non-Proliferation Treaty. A treaty disallowing the development of nuclear weapons by anybody except the five major powers and regulating the monitoring of peaceful use of atomic and nuclear energy, signed in 1969 and renewed (for an indefinite amount of time) in 1995.

NRP National Religious Party (in the Knesset)

NSC National Security Council

NST national security team

NWFZ nuclear weapons free zone. An agreement wherein all states in a region agree to forgo development, production, or possession of nuclear weapons.

OECD Organization of Economic Cooperation and Development. An organization of thirty economically advanced democratic states committed to economic openness, development, and democracy.

PA Palestinian Authority. The governing Palestinian body after the Oslo Accord of 1993.

PCI parliamentary commission of inquiry. Established by the Knesset to investigate policy problems in various areas of government.

PFLP Popular Front for the Liberation of Palestine

PGM precision-guided munition

PLO Palestinian Liberation Organization

PNC Palestinian National Council

POW prisoner of war

QHAIC Project on Quantitative History of the Arab-Israeli Conflict started at the Jaffee Center for Strategic Studies, Tel Aviv University, in 1995. Data for this project are available online at http://psfaculty.ucdavis.edu/zmaoz/quanthist.html.

R&D research and development

RAFAEL Israel's Weapons Development Authority (Hebrew acronym)

RCC Revolutionary Command Council. The council of the Free Officers in Egypt, which overthrew the monarchy in July 1952.

RMA Revolution in Military Affairs. A series of technological breakthroughs in munitions, delivery systems, information warfare, and space-based guidance that is considered to have revolutionized the art of war.

RMSE root mean square error

SAM surface-to-air missiles

SCSD Subcommittee on the Security Doctrine. A subcommittee of the Knesset CFSA that focuses on the Israeli security doctrine (and force structure).

SCSS Subcommittee on Secret Services. A subcommittee of the Knesset CFSA that focuses on the Israeli secret services (intelligence agencies).

SHABAK Israeli General Secret Service. Security organization responsible for internal security (Hebrew acronym).

SigInt signal intelligence. Collection of intelligence from communications and computer traffic.

SLA   Southern Lebanese Army. A paramilitary group made up of Southern Lebanese Christians supported by Israel during the 1983–2000 period.

SLBM   submarine-launched ballistic missiles

SNT   single negotiating text

SOP   standard operating procedure

SOU   special operations unit

SSM   surface-to-surface missile

UAR   United Arab Republic

UN   United Nations

UNDOF   United Nations Disengagement Observer Force. A UN force monitoring the implementation of the 1974 Israeli-Syrian disengagement agreement.

UNEF   United Nations Emergency Force. Stationed in the Sinai during the 1957–67 period.

UNIFIL United Nations Interim Force in Lebanon. Inserted into Southern Lebanon in 1978 following the Israeli Operation Litany.

UNSCOM United Nations Special Commission to Iraq. The organization that was charged with the inspection and dismantlement of Iraq's WMDs after the 1991 Gulf War.

UNS   Unit for National Security. A staff group established in the Israeli Defense Ministry by Ariel Sharon in 1981.

UNTSO   United Nations Truce Supervision Organization. A UN group established to supervise the implementation of the armistice agreements signed in 1948–49 between Israel and the Arab states

VARASH Committee of the Heads of Intelligence Services (AMAN, Mossad, SHABAK). Responsible for intelligence coordination (Hebrew acronym).

VisInt visual intelligence. Principally, aerial and satellite photography.

WMD   weapon of mass destruction. Includes chemical, biological, and nuclear weapons and long-range delivery systems (i.e., SSMs).

WMDFZ   weapons of mass destruction free zone. A regional agreement barring the development or deployment of WMDs in a given region.

References

Reference material to the Preface and Afterword appear at the end of the References.

Abu Iyad (Khalaf Salah). 1983. *Without a Homeland: Conversations with Eric Rouleau* (in Hebrew). Tel Aviv: Mifrasim.

Achen, Christopher, and Duncan Snidal. 1989. Rational Deterrence Theory and Comparative Case Studies. *World Politics* 41 (2): 143–69.

Adan, Avraham. 1980. *On the Banks of Suez: An Israeli General's Account of the Yom Kippur War*. San Rafael, CA: Presidio Press.

Agha, Hussein, and Robert Malley. 2002. Camp David and After: An Exchange. *New York Review of Books*, June 13. Available online at http://www.nybooks.com/articles/15502.

———. 2001. Camp David: The Tragedy of Errors. *New York Review of Books*, August 9. Available online at http://nybooks.com/articles/14380.

Ajami, Fouad. 1998. *The Dream Palace of the Arabs: A Generation's Odyssey*. New York: Pantheon.

Allison, Graham T., and Philip Zelikow. 1999. *Essence of Decision: Explaining the Cuban Missile Crisis*. New York: Longman.

Allon, Gideon. 1994. The Secret Five. *Ha'aretz* (in Hebrew), December 12 (Weekend Supplement).

Allon, Yigal. 1968. *A Curtain of Sand* (in Hebrew). Tel-Aviv: Ha'Kibbutz Ha'Meuchad.

Almog, Doron. 2004. Cumulative Deterrence and the War on Terrorism. Mimeograph. Cambridge, MA: Belfer Center for Science and International Affairs. Available online at http://bcsia.ksg.harvard.edu/person.cfm?item_id=846&ln=fellow&program=ISP.

———. 1995. The Israeli Strategy of Deterrence as a Model of Accumulated Deterrence. MA thesis, University of Haifa.

Almog, Oz. 1997. *The Sabra: A Portrait* (in Hebrew). Tel Aviv: Am Oved.

Alon, Hanan. 1980. *Countering Palestinian Terrorism in Israel: Towards a Policy of Countermeasures*. Santa Monica, CA: Rand.

Alper, Joseph, ed. 1992. *War in the Gulf: Implications for Israel*. Boulder and Jerusalem: Westview Press and Jerusalem Post Press.

Amery, Julian. 1991. The Suez Group. In Selwyn Ilan Toren and Moshe Shemesh, eds.,

The Suez-Sinai Crisis, 1956: Retrospective and Reappraisal, 110–26. London: Frank Cass.

Aras, Bulent. 2000. Turkish-Israeli-Iranian Relations in the Nineties: Impact on the Middle East. *Middle East Policy* 7 (3): 151–64.

Arens, Moshe. 1995. *War and Peace in the Middle East* (in Hebrew). Tel-Aviv: Yediot Aharonot.

Arian, Asher. 2004. *Israeli Public Opinion on National Security, 2004.* Memorandum 71 (August). Tel Aviv: Jaffee Center for Strategic Studies.

———. 2003. *Israeli Public Opinion on National Security, 2003.* Memorandum 67 (October). Tel Aviv: Jaffee Center for Strategic Studies.

———. 2002. *Israeli Public Opinion on National Security, 2002.* Memorandum 61 (July). Tel Aviv: Jaffee Center for Strategic Studies.

———. 2001. *Israeli Public Opinion on National Security, 2001.* Memorandum 60 (August). Tel Aviv: Jaffee Center for Strategic Studies.

———. 2000. *Israeli Public Opinion on National Security, 2000.* Memorandum 56 (July). Tel Aviv: Jaffee Center for Strategic Studies.

———. 1999. *Israeli Public Opinion on National Security, 1999.* Memorandum 53 (August). Tel Aviv: Jaffee Center for Strategic Studies.

———. 1998. *Israeli Public Opinion on National Security, 1999.* Memorandum 49 (July), Tel Aviv: Jaffee Center for Strategic Studies.

———. 1997. *Israeli Public Opinion on National Security, 1997.* Memorandum 47 (April). Tel Aviv: Jaffee Center for Strategic Studies.

———. 1995. *Security Threatened: Surveying Israeli Opinion on War and Peace.* New York: Cambridge University Press.

———. 1985. *Israeli Public Opinion and the War in Lebanon.* Memorandum 15 (October). Tel Aviv: Jaffee Center for Strategic Studies.

Arnon, Aryeh, and Jimmy Weinbladt. 2001. Sovereignty and Economic Development: The Case of Israel and Palestine. *Economic Journal* 111 (2): F291–F308.

Aronson, Shlomo. 1999. *David Ben Gurion: Leader of the Decaying Renaissance* (in Hebrew). Beer-Sheba: Ben Gurion University Press.

———. 1984. The Nuclear Dimension of the Arab-Israeli Conflict: The Case of the Yom Kippur War. *Jerusalem Journal of International Relations* 7 (1–2): 107–41.

———. 1978. *Conflict and Bargaining in the Middle East: An Israeli Perspective.* Baltimore: Johns Hopkins University Press.

Aronson, Shlomo, with Oded Brosh. 1992. *The Politics and Strategy of Nuclear Weapons in the Middle East: Opacity, Theory, and Reality, 1960–1991, An Israeli Perspective.* Albany: State University of New York Press.

Aronson, Shlomo, and Dan Horowitz. 1971. The Strategy of Controlled Retaliation: The Israeli Model. *State and Government* (in Hebrew) 1 (1): 77–99.

Astorino, Allison. 1994. Prerequisites of Progress: Decisions and Decision Makers in the Arab-Israeli Conflict. PhD diss., New York University.

Astorino-Courtois, Allison. 1998. Clarifying Decisions: Assessing the Impact of Decision Structures on Foreign Policy Choices during the 1970 Jordanian Civil War. *International Studies Quarterly* 42 (4): 733–54.

Atherton, Roy. 1990. Interview with Zeev Maoz. May. New York.

Avnery, Uri. 1986. *My Friend, the Enemy.* London: Zed Books.

Ayubi, Shaheen. 1991. *Nasser and Sadat: Decision Making and Foreign Policy.* Wakefield, NH: Longwood Academic.

AzoulaY-Katz, Orly. 1996. *The Man Who Did Not Know How to Win* (in Hebrew). Tel-Aviv: Yediot Aharonot.

Baghat, Gawdat. 2003. Proliferation of Weapons of Mass Destruction: Iraq and Iran. *Journal of Social, Political, and Economic Studies* 28 (4): 423–49.

Baker, James A., III, with Thomas M. Defrank. 1995. *The Politics of Diplomacy: Revolution, War, and Peace, 1989–1992*. New York: G. P. Putnam's Sons.

Baker Institute. 1998. The Prospects for the Israeli-Syrian Peace Negotiations. *Baker Institute Study* No. 8 (June). Houston: James A. Baker III Institute for Public Policy.

Ball, George W. 1977. How to Save Israel in Spite of Itself. *Foreign Affairs* 55 (3): 453–71.

Barak, Ehud. 2003. The Departure from Lebanon: A Test-Case of Civil Military Relations. In Ram Erez, ed., *Civil-Military Relations in Israel: Influences and Restraints*, 29–38. Memorandum 68 (November). Tel Aviv: Jaffee Center for Strategic Studies.

Baram, Amazia. 1992. Israeli Deterrence, Iraqi Responses. *Orbis* 36 (3): 385–403.

Barbieri, Katherine, Omar M. K. Keshik, and Brian Pollins. 2003. BKP Trade Data 0.9. http://psweb.sbs.ohio-state.edu/faculty/bpollins/papers.htm.

Bar Joseph, Uri. 2004. The Paradox of Israeli Power. *Survival* 46 (4): 137–56.

———. 2001. *The Watchman Fell Asleep: The Surprise of Yom Kippur and Its Sources* (in Hebrew). Tel-Aviv: Zmora-Bitan.

———. 1998. Variations on a Theme: The Conceptualization of Deterrence in Israeli Strategic Thinking. *Security Studies* 7 (3): 145–81.

———. 1996. Rotem: The Forgotten Crisis on the Road to the 1967 War. *Journal of Contemporary History* 31 (4): 547–66.

———. 1995. *Intelligence Intervention in the Politics of Democratic States: The United States, Israel, and Britain*. University Park: Pennsylvania State University Press.

———. 1987. *The Best of Enemies: Israel and Transjordan in the War of 1948*. London: Frank Cass.

———. 1982. The Hidden Debate: The Formation of Nuclear Doctrines in the Middle East. *Journal of Strategic Studies* 5 (2): 200–225.

Barletta, Michael, and Christina Ellington. 1998. *Israel's Nuclear Posture Review*. CNS Issue Brief on WMD in the Middle East. Monterey, CA: Monterey Institute of International Studies. http://cns.miis.edu/research/wmdme/israelnc.htm.

Bar Lev, Omer. 1999. *Security Arrangements in the Golan in Light of the Modern Battlefield* (in Hebrew). Tel Aviv: Sifriat Poalim.

Barnaby, Frank. 1989. *The Invisible Bomb: The Nuclear Arms Race in the Middle East*. London: I. B. Tauris.

Barnett, Michael. 1992. *Confronting the Costs of War: Military Power, State, and Society in Egypt and Israel*. Princeton: Princeton University Press.

Bar-On, Mordechai. 1992. *At the Gates of Gaza: The Security and Foreign Policy of Israel, 1955–1957* (in Hebrew). Tel-Aviv: Am Oved.

———. 1991. *Challenge and Quarrel: The Road to Sinai, 1955–57* (in Hebrew). Beer-Sheva: Beer-Sheva University Press.

Bar-Simantov, Yaacov. 1988. Ben-Gurion and Sharett: Conflict Management and Great Power Constraints on Israeli Foreign Policy. *Middle Eastern Studies* 24 (3): 330–56.

———. 1984. *Linkage Politics in the Middle East: Syria between Domestic and External Conflict*. Boulder: Westview Press.

———. 1980. *The Arab-Israeli War of Attrition*. New York: Columbia University Press.

Bartov, Hanoch. 1978. *Dado: Twenty Years and Twenty More Days* (in Hebrew). 2 vols. Tel-Aviv: Zmorah Bitan Modan.

Bar Yaacov, Nissim. 1967. *The Israel-Syria Armistice: Problems of Implementation, 1949–1966*. Jerusalem: Magness Press.

Barzilai, Amnon. 1999. The Recommendations of Adviser Ivry for Updating the Security Conceptions Were Shelved. *Ha'aretz*, August 8, A3.

———. 1998. The Defense Minister: Israeli Governments Did Not Want a Written Security Conception to Preserve Their Room for Maneuver. *Ha'aretz*, June 30, A3.

Barzilai, Gad. 2003. *Communities and Law: Politics and Culture of Legal Identities*. Ann Arbor: University of Michigan Press.

———. 1996. *Wars, Internal Conflict, and Political Order: A Jewish Democracy in the Middle East*. Albany: State University of New York Press.

Barzilai, Gad, and Bruce Russett. 1990. The Political Economy of Israeli Military Action. In Asher Arian and Michal Shamir, eds., *The Elections in Israel, 1988*, 13–35. Boulder: Westview Press.

Barzilai, Gad, Ephraim Yuchtman-Yaar, and Zeev Segal. 1994. *The Supreme Court and the Israeli Public* (in Hebrew). Tel Aviv: Papyrus, Tel Aviv University Press.

Bar-Zohar, Michael. 1987. *Ben-Gurion* (in Hebrew). 3 vols. Tel Aviv: Zmora-Bitan.

Beattie, Kirk J. 1994. *Egypt during the Nasser Years: Ideology, Politics, and Civil Society*. Boulder: Westview Press.

Beilin, Yossi. 1998. *The Guide for Withdrawal from Lebanon* (in Hebrew). Tel Aviv: Ha'Kibbutz Ha'Meuchad.

———. 1997. *Touching Peace* (in Hebrew). Tel Aviv: Yediot Aharonot.

Bellof, Lord. 1989. The Crisis and Its Consequences for British Conservative Party. In Wm. Roger Louis and Roger Owen, eds., *Suez, 1956: The Crisis and Its Consequences*, 319–34. Oxford: Clarendon Press.

Ben, Aluf. 2000a. Barak: Shamir, Rabin, Peres, and Netanyahu Agreed to Full Withdrawal to the 4 June 1967 Lines. *Ha'aretz* (in Hebrew), February 28.

———. 2000b. A Letter from Netanyahu to Asad Reveals: Netanyahu Was Willing to Concede the Golan Height. *Ha'aretz* (in Hebrew), January 2.

———. 1997. The Golan File. *Ha'aretz* (in Hebrew), January 4.

Ben David, Dan. 2003. Inequality and Growth in Israel. *Economic Quarterly* (in Hebrew) 50 (1): 27–104.

Ben-Eliezer, Uri. 2003. The Military Society and the Civil Society in Israel: Expressions of Anti-Militarism and Neo-Militarism in a Post-Hegemonic Era. In Majd Al Haj and Uri Ben Eliezer, eds., *In the Name of Security: The Sociology of Peace and War in Israel in Challenging Times* (in Hebrew), 29–76. Haifa: University of Haifa Press.

———. 2000. Do the Generals Govern Israel? The Military-Political Nexus and the Legitimacy for War in a Nations in Arms. In Hanna Herzog, ed., *Reflection of a Society* (in Hebrew), 235–68. Tel Aviv: Ramot.

———. 1998. *The Making of Israeli Militarism*. Bloomington: Indiana University Press.

———. 1997. Rethinking the Civil-Military Relations Paradigm: The Inverse Relations between Militarism and Praetorianism through the Example of Israel. *Comparative Political Studies* 30 (3): 356–74.

Ben Eliyahu, Eytan. 2003. Missile Technology and the IAF. Lecture delivered at the Science, Technology, and National Security Conference, Tel Aviv University, March 25. (Lecture transcript in Hebrew available from author.)

Bengio, Ofrah. 1989. *The Kurdish Rebellion against Iraq* (in Hebrew). Tel-Aviv: Ha'Kibbutz Ha'Meuchad.

Ben Gurion, David. 1986. *War Diary* (in Hebrew). 2d ed. Tel Aviv: Defense Ministry Publishing House.

———. 1971. *Uniqueness and Mission* (in Hebrew). Tel Aviv: Ma'arachot.

———. 1969. *The Renewed State of Israel* (in Hebrew). 2 vols. Tel-Aviv: Am Oved.

————. 1959. *The Sinai Campaign* (in Hebrew). Tel-Aviv: Am Oved.

————. 1956. *The Foreign Policy [of Israel]* (in Hebrew). Tel Aviv: Ayanot Publishing.

Ben-Horin, Yoav, and Barry Posen. 1981. *Israel's Strategic Doctrine*. Santa Monica, CA: Rand.

Ben Israel, Isaac. 2001. Security, Technology, and the Future Battlefield. In Hagai Golan, ed., *Israel's Security Web: Core Issues of Israel's National Security in Its Sixth Decade*, 269–327. Tel Aviv: Ma'arachot.

————. 1999. *The Philosophy of Intelligence* (in Hebrew). Tel Aviv: Defense Ministry Publishing House.

Ben Meir, Yehuda. 1995. *Civil-Military Relations in Israel*. New York: Columbia University Press.

Ben Porat, Yesha'ayahu. 1996. *Talks with Yossi Beilin*. Tel Aviv: Ha'Kibbutz Ha'Meuchad.

Ben Porat, Yesha'ayahu, et al. 1974. *The Default* (in Hebrew). Tel-Aviv: Special Edition Press.

Ben Porat, Yoel. 1991. *Closure* (in Hebrew). Tel-Aviv: Edanim.

Ben-Tzur, Avraham. 1975. *Soviet Factors and the Six Day War: The Influence of Power Struggles in the Kremlin on the Middle East* (in Hebrew). Tel-Aviv: Sifriat Poalim.

Benziman, Uzi. 1985. *Sharon: An Israeli Caesar* (in Hebrew). Tel-Aviv: Adam.

————. 1981. *Prime Minister under Siege* (in Hebrew). Tel-Aviv: Adam.

Ben-Zvi, Abraham. 1998. *Decade of Transition: Eisenhower, Kennedy, and the Origins of the American-Israeli Alliance*. New York: Columbia University Press.

————. 1976. Hindsight and Foresight: A Conceptual Framework for the Analysis of Surprise Attacks. *World Politics* 28 (3): 381–95.

Beres, Louis Rene. 2004. Israel and the Bomb. *International Security* 29 (1): 175–76.

Berglas, Eytan. 1986. Defense and the Economy. In Yoram Ben Porath, ed., *The Israeli Economy: Maturing through Crises*, 173–91. Cambridge, MA: Harvard University Press.

Bialer, Uri. 1989. *Between East and West: Israel's Foreign Policy Orientation, 1948–1956*. Cambridge: Cambridge University Press.

————. 1971. David Ben Gurion and Moshe Sharett: The Crystallization of Two Political Perspectives on the Arab-Israeli Conflict. *State and Government* (in Hebrew) 1 (2): 85–101.

Black, Ian, and Benny Morris. 1991. *Israel's Secret Wars: A History of Israel's Intelligence Services*. London: Futura.

Blechman, Barry M. 1972. The Impact of Israel's Reprisals on the Behavior of Arab States. *Journal of Conflict Resolution* 16 (2): 155–81.

Bonen, Zeev. 2003. Missile Technology Development by Israeli Defense Industries. Lecture delivered at the Science, Technology, and National Security Conference, Tel Aviv University, March 25. (Lecture transcript in Hebrew available from author.)

Bowie, Robert. 1989. Eisenhower, Dulles, and the Suez Crisis. In Wm Roger Louis and Roger Owen, eds., *Suez, 1956: The Crisis and Its Consequences*, 189–214. Oxford: Clarendon Press.

Braun, Arie. 1997. *Personal Imprint: Moshe Dayan in the Six Day War and After*. Tel Aviv: Ma'arachot.

————. 1992. *Moshe Dayan in the Yom Kippur War* (in Hebrew). Tel-Aviv: Yediot Aharonot.

Brecher, Michael. 1975. *Decisions in Israel's Foreign Policy*. Oxford: Oxford University Press.

————. 1972. *The Foreign Policy System of Israel: Setting, Images, Process*. Oxford: Oxford University Press.

Brecher, Michael, with Benjamin Geist. 1980. *Decisions in Crisis: Israel, 1967 and 1973*. Berkeley and Los Angeles: University of California Press.

Brom, Shlomo. 2003. The Implications of the USA-Iraq War (2003) for the Balance of Forces in the Middle East. Lecture delivered at the USA-Iraq War and International Relations Workshop, Israeli Association of International Studies, Tel Aviv University, May 4.

————. 1999. *Israel and South Lebanon Prior to Peace Agreement with Syria* (in Hebrew). Jaffee Center for Strategic Studies—Special Studies (September). Tel Aviv: Jaffee Center for Strategic Studies.

Brom, Shlomo, and Yiftah Shapir. 2000. *The Middle East Military Balance*. Cambridge, MA: MIT Press.

Brookings Institution. 1975. *Toward Peace in the Middle East: A Report of a Study Group*. Washington, DC: Brookings Institution.

Brynen, Rex. 1990. *Sanctuary and Survival: The PLO in Lebanon*. Boulder: Westview Press.

Brzeszinski, Zbigniew, François Duchêne, and Kiichi Saeki. 1975. Peace in an International Framework. *Foreign Policy* 19 (2): 3–17.

B'Tselem. 2003. Fatalities in the Al Aqsa Intifada: Data by month. http://www.btse lem.org.

————. 2002. *Land Grab: Israel's Settlement Policy in the West Bank*. May. Available online at http://www.btselem.org/Download/Land_Grab_Eng.pdf.

Bukay, David. 1993. *Inter-Arab Relations and the Arab-Israeli Conflict*. PhD diss., University of Haifa.

Bulmer, Elisabeth Ruppert. 2001. The Impact of Future Labor Policy Options on the Palestinian Labor Market. World Bank (June). Available on line at: http://www -wds.worldbank.org/servlet/WDSContentServer/WDSP/IB/2002/09/07/00009494 6_02081604154435/Rendered/PDF/multiopage.pdf.

Bush, George W. 2002. Elements of a Performance-Based Road Map to a Permanent Two-State Solution to the Israeli-Palestinian Conflict. September 17. http://www.mideastweb.org/quartetrm2.htm.

Camp David. 1978. Egyptian-Israeli Peace Accords. Available online from the Israeli Ministry of Foreign Affairs at http://www.mfa.gov.il/mfa/go.asp?MFAH00ieo.

Carter, Jimmy. 1982. *Keeping Faith: Memoirs of a President*. New York: Bantam.

Cohen, Avner. 2005. *The Last Taboo* (in Hebrew). Tel-Aviv: Zmora-Bitan.

————. 2003. The Last Nuclear Moment. *New York Times*, October 6, A17.

————. 2000. Nuclear Arms in Crisis under Secrecy: Israel and the Lessons of the 1967 and 1973 Wars. In Peter R. Lavoy, Scott D. Sagan, and James J. Wirtz, eds., *Planning the Unthinkable: How New Powers Will Use Nuclear, Biological, and Chemical Weapons*, 104–24. Ithaca, NY: Cornell University Press.

————. 1998. *Israel and the Bomb*. New York: Columbia University Press.

Cohen, Avner, and Benjamin Frankel. 1990. Opaque Nuclear Proliferation. *Journal of Strategic Studies* 13 (3): 14–44.

Cohen, Eliot A. 1997. A Revolution in Warfare. *Foreign Affairs* 75 (2): 37–54.

Cohen, Eliot A., Michael J. Eisenstadt, and Andrew J. Bacevich. 1998. *Israel's Security Revolution*. Washington, DC: Washington Institute for Near Eastern Policy.

Cohen, Stuart A. 2003. Changing Societal-Military Relations in Israel: The Operational Implications. In Majd Al Haj and Uri Ben Eliezer, eds., *In the Name of Security: The Sociology of Peace and War in Israel in Challenging Times*, 103–24. Haifa: University of Haifa Press.

————. 1997. Towards a New Portrait of a (New) Israeli Soldier. *Israel Affairs* 3 (2): 77–117.

————, ed. 2000. *Democratic Societies and Their Armed Forces: Israel's in Comparative Perspective*. London: Frank Cass.

Cordesman, Anthony H. 2004. *The Military Balance in the Middle East: The Arab-Israeli Balance*. Washington, DC: Center for Strategic and International Studies.

————. 2002. *Peace and War: The Arab-Israeli Military Balance Enters the 21st Century*. Westport, CT: Praeger.

————. 1999. *Iran's Military Forces in Transition: Conventional Threats and Weapons of Mass Destruction*. Westport, CT: Praeger.

————. 1996. *Perilous Prospect: The Peace Process and the Arab-Israeli Military Balance*. Boulder: Westview Press.

————. 1994. *Iran and Iraq: The Threat from the Northern Gulf*. Boulder: Westview Press.

————. 1993. *After the Storm: The Changing Military Balance in the Middle East*. Boulder: Westview Press.

Correlates of War Project. 2004. National Material Capabilities Dataset, 1816–2001. http://cow2.la.psu.edu/.

Dawisha, Adeeb. 1980. *Syria and the Lebanese Crisis*. New York: St. Martin's Press.

Dayan, Moshe. 1981. *Breakthrough: A Personal Account of the Israel-Egypt Peace Negotiations*. New York: Alfred A. Knopf.

————. 1976. *Story of My Life* (in Hebrew). Tel-Aviv: Yediot Aharonot.

————. 1967. *Diary of the Sinai Campaign*. New York: Schocken.

————. 1959. Military Action during Peacetime. *Ma'arachot* (in Hebrew), no. 118–19:54–61.

————. 1955. Military Action during Peacetime. *Ba'Mahaneh* (in Hebrew), September 14 and 21.

De Atkine, Norvell. 2002. Why Arab Armies Lose Wars. In Barry Rubin and Thomas A. Keany, eds., *Armed Forces in the Middle East: Politics and Strategy*, 12–35. London: Frank Cass.

Dowty, Alan. 1984. *Middle East Crisis: U.S. Decision Making in 1958, 1970, and 1973*. Los Angeles and Berkeley: University of California Press.

Dror, Yehezkel. 1998. *A Memorandum to the Prime Minister*. Jerusalem: Akademon Press.

————. 1989. *A Grand Strategy for Israel* Jerusalem: Akademon Press.

Drucker, Raviv. 2002. *Hara-kiri: Ehud Barak—the Failure*. Tel Aviv Yediot Aharonot.

Dupuy, Trevor. 1978. *Elusive Victory: The Arab-Israeli Wars, 1947–1974*. New York: Harper and Row.

Dupuy, Trevor N., and Paul Martell. 1986. *Flawed Victory: The Arab-Israeli Conflict and the 1982 War in Lebanon*. Fairfax, VA: Hero Books.

Eban, Abba. 1977. *Abba Eban: An Autobiography*. London: Widenfeld and Nicholson.

————. 1973. *My Country: The Story of Modern Israel*. London: Widenfeld and Nicholson.

Edelist, Ran. 2003. *Ehud Barak: Fighting the Demons*. Tel Aviv: Yediot Aharonot.

Eisenberg, Laura Zittrain. 1992. Passive Belligerency: Israel and the 1991 Gulf War. *Journal of Strategic Studies* 15 (3): 299–320.

Erez, Ram, ed. 2003. *Civil-Military Relations in Israel: Influences and Restraints* (in Hebrew). Memorandum 68 (November). Tel Aviv: Jaffee Center for Strategic Studies.

Erlich, Reuven. 2000. *The Lebanese Blessing: The Policy of the Zionist Movement and of the State of Israel vis-à-vis Lebanon, 1918–1958* (in Hebrew). Tel Aviv: Ma'arachot.

Evron, Joseph. 1986. *Suez 1956: A Second Look* (in Hebrew). Tel-Aviv: Modan.

Evron, Yair. 1998. *Weapons of Mass Destruction in the Middle East*. Washington, DC: Henry Stimson Center.

———. 1994. *Israel's Nuclear Dilemma*. Ithaca, NY: Cornell University Press.

———. 1987. *War and Intervention in Lebanon: The Israeli-Syrian Deterrence Dialogue*. London: Croom Helm.

———. 1974. Israel and the Atom: The Uses and Misuses of Ambiguity. *Orbis* 17 (4): 1326–423.

Fahmy, Ismail. 1983. *Negotiating for Peace in the Middle East*. London: Croom Helm.

Farid, Abdel Magid. 1994. *Nasser: The Final Years*. Reading, Berkshire: Ithaca Press.

Farr, Warner D. 1999. The Third Temple Holy of Holies: Israel's Nuclear Weapons. In *The Counterproliferation Papers, Future Warfare Series* No. 2. Maxwell, AL: U.S. Air War College. Available online at http://www.fas.org/nuke/guide/israel/nuke/farr.htm.

Fearon, James D. 1991. Counterfactuals and Hypothesis-Testing in Political Science. *World Politics* 43 (2): 169–95.

Federation of American Scientists. 2004. Nuclear Forces Guide. http://fas.org/nuke/guide/index.html.

Feldman, Shai. 1997. *Nuclear Proliferation and Arms Control in the Middle East*. Cambridge, MA: MIT Press.

———. 1991. Israeli Deterrence: The Test of the Gulf War. In Joseph Alpher, ed., *War in the Gulf: Implications for Israel* (in Hebrew), 170–89. Tel-Aviv: Jaffee Center for Strategic Studies.

———. 1983. *Israeli Nuclear Deterrence: A Strategy for the 1980s*. New York: Columbia University Press.

Feldman, Shai, and Heda Rechnitz-Kijner. 1984. *Deception, Consensus, and War: Israel's Intervention in Lebanon*. Memorandum 27 (October). Tel Aviv: Jaffee Center for Strategic Studies.

Feldman Shai, and Yiftah Shapir. 2004. *The Middle East Strategic Balance*. Sussex: Sussex Academic Press.

Flapan, Simha. 1987. *The Birth of Israel: Myths and Realities*. New York: Pantheon.

Foundation for Middle East Peace. 2004. Report on Israeli Settlement in the Occupied Territories. Available online at: http://www.fmep.org/reports/2004/is_v14n1.pdf.

Friedlander, Dov, and Calvin Goldscheider. 1979. *The Population of Israel*. New York: Columbia University Press.

Friedman, Lawrence L., and Ephraim Karsh. 1993. *The Gulf Conflict: Diplomacy and War in the New World*. Princeton: Princeton University Press.

Gamassy, Abd el Ghani. 1993. *The Ramadan War*. Cairo: American University in Cairo Press.

Garfinkle, Adam. 1992. *Israel and Jordan in the Shadow of War: Functional Ties and Futile Diplomacy in a Small Place*. New York: St. Martin's Press.

Gaubatz, Kurt Taylor. 1999. *Elections and War: The Electoral Incentive in the Democratic Politics of War and Peace*. Stanford: Stanford University Press.

Gawrych, George W. 2000. *The Albatross of Decisive Victory: War and Policy between Egypt and Israel in the 1967 and 1973 Arab-Israeli Wars*. Westport, CT: Greenwood Press.

Gazit, Mordechai. 1983. *The Peace Process, 1969–1973: Efforts and Contacts*. Jerusalem: Magness Press.

Gazit, Shlomo. 2003. *Between Warning and Surprise: On Shaping National Intelligence Estimates in Israel* (in Hebrew). Memorandum 66 (October). Tel Aviv: Jaffee Center for Strategic Studies.

———. 1999. *Trapped* (in Hebrew). Tel Aviv: Zmora Bitan.

Gelber, Yoav. 2003. The Status of Zionism and Israeli History in Israeli Universities. In Anita Shapira and Derek J. Penslar, eds., *Israeli Historical Revisionism: From Left to Right*, 155–70. Portland, OR: Frank Cass.

———. 1994. Introduction: The Era of Retaliation. In Motti Golani, ed., *"Black Arrow": The Gaza Raid and Israeli Retaliation Policy in the 1950s* (in Hebrew), 13–16. Tel-Aviv: Ma'arachot.

George, Alexander L. 1991. *Forceful Persuasion: Coercive Diplomacy as an Alternative to War*. Washington, DC: United States Institute of Peace.

George, Alexander L., and William Simmons. 1994. *The Limits of Coercive Diplomacy*. 2d ed. Boulder: Westview Press.

George, Alexander L., and Richard Smoke. 1989. Deterrence and Foreign Policy. *World Politics* 41 (2): 170–82.

Gilboa, Amos. 1996. Main Armies in the Middle East. In Ephraim Kam and Yiftah Shapir, eds., *The Middle East Strategic Balance, 1993–1994*, 130–50. Jerusalem and Boulder: Jerusalem Post and Westview Press.

Gilboa, Moshe A. 1969. *Six Years, Six Days: Origins and History of the Six Day War* (in Hebrew). Tel-Aviv: Am Oved.

Glubb, John. 1978. *Arabian Adventures: Ten Years of Joyful Service*. London: Cassel.

Gochman, Charles S., and Zeev Maoz. 1984. Militarized Interstate Disputes, 1816–1976: Procedures, Patterns, and Insights. *Journal of Conflict Resolution* 28 (4): 585–615.

Goemans, Hank E. 2000. *War and Punishment: The Causes of War Termination and the First World War*. Princeton: Princeton University Press.

Golan, Galia. 1990. *Soviet Policies in the Middle East from World War Two to Gorbachev*. Cambridge: Cambridge University Press.

Golan, Matti. 1976. *The Secret Conversations of Henry Kissinger*. New York: Quadrangle.

Golan, Shimon. 2000. *Hot Border, Cold War: The Crystallization of Israel's Security Policy, 1949–1953* (in Hebrew). Tel Aviv: Ma'arachot.

Golani, Motti. 2002. *Wars Don't Just Happen: On Memory, Power, and Choice* (in Hebrew). Tel Aviv: Modan.

———. 1997. *There Will Be War Next Summer . . .* (in Hebrew). 2 vols. Tel-Aviv: Ma'arachot.

———, ed. 1994. *"Black Arrow": The Gaza Raid and Israeli Retaliation Policy in the 1950s* (in Hebrew). Tel-Aviv: Ma'arachot.

Gordon, Shmuel. 2003. *Dimensions of Quality: A New Approach to Net Assessment of Airpower*. Memorandum 64. (May). Tel Aviv: Jaffee Center for Strategic Studies.

———. 2002. *Israel against Terrorism* (in Hebrew). Tel Aviv: Epi Meltzer.

———. 2000. The Air Force and the Yom Kippur War: New Lessons. In R. P. Kumaraswamy, ed., *Revisiting the Yom Kippur War*, 221–37. London: Frank Cass.

Gorst, Anthony. 2000. A "Modern" Major General: General Sir Gerald Templer, Chief of the Imperial General Staff. In Saul Kelly and Anthony Gorst, eds., *Whitehall and the Suez Crisis*, 29–45. London: Frank Cass.

Gur, Mordechai. 1987. The Six Day War: Reflections after Twenty Years (in Hebrew). *Ba'Mahane*, no. 309.

Haber, Eitan. 1987. *Today War Will Break Out: The Memoirs of Brig. Gen. Israel Lior, Military Aide de-Camp to Prime Ministers Levi Eshkol and Golda Meir*. Tel-Aviv: Edanim.

Haber, Eitan, Zeev Schiff, and Ehud Yaari. 1979. *Year of the Dove*. New York: Bantam.

Hagelin, Björn, Mark Bromely, and Simeon T. Wezman. 2004. International Arms Transfers. In *SIPRI Yearbook, 2004*. Oxford: Oxford University Press.

Hahn, Peter L. 1991. *The United States, Great Britain, and Egypt, 1945–1956: Strategy and Diplomacy in the Early Cold War*. Chapel Hill and London: University of North Carolina Press.

Haig, Alexander M. 1984. *CAVEAT: Realism, Reagan, and Foreign Policy*. New York: Macmillan.

Hamza, Khidhir, with Jeff Stein. 2000. *Saddam's Bombmaker*. New York: Scribner.

Handel, Michael I. 1995. The Evolution of Israel's Strategy: The Psychology of Insecurity and the Search for Absolute Security. In Williamson Murray, MacGregor Kox, and Alvin Bernstein, eds., *The Making of Strategy: Rulers, States, and War*, 534–78. New York: Cambridge University Press.

———. 1973. *Israel's Political-Military Doctrine*. Cambridge, MA: Harvard Studies in International Affairs.

Handwerker, Haim. 2002. Twenty-Four Years before Sadat. *Ha'aretz*, February 1 (Weekend Edition).

Harik, Judith P. 2004. *Hezbollah: The Changing Face of Terrorism*. London: I. B. Tauris.

Harkabi, Yehoshafat. 1975. *Arab Attitudes and Israel's Response*. New York: Free Press.

———. 1972. *Arab Attitudes to Israel*. London: Vallentine, Mitchell.

Hart, Alan. 1989. *Arafat: A Political Bibliography*. Bloomington: Indiana University Press.

Heikal, Mohammed Hassanin. 1978. *The Sphinx and the Commissar: The Rise and Fall of Soviet Influence in the Arab World*. London: Collins.

———. 1975. *The Road to Ramadan*. New York: Penguin.

Heller, Mark. 2003. Prospects of Creating a Regional Structure in the Middle East. *Journal of Strategic Studies* 26 (3): 125–36.

Helpman, Elhanan. 1998. Israeli Economic Growth: An International Comparison. In Hanna Herzog, ed., *Reflection of a Society* (in Hebrew), 25–36. Tel Aviv: Ramot.

Henry, Clement M., and Robert Springborg. 2001. *Globalization and the Politics of Development in the Middle East*. New York: Cambridge University Press.

Hersh, Seymour. 1991. *The Samson Option*. New York: Random House.

———. 1983. *The Price of Power: Kissinger in the White House*. New York: Summit Books.

Herzog, Haim. 1975. *The War of Atonement*. Boston: Little, Brown.

Heston, Alan, Robert Summers, and Bettina Aten. 2002. Penn World Table, Version 6.1. Center for International Comparisons at the University of Pennsylvania (CICUP), October. http://pwt.econ.upenn.edu/php_site/pwt_index.php.

Hinnebusch, Raymond. 2003. *The International Politics of the Middle East*. Manchester: Manchester University Press.

Hiro, Dilip. 1992. *Desert Shield to Desert Storm: The Second Gulf War*. London: HarperCollins.

Hirshfeld, Yair. 2000. *Oslo: A Formula for Peace. Negotiations on the Oslo Agreement—The Strategy and Implementation* (in Hebrew). Tel Aviv: Am Oved.

Hoffmann, Stanley. 1975. A New Policy for Israel. *Foreign Affairs*, 53 (3): 405–31.

Hofnung, Menahem. 1996. *Democracy, Law, and National Security in Israel*. Aldershot, UK: Darthmouth.

Hourani, Albert. 1989. Conclusion. In Wm. Roger Louis and Roger Owen, eds., *Suez, 1956: The Crisis and Its Consequences*, 392–410. Oxford: Clarendon Press.

Hussein, Bin Talal. 1962. *Uneasy Lies the Head*. London: Heineman.

Ikle, Fred Charles. 1971. *Every War Must End*. New York: Columbia University Press.

Ilan, Amitzur. 1996. *The Origins of the Arab-Israeli Arms Race: Arms, Embargo, Military Power, and Decision in the 1948 Palestine War*. Hounmills, Hampshire: Macmillan.

Inbar, Ephraim. 1999. *Rabin and Israel's National Security*. Baltimore: Johns Hopkins University Press.

———. 1998. Israel's National Security, 1973–96. *Annals of the American Academy of Political and Social Science* 555:62–81.

Israel Defense Forces (IDF). 2003. Israeli Civilian and Security Forces Casualties Since September 2000. http://www.idf.il/daily_statistics/english/1.doc.

Israeli, Raphael. 1985. *Man of Defiance: A Political Biography of Anwar Sadat*. London: Widenfeld and Nicolson.

———. 1979. *The Public Diary of President Sadat*. Leiden: Brill.

Jaber, Fouad. 1971. *Israel and Nuclear Weapons*. London: Chatto and Windus.

Jaber, Hala. 1997. *Hezbollah: Born with a Vengeance*. New York: Columbia University Press.

James, Robert Rhodes. 1990. Eden. In Selwyn Ilan Toren and Moshe Shemesh, eds., *The Suez-Sinai Crisis, 1956: Retrospective and Reappraisal*, 100–109. London: Frank Cass.

Jentelson, Bruce W., and Ariel E. Levite. 1992. The Analysis of Protracted Foreign Military Intervention. In Ariel E. Levite, Bruce W. Jentelson, and Larry Berman, eds., *Foreign Military Intervention: The Dynamics of Protracted Conflict*, 1–22. New York: Columbia University Press.

Jervis, Robert. 1989. Rational Deterrence: Theory and Evidence. *World Politics* 41 (2): 183–207.

———. 1985a. *The Illogic of American Nuclear Strategy*. Ithaca, NY: Cornell University Press.

———. 1985b. Perceiving and Coping with Threat. In Robert Jervis, Richard Ned Lebow, and Janice Stein, eds., *Psychology and Deterrence*, 13–33. Baltimore: Johns Hopkins University Press.

———. 1976. *Perception and Misperception in International Politics*. Princeton: Princeton University Press.

Kafkafi, Eyal. 1994. *An Optional War: To Sinai and Back, 1956–57* (in Hebrew). Tel-Aviv: Yad Tabenkin/Gallili Institute.

Kahalani, Avigdor. 1984. *The Heights of Courage: A Tank Leader's War on the Golan*. Westport, CT: Greenwood Press.

Kahneman, Daniel, and Amos Tversky. 1979. Prospect Theory: An Analysis of Decisions under Risk. *Econometrica* 47 (2): 263–91.

Kalb, Marvin, and Bernard Kalb. 1974. *Kissinger*. Boston: Little, Brown.

Kam, Ephraim. 2004. *From Terror to Nuclear Bomb: The Significance of the Iranian Threat* (in Hebrew). Tel Aviv: Defense Ministry Publishing House.

———. 1987. *Surprise Attack*. Cambridge, MA: Harvard University Press.

———, ed. 1974. *Hussein Starts the War* (in Hebrew). Tel-Aviv: Ma'arachot.

Kaplan, Edward H., Alex Mintz, and Shaul Mishal. 2004. Tactical Prevention of Suicide Bombings in Israel. Paper presented at the annual meeting of the Peace Science Society (International), Houston, TX, November.

Karatnycky, Adrian. 2002. The 2001–2002 Freedom House Survey of Freedom: The Democracy Gap. http://www.freedomhouse.org/research/freeworld/2002/essays.htm.

Karmon, Eli. 1996. Cooperation between Palestinian and European Terrorist Groups (in Hebrew). PhD diss., University of Haifa.

Karsh, Efraim. 1997. *Fabricating Israel's History: The "New" Historians*. Portland, OR: Frank Cass.

Kelly, Saul, and Anthony Gorst, eds. 2000. *Whitehall and the Suez Crisis*. London: Frank Cass.

Kennedy, Paul. 1987. *The Rise and Fall of the Great Powers*. New York: Random House.

Kerr, Malcolm. 1971. *The Arab Cold War: Gamal Abd al-Nasir and His Rivals*. Oxford: Oxford University Press.

Khadduri, Majid, and Edmund Ghareeb. 1997. *War in the Gulf, 1990–91: The Iraq-Kuwait Conflict and Its Implications*. New York: Oxford University Press.

Khalidi, Rashid. 2002. Toward a Clear Palestinian Strategy. *Journal of Palestine Studies* 31 (4): 5–12.

Khouri, Fred J. 1968. *The Arab-Israeli Dilemma*. Syracuse: Syracuse University Press.

Kimche, David, and Dan Bawly. 1968. *The Sandstorm*. New York: Stein and Day.

Kimmerling, Baruch. 2003. *Politicide: Ariel Sharon's War against the Palestinians*. London and New York: Verso.

———. 1993. Patterns of Militarism in Israel. *Archives Europennes de Sociologie* 34 (2): 196–223.

———. 1985. *The Interrupted System: Israeli Civilians in War and Routine Times*. New Brunswick, NJ: Transaction Books.

Kimmerling, Baruch, and Joel S. Migdal. 2003. *The Palestinian People*. Cambridge, MA: Harvard University Press.

Kiss, Naomi. 1977. The Impact of Public Policy on Public Opinion: Israel, 1967–1974. *State Government and International Relations* (in Hebrew) 8 (1): 36–60.

Kissinger, Henry A. 1982. *Years of Upheaval*. Boston: Little, Brown.

———. 1979. *White House Years*. Boston: Little, Brown.

Klein, Zvi. 1976. The Yom Kippur War: Surprise or Trap? *State, Government, and International Relations* (in Hebrew) 6 (1): 127–41.

Klieman, Aharon S. 1990. *Israel and the World after 40 Years*. New York: Pergamon-Brassey.

———. 1986. *Unpeaceful Coexistence*. Tel Aviv: Maariv.

———. 1985. *Israel's Global Reach: Arms Sales as Diplomacy*. New York: Pergamon-Brassey.

Kober, Avi. 1995. *Military Decision in the Arab-Israeli Wars, 1948–1982* (in Hebrew). Tel Aviv: Ma'arachot.

Korn, David A. 1992. *Stalemate: The War of Attrition and Great Power Diplomacy in the Middle East, 1967–1970*. Boulder: Westview Press.

Krause, Keith. 2003. State Making and Region Building: The Interplay of Domestic and Regional Security in the Middle East. *Journal of Strategic Studies* 26 (3): 99–124.

Kretzmer, David. 2002. *The Occupation of Justice*. Albany: State University of New York Press.

Kuperman, Ranan D. 2003. The Effect of Domestic and Foreign Pressure on Israeli Decisions to Use Limited Military Force. *Journal of Peace Research* 40 (5): 677–94.

———. 2001. Rules of Military Retaliation and Their Practice by the State of Israel. *International Interactions* 27 (3): 297–326.

———. 1999. Dynamics of a Policy: A Comparison of Israel's Military Actions Across Time. PhD diss., Tel-Aviv University.

Kurz, Anat, with Nachman Tal. 1997. *Hamas: Radical Islam in a National Struggle*. Memorandum 48. Tel-Aviv: Jaffee Center for Strategic Studies.

Kyle, Keith. 1989. Britain and the Crisis, 1955–56. In Wm. Roger Louis and Roger Owen, eds., *Suez, 1956: The Crisis and Its Consequences*, 103–30. Oxford: Clarendon Press.

Lacouture, Jean. 1973. *Nasser: A Biography*. New York: Alfred A. Knopf.

Landau, Emily. 2001. *Egypt and Israel in ACRS: Bilateral Concerns in an Arms Control Process*. Memorandum 59. Tel-Aviv: Jaffee Center for Strategic Studies.

Landau, Emily, and Tamar Malz. 2003. Assessing Regional Security Dialogue through the Agent-Structure Lens: Reflections on ACRS. *Journal of Strategic Studies* 26 (3): 155–80.

Lanir, Zvi. 1983. *Fundamental Surprise: The National Intelligence Crisis* (in Hebrew). Tel-Aviv: Am Oved.

Lawson, Fred H. 1996. *Why Syria Goes to War: Thirty Years of Confrontation*. Ithaca, NY: Cornell University Press.

Lebow, Richard Ned. 2000. What's So Different about a Counterfactual? *World Politics* 52 (4): 550–73.

———. 1981. *Between Peace and War: The Nature of International Crisis*. Baltimore: Johns Hopkins University Press.

Lebow, Richard Ned, and Janice Gross Stein. 1989. Rational Deterrence Theory: I Think, Therefore I Deter. *World Politics* 41 (2): 208–24.

Leeuw, Frans L. 1995. Policy Theories, Knowledge Utilization, and Evaluation. In Ray C. Rist, ed., *Policy Evaluation: Linking Theory to Practice*, 19–37. Aldershot, UK: Edward Elgar.

Lesch, Ann M., and Mark Tessler. 1989. *Egypt, Israel, and the Palestinians: From Camp David to Intifada*. Bloomington: Indiana University Press.

Levite, Ariel. 1989. *Offense and Defense in Israel's Military Doctrine*. Boulder: Westview Press.

———. 1983. *Intelligence and Strategic Surprise*. New York: Columbia University Press.

Levite, Ariel E., Bruce W. Jentelson, and Larry Berman, eds. 1992. *Foreign Military Intervention: The Dynamics of Protracted Conflict*. New York: Columbia University Press.

Levite, Ariel, and Emily Landau. 1994. *Israel's Nuclear Image: Arab Perceptions of Israel's Nuclear Posture* (in Hebrew). Tel-Aviv: Papyrus, Tel-Aviv University Press.

Levitzky, Nomi. 2001. *His Honor: Aharon Barak—A Biography* (in Hebrew). Tel Aviv: Keter.

Levy, Jack S. 1998. The Causes of War and the Conditions of Peace. *Annual Review of Political Science* 1:139–66.

———. 1989a. The Causes of War: A Review of Theories and Evidence. In Philip E. Tetlock, Jo L. Husbands, Robert Jervis, Paul Stern, and Charles Tilly, eds., *Society, Behavior, and Nuclear War*, 209–333. New York: Oxford University Press.

———. 1989b. The Diversionary Theory of War: A Critique. In Manus I. Midlarsky, ed., *Handbook of War Studies*, 259–88. Boston: Unwin Hymann.

———. 1987. Declining Power and the Preventive Motivation for War. *World Politics* 40 (1): 82–107.

Levy, Jack S., and J. R. Gochal. 2001. Democracy and Preventive War: Israel and the 1956 Sinai Campaign. *Security Studies* 11 (2): 1–49.

Levy, Yagil. 2003. *The Other Army of Israel* (in Hebrew). Tel Aviv: Am Oved.

———. 1997. *Trial and Error: Israel's Route from War to De-Escalation*. Albany: State University of New York Press.

Lieberman, Eli. 1995. *Deterrence Theory: Success or Failure in the Arab-Israeli Wars?* Mac-Nair Paper 45. Washington, DC: National Defense University. Available online at http://www.ndu.edu/inss/McNair/mcnair45/mcnair45.pdf.

Lifschitz, Yaacov. 2003. *The Economics of Producing Defense: Illustrated by the Case of Israel*. Boston: Kluwer Academic Publishers.

———. 1995. *The Defense Industries: Asset or Burden?* (in Hebrew). Jerusalem: Jerusalem Institute for Israel Studies.

Linn, Ruth. 1996. *Conscience at War: The Israeli Soldier as Moral Critic*. Albany: State University of New York Press.

Lissak, Moshe. 1993. Civilian Components in the National Security Doctrine. In Avner Yaniv, ed., *National Security and Democracy in Israel*, 55–80. Boulder: Lynne Rienner.

Lorbar, Azriel. 1998. The Missile Threat to Israel. In Aryeh Stav, ed., *Ballistic Missiles: The Threat and the Response* (in Hebrew), 3–13. Tel-Aviv: Yediot Aharonot.

Lucas, W. Scott. 2000. Cadogan's Last Fling: Sir Alexander Cadogan, Chairman of the Board of Governors of the BBC. In Saul Kelly and Anthony Gorst, eds., *Whitehall and the Suez Crisis*, 110–35. London: Frank Cass.

Luttwak, Edward N. 2001. *Strategy: The Logic of War and Peace*. Cambridge, MA: Harvard University Press.

MacFarquhar, Neil. 2002. Mideast Turmoil: Arab League; Arabs Approve an Offer to Israel with Conditions It Has Rejected. *New York Times* (March 29), 1A.

Maoz, Moshe. 1995. *Syria and Israel: From War to Peacemaking*. London: Oxford University Press.

———. 1985. *Palestinian Leadership on the West Bank* (in Hebrew). Tel Aviv: Reshafim.

Maoz, Zeev. 2005. Dyadic MID Dataset (Version 2.0). http://psfaculty.ucdavis.edu/zmaoz/dyadmid.html.

———. 2004a. Pacifism and Fightaholism in International Politics: A Structural History of National and Dyadic Conflict, 1816–1992. *International Studies Review* 6 (1): 107–33.

———. 2004b. The Revolution in Military Affairs in the Middle East. Paper presented at the Changing Nature of Warfare Conference, Center for Naval Analyses, Alexandria, VA, May 25–26.

———. 2004c. Defending Israel from Its Friends? A Reply to Professor Beres. *International Security* 29 (1): 175–78.

———. 2004d. Intelligence Failures: Types, Causes, and Preventive Measures. Mimeograph. University of California, Davis.

———. 2003a. The Mixed Blessing of Israel's Nuclear Policy. *International Security* 27 (3): 44–77.

———. 2003b. Domestic Politics and Regional Security: Theoretical Perspectives and Middle East Patterns. *Journal of Strategic Studies* 26 (3): 19–48.

———. 2001. Israeli Intervention in Intra-Arab Affairs. In Abraham Ben-Zvi and Aharon Klieman, eds., *Studies in Israeli Diplomacy, Zionism, and International Relations*, 137–76. London: Frank Cass.

———. 1997a. Decisional Stress, Individual Choice, and Policy Outcomes: The Arab-Israeli Conflict, 1970–1975. In Nehemia Geva and Alex Mintz, eds., *Foreign Policy Decisionmaking: The Cognitive-Rational Debate*, 141–77. Boulder: Lynne Rienner.

———. 1997b. Regional Security in the Middle East: Past Trends, Present Realities, and Future Challenges. *Journal of Strategic Studies* 19 (1): 3–47.

———. 1996a. The Evolution of the Middle East Military Balance, 1980–1995. In Ephraim Kam, ed., *The Middle East Military Balance, 1994–95*, 66–92. Jerusalem and Boulder: Jerusalem Post and Westview Press.

———. 1996b. The "Over My Dead Body" Syndrome in Israel's Foreign Policy. *Ha'aretz*, November 15, B3.

———. 1990a. *National Choices and International Processes*. Cambridge: Cambridge University Press.

————. 1990b. *Paradoxes of War: On the Art of National Self-Entrapment*. Boston: Unwin Hyman.

————. 1990c. Framing the National Interest: The Manipulation of Foreign Policy Decisions in Group Settings. *World Politics* 43 (1): 77–110.

————. 1989. Power, Capabilities, and Paradoxical Conflict Outcomes. *World Politics* 41 (2): 239–66.

————. 1986. Multiple Paths to Choice: An Approach for the Analysis of Foreign Policy Decision Making. In I. N. Gallhofer, W. E. Saris, and Marianne Melman, eds., *Text Analysis Procedures for the Study of Decision Making*, 69–96. Amsterdam: Sociometric Research Foundation.

————. 1982a. *Paths to Conflict: International Dispute Initiation, 1816–1976*. Boulder: Westview Press.

————. 1982b. Crisis Initiation: A Theoretical Exploration of a Neglected Topic in International Crisis Theory. *Review of International Studies* 8 (4): 215–32.

————. 1981. The Decision to Raid Entebbe: Decision Analysis Applied to Crisis Behavior. *Journal of Conflict Resolution* 31 (4): 677–707.

Maoz, Zeev, and Allison Astorino. 1992a. Waging War, Waging Peace: Decision Making and Bargaining in the Arab-Israeli Conflict, 1970–1973. *International Studies Quarterly* 36 (4): 373–99.

————. 1992b. The Cognitive Structure of Peacemaking: Egypt and Israel, 1970–78. *Political Psychology* 13 (4): 647–62.

Maoz, Zeev, and Dan S. Felsenthal. 1987. Self-Binding Commitments, the Inducement of Trust, Choice, and the Theory of International Cooperation. *International Studies Quarterly* 31 (2): 177–200.

Maoz, Zeev, and Ben D. Mor. 2002a. *Bound by Struggle: The Strategic Evolution of Enduring International Rivalries*. Ann Arbor: University of Michigan Press.

————. 2002b. Web site of *Bound by Struggle*. Israeli-Syrian Rivalry, 1949–1998. http://spirit.tau.ac.il/poli/faculty/maoz/israel-syria.doc.

Mardor, Munya. 1981. *Rafael* (in Hebrew). Tel-Aviv: Defense Ministry Publishing House.

Margalit, Dan. 1971. *A Dispatch from the White House* (in Hebrew). Tel-Aviv: Otpaz.

Mark, Melvin M., Gary T. Henry, and George Julnes. 2000. *Evaluation: An Integrated Framework for Improving Public and Nonprofit Policies and Programs*. San Francisco: Jossey Bass.

Marshall, Monty G., and Keith Jaggers. 2004. Polity IV Project. Center for International Development and Conflict Management, University of Maryland. Available online at http://www.cidcm.umd.edu/inscr/polity/.

Martin, Andre. 1991. Military and Political Contradictions of the Suez Affair: A French Perspective. In Selwyn Ilan Toren and Moshe Shemesh, eds., *The Suez-Sinai Crisis, 1956: Retrospective and Reappraisal*, 54–59. London: Frank Cass.

May, Ernest. 1973. *"Lessons" of the Past: The Uses and Misuses of History in American Foreign Policy*. New York: Oxford University Press.

Mearsheimer, John D. 1983. *Conventional Deterrence*. Ithaca, NY: Cornell University Press.

Medzini, Myron. 1990. *The Proud Jewess: Golda Meir and the Vision of Israel* (in Hebrew). Tel-Aviv: Edanim.

Meir, Golda. 1975. *My Life*. Jerusalem: Steimatsky's Agency.

Meital, Yoram. 1997. *Egypt's Struggle for Peace: Continuity and Change, 1967–1977*. Gainesville: University Press of Florida.

Melman, Yossi, and Dan Raviv. 1989. *Imperfect Spies: The History of Israeli Intelligence*. London: Sidgwick and Jacobson.

Mendelsohn, Barak. 2003. Israeli Self-Defeating Deterrence in the Gulf War. *Journal of Strategic Studies* 26 (4): 83–107.

———. 1999. Israeli Deterrence in the Gulf War (in Hebrew). MA thesis, Tel-Aviv University.

Merom, Gil. 2003. *How Democracies Lose Small Wars: State, Society, and the Failures of France in Algeria, Israel in Lebanon, and the United States in Vietnam.* Cambridge: Cambridge University Press.

Michelson, Benny. 1994. The Gaza Raid: The Planning, the Operation, and the Lessons. In Motti Golani, ed., *"Black Arrow": The Gaza Raid and Israel's Retaliation Policy in the 1950s* (in Hebrew), 11–25. Tel-Aviv.

———. 1984. Operation "Inferno": A Battle on the East Bank of the Jordan, March 1968. *Ma'arachot* (in Hebrew), no. 292–93:18–32.

Mideast Mirror. 2000. Israel's Intransigence Blamed for Failure of Assad-Clinton Summit. *Mideast Mirror,* March 27.

Miller, Benjamin. 1995. *When Opponents Cooperate: Great Power Conflict and Collaboration in World Politics.* Ann Arbor: University of Michigan Press.

Milstein, Uri. 1999. *The General Security Doctrine: The Principle of Survival* (in Hebrew). Tel Aviv: Sridut.

Mintz, Alex. 1984. The Military-Industrial Complex: The Israeli Case. In Moshe Lissak, ed., *The Israeli Society and Its Defense Establishment: The Social and Political Impact of a Protracted Violent Conflict,* 103–27. London: Frank Cass.

Mishal, Shaul. 1986. *The PLO under Arafat: Between Gun and Olive Branch.* New Haven: Yale University Press.

Mishal, Shaul, and Abraham Sela. 2000. *The Palestinian Hamas: Vision, Violence, and Coexistence.* New York: Columbia University Press.

Mohr, Lawrence B. 1995. *Impact Analysis for Program Evaluation.* Thousand Oaks, CA: Sage.

Monterey Institute of International Studies. 2004. Weapons of Mass Destruction in the Middle East. http://cns.miis.edu/research/wmdme/israelnc.htm.

Mor, Ben D. 1993. *Crisis Decision and Interaction: A Model of International Crisis Behavior.* Westport, CT: Praeger.

———. 1991. Nasser's Decision Making in the 1967 Middle East Crisis: A Rational Choice Explanation. *Journal of Peace Research* 28 (4): 359–75.

Morgan, Patrick M. 2003. *Deterrence Now.* Cambridge: Cambridge University Press.

Morris, Benny. 2004. *The Birth of the Palestinian Refugee Problem Revisited.* Cambridge: Cambridge University Press.

———. 2002. Camp David and After: An Exchange (Interview with Ehud Barak). *New York Review of Books,* June 13.

———. 2001. *Righteous Victims: A History of the Zionist-Arab Conflict, 1881–2001.* New York: Vintage Books.

———. 1993. *Israel's Border Wars, 1949–1956.* Oxford: Oxford University Press.

———. 1990. *1948 and After: Israel and the Palestinians.* Oxford: Clarendon Press.

Mu'alem, Walid. 1997. Interview: Syrian-Israeli Negotiations. *Journal of Palestine Studies* 26 (2): 81–94.

Muhamedou, Mohammad-Mahmoud. 1998. *Iraq and the Second Gulf War: State Building and Regime Security.* San Francisco and London: Austin and Winfeld.

Nachmias, David. 1979. *Public Policy Evaluation: Approaches and Methods.* New York: St. Martin's Press.

Nagel, Stuart. 1998. *Public Policy Evaluation: Making Super-Optimum Decisions.* Aldershot, UK: Ashgate.

Nakdimon, Shlomo. 2001. Saddam Is Still Here. *Yediot Aharonot*, January 14.

———. 1996. *A Hopeless Hope: The Rise and Fall of the Israeli-Kurdish Alliance, 1963–1975*. Tel-Aviv: Yediot Aharonot.

———. 1995. Black Hole: The United States, Israel, and Iraqi Weapons of Mass Destruction, 1981–1991 (in Hebrew). Manuscript.

———. 1982. *Low Probability: The Story of the Drama Preceding the Yom Kippur War, and What Followed* (in Hebrew). Tel-Aviv: Revivim Press.

Naor, Aryeh. 1993. *Begin in Power: A Personal Testimony* (in Hebrew). Tel Aviv: Yediot Aharonot.

———. 1988. *The Writing on the Wall: Where the Likud Is Leading?* (in Hebrew). Tel Aviv: Edanim.

———. 1986. *A Cabinet at War: The Performance of the Likud Government during the Lebanon War, 1982* (in Hebrew). Tel Aviv: Lahav.

Netanyahu, Benjamin. 2000. *A Durable Peace: Israel and Its Place among the Nations*. New York: Warner Books.

Nutting, Anthony. 1972. *Nasser*. New York: Dutton.

O'Balance, Edgar. 2000. *Sudan: Civil War and Terrorism, 1956–99*. New York: St. Martin's Press.

———. 1973. *The Kurdish Revolt*. London: Faber and Faber.

Oren, Michael. 2002. *Six Days of War: June 1967 and the Making of the Modern Middle East*. New York: Oxford University Press.

———. 1994. Did the Gaza Raid Cause a Shift in Egyptian Policy? In Motti Golani, ed., *"Black Arrow:" The Gaza Raid and Israeli Retaliation Policy in the 1950s* (in Hebrew), 35–48. Tel-Aviv: Ma'arachot.

Organization of Economic Cooperation and Development (OECD). 2003. *Literacy Skills for the World of Tomorrow: Further Results from PISA 2000*. Available online at http://www.pisa.oecd.org/Docs/download/pisaplus_eng01.pdf.

Organski, A. F. K. 1988. *The Thirty-Six Billion Dollar Bargain*. New York: Columbia University Press.

Ostfeld, Zehava. 1994. *An Army Is Born: Principal Stages in the Building of the Army under the Leadership of David Ben-Gurion* (in Hebrew). Tel Aviv: Defense Ministry Publishing House.

Pa'il, Meir. 1998. Israel's Wars: Toward the 50th Anniversary of the State of Israel. In Sara Aharoni and Meir Aharoni, eds., *People and Deeds in Israel* (in Hebrew). Tel Aviv: Miksam.

Palestinian National Authority. 2003. Al Aqsa Intifada: Daily Documentation. http://www.pnic.gov.ps/arabic/quds/quds_en.html.

Pape, Robert E. 2003. The Strategic Logic of Suicide Terrorism. *American Political Science Review* 97 (3): 343–61.

Pappe, Ilan. 1992. *The Making of the Arab-Israeli Conflict*. London: I. B. Tauris.

Parker, Richard B. 1993. *The Politics of Miscalculation in the Middle East*. Bloomington: Indiana University Press.

Pedatzur, Reuven. 1996. *The Triumph of Confusion: Israel's Policy in the Occupied Territories Following the Six Day War* (in Hebrew). Tel Aviv: Bitan.

Peres, Shimon. 1995. *Battling for Peace*. London: Widenfeld and Nicolson.

———. 1993. *The New Middle East*. New York: Henry Holt.

Peretz, Don. 1990. *Intifada: The Palestinian Uprising*. Boulder: Westview Press.

Peri, Yoram. 2003. The Democratic Putsch in the 1999 Elections. In Majd Al Haj and Uri Ben Eliezer, eds., *In the Name of Security: The Sociology of Peace and War in Israel in Challenging Times*, 125–44. Haifa: University of Haifa Press.

————. 1983. *Between Battles and Ballots: Israeli Military in Politics*. Cambridge: Cambridge University Press.

Perlmutter, Amos. 1969. *Military and Politics in Israel: State Building and Role Expansion*. New York: Praeger.

Pillar, Paul. 1983. *Negotiating Peace: War Termination as a Bargaining Process*. Princeton: Princeton University Press.

Pipes, Daniel. 1990. *Greater Syria: The History of an Ambition*. New York: Oxford University Press.

Podeh, Elie. 1995. *The Quest for Hegemony in the Arab World : The Struggle over the Baghdad Pact*. New York: E. J. Brill.

Pollack, Kenneth M. 2002. *Arabs at War: Military Effectiveness, 1948–1991*. Lincoln: University of Nebraska Press.

Pressman, Jeremy. 2003. Visions in Collision: What Happened in Camp David and Taba. *International Security* 28 (2): 5–43.

Pundak, Ron. 2001. From Oslo to Taba: What Went Wrong? *Survival* 43 (3): 31–45.

Quandt, William B. 2001. *Peace Process: American Diplomacy and the Arab-Israeli Conflict since 1967*. Los Angeles: University of California Press.

————. 1986. *Camp David: Peace Making and Politics*. Washington, DC: Brookings Institution Press.

————. 1977. *Decade of Decisions: American Foreign Policy toward the Arab-Israeli Conflict, 1967–1976*. Los Angeles: University of California Press.

Rabani, Mouin. 2001. Rocks and Rockets: Oslo's Inevitable Conclusion. *Journal of Palestine Studies* 30 (1): 68–81.

Rabil, Robert G. 2003. *Embattled Neighbors: Syria, Israel, and Lebanon*. Boulder: Lynne Rienner.

Rabin, Yitzhak. 1979. *Service Ledger* (in Hebrew). Tel-Aviv: Yediot Aharonot.

Rabinovich, Itamar. 1998. *The Brink of Peace* (in Hebrew). Tel-Aviv: Yediot Aharonot.

————. 1991. *The Road Not Taken: Early Arab-Israeli Negotiations*. New York and Oxford: Oxford University Press.

————. 1984. *The War for Lebanon*. Ithaca, NY: Cornell University Press.

Rafael, Gideon. 1981. *Destination Peace: Three Decades of Israeli Foreign Policy*. London: Widenfeld and Nicolson.

Rathmell, Andrew. 1995. *Secret War in the Middle East: The Covert Struggle for Syria, 1949–1961*. London: I. B. Tauris.

Reich, Bernard. 1992. Israel and the Persian Gulf Crisis. In Ibrahim Ibrahim, ed., *The Gulf Crisis: Background and Consequences*, 221–40. Washington, DC: Center for Contemporary Arab Studies, Georgetown University.

Riad, Mahmoud. 1981. *The Struggle for Peace in the Middle East*. London and New York: Quartet Books.

Richards, Alan, and John Waterbury. 1996. *A Political Economy of the Middle East*. Boulder: Westview Press.

Rosen, Steven J. 1972. War Power and the Willingness to Suffer. In Bruce Russett, ed., *Peace, War, and Numbers*, 167–84. Beverly Hills: Sage.

Ross, Dennis. 2004. *The Missing Peace: The Inside Story for the Fight for Middle East Peace*. New York: Farrar, Straus, and Giroux.

————. 2001. Camp David: An Exchange. *New York Review of Books*, September 20.

Roy, Sara. 2002. Why Peace Failed: An Oslo Autopsy. *Current History* 101 (1): 8–16.

Rubin, Barry. 2002. *The Tragedy of the Middle East*. Cambridge: Cambridge University Press.

Sachar, Howard. 1981. *Egypt and Israel*. New York: Richard Marek.

Sadat, Anwar. 1977. *In Search of Identity: An Autobiography*. New York: Harper and Row.

Safran, Nadav. 1969. *From War to War: The Arab-Israeli Confrontation, 1948–1967*. New York: Pegasus.

Sagie, Uri. 1998. *Lights in the Fog*. Tel Aviv: Yediot Aharonot.

Savir, Uri. 1998. *The Process*. New York: Random House.

Sayed-Ahmed, Mohammad Abd el-Wahab. 1989. *Nasser and American Foreign Policy, 1952–1956*. London: LAAM.

Sayigh, Yezid. 2001. Arafat and the Anatomy of a Revolt. *Survival* 43 (3): 47–60.

———. 1997. *Armed Struggle and the Search for a State: The Palestinian National Movement, 1949–1993*. Oxford: Clarendon.

Schelling, Thomas C. 1966. *Arms and Influence*. New Haven: Yale University Press.

———. 1960. *The Strategy of Conflict*. Cambridge, MA: Harvard University Press.

Schiff, Zeev. 2001. Comments on the Balance of National Strength and Security. In Uzi Arad, ed., *The Balance of National Strength and Security* (in Hebrew), 246–49. Tel Aviv: Yediot Aharonot.

———. 1999. The Historical Miss of Netanyahu. *Ha'aretz*, July 7, B1.

———. 1970. *Phantom over the Nile: The Story of the Israeli Air Corps* (in Hebrew). Tel-Aviv: Shikmona.

Schiff, Zeev, and Ehud Yaari. 1990. *Intifada* (in Hebrew). Tel-Aviv: Schocken.

———. 1984. *Israel's Lebanon War*. New York: Simon and Schuster.

Schmidt, Dana Adams. 1964. *Journey among Brave Men*. Boston: Little, Brown.

Schueftan, Dan. 1989. *Attrition: Egypt's Postwar Political Strategy, 1967–1970* (in Hebrew). Tel-Aviv: Ma'arachot.

———. 1987. *The Jordanian Option: Israel, Jordan, and the Palestinians* (in Hebrew). Tel Aviv: Ha'Kibbutz Ha'Meuchad.

Seale, Patrick. 1988. *Asad: The Struggle for the Middle East*. Berkeley and Los Angeles: University of California Press.

———. 1986. *The Struggle for Syria: A Study of Post-War Arab Politics*. London: I. B. Tauris.

Segev, Shmuel. 1989. *The Iranian Triangle*. New York: Free Press.

Segev, Tom. 1984. *1949: The New Israelis*. Jerusalem: Domino Press.

Sela, Abraham. 1998. *The Decline of the Arab-Israeli Conflict: Middle East Politics and the Quest for Regional Order*. Albany: State University of New York Press.

Sellers, J. A. 1990. Military Lessons: The British Perspective. In Selwyn Ilan Toren and Moshe Shemesh, eds., *The Suez-Sinai Crisis, 1956: Retrospective and Reappraisal*, 17–53. London: Frank Cass.

Shafir, Gershon, and Yoav Peled. 2001. *Being Israeli: The Dynamics of Multiple Citizenship*. Cambridge: Cambridge University Press.

Shaham, David. 1998. *Israel: Fifty Years* (in Hebrew). Tel Aviv: Am Oved.

Shalev, Aryeh. 1994. *Israel and Syria: Peace and Security on the Golan*. Boulder: Westview Press.

———. 1993. *The Israel-Syria Armistice Regime, 1949–1955*. Jerusalem and Boulder: Jerusalem Post and Westview Press.

———. 1990. *The Intifada: Causes and Effects* (in Hebrew). Tel-Aviv: Papyrus.

Shalev, Michael. 1992. *Labour and the Political Economy in Israel*. New York: Oxford University Press.

Shaliyeh, Emile. 1988. *In Search of Leadership: West Bank Politics since 1967*. Washington, DC: Brookings Institution Press.

Shalom, Zaki. 2002. *David Ben Gurion, the State of Israel, and the Arab World, 1949–56*. Sussex: Sussex Academic Press.

————. 1996. *Policy in the Shadow of Controversy: Israel's Current Security Policy, 1949–1956* (in Hebrew). Tel Aviv: Defense Ministry Publishing House.

Shamir, Itzhak. 1994. *Summing Up: An Autobiography*. Boston: Little, Brown.

Shamir, Michal, and Asher Arian. 1999. Collective Identity and Electoral Competition in Israel. *American Political Science Review* 93 (2): 265–77.

Shamir, Yaacov, and Michal Shamir. 2000. *The Anatomy of Public Opinion*. Ann Arbor: University of Michigan Press.

Shapir, Yiftah. 2004. Military Forces in the Middle East. In Shai Feldman and Yiftah Shapir, eds., *The Middle East Military Balance, 2003–2004*, 171–261. London: Sussex Academic Publishing. Also available online at http://www.tau.ac.il/jcss/ balance/ index.html.

————. 1996. Ballistic Missiles in the Middle East. In Ephraim Kam and Yiftah Shapir, eds., *The Middle East Strategic Balance, 1993–1994*, 151–70. Jerusalem and Boulder: Jerusalem Post and Westview Press.

Shapira, Anita. 2003. The Strategies of Historical Revisionism. In Anita Shapira and Derek J. Penslar, eds., *Israeli Historical Revisionism: From Left to Right*. Portland, OR: Frank Cass.

Shapira, Shimon. 2000. *Hizballah: Between Iran and Lebanon* (in Hebrew). Tel Aviv: Ha'Kibbutz Ha'meuchad.

Sharabi, Hisham. 1970. Prelude to War: The Crisis of May–June, 1967. In Ibrahim Abu Lughod, ed., *The Arab-Israeli Confrontation of 1967: An Arab Perspective*, 49–65. Evanston, IL: Northwestern University Press.

Sharef, Zeev. 1959. *Three Days* (in Hebrew). Tel Aviv: Am Oved.

Sharett, Moshe. 1978. *Personal Diary* (in Hebrew). 8 vols. Tel-Aviv: Am Oved.

————. 1958. *In the Gates of Nations* (in Hebrew). Tel Aviv: Am Oved.

Sharon, Ariel. 1989. *Warrior: The Autobiography of Ariel Sharon*. New York: Simon and Schuster.

Shavit, Ari. 2001. End of a Journey: Interview with Shlomo Ben-Ami. *Ha'aretz Magazine* (in Hebrew), September 14, 10–15, 29.

Shazly, Sa'ad. 1986. *The Arab Military Option*. San Francisco: American Mideast Research.

————. 1980. *The Crossing of the Canal*. San Francisco: American Mideast Research.

Sheehan, Edward R. 1976. *The Arabs, Israelis, and Kissinger: A Secret History of American Diplomacy in the Middle East*. New York: Readers' Digest Press.

Sheffer, Gabriel. 1996. *Moshe Sharett: Biography of a Political Moderate*. New York: Oxford University Press.

————. 1988. Sharett, Ben-Gurion, and the 1956 War of Choice. *State, Government, and International Relations* (in Hebrew) 27 (1): 5–32.

————. 1980. *Resolution versus Management of the Middle Eastern Conflict: Moshe Sharett and David Ben Gurion*. Jerusalem: Magnes Press.

Shelah, Ofer. 2003. *The Israeli Army: A Radical Proposal* (in Hebrew). Tel Aviv: Kinneret, Zmora-Bitan.

Sher, Gilead. 2003. *Just Beyond Reach: The Peace Negotiations, 1999–2001* (in Hebrew). Tel Aviv: Yediot Aharonot.

Shiffer, Shimon. 1984. *Snowball: The Secrets of the Lebanon War* (in Hebrew). Tel Aviv: Yediot Aharont Press.

Shikaki, Khalil. 2004. A Palestinian Perspective on the Failure of the Permanent Status Negotiations. Mimeograph. Ramallah: Bir Zeit University.

Shimoni, Yaacov. 1977. *The Arab States: Their Contemporary History and Politics* (in Hebrew). Tel-Aviv: Am Oved.

Shimshoni, Jonathan. 1988. *Israel and Conventional Deterrence*. Ithaca, NY: Cornell University Press.

Shlaim, Avi. 2000. *The Iron Wall*. New York: W. W. Norton.

———. 1988. *Collusion across the Jordan: King Abdullah, the Zionist Movement, and the Partition of Palestine*. Oxford: Oxford University Press.

———. 1976. Failures in National Intelligence Estimates: The Case of the Yom Kippur War. *World Politics* 28 (3): 348–80.

Shlaim, Avi, and Raymond Tanter. 1978. Decision Process, Choice, and Consequences: Israel's Deep Penetration Bombing in Egypt, 1970. *World Politics* 30 (4): 483–516.

Shoham, Danny. 2001. *Chemical and Biological Weapons in the Arab Countries and Iran: An Existential Threat to Israel?* (in Hebrew). Shaarei Tikva: Ariel Center for Policy Research.

———. 2000. The Chemical-Biological Threat on Israel. In Arieh Stav, ed., *Ballistic Missiles: The Threat and the Response* (in Hebrew), 58–76. Tel-Aviv: Yediot Aharonot.

———. 1998. Ballistic Missiles, Long Range Artillery Rockets, and Missile Launchers in the Middle East. In Aryeh Stav, ed., *Ballistic Missiles: The Threat and the Response* (in Hebrew), 295–99. Tel-Aviv: Yediot Aharonot.

Shultz, George P. 1993. *Turmoil and Triumph: My Years as Secretary of State*. New York: Maxwell Macmillan.

Sick, Gary. 1995. Iran: The Adolescent Revolution. *Journal of International Affairs* 49 (1): 145–66.

Singer, J. David. 1987. Reconstructing the Correlates of War Dataset on Material Capabilities of States, 1816–1985. *International Interactions* 14: 115–32.

Singer, J. David, Stuart Bremer, and John Stuckey. 1972. Capability Distribution, Uncertainty, and Major Power War, 1820–1965. In Bruce Russett, ed., *Peace, War, and Numbers*, 19–48. Beverly Hills, CA: Sage.

Sisco, Joseph. 1990. Interview with Zeev Maoz and Allison Astorino. Washington, DC, July 10.

Small, Melvin, and J. David Singer. 1982. *Resort to Arms: International and Civil Wars, 1816–1980*. Beverly Hills, CA: Sage Publications.

Snyder, Jed C. 1983. The Road to Osirak: Baghdad's Quest for the Bomb. *Middle East Journal* 37 (4): 565–94.

Sobelman, Daniel. 2003. *New Ground Rules: Israel and the Hizballah after the Withdrawal from Lebanon* (in Hebrew). Memorandum 65. Tel Aviv: Jaffee Center for Strategic Studies.

Solingen, Etel. 1998. *Regional Orders at Century's Dawn: Global and Domestic Influences on Grand Strategy*. Princeton: Princeton University Press.

Sontag, Deborah. 2001. Quest for Mideast Peace: How and Why It Failed. *New York Times*, July 26, A1.

Spiegel, Steven L. 2003. Regional Security and the Level-of-Analysis Problem. *Journal of Strategic Studies* 26 (3): 75–98.

———. 1985. *The Other Arab-Israeli Conflict: Making America's Middle East Policy from Truman to Reagan*. Chicago: University of Chicago Press.

Stein, Janice Gross. 1991a. The Arab-Israeli War of 1967: Inadvertent War through Miscalculated Escalation. In Alexander L. George, ed., *Avoiding War: Problems of Crisis Management*, 126–60. Boulder: Westview Press.

———. 1991b. Reassurance in International Conflict Management. *Political Science Quarterly* 106 (4): 431–51.

———. 1989. Getting to the Table: The Triggers, Functions, Stages, and Consequences of Prenegotiation. *International Journal* 44 (2): 231–36.

———. 1985. The View from Cairo. In Robert Jervis, Richard Ned Lebow, and Janice Gross-Stein, eds., *Psychology and Deterrence*, 34–56. Baltimore: Johns Hopkins University Press.

Stein, Janice, and Raymond Tanter. 1980. *Rational Decision Making: Israel's Security Choices, 1967*. Columbus: Ohio State University Press.

Stein, Kenneth W. 1999. *Heroic Diplomacy: Sadat, Kissinger, Carter, Begin, and the Quest for Arab-Israeli Peace*. New York: Routledge.

Steinberg, Gerald. 2000. Parameters of Stable Deterrence in a Proliferated Middle East: Lessons from the 1991 Gulf War. *Non-Proliferation Review* 7 (3): 45–62.

Steinitz, Yuval. 2004a. *Report of the Knesset Subcommittee of Inquiry of the Intelligence System following the War in Iraq* (in Hebrew). Jerusalem: Knessett. Available online at http://www.knesset.gov.il/docs/heb/intelligence_irak_report.pdf.

———. 2004b. The Necessary Revolution in Israel's Security Conception. Lecture at the Center for Research on National Security, University of Haifa, March 2. Available online at mms://vod4.haifa.ac.il/M/NationalSecurityStudiesCenter/Yuval Shteinitz02032004.wmv.

———. 2002. The Sea as Israel's Strategic Depth. *Ma'arachot* (in Hebrew), 383:12–13. Available online at http://steinitz.likudnik.co.il/Front/NewsNet/reports.asp?reportld=463.

Stockholm International Peach Research Institute (SIPRI) 2004. *Military Expenditures and Arms Control*. http://www.sipri.org.

Tal, David. 1998. *The Current Security Conception of Israel: Its Origins and Development, 1949–1956* (in Hebrew). Sdeh Boker: Ben Gurion University Press.

Tal, Israel. 2000. *National Security: The Israeli Experience*. Westport, CT: Preager.

Tal, Rami 1997. Interview with Moshe Dayan (1976–77). *Yediot Aharonot* (in Hebrew), April 18 (Weekend Edition).

Tamir, Abraham. 1988. *A Soldier in Pursuit of Peace* (in Hebrew). Tel-Aviv: Yediot Aharonot.

Tanter, Raymond. 1990. *Who's at the Helm? Lessons of Lebanon*. Boulder: Westview Press.

Telhami, Shibley. 1990. *Power and Leadership in International Bargaining: The Road to the Camp David Accords*. New York: Columbia University Press.

Tessler, Mark. 1994. *A History of the Israeli-Palestinian Conflict*. Bloomington: Indiana University Press.

Tetlock, Philip E., and Aaron Belkin. 1996. *Thought Experiments in World Politics: Logical, Methodological, and Psychological Perspectives*. Princeton: Princeton University Press.

Tevet, Shabtai. 1987. *Ben Gurion and the Palestinian Arabs: From Peace to War*. London: Oxford University Press.

———. 1985. *Ben Gurion: The Burning Ground, 1886–1948*. Boston: Houghton Mifflin.

———. 1976. *David's Envy: The Life of David Ben Gurion* (in Hebrew). 3 vols. Jerusalem: Shocken.

———. 1971. *Moshe Dayan: A Biography* (in Hebrew). Tel-Aviv: Schocken.

———. 1968. *The Tanks of Tammuz*. New York: Viking.

Thornhill, Michael T. 2000. Alternatives to Nasser: Humprey, Trevelyan, Ambassador to Egypt. In Saul Kelly and Anthony Gorst, eds., *Whitehall and the Suez Crisis*, 11–28. London: Frank Cass.

Toren, Ilan. 1990. The Sinai Campaign as a "War of No Alternative": Ben-Gurion's View of the Israeli-Egyptian Conflict. In Selwyn Ilan Toren and Moshe Shemesh, eds., *The Suez-Sinai Crisis, 1956: Retrospective and Reappraisal,* 180–95. London: Frank Cass.

Touval, Saadia. 1982. *The Peace Brokers: Mediators in the Arab-Israeli Conflict, 1948–1979.* Princeton: Princeton University Press.

Tov, Imri. 1998. *The Price of Defense Power: The Economy of Defense—The Case of Israel* (in Hebrew). Tel Aviv: Defense Department Publishing House.

Trimberger, Ellen Kay. 1978. *Revolution from Above.* New Brunswick, NJ: Transaction Books.

Tsur, Yaacov. 1968. *Paris Diary: The Diplomatic Campaign in France, 1953–1956* (in Hebrew). Tel Aviv: Am Oved.

Ullman, Richard. 1975. After Rabat: Middle East Risks and U.S. Roles. *Foreign Affairs* 53 (2): 284–96.

UN Development Programme (UNDP). 2003. *Human Development Report, 2003.* Oxford: Oxford University Press. Available online at http://hdr.undp.org/reports/global/2003/ (cited as UNDP 2003).

UNESCO Institute for Statistics. 2004. Science and Technology Statistics, 2004. Available online at http://www.uis.unesco.org/.

Vaisse, Maurice. 1989. Post-Suez France. In Wm. Roger Louis and Roger Owen, eds., *Suez, 1956: The Crisis and Its Consequences,* 335–40. Oxford: Clarendon Press.

Vance, Cyrus. 1983. *Hard Choices.* New York: Simon and Schuster.

Van Creveld, Martin. 1998. *The Sword and the Olive: A Critical History of the Israeli Defense Force.* New York: Public Affairs Press.

———. 1990. *The Transformation of War.* New York: Free Press.

———. 1987. *Command in War.* Cambridge, MA: Harvard University Press.

———. 1975. *Military Lessons of the Yom Kippur War: Historical Perspectives.* Beverly Hills: Sage.

Vertzberger, Yaacov Y. I. 1998. *Risk Taking and Decisionmaking: Foreign Military Intervention Decisions.* Stanford: Stanford University Press.

Wald, Emmanuel. 1992. *The Wald Report: The Decline of Israeli National Security since 1967.* Boulder: Westview Press.

———. 1987. *The Curse of the Broken Tools: The Twilight of Israeli Political and Military Power, 1967–1982* (in Hebrew). Tel Aviv: Schoken.

Walzer, Michael. 1977. *Just and Unjust Wars: A Moral Argument with Historical Illustrations.* New York: Basic Books.

Ward, Michael D., and Alex Mintz. 1989. The Political Economy of Defense Spending in Israel. *American Political Science Review* 83 (2): 521–33.

Waterbury, John. 1983. *The Egypt of Nasser and Sadat: The Political Economy of Two Regimes.* Princeton: Princeton University Press.

Watson, Adam. 1989. The Aftermath of Suez: Consequences for French Decolonization. In Wm. Roger Louis and Roger Owen, eds., *Suez, 1956: The Crisis and Its Consequences,* 341–46. Oxford: Clarendon Press.

Weinberger, Naomi J. 1986. *Syrian Intervention in Lebanon: The 1975–76 Civil War.* New York: Oxford University Press.

Weizman, Ezer. 1981. *The Battle for Peace.* New York: Bantam.

———. 1975. *On Eagle's Wings* (in Hebrew). Tel-Aviv: Yediot Aharonot.

Whetten, Lawrence. 1974. *The Canal War.* Cambridge, MA: MIT Press.

Wildavsky, Aaron B. 1974. *The Politics of the Budgetary Process.* Boston: Little, Brown.

World Bank. 2003. *Twenty Seven Months: Intifada, Closures, and Palestinian Economic*

Crisis. Jerusalem. May. Available online at http://www-wds.worldbank.org/servlet/WDSContentServer/WDSP/IB/2003/07/14/000160016_20030714162552/Rendered/PDF/263141270monthsoIntifada10Closures.pdf.

———. 2002. *Fifteen Months: Intifada, Closures, and Palestinian Economic Crisis.* Jerusalem. March. Available online at http://www-wds.worldbank.org/servlet/WDSContentServer/WDSP/IB/2002/10/25/000094946_02101004010263/Rendered/PDF/multiopage.pdf.

———. 1999. *Development under Adversity: The Palestinian Economy in Transition.* Jerusalem: Palestinian Economic Research Institute and the World Bank. Available online at http://www-wds.worldbank.org/servlet/WDSContentServer/WDSP/IB/2000/08/15/000094946_0004200546516/Rendered/PDF/multi_page.pdf.

Yaacobi, Gad. 1990a. *On the Razor's Edge* (in Hebrew). Tel-Aviv: Yediot Aharonot (Edanim).

———. 1990b. Interview with Zeev Maoz. May 15.

Yaari, Ehud. 1975. *Egypt and the Fidayeen, 1953–1956* (in Hebrew). Givat Haviva: Center for Arab and Afro-Asian Studies.

Yaniv, Avner. 1995. *Politics and Strategy in Israel* (in Hebrew). Tel-Aviv: Sifriat Po'alim.

———. 1993. Introduction. In Avner Yaniv, ed., *National Security and Democracy in Israel,* 1–10. Boulder: Lynne Rienner.

———. 1987a. *Deterrence without the Bomb: The Politics of Israeli Strategy.* Lexington, MA: Lexington Books.

———. 1987b. *Dilemmas of Security: Politics, Strategy, and the Israeli Experience in Lebanon.* New York: Oxford University Press.

Yaniv, Avner, and Robert J. Lieber. 1983. Personal Whim or Strategic Imperative? The Israeli Invasion of Lebanon. *International Security* 8 (2): 117–42.

Young, John W. 2000. Conclusion. In Saul Kelly and Anthony Gorst, eds., *Whitehall and the Suez Crisis,* 221–31. London: Frank Cass.

Zak, Moshe. 1996. *Hussein Makes Peace: Thirty Years and Another Year on the Road to Peace* (in Hebrew). Ramat Gan: Bar Ilan University Press.

Zeira, Eli. 1993. *The Yom Kippur War: Myth versus Reality* (in Hebrew). Tel-Aviv: Edanim.

Zisser, Eyal. 2002. The Syrian Army on the Domestic and External Fronts. In Barry Rubin and Thomas A Kearny, eds., *Armed Forces in the Middle East: Politics and Strategy,* 101–20. London: Frank Cass.

BIBLIOGRAPHY (PREFACE AND AFTERWORD)

Ben Israel, Isaac. 2007. *The First Missile War* (in Hebrew). Tel Aviv: Hartog School of Government and Policy.

B'Tselem. 2008. Statistics on the Al Aqsa Intifada. http://www.btselem.org/English/Statistics/Index.asp (accessed April 18, 2008).

Cordesman, Anthony H. 2006. Preliminary "Lessons" of the Israel-Hezbollah War. Washington, DC: Center for Strategic and International Studies. http://www.mafhoum.com/press9/284P51.pdf (accessed April 9, 2008).

Defense and Foreign Affairs. 2007. Hizballah Concludes Largest-Ever Military Exercises in South Lebanon. *Defense and Foreign Affairs.* Accessed through Lexis Nexis Academic.

Harel, Amos, and Avi Issacharoff. 2008. *Spider Web: The Story of the Second Lebanon War* (in Hebrew). Tel Aviv: Yediot Aharonot.

ITIC (Intelligence and Terrorism Information Center). 2008. Characteristics of Terrorist Activities against Israel in 2006 (in Hebrew). Ramat Hasharon: Intelligence and Terrorism Information Center. http://www.terrorism-info.org.il/malam_multi media/Hebrew/heb_n/pdf/terrorism_2006h.pdf (accessed April 18, 2008).

Janis, Irving L. 1982. *Groupthink*. 2d ed. Boston: Houghton Mifflin.

Makovsky, David, and Jeffrey White. 2006. Lessons and Implications of the Israel-Hizballah War: A Preliminary Assessment. Washington: Washington Institute for Near East Policy. http://www.washingtoninstitute.org/pubPDFs/PolicyFocus60.pdf (accessed April 9, 2008).

Maoz, Zeev. 2007. Evaluating Israel's Strategy of Low-Intensity Conflict, 1949–2006. *Security Studies* 16 (3): 319–49.

Maoz, Zeev. 2006. Israel's Nonstrategy of Peace. *Tikkun* 21(3): 49–63.

National Intelligence Council. 2007. Iran: Nuclear Intentions and Capabilities. Washington, DC: U.S. National Intelligence Council. http://www.dni.gov/press _releases/20071203_release.pdf (accessed April 28, 2008).

Norton, Augustus Richard. 2007. The Role of Hezbollah in Lebanese Domestic Politics. *International Spectator* 42 (4): 475–91.

Perthes, Volker. 2007. Analytical Perspectives on the War in Lebanon. *International Spectator* 42 (1): 115–19.

PHRMG (Palestinian Human Rights Monitoring Group). 2007. Al Aqsa Intifada. http://www.phrmg.org/aqsa.htm (accessed April 18, 2008).

Salem, Paul. 2008. The After-Effects of the 2006 Israel-Hezbollah War. *Contemporary Asian Affairs* 1 (1): 15–24.

Shavit, Yossi, Epi Yaar, Tamar Herman, and Irit Adler. 2006. Feelings and Positions of Israeli Public during the Fighting in the North: Daily Surveys 19/7–13/8. Tel Aviv: B. I. Cohen Institute for Public Opinion Research. http://www.bicohen.tau.ac.il/ (accessed April 25, 2008).

Shelah, Ofer, and Yechiel Limor. 2007. *Prisoners in Lebanon: The Truth about the Second Lebanon War* (in Hebrew). Tel Aviv: Yediot Aharonot.

Telhami, Shibley. 2007. Lebanese Identity and Israeli Security in the Shadows of the 2006 War. *Current History* (January 2007): 21–26.

Vinograd Inquiry Commission. 2008. Final Report (in Hebrew). Available online at http://www.vaadatwino.org.il/reports.html#null (issued January 2008; accessed April 8, 2008).

Vinograd Inquiry Commission. 2007. Interim Report (in Hebrew). Available online at http://www.vaadatwino.org.il/reports.html#null. (issued April 2007; accessed April 8, 2008).

Author Index

695

Subject Index